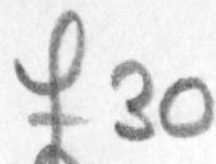

CASS SERIES ON SOVIET (RUSSIAN)

FROM THE DON TO

CASS SERIES ON SOVIET (RUSSIAN) MILITARY EXPERIENCE
Series Editor: David M. Glantz
ISSN 1462-0944

This series focuses on Soviet military experiences in specific campaigns or operations.

1. David M. Glantz, *From the Don to the Dnepr, Soviet Offensive Operations, December 1942 to August 1943* (ISBN 0 7146 3350 X cloth, 0 7146 4064 6 paper)

2. David Glantz, *The Initial Period of War on the Eastern Front: 22 June–August 1941* (ISBN 0 7146 3375 5 cloth, 0 7146 4298 3 paper)

3. Carl van Dyke, *The Soviet Invasion of Finland, 1930–40* (ISBN 0 7146 4653 5 cloth, 0 7146 4314 9 paper)

CASS SERIES ON SOVIET (RUSSIAN) STUDY OF WAR
Series Editor: David M. Glantz
ISSN 1462-0960

This series examines what Soviet military theorists and commanders have learned from the study of their own military operations.

1. Harold S. Orenstein, translator and editor, *Soviet Documents on the Use of War Experience*, Volume I, *The Initial Period of War 1941*, with an Introduction by David M. Glantz (ISBN 0 7146 3392 5 cloth)

2. Harold S. Orenstein, translator and editor, *Soviet Documents on the Use of War Experience*, Volume II, *The Winter Campaign 1941–1942*, with an Introduction by David M. Glantz (ISBN 0 7146 3393 3 cloth)

3. Joseph G. Welsh, translator, *Red Armor Combat Orders: Combat Regulations for Tank and Mechanized Forces 1944*, edited and with an Introduction by Richard N. Armstrong (ISBN 0 7146 3401 8 cloth)

4. Harold S. Orenstein, translator and editor, *Soviet Documents on the Use of War Experience*, Volume III, *Military Operations 1941 and 1942*, with an Introduction by David M. Glantz (ISBN 0 7146 3402 6 cloth)

5. William A. Burhans, translator, *The Nature of the Operations of Modern Armies* by V.K. Triandafillov, edited by Jacob W. Kipp, with an Introduction by James J. Schneider (ISBN 0 7146 4501 X cloth, 0 7146 4118 9 paper)

6. Harold S. Orenstein, translator, *The Evolution of Soviet Operational Art, 1927–1991: The Documentary Basis*, Volume I, *Operational Art, 1927–1964*, with an Introduction by David M. Glantz (ISBN 0 7146 4547 8 cloth, 0 7146 4228 2 paper)

7. Harold S. Orenstein, translator, *The Evolution of Soviet Operational Art, 1927–1991: The Documentary Basis*, Volume II, *Operational Art, 1965–1991*, with an Introduction by David M. Glantz (ISBN 0 7146 4548 6 cloth, 0 7146 4229 0 paper)

8. Richard N. Armstrong and Joseph G. Welsh, *Winter Warfare: Red Army Orders and Experiences* (ISBN 0 7146 4699 7 cloth, 0 7146 4237 1 paper)

9. Lester W. Grau, *The Bear Went Over the Mountain: Soviet Combat Tactics in Afghanistan* (ISBN 0 7146 4874 4 cloth, 0 7146 4413 7 paper)

FROM THE DON TO THE DNEPR

Soviet Offensive Operations December 1942–August 1943

DAVID M. GLANTZ

FRANK CASS
LONDON • PORTLAND, OR

First published in 1991 in Great Britain by
FRANK CASS PUBLISHERS
Newbury House, 900 Eastern Avenue
London, IG2 7HH

and in the United States of America by
FRANK CASS PUBLISHERS
c/o ISBS, 5804 N.E. Hassalo Street
Portland, Oregon, 97213-3644

Website http://www.frankcass.com

Reprinted 1998

The views expressed here are those of the author. They should not necessarily be construed as those of the US Department of Defense or the United States Army.

British Library Cataloguing-in-Publication Data

Glantz, David M.
From the Don to the Dnepr: Soviet offensive operations
December 1942–August 1943.
I. World War 2. Military operations by Soviet military forces
I. Title
940.541247

ISBN 0–7146–3350–X (cloth)
ISBN 0–7146–4064–6 (paper)
ISSN 1462–0944

Library of Congress Cataloging-in-Publication Data

Glantz, David M.
From the Don to the Dnepr: Soviet offensive operations, December 1941–August 1943/
David M. Glantz.
p. cm.
Includes bibliographical references.
ISBN 0–7146–3350–X (cloth) ISBN 0–7146–4064–6 (paper)
1. World War, 1939–1945–Russian S.F.S.R.–Don River Region.
2. World War, 1939–1945 – Campaigns – Donets Basin (Ukraine and R.S.F.S.R.) 3. Don River Region (R.S.F.S.R.)–History. 4. Donets Basin (Ukraine and R.S.F.S.R.)–History.
4. Donets Basin (Ukraine and R.S.F.S.R.)–History. I. Title
D764.7.D6G53 1990 89–71291
940.54'217770–dc20 CIP

Printed in Great Britain by
Bookcraft (Bath) Ltd, Midsomer Norton, Somerset

To my wife and children whose support and tolerance made this work possible

Contents

List of Illustrations

List of Maps

Abbreviations

A	Army
A.ABT.	Armee Abteilung (Army detachment)
A.G.	Army group
ABN	Airborne
AC	Army corps
CD	Cavalry division
CC	Cavalry corps
(G)	German
GA	Guards army
GAD	Guards airborne division
GCC	Guards cavalry corps
GCD	Guards cavalry division
GMC	Guards mechanized corps
GMB	Guards mechanized brigade
GRC	Guards rifle corps
GRD	Guards rifle division
GTA	Guards tank army
GTC	Guards tank corps
GTB	Guards tank brigade
(I)	Italian
ID	Infantry division
IR	Infantry regiment
MB	Mechanized brigade
MC	Mechanized corps
MD	Motorized division
PA	Panzer army
PC	Panzer corps
PD	Panzer division
PGD	Panzer grenadier division
POL.RGT.	Police regiment
PR	Panzer regiment
(R)	Rumanian
RB	Rifle brigade
RC	Rifle corps
RD	Rifle division
RR	Rifle regiment
TA	Tank army
TB	Tank brigade
TC	Tank corps

On maps, numerals with no abbreviations attached are divisions (German and Soviet)

Preface

This study examines how the Soviets planned and conducted four offensive operations during the period from December 1942 to August 1943. The first three of these offensives, each conducted by a single *front* under *STAVKA* (High Command) supervision, took place in the flush of optimism after the successful Soviet encirclement of German forces at Stalingrad in November 1942, while the Soviets were still pondering the lessons of that victory. The fourth, and largest, occurred in August 1943, after the abortive German Kursk offensive at a time when Soviet planning techniques, Soviet force structure, and Soviet capabilities for effectively employing such a force had measurably improved.

One theme emerges as central throughout the period addressed in the study—how a nation's armed forces educate themselves in the conduct of war during wartime when its very survival is threatened. It was a most difficult and costly education, but also one which the Soviet armed force had to master if it was to survive.

Following the dictum of Clausewitz, that in the absence of personal war experience one best gains insights into war by examining a nation's military experience, the Soviets consider their experience during the Great Patriotic War as a rich repository of knowledge and inspiration which contemporary military theorists and professional officers must tap. In terms of scale, scope, and intensity, no modern wars have matched the conflict on the Eastern Front. It was an arena where, for four years, two nations' armies developed, tested, and experimented with a wide variety of strategic, operational, and tactical techniques, many of which are basic to the conduct of war regardless of changing times and technology. At a time when the Soviets are reinvestigating the nuances of conventional war it is particularly appropriate that they study those techniques and reconsider their validity in light of recent technological progress.

For years the Soviets have investigated these experiences in immense detail and with the critical eye of a military scholar, determined to educate the Soviet officer corps to a clearer understanding of the nature of war in all of its aspects. It is the didactic nature of that work that impels the Soviets to a remarkable degree of candor about their successes and their failures.

These studies provide a glimpse of that Soviet realm of study in the hope that Westerners interested in military affairs will find these materials concerning the conduct of modern war of value.

1

INTRODUCTION
The Red Army 1941–1942
Tragedy and Rebirth of an Army

On the morning of 22 June 1941 Nazi Germany unleashed a sudden and massive offensive to destroy the Soviet state. The ambitious German undertaking, based on the premise that the bulk of the Soviet Army could be annihilated in the immediate border regions by use of blitzkrieg conducted on a large scale, caught the Soviets only partially prepared for war. Force reconstruction and reequipment programs were underway but incomplete. Although the Soviets had ample warning, for as yet inexplicable reasons, Stalin forbade the Soviet military to take prudent defensive precautions, thus granting the Germans the equivalent of strategic, operational, and tactical surprise. The German hammer blows staggered the Soviet armed forces and almost resulted in their destruction. By Soviet admission:

> our pre-war views on the conduct of armed struggle in the initial period of war did not investigate the possibility of the concealed timely deployment and simultaneous action of enemy armed forces on the land, in the air and at sea. Mistakes in theory had a negative effect on resolving the practical questions of covering the state borders and deploying the armed forces which, along with other reasons, caused serious misfortunes in the war.
>
> There were many problems in working out command and control and organizing communications with operational large units. The assertion that the defense found fullest expression only in the realm of army operations was incorrect, as was the view that the struggle for air superiority must be realized on the scale of front and army operations. The complicated views at the beginning of the war concerning the organization of the army and forces of the rear did not fully meet the demands of the theory of deep offensive operations and battle. Operational and forces rear services remained cumbersome and immobile.
>
> There were also serious deficiencies in the theoretical training of commanders and in the combat training of forces . . . .[1]

These Soviet admissions, as frank as they were, understated the scale of the problem. In the initial months of the war, Soviet commanders at higher levels displayed an ineptness only partially compensated for by the fervor of junior officers and the stoicism of the hard pressed troops. *Front* and army commanders, unable to construct coherent defenses against the Germans' armored thrusts, displayed an alarming propensity for launching costly uncoordinated counterattacks predestined to failure. Only looming disaster drove the Soviet high command to action in a war which quickly became one of survival.

Ultimately, the Soviet Army successfully met this great challenge and triumphed, but only after years of death, frustration, and an agonizing process of military reeducation conducted during wartime. Throughout the war new generations of commanders emerged, new equipment was developed and fielded, and military theories matured after their late 1930s hiatus. In essence, the concept of deep operations, articulated in the 1936 *Field Service Regulation* but unrealized in the late 1930s, became the focal point of Soviet offensive theory and the means of converting tactical success into operational and even strategic success. By late 1943, the Soviets had wed their military theory and their force structure into a successful formula for achieving victory. During the ensuing two years of war the Soviets experimented with operational techniques, refined their force structure, and worked to overcome resource and logistical constraints. This second great renaissance in Soviet military thought and practice, often ignored in the West because of the Soviet disasters of 1941 and 1942 as related in the works of victorious German generals, is today viewed by the Soviets as the most important period in Soviet military affairs, a vast laboratory for military analysis and a repository of experience that can be and is tapped for inspiration and concrete advice.

For the sake of analysis, the Soviets subdivide their "Great Patriotic War" into three distinct periods, each characterized by broad unifying themes concerning Soviet fortunes in war and the state of military art. The first period of war (June 1941–November 1942) found the Soviets on the strategic defense punctuated by several Soviet attempts to undertake offensive operations on several important directions. The second period (December 1942–December 1943) was one of transition from defensive operations to a general Soviet offensive designed to wrest the strategic initiative from the Germans. The third period (1944–1945) was a period of general Soviet offensives culminating in the achievement of total victory.

The first and most difficult period commenced in June 1941 with the German invasion and the series of border battles during which the Germans swallowed up large segments of deployed Soviet forces. The large scale encirclements at Minsk, Bryansk, Vyaz'ma and Smolensk culminated in the fall of 1941, when German forces tried to cap their victorious advance with the seizure of Moscow by one last envelopment. German failure to take Moscow prompted the first major Soviet attempt to regain the strategic initiative. A desperate Soviet winter offensive in the Moscow environs, broadened into an attempt to expand the offensive across the front from Leningrad to Rostov and the Crimea, foundered because of insufficient Soviet forces and materiel, and left the Soviets vulnerable to renewed German strategic thrusts in the summer of 1942. The ill-fated and costly Soviet offensive failure at Khar'kov in May 1942 was followed by the general German offensive in south Russia which, by late fall, reached the Volga at Stalingrad and the passes of the Caucasus Mountains. Like the 1941 German offensive campaign, by late fall the Germans were overextended while the Soviets again husbanded their resources for a counterattack. Unlike 1941, by 1942 the Soviets had undertaken organizational and theoretical measures to better parry the German offensive as it ran out of steam on the banks of the Volga River. The November Soviet offensive around Stalingrad saw the strategic initiative pass into Soviet hands and marked the end of the first period of war.

The German attack in 1941 smashed the large and complex Soviet force structure and clearly demonstrated that the Soviet officer corps was incapable of efficiently commanding and controlling so elaborate a force. Likewise, Soviet industry had been unable to supply the necessary weaponry to so extensive a force. Thus, by late summer 1941 the Soviets had dismantled that portion of their force structure the Germans had not already destroyed. The Soviets severely truncated the size of all units in order to improve span of control and concentrated scarce artillery and armor assets under High Command control. The Soviets abolished rifle corps and created smaller armies comprised of rifle divisions and rifle brigades. Rifle divisions were reduced in strength; and smaller, more easily controlled rifle brigades were formed to supplement rifle divisions. The Soviets abolished their mechanized corps and the corps' component mechanized and tank divisions and consolidated armor assets in a handful of small tank brigades earmarked to support the smaller armies. Field, antitank, and antiaircraft artillery were withdrawn from rifle divisions, corps, and armies and formed into battalions, regiments, and brigades under High Command control to reinforce armies operating along specific directions. The Soviets created numerous light cavalry divisions, united into cavalry corps in order to compensate for shortages in armor and provide some mobile offensive capability for the basically footbound Soviet army.[2]

These measures, along with improvements in strategic and operational command and control, provided the basis for Soviet offensive successes in the winter of 1941–42. But it was clear that further improvements were necessary if the Soviets hoped to expand their limited offensive capabilities. In particular, larger and more effective mechanized formations were essential for developing tactical success into operational success. Thus in the spring of 1942, while larger artillery units were evolving, and Soviet riflemen were being reequipped with an array of automatic weapons, the Soviets created new tank corps designated to exploit success in army operations. Later, in the summer, tank armies of mixed composition (rifle, cavalry and infantry forces) were formed to conduct larger scale exploitation and in early fall, mechanized corps were formed which combined heavy armor and large numbers of mechanized infantry (often scarce in tank corps). Although the new composite tank armies proved unwieldy and difficult to coordinate, the tank and mechanized corps provided the offensive punch necessary for the Soviets to unleash the successful Stalingrad counteroffensive in November 1942. These structural changes combined with increased Soviet production of the weapons of war and revitalized Soviet military theory to produce the turnabout in Soviet battlefield fortunes in the late fall of 1942.

Soviet emphasis on implementing practical measures necessary to achieve victory eclipsed Soviet theoretical military doctrine during the first period of war, and during the war in general. Under Stalin's leadership, the General Staff made tremendous efforts to investigate strategic, operational, and tactical methods for preparing and conducting operations. The Soviets gathered, studied and analyzed battlefield experiences and converted them into directives, instructions and coherent regulations governing the conduct of war.[3] This practical work paralleled similar measures undertaken to mobilize the will and resources of the nation for war. While ideology remained a strong ingredient, and party control remained preeminent, the Soviets tapped memories of past "Russian" military glories to inspire the nation. A pantheon of Russian heroes – Peter the Great, Suvorov, Kutuzov – and others reemerged, and their memories were commemorated in new military decorations for Soviet war heroes. New ranks and titles adorned the Soviet officers corps and reinforced the older Soviet class discipline even while echoes of "holy" mother Russia could be heard. If the nature of Soviet military doctrine remained constant during wartime the tone of that doctrine perceptibly changed; driven by the necessity of survival and attaining victory in war.

The foremost strategic problem for the Soviet High Command during the first period of the war was that of conducting a successful strategic defense. Specifically, the Soviets had to halt the German general offensive, deprive the Germans of their initial advantages resulting from surprise and superiority in operational and tactical skills, establish defenses along a huge front, including around Moscow and Leningrad, and prepare to conduct critical counteroffensives. All this had to be done over tremendous distances in spite of huge losses in manpower, equipment, territory and in the nation's productive base.

The Red Army conducted strategic defensive operations simultaneously along several strategic directions, using several *fronts* cooperating according to *STAVKA* plans. This practice clashed with prewar views which supposed that single *fronts* would conduct strategic defensive operations, and produced new concepts governing operations by groups of *fronts*. These operations were aimed at inflicting maximum casualties on the Germans, weakening and bleeding their main offensive groups while stopping their offensive, denying them possession of the most important economic and political regions, and creating conditions suitable for the launching of counteroffensives. Such defensive operations raged along frontages of from 200 to 800 kilometers to depths of from 100 to 600 kilometers, over periods ranging from 20 to 100 days.

Strategic reserves played a significant role in the strategic defense by establishing new defense lines, liquidating enemy penetrations, and providing forces necessary to launch counteroffensives. During this period of the war the *STAVKA* retained between two and ten reserve armies under its direct control, and these reserves were instrumental in launching the winter counteroffensive around Moscow in 1941–42 and the abortive Khar'kov offensive in May 1942. Strategic offensives, usually begun in the form of counteroffensive, occurred on frontages of up to 550 kilometers and penetrated to depths of up to 250 kilometers.[4] All were overly ambitious, and because of force and logistical inadequacies fell far short of expectations. The Soviet High Command still had to learn the art of the possible.

Strict centralization of command and control at the highest level made successful strategic defense possible. Early attempts to create three theaters of military operations covering the three main strategic directions (northwest, west, and southwest) failed during the disastrous operations in the summer of 1941. Consequently, to provide "uninterrupted and qualified command and control" Stalin created the *STAVKA* of the Supreme High Command (*STAVKA* VGK). Organized first on 23 June 1941, by 8 August the composition was fixed with Stalin himself as Supreme High Commander.[5] The *STAVKA,* either directly or through its representatives, familiarized commanders of directions* and *fronts* with the aims of each operation, provided forces and weaponry, designated missions, and organized cooperation between *fronts* and other large units. It also provided a link between political and military leaders and as such provided clear political control over the conduct of the war.

In the operational arena the Soviets amassed considerable experience in conducting *front* and army defensive operations. Fronts covered operational directions in accordance with *STAVKA* plans while armies defended according to *front* plans. In violation of pre-war concepts shortages

*Strategic directions roughly corresponded to a modern Theater of Military Operations (TVD). Several *fronts* operated along a strategic direction. Individual *fronts* operated along an operational direction.

of men and materiel forced the deployment of the bulk of forces in a single operational echelon with only small reserves. These shallow, poorly prepared defenses were easily pierced by concentrated German armor supported by aviation. As Soviet mobilization progressed, and weapons production improved, weapons densities increased and defenses deepened. By the fall of 1942 combined arms armies created army artillery groups, air defense groups, and artillery and antitank reserves. The army's defensive depth increased to as much as 20 kilometers, the average operational density to 10 kilometers of frontage per rifle division, and the average weapons density to 15–25 guns per 1 kilometer of frontage. By late 1942 army and *front* defensive depths averaged 15 and 30 kilometers, respectively, with the first defensive belt best developed, consisting of battalion defensive regions. However, the fragmented nature of the defense isolated subunits and hindered maneuver of forces along the front and in its depths. The Soviets emphasized improvements in antitank defenses which had been ineffective early in the war due to the paucity of weapons and the tendency of commanders to scatter them evenly across the front. Heavy caliber artillery and aviation were ineffective against tanks for the same reason. Although antitank artillery remained in scarce supply (less than 4 guns per kilometer), by mid-1942 the Soviets began creating antitank regions (strong points) echeloned in depth along likely tank axes of advance. The detachment of antitank reserves from *front* and army commands to lower command echelons also increased the density and mobility of antitank defenses. After the summer of 1941, artillery customarily engaged enemy armor units to supplement antitank defenses (often in a direct fire role).[6]

Offensive experiences in 1941–42 provided the Soviets with the basis for improving their operational techniques in 1943. In the largest offensive, the winter campaign of 1941–42, *fronts* advanced in sectors of from 300–400 kilometers and armies in sectors of 20–80 kilometers with objectives at depths of 120–250 kilometers for *fronts* and 30–35 kilometers for armies. These objectives were to be secured over a period of 6–8 days. The tendency on the part of Soviet commanders to disperse attacking forces over a wide front prompted *STAVKA* corrective action during the winter offensive. *STAVKA* Directive No. 3 (10 January 1942) required creation of shock groups on main attack directions at all levels of command.[7] The directive established penetration sectors of 30 kilometers for *fronts* and 15 kilometers for armies. This permitted creation of higher artillery densities on main attack directions (from 7–12 guns/mortars per kilometer in summer–autumn 1941 to 45–65 guns/mortars in the summer of 1942). The operational formation of *fronts* in the entire first period of war was single echelon, at first with a two or three rifle division reserve, and later with a tank or cavalry corps in reserve. Armies also formed in single echelon. However, in 1942 a growth in forces allowed armies to deploy in two echelons with a combined arms reserve, mobile forces, artillery groups and antitank, tank, and engineer reserves. The depth of the army operational formation increased to 15–20 kilometers and in some instances, 30–40 kilometers.[8]

The operational role of armor increased both in a defensive role and on the offensive. The Soviets used the small tank brigades of 1941–42 in concert with cavalry (and air assault forces) to stiffen the infantry, launch counterattacks or spearhead pursuits. However, these mobile forces had limited sustaining power, and they were difficult to resupply and coordinate with foot infantry. In 1942, the new tank armies, tank corps, and mechanized corps provided better means for countering German armored thrusts and exploiting success while functioning as mobile groups of *fronts* and armies.* However, their composition was unbalanced by a marked shortage of mechanized infantry. Hence, they were difficult to coordinate with other types of forces; they were vulnerable when isolated from their supporting infantry, and Soviet commanders simply had not learned how to use them properly. A special order of the People's Commissariat of Defense (Order No. 325, 16 October 1942) pondered mobile group failures (such as the debacle at Khar'kov in May 1942), directed that tank and mechanized corps be used as single entities for powerful attacks or counterattacks, and prohibited the fragmented use of those valuable operational formations.[9]

At the outbreak of war, Soviet tactics suffered from the same general malaise as operational art. Understrength divisions of 5000–6000 men, defending in extended sectors of 14–20 kilometers, were forced to deploy in single echelon defenses to a depth of only 4–6 kilometers. The small reserves had little capability for sustained counterattack, and infantry support groups were weak. Inadequate tactical densities of .5 battalions and 3 guns/mortars per kilometer of frontage resulted. Division defenses consisted of noncontiguous battalion defense regions and had little engineer support or antitank defenses. By late 1941 more extensive engineer support permitted construction of trenches and the evolution of a truly interconnected first defensive position. Increases in manpower and weaponry further improved the defenses in 1942. Divisions began creating second echelons, tank and antitank reserves, and stronger artillery groups. Second echelons of rifle regiments and rifle divisions created battalion defense regions which later would become second and third defensive positions. Meanwhile, division defenses remained shallow (one defensive belt) and weak in antitank means. By the end of the first period

*Mobile groups were designed to undertake operational maneuver to exploit tactical success into the operational depths of the enemy defenses.

of war, tactical densities rose to 1 battalion and 20 guns/mortars per kilometer of front.[10]

Soviet offensive tactics deviated from those recommended in prewar regulations. Rifle divisions at first deployed in the recommended two echelon formation meaning that only eight of twenty-seven rifle companies actually participated directly in the attack. Because of the weakness of rifle divisions and the shallow enemy defenses this combat formation was futile as well as vulnerable to enemy air and artillery fire. Thus Commissariat of Defense Order No. 306 of 8 October 1942 required use of a single echelon combat formation in all units from company to division and creation of a reserve of 1/9th of the force.[11] This effectively mandated forward use of 80 percent of a division's combat power and facilitated achievement of penetrations, but it also made it difficult to sustain the attack. By the winter of 1941–42, rifle divisions attacked in sectors of from 5–6 kilometers to achieve objectives from 5 to 12 kilometers deep. After January 1942, when enemy defenses became deeper, rifle divisions attacked in sectors of 3–4 kilometers against objectives 5–7 kilometers deep which, in reality, took several days to secure. Tactical densities increased from 1–2 rifle battalions, 20–30 guns/mortars and 2–3 tanks per kilometer of frontage during the winter of 1941–1942 to 2–4 battalions, 30–40 guns/mortars, and 10–14 tanks per kilometer of frontage in the summer of 1942.[12]

Fire support in each division increased with the creation of infantry support artillery groups (PP) and, in some instances, long range action artillery groups (DD). Centralized artillery preparations before the attack were followed by decentralized support of each rifle battalion by one artillery battery during the attack. Armor support for attacking units in 1941 was poor and resulted in heavy tank losses. After Order No. 325 was issued in October 1942, the Soviets used tank brigades and separate tank battalions as complete single units to support attacking infantry, but only after proper reconnaissance and coordination with appropriate infantry/artillery and aviation commanders. After the spring of 1942, the rifle division received increased engineer support; and air support, virtually nonexistent before that time, began to contribute to preattack preparations and provide some tactical air support as well.

The first period of war was a harsh and costly experience for the Soviet nation and the military in particular. It pointed out vividly the gap between the promises of 1936 and the realities of 1941. But it was a necessary stage for future victory. The division, army and *front* commanders who emerged in 1942 would lead their units and the Red Army to victory in 1945. The rules, regulations and theoretical principles which emerged by 1942 would be adjusted in 1943 and perfected in 1944–45. The military weaponry flowing off Soviet assembly lines in 1942 would flood the theater by 1944 and swamp the best of German equipment by war's end. The prerequisites for eventual victory were established in 1942 and would be capitalized upon in 1943. The best indication of Soviet progress was the offensive that the Soviets unleashed in November 1942 to mark the opening of the second period of war – the offensive at Stalingrad.

2

OPERATION "LITTLE SATURN"
The Soviet Offensive on the Middle Don
December 1942

Strategic and Operational Context

The Situation in November 1942

In November 1942 Stalin struck at overextended German, Rumanian, Hungarian, and Italian forces in the Stalingrad area using several reserve armies released from *STAVKA* control, one tank army, and the majority of his tank and mechanized corps. The success of the ensuing operation exceeded Stalin's expectations and trapped the German 6th Army and a major portion of the 4th Panzer Army at Stalingrad. This first successful Soviet encirclement operation wrested the strategic initiative from German hands. After the encirclement Stalin attempted simultaneously to reduce surrounded German forces at Stalingrad, defeat German relief attempts, and expand the Soviet offensive to encompass the entire southern wing of the Eastern Front – in essence to destroy German Army Group "Don" (see Map 1).

The Soviet Stalingrad counteroffensive began on 19 November 1943 and by 23 November had encircled German 6th Army and the bulk of 4th Panzer Army and severely damaged the Rumanian 3d and 4th Armies.[1] Initial Soviet estimates placed German strength in the Stalingrad pocket at 90,000 men, an estimate that proved woefully low. At the time the trap snapped shut around 6th Army, a representative of the Soviet *STAVKA*, General A.M. Vasilevsky, conferred with the Stalingrad and Don Front commanders.[2] Vasilevsky then reported to the *STAVKA* on the military situation in the Stalingrad area and recommended that they give priority to the creation of a dense inner encirclement around German forces and to the subsequent reduction of the pocket. Vasilevsky defined three requirements: First and foremost, Stalingrad had to be reduced. Implied in that task was the necessity of preventing German attempts to relieve Stalingrad by Soviet erection of an outer line of encirclement, preferably one capable of launching spoiling attacks in order to preempt German counterattacks. Once the Soviets addressed these two priority tasks, they

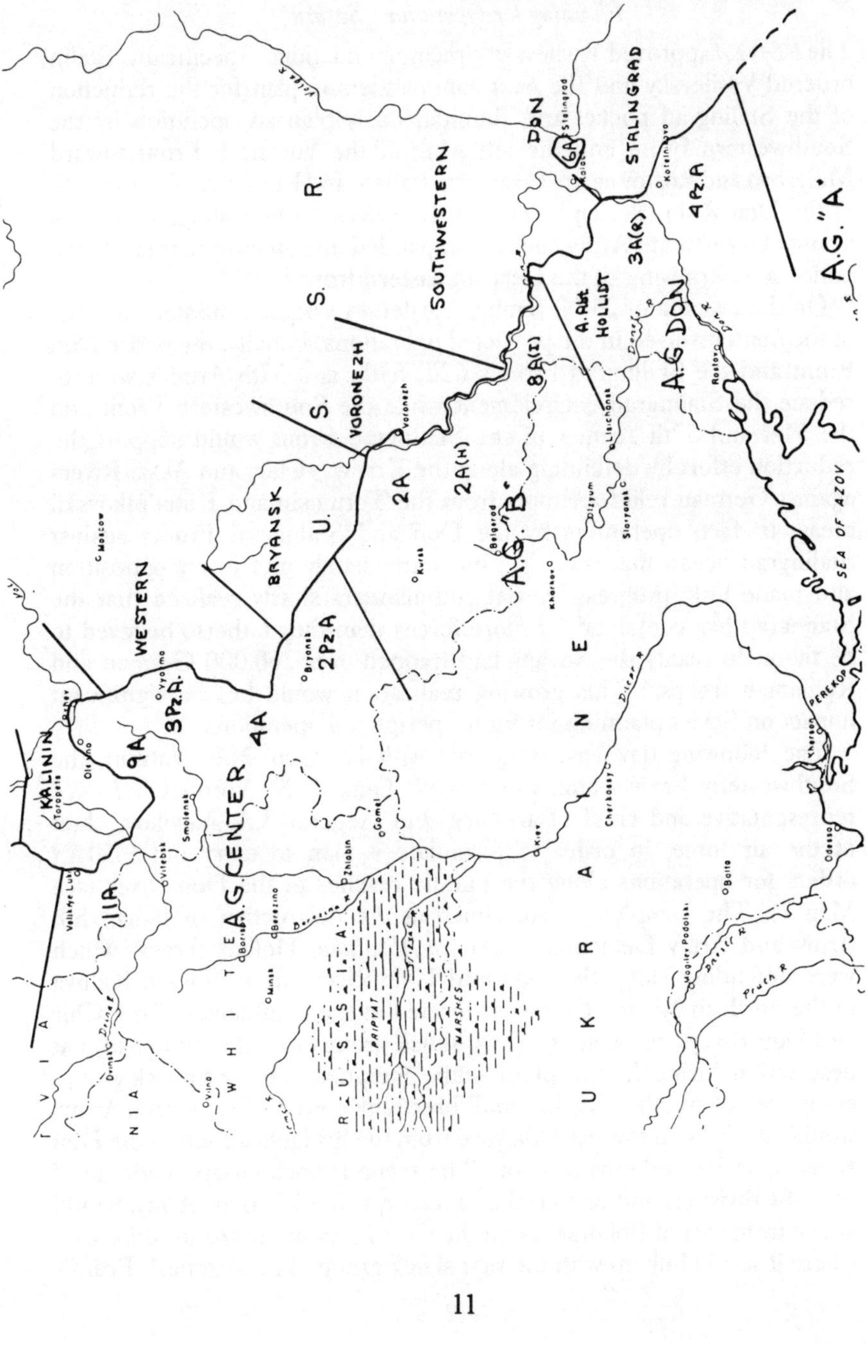

MAP 1. SITUATION ON THE EASTERN FRONT, 1 DECEMBER 1942

could undertake the third priority task, to expand the offensive westward in order to capitalize on the catastrophic German losses.

Planning for Operation "Saturn"

The *STAVKA* approved Vasilevsky's recommendations. Specifically, Stalin ordered Vasilevsky and the *front* commanders to plan for the reduction of the Stalingrad pocket and simultaneously plan an operation by the Southwestern Front and the left wing of the Voronezh Front toward Millerovo and Rostov against German, Italian, and Rumanian forces south of the Don River. Perhaps, thought the *STAVKA,* the Stalingrad success against German 6th Army could be expanded into an envelopment of the entire southern wing of the German eastern front.[3]

On the evening of 24 November Vasilevsky assigned missions to each of the *fronts* involved in the projected operations. Initially, the entire Don Front and the Stalingrad Front's 62d, 64th, and 57th Armies were to reduce the Stalingrad encirclement while the Southwestern Front and the 51st and 57th Armies of the Stalingrad Front would support the reduction effort by defending along the Krivaya, Chir, and Aksai Rivers against German relief attempts from the Tormosin and Kotel'nikovskii areas. In fact, operations by the Don and Stalingrad Fronts against Stalingrad began that very day, but immediately met heavy opposition and made little progress. Soviet commanders slowly realized that the Stalingrad bag contained far more forces than they hitherto believed to be there. In reality the Soviets had trapped over 260,000 German and Rumanian troops.[4] This growing realization would have a significant impact on Soviet planning for future peripheral operations.

The following day Vasilevsky met with Lt. Gen. N.F. Vatutin, the Southwestern Front commander; Col. Gen. N.N. Voronev, *STAVKA* representative and chief of artillery; and General A.A. Novikov, chief of the air force, in order to formulate a plan to carry out *STAVKA* orders for operations along the middle reaches of the Don River (see Map 2). The completed plan aimed at the destruction of Italian 8th Army and Army Detachment (*Armee Abteilung*) Hollidt forces, which were defending along the Don and Chir Rivers from Novaya Kalitva in the north to Nizhne Chirskaya located at the confluence of the Chir and Don Rivers in the south. Two shock groups would accomplish that destruction during the first phase of the operation. The first shock group, comprised of six rifle divisions and three tank corps of 1st Guards Army, would attack south toward Millerovo from the bridgehead across the Don River opposite Verkhnyi Mamon. The second shock group, made up of five rifle divisions and one mechanized corps of 3d Guards Army, would attack from east of Bokovskaya on the Chir River westward to Millerovo, where it would link up with the first shock group. The Voronezh Front's

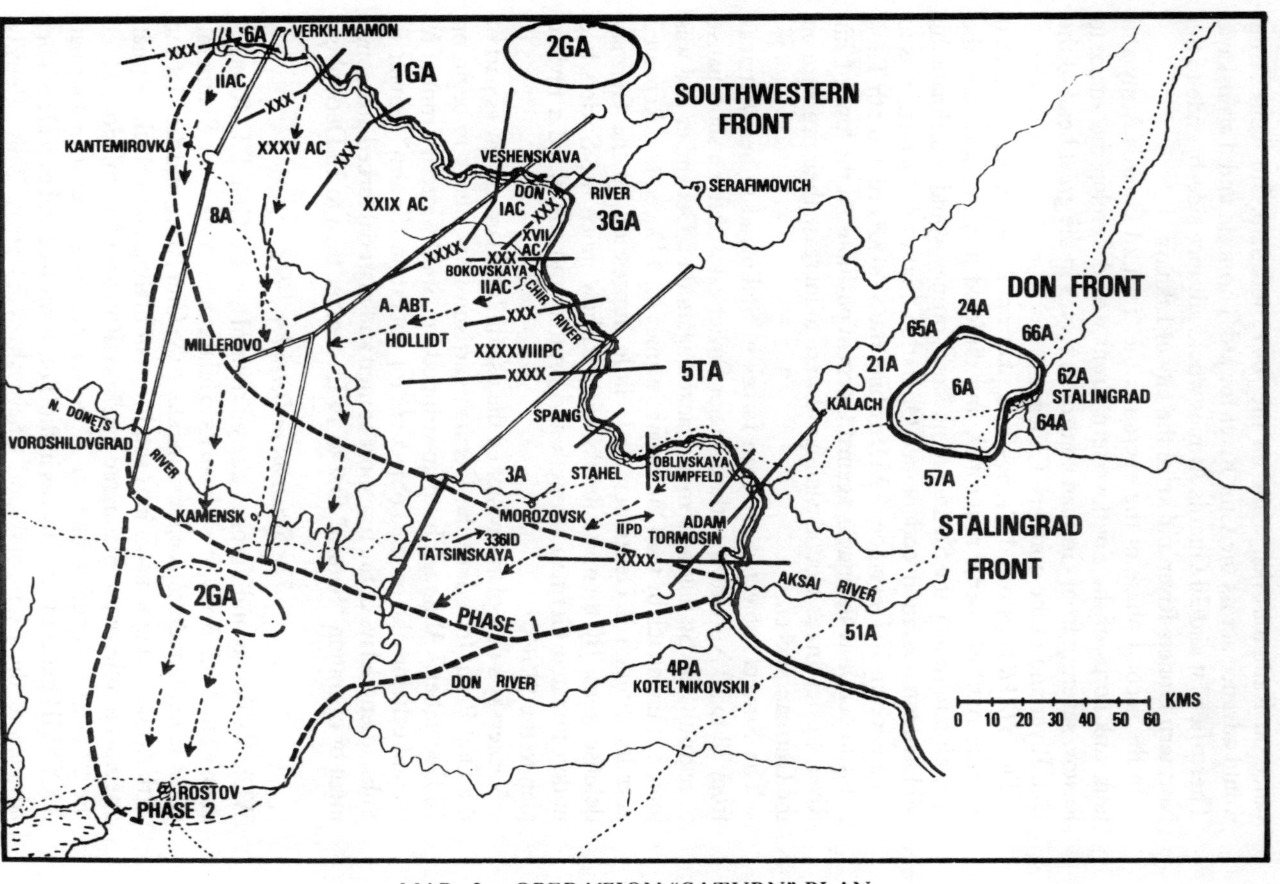

MAP 2. OPERATION "SATURN" PLAN

6th Army would cover the Southwestern Front's right flank with an advance on Kantemirovka, while on the *front's* left flank 5th Tank Army would advance across the Chir River toward Tormosin and Tatsinskaya. Thereafter 1st and 3d Guards Armies would advance side-by-side to the Northern Donets River and seize the city of Likhaya.

In the second phase of the operation the fresh 2d Guards Army and four tank corps of the Southwestern Front would develop the attack to Rostov, severing from German control its forces in the great bend of the Don River and in the northern Caucasus.[5]

The *STAVKA* approved Vasilevsky's plan on 2 December, promised him the reinforcements requested, and directed him to coordinate the operation to reduce the Stalingrad pocket. Voronev would coordinate the Middle Don operation, codenamed Operation "Saturn." "Saturn" was to commence on 10 December.[6] Meanwhile, the *STAVKA* ordered 5th Tank Army to continue its attacks against German positions on the lower Chir River. Soviet forces around Stalingrad were to increase their pressure on the German pocket.

The Soviets subjected German forces in Stalingrad to heavy attacks from 28 to 30 November without major Soviet gains. After a short pause to regroup, the Stalingrad Front attacked again on 2 December and was joined in the attack by the Don Front's armies on 4 December. Repeated assaults through 8 December made little impression on the German defense lines. By then, Vasilevsky realized how much the Soviets had underestimated German strength and drafted and submitted a revised plan to the *STAVKA*.

Vasilevsky's new plan envisioned the use of 2d Guards Army as part of the Don Front to reduce the German garrison in an attack to begin on 18 December.[7] Although his plan stripped the Southwestern Front of its second echelon, the original objectives for operation "Saturn" remained. Subsequent delays in the transport of men and material forced postponement of operation "Saturn" first to 14 December then to 16 December.

The Situation in December 1942

While Vasilevsky and Voronev altered their plans, Lt. Gen. P.L. Romanenko's 5th Tank Army, fresh from its exhilarating victory in the Stalingrad encirclement, undertook operations along the Chir River, and the 51st and 57th Armies occupied positions southwest of Stalingrad to block German attempts to relieve the Stalingrad garrison. Romanenko's mission, which the *STAVKA* assigned to him on 27 November, was to destroy German XXXXVIII Panzer Corps forces in the Tormosin area and by 5 December advance to the Morozovsk and Chernyshkovskii areas. This offensive would eliminate the threat posed by German forces in the bridgehead they held across the Chir River at Nizhne–Chirskaya.

Romanenko's army consisted of six rifle divisions, two cavalry divisions, one tank corps, one separate tank brigade, and eight artillery regiments reinforced by four additional rifle divisions from 21st and 65th Armies. Its strength was about 70,000 men, 182 tanks, and 1,213 guns and mortars.[8] With this force Romanenko was to attack in a 60 kilometer sector from Oblivskaya to Rychkovskii against units of the German XXXXVIII Panzer Corps, which consisted of the 336th Infantry Division, the 7th Luftwaffe Field Division, the 11th Panzer Division, and the 403d Security Division.[9]

5th Tank Army opened its attacks on 2 December with infantry assaults on German positions at Oblivskaya, Surokovino, Rychkovskii, and Nizhne–Chirskaya. By nightfall on 3 December, with heavy losses, Soviet forces gained a bridgehead at Nizhnyaya Kalinovka but were unable to reduce the German bridgehead at Rychkovskii. That evening, Romanenko halted the assaults and regrouped his forces.

By 7 December the Soviets had completed regrouping and renewed their attacks using the 333d, 119th, and 258th Rifle Divisions in the Lisinskii–Surokovino sector, backed up by 1st Tank Corps (with a strength of 72 tanks), 3d Guards Cavalry Corps, and the 216th Tank Brigade. At 1600 hours the 1st Tank Corps and 333d Rifle Division secured Sysoyevskii and State Farm 79, while left flank army units reached Ostrovskii and Lisinskii. A masterful counterattack by German 11th Panzer Division and the 336th Infantry Division blunted the assault and drove Soviet forces back to their starting positions by 10 December. Although the 5th Tank Army assaults were poorly coordinated and failed to dislodge the Germans from the Tormosin region, they did tie down German forces and prevent a German counteroffensive from the Nizhne–Chirskaya area. As a result of 5th Tank Army's failures, on 9 December the *STAVKA* created 5th Shock Army (from 10th Reserve Army) and ordered it to join 5th Tank Army in attacks beginning on 11 December toward Tormosin and Tatsinskaya.[10] However, in the immediate future all such attacks failed.

On 11 December Vasilevsky received *STAVKA* approval for his plan to reduce Stalingrad (codenamed "Kol'tso"). The attack would begin on 18 December after 2d Guards Army had been fully deployed into the Stalingrad area. However, no sooner did the *STAVKA* approve the plan than the conditions changed. A strong German force (LVI Panzer Corps of 4th Panzer Army) began operations from Kotel'nikovskii toward the Aksai River and Stalingrad from the southwest.

The Genesis of Operation "Little Saturn"

The simultaneous news of 5th Tank Army's failures on the Chir River and the new German advance alarmed Vasilevsky who feared that his priority

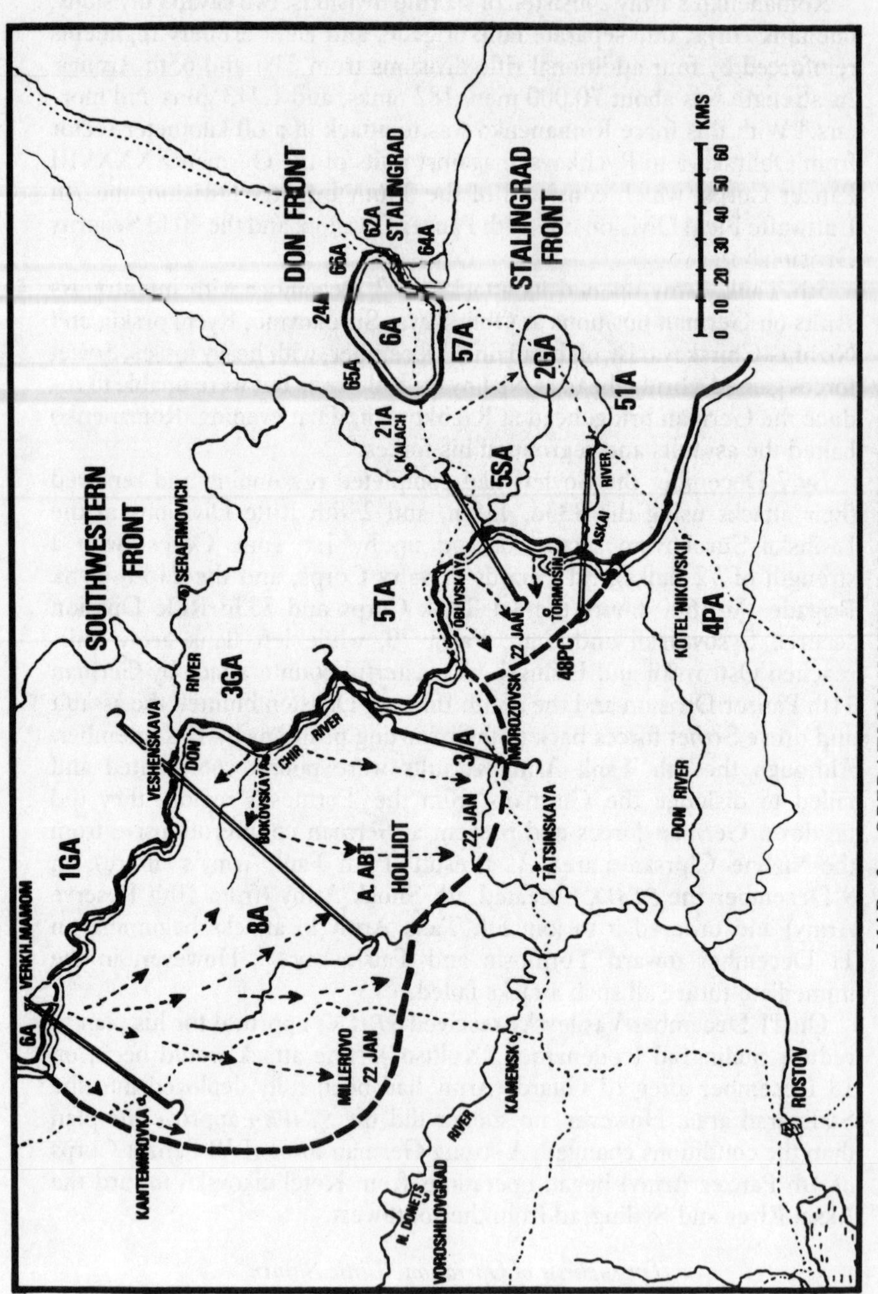

MAP 3. OPERATION "LITTLE SATURN" PLAN

mission of preventing German relief of Stalingrad might be in jeopardy if he did not act. Consequently, on 13 December Vasilevsky requested *STAVKA* permission to postpone Operation "Kol'tso" and instead, move 2d Guards Army southward to reinforce 51st and 57th Armies and deal with the threat of German LVI Panzer Corps. The *STAVKA* reluctantly approved his request, a decision which forced a revision of other Soviet plans as well.[11] Specifically, Operation "Saturn" was no longer feasible. That evening the *STAVKA* truncated the missions of units involved in "Saturn," thus giving birth to Operation "Little Saturn."

In essence, the new plan for Operation "Little Saturn" involved a shallower envelopment of Italian 8th Army and Army Detachment Hollidt by changing the attack direction of the Southwestern Front's armies to the southeast (see Map 3). Instead of attacking through Millerovo to Rostov, the new attacks would terminate at Morozovsk and Tormosin. Stalin's message to his commanders read:

> (To: Comrades Voronov, Golikov and Vatutin.)
>
> *First*: Operation "Saturn" aimed at Kamensk–Rostov was conceived when the overall situation was in our favour, when the Germans had no more reserves in the Bokovsk–Morozovsk–Nizhne Chirskaya area, when the [5th] tank army had made successful attacks in the direction of Morozovsk, and when it appeared that an attack from the north would be supported at the same time by an offensive from the east aimed at Likhaya. Under these circumstances it was proposed that 2d Guards Army should be swung into the area of Kalach and used to develop a successful advance in the direction of Rostov–Taganrog.
>
> *Second*: Recently, however, the situation has not developed in our favor. Romanenko [5th Tank] and Lelyushenko [3rd Guards Army] are on the defensive and cannot advance since the enemy has brought in from the west a number of infantry divisions and tank formations, which are containing the Soviet forces. Consequently, an attack from the north would not meet with direct support from the east by Romanenko, as a consequence of which an offensive in the direction of Kamensk–Rostov would meet with no success. I have to say that 2nd Guards Army can no longer be used for Operation "Saturn" since it is operating on another front.
>
> *Third*: In view of all this, it is essential to revise Operation "Saturn." The revision lies in the fact that the main blow will be aimed not at the south, but towards the southeast in the direction of Nizhnii–Astakhov, to exit at Morozovsk in order to take the enemy grouping at Bokovsk–Morozovsk in a pincer movement, to break into his rear and to destroy these forces with a simultaneous

blow from the east with the forces of Romanenko and Lelyushenko and from the north-west with the forces of Kuznetsov and mobile formations subordinated to his command. Filippov [Golikov: Voronezh Front] has as his assignment to help. Kuznetsov to liquidate the Italians [8th Army], get to the river Boguchar in the area of Kremenkov to set up a major covering force against possible enemy attacks from the west.

Fourth: The breakthrough will proceed in those sectors which were projected under Operation "Saturn." After the breakthrough, the blow will be turned to the south-east in the direction of Nizhnii–Astakhov–Morozovsk, breaking into the rear of the enemy forces facing Romanenko and Lelyushenko. The operation will begin December 16. The operation has the codename "Little Saturn."

Fifth: You must now operate without the 6th Mechanized Corps, meanwhile tank regiments are on their way to you. This is because the 6th Mechanized Corps has been handed to the Stalingrad Front for use against the Kotelnikovskii enemy concentration. In place of 6th Mechanized Corps you can get a tank corps from Filippov, 25th or 17th [Tank Corps].

Vasil'yev (Stalin)[12]

In accordance with this directive Voronev, Lt. General F.I. Golikov, commander of the Voronezh Front, and Vatutin altered their plans. During the discussions among the commanders Vatutin consistently and persuasively argued for a return to the original objectives of Plan "Saturn" and requested that 17th Tank Corps be made available to his 1st Guards Army rather than to 6th Army. After considerable argument, on 14 December the *STAVKA* ordered Vatutin to comply with the *STAVKA* guidance for Operation "Little Saturn."[13]

Initial Front Planning

Under Voronev's supervision the *front* commanders worked out the missions they would fulfill (see Map 4). Vatutin's Southwestern Front's 1st Guards Army and 3d Guards Army, in cooperation with the Voronezh Front's 6th Army, would surround and destroy Italian 8th Army and Army Detachment Hollidt and develop the offensive through Nizhnii–Astakhov to Morozovsk. The Voronezh Front's 6th Army, by the fourth day of the operation, was to secure the operation from German attacks from the west. Vatutin shifted 1st Guards Army's main attack eastward and reinforced its shock group with three tank corps, all of which would attack from the Osetrovka bridgehead. To avoid a major regrouping of forces, both *fronts* would attack in the same sectors as were designated in plan "Saturn."[14]

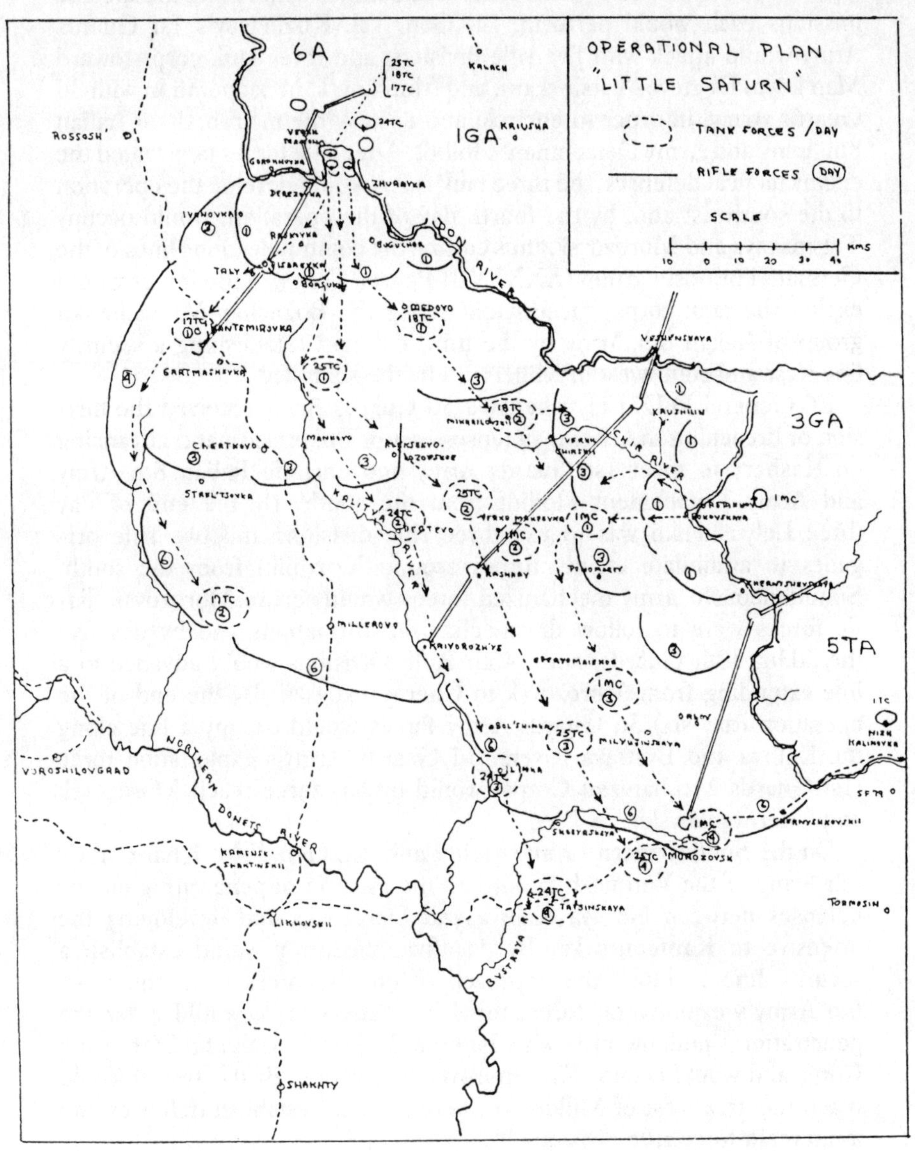

MAP 4. OPERATIONAL PLAN "LITTLE SATURN"

Vatutin coordinated with his army commanders concerning the specific missions each would perform. Lt. Gen. V.I. Kuznetsov's 1st Guards Army would attack with five rifle divisions and three tank corps toward Man'kovo, Degtevo, Tatsinskaya, and Morozovsk, in cooperation with 3d Guards Army, in order to encircle and destroy the main body of Italian 8th Army and Army Detachment Hollidt. After rifle forces penetrated the enemy tactical defenses, the three tank corps would develop the operation to the southeast and, by the fourth day of the operation, would occupy Tatsinskaya and Morozovsk, thus cutting the communications lines of the German Tormosin group (XXXXVIII Panzer Corps). Rifle forces would exploit the tank corps' success, encircling the Boguchar–Mikhailovskii group of Italian 8th Army by the third day and establishing a security line west and southwest of Millervoro by the sixth day.

Lt. General D.D. Lelyushenko's 3d Guards Army received the mission of breaching the enemy defenses east of Bokovskaya and advancing on Kashary to meet 1st Guards Army and encircle Italian 8th Army and Army Detachment Hollidt from the south. By the end of day three Lelyushenko was to use three rifle divisions and two rifle brigades to annihilate enemy forces around Kruzhilin from the south. Simultaneously, army mechanized forces would secure Morozovsk. Rifle forces were to follow the mechanized formations and by day five the 203d, 50th Guards, and 346th Rifle Divisions would advance to a line extending from Morozovsk to Chernyshkovskii. By the end of the operation (day six) 3d Guards Army forces would occupy a line along the Kalitva and Bystraya Rivers. 3d Guards Army's exploitation force (1st Guards Mechanized Corps) would by day three reach Morozovsk and Chernyshkovskii.[15]

On the Southwestern Front's right flank, Lt. Gen. F.M. Kharitonov's 6th Army of the Voronezh Front had the mission of penetrating enemy defenses between Novaya Kalitva and Derezovka and developing the offensive to Kantemirovka. By day five, the army would establish a security line to block the approach of enemy forces from the west. 6th Army's exploitation force, the 17th Tank Corps, would enter the penetration simultaneously with 1st Guards Army's 18th and 25th Tank Corps and would occupy Kantemirovka by day one. By day two, it would reach the area west of Millerovo where it would establish defenses and await main force rifle divisions.[16]

To the south, Romanenko's 5th Tank Army was to cooperate with Lt. Gen. M.M. Popov's 5th Shock Army to destroy enemy units in the Nizhne Chirskaya and Tormosin areas and to block a German advance from that region toward Stalingrad. Subsequently, the army would advance through Morozovsk and I'linka to the Tatsinskaya–Likhaya region. In addition, 5th Tank Army's 346th Rifle Division would cooperate

1. Colonel General N.F. Vatutin, Southwestern Front commander, December 1942.

with 3d Guards Army and would envelop Chernyshevskaya from the south.

Subsequent Front Planning

These initial missions, like earlier ones, quickly fell victim to changing circumstances. German progress toward Stalingrad on the Kotel'nikovskii axis increased the importance and urgency of the Middle Don offensive. Consequently, on 15 December the *STAVKA* altered 1st Guards Army's mission by placing more stringent time requirements on the advancing forces. According to this revision, by the third day of operations, 1st Guards Army was to use its 4th Guards Rifle Corps to establish a security line running south of Chertkovo, and southeast along the Kalitva River to the region northeast and east of Millerovo. By the fourth day, 4th Guards Rifle Corps would concentrate for an advance eastward to link up with 3d Guards Army or southward toward Millerovo.

The new orders affected the mission of two of 1st Guards Army's tank corps as well. 18th Tank Corps, by the second day, was to reach Mikhailovskii and Verkhne–Chirskii and cooperate with 6th Guards Rifle Corps and the 153d Rifle Division in destroying Italian troops south of the Don River. Subsequently, the corps would advance toward either Chernyshkovskii or Kruzhilin. 25th Tank Corps was to reach the area north of Man'kovo by day one and then advance to Morozovsk.

In essence, these major and minor alterations to the original Plan "Saturn" reduced the importance of the operation from one with strategic aims of its own (the seizure of Rostov) to one which would assist in the reduction of enemy forces at Stalingrad. Only the immediate tasks remained essentially unaltered.

The operational timing for "Little Saturn" was critical to its overall success and was representative of the detail with which the Soviets planned operations at that stage of the war. While the *fronts* established parameters for the accomplishment of close missions (three days) and distant missions (six days) they also thoroughly planned the timed development of the operation on each day which worked out as follows:

Day 1

penetration of tactical defenses

introduction of 17th, 18th, and 25th Tank Corps in order to widen the penetration

advance of rifle units to a depth of 20–30 kilometers

exploitations of tank/mechanized units to a depth of 40–60 kilometers

encirclement of the Kruzhilin and Bokovskaya enemy groups by 3d Guards Army.

Day 2

introduction of 24th Tank Corps and 1st Guards Mechanized Corps encirclement of the main Italian force by 1st Guards Army's 6th Guards Rifle Corps and 18th Tank Corps

advance of:

18th, 25th, and 24th Tank Corps to Verkhne–Chirskii and Degtevo regions

3d Guards Army (three rifle divisions) to Kruzhilin

3rd Guards Army (two rifle divisions) south toward Morozovsk

1st Guards Mechanized Corps to west of Ponomarov

17th Tank Corps through Taly and Kantemirovka to area west of Millerovo

Day 3

destruction of the enemy at Chertkovo, Man'kovo, and Verkhne–Chirskii by 18th Tank Corps, 6th Guards Rifle Corps, and 153d Rifle Division

destruction by 3d Guards Army of the enemy at Kruzhilin

advance of:

17th Tank Corps, 24th Tank Corps, and 25th Tank Corps to a line from Millerovo to I'linka

1st Guards Mechanized Corps to Chernyshkovskii

1st Guards Army main force to Degtevo

establishment of a 6th Army security line through Chertkovo and southeast along the Kalitva River

Day 4

complete the destruction of enemy forces south of the Don River by 1st Guards Army and 3d Guards Army

advance of:

24th Tank Corps to Tatsinskaya

25th Tank Corps to Morozovsk

1st Guards Mechanized Corps to Morozovsk and Chernyshkovskii

14th Rifle Corps and 203d Rifle Division (3d Guards Army) to support the tank and mechanized corps

6th Army to a line from Novaya Kalitva west of Kantemirovka and Millerovo

1st Guards Army (two rifle divisions) to a line through Chertkovo and along the Kalitva River

The overall depth of tank corps missions ranged from 150 kilometers for 17th Tank Corps to 250 kilometers for 25th Tank Corps. The corps would traverse this distance in a period of from two to four days, respectively. Rifle units would destroy main enemy units within four days and, in six days, would reach a line running from Ivanovka, Chertkovo, I'linka, Tatsinskaya, and Morozovsk to Chernyshkovskii.

Area of Operations

Operation "Little Saturn" would take place in a rectangular region 140 kilometers wide and 210 kilometers deep, bounded on the north by the Don River, on the south by the Northern Donets River, on the east by the Chir River, and on the west by the Derkul River (see Maps 5–6). The Russians characterized the terrain throughout the region as open hilly plateau land with sparse vegetation. Western Europeans would call it flat. Numerous tributaries of the major rivers crisscrossed the area, and frequent deep gullies or gorges (*balkis*) scarred its landscape. Often these *balkis* had steep banks and were well suited to serve as anti-tank obstacles or natural cover for anti-tank defenses. Although the region appeared ideally suited for armored operations, much of it was inaccessible for mechanized units and, moreover, severely compartmentalized.

There were many rivers in the region, but aside from the four major ones on its perimeter, most were dry or shallow. In December all small rivers were frozen except the Bogucharka, which had to be bridged. All other rivers could be crossed by all types of forces. The Don and Northern Donets Rivers, normally unfordable, had frozen surfaces in December, but the ice could be, and often was, broken up by explosive charges. The Don ranged from 200–350 meters in width from Novaya Kalitva to Veshenskaya with higher ground being located on the south (west) bank of the river. Engineer work was necessary in order for forces to cross the rivers on the thin or broken ice.

The transportation and communications network in the region was poorly developed, so existing rail lines were extremely important. The main rail line north of the Don River ran from Povorino to Liski and from Povorino to Stalingrad at a distance of 100 to 150 kilometers from the river. The nearest railhead to the river was at Kalach, 70 kilometers from the front lines. A more extensive rail net served the region south of the Don River. There, the most important lines ran from Rossosh south through Millerovo to Likhaya, from Voroshilovgrad to Millerovo and from Likhaya through Tatsinskaya and Morozovsk to the region north of Tormosin.

A dense network of dirt roads served the region, but there were no paved roads. Most of these roads ran along valleys and gorges, and they were dotted with villages and towns. All of these villages represented severe obstacles for military movements, especially if defended.

The weather in December 1942 in the great bend of the Don River was favorable for combat by warmly dressed troops. Temperatures ranged from 0–10 degrees centigrade and never fell below –20 degrees centigrade. Snow cover was light (less than 15 centimeters), and there were no heavy snow drifts. Consequently, road and cross country mobility was good for both sides.[17]

OPERATION "LITTLE SATURN"

MAP 5. MIDDLE DON, AREA OF OPERATIONS

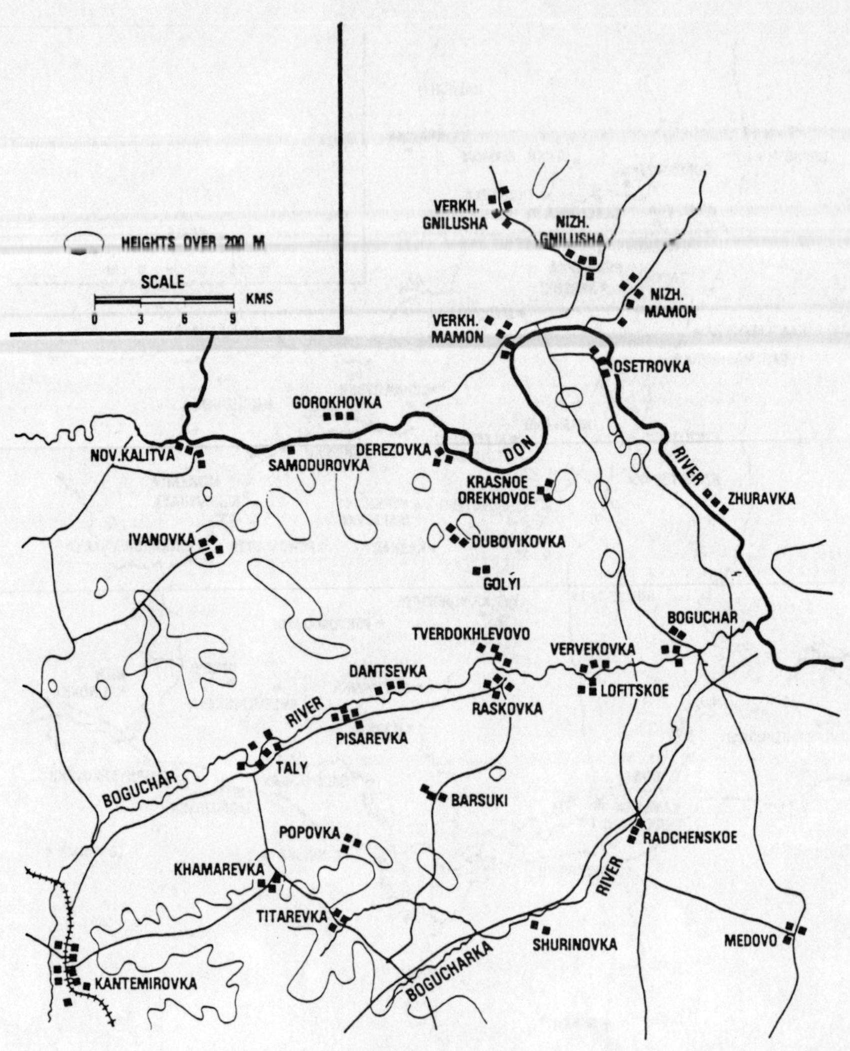

MAP 6. MIDDLE DON, AREA OF OPERATIONS, DON RIVER BRIDGEHEAD

OPERATION "LITTLE SATURN"

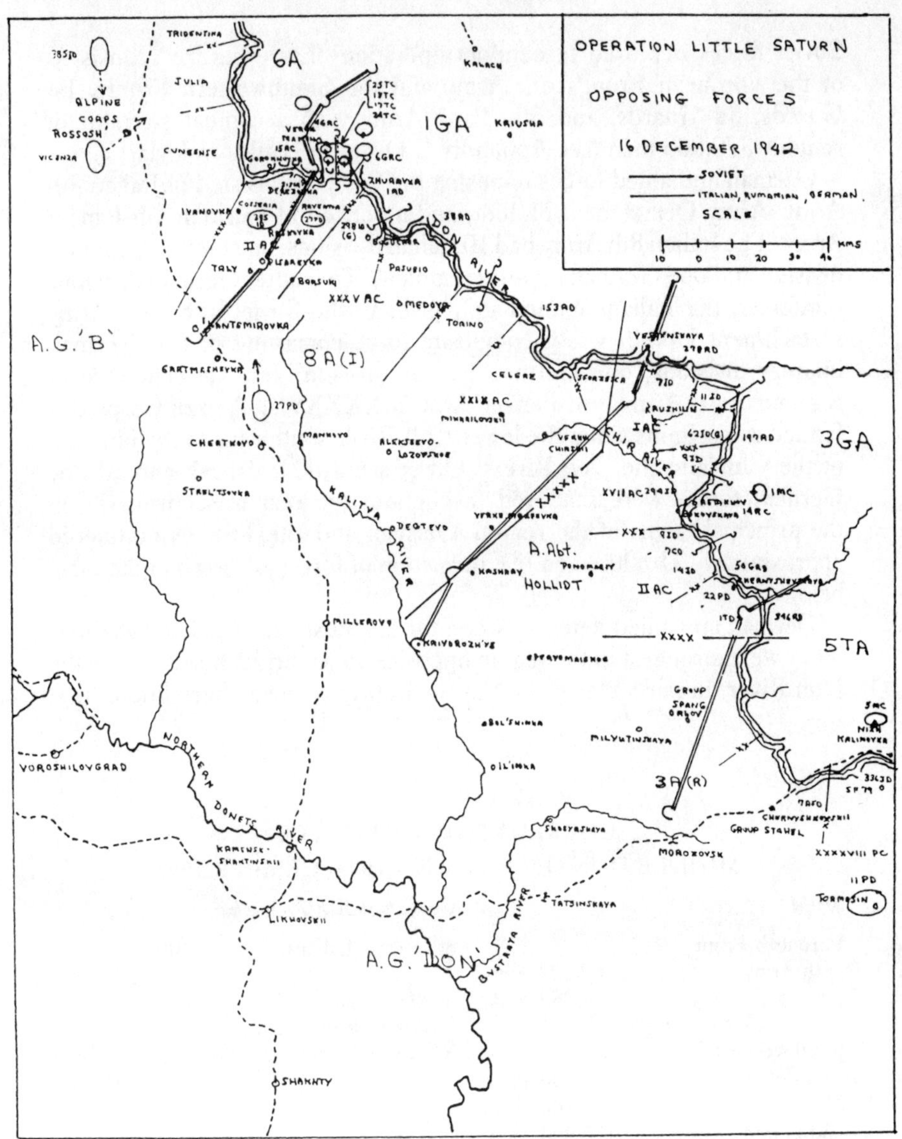

MAP 7. MIDDLE DON, OPPOSING FORCES, 16 DECEMBER 1942

Opposing Forces

Soviet forces deployed to conduct operation "Little Saturn" consisted of the Voronezh Front's 6th Army and the Southwestern Front's 1st Guards, 3d Guards, and 5th Tank Army with a combat strength of roughly 370,000 men (see Appendix 1, Order of Battle, and Map 7).

German and allied forces opposing the Soviets consisted of Italian 8th Army, Army Detachment Hollidt, and a portion of German 4th Panzer Army. The Italian 8th Army had 10 Italian divisions, one German infantry division and one German infantry regiment. Two other German divisions reinforced the Italians immediately prior to the Soviet offensive. Army Detachment Hollidt was a composite force consisting of two German infantry divisions, one German panzer division, and the remnants of Rumanian 3d Army. 4th Panzer Army's XXXXVIII Panzer Corps defended in positions along the lower Chir River southward to the junction of the Chir and the Don Rivers. Other security, logistical, and ad hoc German forces were scattered throughout the rear area, primarily in the principal towns of the region. German and allied forces numbered approximately 210,000 men.[18] Correlation of forces is shown in the table below.

German and allied defenses were, for the most part, rigid and shallow. They were strongest in the region opposite Soviet bridgeheads across the Don River, in particular from Novaya Kalitva to Boguchar. There, first

CORRELATION OF FORCES
MIDDLE DON OPERATION – 16 DECEMBER 1942

Soviet		*German/Italian/Rumanian*	
Voronezh Front		8th Army (Italian)	100,000 men
6th Army	60,200 men		50 tanks
	250 tanks	*A. Abt.* Hollidt/	
		3d Army (Rumanian)/	
Southwestern Front		XXXXVIII Panzer Corps	110,000 men
1st Guards Army	110,700 men		70 tanks
	504 tanks		
3d Guards Army	110,000 men		
	234 tanks		
5th Tank Army	90,000 men		
	182 tanks		
Total	370,000 men	1.8:1	210,000 men
Strength	1,170 tanks	10:1	120 tanks

defensive positions were 5–6 kilometers deep and based on a well organized fire system interspersed with engineer obstacles. Italian and German divisions defended 15–25 kilometer sectors and generally deployed with four battalions in the first defense line and two battalions in the second.

Regimental defenses were 2–3 kilometers deep and consisted of platoon and company strong points prepared for all round defense. There were no second defensive positions or rear positions, and most sectors lacked any mobile reserve. Infantry platoons reinforced by anti-tank guns, mortars, engineers, and flame thrower elements usually manned strong points organized for all round defense supported by machine gun or rifle fire from adjacent trenches. Most strong points were located in villages or on heights and were constructed of earth and timber pill boxes. Anti-personnel and anti-tank obstacles and single and double rows of barbed wire covered the positions, and the defenders placed anti-tank mines on all armored approaches to the strong points. Each strong point covered a distance of 1–1.5 kilometers, and multiple strong points covered one another throughout the depth of the tactical defense. Artillery was located along roads and near villages. Most anti-tank guns were located forward within each of the strong points or in the depth of the battalion defensive position.

The Italians and Germans created major strong points around larger towns, using stone walls and buildings in order to anchor the defense. One to two infantry companies with ten to sixteen mortars, and two to four batteries of 75 mm and 105 mm guns manned each major strong point. Artillery and mortar fire from division or corps artillery provided additional cover.[19]

The major flaw in defenses along the south bank of the Don River was that they lacked depth and mobile operational reserves. Once the defense was penetrated, only rapid withdrawal could ensue. Defenses were even weaker in Army Detachment Hollidt's sector along the Chir River, because German and allied units had occupied the positions only since late November. Here there were no solid permanent fortifications, nor was there an elaborate system of strong points. Instead, there were full depth trenches with light overhead cover, dugouts, mine fields, barbed wire, and a few earth and timber strong points. Defenses in this region were strongest in the Bokovskaya, Krasnokutskaya, and Chernyshevskaya sectors which were occupied by German divisions.

The Soviets had a significant artillery and armor superiority over the defending German and allied forces. Each Italian and German division had an artillery regiment. In addition, the 9th Artillery Group of Italian 8th Army provided support throughout the Italian corps' sectors. In Italian 8th Army's sector (less the Alpine Corps), the artillery and mortar strength by Italian count was 355 tubes (less German strength) against

2. Soviet infantry advancing.

3. Assault at dusk.

over 2,000 for the Soviets. The discrepancy in armor was even more marked – the Italians had but fifty tanks, and these were not deployed in the region where the Soviets committed the bulk of their armor (700 tanks).[20] Similar disparities in strength existed in Army Detachment Hollidt's sector and XXXXVIII Panzer Corps' sector although in these sectors Soviet armored superiority was not as pronounced.

Army Planning

Army commanders began their planning in accordance with the missions assigned them by *front*. Army planning was a dynamic process that involved frequent consultation between army commanders and supporting unit staffs. Detailed army level planning for operation "Little Saturn" commenced on 14 December and continued virtually up to the time of the attack (16 December). During this short period army commanders addressed questions of task organization, operational formation for combat, cooperation between units and coordination of supporting arms.

6th Army

Vatutin ordered Kharitonov's 6th Army to force the Don River between Novaya Kalitva and Derzovka and develop the offensive to the southwest in order to secure the right flank of 1st Guards Army. Kharitonov deployed his army with a heavy first echelon of four rifle divisions (the 172d, 267th, and 305th of 15th Rifle Corps and the 127th Rifle Division), a light second echelon of one rifle division (106th) and an exploitation echelon (17th Tank Corps). His rifle corps and rifle divisions deployed in a single echelon of regiments and the subordinate rifle regiments in two echelons of battalions.

Kharitonov decided to conduct his main attack on the army's left flank with the 15th Rifle Corps and the 127th Rifle Division as the army shock group. The shock group would attack between Novaya Kalitva and the woods east of Derezovka, overcome the enemy main defensive positions, and secure Novaya Kalitva and Pisarovka by the evening of the first day. Subsequently, the 15th Rifle Corps, led by Major General P.P. Poluboyarov's 17th Tank Corps, would develop the offensive toward Taly and Ivanovka. By the end of the fourth day 15th Rifle Corps would reach positions west of Kantemirovka with the 127th Rifle Division covering its right flank. Poluboyarov's tank corps would begin an exploitation from the Taly area at the end of the first day and, by the end of the second day, it would establish defensive positions at Voloshino west of Millerovo.

4. Infantry advancing under air cover.

5. Pursuit in the steppes.

6th Army created high tactical force densities in its main attack sector to generate a rapid advance by concentrating four rifle divisions, one tank corps, one tank brigade, two tank regiments, eight artillery regiments, and five multiple rocket launcher battalions in a nine kilometer penetration sector. This resulted in tactical densities of one rifle division per 2.25 kilometers of front and twelve infantry support tanks and sixty-two guns and mortars per kilometer of front. The remaining division of 6th Army deployed on an extended 18 kilometer front.[21]

1st Guards Army

Kuznetsov's 1st Guards Army was ordered to penetrate enemy defenses in the Verkhnii Mamon bridgehead sector; develop the offensive to Chertkovo and Degtevo; and, with 3d Guards Army, encircle Italian 8th Army. Subsequently, his tank corps (18th, 24th, and 25th) would exploit to Tatsinskaya and Morozovsk. Kuznetsov created a strong first echelon of six rifle divisions (4th Guards Rifle Corps' 195th, 41st Guards Rifle Divisions; 6th Guards Rifle Corps' 1st, 44th Guards Rifle Divisions: 38th and 153d Rifle divisions), a weak second echelon of one rifle division (35th Guards), and a strong exploitation echelon (18th, 24th, 25th Tank Corps). His rifle corps formed in a single echelon of divisions; but his rifle divisions and regiments, because of the heavy defenses, formed in two echelons.

Kuznetsov decided to launch his main attack on the army right flank where he concentrated the 4th Guards Rifle Corps and most of 6th Guards Rifle Corps. The 4th Guards Rifle Corps was to establish a security line from Chertkovo southeast to the Kalitva River by the third day of the operation, while the 6th Guards Rifle Corps would cooperate with the 153d Rifle Division and 18th Tank Corps to surround and destroy enemy units at Boguchar, Meshkov, and Mikhailovskii by the end of the fourth day. 6th Guards Rifle Corps would then advance on either Nizhnii–Astakhov or Millerovo and the 153d Rifle Division would revert to army reserve.

Kuznetsov planned to commit his mobile forces in a time-phased sequence. Major General B.S. Bakharov's 18th and Major General P.P. Pavlov's 25th Tank Corps would join battle at the end of the first day to complete the penetration of the tactical defenses, and on the following day, joined by Major General V.M. Badanov's 24th Tank Corps, the tank corps would begin the exploitation. While the bulk of army forces swept southeast, two rifle divisions (195th and 41st Guards) would cover the army right flank in close coordination with 6th Army units.

Kuznetsov concentrated five rifle divisions and three tank corps in his 18 kilometer penetration sector. His two remaining rifle divisions deployed on a 127 kilometer front. This concentration created tactical densities of one rifle division per 3.5 kilometers of front and six infantry support tanks and 75 guns and mortars per kilometer of front. In fact, Kuznetsov's superiority was 4:1 in battalions; 7.3:1 in machine guns; over 7:1 in artillery; and up to 10:1 in tanks.[22]

3d Guards Army

Lelyushenko's army was to penetrate enemy defenses in the Bokovskaya sector, advance to Verkhne–Chirskii, Pervomaiskoye and Bol'shinka, encircle the enemy Kruzhilin group, and subsequently develop the offensive southward. His exploitation force (1st Guards Mechanized Corps and 22d Motorized Rifle Brigade) would advance on Verhkne–Chirskii and Kashary, and then spearhead the advance southward.

Lelyushenko deployed seven rifle divisions (278th, 197th, 159th, 203d, 266th, 14th Guards, 50th Guards), one rifle brigade (94th), and three tank regiments in first echelon and one rifle brigade (90th) and one tank brigade in second echelon. Lieutenant General I.N. Russiyanov's 1st Guards Mechanized Corps served as the exploitation echelon. Rifle corps and divisions formed in single echelon and rifle regiments in two echelons.

14th Guards Rifle Corps with four rifle divisions was to launch the army main attack in the Bokovskaya sector. After penetrating the tactical defenses, by the end of the first day 14th Guards Rifle Corps and 22d Motorized Rifle Brigade would encircle the enemy Kruzhilin group. On the second day 22d Motorized Rifle Brigade would dispatch its forward detachment westward to link up with 1st Guards Army's tank forces. Two 3d Guards Army rifle divisions (203d and 50th Guards) would advance southward along the west bank of the Chir River and envelop Chernyshevskaya while one rifle division (278th) and one tank brigade would launch a secondary attack from the Don River southwest toward Kruzhilin.

1st Guards Mechanized Corps would advance westward in the 14th Guards Rifle Corps' sector on the first day. The following day it would turn southeast and advance toward Ponomarev, Milyutinskaya and Morozovsk. By evening on the fourth day the corps' main force was to reach Morozovsk while one of its brigades enveloped Chernyshevskaya from the southwest. After army rifle forces destroyed the axis forces around Kruzhilin, they would advance southwest to support the mobile forces.

Lelyushenko concentrated four rifle divisions, his mechanized corps, one motorized rifle brigade, and one rifle brigade in his 14 kilometer main attack sector. His remaining three divisions occupied a 75 kilometer sector. This concentration produced tactical densities in the penetration sector of one rifle division per 3 kilometers of front and 7–8 infantry support tanks and 70 guns and mortars per kilometer of front.[23]

5th Tank Army

On the Southwestern Front's left flank, Romanenko's 5th Tank Army again prepared to assault German positions on the Chir River. His force was to attack Nizhne–Chirskaya and Tormosin in cooperation with 5th Shock Army. Subsequently, both armies would develop the offensive westward to Morozovsk and Likhaya in conjunction with 3d Guards Army. Romanenko formed his army in a single echelon of rifle divisions (no rifle corps) and designated Major General M.V. Volkov's newly assigned 5th Mechanized Corps and 8th Cavalry Corps to exploit the rifle forces' success.

Artillery Support

The *STAVKA* allocated Vatutin and Golikov fifty-six artillery regiments and nine regiments and six separate battalions of multiple rocket launchers (*Katushas*) from the *STAVKA* reserves to supplement the existing twenty-six divisional artillery regiments. However, it remained to be seen how many of these units could actually deploy forward given the weak transportation net, and how well the Soviets could supply them once they deployed forward. The Soviets allocated the artillery to armies on the following basis:[24]

Army	*Reinforcing Regiments*	*Total Regiments*
6th	15	19
1st Guards	10* (12 battalions)	17
3rd Guards	17	25
5th Tank Army	14	21
Total	56	82

*eight not present for the attack

This quantity of artillery (about 5,600 tubes) provided Soviet forces a superiority in field guns of about 7:1, in mortars of about 4:1, and in anti-tank guns of about 3:1.[25] However, the allocation of the artillery was unbalanced and did not properly weight the main attack. 1st Guards Army had but seventeen regiments, less than each of the other three armies. Moreover, eight of the army's regiments failed to arrive by the time of the assault (only two of 9th Artillery Division's regiments arrived on time). Thus, 1st Guards Army began the attack against the most heavily defended enemy sector with the lowest artillery densities in the Southwestern Front.

Army commanders attached most of their reinforcing artillery to individual rifle corps or rifle divisions. 1st and 3d Guards armies created small army artillery groups (AAGs) of one to two artillery regiments and an anti-tank reserve of ad hoc composition. 6th Army organized no army artillery group but, instead, created long-range artillery groups of one to two regiments in the 15th Rifle Corps and in the 127th Rifle Division. Anti-tank reserves of 6th Army were within the 15th Rifle Corps and 127th Rifle Division.

The *front* chiefs of artillery de-centralized control of army's artillery and each corps and division coordinated its own fires. Ultimately, this lack of centralization inhibited the massing of fires; and further unbalanced artillery support. For example, 1st Guards Army's 44th Guards, 38th Guards, and 1st Rifle Divisions had infantry support groups of one or two artillery regiments while each 6th Army first echelon division had three or four regiments firing in support.[26]

The Soviets planned a ninety minute artillery preparation prior to the attack. Divisional artillery groups were to fire to a depth of 6 kilometers and army artillery groups to a depth of 12–14 kilometers. The preparation was to begin with a five minute barrage by all weapons and end with a fifteen minute barrage. In between the barrages would be seventy-five minutes of aimed fire delivered against targets detected during the reconnaissance or identified at the last minute.[27] The Soviets attached the bulk of their tank destroyer artillery units to tank and mechanized forces, and for several days prior to the attack those units trained with units they would support. Tank destroyer units participated in the preparation and supported the attack as well. Although the bulk of army artillery was decentralized, army commanders did retain centralized control over multiple rocket launcher units. Army reconnaissance sought to identify precise targets for these units to engage during the initial and final stages of the preparation. In addition, the Soviets used them to strike enemy command posts, to support the introduction of the mobile groups, and to prevent enemy maneuver and counterattacks.

Transportation and supply problems hindered the deployment of artillery units and inhibited their ability to deliver effective fire. The poor road net slowed the forward movement of artillery, and the shortage of trucks (*STAVKA* transport regiments were at 50 to 60 percent strength) created a shortage of ammunition which persisted throughout the operation.[28] Artillery units deployed into forward firing positions at night during the four days preceding the attack. All deployments were supposed to be completed one day prior to the preparation which was scheduled to begin at 0800 on 16 December. A limited number of guns conducted registration for all of the artillery, and wire laying and survey were also done in advance.

The Soviets used anti-aircraft units to protect key troop assembly areas, artillery concentrations, command posts, and airfields.[29] They also attached anti-tank and anti-aircraft artillery units to tank and mechanized forces in order to improve their survivability in the depth of the enemy defenses.[30] Anti-aircraft and anti-tank artillery units generally suffered from the same general deficiencies in ammunition supply that other artillery units suffered from.

Air Support

Air armies concentrated their support in *front* and army main attack sectors. Maj. Gen. K.N. Smirnov's 2d Air Army supported the Voronezh Front's 6th Army while Maj. Gen. S.A. Krasovsky's 17th Air Army supported the Southwestern Front. The two air armies consisted of twelve aviation divisions with 309 combat aircraft* and 106 PO-2 and P-5 reconnaissance and liaison aircraft which also served as night bombers.[31]

Before the offensive began, aircraft struck at enemy airfields and railroad stations to disrupt enemy resupply and troop movements. Bombers and assault aviation aircraft concentrated their preoffensive efforts on daylight raids against targets in the Tatsinskaya, Morozovsk, and Likhaya regions. Night bombers struck enemy headquarters and reserve concentrations. During the preparation, bombers and assault aircraft would strike command and control points, enemy troop concentrations, artillery positions, and strong points. Some fighter aircraft units were to provide cover for advancing infantry and support the introduction of the tank and mechanized corps into the penetration. Remaining aircraft would engage targets under the army commanders' control and bombers would continue to strike deeper targets and block the movement of enemy reserves. During the exploitation phase assault aviation was to concentrate on striking withdrawing enemy forces to hasten their collapse.

Front and air army commanders supervised the development of the aviation support plan. Control of all aircraft would be centralized during the preparation and penetration phases. Thereafter, when mechanized and tank forces entered the penetration and during exploitation, control of aircraft would be decentralized; and air units would be subordinate to army commanders. During this phase, 1st and 3d Guards Armies would each be supported by one mixed aviation corps. Operational groups (with radios) from the aviation corps would deploy to army command posts to establish liaison and communications between supporting and supported units.

Bomber units would remain under the centralized control of the air army commanders throughout the operation. When the tank and mechanized corps began their exploitation, part of the aviation assets would be directly subordinate to them. While this provided some close support for

*72 bombers, 135 assault aircraft, and 97 fighters

mobile forces, it also prevented subsequent concentrated use of those air assets. To provide better air support, the Soviets built airfields closer to the front and moved aircraft into them.[32]

Command, Control and Communications

The *STAVKA* supervised planning for Operation "Little Saturn" through its representatives (initially Vasilevsky and, after 3 December, Voronov). Planners conferred with one another by using a direct telephone line between the *STAVKA* and the *front* command posts and through personal contact. A 3 December meeting of Voronov, Vatutin, Golikov, Kharitonev, and Kuznetsov worked out the details of *front* and army missions, coordination between *fronts*, support for the Don River crossing, masking of preparations, anti-aircraft defense, and the order of commitment of exploiting forces. Although the concept of the operation later changed, this had little effect on lower level army preparations, which continued unabated after 4 December. The *front* commanders personally reviewed all army commanders' plans.

During the planning phase the *front* commanders and their staffs communicated with their armies in person or by written message, and radio and wire communications were strictly forbidden. After operations commenced the Soviets relied primarily on radio and wire links to communicate with rifle forces and special radio stations mounted on vehicles to communicate with mobile groups. However, the long distances required use of numerous relay stations to keep those communications intact.

Although army commanders retained control over mobile forces operating in their sectors, the *front* commanders retained overall direction of these mobile forces. This dual control, necessitated by the fluid situation and facilitated by the use of radios, ultimately caused some confusion. Overall the Soviets rigidly centralized command and control during the penetration phase of the operation but decentralized command and control thereafter. Throughout the operation inadequate supplies of communications equipment and the inability of officers to use it properly had an adverse effect on command and control.

Security

The Soviets stressed strict secrecy during planning, concentration, and regrouping of forces at all levels of command. Only key personnel knew the contents of operational plans and all *front* orders were delivered orally or by liaison officers. Commanders or chiefs of staff wrote all documents by hand in a single copy. The Soviets prohibited telephone and wire communications and permitted radio operators only to receive transmissions. All movement to assembly areas occurred at night or during fog or snowstorms, and *front* commanders mandated strict light discipline. In order to deceive the enemy, armies moved units and conducted reconnaissance on secondary directions where the enemy could observe it. Because of these measures the Soviets were certain that, although the enemy knew of general offensive preparations, he did not know the time, location, or form of the attack.[33]

Engineer Support

A large scale offensive launched out of small bridgeheads across several major rivers required considerable engineer support. Additional bridging was necessary to build up the forces within the bridgeheads and then support operations once the bridgeheads expanded. Consequently, engineers secretly built six bridges across the Don River into the Osetrovka bridgehead, prepared twelve special reinforced ice crossings, and used local materials (from houses in villages) to build sleds and boats necessary to transport artillery and supplies across the river. They also constructed several 8 to 10 meter portable bridges for use in crossing smaller rivers in close proximity to the Don (primarily the Bogucharka River). 1st Guards Army assigned engineer battalions equipped with track bridge carrying trucks to support the 18th and 25th Tank Corps.[34]

The Soviets also planned extensive engineer support for the assault against enemy defensive positions. Armies established and trained shock teams and obstacle clearing detachments to operate in advance of the infantry. These units would assist divisional sappers in clearing passage through minefields and wire obstacles and would mark minefields left in the rear of advancing forces. Destruction groups, made up of sappers equipped with explosives, were formed to destroy bypassed enemy strong-points. In addition to these combat tasks, the engineers prepared army, corps, and division command posts, observation posts, and artillery firing positions.

Logistical Support

One of the most difficult problems Soviet staff planners faced in this, and in subsequent operations, was that of providing logistical support. Supplies for the Southwestern Front, and for the Voronezh and Don Fronts as well, came to Kalach, 70 kilometers from the front, by single rail line from stockpiles and depots 150–200 kilometers away. The shortage of rail lines forced the Soviets to use a limited number of dirt roads to supplement the rail lines. In turn, a shortage of vehicles, heavier than usual vehicular traffic, and occasional December thaws combined to produce chaotic and undependable road conditions which reduced the quantity of supplies reaching the front.

The Southwestern Front organized one main supply distribution point and created forward supply dumps along the railroad. The main army supply dumps were served by three army railheads; and, to facilitate resupply, each army received priority use of a specific rail sector. There were also forward dumps for each type of supply located in the immediate army area. Through this system the Soviets amassed adequate supplies for the initial stage of the operation.[35] However, if the operation exceeded the six day planning figure, a severe strain on the logistical system would result. In fact, the distribution system prevented adequate supply of artillery ammunition for the preparation and adequate resupply of units throughout the offensive.[36]

Slow or tardy assembly of units also occurred because of transportation difficulties. When the offensive began concentration of units was incomplete. By that time most of the 9th Artillery Division, several tank regiments, and the rear service units of several new 1st Guards Army formations had not yet arrived. In addition, the Soviets had not completed many aspects of the supply plan.

Preoffensive Training

The troop training period for Operation "Little Saturn" began on 27 November when units learned that some sort of attack would occur. It accelerated after 3 December when Plan "Saturn" emerged and became even more focused after 13 December when "Little Saturn" took concrete form. Early in this period (1–3 December) the Southwestern Front received two new rifle corps (six rifle divisions), three tank corps, and a large number of support units. This involved considerable work to build unit cohesion. After 5 December, when Plan "Saturn" emerged and army commanders issued corps and division commanders their mission, units began systematic troop preparations.

Front directives ordered training and actual practical exercises in such matters as concentration of forces; cooperation of armor, infantry, and air units; consolidation of secured lines; repulse of tank attacks; anti-aircraft defense using individual weapons; field radio communications; encirclement maneuvers; and winter operations (in particular, equipment maintenance). In addition, the Soviets trained special teams to penetrate enemy defenses during battle to disorganize enemy command and control and disrupt his communications. Each of these teams had a specially trained "navigator" officer to guide it to its assigned objective. Commanders at all levels and in every type of force conducted a personal reconnaissance of their area of operations. Division commanders did so personally with regimental commanders, and regimental commanders did the same with battalion commanders. General Kuznetsov of 1st Guards Army conducted personal reconnaissance with his units down to regimental level. In the rear area the tank corps conducted map and field exercises which simulated the actual operational plan. For example, 25th Tank Corps arranged eight tactical staff rides and five tactical exercises.[37]

Conclusions

Soviet planners of operation "Little Saturn" sought to destroy Italian 8th Army and Army Detachment Hollidt and to prevent German interference with the all important Stalingrad reduction operation. They concluded that the best way to achieve those aims was to conduct an envelopment operation against enemy forces along the Don and Chir rivers by rapidly penetrating enemy tactical defenses and by committing mobile forces to advance rapidly into the depth of the enemy defenses. During the exploitation, mobile forces would advance parallel to the front and disrupt enemy command and control. The operation would last five to six days with rifle forces advancing 20–30 kilometers per day and mobile forces 50–70 kilometers per day. Ultimately Soviet forces would cut critical German lines of communications and draw German forces away from the Stalingrad battle. *STAVKA* control of the operation would produce comprehensive planning and would insure the operation remained focused on strategic objectives. Despite the careful preparations, logistical problems would remain the most serious impediment to both the planning and the conduct of the operation.

On 11 December, with planning in its final phase, the reconnaissance phase of the operation began.

The Reconnaissance Phase (11–15 December)

The Soviets conducted reconnaissance from 11–15 December throughout the entire Southwestern Front sector by using companies and battalions of first echelon rifle divisions to create new bridgeheads or expand existing bridgeheads, to determine the location and strength of enemy defenses, and to confuse the enemy regarding the location of the Soviet main attack.[38]

In 6th Army sector, 127th Rifle Division's battalions destroyed Italian security posts and penetrated the Italian forward defensive sector. Although Italian and German counterattacks ultimately forced the Soviets to commit the entire 127th Rifle Division the Soviets retained the expanded bridgehead.[39] 6th Army used this new bridgehead as a jumping-off position for first echelon battalions and moved the 82d and 212th Tank Regiments and additional artillery into the bridgehead to support the army attack.

A reconnaissance battalion of 1st Guards Army's 195th Rifle Division attacked at 0445 11 December and seized the fortified heights east of Krasnoye–Orekhovoye. After repelling repeated enemy counterattacks, on the evening of 14 December an entire rifle regiment moved into the bridgehead where, after being subjected to heavy bombing, it was joined on the night of 15 December by a second rifle regiment.[40] By 0500 on 16 December both regiments were prepared for the attack. Reconnaissance efforts in other sectors produced similar results.

The Soviet reconnaissance prompted changes in enemy troop dispositions. From 13 to 15 December the German 385th Infantry and 27th Panzer Divisions moved forward to reinforce Italian defenses, and the German 387th Infantry Division accelerated its movement into the Italian army sector from the north. On 14 December elements of the German 537th Infantry Regiment (385th Infantry Division) occupied positions in the Samodurovka area while the German 318th Infantry Regiment tried repeatedly to reduce the Soviet Derezovka bridgehead. In essence, two regiments of the German 385th Infantry Division and the 318th Infantry Regiment took over the forward defenses of the Cosseria Division and part of Ravenna Division. The Italian units then deployed to new positions in the rear to serve as a reserve and to launch counterattacks to support the Germans.

By the morning of 16 December other German units had arrived to bolster the Italian defenses. Group Schuldt (with two SS Police battalions) was at Kantemirovka, Group Fegelein (two SS battalions, one battery of assault guns, and the 15th Police Regiment) was west of Kantemirovka, the 27th Panzer Division was supporting the Ravenna Division, and one battalion of the 298th Infantry Division was supporting the Pasubio Division.[41] In addition, by 18 December the 387th Infantry Division was to move into a sector just north of Kantemirovka.

The Penetration Operation (16–18 December)

The First Day: 16 December 1942

The Soviet offensive began at 0800 on 16 December with a ninety minute artillery preparation fired throughout all of 1st Guards Army's Sector (see Map 8). Thick fog rising from the Don Valley prevented observation and adjustment of artillery fire and forced the Soviets to resort to unaimed area fire. This fire left many enemy firing positions and strong points untouched. In 3d Guards Army sector poor visibility caused the Soviets to fire the preparation late and for a total of only fifty minutes. In addition, poor weather forced the Soviets to cancel the aviation offensive

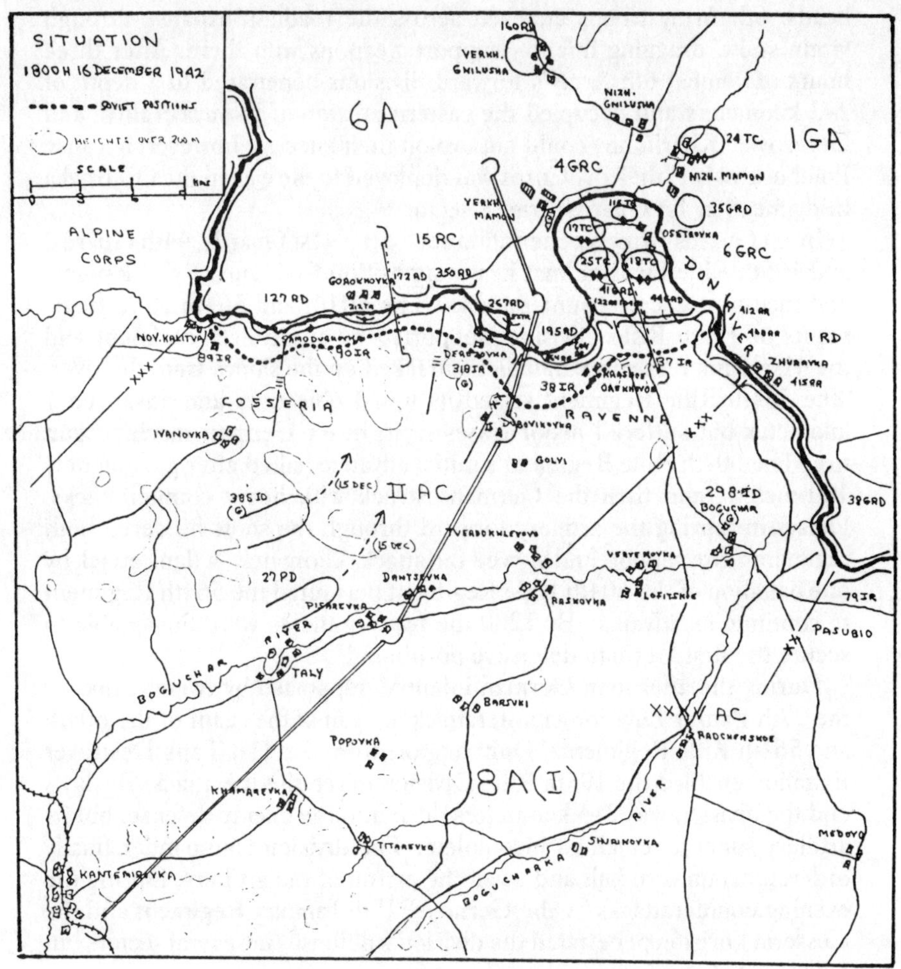

MAP 8. MIDDLE DON, SITUATION, 1800 16 DECEMBER 1942

throughout the *front* sector. Aircraft were unable to operate until midday on 16 December.

Despite the problems with the preparation, the Soviet infantry advanced at 0930 as the artillery shifted its fires to the enemy's second defensive positions. 6th and 1st Guards Army forces crossed the ice of the

Don River and advanced from the Samodurovka and Osetrovka bridgeheads. 6th Army troops attacked across the roadless expanse through virgin snow, dragging infantry support weapons with them. After three hours of combat 6th Army's forward divisions penetrated to a depth of 2–3 kilometers and occupied the eastern portion of Novaya Kalitva and Derezovka. Kharitonov could not exploit their success, however, because Poluboyarov's 17th Tank Corps was deployed to the east in the Osetrovka bridgehead in 1st Guards Army's sector.[42]

In 1st Guards Army's penetration sector the 41st Guards, 44th Guards, and 195th Rifle Division met heavy opposition from enemy firing points and incessant enemy counterattacks. The 604th and 564th Rifle Regiments of 195th Rifle Division, supported by an artillery regiment and the 41st Tank Destroyer Battalion, attacked up the slopes from the river. The 564th Rifle Regiment seized its initial objectives and advanced 1 kilometer but suffered major losses from heavy German machine gun fire. The 604th Rifle Regiment's initial advance halted after gaining only 100 meters, and then the Germans struck with heavy counterattacks. Delays in moving the artillery forward through the snow hindered both regiments' fire support and slowed the attack. Ultimately, a flank attack by one battalion of the 604th Rifle Regiment permitted the 564th Regiment to continue its advance. By 1200 the two regiments were finally able to secure the first German defensive positions.[43]

During the afternoon German infantry, supported by twenty tanks of the 27th Panzer Division counterattacked against the seam of the 604th and 564th Rifle Regiments. Only support from the 41st Tank Destroyer Battalion enabled the 195th Rifle Division to repulse the attack. By day's end the division was 2–4 kilometers deep into the enemy defense, but its artillery support remained incomplete. The division commander finally ordered his units to halt and await the arrival of the artillery. During the evening counterattacks by the German 318th Infantry Regiment and the Cosseria Division penetrated the division's defenses in several sectors but failed to dislodge it from its positions.[44]

Further east other 1st Guards Army divisions fared worse than the 195th. The 41st Guards Rifle Division attacked with its 122d and 124th Rifle Regiments in first echelon, supported by an artillery regiment and four batteries of the 407th Tank Destroyer regiment. On the right flank the 122d Guards Rifle Regiment attacked across 300–400 meters of snow-covered ground toward Krasnoye–Orekhovoye and secured the first enemy trench line. On the left the 124th Guards Rifle Regiment seized the first heights to its front, but was halted by fire from enemy artillery units which had not been knocked out by the preparation. The division committed its second echelon 126th Rifle Regiment but still was unable to secure the enemy positions. In the course of 16 December the

41st, and 44th Guards Rifle Divisions as well, struggled forward to a depth of only 300 to 2000 meters.[45] 1st Rifle Division had an equally difficult time in its attack sector on the army left flank along the Don River opposite German positions at Zhuravka.

With the army attacks stalled, Vatutin ordered Kuznetsov to commit the forward elements of the 18th, 25th, and 17th Tank Corps to assist the infantry in penetrating the defenses. On 16 December, the tank strength of the three corps was: 17th Tank Corps, 168; 18th Tank Corps, 160; 25th Tank Corps, 160 tanks. At 1100 the lead brigade of 18th and 25th Tank Corps advanced without sufficient engineer reconnaissance and lost twenty-seven tanks to exploding mines.[46] The tank units were forced to halt while sappers cleared lanes through the minefields. Kuznetsov decided to commit his armor the next day with individual tank brigades designated to support each rifle division in the reduction of enemy strong points.

Lelyushenko's 3d Guards Army forces had even less success on 16 December than those of Kharitonov and Kuznetsov. After the abbreviated artillery preparation, Soviet infantry attacked without the support of aimed artillery fire or air strikes. 14th Rifle Corps' divisions struck German 62d and 294th Infantry Divisions' defenses at Krasnokutskaya and Bokovskaya. Combat in the 203d Rifle Division's sector was representative of the first day's action in 3d Guards Army's sector. In the division's sector opposite Krasnokutskaya, the Chir River was 20–30 meters wide and covered by thick ice. The steep, snow-covered western bank was sprinkled with buildings that the Germans had converted into strong points. However, dense high brush covered the Soviet approaches to the river and provided some protection for advancing Soviet forces. The 619th and 592d Rifle Regiments of the division were to lead the attack, supported by the 1243d Tank Destroyer Regiment and two sapper battalions. The two regiments were to cross the river, secure Krasnokutskaya Station, and penetrate German tactical defense. After the fifty minute artillery preparation, the two regiments assaulted through lanes cut to the river by the sappers. Using wooden ladders, facines, and axes, they crossed the river; mounted its western bank; and, covered by machine gun fire, gained a lodgement in Krasnokutskaya. In bitter house-to-house fighting, the 2d Battalion, 592d Rifle Regiment finally penetrated to the railroad station.

Meanwhile, on the 592d Rifle Regiment's left flank, the 610th Rifle Regiment occupied a hill south of Krasnokutskaya and repulsed a battalion-sized German counterattack. At 1300 the 610th Rifle Regiment was attacked by an enemy company to its front and by another force supported by tanks advancing on its left flank. At 1500 a third counterattack supported by German aircraft and tanks forced the regiment to deploy all of its battalions on line. The heavy enemy attacks forced some Soviet troops to break formation and run, only to be cut down by enemy tank fire. Since defensive supporting fires were insufficient to stop the German tank attack, the division commander called for artillery support from the neighboring 50th Guards Rifle Division. However, that division was itself under heavy attack and unable to provide help. Only by the use of a battery of 45mm anti-tank guns and direct fire from supporting artillery did the Soviets finally halt the German attack. That evening at 2100 the 592d Rifle Regiment in Krasnokutskaya had one battalion cut off in a counter-attack by Rumanian units and elements of the 22d Panzer Division. As a result of the intense enemy pressure and heavy losses, the remainder of the regiment withdrew across the Don River to its initial attack positions.[47]

To the south, on the 203d Rifle Division's left flank, the 50th Guards Rifle Division assaulted across the Chir River. Despite capturing the first German trenches, the division could advance no further; and it also had its hands full repulsing strong German counterattacks. Lelyushenko watched from his army observation point located nearby as the attacks disappeared into the fog.[48] Disheartened by the lack of progress in this and in other sectors, he resolved to do better on the second day.

Thus, on 15 December a combination of circumstances disrupted Soviet efforts to accomplish their missions. Weather conditions impeded the artillery preparation and the air offensive, although the fog did provide some cover for the infantry assault. Supply difficulties and movement problems inhibited full concentration of artillery in the most critical sectors. Although reconnaissance provided Soviet commanders with a fair picture of enemy dispositions, the Soviets were unaware of the full extent of enemy reinforcements in the Verkhne-Mamon sector. Thus, instead of facing just the Italian Cosseria and Ravenna Divisions and the German 318th Infantry Regiment and 298th Infantry Division, they also faced the German 385th Infantry and 27th Panzer Divisions, in essence a defense twice as strong as anticipated. The ensuing lack of success led to premature commitment of the lead tank brigades, a move which also aborted when these brigades ran into enemy minefields. 3d Guards Army's assault units were similarly stymied in the critical Bokovskaya and Krasnokutskaya sectors. In other areas smaller Soviet forces made limited gains which, because of German reinforcements (Pasubio sector) or because of the limited size of the Soviet force, the Soviets could not exploit.

Already, by the end of the first day the Soviets were seriously behind schedule in fulfilling their offensive timetable. On the evening of 16–17 December commanders made adjustments to correct the situation. In particular, they prepared for the systematic use of tank forces cooperating with infantry to achieve the penetrations necessary for the offensive to develop successfully.

The Second Day: 17 December 1942

On the morning of 17 December, after a renewed artillery preparation, the Soviet infantry resumed its advance, this time accompanied by tanks from the 17th, 18th, and 25th Tank Corps, against German and Italian defenses anchored on a string of strongpoints running from Novaya Kalitva to Boguchar on the Don River (see Map 9).[49] Soviet divisional artillery supported the infantry and tank assault because the 9th Artillery Division regiments were still unavailable. The Soviets committed their tank corps consecutively. The tank brigades of Bakharov's 18th Tank Corps and Pavlov's 25th Tank Corps advanced first, followed by the corps' motorized rifle brigades. Then Poluboyarov committed his tank brigades on the right flank of the 18th and 25th Tank Corps toward Dubovikovka and Golyi. Badanov's 24th Tank Corps followed in the wake of these units. (24th Tank Corps had 159 tanks.) By late afternoon, Soviet air forces were finally able to lend their support to attacking Soviet forces.

While 6th Army's right flank divisions (127th, 172d, and 350th), supported by two tank regiments, advanced from Samodurovka and Derezovka toward Ivanovka, the 267th Rifle Division led by tanks of the 17th Tank Corps' 67th Tank Brigade pushed on toward Dubovikovka against heavy enemy resistance. 195th Rifle Division's 564th Rifle Regiment supported the 267th Rifle Division's attack on Dubovikovka while the remainder of the 195th advanced toward Golyi. On the 195th Rifle Division's left flank, the 41st Guards Rifle Division struck enemy strongpoints east of Golyi with its 126th Rifle Regiment while the 122d and 124th Rifle Regiments overcame weaker enemy resistance further east.

The Germans repulsed the first 267th Rifle Division and 67th Tank Brigade assaults on Dubovikovka. Consequentially, the 67th Tank Brigade blockaded the northeast side of the village with a rifle/machine gun battalion and moved to attack the strong point from the east and south. The 267th Rifle Division left one regiment to cover the front and sent two regiments on skis to accompany the flank attack of the armor. The joint attack by infantry on skis and by tanks with their sirens blaring dislodged the enemy from Dubovikovka. The 195th Rifle Division's 564th Rifle Regiment added its weight to the 267th's assault and shortly thereafter the division's 604th Rifle Regiment took Golyi.[50] The joint attack of the 267th and 195th Rifle Divisions and 17th Tank Corps unhinged the German–Italian defenses and permitted full commitment of Poluboyarov's

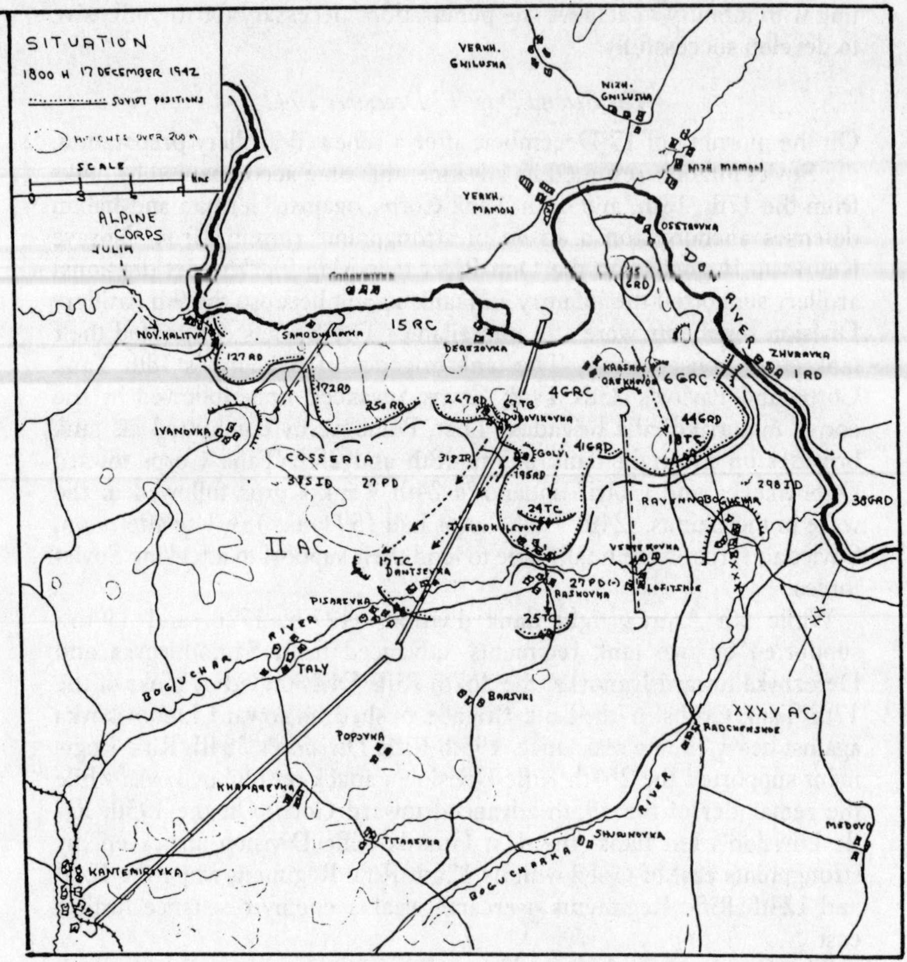

MAP 9. MIDDLE, DON, SITUATION, 1800 17 DECEMBER 1942

tank corps to an advance toward Pisarevka on the Boguchar River. Late on 17 December the 195th Rifle Division ordered its second echelon 573d Rifle Regiment to support the 17th Tank Corps' advance to the Boguchar River.

On the 195th Rifle Division's left flank, the 41st Guards Rifle Division, supported by the 25th Tank Corps' lead tank brigade, crushed German defenses and pushed German forces toward Tverdakhlevovo on the Boguchar River. By nightfall lead elements of 25th Tank Corps passed through Raskovka, on the south bank of the river. Meanwhile, the

44th Guards Rifle Division, with 18th Tank Corps in support, overcame heavy German opposition and pressed the German 298th Infantry Division back toward Boguchar.[51] The 1st Rifle Division continued to assault German positions opposite Zhuravka with only limited success.

By the evening of 17 December, after two days of heavy combat, 6th and 1st Guards Army's assault units had successfully penetrated the central sector of the German and Italian tactical defenses. The German 385th Infantry and Italian Cosseria Divisions, supported by elements of 27th Panzer Division, fought delaying actions back toward Ivanovka and Pisarevka, while the 298th Infantry and Ravenna Divisions, with other elements of 27th Panzer Division, defended to the southeast in positions around Boguchar and along the Boguchar River valley. Poluboyarov's 17th Tank Corps and Pavlov's 25th Tank Corps, supported by the 195th and 41st Guards Rifle Divisions, poured into the breach in the enemy defenses toward and across the Boguchar River. Badanov's 24th Tank Corps followed to begin a deep exploitation on 18 December.

Lelyushenko's 3rd Guards Army opened action on 17 December with a thirty minute artillery preparation concentrated on German positions in the Bokovskaya and Krasnokutskaya sectors after which his infantry forces resumed their assaults. Again, 14th Rifle Corps' divisions seized individual enemy strong points but could not fully smash through the tactical defenses. The 50th Guards Rifle Division seized the villagers of Fomin and Orekhov but was forced by heavy German counterattacks to relinquish them. Lelyushenko then committed the three brigades (1st, 2d, 3d Guards) of Russyanov's 1st Guards Mechanized Corps to reinforce the assault. The brigades managed to secure Astakov, but could advance no further. However, in heavy fighting the 20th Tank Regiment seized Staryi Zemstov (1 kilometer southeast of Bokovskaya) thus paving the way for the 1st Guards Mechanized Corps to outflank German positions at Bokovskaya from the northeast on the following day.[52]

On the evening of 17 December Vatutin ordered 6th and 1st Guards Armies to maintain pressure on the enemy throughout the night. Consequently, in the central sector where enemy resistance had waned 17th Tank Corps and 267th Rifle Division advanced to Pisarevka and the 25th Tank Corps and the 41st Guards Rifle Division crossed the Boguchar River and seized Barsuki in the army's rear. Having finally gained operating room for his tank forces, Vatutin ordered full exploitation to begin on the morning of 18 December.

The Third Day: 18 December 1942

At dawn 6th and 1st Guards Army, warding off attacks on their flanks, resumed the offensive (see Map 10). As rocket artillery units fired

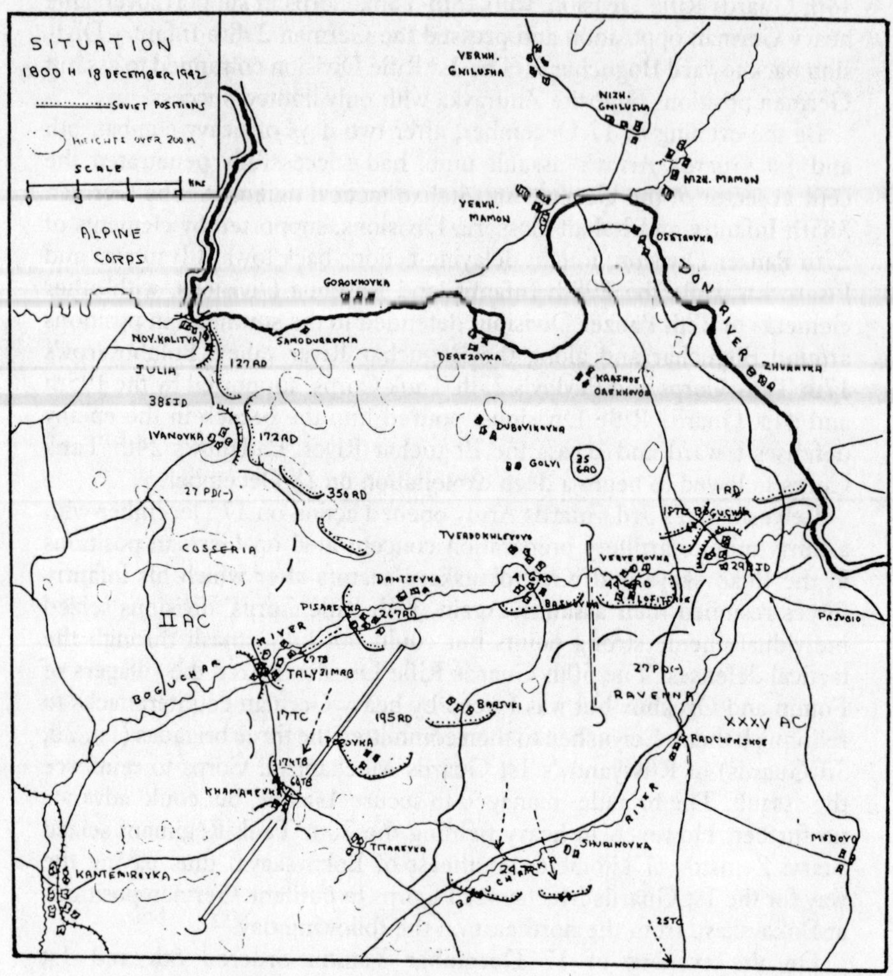

MAP 10. MIDDLE DON, SITUATION, 1800 18 DECEMBER 1942

concentrations on counterattacking enemy units to cover the advance, mobile forces led the attack to the south and southwest. Soviet forces again made their best progress in the central sector of the front where they crossed the Boguchar River and advanced to Taly and Shurinovka. The German 385th Infantry Division, now supported by Alpine Division Julia which had moved in to the Novaya Kalitva area from the north, and by 27th Panzer Division elements and the 14th SS Police Regiment, offered heavy resistance on the west side of the penetration but were threatened with envelopment by Poluboyarov's tank corps which moved against their southern flank. The 298th Infantry and 27th Panzer Divisions together with Ravenna Division units held on to defenses around the town of Boguchar and withdrew their left flank back toward the Bogucharka River, through an area now strewn with the human remnants of withdrawing Italian units and discarded equipment.[53] Soviet 38th Guards Rifle Division pressure on Pasubio Division defensive positions threatened the right flank of the German defenses at Boguchar.

Meanwhile Kharitonov's 6th Army divisions swung westward toward Ivanovka; and 17th Tank Corps' brigades, with the 267th Rifle Division trailing behind, advanced up the Boguchar Valley. At Taly, the corps ran into two Italian infantry battalions occupying defensive positions. The right column of Poluboyarov's tank corps composed of the 67th Tank and 31st Motorized Rifle Brigades, battled for Taly until noon on 19 December while other elements of the brigades bypassed the village and pushed on toward Kantemirovka. Poluboyarov's left column (174th Tank and 66th Tank Brigade) enveloped and secured Pisarevka, and during the night of 18–19 December the 66th Tank Brigade raced on toward Kantemirovka.[54] Meanwhile, the 127th, 172d, and 350th Rifle Divisions pushed against heavy resistance toward Ivanovka, thus lengthening the west flank of the penetration.

In 1st Guards Army sector the Soviet advance continued across the Boguchar River against slackening resistance. Italian and German troops had occupied hastily constructed defensive positions along the Boguchar. The 195th Rifle Division outflanked a portion of these defenses, and the main forces of 25th and 24th Tank Corps passed through the infantry lines and began the exploitation southward. The 41st Guards Rifle Division, on the 195th Rifle Division's left flank, consolidated its positions at Barsuki and also assisted the passage of lines by the tank corps. The German defenders, however, continued heavy resistance in the eastern portions of the Boguchar defensive sector. The 44th Guards and 1st Rifle Divisions, supported by the 18th Tank Corps, repeatedly assaulted German positions and by the evening of 18 December the 44th Guards Rifle Division had secured Lofitskoye and threatened Radchenskoye on the German 298th Infantry Division's left flank. This incessant pressure combined with threats against Pasubio Division on the 298th Infantry Division's right flank forced the 298th Infantry as well as remnants of 27th Panzer and Ravenna Division, to begin a withdrawal southward to Medovo.[55]

By the evening of 18 December Soviet forces had thoroughly ruptured enemy defenses opposite Verkhnii–Mamon. German and Italian forces (385th Infantry Division, 27th Panzer Division, Julia Division, Cosseria Division remnants, and lead units of 387th Infantry Division) held firmly to the western shoulder of the penetration but were themselves outflanked

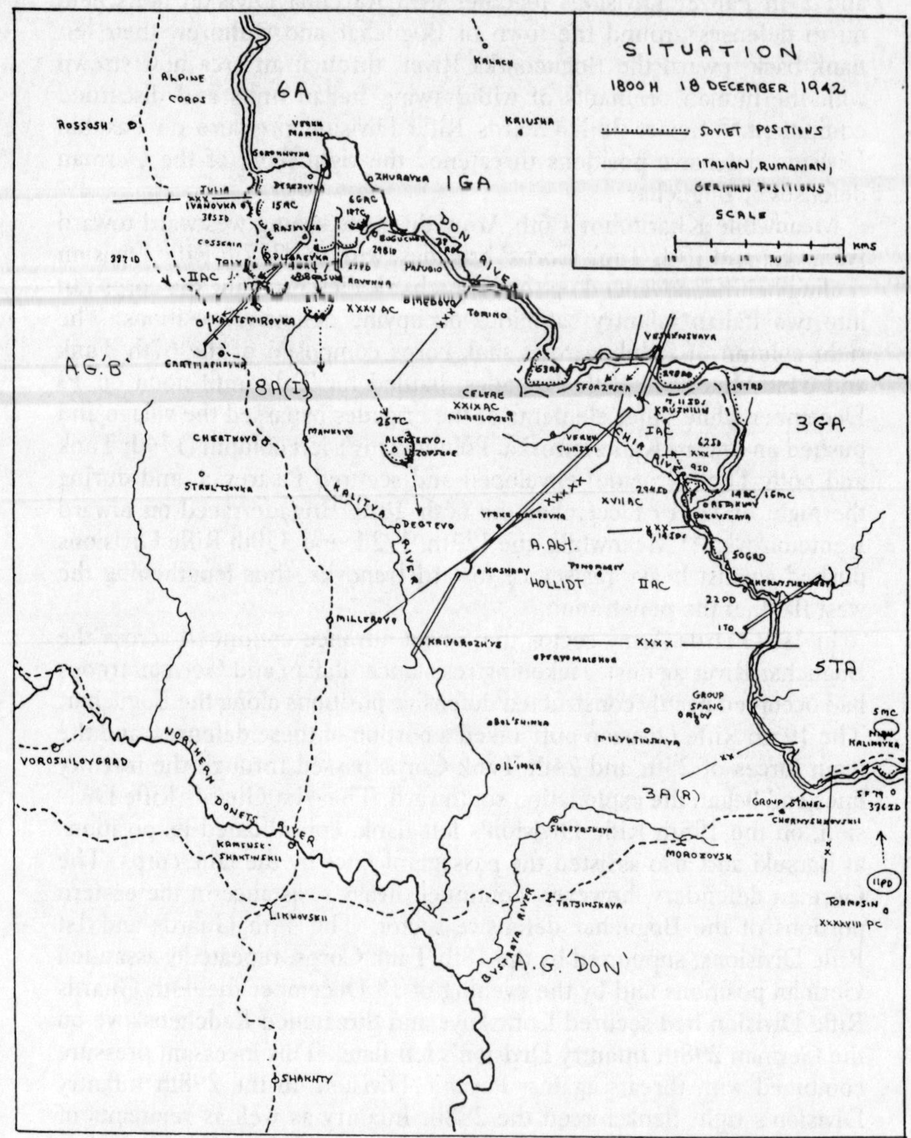

MAP 11. MIDDLE DON, SITUATION, 1800 18 DECEMBER 1942

in the direction of Kantemirovka. Soviet assaults from three sides forced the 298th Infantry Division, elements of 27th Panzer Division, and remnants of the Ravenna Division to withdraw southeast. Only scattered and shattered Italian forces remained in the central sector. Through these units passed the armor of the 18th, 25th, and 24th Tank Corps, followed by infantry formations which marched rapidly due south and southeast. Clearly, only the arrival of German reserves could stem the Soviet offensive torrent.

On 18 December enemy defenses also began to erode in 3d Guards Army sector (see Map 11). 14th Guards Rifle Corps' divisions, supported by the brigades of Russiyanov's mechanized corps, widened the small penetration northeast of Bokovskaya and capitalized on the collapse of 1st Rumanian Army Corps to advance northwestward toward Kruzhilin. In heavy fighting the 14th Guards Rifle Corps and 20th Guards Tank Regiment finally cleared Bokovskaya of German forces. Other brigades of Russiyanov's corps supported by rifle divisions moved northwest along the Chir River's north bank toward Kruzhilin, which was already under assault from the north and east by the Soviet 278th and 197th Rifle Divisions.[56] Rumanian 1st Army Corps units withdrew in disarray under the pressure, and the German 62d and 294th Infantry Divisions pivoted their defenses southwest of Bokovskaya to face the growing threat from the north.

In the Krasnokutskaya sector, however, the 203d Rifle Division continued to no avail its attempts to overcome German resistance, and farther south the 50th Guards Rifle Division made only limited progress. The collapse of Rumanian and German defenses in the northern sector of Army Detachment Hollidt spelled doom for 1st Rumanian Army Corps and German 62d Infantry Division and threatened to roll up the army detachment from the north. However, the firmness of German defenses between Krasnokutskaya and Chernyskevskaya permitted an orderly withdrawal of forces from this area southward toward arriving German reinforcements and bought time necessary for the construction of a coherent defense line in the Morozovsk region. The burning question was whether advancing Soviet tank corps could reach the Morozovsk–Tatsinskaya region in sufficient time and with sufficient strength to preempt creation of those defenses or disrupt them before they became strong enough to hold the Soviet tide.

Meanwhile, on the Southwestern Front's right wing Romanenko's 5th Tank Army resumed offensive operations. From 12 to 18 December Volkov's 5th Mechanized Corps and 321st Rifle Division forced the Chir River and, in heavy battles with XXXXVIII Panzer Corps' 11th Panzer and 336th Infantry Divisions, secured a bridgehead 15 kilometers wide and 5 kilometers deep near Dal'nepodgorovskii.[57] However, despite repeated attempts to extend the bridgehead, Romanenko's forces could not penetrate any deeper into German defenses.

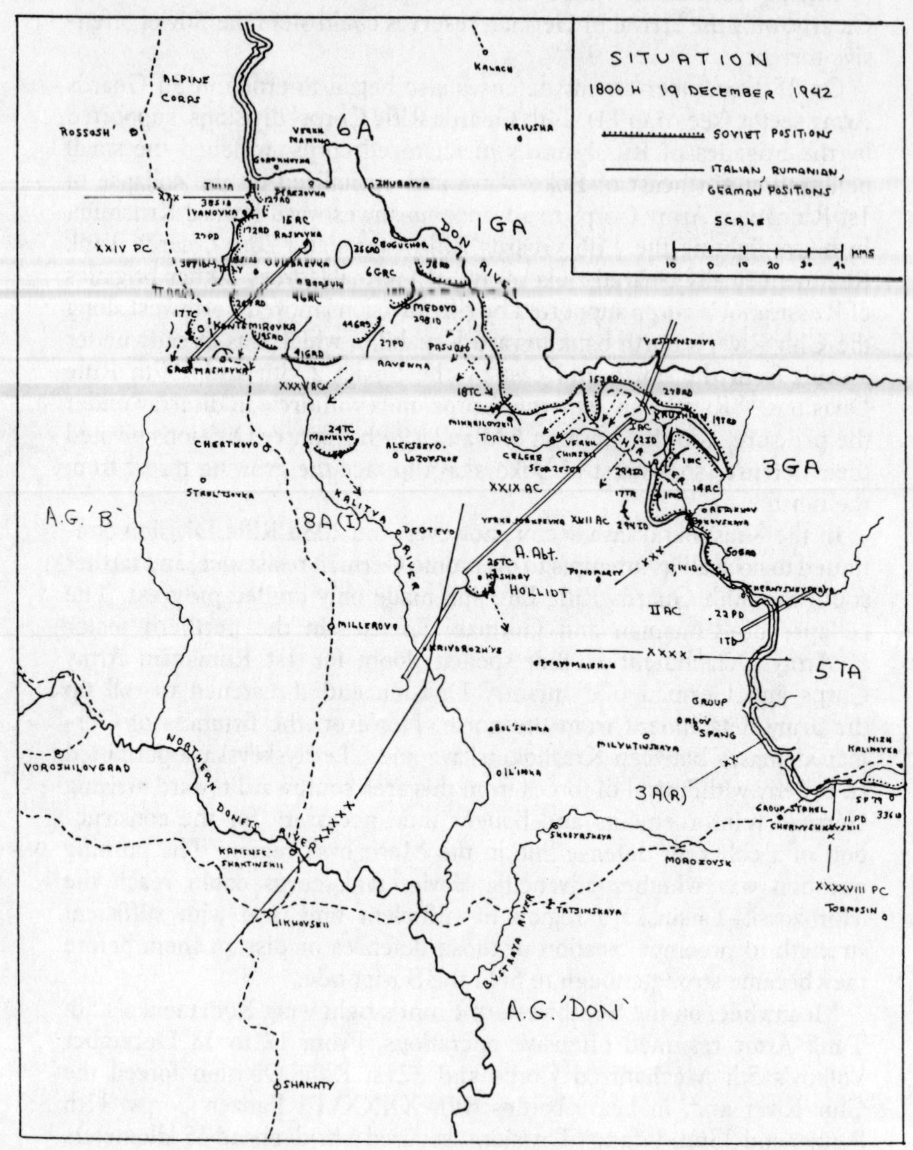

MAP 12. MIDDLE DON, SITUATION, 1800 19 DECEMBER 1942

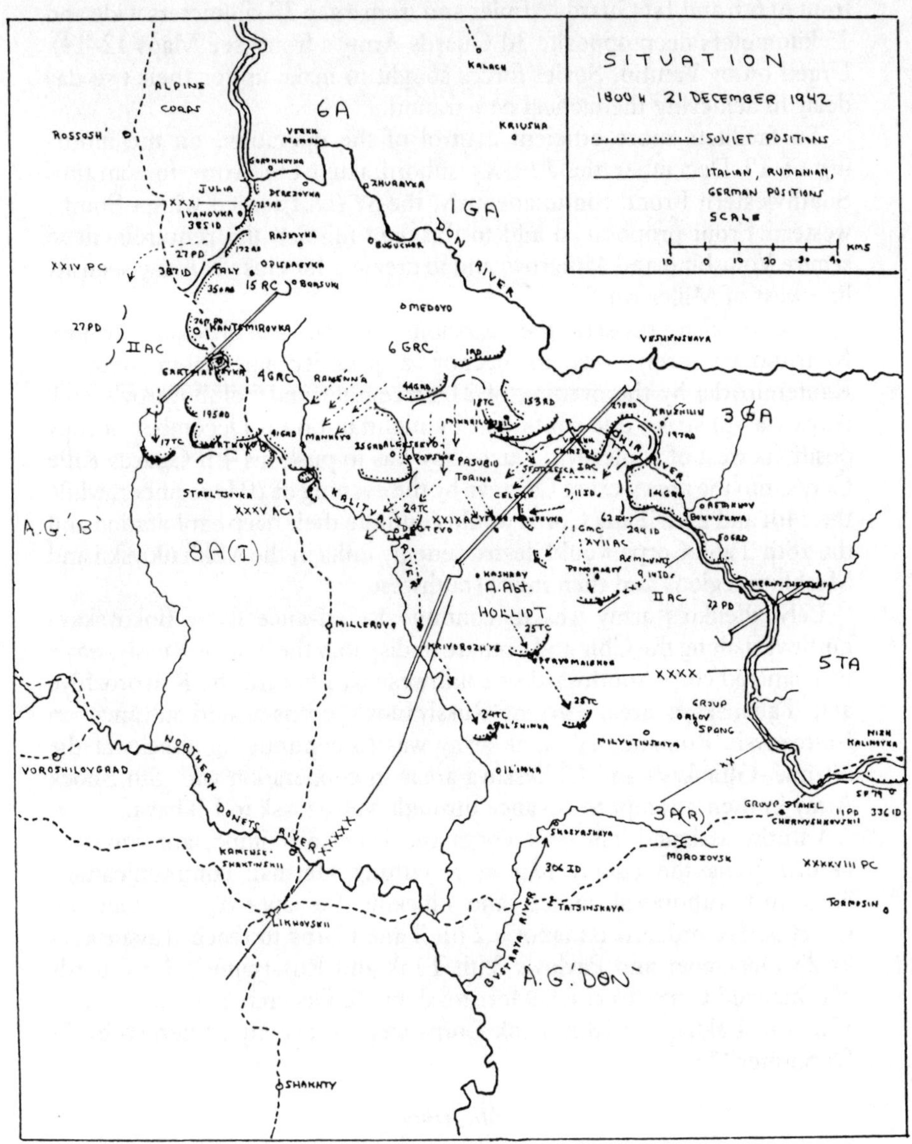

MAP 13. MIDDLE DON, SITUATION, 1800 21 DECEMBER 1942

The Exploitation Phase (19–23 December)

Planning Adjustments

On 19 December Soviet forces began full exploitation operations from a gap in enemy defenses 60 kilometers wide and 40 kilometers deep in front of 6th and 1st Guards Armies and from a gap 20 kilometers wide and 15 kilometers deep opposite 3d Guards Army's front (see Maps 12–14). Urged on by Vatutin, Soviet forces sought to make up for their two day delay in achieving the tactical penetration.

To facilitate more efficient control of the operation, on the morning of 19 December the *STAVKA* subordinated 6th Army to Vatutin's Southwestern Front. Simultaneously, the *STAVKA* agreed with a Southwestern Front proposal to add to the *front* mission the requirement to secure Voloshino and Millerovo and to create a 1st Guards Army security line west of Millerovo.[58]

Vatutin also revised the missions of his subordinate armies. Kharitonov's army was to occupy a security line from west of Kantemirovka by the evening of 21 December and Poluboyarov's tank corps was to strike due south and by nightfall on 20 December occupy positions west of Millerovo. Kuznetsov was to push his 4th Guards Rifle Corps into the area west of Degtevo by the evening of 20 December, while the 24th and 25th Tank Corps would continue their deep exploitation and the 18th Tank Corps would destroy enemy units in the Mikhailovskii and Meshkov regions and then move southwest.

Lelyushenko's army was to continue its advance from Bokovskaya northwest along the Chir and prepare to dispatch the bulk of Russiyanov's mechanized corps southward or southwestward toward the Krivorozh'ye and Tatsinskaya area. Part of Russiyanov's corps would advance on Morozovsk. Romanenko's tank army was to continue its attacks at the Nizhne–Ghirskaya and Oblivskaya areas in cooperation with 5th Shock Army in their attempt to advance through Morozovsk to Likhaya.

Vatutin assigned his tank corps the especially important missions of disrupting the enemy rear area, cutting German communications lines and withdrawal routes, and blocking the approach of German reserves. He ordered Badanov's 24th Tank Corps to reach Tatsinskaya by 23 December and Pavlov's 25th Tank and Russiyanov's 1st Guards Mechanized Corps to reach Morozovsk by 22 December. Poluboyarov's 17th and Bakharov's 18th Tank Corps were to occupy Millerovo by 24 December.[59]

6th Army

Before dawn on 19 December, Poluboyarov's tank corps and 6th Army rifle units advanced on the important rail center of Kantemirovka to cut the vital German north-south rail communications. After reducing enemy defenses at Pisarevka, the 174th Tank Brigade approached Kantemirovka from the southeast and the 66th Tank Brigade neared the eastern approaches to the city. After three hours of assault preparations the two brigades were to attack and seize the city from the hastily assembled enemy garrison of SS battalions, police units, and remnants of Italian units. The Soviet assault began at first light and by 1000 the 66th Tank Brigade had broken into the city center and, with assistance from the 174th Tank Brigade, had seized the rail station. After noon the northern column of 17th Tank Corps advanced on the city from the north, and the 31st Motorized Rifle Brigade cleared the northwestern and northern areas of the city. Late in the afternoon, the 67th Tank Brigade arrived from Taly in time to join the final Soviet assault which secured Kantemirovka by evening. The fall of Kantemirovka severed the lateral communication of German Army Group "B." In addition, the Soviets captured large stocks of supplies and several railroad trains as well as 600 former Soviet POWs who the Soviets immediately organized into a rifle regiment.[60] The following morning 17th Tank Corps units and the POW regiment dug in on the western outskirts of Kantemirovka to await the arrival of 6th Army rifle forces. Meanwhile, commanders planned to resume the offensive, and repair units worked to restore the full operational armored strength of the corps.

6th Army's 267th Rifle Division arrived in Kantemirovka on 21 December and took over 17th Tank Corps defenses. That evening Poluboyarov's tank corps resumed its operations to the south. The 66th Tank Brigade, as the corps forward detachment, raced 110 kilometers south in twenty-eight hours, overcame scattered small enemy detachments, and routed enemy rear service units defending Voloshino.* Early on 22 December the tank corps' main forces arrived and took inventory of the large amounts of captured supplies in the town's warehouses. After securing Voloshino 17th Tank Corps units set up defenses to block the approach of German units from the west and to permit 6th Army to consolidate its gains. Meanwhile, Poluboyarov dispatched his 31st Motorized Rifle Brigade eastward to cut enemy withdrawal routes from Millerovo and to assist 1st Guards Army's efforts to capture that city, which, by 23 December, was defended by the German 3d Mountain Division, which had occupied a hedgehog defense around the city. Poluboyarov's forces also conducted reconnaissance westward toward Belovodsk until the arrival of the German 19th Panzer Division in that sector halted such activities.[61]

6th Army's 15th Rifle Corps capitalized on 17th Tank Corps' success and established a security line west and northwest of Kantemirovka. The 127th Rifle Division advanced westward toward Novaya Kalitva, but heavy German resistance limited its advance to only meters per day. The

*The forward detachment was used by mobile forces and later in the war by rifle forces to lead pursuits, to seize key terrain, to preempt defenses, and to maintain the momentum of the advance. It usually consisted of a brigade for a corps or a battalion for a brigade and it was reinforced with appropriate support forces.

172d and 350th Rifle Divisions struggled against the German 385th and 387th Infantry Division defenses southwest of Ivanovka but also made little progress. Moreover, German counterattacks forced 6th Army on 25 December to commit its reserve 160th Rifle Division to combat. By 25 December 15th Rifle Corps' units had finally erected a security line from Novaya Kalitva west of Kantemirovka to Strel'tsovka.[62]

The Germans reacted to the Soviet seizure of Kantemirovka by shifting the weakened 27th Panzer Division (with fewer than 10 tanks) and Group Fegelein (387th Infantry Division) to cover the area west of the city (21 December). 19th Panzer Division also moved into the area from the north to occupy defensive positions running from north to south along the Derkul River, and to prepare relief attempts for Italian and German units encircled at Chertkovo and Gartmashevka in the Soviet rear area.[63]

1st Guards Army

In the Southwestern Front's main attack sectors the Soviet tank and mechanized corps developed their deep operations and 1st Guards and 3d Guards Armies sought to capitalize on the progress of these mobile forces by completing the liquidation of enemy forces in their sectors. 18th Tank Corps and 1st Guards Mechanized Corps, operating in tandem with the 6th Guards and 14th Rifle Corps, sought to complete the tactical envelopment of enemy forces in the immediate area south of the Don River. After the envelopment was complete, the two mobile corps were to join the advance of other *front* mobile forces toward Millerovo and Morozovsk.

On 19 December 24th and 25th Tank Corps struck southward passing through and around withdrawing Italian combat units and German and Italian rear service units. Soon both corps were separated by a considerable distance from their supporting artillery and infantry. Although the corps did have considerable initial air cover, that cover diminished as the corps plunged into the operational depths, and German air activity intensified. German bombers struck repeatedly at the tank columns, especially against 24th Tank Corps in the Skosyrskaya area on 23 December and against 25th Tank Corps at Milyutinskaya and Uryupin on 23 and 24 December. Despite the damage of air attacks the corps continued their advance. Logistical problems also became a serious obstacle to the successful fulfilment of corps' missions. Separated from their supply points by almost 300 kilometers and by numerous bypassed enemy forces, fuel and ammunition shortages developed despite the corps' careful preparations. In addition, maintenance problems reduced the two corps' tank strength by 40 to 60 percent by 23 December.[64]

By the evening of 19 December Badanov's 24th Tank Corps had advanced 55 kilometers and reached Man'kovo. Continuing his rapid march Badanov reached Degtevo on 21 December, Bol'shinka by 22 December, and German defenses at Skosyrskaya on 23 December. By that time logistical problems, maintenance difficulties, and enemy air attacks had reduced his corps' tank strength to under 100 tanks. Despite the difficulties Badanov prepared to strike Skosyrskaya and Tatsinskaya on 24 December.[65]

Pavlov's 25th Tank Corps reached Kashary by noon on 19 December. Through 19 and 20 December his corps battled Italian units which were attempting to withdraw across his front toward the southwest. These heavy battles ended late on 20 December, and Italian forces infiltrated westward toward Millerovo, northwest toward the advancing 18th Tank Corps, and southwest toward Morozovsk. The intense and frequent battles and the strain of the long march significantly reduced Pavlov's tank strength. Nevertheless, on the late evening of 20 December, his corps resumed its advance toward Morozovsk. It bypassed isolated enemy units; passed through Pervomaiskoye; and, late on 21 December, reached the Uryupin area. Uryupin was defended by advanced elements of the German 306th Infantry Division and the 8th Air Force Field Division (Luftwaffe Field Division). In costly battles with these German forces on 23 and 24 December Pavlov seized Uryupin, but his corps' combat strength was so eroded that it could advance no further.[66]

1st Guards Army's 4th Guards Rifle Corps followed in the wake of 24th and 25th Tank Corps in order to secure Chertkovo and Millerovo and extend the security line of 6th Army further to the southeast. The 195th Rifle Division crossed the Boguchar River against little organized resistance on 19 December and without halting occupied Titarevka and Popovka. The major problems the division encountered were coping with "the totally beaten enemy (who) rushed about in the windblown, frosty weather of the trans-Don region as if caught in a trap" and handling the vast number of prisoners which fell into its hands, a problem succinctly described as follows:

> The trans-Don steppe at that time became an impressive spectacle; hundreds of columns of prisoners in an undying stream flowed to the east under escort of Soviet troops.[67]

Late on 19 December the division continued its advance southward toward Chertkovo and Millerovo with the 41st Guards Rifle Division on its left flank. The division's forward detachment, the 3d Battalion, 604th Rifle Regiment, successfully cut the rail line between Kantemirovka to Millerovo, but the next day the 195th encountered heavy resistance at Gartmashevka station, a major enemy supply base. The division commander left the 604th Rifle Regiment and a battalion of the 41st Guards Rifle Division to reduce Gartmashevka, and the remainder of the division bypassed Gartmashevka, advanced toward the southwest, and by 22 December cut the main enemy supply route running westward from Chertkovo. The 41st Guards Rifle Division encircled Chertkovo with its two regiments, and the 195th Rifle Division continued its march southwest to the Derkul River. The 195th occupied defensive positions along the Derkul River on 6th Army's left flank and prepared to repel German attempts to relieve encircled forces at Chertkovo and Gartmashevka.[68] Kuznetsov dispatched the 106th Rifle Brigade to strengthen the 195th Rifle Division's defenses. Meanwhile, the portion of the 41st Guards Rifle Division not engaged at Chertkovo occupied defensive positions on the 195th Rifle Division's left flank near Strel'tsovka.

While the 195th Rifle Division and portions of the 41st Guards Rifle Division established the defensive line along the Derkul River, the 41st Rifle Division commander formed an operational group to reduce the Chertkovo garrison. The strong enemy garrison of about 10,000 men made numerous attempts to break out. These attempts and subsequent operations by the 19th Panzer Division to relieve the garrison occupied the 41st Guards Rifle Division's attentions throughout the remainder of operation "Little Saturn."

1st Guards Army second echelon division (the 35th Guards) had been assigned the complex mission of dealing with bypassed and surrounded enemy forces in 1st Guards Army's sector and protecting 4th Guards Rifle Corps' units from attack by those withdrawing enemy forces. Kuznetsov committed the 35th Guards Rifle Division to action on the morning of 21 December while other 4th Guards Rifle Corps divisions were moving to invest Chertkovo and Millerovo. Colonel I. Ya. Kulagin's division deployed on a line extending west and north of Alekseyevo–Lozovskoye, and it immediately encountered withdrawing enemy units. Italian units from the Pasubio, Torino, and Celere Divisions, forced out of the Medovo and Mikhailovskii area, frantically fled westward seeking refuge at Chertkovo and Millerovo. These units, in company and battalion strength, struck 35th Guards Rifle Division rear service units and rifle battalions deployed to intercept them. A complicated fluid battle ensued between thousands of fleeing men in groups of every size, and the 35th Guards Rifle Division deployed in netlike fashion across enemy escape routes.

POW and other intelligence reports indicated that 25,000 Italians and 1,500 Germans were attempting to pass through the 35th Guards Rifle Division sector. Although the Italian and German units [Ravenna, Celere, Sforzesca, Pasubio, Torino, 298th German divisions] were worn down by earlier battles, their huge mass posed a serious threat to Kulagin's division. To meet this threat he posted his 102d Guards and 101st Guards Rifle Regiments northeast of Alekseyevo–Lozovskoye in positions facing east while the 100th Guards Rifle Regiment blocked enemy units south of the town. A heated two day series of meeting battles resulted, involving intense but scattered combat with desperate enemy units. In the course of one day (21 December) the 102d and 101st Guards Rifle Regiments took 4,500 prisoners including 200 officers. The 2d Battalion, 100th Guards Rifle Regiment, repelled the attacks and ultimately accepted the surrender of the Rumanian 37th Infantry Regiment, capturing 720 prisoners, 700 rifles, 34 machine guns, 4 mortars, and 6 field guns. The encircled enemy forces suffered heavy casualties from artillery fire; and many Italian officers, out of concern for their men's fate, surrendered. A few did not. On 22 December the 102d Guards Rifle Regiment intercepted and captured an enemy column and took another 2,100 prisoners. However, by the evening of 22 December resistance had slackened and Soviet units encountered only isolated groups the following day.[69]

Enemy units which failed to break out often resisted fanatically in isolated strong points. Near Arbuzovka, north of Alekseyevo–Lozovskoye, almost 6,000 men of the 298th Infantry Division (German) and a Blackshirt brigade occupied an all round defense. Fifteen times on 23 December these forces attempted to break through the cordon which the 35th Guards Rifle Division had erected around them. On Christmas morning the 44th Guards Rifle Division of 6th Guards Rifle Corps reinforced the 35th Guards Rifle Division, and together the two Soviet divisions assaulted the surrounded enemy after a 30-minute artillery preparation. By midmorning the Soviets had killed 2,000 of the enemy and had taken another 2,773 prisoners. In four days of heavy fighting the 35th Guards Rifle Division recorded enemy losses amounting to 1 general killed, 9,996 soldiers killed, and 10,443 prisoners, for a total of 20,440 men.[70] On 26 December, having successfully dealt with most bypassed enemy forces, the 35th Guards Rifle Division shifted to 4th Guards Rifle Corps control and moved southwest to join the 41st Guards Rifle Division in its operation to reduce Chertkovo.

Although the Soviets killed or captured many bypassed encircled Italians and Germans, many enemy groups successfully moved westward through Soviet lines. Large gaps existed between the advancing 24th and 25th Tank Corps and between the tank corps and the follow-on rifle divisions. Moreover, the two tank corps lacked infantry strength sufficient to cordon off the area and had no capacity for dealing with prisoners. The tank corps' focus remained fixed forward. In addition, as Soviet rifle divisions marched southward and southwestward a large gap formed between 4th Guards and 6th Guards Rifle Corps. The 35th Guards Rifle Division was unable to fill that gap entirely. Thus, hundreds or even thousands of men fled westward in semi-organized fashion and joined the encirclements at Gartmashevka and Chertkovo. Other enemy forces further east moved south toward

Morozovsk through gaps in the ranks of the advancing Soviet 3d Guards Army.

While the 35th Guards Rifle Division blocked escape routes to the west, 6th Guards Rifle Corps units, cooperating with the brigades of 18th Tank Corps, swept toward Medovo south of the Don River, pushing German and Italian forces in their path. Bakharov's 18th Tank Corps crushed German resistance at Vervekovka, crossed the Bogucharka River, and, by day's end on 19 December, seized Meshkov, just northwest of Mikhailovskii, thus cutting off the westward withdrawal of Italian units along the Don River. Units of the German 298th Infantry Division resisted south of Meshkov, and Italian forces launched repeated although futile counterattacks to break 18th Tank Corps' grip on the key town. The 18th Tank Corps remained on the defense at Meshkov until relieved on 21 December by the 1st and 44th Guards Rifle Divisions. Once released from its defensive tasks, on 22 December Bakharov's tank corps raced southeast and occupied Verkhne–Chirskii where it slammed the door on the retreat of all remaining Italian and Rumanian forces still defending south of the Don River. Thereafter Vatutin ordered Bakharov to move his corps through Kashary to Millerovo, there to join forces with 4th Guards Rifle Corps and seize that key city.[71] Spurred on by Vatutin's orders, the 6th Guards Rifle Corps completed the liquidation of bypassed enemy units in cooperation with 35th Guards Rifle Division located in its blocking positions to the west. By 25 December almost 15,000 prisoners had fallen into Soviet hands.[72]

3d Guards Army

Meanwhile, on 19 December Lelyushenko's 3d Guards Army developed its penetration toward Kruzhilin and strove to smash German defensive positions around Krasnokutskaya and Chernyshevskaya. 1st Guards Mechanized Corps' 1st Guards Mechanized Brigade and the 197th Rifle Division encircled the Rumanian 7th Infantry Division in Kruzhilin and on the next day took the town, killing 2,000 enemy and taking many prisoners and 30 field guns.[73] Farther south, the 2d and 3d Guards Mechanized Brigades met lead units of 1st Guards Army at Kashary thus effecting the total encirclement and isolation of Italian 8th Army, three divisions of the Rumanian 3d Army, and the German 62d Infantry Division. The entire Rumanian 1st Army Corps collapsed after the Soviet 278th Rifle Division crushed defenses of the Rumanian 11th Infantry Division and drove it westward into the sector of the Italian Sforzesca Division. The remnants of the German 62d Infantry Division, with units on both its left and right flank demolished, withdrew southward west of Bokovskaya pursued by the Soviet 266th Rifle Division and 94th Rifle Brigade. Simultaneously, the Soviet 17th Guards Tank Regiment plunged through German defenses north of Bokovskaya and occupied positions near Krasnaya Zarya in the German rear. It held these positions for two days thus blocking the orderly withdrawal of Rumanian and German units.[74]

For two days a complex and intense battle raged west of Bokovskaya and around Kruzhilin as Soviet divisions engaged encircled and withdrawing Rumanian, German, and Italian units. Simultaneously, Soviet mechanized forces disengaged from battle and swung to the southwest to cut enemy withdrawal routes and resume the advance on Morozovsk. Soviet forces fought in decentralized fashion, supported by regimental artillery groups which often used only direct fire techniques. Attached artillery remained under corps and army control for use in repulsing enemy counterattacks, and supporting aviation struck at withdrawing enemy troop concentrations. The enemy often left manned strong points which the Soviets had to reduce by using reserves and second echelon units.*

As the Axis defenses north of Bokovskaya evaporated, those south of Bokovskaya also began to crumble. On 19 December in the strong German defensive sector between Krasnokutskaya and Chernyshevskaya, the 50th Guards Rifle Division achieved its first success in days by advancing 2 kilometers and seizing the village of Fomin. Two days later, on the 50th Division's right flank, the 14th Guards Rifle Division and 2d Guards Mechanized Brigade also cracked German defenses. As the entire German defensive zone threatened to collapse, the German 294th Infantry and 22d Panzer Divisions operating further south prepared to abandon their defenses and conduct a delaying action southward toward Morozovsk in the hope of joining German reinforcements. Finally, on 23 December, one week after the initial Soviet assault on the town, the 203d Rifle Division seized Krasnokutskaya. The following day the division also began to pursue withdrawing enemy units.

To the west, in the German rear area, on 23 December 1st Guards Mechanized Corps' brigades wheeled southeast, and Russiyanov's forward detachments occupied Milyutinskaya. The 22d Motorized Rifle Brigade passed through Kashary, linked up with 18th Tank Corps, and then moved southeast to join Russiyanov's mechanized corps and occupy blocking positions southwest of Chernyshevskaya. Lelyushenko's northernmost rifle divisions completed the task of reducing enemy forces around Kruzhilin, then wheeled to the south and followed in the wake of the Soviet mobile units. Lelyushenko's 14th Rifle Corps pursued columns of enemy forces and occasionally battled resisting German units. On the evening of 23 December its divisions spread westward from

*For example, the town of Taly, which the 846th Rifle Regiment, 267th Rifle Division, reduced, and also the towns of Kruzhilin and Verkhne–Chirskii.

Krasnokutskaya, while other 3d Guards Army divisions neared Kashary and Pervomaiskoye.[75]

German and allied forces on the left wing of Army Detachment Hollidt were in total disarray. Columns of Italian units blocked from moving westward to Millerovo instead fled up the east bank of the Kalitva Valley, dodging Soviet mobile columns in a desperate search for safety. Rumanian remnants mixed in with Italian units or fled due south toward Morozovsk. The German 294th Infantry Division conducted an orderly but harried withdrawal from the Bokovskaya–Krasnokutskaya area. Meanwhile, the 22d Panzer Division and Rumanian forces struggled to hold back an advance by 50th Guards Rifle Division and 5th Tank Army's 346th Rifle Division around Chernyshevskaya until other units had safely passed to the south. The makeshift German Groups Spang and Stahel kept a wary eye on the withdrawal from positions along the Chir River and simultaneously watched for movement by Soviet 5th Tank Army to their front.[76] 5th Tank Army had attacked on 22 December, east of Oblivskaya, but faced with the opposition of XXXXVIII Panzer Corps' 11th Panzer and 336th Infantry Divisions, it failed to achieve any measurable success.

German Countermeasures

Meanwhile, German Army Groups "B" and Don searched for forces to shift into the gap caused by the dissolution of Italian 8th Army. The threat posed by Soviet 24th and 25th Tank Corps to Tatsinskaya and Morozovsk increased the urgency of the situation, for a loss of either or both of those locations would cut the main supply lines from the rear to the German XXXXVIII Panzer Corps at Tormosin and, even more important, cut off air resupply of the Stalingrad garrison, for the primary resupply airfield for Stalingrad was at Tatsinskaya.

Consequently, German Army Group "B" ordered 19th Panzer Division to move to the Derkul River west of Strel'tsovka, to stop any westward expansion of the Soviet offensive and, if possible, to relieve forces encircled at Chertkovo. On 25 December 19th Panzer Division's lead units deployed into positions along the Derkul River west of Chertkovo and south of 27th Panzer Division's defensive line and prepared to counterattack eastward.* Two days earlier, the German 3d Mountain Division had deployed into Millerovo and had begun constructing all round defenses to halt the growing tide of 1st Guards Army forces rolling toward the Northern Donets River. Army Group "B" established a new headquarters to fill the vacuum created by the collapse of Italian

*German units west of Kantemirovka and along the Derkul River were under XXIV Panzer Corps control.

8th Army. This new headquarters, formed from the nucleus of the German XXX Army Corps and designated Army Detachment Fretter Pico, established its headquarters at Voroshilovgrad and began gathering units to defend the region between Hungarian 2d Army (and Italian Alpine Corps) and Army Detachment Hollidt.

Army Detachment Fretter–Pico assumed command of German and Italian forces defending from Novaya Kalitva south to Millerovo. In addition, it directed the German 304th Infantry Division, then enroute to the area, to occupy positions between Millerovo and the Northern Donets River and to reestablish land communications with the 3d Mountain Division isolated in Millerovo. In addition, the remnants of II Italian Corps gathered at Voroshilovgrad.[77] Farther east the German 306th Infantry and 8th Air Force Field Divisions screened the region from Tatsinskaya to Chernyshkovskii and faced the advancing Soviet 24th and 25th Tank and 1st Guards Mechanized Corps. These German forces would join withdrawing XVII Army Corps' forces (294th Infantry Division and 22d Panzer Division) to defend the critical northern approaches to Tatsinskaya and Morozovsk.

With these redeployments underway, the last phase of the operation began, characterized by Soviet attempts to expand the offensive across the Chernyshkovskii–Likhaya rail line and German efforts to prevent that disastrous consequence from occurring. This phase of the operation became a desperate struggle between fatigued Soviet forces operating at the frayed end of a long logistical umbilical cord and a patchwork of elite German units fighting side-by-side with partially trained units and ad hoc temporary formations. The advance of Badanov's 24th Tank Corps into Tatsinskaya on 24 December signaled the beginning of the last phase.

The Battle of Tatsinskaya (24–29 December)

Badanov's three tank brigades had cleared Skosyrskaya of German 306th Infantry Division forces by 2200 on 23 December, and the Germans withdrew toward Morozovsk (see Map 14). Badanov now faced a dilemma. He could halt his unit overnight in order to resupply, give his troops a rest, and await the arrival of his 24th Motorized Rifle Brigade,* thus losing the element of surprise, or he could advance immediately on Tatsinskaya and catch the small German garrison by surprise. Badanov realized the importance of seizing the critical supply center and chose to

*This brigade brought up the rear and collected those tanks and vehicles which fell behind Badanov's lead columns.

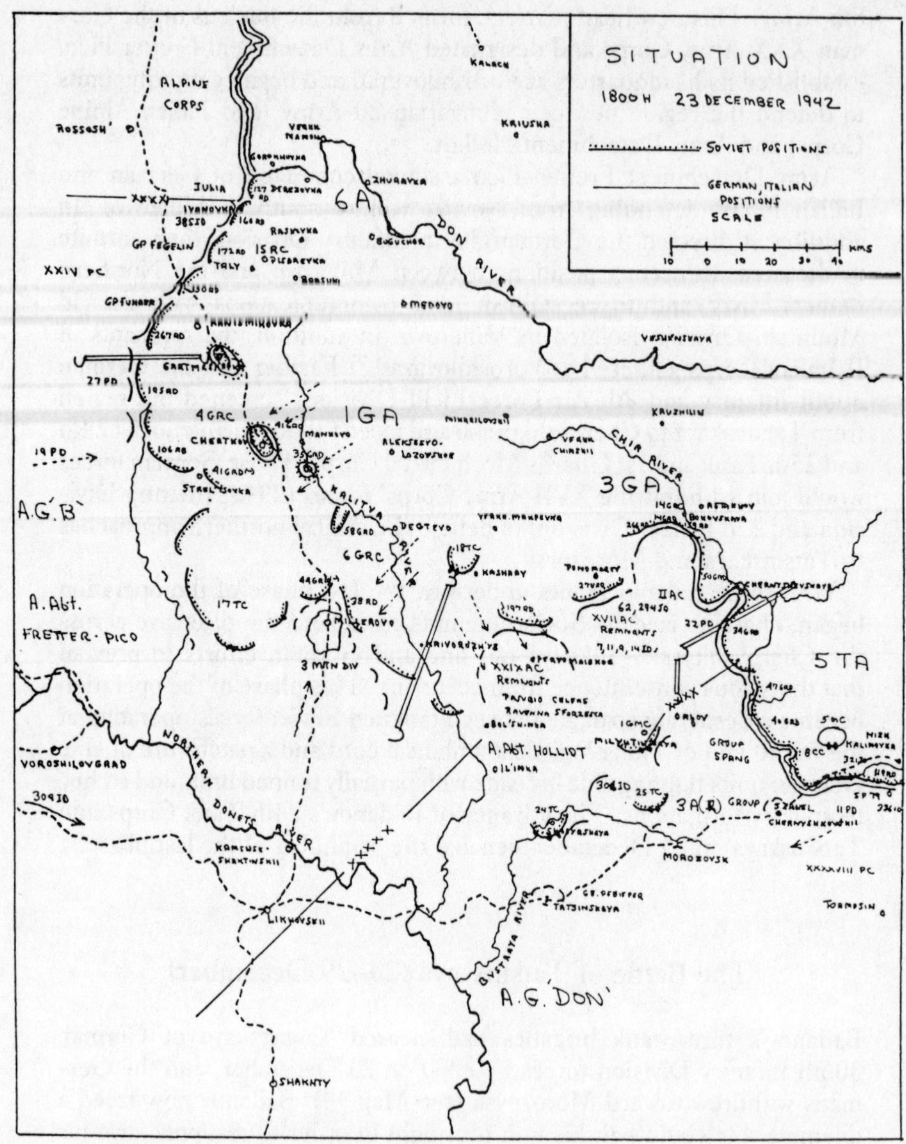

MAP 14. MIDDLE DON, SITUATION, 1800 23 DECEMBER 1942

advance on the night of 23–24 December after a three to four hour rest but before his 24th Motorized Rifle Brigade rejoined his main force.

Badanov's reconnaissance units moved southward and selected brigade attack positions outside of Tatsinskaya which the tank brigades occupied at 0700 24 December. Heavy morning fog covered the Soviet

OPERATION "LITTLE SATURN"

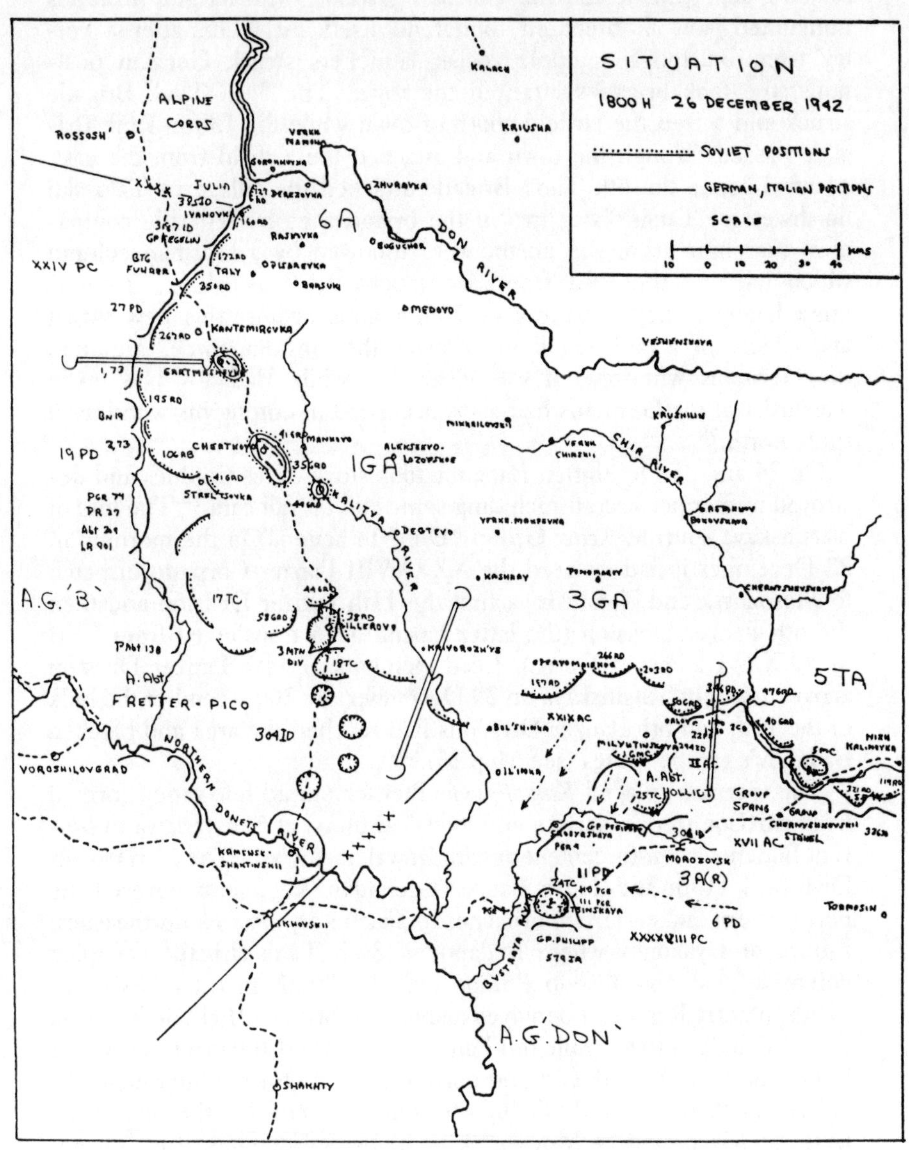

MAP 15. MIDDLE DON, SITUATION, 1800 26 DECEMBER 1942

forward deployment; and the German garrison, with its gun positions unmanned, was ill prepared to defend itself. At 0730, after a volley from Badanov's multiple rocket launchers struck German positions, the tank brigades attacked the town. The 54th Tank Brigade struck and seized the airfield south of town while the 130th Tank Brigade passed through the town and attacked the airfield from the east. Meanwhile, as the 4th Tank Brigade attacked the village of Talovskii northwest of Tatsinskaya, two of the brigades motorized rifle companies, marching from the north, were followed by a German column which had cut the road from Skosyrskaya to Tatsinskaya. Badanov immediately turned a battery of 76mm guns against this new threat and called for a tank battalion to strike the German force. Although the Germans withdrew, it was clear that while Badanov had taken Tatsinskaya, the Germans had also succeeded in cutting his withdrawal route north.[78]

On 24 and 25 December, Badanov took stock of his trophies and destroyed numerous aircraft including some still on rail cars.[79] The loss of Tatsinskaya spurred Army Group "Don" to action. On the morning of 23 December it had ordered the XXXXVIII Panzer Corps to dispatch to Morozovsk and Tatsinskaya first the 11th Panzer Division and then the 6th Panzer Division (the latter having been transferred from LVII to XXXXVIII Panzer Corps). Lead elements of 11th Panzer Division arrived north of Tatsinskaya on 24 December. By 26 December the bulk of the 11th and 6th Panzer Divisions had reached the area and blocked Badanov's escape routes (see Map 15).[80]

The Germans placed *Kampfgruppe* Pfeiffer (an ad hoc group formed from garrison troops, service and logistical units) at Skosyrskaya to prevent Badanov's reinforcement or withdrawal northward. The 11th Panzer Division's 110th and 111th Panzer Grenadier Regiments covered the northeastern and eastern approaches to Tatsinskaya and its northeastern suburb of Dyakonov where Badanov's 130th Tank Brigade occupied defensive positions. Group Philipp and the 306th Infantry Division's 579th Infantry Regiment deployed against the Soviet airfield defenses on the south side of town while 6th Panzer Division's 4th Panzer Grenadier Regiment concentrated west and northwest of the town. Other elements of the 6th Panzer and 306th Infantry Divisions covered the line of the Bystraya River west of Morozovsk to block Soviet units from sweeping west around XVII Army Corps defenses to assist Badanov. XVII Army Corps' 22d Panzer and 294th Infantry Divisions defended with Rumanian units along the Gnilaya River from Mikhailovka, 10 kilometers north of Morozovsk, to the Chir River, but the Soviet 25th Tank Corps was already at Milyutinskaya and Uryupin past the XVII Army Corps' left flank.[81]

From 24 to 28 December Badanov's troops held off German probing attacks as the Soviet fuel and ammunition stocks dwindled. His tank force, down to a strength of 58 tanks (39 T-34, 19 T-20), was immobilized by the fuel shortages. Badanov created an all round defense anchored on his dug-in tanks and artillery, and waited for assistance. On 26 December the 24th Motorized Rifle Brigade, with six vehicles and five tanks in the lead battalion, cut through German lines into Tatsinskaya. Thereafter, the door into the city slammed shut, and no more reinforcements would arrive. The 24th Motorized Rifle Brigade took up positions at Dyakonov northeast of the town, where it replaced the 130th Tank Brigade which Badanov then placed in reserve. Meanwhile, to maintain the limited mobility of his force, Badanov's forces mixed captured aviation fuel and aviation lubricants to fuel his tanks.* Despite Badanov's defensive measures, on 27 December the German noose tightened around his corps as the 110th and 111th Panzer Grenadier Regiments took Dyakonov and Group Philipp took the airfield and drove Badanov's forces into the city proper.[82]

The *STAVKA,* concerned about Badanov's fate (having just rewarded the corps with the new honorific title of 2d Guards Tank Corps), ordered Vatutin to send Badanov necessary assistance. Badanov's requests for assistance punctuated the exchange of messages between the *STAVKA* and Vatutin over Badanov's fate. Vatutin did order the 25th Tank and 1st Guards Mechanized Corps to assist Badanov. But 25th Tank Corps, after heavy fighting at Uryupin and north of Morozovsk, was itself down to strength of 25 tanks. 1st Guards Mechanized Corps, located farther east, also faced growing German opposition and was seriously weakened. Although both corps ultimately moved westward with supporting rifle forces, they were unable to help Badanov. Finally, with the German noose tightening around Badanov's corps, on the night of 28 December Vatutin gave Badanov permission to abandon Tatsinskaya (see Map 16). Badanov concentrated his meager forces in the northwest sector of town in the darkness of the early morning hours; and, under the cover of the last volley from his multiple rocket launchers, at 0430 his troops broke out toward I'linka. In the process they lost much of their remaining equipment. At I'linka the corps rejoined its rear service units which had lagged behind in the original march into Tatsinskaya.[83] On 30 December, as 24th Tank Corps (now 2d Guards Tank Corps) took up new defensive positions, heavy battle could be heard in the direction of Kostino along the Bystraya River as the 25th Tank and 1st Guards Mechanized Corps with rifle units of 3d Guards Army began a desperate struggle to penetrate German lines and advance on Tatsinskaya.

*The Soviets also made feeble efforts to resupply Badanov's force by parachute airdrop.

German Restoration of the Front (24–30 December)

The fighting around Tatsinskaya was characteristic of the series of struggles that occurred along the advanced positions of 6th, 1st Guards, and 3d Guards Army after 23 December. Newly arrived reinforcements

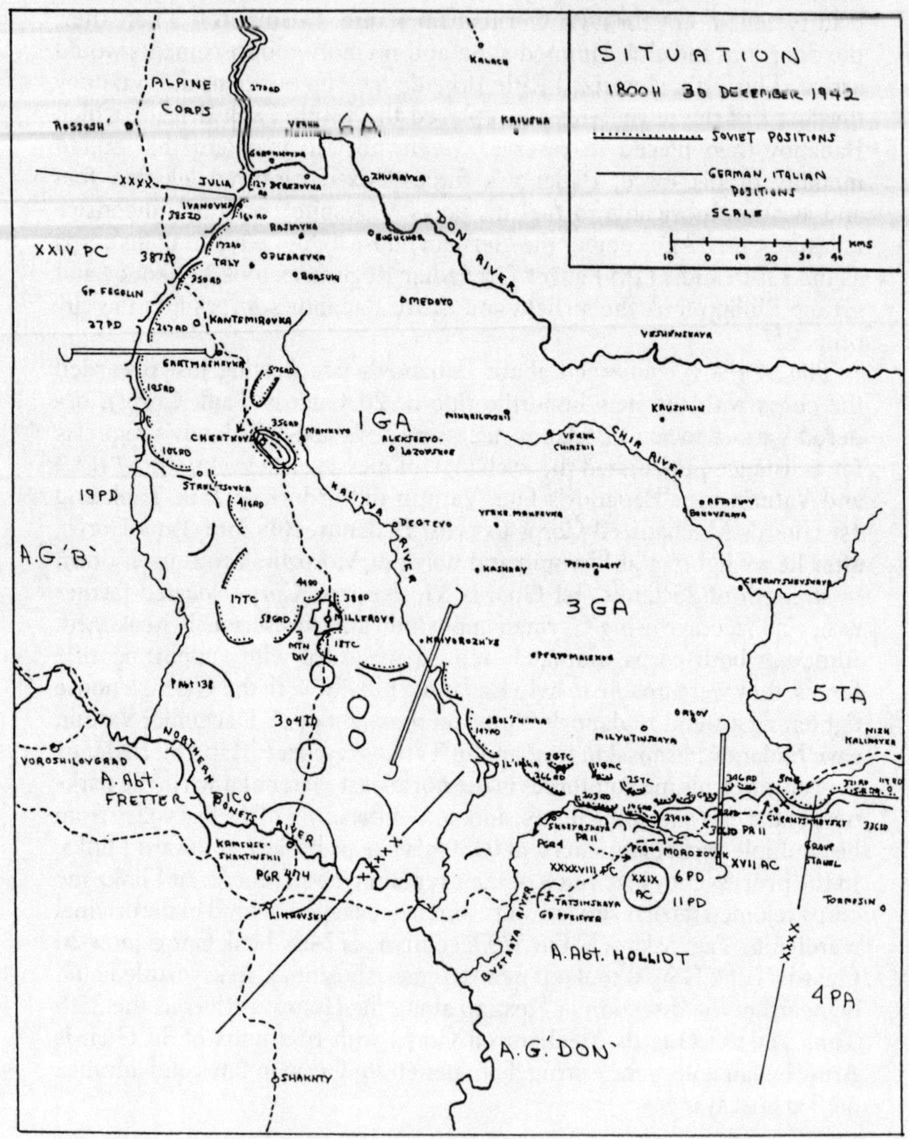

MAP 16. MIDDLE DON, SITUATION, 1800 30 DECEMBER 1942

stabilized German defensive positions and tried, in isolated instances, to deflect or drive back the advanced Soviet units and rescue forces encircled behind Soviet lines. Equally determined Soviet commanders sought to continue the advance in order to fulfill their assigned missions. It became clear, however, that Soviet forward units would require reinforcement if the offensive was to develop further. That reinforcement would not be forthcoming, since on 24 December 2d Guards and 51st Armies began their own offensive southwest of Stalingrad against the German LVII Panzer Corps (4th Panzer Army).

On 24 December Soviet Southwestern Front's positions extended 340 kilometers from the Don River near Novaya Kalitva, west of Kantemirovka and Chertkovo, to Millerovo and along the Kalitva and Bystraya Rivers through I'linka to north of Morozovsk and Chernyshkovskii. Soviet units deployed along this long front were by now clearly overextended. In spite of that overextension the *STAVKA* ordered the Southwestern Front to continue its offensive.

On 24 December General Vatutin assigned new missions to his armies. 6th and 1st Guards Armies were to defend their positions, reduce surrounded enemy forces at Gartmashevka, Chertkovo, and Millerovo, and extend their lines in the south from Voloshino through I'linka to Morozovsk and Chernyshkovskii. 18th Tank Corps was to join other *front* mobile forces and 3d Guards Army units in Skosyrskaya and along the Bystraya River for an attack on Tatsinskaya and Morozovsk. Following the relief of Badanov's force in Tatsinskaya and the fall of Morozovsk, mobile forces would join with 5th Tank and 5th Shock Armies (the latter subordinated to the Southwestern Front on 26 December) to liquidate German XXXXVIII Panzer Corps in the Tormosin area.[84]

The subsequent events at Tatsinskaya forced Vatutin to scrap these plans. Instead, he ordered 18th Tank Corps, 6th and 1st Guards Armies to hold their defensive positions while 3d Guards Army broke through German defenses on the Bystraya River (see Map 15). 6th Army defensive lines south of Novaya Kalitva held firm as did the 195th Rifle Division's defenses farther south. West of Chertkovo the 19th Panzer Division struck hard at 41st Guards Rifle Division positions on 26 December. Although the Germans drove as far east as Strel'tsovka, the 41st Guards with 17th Tank Corps' reinforcements successfully blocked the road to Chertkovo. While the Germans resupplied the Chertkovo garrison by air, the 19th Panzer Division made repeated attempts to break through. On 15 January the garrison tried to break out but failed in the attempt. In the last days of December the 57th Guards Rifle Division joined the Soviet force blockading Chertkovo (35th Guards Rifle Division), and on 17 January the Chertkovo garrison finally surrendered.[85]

Stalemate also ensued in the Millerovo area. The German 3d Mountain Division firmly hung onto its defensive positions against 17th and 18th Tank Corps units reinforced by the 44th Guards, 38th Guards, and 58th Guards Rifle Divisions. The German 304th Infantry Division, unable to break through to Millerovo, occupied defensive strong points north of the Northern Donets River and on the south bank of the Kalitva River eastward toward I'linka. In mid-January 3d Mountain Division abandoned Millerovo and broke out of encirclement.

The heaviest fighting in the Southwestern Front sector occurred along the Bystraya River north of Morozovsk. Lelyushenko ordered his 3d Guards Army units to speed up their movement on Morozovsk and Tatsinskaya to assist the beleaguered Badanov. The 50th Guards Rifle Division and 5th Tank Army's 346th Rifle Division cleared the Chernyshevskaya area of enemy on 24 and 25 December. Then, assisted by the 22d Guards Motorized Brigade and elements of 1st Guards Mechanized Corps, the 50th Guards Rifle Division and the 159th Rifle Division on its right flank pushed the German 294th Infantry and 22d Panzer Divisions back toward Morozovsk. By 29 December these Soviet units had approached within 10 kilometers of Morozovsk, but the German XVII Army Corps (294th Infantry and 22d Panzer Divisions), the 306th Infantry Division, and 8th Air Force Field Division halted their advance.[86] A stalemate, which lasted into January, then ensued along the Bystraya River north of Morozovsk.

While 3d Guards and 5th Tank Army elements advanced on Morozovsk, 3d Guards Army's main force lunged toward Tatsinskaya. On 25 December Lelyushenko ordered the 14th Guards Rifle Corps (203d, 14th Guards, and 266th Rifle Divisions) and the 197th Rifle Division to concentrate by 27 December along the Bystraya River (see Map 16). There, the units would join 1st Guards Mechanized Corps and 25th Tank Corps for an assault on Tatsinskaya. After a grueling march, the exhausted 14th Guards Rifle Corps units took up positions north of the river late on 27 December. Early the next morning the 203d Rifle Division advanced southwest against German units defending Skosyrskaya. Short of ammunition and worn down to a fraction of its strength, the division was struck by counterattacks by 6th Panzer and 11th Panzer Divisions on 28 and 29 December. The German attacks drove the 203d Rifle Divisions back across the Bystraya River, inflicted heavy losses on the division and cut off one regiment of the neighboring 266th Rifle Division (on the 203d Rifle Division's right flank). On the evening of 29 December a German 6th Panzer Division night attack overran the 203d Rifle Division defensive positions and forced another Soviet withdrawal. Total collapse of the unit was avoided when a battery of the 419th Separate Anti-Tank Battalion repulsed the enemy attack. By this time the 203d Rifle Division was totally out of ammunition.[87]

Meanwhile, the 25th Tank and 1st Guards Mechanized Corps arrived on the Bystraya; and, on the next day, Lelyushenko placed the two corps under the overall command of Badanov, who had just broken out of encirclement at Tatsinskaya. The gesture was futile since the combined strength of the three mobile corps was just over 50 tanks.[88] Supporting rifle units had suffered similar casualties and the 203d Rifle Division was reduced to a strength of ten to fifteen men per rifle company.[89] While 3d Guards Army tried in vain to penetrate German defenses along the Bystraya River from Skosyrskaya to Morozovsk, 5th Tank Army on the Southwestern Front's left flank, on 28 December lunged across the Chir River toward Chernyshkovskii. In heavy fighting the 5th Mechanized Corps, 8th Cavalry Corps, and 112th Rifle Division of Romanenko's tank army pushed Group Stahel back to the outskirts of the city. Only the arrival of 11th Panzer Division's 11th Panzer Regiment, hastily summoned from Tatsinskaya, restored German defenses east of Chernyshkovskii.

Throughout the period from 26 to 30 December elements of XXIX Army Corps, consisting of remnants of Italian and Rumanian forces, filtered southward through German lines and gathered in assembly areas southwest of Morozovsk.[90] By 30 December Operation "Little Saturn" had virtually ended, and the front had been temporarily stabilized on a line from Novaya Kalitva, west of Chertkovo and Voloshino, north of Millerovo, Il'inka and Skosyrskaya, to Chernyshkovskii. The Soviet offensive drive had burned itself out. Rifle forces were worn down and fatigued, tank units virtually devoid of armor, and logistical lines strained to a breaking point. German units switched from other sectors of the front would temporarily hold Soviet forces in check until the Soviets replenished their supplies, reinforced their forward units, regrouped, and resumed the offensive westward in mid-January.

Conclusions

The Soviet High Command achieved its principal objectives in Operation "Little Saturn." Soviet armies succeeded in destroying the bulk of Italian 8th Army and Army Detachment Hollidt and cleared the Kalitva and Chir River valleys of enemy forces. In doing so they cut German resupply lines to Stalingrad and smashed German hopes of relieving the beleaguered Stalingrad defenders.

Axis losses bore mute testimony to the scale of their defeat. The Italian Army suffered 84,830 killed, missing, and captured from 11 December

1942 to 31 January 1943. Another 29,690 were wounded or victims of frost-bite.[91] Only the Alpine Corps emerged from the operation unscathed. Italian units operating south of the Don River lost virtually all of their equipment as well. Remnants of Rumanian 3d Army, the 7th, 11th, 9th, and 14th Infantry Divisions and the 7th Cavalry Division suffered heavy casualties and were erased from the enemy order of battle. Both the Italian and Rumanian forces ceased to be a factor in fighting on the Eastern Front. German units, including the 385th, 387th, 62d, and 294th Infantry Divisions; the 318th Infantry Regiment; and the 22d and 27th Panzer Divisions, while maintaining their cohesion, likewise suffered grievous losses. Reinforcing units, including the 19th, 11th, and 6th Panzer Divisions; 3d Mountain Division; and 304th and 306th Infantry Divisions, were worn down in constant heavy fighting and were sorely pressed to hold back the Soviet tide.

While inflicting these staggering losses, the Soviets themselves suffered heavy losses in men and equipment. The tank and mechanized corps, which began the operation with between 159 and 168 tanks each, ended the operation with between 10 and 20 percent of their original strength. The wear and tear of twelve days of operations and an advance of up to 200 kilometers accounted for between 40 and 60 percent of the losses while combat losses inflicted by enemy ground and air forces accounted for a sizable portion of the remaining tank strength.[92] Soviet rifle units suffered heavy losses, in particular during the initial assaults across the Don and Chir Rivers, during the heated battles to reduce encircled enemy forces and block their withdrawal, and during the heavy fighting from 24 to 30 December against German forces trying to restore their defensive lines. The 203d Rifle Division's condition was representative of the state of other units. Its ten to fifteen men per rifle company translated into a division strength of under 1000 men by the end of the operation – a probable loss as high as 70 percent of the division's initial effective strength (probably around 7–8,000 men). In addition, only two-thirds of the division's machine guns and 45mm guns survived the operation, and there was no ammunition for these.

Losses afflicted all ranks as well. The Chief of Staff of the Southwestern Front, Major General G.D. Stel'makh, and the 3d Guards Army Chief of Staff, Major General I.P. Krupennikov, riding in tanks with the 1st Guards Mechanized Corps to obtain a first-hand grasp of the situation and to assign missions to their mobile units, were intercepted by German troops on 20 December. Stel'makh was killed and Krupennikov captured. Major General P.P. Privalov, the 15th Rifle Corps commander, and his artillery commander, Colonel Lyabinov, were wounded and taken prisoner on 22 December during the fluid fighting along the Kantemirovka–Smyaglevsk road.[93]

Although the Soviets achieved their principal objectives they did not succeed in all elements of their plan. Soviet plans called for their tank forces to secure *front* objectives by the fourth day of the operation, 20 December, and for rifle forces to consolidate those gains by the sixth day, 22 December. The operation fell short of these goals. The 17th Tank Corps secured its objective in the Voloshino area on 22 December, four days late. The 24th Tank Corps reached and occupied its objective of Tatsinskaya on 24 December, also four days behind schedule, and thereafter it was unable to hold its objective. The 25th Tank Corps and 1st Guards Mechanized Corps reached the approaches to Morozovsk but were unable to secure the city proper.

Likewise, Soviet rifle forces consolidated the gains of the mobile forces behind schedule. 6th Army occupied most of its designated security line by 23 December. First Guards Army, unable to secure the key city of Millerovo, was forced to truncate its security line and detach large forces to watch the enemy forces encircled in that city and elsewhere in their rear area. Third Guards Army consolidated its positions 10–20 kilometers short of its objectives of Tatsinskaya and Morozovsk also well behind schedule. In the end it scarcely made any difference whether the Soviets cut the rail line, for by the end of December, German forces in the Tormosin area were forced to withdraw west of Chernyshkovskii by the pressure of Soviet 5th Tank and 5th Shock Armies.

The failure to hold Tatsinskaya was a major disappointment for the Soviets. German recapture of the airfield permitted its renewed use to supply the Stalingrad garrison. Yet, the temporary seizure of the town by Badanov's 24th Tank Corps did seriously disrupt German resupply efforts for four days. Thus, the Soviet offensive, even though it fell behind schedule because of tactical difficulties, was an operational and strategic victory. Large German, Italian, and Rumanian forces were destroyed or neutralized; and the German command had to shift scarce forces from other sectors of the front in order to stave off even greater disaster. Early in the operation the German XXXXVIII Panzer Corps was forced to abandon any hope, however remote, of launching a relief effort toward Stalingrad because of the disjointed and ineffective (though disconcerting) attacks of Soviet 5th Tank Army. After Soviet 6th, 1st Guards, and 3d Guards Armies ruptured the defenses of Italian 8th Army and Army Detachment Hollidt, the Germans had to shift additional forces into the growing vacuum. 11th Panzer Division's transfer to Morozovsk and Tatsinskaya paved the way for 5th Tank and 5th Shock Armies' successes in late December against the XXXXVIII Panzer Corps. 6th Panzer Division's transfer from LVII Panzer Corps to Morozovsk critically weakened the German Kotel'nikovskii force operating to relieve Stalingrad from the southwest. Other units thrown into the sector (19th Panzer Division,

206th, 304th Infantry Divisions, and 3d Mountain Division) inevitably weakened other sectors. In addition, German units shifted during the operation (6th, 11th, 19th, 22d, 27th Panzer Divisions) were worn down by those operations and scarcely able to deal effectively with future Soviet offensives. Operation "Little Saturn" in effect negated what little hope remained in the German camp for relieving the Stalingrad cauldron and forced German forces to abandon forever their positions between the lower Don and Donets River. Moreover, the operation posed a serious threat to large German forces overextended in the Caucasus region.

In accomplishing these achievements, the Soviets experienced some severe operational and tactical problems that worked against their achievement of complete operational success. Foremost among these problems were:

– an inability to penetrate the tactical defense in the required time period
– inadequate and inaccurate artillery support during the penetration operation
– recurring logistical problems which hindered sustained operations
– difficulty in coordinating tank and rifle units or tank units with other tank units during deep operations

The Soviets experienced considerable problems while attempting to penetrate the enemy defenses in all main attack sectors. This was due in part to deployment problems and intelligence failures and in part to atmospheric conditions beyond the control of planners. In the Verkhnyi Mamon area, Soviet intelligence correctly assessed the number and strength of opposing Italian divisions. It also recognized the possibility of rapid reinforcement by the German 385th Infantry and 27th Panzer Divisions. It did not, however, detect the actual movement of these German units into the first echelon of the defense on 15–16 December and the placement of many of the Italian units in second echelon. Likewise, the Soviets did not seem to anticipate the rapidity with which other German reinforcements deployed forward (387th Infantry Division, 14th SS Police Regiment). Of course, in part, the extended penetration battle itself bought time for some of these units to deploy forward.

Artillery and tank support for the attack was weaker than planned, generally because of the difficulty the Soviets experienced in moving forces forward. Initial Soviet allocation of artillery support did not concentrate maximum artillery in the main attack sectors of 1st Guards Army and 3d Guards Army. Although planned supporting artillery was adequate, the bulk of the 9th Artillery Division's regiments arrived late; and the absence of haulage once the firing units arrived delayed their employment even longer. To compound these problems, the heavy fog of

16 December rendered aimed artillery fire useless. Since the preparation involved only thirty minutes of barrage fire and sixty minutes of aimed fire, ensuing artillery support did not do the expected damage to enemy positions. In actuality, the most extensive damage to enemy positions was done by artillery (usually divisional) firing over open sights, prior to and during the assault.

In many sectors (but particularly that of 1st Guards Army) the infantry support tanks which were supposed to cut lanes through minefields and destroy bunkers were also delayed in their movement forward. Thus the infantry attacked only partially destroyed enemy positions with limited artillery and virtually no tank support. Consequently, enemy artillery and machine gun fire took a heavy toll on Soviet troops. The Soviet tank corps, committed on the first day of operations to provide additional support for the infantry, ran upon minefields, suffered losses, and had to be withdrawn until sappers could complete cutting lanes through those fields. Ultimately, better combination of infantry, artillery and an increased number of tanks on 17 December ruptured the tactical defenses. Yet the two day delay in effecting the penetration had a telling effect on the subsequent development of the offensive.

Once the defenses were ruptured, Soviet mobile forces lunged deep. The lack of immediately available mobile operational reserves deprived the Italian 8th Army commander of a means to respond. The footbound Italian infantry (as well as the Rumanians) were virtually helpless against Soviet mobile forces once they broke into the operational depth. In the absence of mobile reserves the majority of German units formed hedgehog defenses or delayed in successive positions normally along the hinge and flanks of the penetration (385th Infantry Division, 62d Infantry Division, 294th Infantry Division). Other Italian and Rumanian units along with some German units (298th Infantry Division) were penetrated and outflanked on both flanks. Many of these units were paralyzed and surrendered. Others fled southwest or south in semi-organised fashion, and most ultimately suffered huge if not total losses.

The combat effectiveness of Soviet mobile forces during the exploitation phase of the operation suffered by virtue of their use in heavy fighting to penetrate the enemy tactical defenses. Initial losses incurred by 18th Tank and 25th Tank Corps in the minefields on 16 December amounted to just short of 20 percent of their strength. Subsequent losses may have reduced the tank strength of 17th, 18th, and 25th Tank Corps by as much as 25 percent by the time they finally broke into the operational depth.

Mobile forces, once they reached to operational depths, performed well, in particular Badanov's 24th Tank Corps. Commanders skillfully and doggedly maneuvered their units toward assigned objectives and avoided undue losses in engagements with enemy troops which could be bypassed.

Soviet critiques of the operations, however, rue the absence of close coordination between air forces and the mobile groups. In the absence of air support, enemy air exacted a significant toll of armored vehicles. Antiaircraft support of the tank corps (usually one regiment) was also too light and antitank attachments to the corps were inadequate to deal with the antitank threat both during the penetration and during deep operations. While 17th Tank Corps had a full tank destroyer brigade attached to it, 25th Tank Corps and 1st Guards Mechanized Corps lacked requisite antitank support. Soviet after action reports recommended attachment of one tank destroyer regiment to each corps, if possible, with the guns towed by "Willys" jeeps which "could follow tanks anywhere."[94]

A more important operational deficiency was the inability of tank and mechanized corps to coordinate their actions with one another when operating in the depth of enemy defenses. The 25th Tank, 24th Tank, and 1st Guards Mechanized Corps had virtually no communications with one another until they reached the Tatsinskaya–Morozovsk rail line, thus any coordination had to be effected through higher headquarters and was not timely enough to affect the situation. The limited radius of operations of existing radios compounded this problem. Tank and mechanized corps were thus often out of communication with higher headquarters during critical periods in the advance. After action reports recommended creation of relay stations and units of liaison aircraft to improve communications.

The "Little Saturn" operation thoroughly discredited the idea of using multiple tank and mechanized corps on separate directions without a single control headquarters in the immediate vicinity of the units. Thus,

> this suggests the conclusion that, in order to intensify and assure the continuous effectiveness of a thrust throughout the entire depth of the operation, it is necessary to merge tank and mechanized corps into one mobile group, consisting of several corps (not less than two) and to commit this group to breakthrough by echelons – in two or even three echelons – in any one direction. It is considerably more difficult than in the case of infantry to form and to weld together an improvised HQ team and the command of a mobile group of this kind directly before an operation. Hence, while they are in the process of being formed and welded together, formations and their commanders should receive their control organs, and go through their battle training as component parts of large mobile groups. . . .
>
> The operation carried out by the Southwest Front in the area of the middle reaches of the river Don serves as an example of such an employment of mobile troops. The experience has shown that an operation of this kind can be accomplished only by a group of corps placed under a unified command or merged into one tank army.[95]

This judgement echoed the essence of Stalin's message to Vatutin on 26 December, when he said, in part,

> In general, you must bear in mind that it is better to push tank corps along extended advances in pairs, rather than singly, so as not to get into Badanov's position.[96]

The fate of Badanov's corps had an immediate impact on command and control. Upon his return to Soviet lines on 29 December, he received control of the remnants of 24th and 25th Tank and 1st Guards Mechanized Corps (although by this time their combined strength was less than that of a single tank brigade). More important, in January 1943, the *STAVKA* approved the Table of Organization (establishment) of a new type tank army, five of which would appear in the summer, and two of which would be used in an offensive role in the Belgorod–Khar'kov offensive operation. In the interim the Soviets would attempt to use closer knit *ad hoc* mobile groups in offensive operations.

While tank and mechanized corps had difficulty coordinating among themselves they also operated outside of the supporting range of rifle forces. Thus, from 19 to 21 December 18th Tank Corps, having penetrated to Meshkov, had enemy units cross its rear and virtually isolate the tank corps from its supporting infantry for two days. The 24th Tank Corps, also well in advance of its infantry support, was likewise fatally cut off in Tatsinskaya. The immediate Soviet assessment was that the success of tank corps must be exploited speedily by infantry which had to remain no more than two or three days march from the mobile forces they were to support. The experiences on the Middle Don forced Soviet commanders in the future to assign rifle divisions to cooperate with individual tank corps and to equip those divisions with as many vehicles as possible (a practice evident in the Donbas operation, see Chapter 3).

Logistical support proved a major difficulty for Soviet forces. Mobile forces invariably ran short of supplies, in particular fuel and ammunition. This problem forced them either to voluntarily truncate their force or to reduce their scope of operations. Mechanical failures of tanks and other vehicles accounted for between 40 and 60 percent of armored losses, and the lack of sufficient mobile repair teams made repair of damaged tanks slow and time consuming. This problem occurred in all mobile forces operating along the Middle Don and explained, to a large degree, why the mobile corps were reduced to a strength of twenty-five to fifty tanks each by the end of the operation. The Soviet after action reports recommended careful planning of logistics, reinforcement of the mobile corps by higher level motor transport units, forward movement of supply bases during operations, the creation of salvage and repair points on the route of advance, the use of locally available and captured equipment, the planned organization of protection for LOCs and rear installations, and more widespread air delivery of critical supplies to mobile units (a method used at Tatsinskaya but only on a limited scale).

Subsequent Soviet analysis of the operation indicated that the mobile corps were assigned unrealistically distant objectives and were expected to achieve inordinately high rates of advance (40–80 kms/day) when in reality advances amounted to 25–35 kms/day. This, in part, produced many of the problems the corps experienced. The Soviets concluded that better cooperation between corps could improve the rates of advance in future operations. In the Middle Don operation Soviet planners called for the mobile corps to operate continuously for three to four days. Actually, the corps operated for up to twelve days without rest or systematic resupply. Subsequent operational assessments concluded that the corps were used up after two to three days of precombat preparations and five to seven days of fighting. Thus on the middle Don Soviet mobile corps burned out and ceased to be effective before they fulfilled their missions.

Soviet experiences in operation "Little Saturn" provided a virtual testbed for the future joint use of large mobile forces with standard rifle forces. The faults of the operation were to be expected in an army which was relearning the techniques of modern mobile warfare. Lessons learned on the Don would be applied in future operations after suitable time for reflection. Unfortunately, the frantic offensive dash of Soviet forces across southern Russia in the winter of 1942–1943 did not provide requisite time for the lessons to be fully digested. While the Soviets would make some adjustments, they would relearn many of the same lessons again in February and March 1943. Haste and overoptimism would make the necessary education of the Red Army more difficult and costly.

German, Italian, and Rumanian actions during "Little Saturn" were almost entirely dictated by the exigencies of the situation. Strategically and operationally, Axis options were few in December of 1942. The encirclement of German 6th Army and part of 4th Panzer Army at Stalingrad were realities that the German High Command had to live with and realities which deprived commanders of much of their freedom of action. The focus of German concerns was on relief of the Stalingrad garrison and to that end Army Group Don gathered virtually all of its mobile forces at Tormosin and Kotel'nikovskii, leaving other sectors to fend for themselves. When the Soviets unleashed the offensive torrent across the Don River against Italian 8th Army and Army Detachment Hollidt, German commanders had to improvise. In the end, the German command saved neither German 6th Army nor Italian 8th Army. At best, the Germans restored the front in time to extract Army Group "A" from its precarious position in the Caucasus. This operational juggling of scarce forces was to the credit of Field Marshal Erich von Manstein who, even Hitler admitted, was at his best when the situation was the worst. In addition to Manstein, credit for restoring the front belonged to the individual division commanders of the 294th Infantry, the 385th Infantry, the 11th Panzer, and 6th Panzer Divisions; to individual *kampfgruppen* leaders and to leaders who perished with their units in chaotic struggle – to those encircled at Gartmashevka, at Chertkovo, and at Millerovo. The tactical prowess of these unit commanders (mostly German) achieved local victories that bought time for the ultimate, though temporary, stabilization of the front. Yet these tactical victories could not produce operational success, and in the end it was Soviet forces who faced exhausted German units in a semicircle from Novaya Kalitva to Morozovsk. The exhaustion produced by strenuous, costly tactical successes produced cumulative weakness in German units that led to further Soviet advances. At Stalingrad and on the middle Don there began that steady erosion of German forces that would ultimately spell disaster for German forces later in the war.

Strategically, some have suggested that "Little Saturn" was a mistake and that greater Soviet gains could have been achieved by adherence to the original operation "Saturn."[97] These analysts argue that use of Soviet 2d Guards Army as a second echelon for a Southwestern Front attack could have resulted in a Soviet advance on Rostov and an encirclement of all of German Army Group Don and Army Group "A." Such an encirclement would have rendered relief of the Stalingrad garrison superfluous and would have produced an even larger bag of encircled German units. While consideration of historical "ifs" is often folly, when assessing this "if" it is proper to bear in mind the overall performance of Soviet forces in "Little Saturn." Depriving the Stalingrad Front of 2d Guards Army would have made more possible a successful German linkup with the Stalingrad garrison. It would have committed Soviet forces to an envelopment operation covering up to 400 kilometers of encirclement perimeter, and it would have unleashed larger German forces to operate within that larger area. It would have further taxed Soviet logistics and the mobile forces which, in an operation of just over 100 kilometers depth, wore themselves to a frazzle. Inherently it would have involved a maneuver operation of vaster scope conducted by Soviet commanders who were just then learning the techniques of mobile warfare.

The *STAVKA,* in truncating plan "Saturn" took a more prudent course, and that course paid off. In just over one month, however, the *STAVKA* would seek higher stakes in a far more risky operation to even greater depths. The results of that future operation in the Donbas and against Khar'kov partially answer the question of what course was best for the Soviets at Stalingrad.

3

OPERATION "GALLOP"

The Donbas Operation

29 January – 6 March 1943

Strategic Context

As 1943 opened, the successful Soviet counteroffensive at Stalingrad expanded into a general counteroffensive aimed at pushing German forces as far westward as possible while Soviet forces destroyed the German 6th Army at Stalingrad. The Middle Don operation of December sealed the fate of German 6th Army by disrupting German relief attempts. With these German relief operations thwarted, German concerns focused on bolstering their front and safely extracting their large forces which were increasingly threatened with isolation in the northern Caucasus region.

Throughout January, along the Eastern Front, the Soviets conducted a series of offensives designed to erode German strength and produce a total collapse of German forces in southern Russia. Simultaneously, the Soviets conducted a major operation (*Kol'tso*) to reduce the Stalingrad pocket. German 6th Army's major contribution to German efforts in the south was continued resistance which tied down seven Soviet armies of Rokossovsky's Don Front, armies which could have had a telling effect if used to reinforce operations in other sectors of the front.

While operations to reduce Stalingrad proceeded, new Soviet offensives rippled along the front. On 13 January Golikov's Voronezh Front struck at the Hungarian 2d Army and the remnants of Italian 8th Army along the upper Don River. In the ensuing Ostrogozhsk–Rossosh' operation the Soviets destroyed the Hungarian 2d Army and Italian Alpine Corps and created a major gap south of German 2d Army defending in the Voronezh sector.[1] Simultaneously, the Soviet Southwestern Front resumed a slow, grinding advance westward from Millerovo and Morozovsk toward Starobel'sk and Voroshilovgrad. Further south Yeremenko's (later Malinovsky's) Southern Front pushed toward Rostov while Soviet forces in the northern Caucasus pressured the almost isolated German Army Group "A." 1st Panzer Army of Army Group "A" barely escaped through Rostov to join Army Group Don before the Soviets slammed the door shut on German forces in the northern Caucasus by seizing the city. German 17th Army (of Army Group "A") withdrew slowly into fortified positions on the Kuban and Taman peninsulas and around the city of Novorossiisk.

With Hungarian 2d Army destroyed, by mid-January the *STAVKA* planned a new operation to encircle and destroy German 2d Army in the Voronezh area. On 24 February the 13th Army of the Bryansk Front and three armies of Golikov's Voronezh Front began the Voronezh–Kastornoye operation against German 2d Army.[2] Within days 2d Army, with many of its units encircled, was forced to withdraw westward. It appeared as if the entire southern wing of German forces on the Eastern Front was about to collapse. In a burst of optimism the *STAVKA* pondered plans to accelerate the offensive and force German forces back to the Dnepr River line and perhaps even beyond. Between 20 and 23 January the *STAVKA* approved two plans for operations which it hoped would achieve that aim. The first, codenamed Operation "*Skachok*" (Gallop), sought to liberate the Donbas region and drive German forces across the Dnepr River. The second, codenamed Operation "*Zvezda*" (Star), aimed at liberating Khar'kov and pushing German forces as far as possible to the west. The two *front* operations would occur simultaneously with final Soviet operations to reduce the Stalingrad pocket. Elsewhere on the Eastern Front the Soviets launched supporting offensives.

Operational Context

The Situation in January 1942

While Golikov's offensive against Hungarian 2d Army successfully unfolded in the Ostrogozhsk and Rossosh' areas, Vatutin's Southwestern Front, advancing in tandem with the Southern Front on its left, cleared the Millerovo, Likhaya and Morozovsk regions and pushed German Army Detachment Fretter–Pico and Army Detachment Hollidt westward toward the Northern Donets River. In Mid-January Soviet 6th Army advanced toward Starobel'sk on the banks of the Aydar River; 1st Guards Army marched southwest toward Voroshilovgrad on the Northern Donets River; 3d Guards Army approached the Northern Donets River northeast of Krasnodon; and 5th Tank Army units, supported on their left by 5th

Shock Army of the Southern Front whose main forces were pressuring German units defending Rostov, reached the Northern Donets east of Kamensk.

The Genesis of Operation "Gallop"

Vatutin, understanding the weakened condition of German forces opposing him, developed the concept for an operation launched through Starobel'sk swinging southward toward Mariupol' deep into the rear of Army Group Don. Such an operation could cut off enemy withdrawal routes from the Donbas and lead to the collapse of the entire German defensive structure in southern Russia. On 19 January, Vatutin sent his proposals to the *STAVKA*.[3] The *STAVKA*, realizing that the Hungarian 2d Army and German forces operating in the Ostrogozhsk and Rossosh' areas would be destroyed, approved Vatutin's plan and also considered a follow-on operation in the north, which would become operation Star. Thus the *STAVKA* envisioned a decisive offensive by both the Voronezh and Southwestern Fronts aimed ultimately at securing Kursk, Khar'kov, and the Donbas region. The Donbas operation would begin first. The *STAVKA* ordered the Voronezh and Southwestern Fronts to conduct the operation without an operational pause in order to deny the enemy time to erect fortified defensive positions, in particular along the Oskol and Northern Donets Rivers. The *STAVKA* gave formal approval to Vatutin's plan, codenamed "*Skachok*" (Gallop) on 20 January 1943.[4] The plan called for Soviet mobile forces to reach the Mariupol' area by the seventh day of the operation. By that time they were also to have captured the main crossings over the Dnepr River in the Zaporozh'ye and Dnepropetrovsk regions. The Southern Front would cooperate with Vatutin's forces by destroying German forces in Rostov, by occupying that city as well as the city of Novorossiisk, and by developing the offensive along the northern coast of the Sea of Azov. The offensive would begin on 29 January by which time the *STAVKA* anticipated Southwestern Front forces would be west of Starobel'sk and near the Northern Donets River.[5] Meanwhile, Vatutin's forces were to continue their advance.

As the date of the new offensive neared a 26 January *STAVKA* directive reflected optimism that the operation would succeed, stating:

> As a result of the successful actions of our forces on the Voronezh, right wing of the Southwestern, Don, and North Caucasus Fronts, the opposition of the enemy has been overcome. The enemy defense is penetrated on a wide front. The absence of deep reserves forces the enemy to introduce approaching formations in isolation [piecemeal] and from the march. Many empty places and sectors have formed which are covered by separate small detachments. The right

> wing of the Southwestern Front hangs over the Donbas. Favorable conditions approach for the encirclement and destruction in detail of the Donbas, Caucasus and Black Sea enemy groups.[6]

By this time the Soviets had destroyed Hungarian 2d Army, and the Bryansk and Voronezh Fronts had begun operations in the Voronezh and Kastornoye areas against German 2d Army. On 23 January the *STAVKA* had also sketched out for the Voronezh Front a subsequent operation codenamed Star which would commence on 1 February and which was designed to liberate Belgorod and Khar'kov at the same time that the Southwestern Front cleared the Donbas. At Zhukov's urgings, on 26 January the *STAVKA* added Kursk to the list of Voronezh Front objectives.[7]

Although these operations were evidence of the optimistic view of the *STAVKA* over Soviet offensive prospects there was some concern in the Soviet High Command about the staying power of Soviet forces and their ability to sustain such extensive operations. Both the Voronezh and Southwestern Fronts would conduct these new operations without pause using forces weakened by previous operations and tenuously fed and sustained by overextended supply lines connected to increasingly remote supply points. The expanded offensive sectors required that both *fronts* deploy all of their armies on line with virtually no second echelon or operational reserve available to strengthen the attack. Moreover, unlike the situation at Stalingrad, the *STAVKA* had *no* armies in reserve.[8]

The German Dilemma

While the *STAVKA* ordered its *fronts* to conduct sweeping operations in virtually every sector of the Eastern Front, the German command wrestled with the problem of restoring stability to its southern wing. Field Marshal Erich von Manstein struggled simultaneously to restore the deteriorating situation on the front of Army Group Don and to talk Hitler into authorizing a realistic withdrawal of Army Group "A" units from the north Caucasus, forces which were critically needed by Manstein to restore his precarious situation in the Donbas. Manstein realized that the issue at stake was far larger than just Army Group "A's" survival. Thus he wrote:

> During the battles in and south of the large bend of the Don, the aim of which had been to cover the withdrawal of Army Group "A" from the Caucasus, but in which the larger issue was whether the German southern wing could be preserved at all, a fresh problem was already emerging. The question was whether the southern wing would be able to maintain the Donets area.[9]

By the end of January, while Soviet forces were beginning to push into the gap between Manstein's army group, defending the Donbas, and Army Group "B," defending east of Khar'kov, some reinforcements began arriving in his area. 1st Panzer Army succeeded in moving five divisions from the Caucasus through Rostov into Manstein's sector. After its arrival 1st Panzer Army took responsibility for the defense of the Voroshilovgrad area while 4th Panzer Army and Army Detachment Hollidt defended along the central and southern portion of Manstein's lines in the great bend of the Northern Donets River. The German High Command also dispatched six divisions and two infantry brigades from the west.* Most important among these new units was the full strength and superbly equipped SS Panzer Corps consisting of three SS panzer divisions to which Hitler gave the specific task of defending the important city of Khar'kov. In early February the Germans moved additional divisions south from the areas of the Rzhev–Vyaz'ma and Demyansk salients. Manstein fed these units into the front in order to fill the yawning gaps while he pondered the question of assembling mobile reserves capable of conducting more than just a positional defense.

Opposing Forces

Soviet

The Soviet force structure changed little during the period December 1942 to January 1943. The *STAVKA* concentrated its efforts on applying the lessons learned in the Stalingrad operations and on creating new larger tank armies capable of conducting and sustaining deeper operations. It also continued to develop and field new and larger artillery support units.

Within the operating armies the *STAVKA* began creating intermediate rifle corps headquarters to control the larger number of units which armies controlled. However, the heavy and incessant campaigning of December and January had eroded seriously the infantry strength of rifle units and, more importantly, the tank strength of those mobile forces so critically needed to develop and sustain deep operations. In addition, as Soviet forces marched westward, they were sorely pressed to repair the systematic damage done to communications lines by withdrawing German forces. This damage and the lack of Soviet motor vehicle transport placed a severe strain on logistical networks. Most of the supply bases remained where they had been in mid-December; and the Soviets were

*Including the 320th Infantry Division, 333d Infantry Division, 335th Infantry Division deployed into 1st Panzer Army's sector.

forced to bring up supplies across the poor road network by use of their scarce vehicles, horses, or sheer manpower. Thus the Soviets called upon depleted armies to once again launch deep offensives from overextended supply lines.

The Southwestern Front of General N.F. Vatutin consisted of the 6th, 1st Guards, 3d Guards, and 5th Tank Armies and one mobile group, operating on a frontage of about 250 kilometers (see Appendix 2, Order of Battle). *Front* strength had eroded to a combat strength of about 325,000 men supported by just over 500 tanks. *Front* composition and strength in late January was as follows:[10]

6th Army – Lt General F. M. Kharitonov	40,000 men	40 tanks
1 rifle corps		
4 rifle divisions		
1 rifle brigade		
1 tank brigade		
1 tank regiment		
1st Guards Army – Lt General V. I. Kuznetsov	70,000 men	
2 rifle corps		
7 rifle divisions		
Mobile Group Popov – Lt General M. M. Popov	55,000 men	212 tanks
4 tank corps		
3 rifle divisions		
2 tank brigades		
1 ski brigade		
3d Guards Army – Lt General D. D. Lelyushenko	100,000 men	110 tanks
2 rifle corps		
9 rifle divisions		
3 tank corps		
1 mechanized corps		
1 cavalry corps		
5th Tank Army – Lt General I. T. Shlemin	40,000 men	
3 rifle divisions		
Front Reserve	20,000 men	300 tanks
2 tank corps		
1 cavalry corps		

Soviet rifle divisions in these armies, supposedly at a TOE strength of about 10,000 men, counted only between 6–8,000 men each. Tank corps numbered from 30 to 50 tanks each and their personnel strengths numbered about 50 percent of TOE requirements.[11]

German

German forces facing the Southwestern Front consisted of the right wing of Army Detachment Lanz defending the southern and eastern approaches to Khar'kov and Kupyansk, 1st Panzer Army defending from Kaban'ye, across the Northern Donets River to south of Voroshilovgrad, and the left wing of Army Detachment Hollidt defending from southeast of Voroshilovgrad along the Northern Donets River to northeast of Shakhty. German force composition was as follows:[12]

A. Abt. Lanz	20,000 men	
2 infantry divisions (298th, 320th)		
1st Panzer Army	40,000 men	40 tanks
1 army corps (XXX)		
2 panzer corps (III, XXXX)		
2 infantry divisions (3d Mountain, 335th)		
3 panzer divisions (7th, 19th, 27th)		
A. Abt. Hollidt	100,000 men	60 tanks
2 army corps (XXIX, XVII)		
1 panzer corps (XXXXVIII)		
1 group (Mieth)		
7 infantry divisions (62d, 294th, 304th, 306th, 336th, 384th, 8th Air Force Field Division)		
2 panzer divisions (5th, 22d)		
2 groups (79th, 177th)		
Units enroute		300 tanks (approx)
SS Panzer Corps (3 divisions)		
333d Infantry Division (at Barvenkovo)		

German infantry units were also well below TOE strength as were panzer divisions, since most had been in heavy combat continuously since late November. Tank strength in panzer divisions varied, but at any one time between twenty and forty tanks were available for combat per division.[13] Reinforcements, including the SS Panzer Corps, were at or near full TOE strength. A rough comparison of forces within each sector resulted in the correlation of forces shown in the table below.

CORRELATION OF FORCES
Donbas Operation – 29 January 1942

SOVIET		*GERMAN*	
Southwestern Front			
6th Army	40,000 men 40 tanks	*A. Abt.* Lanz (part)	20,000 men
1st Guards Army	70,000 men	1st Panzer Army	40,000 men 40 tanks (est.)
Mobile Group Popov	55,000 men 212 tanks	*A. Abt.* Hollidt	100,000 men 60 tanks (est.)
3d Guards Army	100,000 men 110 tanks		
5th Tank Army	40,000 men		
Reserves	20,000 men		

OPERATION "GALLOP"

Total Strength	325,000 men*	2×1	160,000 men**
	362 tanks	4×1	100 tanks (est.)

*Reinforced by 300 tanks of 1st Guards and 25th Tank Corps.

**Reinforced by two divisions of SS Panzer Corps with approximately 250 tanks.

The initial Soviet advantage in infantry of 2:1 was exceeded by the Soviet superiority in tanks of up to 4:1. However, mechanical losses and lack of fuel would quickly reduce this Soviet armored superiority. Soon after the Southwestern Front's offensive began, Army Group Don shifted units from right to left in order to bolster defenses in 1st Panzer Army's sector and reduce the overwhelming odds against the German defenders (including 3d Panzer Division, 11th Panzer Division and SS Panzer Grenadier Division "Viking").

Area of Operations

The Southwestern Front was to attack westward across the Aydar and Oskol Rivers then wheel southwest and south across the Northern Donets River and through the Donbas region toward the Dnepr River (see Map 17). The countryside north and south of the Northern Donets River consisted of rolling hills occasionally covered with sparse vegetation. The western banks of the rivers and the southern bank of the Northern Donets were higher than the opposing banks thus offering the tactical advantage to the defender. Marshes and lakes along the river valleys, in particular, along the Northern Donets, inhibited free movement of forces along or across the valleys. South of the towns of Slavyansk, Kramatorsk, and Artemovsk, the hills became more pronounced.

Most roads (all were unpaved) followed the river valleys, and most population centers and communications centers were nestled in the valleys and along these roads. The main roads into the Donbas from the northeast passed either through the large city of Voroshilovgrad or up the Kazenny Torets River past Slavyansk and Kramatorsk and up the Bakhmutka River through Artemovsk. The latter two approaches, because of the steep and eroded valley walls and sprawling built-up areas, were considered by the Germans to be unsuited for an advance by large armored forces. Further west more open country permitted better cross-country movement of armored forces via Barvenkovo or Lozovaya toward the southwest and the Dnepr River. Even these open spaces were crisscrossed with ravines and dry (or frozen) creek beds which inhibited movement of mechanized forces. Snow cover in February was light (less

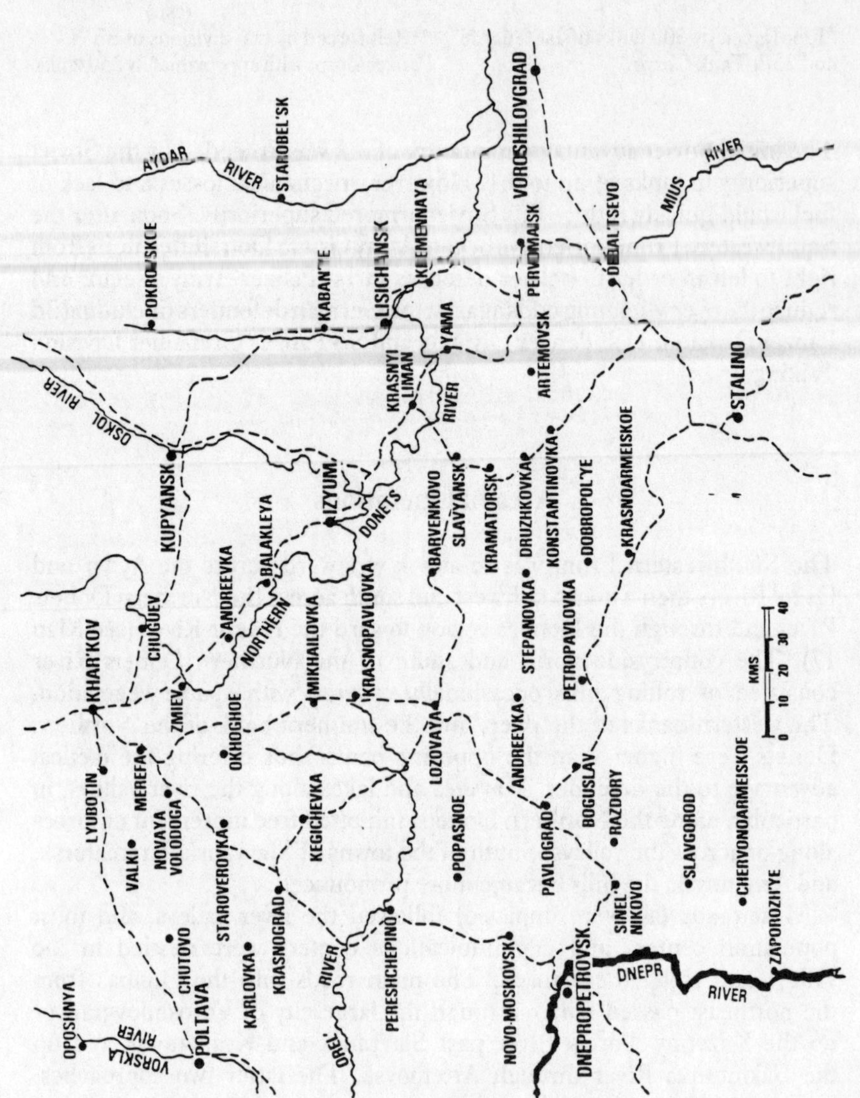

MAP 17. DONBAS AREA OF OPERATIONS

than 10 cm) and temperatures moderate for that time of year by usual Soviet standards (0 to -10 degrees centigrade).

Army Planning

Soviet planning for Operation *Gallop* was hastily done while active offensive operations were taking place (see Map 18). After 21 January *front* headquarters formulated army missions and after 25 January the Voronezh Front pulled mobile units out of combat to regroup and re-equip them while rifle units continued their advance.[14] Meanwhile, army commanders received their missions and planned their attacks.

6th Army

Kharitonov's 6th Army was to attack on 29 January in a 60 kilometer sector with all of his rifle forces organized in a single echelon. His forces would penetrate enemy defenses and advance toward Balakleya and Krasnograd in order to protect the *front* main attack from attack from the north. By the seventh day of the operation the army was to advance 110 kilometers to a line running north and south of Balakleya.[15] The Voronezh Front's 3d Tank Army, attacking on 2 February, would protect 6th Army's northern (right) flank.

Kharitonov would make his main attack in a 20 kilometer sector on the army right flank. There the 15th Rifle Corps' 350th, 172d, and 6th Rifle Divisions would strike westward toward Kupyansk and drive the defending German 298th Infantry Division back toward the Northern Donets River (away from Khar'kov). 6th Army would then encircle both the 298th and 320th Infantry Divisions, defending further south, against the banks of the river and destroy them. A tank brigade, a tank regiment, and three artillery regiments would support the 6th Army assault. The 3d Tank Corps of Popov's Mobile Group would enter combat on 6th Army's left flank in order to exploit toward the southwest and south along with the remainder of Group Popov.

1st Guards Army

Kuznetsov's 1st Guards Army would attack on 30 January in a 130 kilometer sector with the bulk of its rifle units forward. On the army right flank 4th Guards Rifle Corps would attack in a 25 kilometer sector with three rifle divisions abreast to penetrate enemy defenses and advance toward Krasnyi Liman and across the Northern Donets River toward Barvenkovo. After assisting the introduction of Mobile Group Popov, army forces would pivot southward to envelop enemy forces in

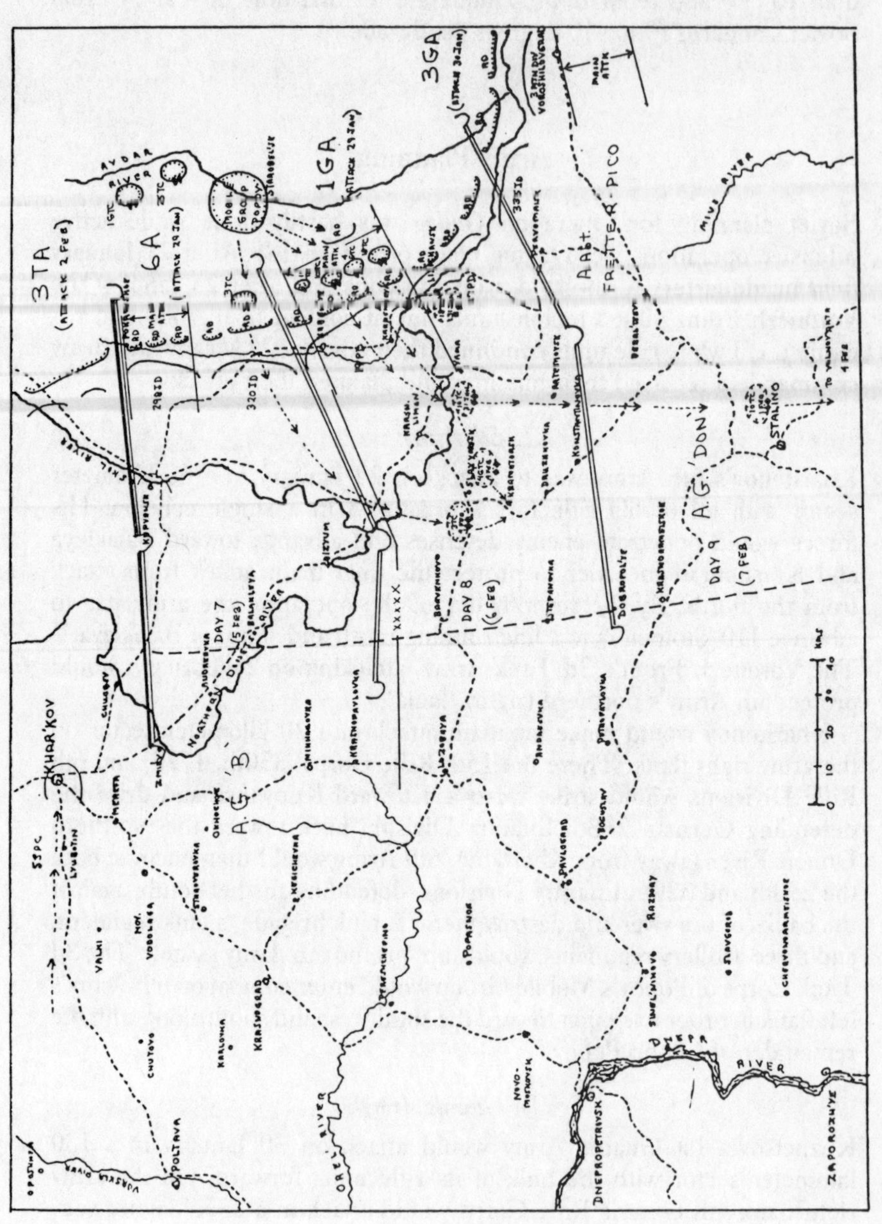

MAP 18. OPERATION "GALLOP" PLAN

the Slavyansk and Artemovsk region. 6th Guards Rifle Corps' three rifle divisions would attack across the Northern Donets River opposite and south of Lisichansk in order to seize the city and assist the wheeling movement of 4th Guards Rifle Corps. By the eighth day of the operation 1st Guards Army units would advance to a line running from Barvenkovo to Krasnoarmeiskii Rudnik.[16]

Mobile Group Popov

The Southwestern Front's Mobile Group, commanded by Lieutenant General M.M. Popov, had the mission of attacking through advancing 6th Army and 1st Guards Army units to Krasnoarmeiskoye and Mariupol' on the Sea of Azov in order to cut off German withdrawal from the Donbas. The mobile group's four tank corps were to advance up to 300 kilometers deep, slice up the enemy defensive formations, pin them into population centers so that rifle forces could destroy them piecemeal, and pave the way for a decisive and rapid advance of *front* main forces.[17] To avoid the problems of deep operations experienced in the Middle Don operation, most tank corps were to cooperate with specific rifle divisions which themselves were reinforced with motor transport or whose men rode on the accompanying tanks. The use of a mobile group command headquarters was designed to remedy earlier command and control and coordination problems.

Popov gave Major General M.D. Sinenko's 3d Tank Corps the mission of cooperating with the 57th Rifle Division in an advance from 6th Army's sector southwestward to Slavyansk which he was to secure by the evening of 4 February. Subsequently, 3d Tank Corps would join 4th Guards Tank Corps in an advance on Kramatorsk. Major General P.P. Poluboyarov's 4th Guards Tank Corps, cooperating with the 38th Guards Rifle Division, would secure crossings over the Northern Donets River, advance on Kramatorsk from the northeast, and occupy the city by 4 February. A shortage of tanks forced Poluboyarov to concentrate all of his remaining armor (forty tanks) in the 14th Guards Tank Brigade. That brigade would conduct the corps attack.[18]

Major General V.G. Burkov's 10th Tank Corps, reinforced by the 11th Tank Brigade, was to attack in cooperation with the 52d Rifle Division and cross the Northern Donets River on the first day of the operation. On the second day the corps would occupy Artemovsk and approach the major city of Stalino from the north. By the fifth day of the operation, 10th Tank Corps was to reach the Volnovakha area deep in Army Group Don's rear.

Popov's last tank corps, General B.S. Bakharov's 18th, was to force the Northern Donets River opposite Lisichansk with the 41st Guards Rifle Division and support that division's attack to seize the city. Thereafter, the corps would move southwest to join other mobile group units. To

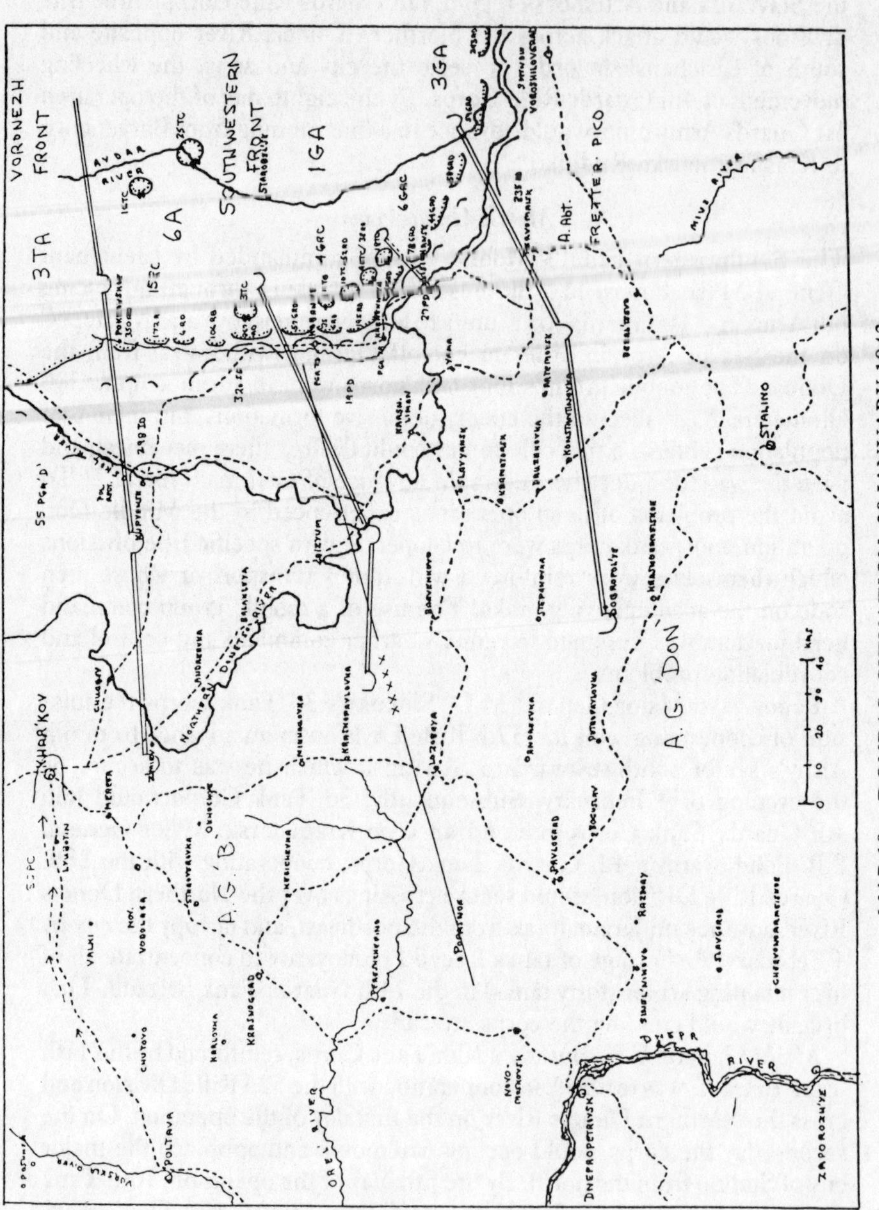

MAP 19. DONBAS. SITUATION. 29 JANUARY 1943

support Mobile Group Popov or exploit other unforeseen opportunities, General Vatutin held two tank corps (1st Guards and 25th Tank Corps) and one cavalry corps (1st Guards Cavalry Corps) in *front* reserve.

3d Guards Army

Simultaneously with the 1st Guards Army attack, Lelyushenko's 3d Guards Army was to attack in a 100 kilometer sector north and south of Voroshilovgrad. Lelyushenko's forces would penetrate German defenses and advance to Stalino to meet 1st Guards Army forces and surround all German forces in the Donbas. Lelyushenko planned to launch his main attack in a 20 kilometer sector on his right flank with five rifle divisions, one tank corps, and one mechanized corps. Rifle units would complete the penetration of enemy defenses by the middle of the first day of operations and then would assist the introduction of the army's mobile group. The two left flank rifle divisions of 3d Guards Army would hold the left bank of the Northern Donets river and a bridgehead on the right bank and prepare to destroy enemy units in Kamensk in cooperation with 5th Tank Army units. Lelyushenko retained one rifle division and one rifle brigade in army reserve. By the ninth day of the operation 3d Guards Army's divisions would reach a line extending from Krasnoarmeiskoye to Yelizavetovka (west of Stalino).[19]

5th Tank Army

Lieutenant General I.T. Shelmin's 5th Tank Army, consisting of just three rifle divisions, was to occupy defensive positions along the Northern Donets River until 8 February in order to protect the left flank of the Southwestern Front. The army would join the offensive only after German troops began to withdraw from the Northern Donets River.

All of the missions assigned to Southwestern Front armies assumed that the armies would continue to operate in existing sectors and that no major changes would be made to their operational formation. 17th Air Army with 274 aircraft would provide air support for the Southwestern Front.[20]

Situation on the Eve of the Offensive

By the evening of 29 January Soviet 6th Army and 1st Guards Army forces had crossed the Aydar River, liberated Starobel'sk and approached the thin German defenses running from north to south along the Krasnaya River and along the west bank of the Northern Donets River (see Map 19). In the northern sector of the *front* zone the German 298th Infantry Division covered the western approaches to Pokrovskoye with small advance elements while the bulk of its forces prepared to defend Kupyansk, 30 kilometers to the west. Further south along the Krasnaya

River, the 320th Infantry Division defended Svatovo on the river's west bank. South along the east bank of the river the 19th Panzer Division defended Kaban'ye and Kremennaya. Near the junction of the Krasnaya and Northern Donets Rivers the 27th Panzer Division defended Rubezhnoye and villages covering the eastern approaches to Lisichansk. These German divisions defended in makeshift fieldworks in sectors of up to 30 kilometers width per division.

South of Lisichansk and through Voroshilovgrad the 335th Infantry Division and 3d Mountain Division occupied stronger defensive positions on the western bank of the Northern Donets River. German XXX Army Corps (Army Detachment Fretter-Pico) controlled the thin defensive lines south of Kaban'ye and sought to defend, if possible, on the Northern Donets River line until reinforcements arrived. During this critical period, while 4th Panzer Army covered the extraction of 1st Panzer Army from the northern Caucasus via Rostov, XXX Army Corps would have to buy time until 1st Panzer Army's arrival.

Conduct of the Offensive (29 January – 20 February)

6th Army's Advance to Zmiyev

On the morning of 29 January Kharitonov's army resumed its offensive spearheaded by 15th Rifle Corps operating toward Kupyansk on the army's right flank (see Maps 20–22). The attack met with immediate success. The 350th Rifle Division rapidly pursued German 298th Infantry Division units to Kupyansk and gained a foothold over the Krasnaya River north and south of the city. The 298th Division stubbornly held onto its positions until late on 2 February when, threatened by Soviet 3d Tank Army's advance into its left rear and the 172d Rifle Division's thrust against its right rear, the division was forced to give up the city. By the time the 298th Infantry Division withdrew, 3d Tank Army's 6th Guards Cavalry Corps and the divisions of Soviet 6th Army had virtually encircled the German division. It began a harried, costly, three day fighting withdrawal to new defense lines along the Northern Donets River at Chuguyev.

In 6th Army's center sector the 172d and 6th Rifle Divisions plunged rapidly forward and penetrated between the German 298th and 320th Infantry Divisions. While the 298th withdrew to and beyond Kupyansk the 320th Infantry Division conducted a delaying operation back toward its headquarters at Izyum. On 5 February the 172d Rifle Division seized Balakleya while the 6th Rifle Division isolated and battled with 320th Infantry Division units between Balakleya and Izyum. On the 6th Army's left flank the 267th Rifle Division and 106th Rifle Brigade encircled German forces in Izyum while other elements of the force outflanked the 320th Infantry Division from the south. Izyum fell to the Soviet 267th Rifle Division on 5 February, but a complex battle of encirclement followed as the German 320th Infantry Division conducted a fighting withdrawal which slowed 6th Army's advance for almost six days.[21]

Meanwhile, Vatutin ordered 6th Army to accelerate its advance in order to bring its units on line with those of 3d Tank Army which were already approaching Khar'kov. Consequently, Kharitonov shifted forces from his right wing to his center to eliminate the bothersome obstacle of the 320th Infantry Division, to reduce Andreyevka (occupied by a battalion *Kampfgruppe* of SS Panzer Division "Leibstandarte Adolf Hitler," sent to assist the 320th Infantry Division), to secure crossings over the Northern Donets River south of Zmiyev, and to cut the critical Khar'kov–Lozovaya rail line in order to deny German reinforcement of Khar'kov from the south.[22]

On the afternoon of 7 February, with regrouping complete, 6th Army divisions renewed their advance while sizeable portions of the 172d Rifle Division, 6th Rifle Division, and 106th Rifle Brigade tried to reduce the 320th Infantry Division pocket which moved slowly westward. By the evening of 8 February Soviet forces had expelled the Germans from Andreyevka, and the 106th Rifle Brigade secured and fortified the town. Further north the 172d Rifle Division ran into stiff resistance on the approaches of Zmiyev, in particular along the rail line into town from Balakleya. Meanwhile, the continued stubborn resistance of the German 320th Infantry Division forced Kharitonov to commit the 350th Rifle Division against it. By now, in a welter of combat, the 320th Rifle was punching west toward the Northern Donets River and freedom. Virtually the entire 6th Army moved to halt it. After a series of bloody small unit engagements the 320th Infantry Division finally broke out westward having lost, by Soviet count, 4000 men east and southeast of Balakleya.[23]

By 10 February 6th Army's 350th Rifle Division finally reached the Northern Donets River but encountered a German bridgehead opposite Zmiyev held firmly by SS Panzer Corps' newly arrived Panzer Division "Leibstandarte Adolf Hitler." Further south the 172d, 6th, and 267th Rifle Divisions safely crossed the Northern Donets River near Andreyevka but still were unable to cut the rail line running south from Khar'kov which was now held by small task forces dispatched by SS Panzer Corps. However, 6th Guards Cavalry Corps of 3d Tank Army passed through 6th Army's lines, crossed the Northern Donets River, and on 10 February, seized the rail line north of Novaya Vodolaga only to be expelled by elements of SS Panzer Division "Das Reich" the next day.

6th Army's advance was on schedule; and Kharitonov, with Vatutin's approval, continued his advance. The appearance of SS Panzer Corps in the Khar'kov area, however, deflected that Soviet advance toward the southwest like water seeking the path of least resistance around an obstacle. This began a trend that would continue with future disastrous consequences for 6th Army as well as 1st Guards Army.

1st Guards Army's Advance to Slavyansk and Lisichansk

Kuznetsov's army began its offensive on the morning of 30 January from positions his army's units had battled for the day before (see Map 19). The 57th and 35th Guards Rifle Divisions struck 19th Panzer Division's units at Kaban'ye late on 29 January while the 195th Rifle Division hit 19th Panzer Division's positions at Kremennaya. After seizing Kaban'ye the Soviet 57th and 35th Guards Rifle Divisions pushed unopposed across the Krasnaya River and advanced on Krasnyi Limon, an important rail junction north of the Northern Donets River. Meanwhile, on 30 January heavy battle raged for possession of Kremennaya. Finally, after very heavy opposition, on the morning of 31 January the 195th Rifle Division and 4th Guards Tank Corps units cleared Kremennaya, and the German 19th Panzer Division withdrew to positions south of the Northern Donets River.[24]

After clearing Kremennaya Poluboyarov's 4th Guards Tank Corps began its exploitation, and the 195th Rifle Division moved across the Krasnaya River to join the 35th Guards Rifle Division in an assault on Krasnyi Liman. Having passed through positions vacated by 19th Panzer Division on 29 January, on the morning of 30 January the 35th Guards Rifle Division units struck Krasnyi Liman with elements of the 195th Rifle Division. These two units enveloped the city from the south while the 11th Tank Brigade and 102d Guards Rifle Regiment struck the city from the north. By the morning of 31 January the 35th Guards Rifle Division had taken the city. Meanwhile, the 57th Rifle Division with 10th Tank Corps tanks swept west past the city toward the Northern Donets River.[25] However, a sudden rise in temperatures caused a temporary thaw that made the advance difficult and hindered the operations of both the tank corps and rear service units.

With the withdrawal of 19th Panzer Division units to positions around Lisichansk, south of the Northern Donets River, the way seemed clear for 4th Guards Rifle Corps units to cross the Northern Donets and push rapidly to Slavyansk (see Map 20). However, the timely arrival of the German 7th Panzer Division in Slavyansk and 3d Panzer Division in the area east of the city filled the gap and stemmed the Soviet advance. On 1 February the 35th Guards Rifle Division with three regiments abreast crossed the river west of Krasnyi Liman and cut the main road running from Khar'kov and Izyum to Slavyansk. Advanced elements of the German 333d Infantry Division, newly arrived from France and assigned the mission of filling the gap west of Slavyansk, withdrew westward toward Barvenkovo.

After replenishing dwindling supplies and solidifying its hold on the highway, the 35th Guards Rifle Division cooperated with 6th Army's 267th Rifle Division in securing Izyum and dispatched forces westward toward Barvenkovo driving elements of the German 333d Infantry Division before them. By noon on 6 February Barvenkovo had fallen to the 35th Guards Rifle Division together with twenty-six rail cars and tons of supplies and equipment. The division then took two days for rest and resupply before resuming its offensive westward.[26]

Meanwhile, the 57th Guards Rifle Division and 195th Rifle Division, after crossing the Northern Donets River, engaged in an unexpectedly heavy battle for Slavyansk (see Map 20). On 2 February the 195th Rifle Division's regiments approached Slavyansk from the north and east. The uncoordinated advance predictably hindered the division's attempt to seize the city from the march. However, 1st Guards Army anticipated little problem in taking the city once the 57th Guards Rifle Division, which was still enroute from the northeast, arrived. Kuznetsov, however, had not reckoned on the timely arrival in the city of the 7th Panzer Division with its thirty-five tanks.

On the morning of 3 February the scattered regiments of the 195th Rifle Division were attacked by German forces advancing from Kramatorsk while elements of the division were still in heavy combat in the north-eastern suburb of Slavyansk. 4th Guards Rifle Corps headquarters promised to support the 195th Rifle Division with 57th Guards Rifle Division and sent the 3d Tank Corps to assist 4th Guards Tank Corps, then approaching Kramatorsk, in the task of distracting the German force in Slavyansk. Meanwhile, the sudden German tank attack by elements of 7th Panzer Division drove 195th Rifle Division forces to defensive positions east and north of the city.[27] Finally, on 4 February the 57th Guards Rifle Division arrived at Slavyansk and took up positions on the 195th Rifle Division's right flank. Further south the 4th Guards Tank Corps dug in at Kramatorsk and awaited the assistance of 3d Tank Corps.

Thus, on 3 February the long and bitter battle for Slavyansk began. Thwarted in their attempts to take the city rapidly, the Soviets, after 4 February poured a steady stream of reinforcements into the area to secure the key position. German 1st Panzer Army, activated at Konstantinovka on 4 February to control the sector, did likewise.[28] For the Soviets Slavyansk was a major obstacle in the fulfillment of their offensive aims. For the Germans Slavyansk became a bulwark, the western anchor of 1st Panzer Army's defense line. German retention of

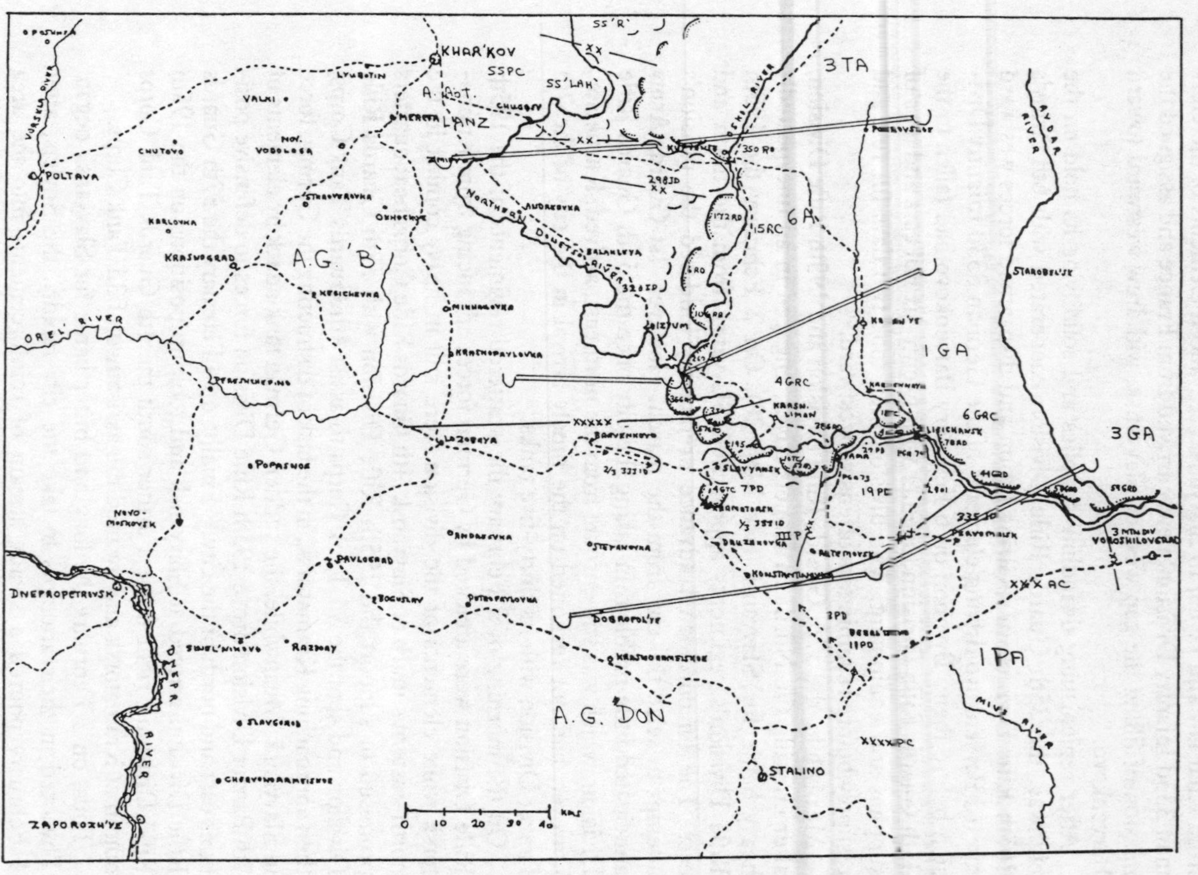

MAP 20. DONBAS, SITUATION, 2–3 FEBRUARY 1943

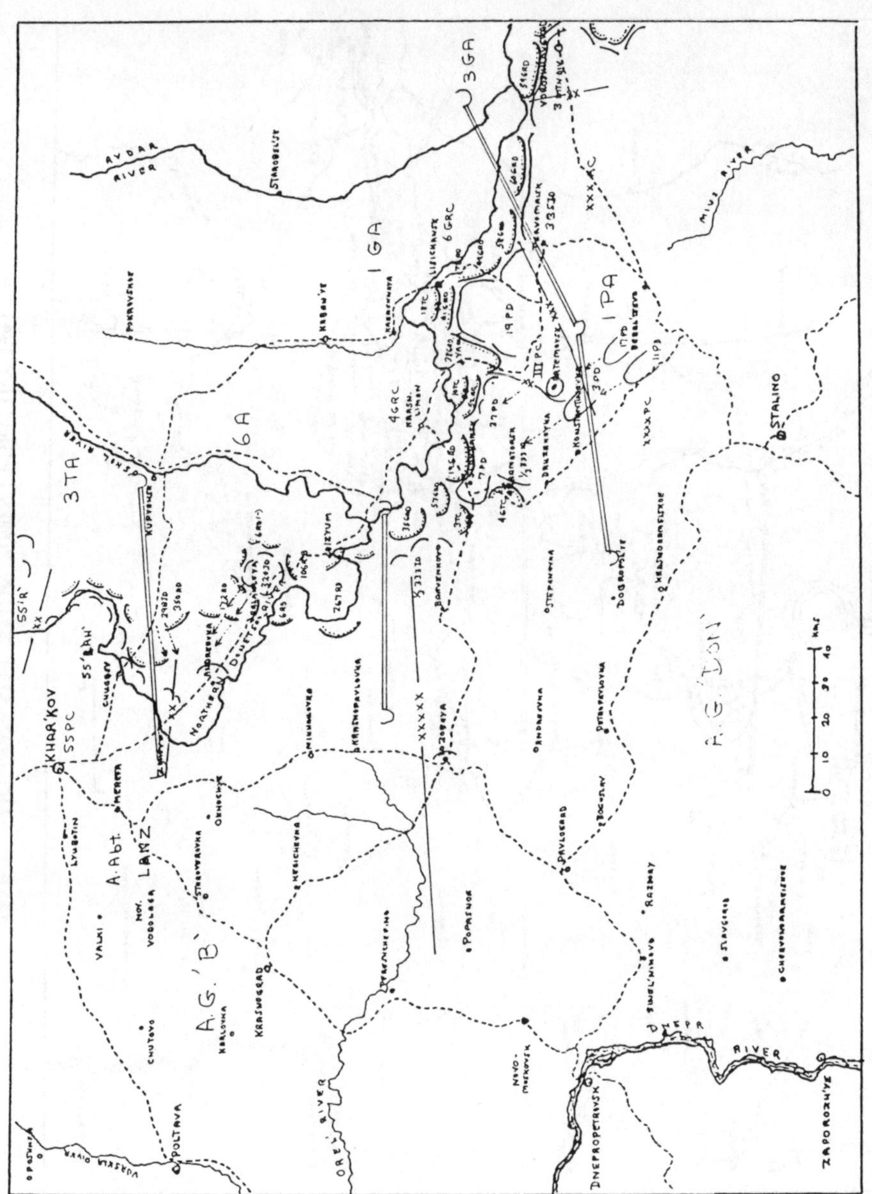

MAP 21. DONBAS, SITUATION, 2000 5 FEBRUARY 1943

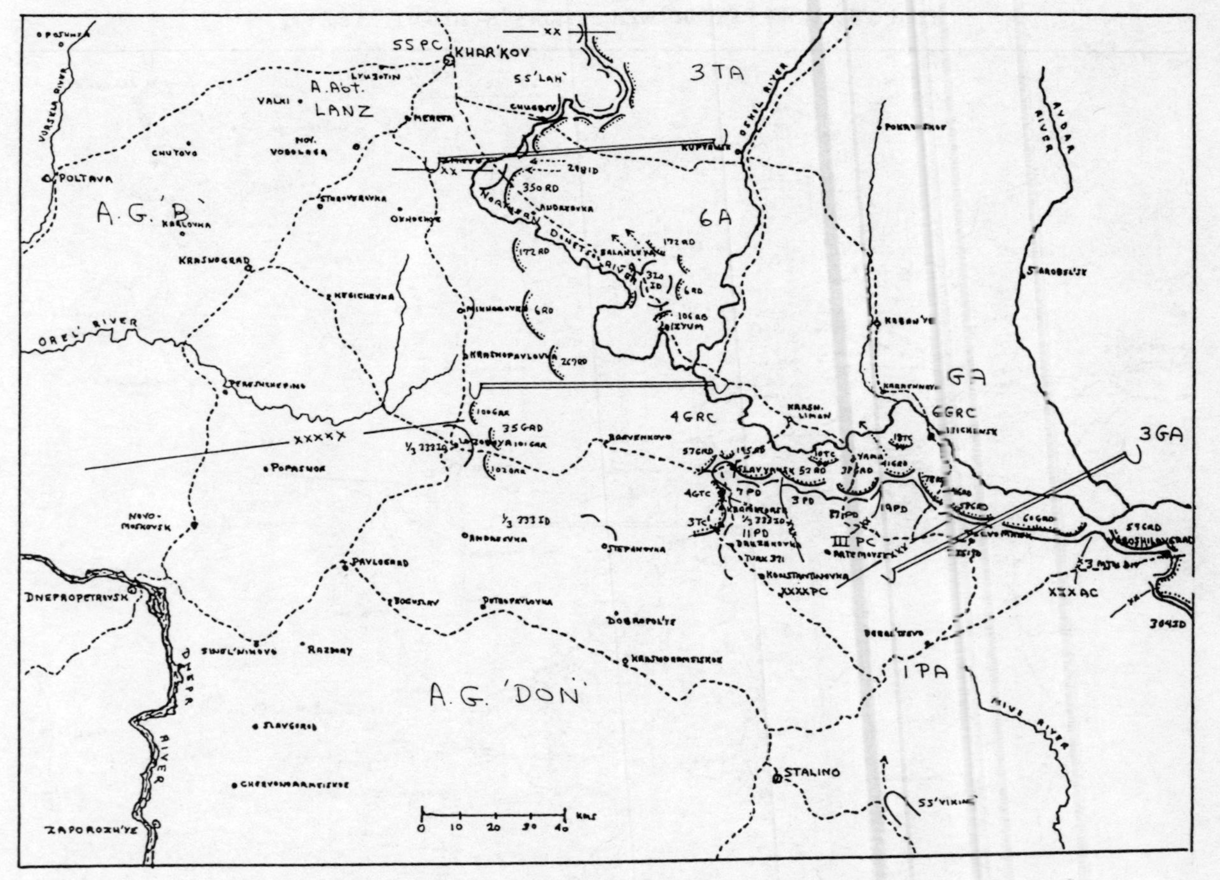

MAP 22. DONBAS, SITUATION, 2000 9 FEBRUARY 1943

Slavyansk dictated that Soviet forces further extend themselves westward and that extension, while threatening to outflank 1st Panzer Army, also provided an opportunity for future German counterattacks.

While 4th Guards Rifle Corps was crossing the Northern Donets River and hammering German positions at Slavyansk, 6th Guards Rifle Corps struck the center of German XXX Army Corps defensive positions at and south of Lisichansk (see Maps 19–22). The 41st Guards Rifle Division, cooperating with 18th Tank Corps armor, and the 78th Guards and 44th Guards Rifle Divisions, struck German units and forced them to withdraw steadily toward the main German defensive positions along the Northern Donets River. After a full day of combat for possession of Rubezhnoye 41st Guards Rifle Division troops pushed the Germans from the town. Using brushwood and planks to help cross the weakened ice surface of the river the division began a heated battle for Lisichansk supported by 18th Tank Corps' tanks. By 1 February the guardsmen had seized a foothold in Lisichansk; but, faced by heavy resistance from elements of 27th Panzer Division and the 19th Panzer Division, the division's advance ground to a halt.[29]

On the 41st Guards Rifle Division's right flank the 38th Guards Rifle Division, after assisting the 4th Guards Tank Corps' 14th Guards Tank Brigade to cross the Northern Donets River and advance on 1 February towards Kramatorsk, struck south against the German XXX Army Corps' left flank near Yama. The 19th Panzer Division blocked the 38th Guards Rifle Division's advance in heavy fighting on 2 February at Yama and Seribryanka. Steady pressure on the Germans built as the 52d Rifle Division, cooperating with Soviet 10th Tank Corps late on 2 February seeped further south along the Bakhmutka River around the German 19th Panzer Division's left flank, an advance that threatened to separate 19th Panzer Division from the 7th Panzer Division on its left flank.

While battles raged for Lisichansk the Soviet 78th Rifle Division and 44th Guards Rifle Division approached the Northern Donets River south of the city. The 78th seized several bridgeheads across the river, but the 901st Training (Lehr) Regiment of 19th Panzer Division, defending the river's western bank, stymied repeated attempts of the 78th to enlarge the bridgeheads. Likewise, further south the 44th Guards Rifle Division crossed the river against the German 335th Infantry Division which occupied more formidable defenses than those existing further north. A foothold gained by the 44th Guards Rifle Division at Krymskaya, 30 kilometers southeast of Lisichansk, became a focal point of conflict as 335th Infantry Division units, with a few tanks in support, conducted repeated counterattacks to reduce the Soviet bridgehead. It could not be reduced nor could, for the moment, the Soviets expand it.[30]

The 6th Guards Rifle Corps resumed its assaults on 19th Panzer Division and 335th Infantry Division defensive positions on 2 February. By 4 and 5 February the 41st Guards Rifle Division and elements of 78th Guards Rifle Division, in heavy street fighting, struggled for possession of Lisichansk. On 6 February 44th Guards Rifle Division joined the attack, and 19th Panzer Division was finally forced to withdraw to new defensive positions running southwest of the city.[31] In the ensuing three days the 19th Panzer Division incessantly shifted forces left and right to stop the Soviet attacks. Finally, on 9 February Soviet pressure slackened as Kuznetsov ordered the 41st Guards Rifle Division to pull out of line and join the 195th and 57th Guards Rifle Division units in their increasingly frustrating attempts to seize Slavyansk, thus initiating a process of moving Soviet forces steadily westward. After 41st Guards Rifle Division's departure from the Lisichansk area, German defense lines stabilized along a line running east to west south of Lisichansk. Thus, by 9 February the Soviet 6th Guards Rifle Corps had firm possession of the south bank of the Northern Donets River, but the 19th Panzer Division and 335th Infantry Division would permit it to advance no further.

Mobile Group Popov's Initial Operations

Popov's Mobile Group, although hindered by shortages of fuel and ammunition, supported the 4th Guards Rifle Corps' and 6th Guards Rifle Corps' assaults (see Maps 19–22). Popov's forces numbered 180 tanks at the time of their commitment to combat, thus each corps attacked in understrength condition.[32] Most corps (like Poluboyarov's 4th Guards) concentrated their remaining armor assets in one of their brigades. The 3rd Tank Corps followed the 38th Guards Rifle Division's advance and, by 4 February, moved into the region northeast of Slavyansk. There it received orders to reinforce 4th Guards Tank Corps units, which had just arrived in Kramatorsk. The 4th Guards Tank Corps had crossed the Northern Donets River on 1 February after the 195th Rifle Division had taken Kremennaya, had passed by 7th Panzer Division's right flank, and had secured Kramatorsk. The following day, under attack from the now alerted German 7th Panzer Division, Poluboyarov's corps dug in at Kramatorsk to await reinforcements from 3d Tank Corps. The 38th Guards Rifle Division, accompanying 4th Guards Tank Corps, was blocked in its forward movement by the newly arrived German 3d Panzer Division which occupied defensive positions east of Slavyansk with its right flank tied in, at first loosely, with 19th Panzer Division further east. 4th Guards Tank Corps, deprived of its supporting infantry, and its tank strength down to thirty-seven tanks, remained in a precarious position at Kramatorsk. To alleviate Poluboyarov's problem somewhat, on 5 February 3d Tank Corps joined his corps at Kramatorsk, thus raising their combined armored strength to sixty tanks.[33] Thus reinforced, Poluboyarov regrouped his forces and transferred seventeen tanks from 14th Guards Tank Brigade to 12th Guards Tank Brigade. The 13th Guards Tank Brigade, as before, remained tankless. In addition, to compensate for Poluboyarov's lack of infantry support Popov reinforced the 4th Guards Tank Corps with two units from his reserve, the 9th Tank Brigade and the 7th Ski Brigade. He also ordered Poluboyarov to prepare for future operations to the south when sufficient rifle forces were available to relieve him at Kramatorsk.

Burkov's 10th Tank Corps, cooperating with the 52d Rifle Division, because of the partial thaw had a difficult march to the Northern Donets River. Roads were in such bad condition that his units had to move cross country, led by tanks using angle irons to clear a path through the mud. His slow advance brought his corps to the river on 1 February. Once across the river Burkov's units ran into the 3d Panzer Division's defenses, and the Germans halted both the 52d Rifle Division's and 10th Tank Corps' forward progress. Burkov's corps remained with the 52d to provide support to the infantry until 11 February when Popov ordered it to reinforce Poluboyarov's force, then operating south of Kramatorsk. Finally, Bakharov's corps cooperated with the 41st Guards Rifle Division's advance to and through Lisichansk. It remained enmeshed with that rifle division in a struggle against 19th Panzer Division until 10 February.

Thus, by 6 February Popov's mobile group had fallen far short of achieving its immediate objectives. The 4th Guards and 3d Tank Corps had penetrated south of Slavyansk, but both were tied up in fighting for Kramatorsk, and neither had the requisite armor strength to conduct a sustained drive elsewhere. The 10th and 18th Tank Corps were bogged down supporting rifle units between Slavyansk and Lisichansk. Compounding Popov's frustration the Germans were shifting new forces, including armor units, into the Slavyansk area. Kuznetsov shared Popov's frustration, for time was running out if 1st Guards Army was to develop the offensive further.

The Battles for Slavyansk and Kramatorsk – 6–10 February

Meanwhile, 4th Guards Rifle Corps units struggled to take Slavyansk against increasing German resistance (see Map 21). By 6 February the 57th Guards Rifle Division operated against German defenses on the northern and western side of the city, and the already battered 195th Rifle Division clung to its footholds in the eastern part of the city and defended against German counterattacks from the southeast. The German 7th Panzer Division with its thirty-five tanks defended the city proper and linked up east of Slavyansk with the 3d Panzer Division whose front extended farther eastward into the Bakhmutka valley. The Soviet 4th Guards and 3d Tank Corps, which occupied Kramatorsk, also threatened Slavyansk from the south.

The German position at Slavyansk, however, was improving as 1st Panzer Army strengthened the defenses by moving reinforcements into the region. On 4 February it assigned to the newly arrived XXXX Panzer Corps the mission of

> while continuing to hold Slavyansk [with 7th Panzer Division], to throw back over the Donets the enemy who had crossed it west of the town and to regain touch with friendly forces in the Izyum area.[34]

The XXXX Panzer Corps had available to it the 7th Panzer Division, most of it encircled at Slavyansk; the 11th Panzer Division (sixteen tanks), which began detraining at Konstantinovka on 5 February; the 333d Infantry Division, which had one regiment detraining at Konstantinovka and two regiments in the Lozovaya and Barvenkovo area after 3 February; and several locally recruited Turkish battalions (the 94th and 371st) located at ruzhkovka, south of Kramatorsk.[35]

While these units could by no means fulfill the ambitious mission assigned them they were capable of conducting a credible defense against the eroding strength of Soviet 4th Guards Rifle Corps and Group Popov. Of course, the larger question was as yet unanswered, that of who or what would fill the large gap between XXXX Panzer Corps and SS Panzer Corps operating to the northwest in the Khar'kov area. The immediate problem facing the XXXX Panzer Corps was to deal with the threat to Slavyansk and the threat posed by 4th Guards Tank Corps and 3d Tank Corps at Kramatorsk. To meet these threats XXXX Panzer Corps ordered the 7th Panzer Division to continue its defense of Slavyansk while the 11th Panzer Division, reinforced by a Turkish battalion and one regiment of 333d Infantry Division, would cover Konstantinovka and prepare to advance north toward Kramatorsk and Slavyansk once all of 11th Panzer Division had arrived in sector.

1st Panzer Army headquarters repeatedly urged XXXX Panzer Corps to seize Kramatorsk and open communications routes into Slavyansk from the south, and ordered 333d Infantry Division forces at Lozovaya and Barvenkovo to concentrate east of Barvenkovo.[36] Pursuant to these orders, on 6 February one mechanized regiment and an artillery battalion of 11th Panzer Division moved north from Konstantinovka towards Kramatorsk but ran into 4th Guards Tank Corps units at Druzhkovka. After losing ten armored personnel carriers and all of its anti-tank guns the task force withdrew to Konstantinovka. A subsequent advance at midday and on the following day supported by 11th Panzer Division's tank regiment forced 4th Guards Tank Corps to withdraw northward from Drushkovka. However, the Soviets still held firmly to Kramatorsk and maintained a toehold in the Druzhkovka area.

While the 7th Panzer Division in Slavyansk held off attacks by the Soviet 195th Rifle Division, 3d Panzer Division elements, advancing northwest drove Soviet forces to new defensive positions in the region northeast of Slavyansk and reopened communications with the 7th Panzer Division defending the city.[37] Further west, the 333d Infantry Division main force reached Barvenkovo and ran into the Soviet 35th Guards Rifle Division. Consequently, the 333d Infantry Division withdrew from Barvenkovo toward Lozovaya, thus ending all immediate prospects for its successful linking up with XXXX Panzer Corps' left flank.

1st Panzer Army, frustrated in its attempts to fulfill its first mission, issued new, less ambitious, orders to XXXX Panzer Corps

> to maintain its link-up [with III Panzer Corps], seize control of the line of the Sukhoy–Torets between Slavyansk and Barvenkovo, and prevent the enemy from advancing in this sector.[38]

With superior Soviet forces confronting XXXX Panzer Corps units from Slavyansk to Kramatorsk and a major gap existing between main corps units and the 333d Infantry Division, the most that the corps could hope to accomplish in the near future was to reestablish firm communications with Slavyansk. Fulfillment of this task became the priority action, and it brought XXXX Panzer Corps units into heavy combat with Soviet 4th Guards Tank Corps, 3d Tank Corps, and 4th Guards Rifle Corps.

After III Panzer Corps' positions in the center of 1st Panzer Army's sector firmed up, the 11th Panzer Division, accompanied by one regiment of the 333d Infantry Division, advanced north along the Krivoy Torets River valley pushing 4th Guards Tank Corps units before them (see Map 22). Although under heavy flanking fire, the 11th Panzer Division took the remainder of Drushkovka and neared the center of Kramatorsk, which was on the west bank of the river. The Germans, however, with their tanks roadbound, and with all bridges blown, were unable to cross to the west bank of the river. German reports of this fighting commented on the low quality of Soviet infantry and the weakness of Soviet artillery, thus pinpointing the problem plaguing Poluboyarov – that of defending Kramatorsk with two understrength tank corps not structured for such a defense. The Germans, however, noted the skill with which the Soviets camouflaged and positioned their tanks for defense in such urban terrain. The Germans claimed to have knocked out forty-five tanks during this series of battles which would amount to most of Poluboyarov's reported armored strength.[39] However, during these days of struggle a trickle of tank reinforcements was reaching Soviet tank corps, just enough to keep the units operational.

While 11th Panzer Division slowly inched its way northwest, the 7th Panzer Division, defending Slavyansk with its infantry, pushed a corridor south with its panzer regiment. Further west the 333d Infantry Division gave up its attempts to retain Barvenkovo and, on 9 February, fell back toward Lozovaya with the Soviet 35th Guards Rifle Division in pursuit. By the morning of 10 February the 35th Guards Rifle Division drove the 333d Infantry Division units out of Lozovaya. With the capture of Lozovaya a key rail line fell into Soviet hands along with large stores of supplies.[40] The 35th Guards Rifle Division consolidated its position and awaited the arrival of new orders (which came on 14 February), while the 333d Infantry Division marched southeast to join the main force of 1st Panzer Army.

Revision of Soviet Plans and the Advance to Krasnoarmeiskoye – 7–10 February

Frustrated in their attempts to develop the offensive in the Slavyansk area, Soviet headquarters issued a stream of new orders designed to restore the momentum of the advance (see Map 22). On 7 February Vatutin noted the limited successes of 4th Guards Rifle Corps but ordered 1st Guards Army to crush enemy resistance and, in cooperation with the mobile group, occupy Slavyansk, Konstantinovka, and Artemovsk. Specifically, 1st Guards Army's 4th Guards Rifle Corps was to occupy Lozovaya and move south into the Krasnoarmeiskoye area while Popov's 4th Guards and 3d Tank Corps would smash the enemy at Slavyansk and Konstantinovka, and the 18th and 10th Tank Corps would break through to Artemovsk. Subsequently, the 4th Guards Tank Corps and 3d Tank Corps would advance on Krasnoarmeiskoye and envelop Stalino from the west. At the same time 6th Guards Rifle Corps would cooperate with 3d Guards Army which was advancing on Voroshilovgrad from the north and east.[41] Bogged down in fighting for Slavyansk and Kramatorsk, 1st Guards Army did seize Lozovaya but did little else before 10 February.

After 10 February a new urgent *STAVKA* directive ordered Vatutin to block a German withdrawal to Dnepropetrovsk and Zaporozh'ye and demanded the *front* undertake all measures to press the German Donets group into the Crimea, to close the passages into the Crimea through Perekop and Sivesh, and then to isolate these German forces from remaining German forces in the Ukraine.[42] Such directives underscored the belief within the *STAVKA* that German forces were preparing to withdraw westward across the Dnepr River, and that heavy German resistance at Slavyansk was designed to cover that withdrawal.

Vatutin translated the *STAVKA* directive into new army missions. Kharitonov's 6th Army was to continue its advance across the Khar'kov–Lozovaya rail line toward Krasnograd and Pereshchepino with the 15th Rifle Corps, supported by the 115th Tank Brigade, making the main attack on the army right flank. Kuznetsov's 1st Guards Army would shift its direction of attack westward, advance toward Sinel'nikovo, and seize Zaporozh'ye on the Dnepr River. Simultaneously, 1st Guards Army would secure Slavyansk and later attack Artemovsk. To facilitate the shifting focus of 1st Guards Army, that army would turn over the Krymskoye sector, on its left flank, to units of Lelyushenko's 3d Guards Army. Thus, 4th Guards Rifle Corps would initiate the advance on Sinel'nikovo, and 6th Guards Rifle Corps would carry out the reduction of Slavyansk.[43] A day before receiving the new *STAVKA* orders, Vatutin issued new orders to Mobile Group Popov. 4th Guards Tank Corps was to turn over its defensive positions at Kramatorsk to 3d Tank Corps; and, after a forced march, on the morning of 11 February it would occupy the rail junction of Krasnoarmeiskoye, 85 kilometers to the south and well into the German rear.

On the night of 11 February, reinforced by the 9th Guards Tank Brigade and 7th Ski Brigade, 4th Guards Tank Corps began its long march south (see Map 23). Simultaneously, Poluboyarov dispatched a battalion of the 7th Ski Brigade to launch a surprise attack on Volnovakha Station to put that railhead out of action, hopefully for 10 to 15 days. The 14th Guards Tank Brigade served as Poluboyarov's forward detachment. The main force, consisting of the 12th Guards Tank Brigade, 9th Tank Brigade, 3d Guards Motorized Rifle Brigade, and 7th Ski Brigade, reinforced by subunits of the 1st Tank Destroyer Brigade, followed the forward detachment. Poluboyarov's operational group traveled with 12th Guards Tank Brigade, which consisted of commanders and staffs to control the operation. The 13th Guards Tank Brigade, as the corps reserve, remained in defensive positions near Kramatorsk to provide cover for Poluboyarov's supply trains and communications routes.[44]

At 0400 on 11 February the 14th Guards Tank Brigade approached Grishino (5 kilometers northwest of Krasnoarmeiskoye), scattered the small German garrison, and occupied the town. By 0900 Poluboyarov's main force had penetrated into and secured Krasnoarmeiskoye. The capture of Krasnoarmeiskoye produced a covey of supplies for the 4th Guards Tank Corps, but, more importantly, it cut the Dnepropetrovsk–Mariupol' rail line, an important lateral communications route of Army Group Don.

German Counterattacks – 12–13 February

German 1st Panzer Army was already reacting to Soviet moves of 8 and 9 February when the surprising news arrived that Grishino had fallen.[45]

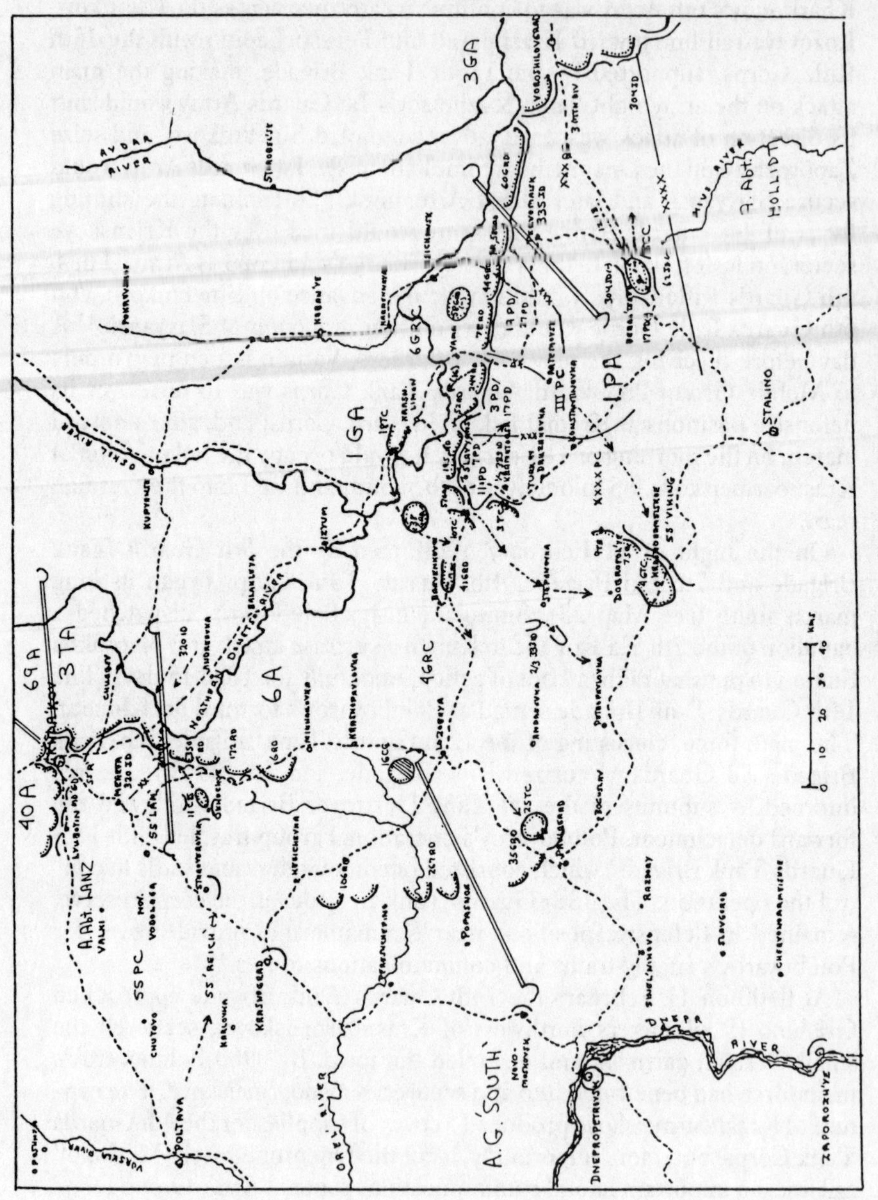

MAP 23. DONBAS, SITUATION, 2000 15 FEBRUARY 1943

Since 8–9 February the Soviets had held firmly to their positions at Kramatorsk and had renewed their attacks on Slavyansk. The 333d Infantry Division had continued its withdrawal southeast from Lozovaya. 1st Panzer Army had at first refused to abandon Slavyansk and, instead, had proposed an attack on Kramatorsk by 11th Panzer Division from the east, 7th Panzer Division from the north, and SS Panzer Grenadier Division "Viking", which had arrived from the Sergeyevka area (with five tanks), from the south. One regiment of the 333d Infantry Division would have covered the corps' left flank along the Samara River. Newly arriving units of the 333d Infantry Division were to deploy directly into Krasnoarmeiskoye.[46] However, the arrival of 4th Guards Tank Corps in Grishino and Krasnoarmeiskoye on the morning of 11 February drastically altered the situation and, hence, German plans to hold Slavyansk and seize Kramatorsk. Having crossed what the Germans felt was the "impassable terrain west of Krivoy Torets" 4th Guards Tank Corps was now on XXXX Panzer Corps' left flank. Moreover, Soviet interdiction of the rail line threatened to seal not only the fate of the army group but also the fate of the entire Eastern Front. Immediately, 1st Panzer Army approved a XXXX Panzer Corps' recommendation to dispatch SS Panzer Grenadier Division "Viking" westward from Artemovsk to Krasnoarmeiskoye in order to expel Soviet forces and reopen the rail line. In addition, the army abandoned plans for an attack on Kramatorsk and instead ordered a concentric attack by SS "Viking" and other units on Krasnoarmeiskoye while the Army maintained a screen along the east bank of Krivoy Torets River.[47] Such a concentric attack, however, clearly required more forces than just SS "Viking" and the by now weakened 333d Infantry Division whose two regiments were in the process of conducting a grueling march (retreat) southeastward toward Krasnoarmeiskoye.

To avoid having to abandon Slavyansk in order to produce the requisite force to strike at Krasnoarmeiskoye, 1st Panzer Army finally adopted a plan to strike out on a foray westward from Slavyansk with 7th and 11th Panzer Divisions, then turn those forces southward toward the rear of Soviet units at Krasnoarmeiskoye (lack of crossings over the Krivoy Torets River precluded an attack further south). Such an attack could also force the Soviets to abandon Kramatorsk and prevent Soviet reinforcement of their mobile forces at Krasnoarmeiskoye by cutting their supply lines. The planned attack of 7th and 11th Panzer Divisions would be under the overall command of the 7th Panzer Division commander (General Hermann Balck) while the 11th Panzer Division commander would supervise the armored thrust westward.[48]

The combined assault of SS "Viking" on Krasnoarmeiskoye and 11th Panzer Division against Soviet positions west of Slavyansk began early on 12 February (see Map 23). SS "Viking" struck hard at the 4th Guards Tank Corps from the south and east and secured a foothold in Krasnoarmeiskoye. The 333d Infantry Division advanced from the northwest in an attempt to break through to the Krasnoarmeiskoye area. Other SS "Viking" units advanced toward Grishino, north of Krasnoarmeiskoye, in order to cut the communications of 4th Guards Tank Corps with its rear units, in particular the 13th Guards Tank Brigade located northeast of the city. However, in heavy street fighting the 4th Guards Tank Corps did manage to halt SS "Viking's" progress within the city and block the division's advance on Grishino.[49]

Meanwhile, after a night march to Slavyansk the 11th and 7th Panzer Division task force (Group Balck) sortied westward from Slavyansk at 1100 hours and advanced 10 kilometers to Cherkasskoye. There, in heavy battles with the 10th Tank Corps (just arrived from east of Slavyansk) and the 41st Guards Rifle Division, the progress of Group Balck ground to a halt. Elements of the 57th Guards Rifle Division, just transferred to Slavyansk, and the 195th Rifle Division, supported by the 41st Tank Destroyer Battalion participated in halting Group Balck.[50] With its advance halted and the element of surprise lost, two days later Group Balck returned to Slavyansk to join the regiment of the 333d Infantry Division in a new advance on Kramatorsk, this time from the north. SS "Viking" and the remainder of the 333d Infantry Division were to continue operations against Krasnoarmeiskoye proper.

Subsequent German operations against Soviet 3d Tank Corps in Kramatorsk achieved only limited success. The 333d Infantry Division occupied the eastern part of the city, but on 13 February Group Balck's advance stalled north of the city. Further south SS "Viking" became bogged down in street fighting for Grishino and Krasnoarmeiskoye while the two regiments of the 333d Infantry Division were deflected in their march southward by the Soviet 10th Tank Corps which was moving toward Krasnoarmeiskoye from the north. Consequently, on 14 February XXXX Panzer Corps ordered SS "Viking" and the 11th Panzer Division to discontinue their attacks and simply seal off Kramatorsk and Krasnoarmeiskoye. 1st Panzer Army also refused XXXX Panzer Corps' request for permission to abandon Slavyansk. XXXX Panzer Corps ordered all units to mount special operations against Soviet mobile forces' supply lines as a temporary expedient while it formulated plans for new, hopefully reinforced attacks.[51]

The Soviet Offensive Shifts Westward

The German thrusts at Slavyansk disrupted the renewed Southwestern Front offensive (see Map 23). The bulk of 1st Guards Army's 4th Guards Rifle Corps remained locked in a struggle to take Slavyansk, and only the

35th Guards Rifle Divisions had advanced toward Sinel'nikovo. The 6th Guards Rifle Corps, on the army left, also had failed in its attempts to break through to Artemovsk. Only 6th Army, on the right wing of the *front*, made any progress when it cut the Khar'kov–Lozovaya rail line north of Krasnopavlovka, broke through German defenses along the Northern Donets River, and on 16 February occupied Zmiyev. Ominously, however, elements of SS Panzer Division "Das Reich" began appearing on 6th Army's right flank along the rail line south of Khar'kov. These newly arrived German units forced 6th Army's advance again to veer off to the southwest. Consequently, the 106th Rifle Brigade and 267th Rifle Division plunged into the yawning gap devoid of German forces between Lozovaya and Krasnograd.

By this time 1st Guards Army had all but two of its nine divisions in first echelon. Moreover, heavy combat had reduced each division to the strength of a full rifle regiment, and artillery in the army was reduced to a total of 417 guns, most of them in the rifle divisions.[52] A majority of this force was tied down in the struggle for Slavyansk and Artemovsk. It was clear that only further concentration of forces in the most critical sectors could produce new offensive successes. Of course, that concentration would involve weakening forces in other sectors. Thus, in response to Vatutin's orders of 12 February Kuznetsov issued new orders which accelerated the westward shift of his forces. The 41st Guards Rifle Division at Slavyansk and the 244th Rifle Division east of Slavyansk were to march to the Lozovaya area to assist the 35th Guards Rifle Division in developing the attack toward Sinel'nikovo and Pavlograd. In addition, Kuznetsov ordered the 38th Guards Rifle Division near Lisichansk to shift to the west and join the 195th and 57th Rifle Division's assaults on Slavyansk.[53]

To assist the hard-pressed and overextended 4th Guards Tank Corps at Krasnoarmeiskoye, Popov ordered the 10th Tank Corps, then east of Slavyansk, to assemble, regroup north of Slavyansk, and then move south to Krasnoarmeiskii Rudnik in order to link up with the 4th Guards Tank Corps. During regrouping Popov outfitted 10th Tank Corps with some new tanks and on 11 February, added the 11th Tank Brigade to the 10th Tank Corps concentration. On 12 February 10th Tank Corps moved south at an excruciatingly slow rate of less than 1 kilometer per hour because of the deep snow. On the afternoon of 12 February 10th Tank Corps' 11th Tank Brigade ran into Group Balck (then on its sortie west of Slavyansk); and the brigade's eleven tanks, supported by 41st Guards Rifle Division troops, were penned into defensive positions at Cherkasskoye. After Group Balck's withdrawal on 13 February, 10th Tank Corps moved on toward Krasnoarmeiskii Rudnik and linked up with 4th Guards Tank Corps on 15 February.[54]

6th Army Advance Towards the Dnepr River

Having received revised orders and reinforcements, Southwestern Front rifle forces and Group Popov sought to continue their offensive (see Maps 23–25). 6th Army's units continued their offensive opposed only by SS Panzer Corps units on their right flank. The 350th Rifle Division consolidated its bridgehead across the Northern Donets River west of Zmiyev, and the 172d and 6th Rifle Divisions successfully advanced against SS Panzer Division "Das Reich" units to within 15 kilometers of Krasnograd by 19 February. On 6th Army's left flank the 267th Rifle Division occupied the important regional center of Pereshchepino on the Orel River and rail line midway between Krasnograd and Dnepropetrovsk, and, by the morning of 20 February, reached the region northwest of Novo-Moskovsk, just 25 kilometers from the Dnepr River and Dnepropetrovsk.[55] The 35th Guards Rifle Division of 1st Guards Army's 4th Guards Rifle Corps brushed aside light opposition and on 17 February occupied Pavlograd. The following day one regiment of the division conducted a night march, seized Novo-Moskovsk, and cut the railroad line to Dnepropetrovsk. Running low on ammunition, the regiment then dug into defensive positions on the outskirts of Novo-Moskovsk. The division's other two regiments approached Sinel'nikovo and joined elements of the 41st Guards Rifle Division and 1st Guards Cavalry Corps in an unsuccessful joint night attack on the town which was defended by elements of the newly arrived German 15th Infantry Division.[56] Early on 19 February the Southwestern Front released the 25th Tank Corps and 1st Guards Cavalry Corps to 6th Army control and lead elements of that tank corps arrived in Sinel'nikovo. The same day Vatutin switched 4th Guards Rifle Corps (35th Guards Rifle Division, 41st Guards Rifle Division, and 244th Rifle Division) from 1st Guards Army to 6th Army control and ordered the 41st Guards and 244th Rifle Divisions to concentrate at Pavlograd.

Battles at Krasnoarmeiskoye and Slavyansk – 15–20 February

While 6th Army with its newly assigned 4th Guards Rifle Corps plunged toward the Dnepr River, the remainder of 1st Guards Army tried to break the deadlock at Slavyansk (see Map 24). Renewed Soviet attempts to take the city dovetailed with the German decision to abandon Slavyansk in order to generate reserves (essentially the 7th Panzer Division) necessary to attack elsewhere.

On 15 February 1st Panzer Army finally approved XXXX Panzer Corps' request to abandon Slavyansk. XXXX Panzer Corps then ordered the 7th Panzer Division to withdraw from Slavyansk and redeploy to the Krasnoarmeiskoye area with the mission of reopening the railroad

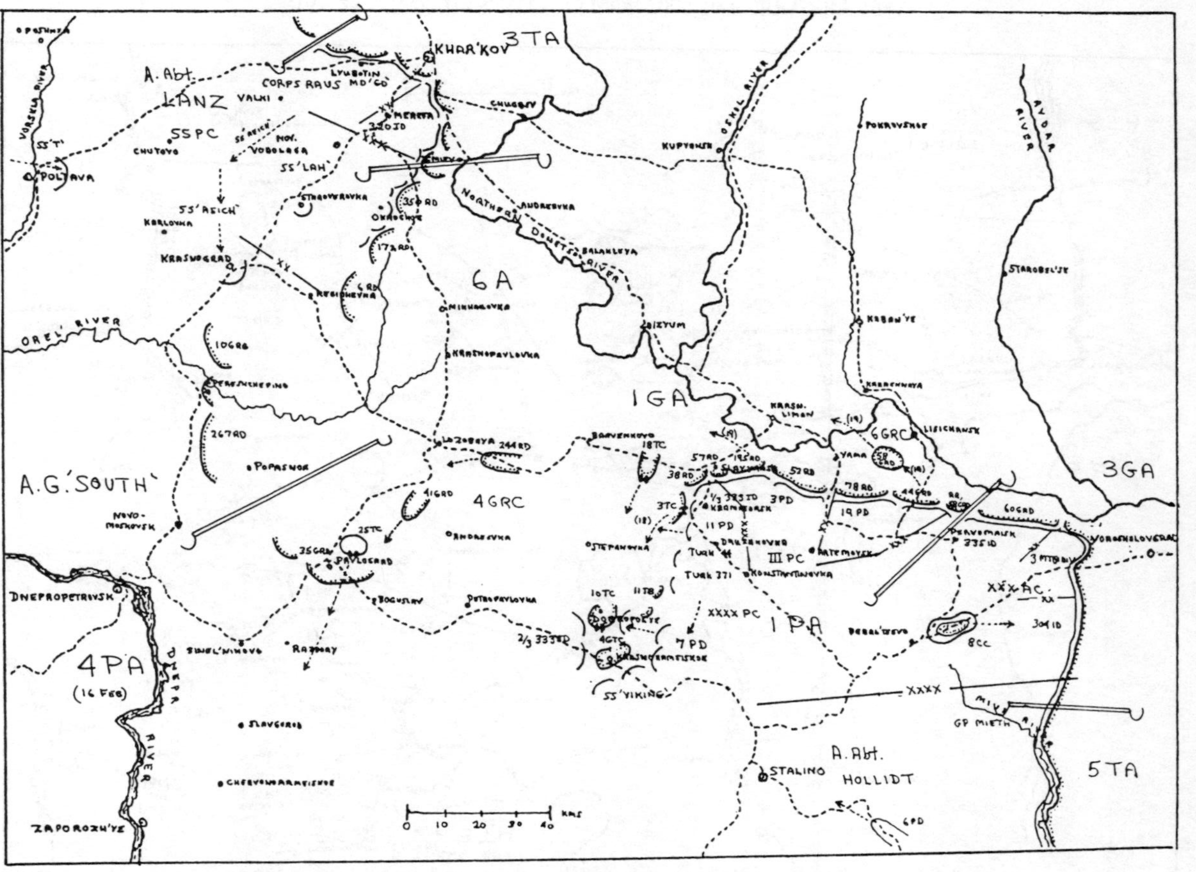

MAP 24. DONBAS, SITUATION, 2000 17 FEBRUARY 1943

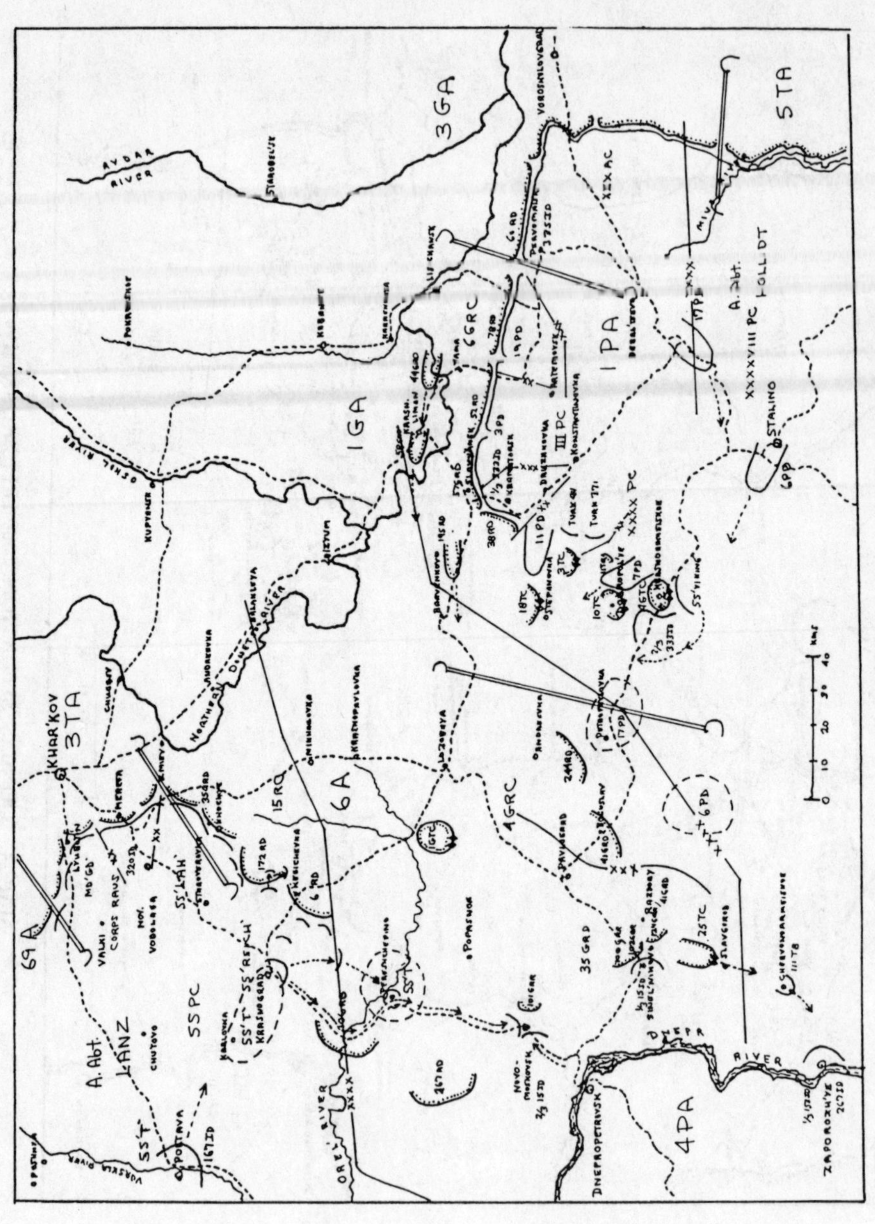

MAP 25. DONBAS, SITUATION, 2000 20 FEBRUARY 1943

between Stalino and Dnepropetrovsk.[57] The following day 7th Panzer left Slavyansk unimpeded, and on 17 February it moved south to positions 15 kilometers east of Krasnoarmeiskoye. Simultaneously, 11th Panzer Division deployed to the Druzhkovka area to prepare for an attack westward into the Soviet mobile group's rear. III Panzer Corps extended its lines to the west and took over defensive positions south of Slavyansk. In addition, SS "Viking" was ordered to continue its attacks against the southern part of Krasnoarmeiskoye while the 333d Infantry Division was to advance on SS "Viking's" left flank against Soviet forces at Krasnoarmeiskoye and Grishino.

Meanwhile, 4th Guards Corps' 57th Guards, 38th Guards, and 195th Rifle Divisions prepared to resume their attacks on Slavyansk just as the Germans withdrew from the town.[58] On 17 February, having occupied the town, the three rifle divisions occupied new defensive positions on its southern outskirts facing III Panzer Corps units. The following day Kuznetsov transferred the 195th Rifle Division to 6th Guards Rifle Corps control to operate in that corps' new sector running from Slavyansk through Barvenkovo to Lozovaya. The 195th Rifle Division was to turn over its defensive sector to 57th Guards Rifle Division and move through Barvenkovo and Lozovaya to Petrokovka (50 kilometers west of Novo-Moskovsk) by 1 March. However, Kuznetsov delayed the move in order for the 195th Rifle Division, 57th Guards Rifle Division, and part of 4th Guards Tank Corps to launch an attack east of Slavyansk to straighten out Soviet defensive lines. Thus, 195th Rifle Division's movement westward did not commence until 19 February.[59] At the same time the 58th Guards and 44th Guards Rifle Divisions also began their movement west, after handing over their positions to 3d Guards Army units.

After the initial attacks by SS Panzer Grenadier Division "Viking" on 12–13 February, the 4th Guards Tank Corps hung grimly onto its positions at Krasnoarmeiskoye until it was reinforced by 10th Tank Corps on 16 February. By 18 February 4th Guards Tank Corps' armored strength was seventeen tanks, and its fuel and ammunition were also running dangerously low.[60] 10th Tank Corps, which occupied positions from Krasnoarmeiskii Rudnik to the northern limits of Krasnoarmeiskoye, had only a few tanks more than 4th Guards Tank Corps. At one point 10th Tank Corps radioed Group Popov headquarters that "no wheel was turning."[61] Poluboyarov organized his tank corps for all round defense of the town (see Map 24). He placed the 14th Guards Tank Brigade and 9th Tank Brigade in defensive positions in the eastern and southeastern sectors of the city, while the 12th Guards Tank Brigade defended on the west and the 3d Guards Tank Brigade in the southern outskirts of the town. 7th Ski Brigade troops reinforced the tank brigades.

At 0830 on 18 February 7th Panzer Division, having completed its redeployment south from Slavyansk under cover of poor visibility, opened its assault on 4th Guards Tank Corps' positions. The initial attack against the 14th Guards Tank Brigade's sector carried into the center and northern outskirts of Krasnoarmeiskoye. The ferocity of the fighting was borne out by German reports claiming the destruction of eleven T-34s. In repeated counterattacks, during which its commander was killed, the 14th Guards Tank Brigade halted 7th Panzer Division's advance in the center of the city. Meanwhile, at 1200 SS Panzer Grenadier Division "Viking" struck 12th Guards Tank Brigade positions in the western portion of the city just as heavy German air attacks hit the Soviet defenses. In heavy fighting, during which the brigade commander was also seriously wounded, SS "Viking's" advance ground to a halt. The German 333d Infantry Division was likewise halted northwest of Krasnoarmeiskoye.[62]

While fighting was in progress Popov ordered reinforcements to move to assist the beleaguered Poluboyarov (see Map 25). On the evening of 18 February Popov ordered the 18th Tank Corps (which had already turned over its sector east of Slavyansk to the 52d Rifle Division) to move on Krasnoarmeiskoye by forced march, to concentrate that night 20 kilometers northwest of Krasnoarmeiskoye, and to strike the German rear at Grishino in coordination with 10th Tank Corps, already defending in the area. Popov also ordered 3d Tank Corps to turn over its positions at Kramatorsk to Soviet infantry and to concentrate by 20 February at Krasnoarmeiskoye. The 5th and 10th Ski Brigades of the mobile group also advanced to assist Poluboyarov.

Meanwhile, Poluboyarov himself tried to affect his fate. On the evening of 18 February he created a special group under the 183d Tank Brigade commander, consisting of the 183d Tank Brigade, 12th Guards Tank Brigade, 11th and 9th Tank Brigades, 14th Motorized Rifle Brigade, and 7th Ski Brigade; and he ordered this group to retake the center of the city.[63] Early on 19 February the group attacked and regained some ground, but in vain, for the opposing 7th Panzer Division and SS "Viking" had already resolved to bypass the city and allow the garrison to be mopped up by the 333d Infantry Division. In a touch of irony, on 19 February General Poluboyarov received an order from the Front Military Council which read: "I order the encirclement and destruction of the enemy at Krasnoarmeiskoye. Fully restore the situation. Do not, in any case, permit an enemy withdrawal."[64] The order illustrated the air of unreality now permeating the *STAVKA* and *front* headquarters.

German assaults on Krasnoarmeiskoye resumed on 19 February. While 7th Panzer Division swept by the city to the north, SS "Viking" and the 333d Infantry Division pressed into the city itself and secured

Grishino. At the same time, to the north the 11th Panzer Division struck westward from Druzhkovka and seized Novo-Alekseyevsky and Aleksandrovka, thereby hitting 3d Tank Corps columns moving to aid Poluboyarov.[65] In essence, 4th Guards Tank Corps was encircled, and German actions ruled out any relief. Moreover, the other mobile group corps sent to aid Poluboyarov were themselves fragmented. As SS "Viking" joined 7th Panzer Division in a drive northward toward Dobropol'ye, the 333d Infantry Division mopped up Soviet forces in Krasnoarmeiskoye. 4th Guards Tank Corps with its remaining twelve tanks resisted until 20 February when supplies finally ran out. On the night of 20–21 February the corps' survivors began infiltrating out of the area toward Barvenkovo to rejoin the corps' 13th Guards Tank Brigade which had remained north to cover supply routes. Reequipped with thirty-two new T-34s, the brigade gathered up the remnants of 4th Guards Tank Corps and eventually rejoined Popov's dwindling force at Barvenkovo.[66] 4th Guards Tank Corps' survivors reached Barvenkovo on 24 February, just in time to join 1st Guards Army's withdrawal to the Northern Donets River.

On the Eve of the Manstein Counteroffensive

The German assault on Krasnoarmeiskoye marked a change in the momentum of battle; but, as the Front Military Council order to Poluboyarov indicated, Soviet headquarters had no idea of that change. An air of unreality and overconfidence had pervaded Soviet headquarters for weeks and colored all aspects of Soviet planning. That mood would spell doom for the Soviet offensive and many of the men participating in it.

The mood of optimism within the *STAVKA* and General Staff was based upon the collective impression on the part of the Soviets of the immense damage done to German and other axis forces since 19 November. Three major armies (German 6th, Italian 8th, and Hungarian 2d) had been erased from the German order of battle in the East. 4th Panzer Army and 2d Army had been badly chewed up, and the remainder of German forces had suffered grievous losses. Surely, the Soviets reasoned, the trickle of reinforcements from the West could not compensate for these losses.

In a sense, Soviet High Command attitudes and actions in the winter of 1942–43 were a repeat, on a grander scale, of similar *STAVKA* behavior that prevailed during the winter of 1941–42 when the *STAVKA* assigned unrealistic missions to overextended armies, missions which, under the circumstances, were condemned to failure if for no other reason than the sheer exhaustion and attrition of Soviet forces. For that matter, the Soviet overoptimistic attitude in both the winter of 1942–43 and the winter of 1941–42 were manifestations of general Soviet confidence in the offensive born of the interwar theoreticians' work and so evident in the costly but foolhardy counterattacks of the summer of 1941 which unavoidably ended in disaster in the teeth of blitzkreig. That rashness – that inability to even consider the necessity for restraint – surfaced again in February 1943. Only by the summer of 1943 would the Soviets fully learn and apply the lessons of restraint – by that time at the expense of the Germans.

As Soviet forces advanced in February 1943, the *STAVKA* reverted to traditional offensive form in word and in deed and continually left unheeded the warnings of commanders who sensed impending disaster. *STAVKA* optimism also colored Soviet assessment of intelligence which was collected in adequate quantities but which was misassessed since the High Command and the *fronts* placed their own rosy interpretation on German intentions.

Both the Southwestern and Voronezh Front commanders believed they were facing a panorama of German forces withdrawing toward the Dnepr River and safety. The Southwestern Front staff, in particular, erroneously assessed the large German regrouping which it detected as being the beginning of a German withdrawal. Front headquarters used that assessment to continue to rationalize the pursuit. Lt. General S. P. Ivanov, *front* chief-of-staff, and Maj. General A. S. Rogov, *front* chief of reconnaissance, signed an intelligence estimate which judged that the concentration of German armored units detected in the Krasnograd and Krasnoarmeiskoye regions on 17 February occurred "to strike a blow to liquidate a penetration of Soviet forces and to free communications for a withdrawal of forces in the Donbas territories across the Dnepr."[67] The estimate concluded that "all information affirms that the enemy will leave the territory of the Don basin and withdraw his forces beyond the Dnepr."[68] General Vatutin underscored that judgement by stating, "Without a doubt the enemy is hurrying to withdraw his forces from the Donbas across the Dnepr."[69] Vatutin was so convinced of this German intent that he ignored repeated warnings from his army commanders that troop fatigue, equipment shortages, and growing enemy strength made it impossible to conduct simultaneous offensives in all sectors of the front. Instead he insisted on pressing to fulfill his mission of encircling and destroying the entire German Donbas group before the beginning of the spring thaw.

On the eve of the looming German counteroffensive (the evening of 19 February and the morning of 20 February) Soviet air reconnaissance observed large German tank concentrations near Krasnograd, noted the forward movement of equipment from Dnepropetrovsk, and detected the regrouping of tank forces from the east toward Krasnoarmeiskoye. Nevertheless, in an estimate dated 1600 20 February Lt. General S. P. Ivanov, chief-of-staff of Southwestern Front, assessed the movements of German XXXXVIII Panzer Corps as a withdrawal from the Donbas to Zaporozh'ye. Based on that conclusion Vatutin ordered 6th Army to continue its advance and demanded that the *front* mobile groups "fulfill their assigned mission at any cost."[70]

The optimism of the Southwestern Front staff and Vatutin affected the attitude and actions of the Voronezh Front as well. A steady stream of information sent from the Southwestern Front to the Voronezh Front spoke of German intentions to withdraw and encouraged the Voronezh Front to speed up its offensive. German SS Panzer Corps' abandonment of Khar'kov on 16 February and its movement to Krasnograd simply reinforced that view. Golikov confirmed this state in comments made in September 1943 when he said, "It is necessary to recognize that at that stage I had an incorrect evaluation of the intent and capabilities of the enemy."[71]

As it had done earlier in the war, the *STAVKA* and General Staff reinforced the *front* commanders' optimism and thus compounded their mistakes. On 21 February Lt. General A.N. Bogolyubov, deputy chief of the operations section of the General Staff, said, "We have exact data that the enemy in the evening is withdrawing in dense columns from the Donbas," when, in fact, those dense columns were about to participate in a violent counterattack.[72] These mistaken conclusions on the part of *fronts* and the *STAVKA* persisted well after the time the Germans delivered their counteroffensive, and they hindered the Soviet forces' ability to deal with the attacks. Thus, the *STAVKA* and *front* commanders misjudged German intentions in general and Manstein's in particular.

The German Counteroffensive (20 February – 6 March)

German Counterattack Planning

Throughout early February, Manstein developed plans to halt the Soviet advance and restore operational freedom to German forces (see Map 25).[73] Those plans capitalized on superior German mobility and command flexibility. By permitting an unhindered Soviet advance in some sectors, by holding tightly to a few critical sectors, and by deliberately taking the calculated risk of reducing German forces to a minimum in other sectors, Manstein intended to generate sufficient operational reserves to mount a coordinated counteroffensive.

In outline Manstein planned to withdraw the headquarters of 4th Panzer Army from its defensive positions east of the Mius River and leave Army Detachment Hollidt to defend that region from south of Voroshilograd to the Sea of Azov. 4th Panzer Army would set up its new headquarters in Dnepropetrovsk where it would assume command of SS

6. Southwestern Front command and staff, February 1943, (from left to right): Major General L. Z. Kotliar; Major General M. V. Rudakov; Major General V. M. Laiok; *front* commander Army General N. F. Vatutin; Lieutenant General A. S. Zheltov, Lieutenant General S. A. Krasovsky; Lieutenant General S. P. Ivanov; Major General V. I. Vozniuk.

Panzer Corps, transferred from Army Detachment Lanz, and XXXXVIII Panzer Corps (6th, 17th Panzer Divisions), moved westward from Army Detachment Hollidt. The two panzer corps would attack the Soviet forces occupying the gap between German forces at Krasnograd and at Krasnoarmeiskoye (Corps Raus and XXXX Panzer Corps). SS Panzer Corps would position its two divisions (SS Panzer Division "Totenkopf" and SS Panzer Division "Das Reich") near Krasnograd and deliver a southeasterly thrust against Soviet forces advancing toward the Dnepr River. The third division of SS Panzer Corps (SS Panzer Division "Leibstandarte Adolf Hitler") would remain under Army Detachment Lanz control with the mission of holding the northern shoulder of the Soviet penetration between Krasnograd and Merefa. XXXXVIII Panzer Corps would deploy its two divisions to the rail line between Boguslav and Petropavlovka to strike the Soviet penetration from the south. SS Panzer Corps' and XXXXVIII Panzer Corps' attacks would converge on Lozovaya in the Soviet rear area. Subsequently, all four divisions would attack in tandem toward the Northern Donets River.

Meanwhile, 1st Panzer Army would hold firm to its defensive positions between Kramatorsk and Voroshilovgrad to tie down as many Soviet 1st Guards Army forces as possible, XXXX Panzer Corps (11th Panzer Division, 7th Panzer Division, SS "Viking") would continue its coordinated offensive against Soviet mobile forces in the Krasnoarmeiskoye area and then advance northward toward Barvenkovo where its attack would line up with the advance of SS Panzer Corps and XXXXVIII Panzer Corps.

7. Infantry advancing through heavy snow.

8. A tank unit commander briefs his officers on the terrain.

After successful restoration of the Northern Donets River line these forces could, with minor regrouping, continue the offensive northward against Soviet forces in the Khar'kov region.

Manstein's task was made more difficult by the fact that the plan was formulated while the Soviet offensive developed, thus Manstein had to anticipate Soviet movements. More important, Manstein had to convince the High Command and Hitler of the plan's feasibility, an especially difficult task since the plan involved a withdrawal by Army Detachment Hollidt to the Mius River. As before, Hitler categorically resisted abandonment of any territory, especially territory of such symbolic and economic importance as the eastern Donbas. In repeated correspondence and conversation with Hitler, Manstein urged acceptance of his plan while punctuating the dialogue with news of the rapidly deteriorating situation. Personal meetings occurred between Manstein and Hitler on 6 February at Rastenburg and on 17 February at Zaparozh'ye, in the latter instance just as lead Soviet tank units were only 30 kilometers distant. The urgency of the situation and Manstein's arguments prevailed. Hitler finally approved Manstein's plan, and on 19 February Manstein ordered 4th Panzer Army to deploy for its counterattack.[74] Simultaneously, Army Detachment Lanz was to protect the northern flank of the attack, and 1st Panzer Army was to hold firm to positions south of Slavyansk and continue the offensive of XXXX Panzer Corps.

Manstein's plan called for the operational use of virtually all of Army Group "South's" scarce armored forces in a concerted drive against exploiting forces of Soviet 6th Army, Mobile Group Popov, and 1st Guards Army. The plan relied on an attack by concentrated forces along converging axes of advance. It capitalized on the offensive strength of the SS Panzer Corps' division and the synergistic effect of the weaker panzer divisions attacking on adjacent axes along converging lines. In essence, it extracted maximum shock effect from units, many of which were of depleted strength, and the plan relied heavily on the flexibility and imagination of German corps, division, regiment, and battalion commanders and staffs.

The final concept of Manstein's counteroffensive involved the use of three shock groups to strike the Soviet penetrating forces in the flank and rear. SS Panzer Corps, advancing from Krasnograd, and XXXXVIII Panzer Corps, from the Chaplino region, would converge on the Pavlograd area to cut off and isolate lead units of Soviet 6th Army. Subsequently, the two panzer corps would combine for an attack on Lozovaya and the Northern Donets River to complete the destruction of Soviet forces in the area. XXXX Panzer Corps of 1st Panzer Army would attack from Krasnoarmeiskoye and Druzhkovka toward Barvenkovo to destroy Popov's Mobile Group and ultimately drive the right wing of 1st Guards Army to the Northern Donets River. The timing of the operation was critical. On 20 February XXXX Panzer Corps had already begun its assault northward, and SS Panzer Corps had attacked the same day. XXXXVIII Panzer Corps units, however, were enroute to their jumping-off positions and would not arrive until 23 February. The earlier attack of SS Panzer Corps would permit both that corps and XXXXVIII Panzer Corps to reach the Lozovaya area roughly simultaneously (about 25 February).

SS Panzer Corps would attack with two SS Panzer Divisions. SS Panzer Division "Das Reich" on 20 February would strike south from Krasnograd via Pereshchepino to Novo Moskovsk and there join forces with two regiments of the 15th Infantry Division which would have advanced from Dnepropetrovsk. The 15th Infantry Division would also defend Sinel'nikovo with one of its regiments. The following day SS "Das Reich" would advance east toward Pavlograd while SS Panzer Division "Totenkopf" would strike eastward from Pereshchepino through Popasnoye. In the following days SS "Das Reich" would advance on Lozovaya from the southwest while SS "Totenkopf" advanced on that same point from the west. At Lozovaya both divisions would join in a concerted attack northward along the rail line toward Merefa. 15th Infantry Division would assist the SS Panzer Corps' advance and mop up bypassed Soviet forces. Meanwhile, SS Panzer Division "Leibstandarte Adolf Hitler" of Army Detachment Lanz would cover SS Panzer Corps' left flank from Krasnograd to the northeast.

XXXXVIII Panzer Corps' two panzer divisions would deploy into the Chaplino area in preparation for their attack northward. Once in position 6th Panzer Division would attack northward from positions east of Boguslav toward the rail line east of Lozovaya, and 17th Panzer Division would attack northward from Petropavlovka toward the rail line midway between Lozovaya and Barvenkovo. XXXXVIII Panzer Corps' divisions would initiate their advance immediately after their arrival in jumping-off positions on about 23 February. XXXX Panzer Corps would continue its attacks initiated on 19 February. SS "Viking," skirting west of Krasnoarmeiskoye, would advance northward through Krivorozh'ye toward Barvenkovo. 7th Panzer Division would advance northward east of Krasnoarmeiskoye through Dobropol'ye toward Barvenkovo while the 11th Panzer Division continued its westward march from Gavrilovka toward Andreyevka where it would turn north in tandem with SS "Viking" and 7th Panzer Division to strike at Barvenkovo. Two regiments of the 333d Infantry Division would complete the reduction of Krasnoarmeiskoye and mop up bypassed Soviet forces, while the division's third regiment blockaded Soviet forces in Kramatorsk.

SS Panzer Corps and XXXXVIII Panzer Corps Counterattack – 20–23 February

While the Germans completed the deployments necessary to initiate this triple pincer attack, Soviet forces continued their advance in accordance with *Front* directives issued in mid-February, urged on by a constant stream of exhortations from the *STAVKA* and *front* headquarters. Soviet euphoria was only mildly blunted when, early on the morning of 20 February, SS Panzer Division "Das Reich" suddenly struck from assembly areas south of Krasnograd (see Map 25). Marching in two columns, SS "Das Reich" brushed aside Soviet units, seized the Orel River crossings at Pereshchepino, and linked up with the two infantry regiments of the 15th Infantry Division at Novo Moskovsk.[75] The 35th Guards Rifle Division abandoned its positions around the city and withdrew eastward across the Samara River. The western column of SS "Das Reich" moved south through Pereshchepino and joined the division's main force.

The southerly plunge of SS "Das Reich" sliced through the rear area of the Soviet 267th Rifle Division and 106th Rifle Brigade, both enroute toward Kremenchug on the Dnepr River, and severed their communications with the rear. Although under orders to continue the advance, elements of the 106th Rifle Brigade struggled with German elements north of Pereshchepino in a futile attempt to restore their communications. Likewise, 267th Rifle Division elements were isolated west and northwest of Novo Moskovsk. Throughout 21 February SS "Das Reich" and 15th Infantry Division units consolidated their positions around Novo Moskovsk and prepared for a new advance on Pavlograd. SS Panzer Regiment "Deutschland" engaged elements of the 267th Rifle Division and 35th Guards Rifle Division northwest and northeast of Novo Moskovsk. Other divisional elements defended SS "Reich's" line of communications. Meanwhile, on 21 February SS "Totenkopf" units completed their movement into the Krasnograd area, and part of the division marched south to Pereshchepino to prepare for an advance on Pavlograd on the following morning.[76]

Although Soviet 6th Army's situation was precarious the *front* still insisted it continue its mission. To that end the *front* staff completed deployment of the new *front* mobile group (25th Tank Corps and 1st Guards Tank Corps) to the Lozovaya-Pavlograd area. *Front* also ordered 6th Army to force a crossing over the Dnepr River on the night of 21–22 February and secure and hold a bridgehead on the right bank of the river. Simultaneously, mobile group units would secure Zaporozh'ye and prepare to advance on Melitopol'. Army right flank units were to secure Poltava by the evening of 23 February.[77]

With its right flank units already sliced off, on 21 February 6th Army continued its offensive. 25th Tank Corps bypassed Sinel'nikovo to the east and moved 20–30 kilometers southeast of the city toward Slavgorod. Its lead brigade (111th Tank Brigade), as the Corps' forward detachment, marched on Chernoarmeiskoye, 25 kilometers from Zaporozh'ye. The 6th Army commander, in order to counter German actions, on 20 and 21 February dispatched tank brigades (16th and 17th Guards Tank Brigades) from 1st Guards Tank Corps to support Soviet units west of Lozovaya and at Pavlograd.[78] While the remainder of the army attacked, the 267th Rifle Division and 106th Rifle Brigade made repeated attempts to open a corridor to 6th Army main elements through SS Panzer Corps positions north of Novo Moskovsk and north of Pereshchepino.

At 0500 on 22 February SS "Das Reich" crossed the Samara River and drove on to Pavlograd smashing the resistance of 35th Guards Rifle Division and destroying six supporting tanks in the process (see Map 26). By 0915 SS "Das Reich's" units reached Pavlograd and drove off the 35th Guards Rifle Division's training battalion. In the afternoon a *kampfgruppe* of the division cleared a path through the 35th Guards Rifle Division to Sinel'nikovo.[79] The Soviet division, having lost communications with 6th Army headquarters, withdrew northward toward Novo Aleksandrovka to unite with division elements withdrawing from Novo Moskovsk and with tank subunits of the 16th Guards Tank Brigade. SS "Das Reich" units linked up with 15th Infantry Division elements at Sinel'nikovo and then made preparations to resume the advance from Pavlograd. The 124th Guards Rifle Regiment of 41st Guards Rifle Division, also operating against Sinel'nikovo, was split away from the 35th Guards Rifle Division by SS "Das Reich" attacks and moved east to occupy new defensive position near Razdory. Its parent unit as well as the 244th Rifle Division had, by 20 February, taken up defensive positions north of Boguslav and Petropavlovka, defending against a German attack from the east against Pavlograd.[80]

While the SS Panzer Division "Das Reich" moved on Pavlograd, SS "Totenkopf" advanced southwest of Pereshchepino, thus widening the breach between Soviet 6th Army main forces and the isolated 267th Rifle Division and 106th Rifle Brigade.

6th Army, its right flank cut off and its center caved in, received new orders from *front* on 22 February to push the mobile group aggressively forward in order to cut off a German withdrawal from the Donbas and to press the 15th Rifle Corps' attack on Krasnograd. While the 267th Rifle Division and 106th Rifle Brigade sought to fight their way out of encirclement southwest of Krasnograd, and the 35th Guards Rifle Division fought for its survival north of Sinel'nikovo, Pavlov's 25th Tank Corps continued its advance. By day's end on 22 February

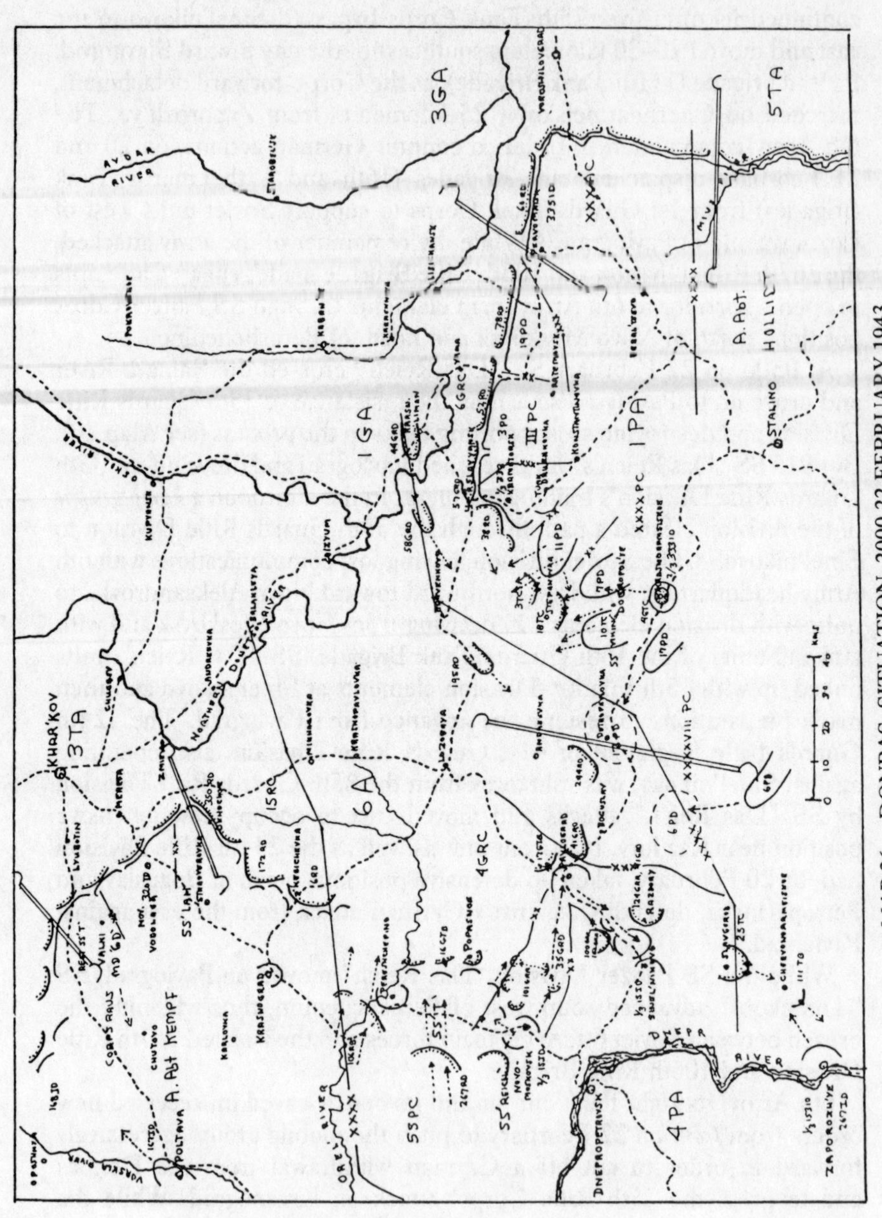

MAP 26. DONBAS, SITUATION, 2000 22 FEBRUARY 1943

Pavlov had seized Slavgorod, and his 111th Tank Brigade had secured Chernoarmeiskoye. One hundred kilometers ahead of 6th Army lines, 25th Tank Corps was running short of fuel, ammunition, and food; and no provision had been made to resupply it by air. The following day the corps' escape route slammed shut as German XXXXVIII Panzer Corps began its offensive. 25th Tank Corps, caught between German forces at Zaporozh'ye (15th Infantry Division), SS "Das Reich," and XXXXVIII Panzer Corps' 6th Panzer Division, literally died on the vine. The 3d Tank Brigade political officer reported, "In the daytime the brigade is subjected to intensive bombardment from the air. We have lost seven tanks and a large number of personnel."[81] Finally ordered to break out by 6th Army, 25th Tank Corps personnel, abandoning their equipment, scattered to the northeast, joining a growing host of Soviet soldiers seeking refuge from the German armored thrusts.

On 23 February Soviet 6th Army's position worsened. SS "Das Reich" consolidated its positions at Pavlograd while the 15th Infantry Division cleared the area east of Sinel'nikovo, drove 41st Guards Rifle Division units from Razdory, and linked up with 6th Panzer Division which had just begun its attack from the southeast. At Pavlograd rear service units of 4th Guards Rifle Corps, elements of 1st Guards Cavalry Corps, and the 17th Guards Tank Brigade of 1st Guards Tank Corps prepared to resist SS "Das Reich's" advance. The 35th Guards Rifle Division moved north across the rail line from Novo Moskovsk to Pavlograd, skirmished with German SS "Totenkopf" units, and assembled off the main roads near Petrovskii and Sergeyevka.

9. Armor on the exploitation.

The German SS Panzer Division "Totenkopf" began its advance on the morning of 23 February, thrusting both northeast and southwest of Popasnoye against the 16th Guards Tank Brigade, the 35th Guards Rifle Division, and remnants of other Soviet units. By nightfall the northern column of the division reached Soviet defensive positions 20 kilometers west of Lozovaya, while the southern column crushed Soviet resistance and reached Vyazovok just northeast of Pavlograd.[82] Soviet units fought desperately to prevent a link-up between SS "Das Reich" and SS "Totenkopf" and to keep withdrawal lines open for units to the south.

While the German vise tightened on Pavlograd XXXXVIII Panzer Corps opened its attack from the southeast. 6th Panzer Division advanced from Chaplino, linked up with 15th Infantry Division units west of Vasil'kovka, and swept north toward 41st Guards Rifle Division defensive positions near Boguslav. Simultaneously, the 17th Panzer Division reached Petropavlovka (south of the 244th Rifle Division's position) and took up positions facing north on both banks of the Samara River. Both units prepared to advance north on 24 February side-by-side with the two SS Panzer Divisions.[83]

Finally, with disaster looming, Vatutin awoke to the true situation. Two days earlier (21 February) he had asked for assistance from the Voronezh Front in the form of a southerly advance by that *front's* left flank armies (3d Tank Army and 69th Army). With permission from the *STAVKA*, Golikov, the Voronezh Front commander, ordered 69th Army and 3d Tank Army to cease their westward advance and turn south to strike from Bogodukhov against the German left flank.[84] Over the next few days, however, neither attack materially affected 6th Army's position.

In light of the total absence of *front* operational reserves Vatutin ordered a speed-up in the transfer of 6th Guards Rifle Corps' divisions from 1st Guards Army's left flank to its right flank in order to shore up the *front's* collapsing center and right flank. Kuznetsov ordered the 58th Guards Rifle Division to occupy all round defensive positions at Lozovaya and conduct reconnaissance to the northwest, west, and south. The 195th and 44th Guards Rifle Divisions, supported by *front* mobile force units, were to occupy defensive positions on a broad front south of the Lozovaya, Barvenkovo, Slavyansk rail line.[85] Notably absent from these directives was an order for the *front's* right wing to go on the defensive.

Expansion of the German Counteroffensive – 24 February

On 24 February 4th Panzer Army units continued their relentless concerted drive against Vatutin's already shattered right flank (see Map 27). SS Panzer Division "Totenkopf's" northern column seized Orel'ka and probed eastward from Mikhailovka against a light screen of 6th Army

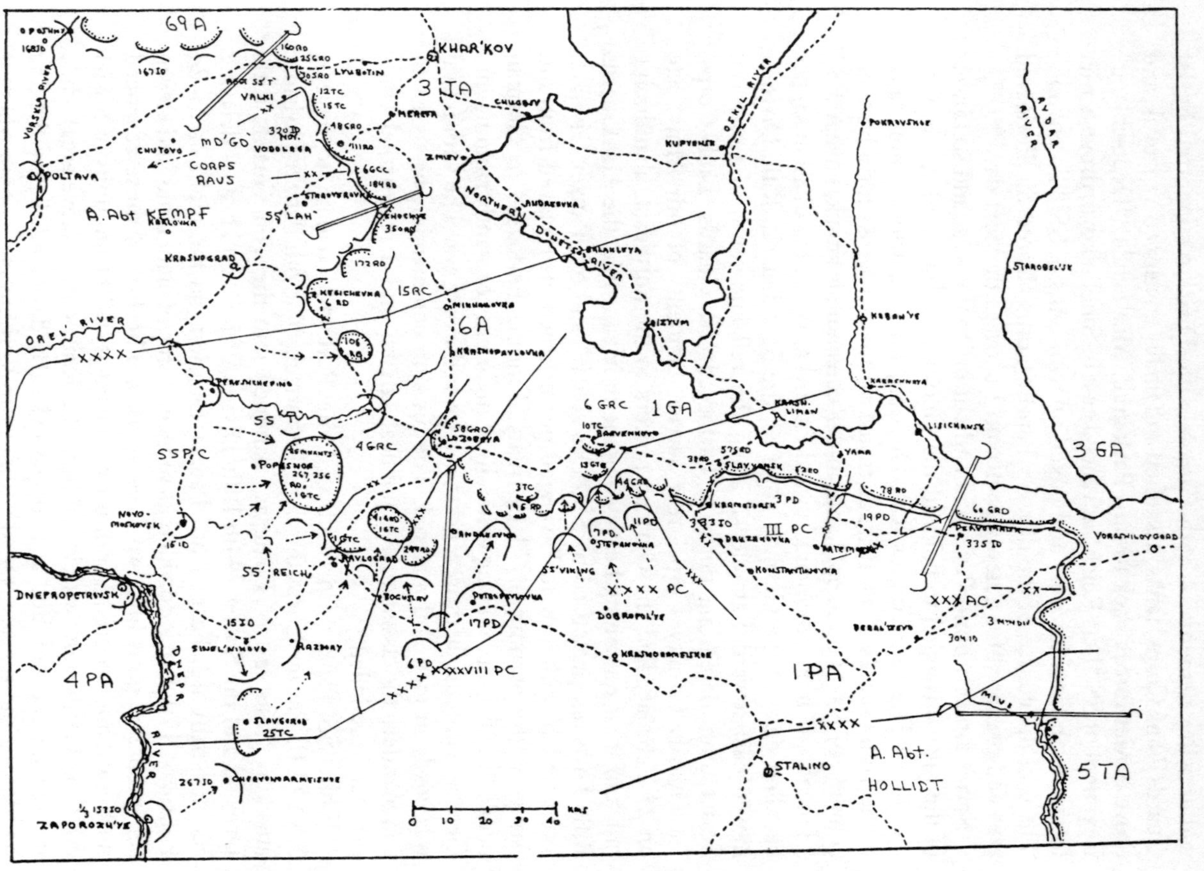

MAP 27. DONBAS, SITUATION, 2000 24 FEBRUARY 1943

units. The SS Panzer Division's southern column repulsed attacks by withdrawing elements of 35th Guards Rifle Division supported by 1st Guards Tank Corps' tanks, assaulted and finally enveloped Vyazovok, and drove Soviet forces back toward Pavlograd. Meanwhile, "Deutschland" Regiment of SS "Das Reich" advanced east of Sinel'nikovo, drove Soviet forces north from Razdory and linked up with units of SS "Totenkopf." Then, in the course of the day, SS Panzer Corps cleared the Pavlograd area and prepared for a new advance on Lozovaya the next day.[86]

Soviet forces around Pavlograd and cut off to the west and southwest of the town struggled to hold off the German advance and regain their own lines. The 35th Guards Rifle Division, still supported by nine tanks of the 16th Guards Tank Brigade thrust northward across the advancing columns of SS "Totenkopf" and, under constant air attack, engaged SS "Totenkopf" units advancing toward Pavlovka. While the division sapper battalion delayed the German advance, the 35th Guards Rifle Division moved east toward Samoilevka along the rail line south of Lozovaya. Soviet units defending north of Pavlograd (1st Guards Tank Corps, 1st Guards Cavalry Corps, rear service elements of 6th Army) late on 24 February fled the German pincers to the northeast, abandoning much of their remaining heavy equipment. Meanwhile, the 41st Guards Rifle Division, pressured by SS "Das Reich" and 6th Panzer Division, attempted to withdraw to Pavlograd per instructions received from 6th Army on the evening of 23 February. Finding Pavlograd in German hands, the division, moving generally at night but constantly running into German columns, withdrew northeast toward Lozovaya. The withdrawal was costly in men and material. The division commander, his assistant commander, the assistant for political affairs, and a regimental commander were killed.[87]

While SS Panzer Corps cleared the Pavlograd region, to its east XXXXVIII Panzer Corps developed its attack. The 6th Panzer Division, attacking from east of Boguslav, slammed into the 41st Guards Rifle Division and the Soviet 244th Rifle Division who then began a delaying action northward. East of 6th Panzer Division, on the night of 23–24 February, 17th Panzer divided its reduced force of eight tanks and eleven self-propelled guns into two *kampfgruppen.* The first of these advanced northward and secured Verkhnyaya Samara at 0900 from units of Soviet 3d Tank Corps (now withdrawn from the Krasnoarmeiskoye area) while the second concentrated at Petropavlovka. By day's end, heavy fighting had forced the *kampfgruppe* to withdraw to Verkhnyaya Samara where it occupied defensive positions for the night.[88]

The 17th Panzer Division units had run into the deploying Soviet 195th Rifle Division. The 195th, on the morning of 24 February, had erected a defensive screen facing south along a front of almost 45 kilometers.

The division's right flank theoretically tied in with the 58th Guards Rifle Division's defensive positions at Lozovaya and its left flank tied in with the 44th and 38th Guards Rifle Divisions which defended the extended front east to Slavyansk.[89] Remnants of Mobile Group, Popov, which had survived battle in the Krasnoarmeiskoye area, provided limited armored support from this overextended defense line. The collision of 195th Rifle Division troops with 17th Panzer Division units initiated the German assaults against Soviet defenses south of Barvenkovo.

XXXX Panzer Corps' Destruction of Mobile Popov – 21–24 February

While the SS Panzer Corps and XXXXVIII Panzer Corps smashed 6th Army and 1st Guards Army's right flank, XXXX Panzer Corps completed the rout of Mobile Group Popov and advanced northward toward Barvenkovo (see Map 25). Popov's situation was desperate. 10th Tank Corps with seventeen tanks occupied defensive positions at Krasnoarmeiskii Rudnik and attempted to parry the advance of SS Panzer Grenadier Division "Viking" and 7th Panzer Division from the south. 3d Tank Corps in the Andreyevka area with twelve tanks faced the advance of 11th Panzer Division from Aleksandrovka and Novo Alekseyevsky, and further south the remnants of 18th Tank Corps (eight tanks) defended at Dobropol'ye.[90] On the night of 20–21 February Popov requested permission from Vatutin to withdraw his tank forces northward to the Stepanovka area. Vatutin scolded Popov for his request, stating that such a movement would permit an enemy withdrawal to Dnepropetrovsk and would also expose the flank and rear of 6th Army. Moreover, Vatutin said Popov's proposal "contradicts the group's mission and the existing conditions whereby the enemy at all costs hurries to withdraw his forces from the Donbas across the Dnepr."[91] Vatutin ordered Popov to fulfill his mission and forbade him to withdraw northward. Popov was to cut all routes westward from Dobropol'ye and Krasnoarmeiskoye and, with a part of his force, begin a pursuit of German forces parallel to Dobropol'ye and Pokrovskoye. The *STAVKA* echoed Vatutin's lack of realism. On 21 February Lt. Gen. Bogolyubov notified the chief-of-staff of the Southern Front that:

> Vatutin's forces were operating extraordinarily successfully. His right flank is located at Pavlograd and the delay of the left flank occurred because of insufficiently active operations of our front.[92]

As if to confirm Popov's worst fears, on 21 February XXXX Panzer Corps resumed its advance, assisted in its movement by a cold spell which froze the previously marshy ground (see Maps 26–27). The 7th Panzer Division, in a two-day engagement, smashed 18th and 10th Tank Corps units at Dobropol'ye, and then, on 22 February, pressed on northward through Krasnoarmeiskii Rudnik while SS Panzer Grenadier Division "Viking" swung in a wide arc west and north through Krivorozh'ye to Novo Petrovka, where it struck 3d Tank Corps. 18th Tank Corps, caught between the advancing German columns, fell back toward new Soviet defense lines being erected by the 44th Guards Rifle Division south of Barvenkovo. 11th Panzer Division moved toward Stepanovka, struck the Soviet 18th Tank Corps and 38th Guards Rifle Division enroute, and forced them to withdraw northward as well. Meanwhile, the 333d Infantry Division continued to chase down survivors of 4th Guards Tank Corps in the Krasnoarmeiskoye area. In the Brody-Cheretino area the Soviet 44th Guards and 38th Guards Rifle Divisions, remnants of 3d, 10th, and 18th Tank Corps, and the 13th Guards Tank Brigade of 4th Guards Tank Corps (a total of thirty-five T-34 and fifteen T-70 tanks) put up heavy resistance to the concerted advance of SS "Viking," 7th Panzer, and 11th Panzer Divisions.[93] The Soviets created numerous small units out of withdrawing forces to bolster the makeshift defense.

By the evening of 24 February the German shock groups had established a virtually continuous front with SS Panzer Corps in the Pavlograd area, XXXXVIII Panzer Corps southeast of Lozovaya, and XXXX Panzer Corps south of Barvenkovo. Having isolated a large portion of 6th Army and eradicated the threat of both Soviet mobile groups (25th Tank Corps and Group Popov), the German command now moved to capitalize on the momentum already achieved to crush the remainder of 6th Army and 1st Guards Army.

By the end of 24 February Vatutin finally realized the parlous position of his forces, and he ordered what remained of the *front's* right wing to go over to the defense. His report to the *STAVKA* that evening finally reflected conditions as they actually existed. He highlighted the heavy personnel losses and pointed out that the *front* lacked rear tank repair facilities (all were forward with the now-smashed corps). Vatutin's report outlined the defensive measures he was undertaking and requested that the *STAVKA* order adjacent *fronts* to launch supporting attacks and also shift air assets from those *fronts* to strike at German armored concentrations.[94] The Germans, however, moved too quickly for any of Vatutin's remedies to be of assistance.

German Advance to Lozovaya and Barvenkovo – 25–27 February

On 25 February SS Panzer Corps struck north from Pavlograd with its two SS Panzer Divisions abreast (see Map 28). SS "Totenkopf's" 3d SS Grenadier Regiment and reconnaissance battalion moved northeast and east from Orel'ka and threatened Soviet 6th Army communications stretching from Lozovaya north toward Merefa. The main force of

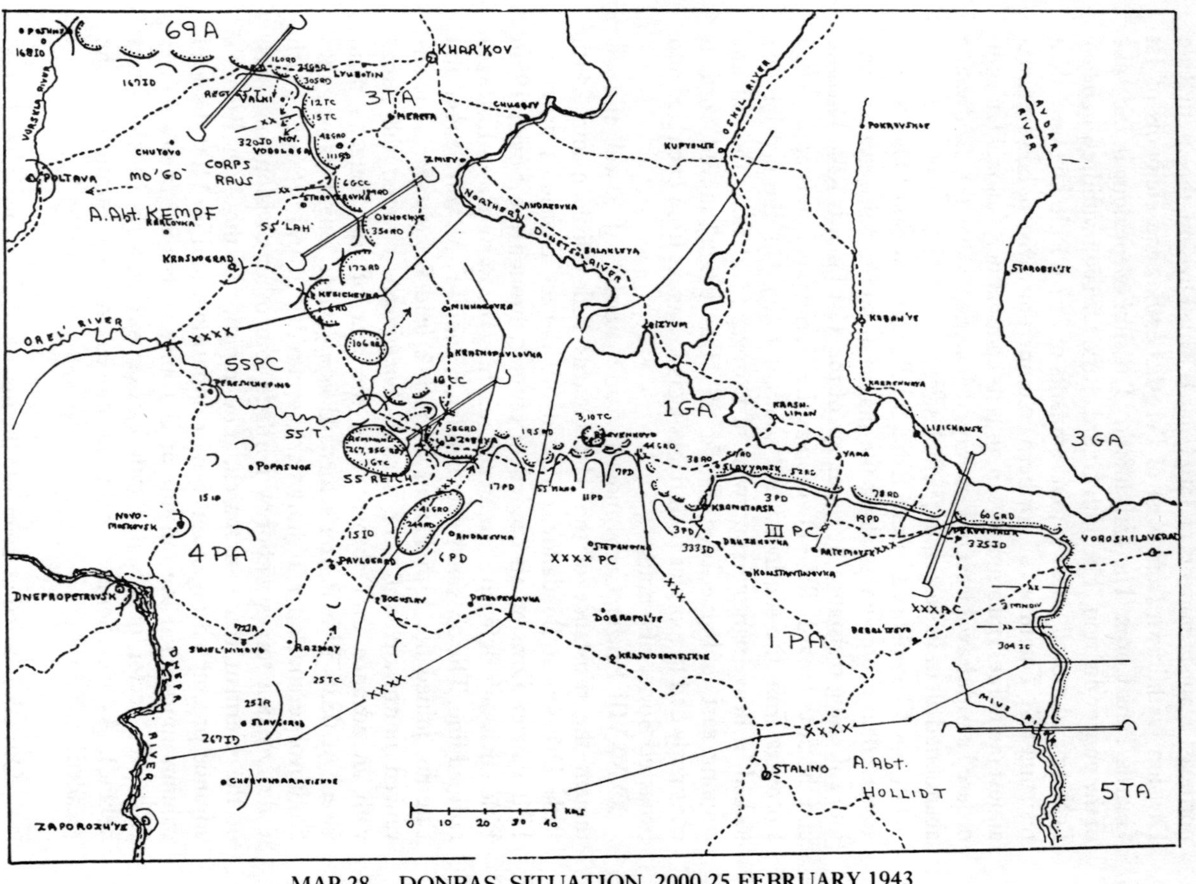

MAP 28. DONBAS, SITUATION, 2000 25 FEBRUARY 1943

SS "Totenkopf" advanced in several columns from Vasil'evka to the northeast against remnants of 35th Guards Rifle Division, the 267th Rifle Division (withdrawn from west of Pereshchepino) and elements of 1st Guards Tank Corps. The 15th Infantry Division swept along in the wake of the panzer division. The 35th Guards Rifle Division withdrew in heavy fighting and moved north to join remnants of 267th Rifle Division, then resisting SS "Totenkopf's" northern column. The division, however, was almost out of fuel and ammunition, thus its commander, Colonel Kulagin, ordered a withdrawal west of Lozovaya. Movement slowed as the division abandoned all of its remaining vehicles.[95]

On SS "Totenkopf's" right flank SS Panzer Division "Das Reich" advanced in two columns along the main rail line to Lozovaya and ran into stiffening resistance by remnants of the 41st Guards Rifle Division and the 58th Guards Rifle Division as the German columns approached Lozovaya from the southwest and south. By nightfall, the division was locked in heavy fighting southwest of Lozovaya and along the rail line running east to Barvenkovo. While SS "Das Reich" moved north it constantly had to monitor both flanks against attacks from encircled and bypassed Soviet rifle units.

XXXXVIII Panzer Corps moved steadily northward as well and, although the resistance of the 41st Guards Rifle Division and 244th Rifle Division at Bogdanovka slowed 6th Panzer Division's progress, 17th Panzer Division succeeded in cutting through the Soviet 195th Rifle Division's defensive screen and reaching the Barvenkovo–Lozovaya railroad line. The division's commander, General F. M. von Senger und Etterlin, joined the 17th Panzer Division's lead *kampfgruppe* as it advanced northward while the second *kampfgruppe* covered the flanks with an advance to Dobrovol'ye in the rear of von Senger's main force. At 0830 17th Panzer's forward *kampfgruppe* fought its way into Dobrovol'ye and, after a short fight, secured it at 0915. Soviet 195th Rifle Division forces withdrew north to join other division units east of the German route of march. The rapidity of the 17th Panzer's advance preempted organized Soviet opposition, and by 1100 the lead column approached the rail line at Burbulatovo Station in 6th Panzer Division's sector of advance (6th Panzer was still 15–20 kilometers behind). As von Senger's columns moved through Burbulatovo, he recalled,

> Our advance led us deep into the mass of the retreating Red forces. I saw long Russian columns battered by unopposed STUKA dive bombers. Then my few tanks would overrun the scattered remnants. Fierce fighting developed between Barbalatovo (sic) and Starya Bliznetsy. The road was blocked by abandoned armored

scout cars, horse drawn vehicles, wounded men and horses, and many dead. It was difficult to get through.[96]

Von Senger's column ran into the headquarters column of the 195th Rifle Division and cut off the Soviet division commander and his staff from his combat regiments. Since communication was lost with the division commander, the division chief-of-staff took over direction of the division, formed a rear guard consisting of several rifle battalions and all the available division artillery, and began a withdrawal to the Northern Donets River. By night movement, although with considerable losses, on 3 March all of the division regiments crossed the Northern Donets River. The division commander followed shortly thereafter.

Having routed a major portion of the 195th Rifle Division, the 17th Panzer Division continued on and occupied a security line further north while other division units moved forward to secure the division's flanks against large bypassed enemy forces. Especially large enemy forces remained on the division's flanks south of Starye Bliznetsy. 17th Panzer Division's drive accounted for destruction of three Soviet tanks, seven guns, two anti-tank guns, eight anti-aircraft guns, ten mortars, and sixty trucks, most from the headquarters element of 195th Rifle Division.[97] The low kill in tanks was indicative of the low strength of the tanks' parent unit, probably 3d Tank Corps (which also lost twelve armored reconnaissance cars).

By the evening of 25 February 17th Panzer Division was still far in advance of 6th Panzer Division, and XXXX Panzer Corps on the right still experienced heavy fighting for the approaches to the Barvenkovo area (see Map 28). There, elements of 38th, 44th, and 52d Guards Rifle Divisions and 3d, 4th, 10th, and 18th Tank Corps under 1st Guards Army control, desperately clung to defensive positions. Kuznetsov had stripped his left flank of units in order to hold on to the Barvenkovo area at all costs. His tank strength, which had risen to fifty, permitted him to offer considerable resistance to XXXX Panzer Corps, although most of his tanks were dug in because they were out of fuel.[98] In order to smash the final Soviet defenses at Barvenkovo 1st Panzer Army ordered a concerted attack by XXXX Panzer Corps and the 333d Infantry Division past Barvenkovo and toward the Northern Donets River. The 333d Infantry Division would concentrate to the rear of XXXX Panzer Corps, and III Panzer Corps would take over the Druzhkovka sector and ultimately join XXXX Panzer Corps' advance with its own attack on Kramatorsk and Slavyansk, now held by a portion of the Soviet 38th and 57th Guards Rifle Divisions.

Heavy fighting raged for Lozovaya on 26 and 27 February (see Maps 29–30). The 58th Guards Rifle Division defended in the city at all costs, reinforced by tanks of 1st Guards Tank Corps and 1st Guards Cavalry

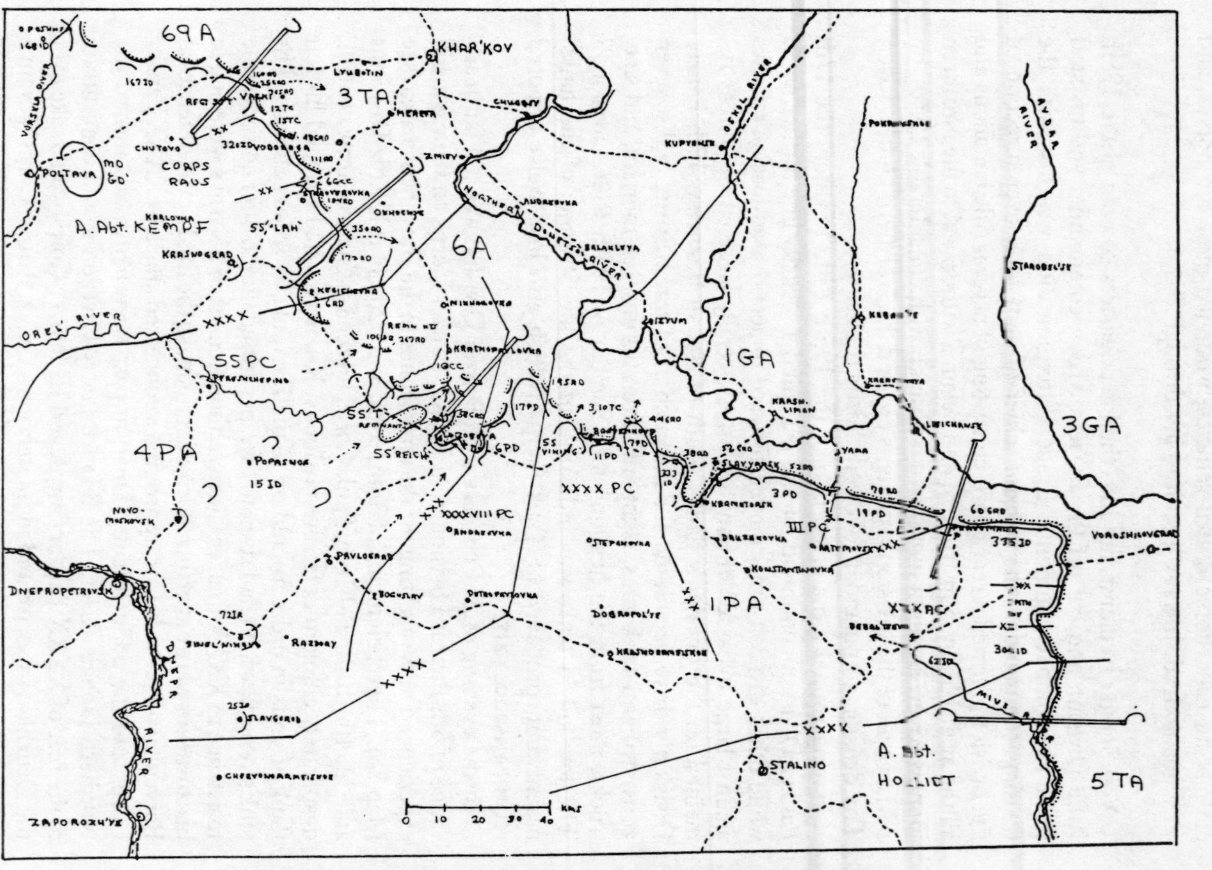

MAP 29. DONBAS, SITUATION, 2000 26 FEBRUARY 1943

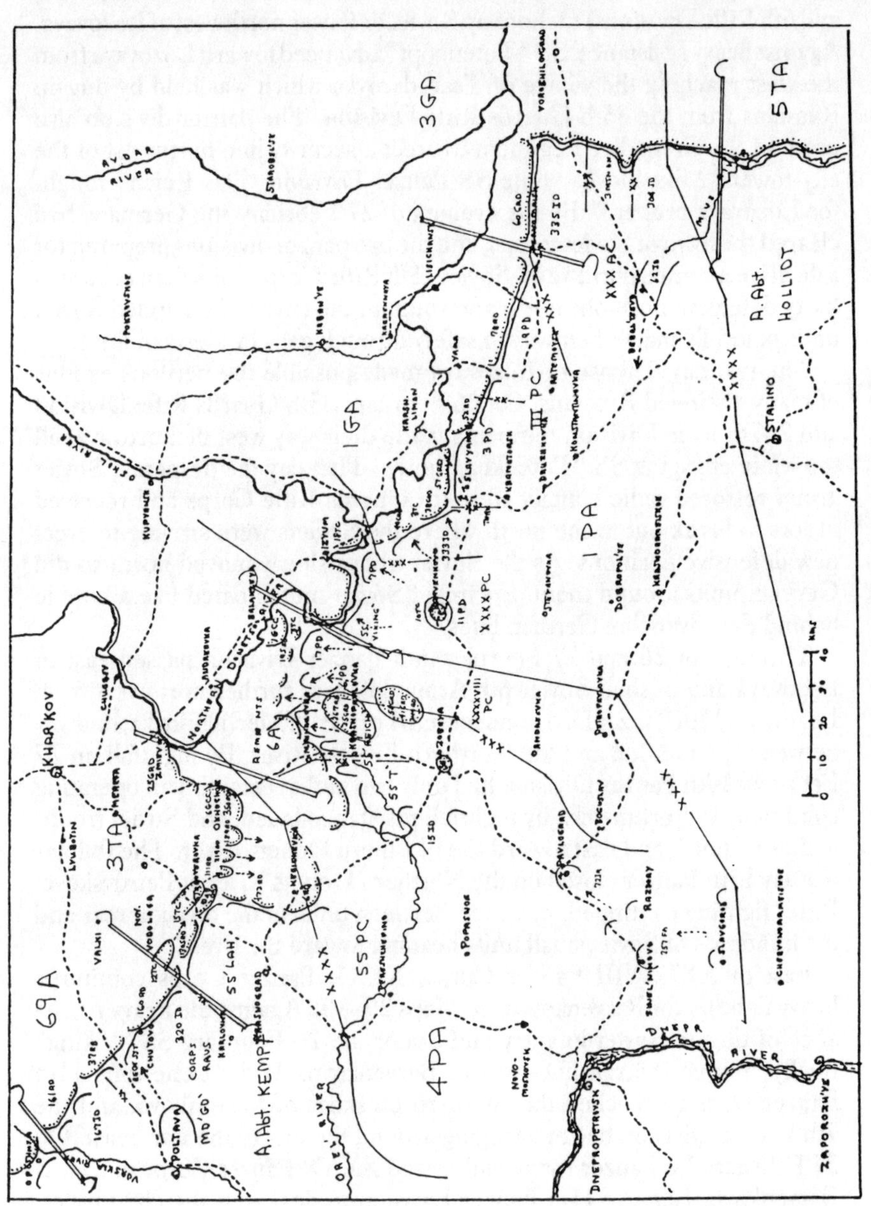

MAP 30. DONBAS, SITUATION, 2000 28 FEBRUARY 1943

Corps. General Kharitonov also ordered 15th Rifle Corps (the 350th, 172d, and 6th Rifle Divisions) to shore up Soviet defenses northwest of Lozovaya. Against heavy resistance, SS "Totenkopf" advanced toward Lozovaya from the west reaching the village of Tsaredarovka which was held by dug-in Russians from the 35th Guards Rifle Division. The panzer division also used 3d SS Grenadier Regiment to erect a security line northwest of the city toward Mikhailovka while SS Panzer Division "Das Reich" fought for Lozovaya proper.[99] By the evening of 27 February the Germans had cleared the town of Soviet troops, and the two panzer divisions prepared for a decisive advance northward. Soviet 15th Rifle Corps units then occupied hasty defensive positions north and south of the city, and encircled Soviet units painfully made their way to safety through gaps in German lines.

The two day defense of Lozovaya made possible the perilous exodus of many encircled Russians. On 26 February 35th Guards Rifle Division and 267th Rifle Division remnants made their way west of Lozovaya, all the while engaging SS "Totenkopf" units. That day the desperate Soviet group restored radio contact with 4th Guards Rifle Corps and received orders to break out to the north where the Soviets were striving to erect new defensive positions. As the Soviet troops slowly moved north so did German units around them. Encircled Soviet units floated like a bubble behind the advancing German lines.

Throughout 26 and 27 February 6th Panzer Division passed east of Lozovaya and pushed Soviet 6th Army defenses further northwest from Lozovaya. 17th Panzer Division secured the town of Mechebilovka, midway between the rail line and the Northern Donets River. By nightfall on 27 February 17th Panzer Division had only two tanks remaining in operating condition.[100] Fortunately, by nightfall resistance faded; and Soviet troops withdrew north and east toward the Northern Donets River. The following day 17th Panzer closed on the Northern Donets River at Petrovskoye. Bitter fighting continued, however, between units in the division rear and the hundreds of Soviet small units heading toward the river.*

East of XXXXVIII Panzer Corps, XXXX Panzer Corps continued heavy fighting for Barvenkovo (see Maps 29–30). Against the heavy resistance of dug-in Soviet infantry and armor, on 26 February SS "Viking" finally crossed the rail line west of Barvenkovo. At the same time 11th Panzer Division reached the southern outskirts of Barvenkovo, and the 7th Panzer Division began swinging around the city to the northeast. On 27 February 1st Panzer Army authorized XXXX Panzer Corps to bypass Barvenkovo. Leaving 11th Panzer Division to deal with the city proper, SS "Viking" headed west around the city toward the Northern Donets River while 7th Panzer Division sped north headed for Izyum.[101] Soviet

*17th Panzer Division strength on 27 February was 1840 men, 10 light and 3 medium howitzers, 6 tanks, and 10 self-propelled anti-tank guns.

resistance at Barvenkovo continued until midday on 28th February when, imperiled by the envelopment by SS "Viking" and 7th Panzer Division and the frontal assaults of 11th Panzer Division, Soviet forces withdrew to Izyum.

German Exploitation to the Northern Donets River – 28 February – 3 March

As evidenced by the slackened resistance in 17th Panzer Division's sector, on 27 February the *STAVKA* and the Southwestern Front, chilled by the prospects of impending defeat, ordered those 1st Guards Army and 6th Army forces who could, to withdraw to the Northern Donets River. Symbolic of the entire operation, however, the *STAVKA* offered up yet another army in sacrifice to the Germans. To cover the withdrawal of 6th Army and to assist in the escape of already encircled units, the *STAVKA* ordered the Voronezh Front to turn its 3d Tank Army sharply south and launch an attack against German units advancing northward between Krasnograd and Lozovaya.[102] 3d Tank Army had already for a week been pressing SS Panzer Division "Leibstandarte Adolf Hitler" back from Merefa toward Krasnograd, but that advance was difficult because 3d Tank Army's strength had ebbed away. Now, reinforced by several new rifle divisions shifted from other sectors, 3d Tank Army was to throw its last tanks into a suicidal advance southward, an advance into the gap between the SS Panzer Division "Leibstandarte Adolf Hitler," defending on the Krasnograd axis, and the two SS Panzer Divisions advancing north from Lozovaya. 3d Tank Army, by forced march, assembled on 28 February and 1 March in the Staroverovka–Okhocheye–Kegichevka area while SS "Leibstandarte Adolf Hitler" monitored its movements southeast (see Map 30).[103]

While 3d Tank Army shifted its forces to the southeast, on 28 February SS Panzer Corps continued its drive from Lozovaya with its two divisions advancing northwest on either side of the rail line from Lozovaya through Krasnopavlovka to Mikhailovka. (SS Panzer Division "Totenkopf's" commander was killed near Mikhailovka when the reconnaissance aircraft he was riding in was shot down by Soviet gunners.) The 15th Infantry Division supported the corps by fighting off the continuing stream of fugitives fleeing northward west of Lozovaya. Among those fugitives were the remnants of 35th Guards Rifle Division and 267th Rifle Division. These units, having successfully bypassed Lozovaya from the west, ran into SS "Totenkopf" and 17th Panzer Division's rear elements south of Mikhailovka; and they struggled to extricate themselves through 17th Panzer Division lines to the Northern Donets River. By 1 March, covered by elements of 1st Guards Cavalry Corps, the remnants of the 35th Guards and 267th Rifle Divisions crossed the Northern Donets

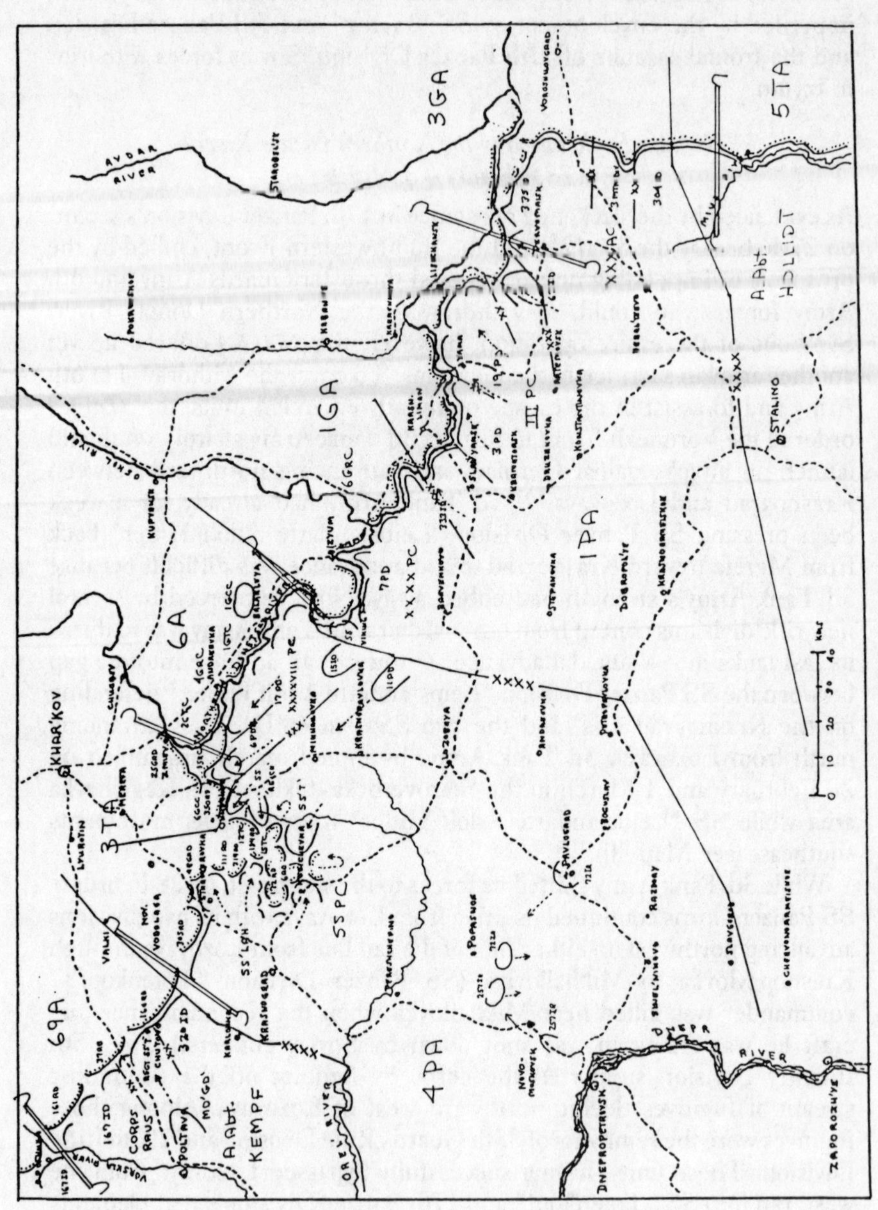

MAP 31. DONBAS, SITUATION, 2000 3 MARCH 1943

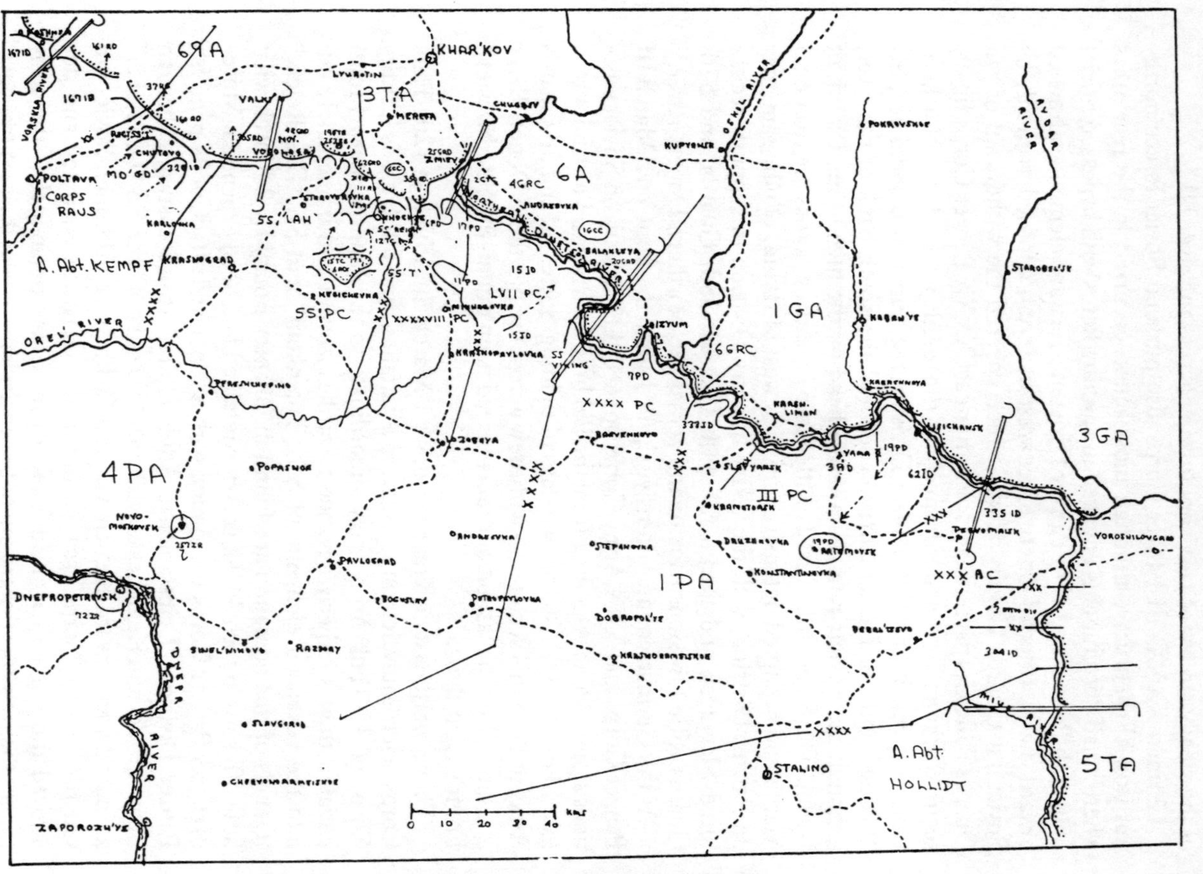

MAP 32. DONBAS, SITUATION, 2000 5 MARCH 1943

River and occupied defensive positions, having been reinforced by part of the steady stream of survivors flowing across the river.[104]

German XXXXVIII Panzer Corps also pursued Soviet forces northward on 28 February, although most action occurred in the rear areas where small detachments engaged in running fights with bypassed Soviet units. 6th Panzer and 17th Panzer Division's forward elements advanced toward the Northern Donets River west of Izyum opposed primarily by Soviet 1st Guards Cavalry Corps which covered the withdrawal of 4th Guards Rifle Corps' remnants. Further east XXXX Panzer Corps finally secured Barvenkovo and advanced to the south bank of the Northern Donets River. While 11th Panzer Division regrouped at Barvenkovo, SS "Viking" and 6th Panzer Division secured the south bank of the river, although the Soviets retained a bridgehead on the high ground south of Izyum. The Soviet 6th Guards Rifle Corps withdrew across the river on 3 March and occupied defensive positions west of Izyum. On the same day 3d Panzer Division, with the 331st Infantry Division in support, recaptured Slavyansk and forced the 44th Guards, 38th Guards, and 57th Guards Rifle Divisions back to and across the Northern Donets River.

As the German counteroffensive rippled along the front, on 2 March III Panzer Corps and XXX Army Corps opened their assault on Soviet positions along a front extending from the Bakhmutka River to Voroshilovgrad (see Maps 31–33). During two days of fighting Soviet 1st and 3d Guards Army units in this sector also withdrew across the Northern Donets River at a time when the last bit of drama played itself out on the Southwestern Front's right flank.

There, northeast of Krasnograd, on 1 March the 15th and 12th Tank Corps, each equivalent in strength to a battalion, and 6th Guards Cavalry Corps of 3d Tank Army (now subordinate to the Southwestern Front) initiated their southerly advance toward Lozovaya and immediately ran into the advanced elements of SS "Totenkopf" and SS "Das Reich." (Details of this operation are found in Chapter Four.) By 2 March what little offensive punch 3d Tank Army retained had been expended. Moreover, SS Panzer Corps responded with a concerted attack of its own. SS Panzer Division "Leibstandarte Adolf Hitler" struck eastward through Staroverovka and Kegichevka while SS "Totenkopf" and SS "Das Reich" advanced west toward Kegichevka and Okhocheye. Although Soviet 6th Guards Cavalry Corps escaped north, the Germans encircled and destroyed the remainder of 3d Tank Army. Some personnel of the army fought their way northward out of the encirclement over the next two days.

The destruction of 3d Tank Army marked the grisly end to the Soviet Donbas operation. Manstein's attention then shifted northward toward the large Soviet salient projecting west of Khar'kov. With a few adjustments to his troop deployments, Manstein ordered his divisions north to repeat against Soviet forces in the Khar'kov area what the Germans had accomplished south of the Northern Donets River.

Conclusions

The Soviet Donbas operation, conceived in January in a blaze of optimism, expired in March as the coherence of the southwestern Front exploded in a mass of sparks under the blows of Manstein's counteroffensive. The heels of German soldiers, the treads of German armor, and the cold waters of the Northern Donets River extinguished those sparks and gave the Soviet High Command a new lesson in the dangers of overconfidence. The Donbas operational failure, combined with subsequent Soviet failures in the Khar'kov area, sobered the Soviet High Command and conditioned them for more realistic actions in the summer of 1943.

In retrospect the optimism of the Soviet High Command in the winter of 1943 seemed justifiable. A series of major offensive operations had encircled German 6th Army at Stalingrad, destroyed Italian 8th and Hungarian 2d Armies, seriously injured German 2d Army, and isolated German 17th Army in the Kuban area. German operational reserves in the months of combat were threadbare, and many German panzer divisions were engaged in the debilitating task of front line defense. These operations reduced by as much as half German strength in the Eastern Front's southern wing. In a situation somewhat analogous to that of the winter of 1942, the Soviet High Command expected at any time German strategic defenses to crack and irrevocably collapse. That collapse had to occur before the spring thaw brought operations to a halt. If two or more operations by admittedly tired forces in reduced strength could produce that collapse the venture was well worth the risk. Moreover, it was within the realm of possibility that Soviet forces facing German 6th Army in the Stalingrad area could lend their weight to the offensives. In the unlikely event that the offensives faltered, the same spring thaw that the Soviets feared would preempt their success would preempt any prospects for a successful German counteroffensive.

In making these judgements the Soviet High Command, and the *front* headquarters and staffs who shared their optimism were mistaken in several important respects. First, they paid inadequate attention to the condition and offensive capabilities of their own forces. Second, German 6th Army tied down significant Soviet forces until early February; and these forces were unable to affect materially the course of the Donbas and Khar'kov operations. Third, the Soviets did not reckon on the reinforcement capabilities of German forces and their ability to use in combat, units whose strength would normally have rendered them unfit for such tasks. Last, and most important, they misjudged the reaction of the German High Command, which, instead of prudently withdrawing, conducted a major skillful counteroffensive, a counteroffensive ironically produced by Hitler's insistence on forward defense blended with Manstein's insistence on operational maneuver. The Soviets paid for these miscalculations by suffering heavy losses and by losing about 30 percent of the gains their forces made in the winter of 1943.[105] More important, the operational initiative swung into German hands to use as they saw fit in the summer of 1943. Soviet analysts hold the *STAVKA* and *front* commands responsible for these errors in judgement.

It is clear that Soviet forces attacking into the Donbas were weaker than those which had initiated the November and December offensives around Stalingrad. The divisions in 1st Guards Army, 6th Army, 3d Guards Army, and 5th Tank Army had been in nearly continuous combat since 16 December 1942; and many operated at from 40–60 percent of TOE strength. More important, high casualties in earlier operations meant that many of the soldiers in these units were new and relatively untrained. It is no coincidence that rifle divisions had in their TOE structure distinct training battalions to process new men into their units, and even these training battalions fought in combat as tactical units. The wear and tear of a long campaign also reduced the supporting weapons strength of rifle divisions which, with a diminution of army fire support, prevented the Soviets from using the heavy artillery support they had available earlier in the winter. (Much of the artillery was still concentrated around Stalingrad.)

Even more serious were the deficiencies in Soviet mobile forces. Being more susceptible to the ravages of time and distance, mobile units (tank corps, brigade and regiments) were below 50 percent authorized strength, and the long distances from supply bases further reduced their effectiveness by denying them adequate supplies of fuel and ammunition. Popov's mobile group, although imposing on paper, seldom constituted more than the equivalent of one or two complete tank corps. Although the *front* commander learned from earlier operations the value of uniting these forces under a single command (a mobile group headquarters), operationally and tactically they fought on separate directions thereby further diminishing their shock value. The long distance the mobile forces traversed had the by now familiar effect of further reducing their actual armor strength (by 40–60 percent); and the *front* passed on to these units newly received tanks in penny-packet fashion, never in quantities large enough to affect the outcome of battle. Air forces provided only marginal support in the operation because the Germans

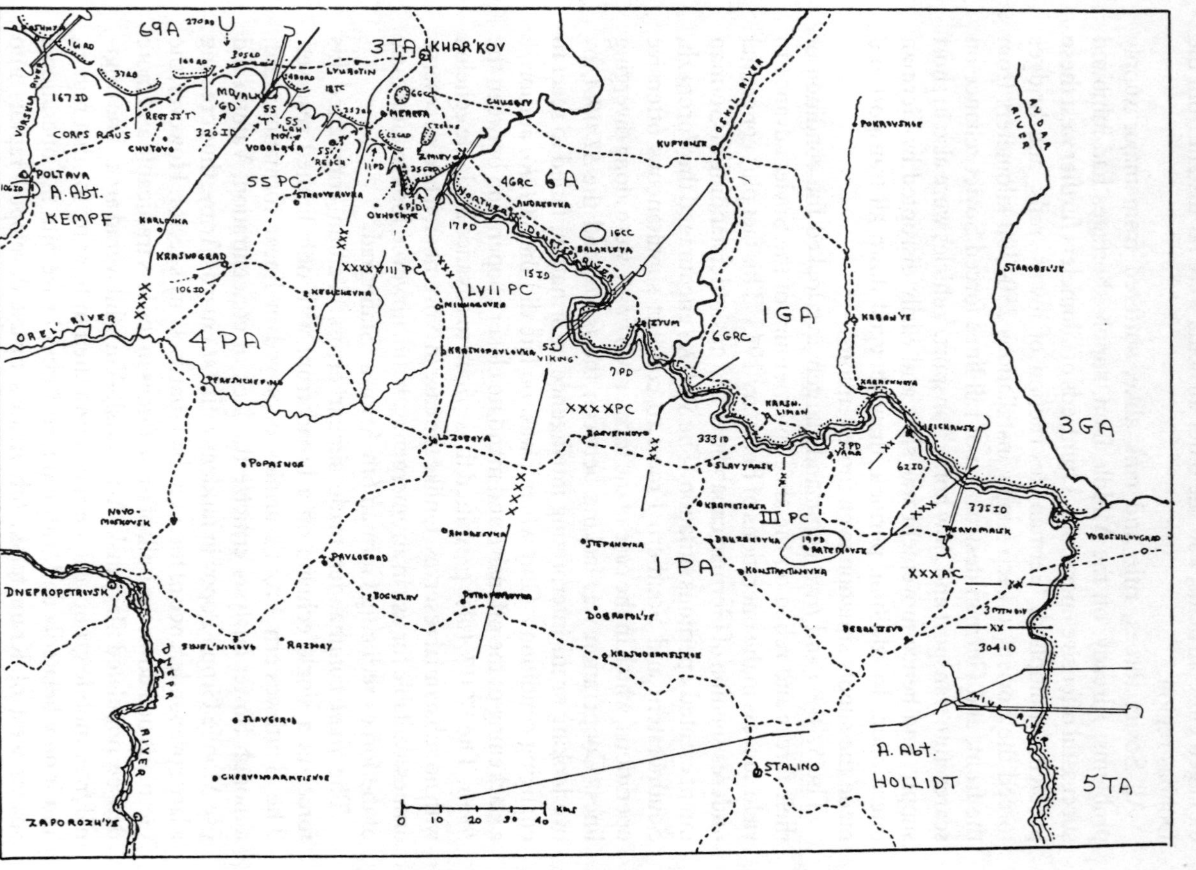

MAP 33. DONBAS, SITUATION, 2000 7 MARCH 1943

damaged close airfields, and the older airfields were far distant from the Donbas region.

All Soviet forces, rifle and tank alike, suffered from major supply problems. Already, on the Middle Don, supply shortages had inhibited successful offensive operations. Hundreds of kilometers further west these problems multiplied. German destruction of towns, rails, and bridges forced the Soviets to keep supply installations 250–300 kilometers from the front; and German destruction of rail lines forced Soviet reliance on scarce auto transport and slow horse transport. Vehicles were also in short supply, and hence movement was slow and easily disrupted by German interdiction. In addition, periodic thaws bogged down all transport and made the supply situation even more tenuous.

The *STAVKA* and *front* commands largely overlooked the condition of their forces and relied on the sheer momentum of the Soviet advance to yield success in the operations of February 1943. This fact plus congenital underestimation of German capabilities and misunderstanding of German intent created a perilous situation. The *STAVKA* encouraged the Voronezh, Southwestern and Southern Fronts to conduct simultaneous offensive operations, which in the case of the former two *fronts*, were along diverging lines. Cooperation was lacking between the *fronts*; and the *STAVKA,* by overlooking or misinterpreting intelligence information, failed to react to changing conditions. Only when it was too late did the *STAVKA* authorize a slackening of the offensive and mandate closer cooperation between the *fronts*. The *STAVKA* also permitted those *fronts* to advance in single echelon with no substantial reserves. Unlike the case in November, it had no reserve armies available for use in an emergency. It did, however, look to future use of the forces reducing German 6th Army at Stalingrad.

The *front* commander made similar errors. Vatutin committed his forces in a single echelon on a broad front with only limited reserves. The Southwestern Front's armies deployed in linear formation; and, although Soviet analysts criticize the lack of concentration, Vatutin did use Mobile Group Popov in tandem with 1st Guards Army, thus creating a large preponderance of forces in 1st Guards Army's sector. However, the Germans tied down the bulk of these forces in the less trafficable and more densely populated Slavyansk–Artemovsk–Voroshilovgrad area. The original *front* mobile group also became enmeshed in fighting for that region, and it only belatedly and with reduced forces broke into the operational spaces west of Kramatorsk. 6th Army's thrust developed rapidly into the depths but along an axis diverging from that of 1st Guards Army. Subsequently, Vatutin shifted his forces from east to west in piecemeal fashion ostensibly to add to the strength of 6th Army. These redeployments, however, simply filled open spaces and neither increased the force of 6th Army's blow nor closed the yawning gap between 1st Guards Army and 6th Army. Belatedly, Vatutin committed his armored reserves, not to reinforce the main mobile group, but rather as a second mobile group. Neither mobile group was able to perform its mission because of its weakness and lack of infantry support. A measure of these groups' ineffectiveness was the necessity in the middle of the operation to commit a ski brigade to their assistance (a process recalling futile Soviet attempts to generate successful exploitation in the winter of 1941–42).

The *front* commander, caught up in the optimistic mood of the *STAVKA* and prodded by often sarcastic *STAVKA* directives, also ignored or misread intelligence indicators on initial enemy movements and made the fatal mistake of allowing subjective judgements concerning German intentions to cloud objective judgements concerning German capabilities. Moreover, Vatutin opposed the advice of his subordinate army commanders, who were much more attuned to the realities of the situation. Like the *STAVKA,* Vatutin did not react quickly enough to avert disaster. As seen from another perspective, he reacted too quickly, adhering steadfastly to his own misconceptions of what the enemy was going to do. Although last minute reactions were too late to alter the outcome of the operation, Vatutin's shift of forces into the Barvenkovo area probably forestalled even greater damage to his *front*.

The German command capitalized on all of these misjudgements, and it is to Manstein that credit must be given for doing so. In the perilous days of February, the prudent commander would have judged the situation for the disaster it was and would have withdrawn beyond the Dnepr River. Manstein, particularly known for his ability to function best in a time of crisis (Hitler's statement) and a master advocate of maneuver warfare, chose not to take the prudent and safer course. Ironically, in a sense, he was assisted by the stubbornness of Hitler who demanded that all territory be held. In the end, both men prevailed. Manstein gave up some territory permanently (to the Mius River) and some territory temporarily (the northern Donbas) but in so doing he created conditions for a counteroffensive that carried German forces back to the Northern Donets River and ultimately through Khar'kov and Belgorod.

Manstein's plan involved the use of forces as fatigued as Soviet forces, moreover, a force deprived of the euphoria produced by a successful advance. Most German divisions had also been in the line since November and were at reduced strength while the panzer divisions were a shell of their former selves. However, Manstein did secure significant reserves which he used to good effect. He used the new infantry divisions to bolster those sectors which had to be held (333d–335th Infantry Division) and to support the operations of panzer units (15th Infantry Division). Most significant was the arrival of SS Panzer Corps in the region. Although elements of the corps were involved in the retrograde to and through

Khar'kov, it is difficult to see how Manstein could have conducted his operations without that corps' participation. In essence, by virtue of its strength, it was the fresh reserve that Soviet forces did not possess.

The German plans worked almost perfectly. Army Detachment Hollidt held the Mius River line and early in the operation shifted requisite forces to 1st Panzer Army to hold the critical Slavyansk–Artemovsk sector as a rock against which waves of Soviet forces would crash and deflect westward and around which the German counterattack would develop. The tenuous threat of Mobile Group Popov after 15 February forced 1st Panzer Army to commit XXXX Panzer Corps in that sector, thus providing a nucleus around which one German shock group could be created for the counterattack. The assembly of operational reserves went smoothly although detected by Soviet reconnaissance. XXXXVIII Panzer Corps and SS Panzer Corps deployed to their shock group attack positions virtually unhindered. Striking in coordinated fashion the three shock groups showed the positive synergetic effect that concentrated forces operating side-by-side along converging axes can have on a less well-organized though more numerous enemy. This was true even though two of these corps, XXXXVIII and XXXX Panzer Corps, consisted of woefully understrength units. Like two tired fighters slumping around the ring in a late round of a boxing match, the one best able to prevail was the one who would bring to bear the last series of coordinated punches. Manstein delivered those last punches. In a perceptive comment on the operation, General von Senger wrote:

> During the two months after the battle of Stalingrad, the Russians pursued the defeated German troops uninterruptedly along a 750 mile front, which in the south attained a depth of 435 miles. This pursuit slowly but surely ground to a halt. The Russian spearheads became thinner and thinner. Assault units continued to the limit of their endurance and beyond the point where they would be supplied. This extension and weakening of the Russian lines during the German withdrawal explains why units with limited combat strength like the 17th Panzer Division were able, after disengaging themselves from the Russians, to recover, halt the enemy, and then throw him back in the exhilarating change of role from pursued to pursuer.[106]

In was Manstein who detected that true state of the Soviet armies' condition and not the Soviet High Command. It was Manstein's forces who capitalized on it and won an operational victory in the Donbas which partially compensated for German strategic defeat in the winter of 1942–43.

4

OPERATION "STAR": The Khar'kov Operation

2 February – 23 March 1943

Operational Context

After planning commenced for Operation Gallop the *STAVKA* displayed its growing optimism by expanding the winter offensive to include operations by Golikov's Voronezh Front. Although Golikov's forces were engaged in heavy fighting with German forces in Kastornoye area, the *STAVKA* planned for a continuation of the offensive westward virtually without an operational pause. The *STAVKA* was willing to undertake a calculated risk that its forces, already worn down by a month of fighting, could, in conjunction with pressure from adjacent *fronts*, produce a final inexorable collapse of German forces on the entire southern wing of the Eastern Front. Thus, while the Southwestern and Southern Fronts planned an operation through the Donbas toward the Dnepr River, the Voronezh Front received orders to advance on Kursk and Khar'kov.

STAVKA sketched out the concept of future Operation *Zvezda* (Star) on 23 January 1943 and ordered Golikov to regroup his forces hastily and launch an attack on 1 February toward the west and southwest to secure Khar'kov and cover the northern flank of the Southwestern Front as well.[1] On 26 January the *STAVKA*, at General G. K. Zhukov's urging, widened the scope of the offensive by including Kursk as an objective. The net effect of this decision was to add about 100 kilometers to the ultimate operational sector of the Voronezh Front. The *STAVKA* also delayed commencement of the operation to 2 February to permit the attacking armies to complete the concentration of their forces.

Opposing Forces

Soviet

The Voronezh Front had at its disposal five armies, two of which (the 38th and 60th) would attack toward Kursk and three (40th, 69th, and 3rd Tank) toward Khar'kov (see Appendix 3, Order of Battle). This study will focus on those forces operating on the Belgorod–Khar'kov direction. Lieutenant General K.S. Moskalenko's 40th Army was the strongest of Golikov's armies. Its eight rifle divisions, one tank corps, and three tank brigades numbered about 90,000 men and 100 tanks.[2] However, in late January, a significant portion of these forces was busy eliminating encircled German forces in the Kastornoye and Staryi Oskol areas and would not be available to participate in the opening stages of the new offensive. Thus, Moskalenko had but five divisions with light armor support available to begin the offensive. Lieutenant General M.I. Kazakov's 69th Army was a new formation only recently elevated to army status. It consisted of the former 18th Rifle Corps reinforced by additional infantry and armor units. On the eve of the Khar'kov operation 69th Army's five rifle divisions, one rifle brigade, one tank brigade, and one tank regiment numbered approximately 40,000 men and fifty tanks.[3]

Lieutenant General P.S. Rybalko's 3d Tank Army was the Voronezh Front's armored fist, although it was a bit dulled by a month of operations. Its armored nucleus was the 12th and 15th Tank Corps supplemented by the mobile but more fragile 6th Guards Cavalry Corps. Its four rifle divisions were supported by one tank brigade and one tank regiment. Rybalko's army included 55,577 men and 165 tanks.[4] Thus, Golikov's Voronezh Front could commit a force of just under 200,000 men and over 300 tanks to crush German forces in the Khar'kov region. Golikov's reserve was small, although in the later stage of the operation, the *STAVKA* would release to his control several rifle divisions, two additional tank corps, and two tank brigades. However, these reserves arrived too late to participate in the offensive.

German

German and allied forces facing the left wing of the Voronezh Front were seriously weakened by earlier defeats. Army Detachment Lanz covered the sector along the west bank of the Oskol River from north of Chernyanka to Kupyansk with only a thin screen of forces. In its northern sector Army Detachment Lanz deployed two regiments of the 168th Infantry Division interspersed with remnants of the Hungarian 10th, 13th and 23rd Infantry Divisions. In the Novyi Oskol–Volokonovka area the large Panzer Grenadier Division "Grossdeutschland" covered a broad front tied in on its right with one regiment (Führer) of SS Panzer Division "Das Reich" deployed on the west bank of the Oskol River opposite the city of Valuiki. Further south the 298th Infantry Division defended at Kupyansk and the 320th Infantry Division south of Kupyansk. By early February Corps Cramer controlled operations of the 168th Infantry Division and Panzer Grenadier Division "Grossdeutschland." Thus, German forces of Army Detachment Lanz attempted to defend a sector of over 150 kilometers with an over-extended force of around 50,000 men.[5] The only hope of succor lay in the expected arrival of the bulk of SS Panzer Corps in the Khar'kov area, a move planned for completion in early February. Correlation of Soviet and German forces is given in the table below.

SOVIET		*GERMAN*	
Voronezh Front		A.Abt. Lanz (part)	50,000 men
40th Army	90,000 men	SS Panzer Corps	20,000 men
	100 tanks	(2 divisions)	200 tanks (est)
69th Army	40,000 men		
	50 tanks		
3d Tank Army	57,600 men		
	165 tanks		
Front Reserves	20,000 men		
	300 tanks*		
Total strength	210,000 men	3×1	70,000 men
	615 tanks	3×1	200 tanks

*2d and 3d Guards Tank Corps – arrived late in operation

Area of Operations

The Voronezh Front would operate across a region cut by two major rivers and containing several major cities (see Maps 34 a and b). The most immediate obstacle was the Oskol River running from north to south across the *frontal* zone into the Northern Donets River south of Izyum. *Front* forces had attempted in late January to occupy bridgeheads on the west bank of the river from which they could launch their offensive. The task was successfully completed in the entire *front* sector by 1 February. That left one major river obstacle to surmount in the advance on Khar'kov, that being the Northern Donets River. While fordable in the region north of Belgorod, further south it formed a formidable barrier astride the road to Khar'kov. Between the Oskol and Northern Donets Rivers the land was rolling, sparsely wooded, and crisscrossed by tributaries of the Northern Donets. In the north these tributaries ran from north to south, but the southwestward line of advance of 40th Army and 69th Army took these forces along but not across these rivers. In the south Soviet forces advanced from east to west along the valleys of the smaller rivers. The only real obstacles in the region were the smaller towns along the dirt roads through the river valleys, towns such as Korocha, Veliko-Mikhailovka, and Veliki Burluk which the Germans invariably converted into strongpoints. Thus, the Soviets would seek to transverse rapidly the open country east of the Northern Donets, secure crossings over the Northern Donets before it could be defended, and advance on Khar'kov.

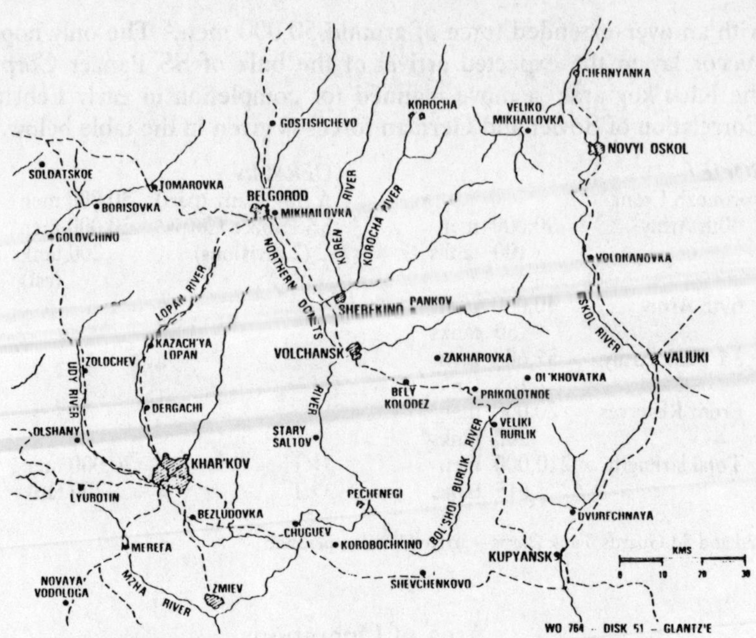

MAP 34a. KHAR'KOV AREA OF OPERATIONS

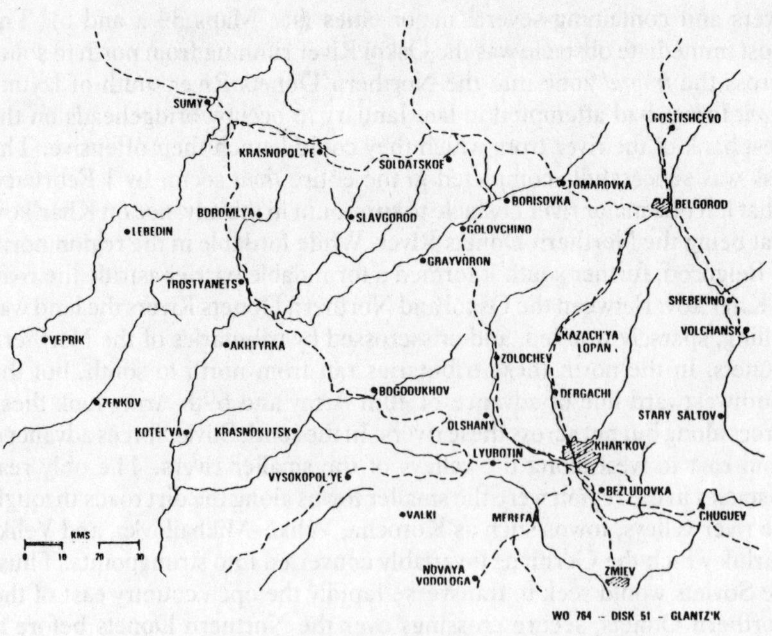

MAP 34b. KHAR'KOV AREA OF OPERATIONS

West of the Northern Donets River were the cities of Belgorod and Khar'kov, both major obstacles if defended. The land west of Belgorod comprised a series of ridges running from northeast to southwest parallel to tributaries of the Vorskla and Psel Rivers. These ridges offered a natural, relatively unhindered advance route around Belgorod and to the southwest into lower terrain in the Akhtyrka, Kotel'va, and Bogodukhov areas. The principal avenue of advance around Belgorod ran along the Vorskla River through the towns of Tomarovka, Borisovka, and Graivoron. These same ridges running southwest of Belgorod would carry advancing troops into and west of Khar'kov.

The eastern approaches to Khar'kov were covered by the Northern Donets River and a series of tributaries running north to southeast of Khar'kov, each of which offered strong possibilities for defense. South of Khar'kov the best approaches to the city ran up the Mzha and Udy Rivers from the Northern Donets. The area along and between these rivers was heavily wooded, sharply hilly, and sprinkled with villages and towns. Moreover, the Mzha River led to the large town of Merefa, and the Udy led directly into Khar'kov. South of the Mzha River the terrain west of the Northern Donets River was open and generally flat. Once west of the Northern Donets valley a force could sweep west and northwest relatively unhindered by terrain until it reached the more densely populated region of Lyubotin, west of Khar'kov. West of the Khar'kov area flat open terrain gently sloped westward and southwest toward Kotel'va and Poltava in the Vorskla River valley.

Roads in the region were all dirt surfaced and subject to deterioration during wet weather or thaws. The major roads ran from north to south from Kursk through Belgorod to Khar'kov and from Sumy southeast through Bogodukhov to Khar'kov. Important rail lines paralleled these roads and, in addition, ran westward from Khar'kov to Poltava. Most major population centers (Belgorod, Khar'kov, Sumy, Trostyanets, Akhtyrka, Bogodukhov, Merefa, and Poltava) were located on or near these communication arteries. Other large towns (Shebekino, Volchansk, Pechenegi, Chuguyev, Zmiyev) nestled on or near the Northern Donets River at key crossing sites over the river. Other large villages were scattered along minor roads in the valleys of the numerous smaller rivers.

Thus, forces defending the Belgorod–Khar'kov region had to make maximum use of the obstacle value of the Northern Donets River and the towns and villages along the natural valley avenues of approach. Moreover, Belgorod and Khar'kov offered excellent defensive possibilities if the enemy chose to attack them directly. However, as compensation, forces could convert these cities into traps if they chose to envelop rather than attack them.

Planning

Front Planning

STAVKA orders to Golikov specified that the Voronezh Front should destroy enemy forces defending in the Tim, Oskol, Volokonovka, and Valuiki areas, rout German operational reserves, and advance to secure Kursk, Belgorod, and Khar'kov (see Map 35).[6] The *front* main attack force (40th, 69th, and 3d Tank Armies) would penetrate German defenses, advance to the southwest, and ultimately converge on the Khar'kov area. These armies would envelop Khar'kov from the west and south and entrap large German forces in the environs of the city. Lieutenant General N.E. Chibisov's 38th Army would advance toward Tomarovka in order to drive German forces westward from Belgorod and protect the main *front* force's right flank. Meanwhile, Lieutenant General I.E. Chernyakovsky's 60th Army would launch a secondary attack from the Kastornoye area to Kursk.

Thus, the overall operation would achieve a depth of advance of 200–250 kilometers and would bring Soviet forces to a line from Rakitnoye through Graivoron, Bogodukhov and Lyubotin, to Merefa. The advance would occur in two stages. During the first stage *front* forces would destroy enemy units along the Oskol River from Stary Oskol to Valuiki and then advance to the Northern Donets River on a front from Belgorod through Volchansk to Pechenegi. In the second stage Soviet forces would secure Khar'kov and then advance to their final objective line.

The *front* main attack force would converge on Khar'kov from the northeast and east. 40th Army would sweep southwest from Stary Oskol through Belgorod to envelop Khar'kov from the northwest. Simultaneously, one rifle division would advance westward to the key road junction of Bogodukhov and cover the army right flank. 69th Army would attack southwest through Volchansk across the Northern Donets River to the northeastern approaches to Khar'kov. 3d Tank Army would advance through Veliki Burluk, cross the Northern Donets River, swing southwest through Chuguyev, and then turn westward and northwestward to Lyubotin in a close enveloping maneuver designed to link up with 40th Army.

In order to project as much as possible of his combat power forward, Golikov formed his *front* into a single operational echelon of armies without a significant second echelon or reserve. He hoped this would produce an advance rapid enough to preempt the Germans from erecting formidable defenses across the Northern Donets River.

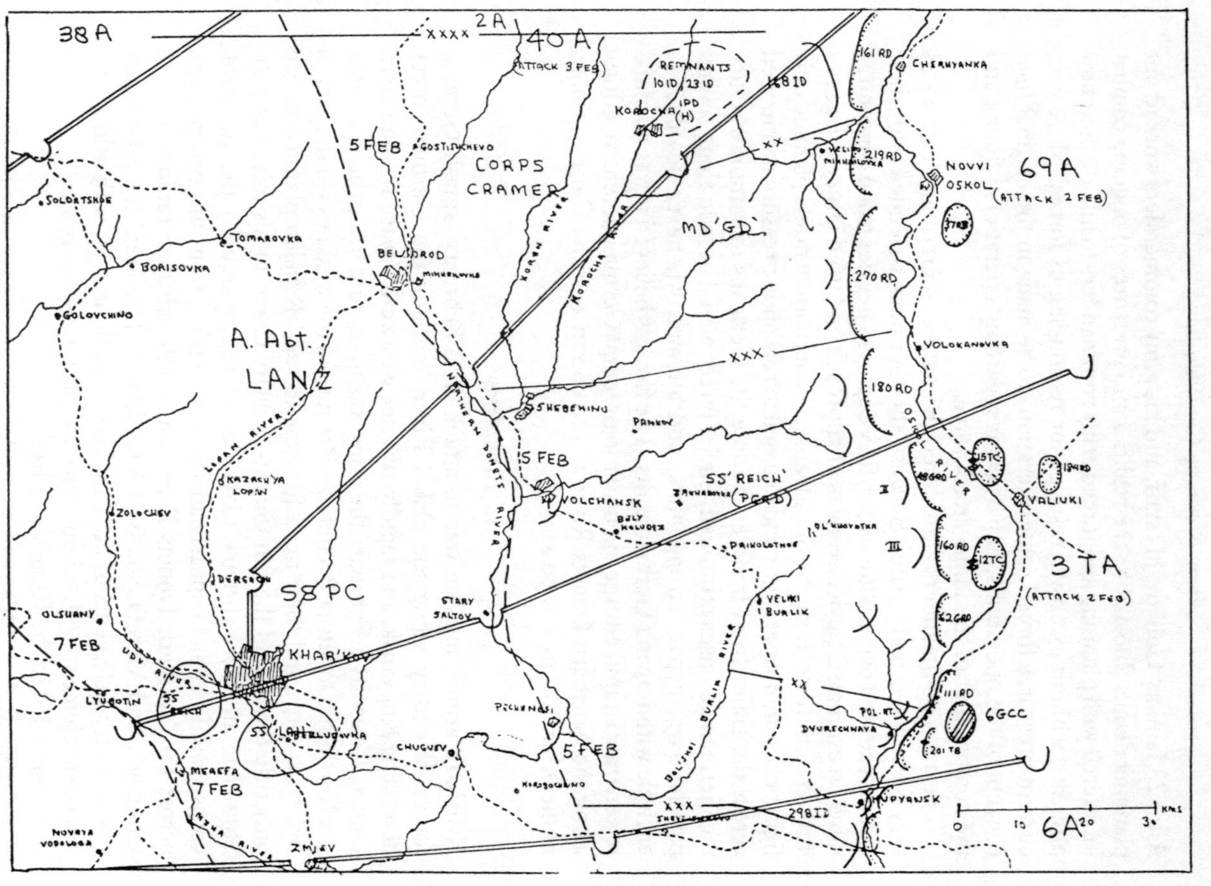

MAP 35. OPERATION "STAR" PLAN

Army Planning Considerations

After 23 January Golikov, his staff, and his army commanders worked out planning details. Inevitably, the realities and pressures of ongoing combat interfered with planning and forced army commanders to initiate their new offensive without extensive resupply or regrouping of forces. Moreover, current pressures forced some alterations to be made in the original *front* concept of the operations, in particular regarding operational timing and the composition of the initial attack force.

The army commanders considered the nature of German defenses as they formulated their plans. Because the Germans defended with their forces scattered over a wide sector, they deployed heavier troop concentrations on estimated Soviet avenues of approach and used larger villages as strongpoints to delay the Soviet advance. Soviet commanders planned only light penetration operations and decided to rely upon pressure maintained across the entire front in order to force the Germans to withdraw. Once the German defenses crumbled, Soviet forces would pursue along several parallel axes; bypass strongpoints; and attempt, whenever possible, to encircle withdrawing German units. The Soviets believed it was essential to generate a rapid advance in order to preempt German defensive efforts along the Northern Donets River and to entrap as many German troops in the Khar'kov area as possible.

3d Tank Army

Rybalko's army's mission was to attack on 2 February, smash German forces defending along the Oskol River, outflank the German forces defending Kupyansk, and rapidly advance westward toward the Northern Donets River. By 5 February the army was to capture bridgeheads across the Northern Donets at Pechenegi. Because of the weakness of the army's two tank corps and their need for time to refit, Rybalko planned to use only rifle forces and the 6th Guards Cavalry Corps in his initial assault. However, after 6 February (day four of the operation) the two tank corps would begin to spearhead the army attack from the bridgeheads across the Northern Donets River and would advance rapidly through Chuguyev and Merefa, south of Khar'kov, to Lyubotin. By 7 February (day five) lead elements of 3d Tank Army would link up with 40th Army advanced elements at Lyubotin and seal off the escape routes of German units encircled in the Khar'kov area.[7]

Rybalko deployed his army in a 60–65 kilometer sector with the main attack sector on his army's left flank and center where the 62d Guards, 111th, and 160th Rifle Divisions would lead the attack followed closely by 6th Guards Cavalry Corps on the left and 12th Tank Corps. On the army right flank the 48th Guards Rifle Division would make a secondary attack toward Ol'khovatka and Prikolotnoye followed by the 15th Tank Corps and 184th Rifle Division in army second echelon. As the army neared the Khar'kov area its offensive sector would shrink to about 40 kilometers. Rybalko ordered his forces to occupy their jumping-off positions on the evening of 1 February.

69th Army

Kazakov's 69th Army was assigned the mission of advancing westward from Novyi Oskoli, securing Shebekino and Volchansk, seizing crossings over the Northern Donets River by 5 February, and advancing directly on Khar'kov from the northeast.[8] 69th Army's sector would also narrow to a width of about 10 kilometers as the army neared the Khar'kov defenses. This truncation of the army sector would permit the army to generate sufficient power to overcome German defenses in the immediate Khar'kov area by 7 February. Kazakov deployed his four rifle divisions in first echelon and the 37th Rifle Brigade in second echelon. The army's tank brigade and tank regiment provided armored support for the rifle divisions. By 1 February all units had secured bridgeheads on the right bank of the Oskol River, and they were to complete attack preparations by the evening of 1 February.

40th Army

Moskalenko of 40th Army planned to use his five available rifle divisions to initiate the attack while his remaining forces (three rifle divisions and 4th Tank Corps) continued to mop up German forces in his army's rear area. Even this smaller force could not redeploy in time to meet *STAVKA* requirements, thus the *STAVKA* postponed the attack time of 40th Army to 3 February. That day 40th Army would advance to penetrate German defenses; move southwestward; and, by 6 February, reach positions northeast of Belgorod. Subsequently, 40th Army would secure Belgorod and sweep southward to envelop Khar'kov from the northwest and west and to link up with 3d Tank Army forces at Lyubotin.[9] In order to generate strong initial momentum for his attack Moskalenko deployed four rifle divisions in his first echelon backed up by only one rifle division and a tank brigade in second echelon. On the third day of the attack he would commit his second echelon forces as a mobile group to lead the advance on Belgorod. By that time two additional rifle divisions should have rejoined the army. Moskalenko also hoped 4th Tank Corps would rejoin the army in time to participate in the final drive on Khar'kov. While 40th Army's main force advanced toward Khar'kov two divisions would peel off westward to occupy Graivoron and Bogodukhov, cover the right flank of the army, and pave the way for 40th Army to redeploy westward after 40th Army secured Khar'kov.

With planning underway the Voronezh Front undertook minimal regrouping of its forces while completing the Ostrogozhsk–Rossosh' and Voronezh–Kastornoye operations. 3d Tank Army and 69th Army completed that regrouping by 31 January, but the 40th and 38th Armies required a delay before they could initiate the new offensive.

Conduct of the Operation: The Soviet Advance to Khar'kov (2–16 February)

Initial Soviet Penetration Operations 2–4 February

On 1 February 3d Tank Army's forward detachments crossed the Oskol River and occupied jumping-off positions for use by the army's main force. These detachments succeeded in advancing several kilometers west of Valuiki, but in the southern portion of the army sector they succeeded in advancing only 300–400 meters against elements of SS Panzer Division "Das Reich," a police regiment defending at Dvurechnaya, and 298th Infantry Division elements defending north of Kupyansk.[10]

At 0600 the following day lead elements of Rybalko's main force rifle divisions attacked to complete the unfinished work of the forward detachments (see Maps 36–37). The 160th Rifle Division thrust 11 kilometers through Borki in the center of the army sector while the 62d Guards Rifle Division on its left brushed aside light opposition and pushed 8 kilometers toward Veliki Burluk. The 48th Guards Rifle Division advanced against heavier resistance toward Ol'khovatka. Meanwhile, 3d Tank Army's left wing made better progress by capitalizing on the successful assault of the neighboring 6th Army which had begun the day before. The 201st Tank Brigade, acting as the forward detachment of the 6th Guards Cavalry Corps, crossed the Oskol River, pried the Police Regiment from its positions at Dvurechnaya, and thrust toward the rail line connecting Volchansk with Kupyansk. The adjacent 111th Rifle Division penetrated deeply between Dvurechnaya and Kupyansk and by day's end pressed back the left flank of the German 298th Infantry Division and cut the rail line running northwest from Kupyansk to Volchansk.[11] The 20 kilometer thrust on 3d Tank Army's left flank created a gap between SS Panzer Division "Das Reich's" regiment and the 298th Infantry Division and threatened the latter with encirclement.

Despite the success in the south Rybalko was dissatisfied with the day's progress. Heavy German resistance in the center and right of the army's sector was bothersome, and intelligence reports indicated that other elements of SS Panzer Corps (SS Panzer Division "Das Reich") were moving forward from Khar'kov. Unless the attacks speeded up these German forces could erect defenses on the Northern Donets River and severely impede 3d Tank Army's progress. Consequently Rybalko decided to commit his two tank corps to action the following day before their refitting was complete. Because of the strong German resistance Rybalko shifted the direction of his advance southwest. Rather than pressing on via Staryi Saltov Rybalko ordered the 12th and 15th Tank Corps to attack toward the Pechenegi area to seize crossings across the Northern Donets River as soon as possible. 6th Guards Cavalry Corps, with its attached tank brigade and the 111th Rifle Division trailing in its wake, would sweep southwest to the rail line from Kupyansk to Chuguyev, cut the German 298th Infantry Division withdrawal routes, and cover the army's left flank. The right wing rifle divisions, the 48th Guards and 160th Rifle Divisions, would deal with SS Panzer Division "Das Reich" forces in the Veliki Burluk area in cooperation with the rifle divisions of 69th Army pressing from the northeast.[12]

On 3 February Rybalko's two tank corps went into action through the sector of the 62d Guards Rifle Division in tandem with 6th Guards Cavalry Corps. 12th Tank Corps, led by forward detachments, advanced in column formation with two tank brigades in first echelon and one tank brigade and its motorized rifle brigade in second echelon. The corps was to attack southwest supported by the 62d Guards Rifle Division to secure crossings over the Northern Donets River in the Chuguyev sector. On its right flank the 15th Tank Corps would advance in similar order with the 160th Rifle Division to secure Veliki Burluk and Northern Donets River crossings at Pechenegi. Meanwhile, 6th Guards Cavalry Corps was to sweep southwest to Skripai.[13] Rybalko's orders reflected his *front* commander's desire that 3d Tank Army's rate of advance be maintained at at least 20–25 kilometers per day.

Although the two tank corps and the cavalry corps made commendable progress on 3 February and crossed the Burlik River, German resistance in the Veliki Burluk area and near Ol'khovatka slowed the advance of Rybalko's right wing divisions and forced him to detach portions of his armored force to deal with the looming threat on his right flank. More ominously, as advanced elements of 12th Tank Corps and 6th Guards Cavalry Corps probed to within 10 kilometers of the Northern Donets River at Pechenegi, SS Panzer Division "Leibstandarte Adolf Hitler" began moving into positions on the west bank of the river and into some bridgeheads on the east bank from Zmiyev northward to beyond Pechenegi.[14]

The following day the 15th Tank Corps and the 48th Guards Rifle Division finally secured a tenuous hold on Veliki Burluk and prepared to relinquish it to the 184th Rifle Division, a unit which German resistance forced Rybalko to commit from his army second echelon. Meanwhile, the lead element of 15th Tank Corps (the 195th Tank Brigade) marching

25 kilometers in advance of its parent unit, reached German positions covering the banks of the Northern Donets River opposite Pechenegi. On the 195th Tank Brigade's left flank lead elements of the 12th Tank Corps seized Vasilenkovo and Annovka east of Korobochkino although the main force of the corps was strung out a considerable distance to the rear, marching with infantry columns of the 160th Rifle Division, which had also slipped south of Veliki Burluk. By the evening 6th Guards Cavalry Corps units, along with elements of the 111th Rifle Division, had secured Shevchenkovo, thus cutting the withdrawal routes of the German 298th Infantry Division, then retreating westward from Kupyansk toward Chuguyev.[15]

German SS Panzer Division "Das Reich" continued to hamper the overall progress of 3d Tank Army by fighting a strong delaying action against the 48th Guards Rifle Division westward through Ol'khovatka to new positions just east of Prikolotnoye. Although forced to relinquish Veliki Burluk to 15th Tank Corps elements on 4 February, SS "Das Reich" units established strong defenses north of the village and halted attempts by the 184th Rifle Division to dislodge them. Simultaneous attempts by 69th Army elements (180th Rifle Division) to seize the town of Belyi Kolodez, located along the key rail line from Prikolotnoye to Volchansk in SS Panzer Division "Das Reich's" rear also failed. SS Panzer Division "Das Reich" held firmly to a salient projecting into the junction of 69th Army's and 3d Tank Army's advance, and that salient seriously interfered with the advance of both Soviet armies. Moreover, once reinforcements arrived, SS "Das Reich" also used the salient to launch offensive operations against 3d Tank Army units which almost upset the entire Voronezh Front's offensive.

While 3d Tank Army launched its assaults westward toward Khar'kov 69th Army opened its attacks toward Volchansk. At 0600 on 2 February Kazakov's lead rifle divisions broke out of the bridgeheads west of the Oskol River and inundated scattered German strongpoints. On the army's right flank the 161st and 219th Rifle Divisions slowly pushed Panzer Grenadier Division "Grossdeutschland" units back toward Veliko-Mikhailovka and initiated a three day struggle to seize that town.[16] The 161st Rifle Division advanced westward and then turned south to envelop Veliko-Mikhailovka from the southwest. Further south the 270th and 180th Rifle Divisions struck the boundary of "Grossdeutschland" Division and SS "Das Reich" and made better progress against weaker resistance. The 270th drove one battalion of "Grossdeutschland" westward toward Bol'she-Troitskoye while the 180th Rifle Division, faced by but one company of "Grossdeutschland," advanced southwest. 69th Army's progress, however, like that of 3d Tank Army, was threatened by the tenacious German defense of major towns which hindered a Soviet advance on a broad front and forced Soviet forces to fall behind their timetable. In 69th Army's sector the town of Veliko-Mikhailovka proved to be a hard nut to crack. Having failed to take the town from the march, fighting for the town continued throughout 3 and 4 February as the two Soviet divisions slowly enveloped the German units defending it. Only after the 161st and 219th Rifle Divisions took all adjacent towns and threatened to cut the only remaining withdrawal route did Panzer Grenadier Division "Grossdeutschland" units withdraw southwest toward Shebekino.

While fighting raged for Veliko-Mikhailovka the 270th and 180th Rifle Divisions surged southwestward, leaving a gap between themselves and the two right flank divisions into which on 5 February Kazakov commited his reserve, the 37th Rifle Brigade. The 270th Rifle Division pushed southwestward against weak opposition until 4 February when its advance abruptly ground to a halt against SS Panzer Division "Das Reich" defenses at Pankov. Likewise, on 4 February the 180th Rifle Division ran into SS Panzer Division "Das Reich" defenses east of Belyi Kolodez where the Germans also brought its progress to a halt.[17] By the evening of 4 February Kazakov had committed all of his units to combat; and, although progress had been satisfactory, further advance could be made only after his two divisions at Veliko-Mikhailovka could be brought up to join a concerted army advance. Unbeknownst to Kazakov his left flank formations were also about to become targets for counterattacks by SS Panzer Division "Das Reich."

Although Moskalenko's 40th Army attacked a day after her sister armies and with reduced forces, German opposition in his sector had been seriously weakened during earlier operations. Thus, Moskalenko's attack met with early success. At 0900 on 3 February Moskalenko's four lead rifle divisions thrust southwest supported by a tank brigade and one rifle division in second echelon. German defenders from the 168th Infantry Division could do no more than delay the advance and hope for reinforcements to halt it. Golikov had ordered Moskalenko to penetrate to a depth of 70 kilometers during the first three days of the attack.

Moskalenko's advance developed rapidly and traversed 15–20 kilometers on the first day of operation. By 5 February his forces were on line with those of 69th Army. 40th Army's left flank divisions (305th and 100th Rifle Divisions) approached Korocha while his right flank divisions moved across the upper reaches of the Northern Donets River, cut the rail line from Belgorod to Kursk, and advanced toward Gostishchevo, north of Belgorod. Already, by the evening of

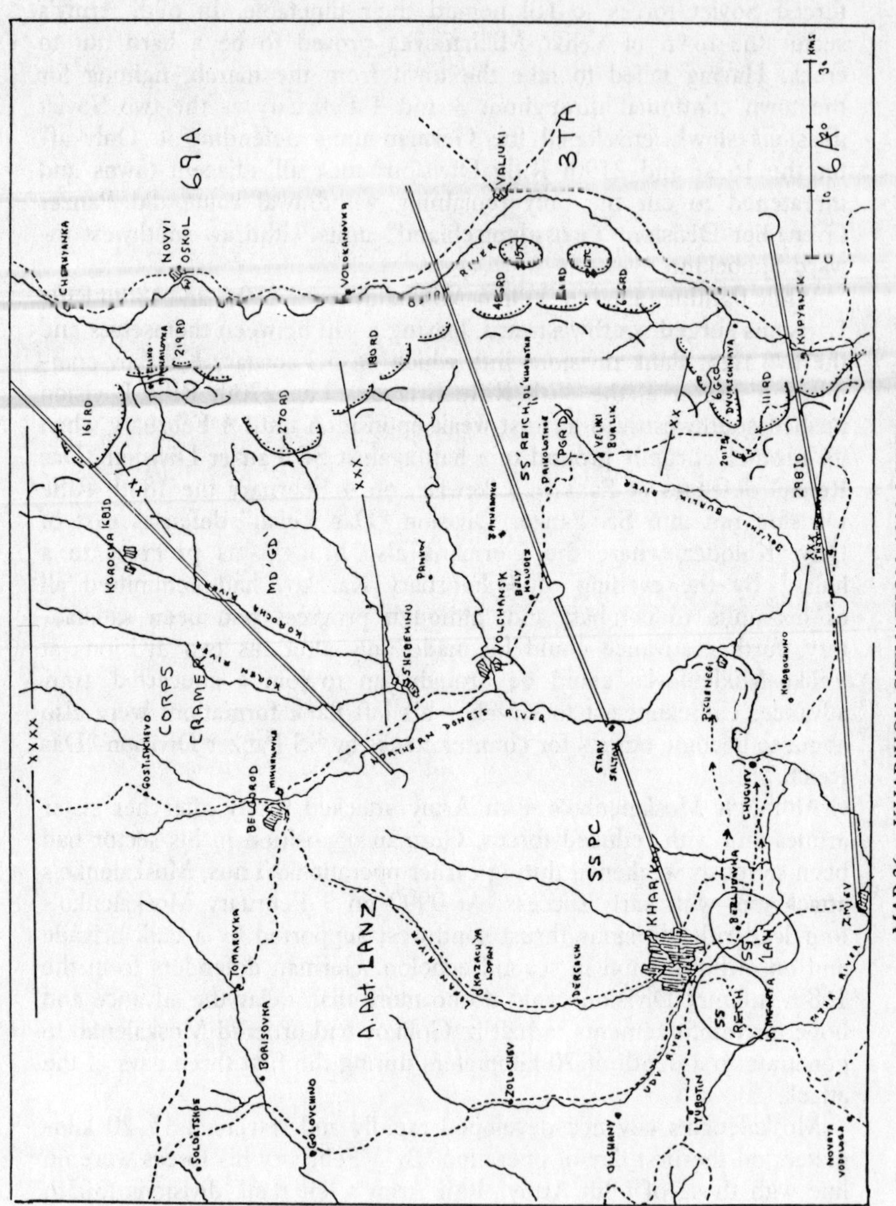

MAP 36. KHAR'KOV, SITUATION, 1800 2 FEBRUARY 1943

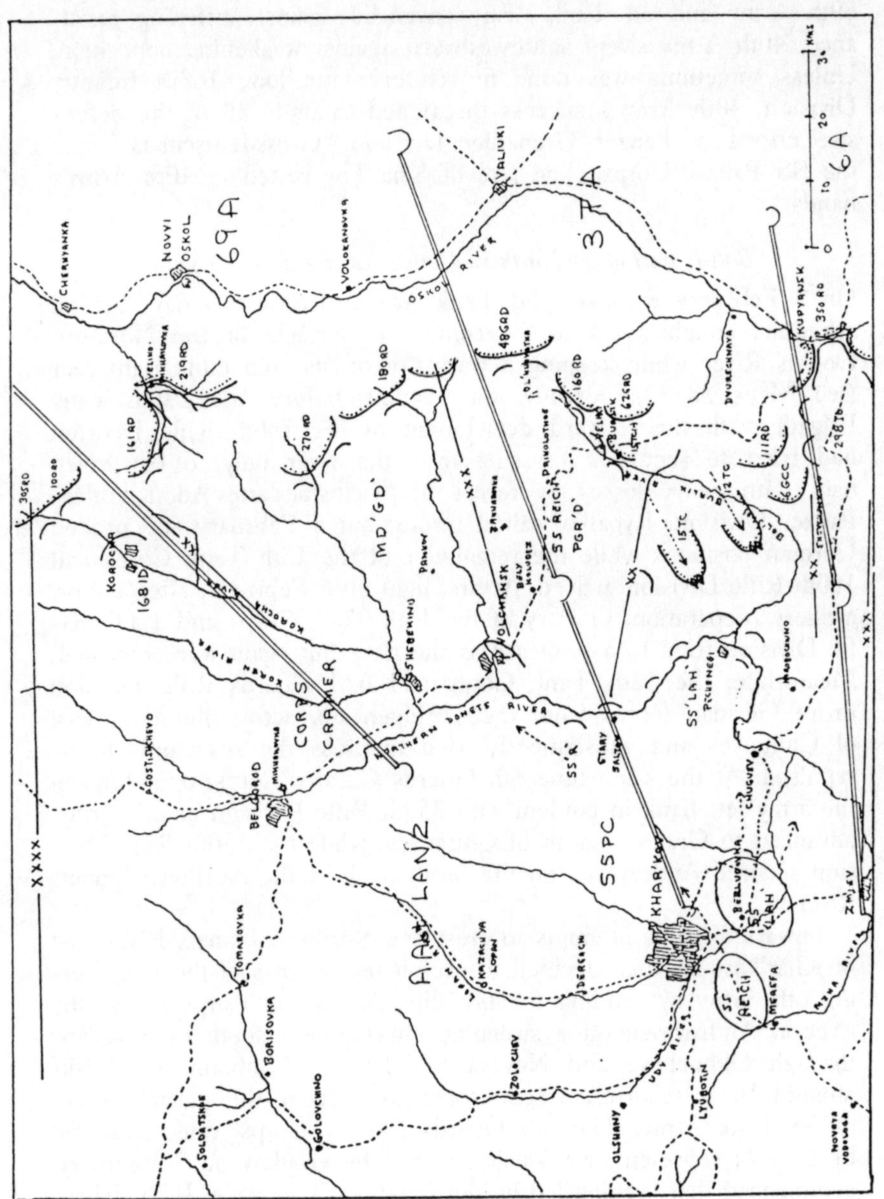

MAP 37. KHAR'KOV, SITUATION, 2000 3 FEBRUARY 1943

4 February, outlines of what was to come were emerging. While 69th Army and 3d Tank Army advanced against stiffening resistance, 40th Army swept southwestward against weakening opposition. Unless something was done to reinforce the lone 168th Infantry Division, 40th Army's success threatened to undo all of the defensive efforts of Panzer Grenadier Division "Grossdeutschland" and the SS Panzer Corps. The fate of Khar'kov rested in 40th Army's hands.

Battles East of the Northern Donets River – 5–9 February

On 5 February Rybalko's 3d Tank Army, already two days behind schedule, sought ways to overcome the obstacle of the Northern Donets River while keeping a wary eye on its vulnerable right rear (see Maps 38–39). Already, the evening before, the 195th Tank Brigade with the forward detachment of the 160th Rifle Division had tried to secure a crossing over the river only to be driven back with heavy losses by forces of "Leibstandarte Adolf Hitler" Panzer Division. Rybalko waited throughout 5 February and probed German positions while the remainder of the 15th Tank Corps and 160th Rifle Division arrived. At first light on 6 February, after a short artillery preparation, infantry of the 15th Tank Corps and 160th Rifle Division tried to assault across the river but again were repulsed. Meanwhile, the 12th Tank Corps and 62d Guards Rifle Division drove German forces from their bridgeheads across the river east of Chuguyev and subsequently tried to cross the river only to be repulsed. At the same time 6th Guards Cavalry Corps, operating on the army left flank in tandem with 350th Rifle Division of 6th Army, advanced to Grakovo south of Chuguyev, while the 350th Rifle Division secured Andreyevka on the north bank of the Northern Donets River.[18]

Thwarted in his attempts to cross the Northern Donets River east of Khar'kov, Rybalko decided to exploit the success of the neighboring 6th Army by sending the 6th Guards Cavalry Corps across the river at Andreyevka on a sweeping envelopment south of Khar'kov through Okhocheye and Novaya Vodolaga to Lyubotin in a risky attempt by a relatively fragile force to redeem the partial failure of 3d Tank Army. The 6th Guards Cavalry Corps' raid, endorsed by *STAVKA* representative Vasilevsky and by Golikov on 7 February, commenced that evening led by the 201st Tank Brigade. By 8 February the corps had crossed the Northern Donets River and secured Bol'shaya Bereka. The next day it reached the Borki–Taranovka area.[19] The Germans reacted quickly. Elements of SS "Das Reich," dispatched south from Khar'kov, engaged the cavalrymen north of

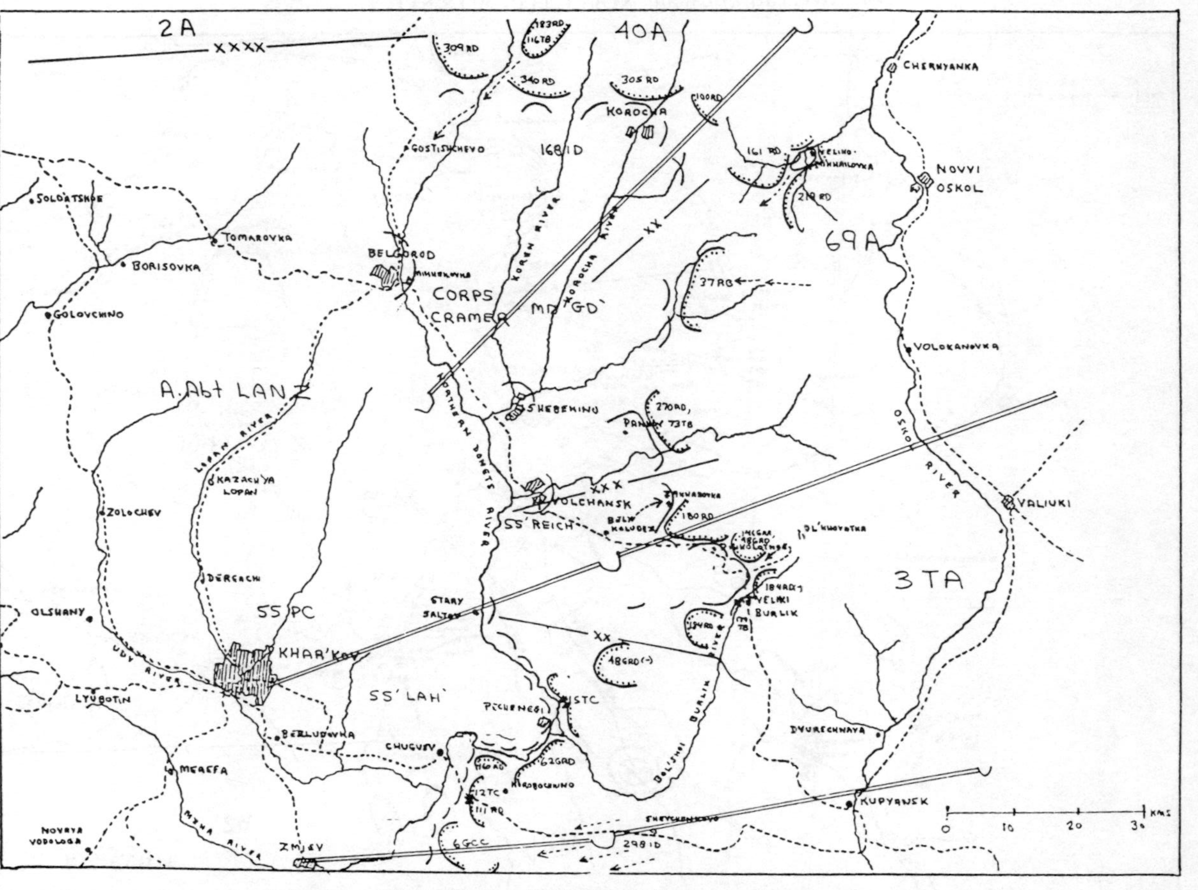

MAP 38. KHAR'KOV, SITUATION, 2000 5 FEBRUARY 1943

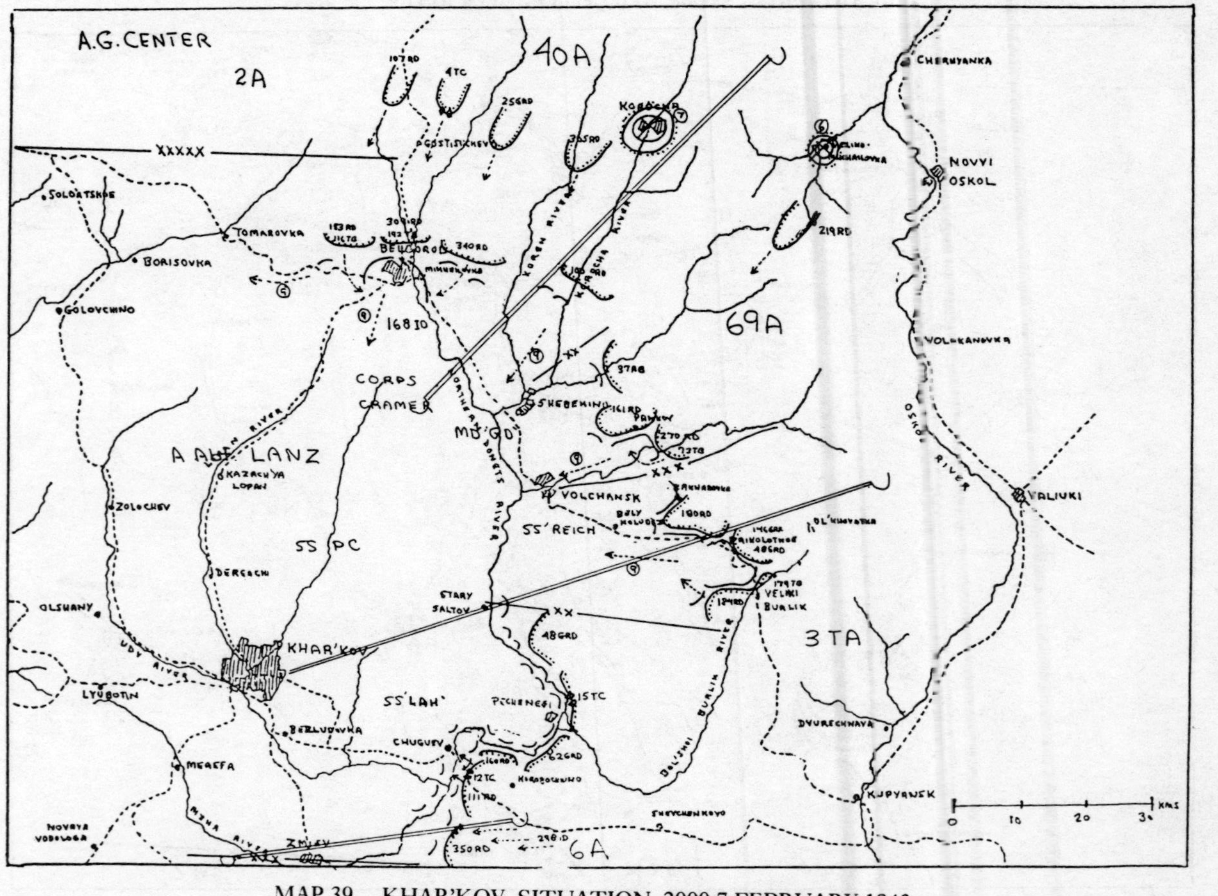

MAP 39. KHAR'KOV, SITUATION, 2000 7 FEBRUARY 1943

Taranovka on 10 February and slowly drove them southward toward Okhocheye.*

After his repeated failures to force the Northern Donets River, on 6 February Rybalko began three days of preparations to launch a concerted assault across the river. The excessive time, attributed by Soviet critics to Rybalko's overcaution, resulted also from the tenuous security situation in his rear and along his right flank.[20] The German 298th Infantry Division was at that time conducting a hazardous withdrawal westward toward German lines at Zmiyev, engaging as it did elements of 3d Tank Army's left wing which damaged but were unable to totally destroy the German division. A more serious situation developed in the Veliki Burluk–Prikolotnoye area.

Early on the morning of 5 February the 48th Guards Rifle Division struck the defensive positions of SS Panzer Division "Das Reich's" "Deutschland" Regiment at Prikolotnoye while, at the same time, the 180th Rifle Division of 69th Army struck "Das Reich's" "Führer" Regiment at Belyi Kolodez. The Germans responded with heavy counterattacks. SS Panzer Division's "Deutschland" Regiment slashed through the 48th Guards Rifle Division lines, split the 146th Guards Rifle Regiment from the division's other regiments which were forced to withdraw south, and advanced to Ol'khovatka by noon on the 5th. Rybalko committed the 184th Rifle Division, 179th Tank Brigade, and 1241st Tank Destroyer Regiment to seal the gap and to try to encircle the attacking SS "Das Reich" units. These forces attacked from Veliki Burluk and from south of Ol'khovatka while the 146th Rifle Regiment of 48th Guards Rifle Division held the northern edge of the penetration. At dawn on 6 February renewed German attacks hit the boundary of the 48th Guards Rifle Division and the 184th Rifle Division.[21] Late that day German forces withdrew to defensive positions near Prikolotnoye, having thrown a distinct scare into Rybalko and his staff. Meanwhile SS Panzer Division's "Führer" Regiment repulsed the 180th Panzer Division's assault on Belyi Kolodez and, at 0800 on 6 February collapsed that division's right flank, forcing it to withdraw 8 kilometers.[22] While the fighting ebbed and flowed, elements of the 184th Rifle Division circled west of German positions into SS Panzer Division "Das Reich's" rear.

After 6 February the situation stabilized on 3d Tank Army's right wing. SS Panzer Division "Das Reich" held its positions and occasionally struck out at Soviet units while Soviet units repeatedly failed in attempts to take Prikolotnoye. Other Soviet forces slowly made their way around the Ger-

*German accounts criticized "Das Reich's" progress on the thawed dirt roads south of Khar'kov, calling the operation the "mud march" of "Das Reich." The thaw did assist 6th Guards Cavalry Corps in extricating itself from a dangerous situation.

man right flank while 69th Army forces (180th Rifle Division) continued to threaten German communication lines at Belyi Kolodez. Although time was on Rybalko's side in his battle with SS Panzer Division "Das Reich," the ensuing four day contest distracted Rybalko from his main task which was to overcome German defense lines on the Northern Donets River and secure Khar'kov. Only on 9 February did German resistance near Prikolotnoye and Belyi Kolodez end. On that day Army Detachment Lanz ordered SS Panzer Division "Das Reich" to withdraw to new defensive positions covering Khar'kov, then threatened by 40th Army which had just taken Belgorod.

While 3d Tank Army sought to penetrate directly to Khar'kov, 69th Army continued its advance on Volchansk. Kazakov's 161st and 219th Rifle Divisions, having finally ended German resistance at Veliko-Mikhailovka, moved southwest and joined the 37th Rifle Brigade, itself committed to first echelon action on 4 February. The advance toward Shebekino was slow but steady as the German Panzer Grenadier Division "Grossdeutschland" conducted a skillful delaying action. The 270th Rifle Division launched new assaults on "Grossdeutschland" units defending around Pankov on the approaches to Volchansk. The 161st Rifle Division joined the 270th Rifle Division and conducted a night assault on a village in the German rear. On 8 February Soviet pressure finally forced "Grossdeutschland" Division to conduct a withdrawal across the Northern Donets River.[23] 69th Army forces occupied Shebekino and Volchansk on 9 February and prepared to continue their advance across the Northern Donets River toward Khar'kov. Further south the 180th Rifle Division, cooperating with 48th Guards Rifle Division of 3d Tank Army took Belyi Kolodez only after SS Panzer Division "Das Reich" units began their orderly withdrawal toward Khar'kov. The 180th followed in the panzer division's wake and closed on the Northern Donets River on the evening of 9 February.

Soviet Seizure of Belgorod

Only the successful advance of 40th Army, which brought great pressure to bear on Army Detachment Lanz's left flank and ultimately threatened to envelop that formation, made possible the advance of 3d Tank Army and 69th Army to the Northern Donets River. Despite the absence of his 4th Tank Corps, Moskalenko continued to make good progress against the German 168th Infantry Division. Golikov, frustrated over Rybalko's and Kazakov's difficulties, urged Moskalenko on with repeated orders to accelerate his offensive. Moskalenko's left flank divisions, the 305th and 100th, reached Korocha on the evening of 5 February and, during the night, enveloped the town from the north and southeast. Fighting raged at Korocha on 6 and 7 February. Finally, when the Soviets threatened the sole withdrawal route of 168th Infantry Division units, the Germans withdrew southwestward toward Shebekino.[24] The 100th Rifle Division initiated the pursuit followed soon after by the 305th Rifle Division.

Meanwhile, 40th Army's main force continued its advance on Belgorod. To compensate for the absence of 4th Tank Corps, Moskalenko on 5 February created a mobile group consisting of the 183d Rifle Division and 116th Tank Brigade and ordered it to operate on the right flank of the 309th Rifle Division and conduct an envelopment of Belgorod from the west. The following day, while the 309th Rifle Division, reinforced by the 192d Tank Brigade, took Gostishchevo, 20 kilometers north of Belgorod, the 183d Rifle Division and its reinforcing tank brigade swung west of the city. On the same day Moskaleno's second echelon forces began arriving. He ordered his 107th Rifle Division to cover the army's right flank by advancing toward Tomarovka while the 25th Guards Rifle Division and 4th Tank Corps reinforced the main body of the army.

Moskalenko's divisions closed in on Belgorod on 7 February.[25] The 183d Rifle Division and 116th Tank Brigade penetrated into the western outskirts of Belgorod while the 309th Rifle Division and 192d Tank Brigade occupied positions northeast of the city. German 168th Infantry Division forces desperately clung to its positions around the city. Further east the 340th Rifle Division drove "Grossdeutschland" units toward Staryi Gorod. A German decision to shift "Grossdeutschland" units into the Belgorod region increased the urgency of Moskalenko's task of taking the city. Consequently, he ordered a combined assault on Belgorod by the 309th, 183d, and 340th Rifle Divisions to begin on the morning of 8 February. On the night of 7–8 February Moskalenko concentrated his artillery and regrouped his units for the assault. Despite strong initial German resistance a bitter night battle with increasingly fragmented German defenders finally forced the Germans to abandon the city. The 168th Infantry Division withdrew toward Tomarovka while Panzer Grenadier Division "Grossdeutschland" withdrew to new positions to the south in order to block a Soviet advance along the main road to Khar'kov.

The Battle for Khar'kov – 10–16 February

German abandonment of Belgorod threatened Army Detachment Lanz's left flank and placed German forces east of the Northern Donets River in jeopardy of envelopment. Consequently, German forces initiated a general withdrawal westward and southwestward across the Northern Donets River to new defense lines covering the close approaches to Khar'kov. East of Khar'kov SS Panzer Division "Leibstandarte Adolf Hitler" began its withdrawal to new defense lines just as 3d Tank Army launched its planned assault across the Northern Donets River. SS Panzer

Division "Das Reich" fell back through Staryi Saltov in order to defend northeastern approaches into the city while Panzer Grenadier Division "Grossdeutschland" faced 40th Army units advancing along the main road from Belgorod into Khar'kov. The 168th Infantry Division continued delaying operations through Tomarovka, Borisovka, and Graivoron, and attempted to fill the growing gap between Army Detachment Lanz and German 2d Army operating further north.

Thus, for the Soviets the first seven to eight days of the offensive were frustrating. 69th Army and 3d Tank Army had advanced about 80 kilometers and reached the Northern Donets River, but well behind schedule. Moreover, these armies now faced determined German resistance in prepared defenses outside the major city of Khar'kov. Only 40th Army's advance had exceeded expectations; and, in reality, only that advance had forced the Germans to give up positions east of the Northern Donets River. The hoped for envelopment of Khar'kov by 40th Army was still possible; but this single envelopment, if successful, would probably permit German forces to conduct an orderly withdrawal from the city if the German High Command permitted such a withdrawal. Thus, on 10 February Golikov's Voronezh Front resumed the offensive, now with the primary aim of taking Khar'kov at all costs.

That day Rybalko finally unleashed 3d Tank Army in an assault across the Northern Donets River (see Maps 40–42). Earlier on the night of 9–10 February the 15th Tank Corps and infantry of the 160th Rifle Division had secured crossing sites near Pechenegi, occupied the town, and rapidly advanced against withdrawing forces of SS Panzer Division "Leibstandarte Adolf Hitler." Meanwhile, Rybalko ordered 12th Tank Corps to strike across the Northern Donets River near Chuguyev – a fateful decision that ultimately resulted in the commitment of both tank corps to operations in the heavily built-up Khar'kov area.[26] The 12th Tank Corps and 62d Guards Rifle Division crossed the river against light opposition, secured Chuguyev, and advanced westward to positions slightly in advance of 15th Tank Corps operating to its north. The 111th and 48th Guards Rifle Divisions covered 3d Tank Army's left and right flanks, respectively.

3d Tank Army's advance soon struck against prepared German defenses north and south of Rogan, 10 kilometers east of Khar'kov, where the Soviets again came to a grinding halt.[27] Rybalko thus formulated a new plan on the evening of 10 February. On 11 and 12 February the 15th Tank Corps, 48th Guards Rifle Division, 160th Rifle Division, and 179th Tank Brigade were to assault German defenses east of Khar'kov while the 12th Tank Corps and the 62d Guards Rifle Division attacked Khar'kov from the southeast. Simultaneously, 6th Guards Cavalry Corps was to strike back at German units from the south and occupy Lyubotin

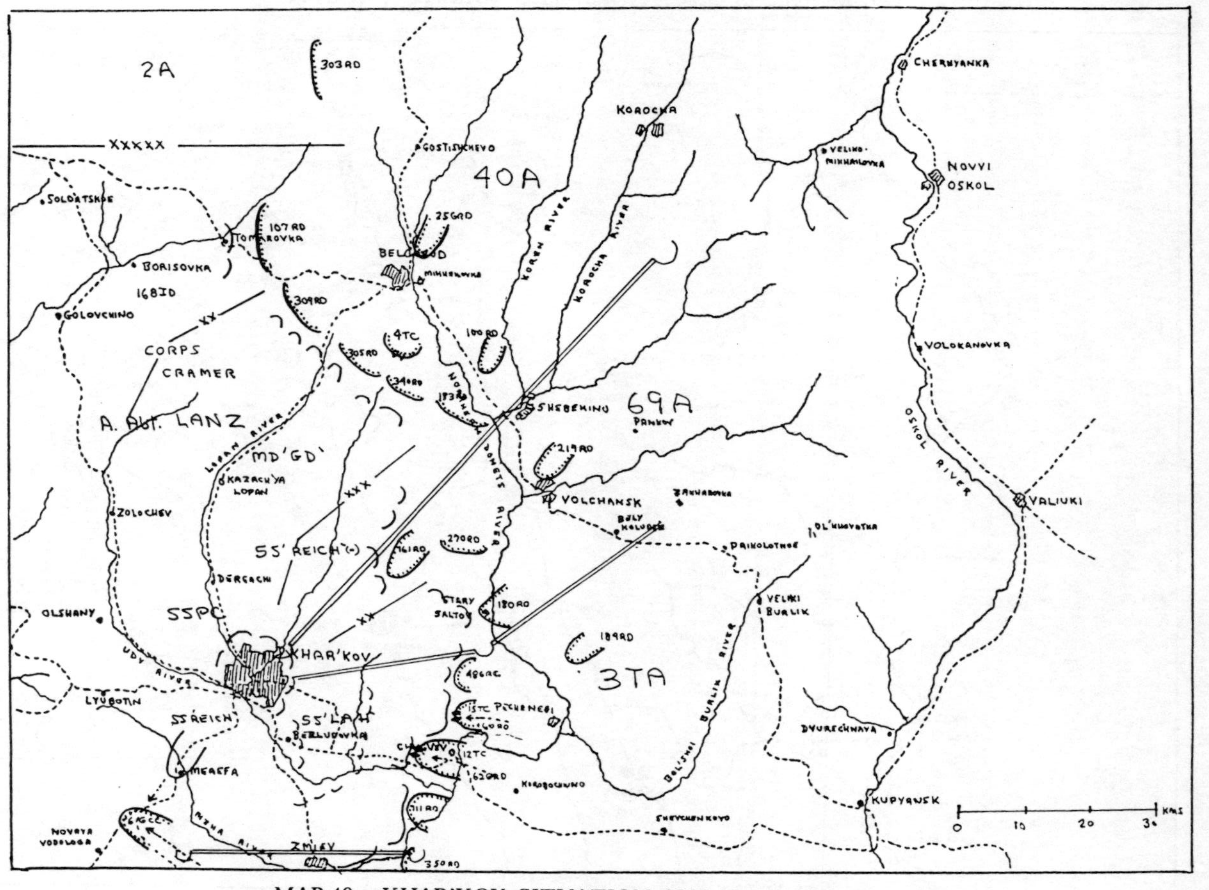

MAP 40. KHAR'KOV, SITUATION, 2000 10 FEBRUARY 1943

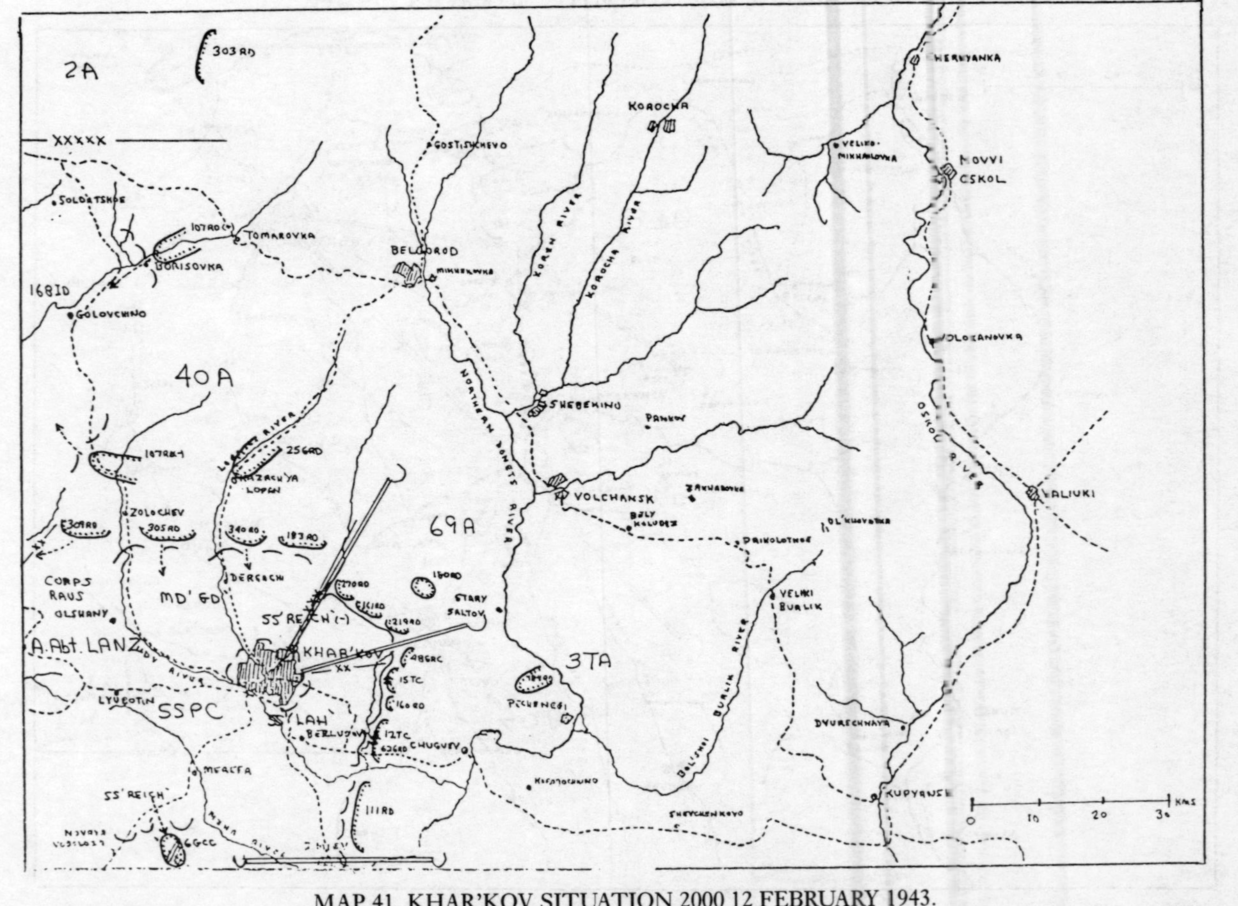

MAP 41. KHAR'KOV SITUATION 2000 12 FEBRUARY 1943.

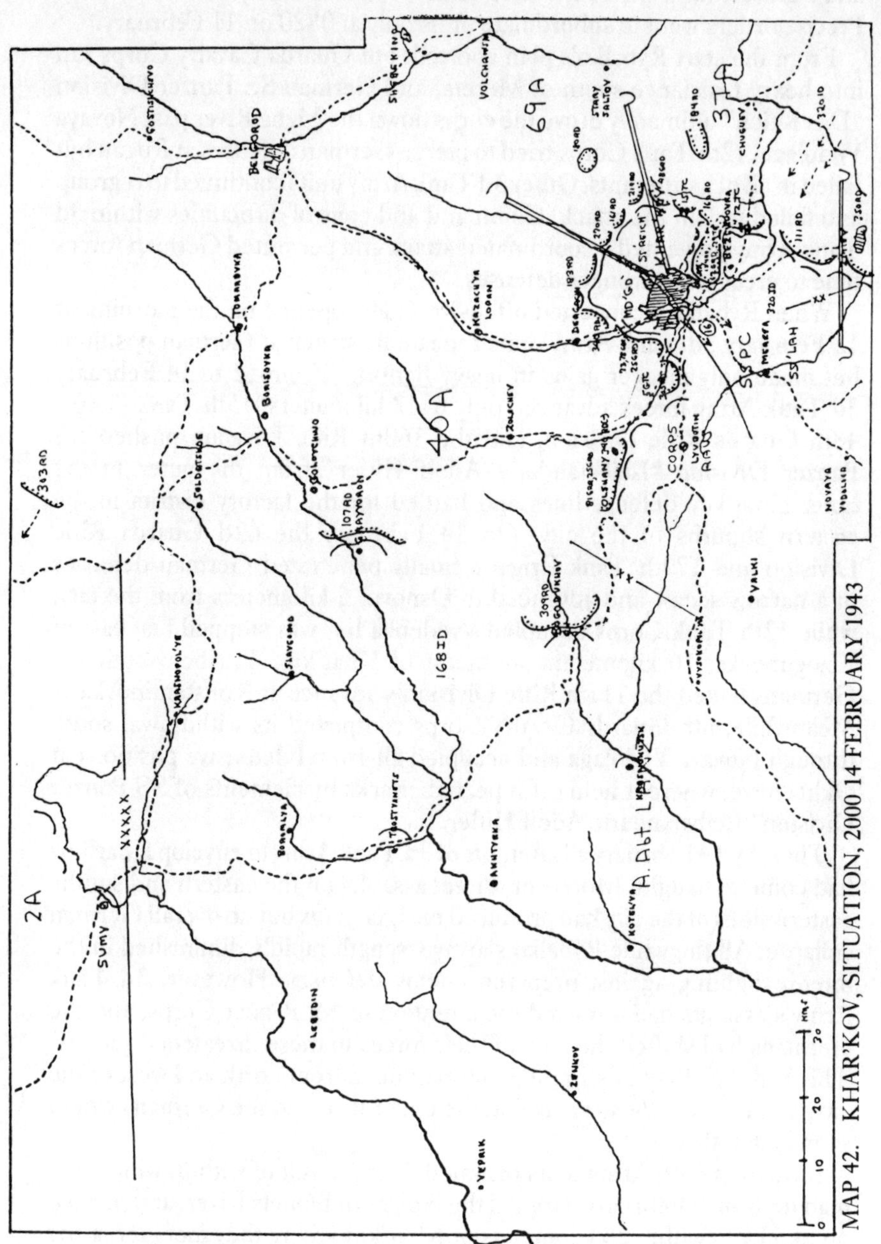

MAP 42. KHAR'KOV, SITUATION, 2000 14 FEBRUARY 1943

and Peresechnaya where it would unite with 40th Army advanced units. Precise orders went to subordinate units only at 0820 on 11 February.

From the start Rybalko's plan aborted. 6th Guards Cavalry Corps ran into heavy resistance south of Merefa, and German SS Panzer Division "Das Reich" ultimately drove the corps down the Mzha River past Novaya Vodolaga. 12th Tank Corps tried to pierce German defenses at Rogan but failed in all of its attempts. Other 3d Tank Army units continued to regroup and failed to join the attack. Command and control difficulties within 3d Tank Army prevented a coordinated attack and permitted German forces time to erect even stronger defenses.

When Rybalko's concerted offensive finally opened on the morning of 12 February 3d Tank Army units repeatedly struck at German positions but made only meager gains in heavy fighting. From 12 to 14 February 3d Tank Army forces advanced only 6–12 kilometers. 15th Tank Corps, 48th Guards Rifle Division, and the 160th Rifle Division pushed SS Panzer Division "Leibstandarte Adolf Hitler" from the outer to the inner Khar'kov defense lines and battled for the factory district in the eastern suburbs of the city. On 14 February the 62d Guards Rifle Division and 179th Tank Brigade finally penetrated German defenses in a narrow sector and advanced to Osnovo, 5 kilometers from the city, while 12th Tank Corps occupied Vvedenka but was stopped just east of Lizogubovka, 10 kilometers southeast of Khar'kov. Further south the Germans halted the 111th Rifle Division's advance at Konstantinovka.[28] Meanwhile, 6th Guards Cavalry Corps completed its withdrawal south through Novaya Vodolaga and occupied all-round defensive positions at Okhocheye, where it held off repeated attacks by elements of SS Panzer Division "Leibstandarte Adolf Hitler."

Thus, by 14 February all attempts of 3d Tank Army to envelop Khar'kov had come to naught. Moreover, direct assaults on the eastern and southeastern sides of the city had produced meager gains but no overall German collapse. All the while Rybalko's army strength rapidly diminished in the intense fighting against prepared enemy defenses. However, 3d Tank Army's assaults had attracted the attention of SS Panzer Corps, and the Germans had shifted the bulk of their forces to these threatened sectors. This had the effect of stripping German units from north and west of the city, and it was in those areas that the major threat to the Germans would soon materialize.

Kazakov's 69th Army units resumed their pursuit of withdrawing German units on 9 February, crossed the Northern Donets River, and pushed on rapidly to within 20 kilometers of Khar'kov where they met increasing resistance from SS Panzer Division "Das Reich." Other units crossed the Northern Donets River at Staryi Saltov and established communications with 3d Tank Army operating on its left flank. Deprived of maneuver space by the shrinking army sector, Kazakov's divisions inched forward against heavy resistance and finally reached the outer German defenses of Khar'kov. The heavy fighting sapped the combat strength of Kazakov's units, many of which Kazakov combined into mixed detachments.[29] Like the case of 3d Tank Army, 69th Army simply was unable to break German defenses on the northeastern approaches to the city.

The only escape from the grinding direct advance on Khar'kov by 3d Tank Army and 69th Army lay with a successful advance by 40th Army. Moskalenko's army, having cleared Belgorod on 9 February, commenced its advance southward toward Khar'kov the next day. Moskalenko ordered his main force, the 25th Guards, 340th, 183d, and 305th Rifle Divisions and the 4th Tank Corps, to attack south along the road and railroad from Belgorod to Khar'kov in order to envelop Khar'kov from the west.[30] The 303d, 107th, and 309th Rifle Divisions advanced westward toward Oboyan, Graivoron, and Bogodukhov in order to cover the northern flank of the Army. The German 168th Infantry Division withdrew southwestward toward Borisovka while Panzer Grenadier Division "Grossdeutschland" withdrew south toward Zolochev and Olshany thus creating a growing gap in German defenses which only reinforcements could fill. To cover as much territory as possible during this withdrawal the Germans defended in small battalion groups supported by tanks and self-propelled guns.

Moskalenko's advance accelerated on 12 February when he committed Major General A. G. Kravchenko's 5th Guards Tank Corps (formerly 4th Tank Corps) to battle. Kravchenko's armor quickly ruptured the German defense lines at Zolochev. Simultaneously, the 25th Guards Rifle Division, introduced from army second echelon, lunged on toward Dergachi in cooperation with 5th Guards Tank Corps. The following day all of Moskalenko's divisions pressed the German defenders back toward Khar'kov. Consequently, at nightfall German forces abandoned Dergachi and withdrew southward into Khar'kov's inner defenses. Further northwest the 107th Rifle Division occupied Borisovka and moved on Graivoron and the 309th Rifle Division advanced toward Bogodukhov. By nightfall on 13 February lead elements of 5th Guards Tank Corps, supported by the 340th Rifle Division reached the northern limits of Khar'kov's defense.[31]

On 14 February the Soviet 40th Army threatened critical German lines of communications running west and southwest from Khar'kov. The 183d Rifle Division seized Sokolniki on the northern outskirts of Khar'kov, and, by evening, entered the city proper. The 340th Rifle Division with elements of the 25th Guards Rifle Division and 5th Guards Tank Corps entered the city's northwestern suburbs. Meanwhile, other Soviet forces drove German forces from Olshany. Moskalenko's spearhead, consisting of 5th Guards Tank Corps, the 305th Rifle Division, and the 6th Guards

Motorized Rifle Brigade, struck south at the main railroad and road at Lyubotin, west of Khar'kov. Further west, the 107th Rifle Division approached 168th Infantry Division positions at Graivoron, and the 309th Rifle Division neared Bogodukhov.[32]

Thus, in four days of battle 40th Army units had advanced 50–70 kilometers, established a security line from Graivoron to Bogodukhov, pinned German forces into their defenses at Khar'kov, and threatened to encircle German forces in the city. The final lunge of 40th Army units at German communication lines at Lyubotin coincided with 3d Tank Army's advance to Osnovo and left only a narrow 10 kilometer corridor through which the German command could resupply its units in Khar'kov. The 168th Infantry Division and Panzer Grenadier Division "Grossdeutschland" of Corps Raus were irrevocably split apart with the former spread out from Graivoron to Bogodukhov and the latter defending the western approaches to Khar'kov. SS Panzer Corps with "Das Reich," "Leibstandarte Adolf Hitler," and the 320th Infantry Division remnants hung grimly onto the eastern and southern approaches to Khar'kov.

With Soviet forces converging on Khar'kov, conflicting decisions disrupted German plans to defend the city. Despite orders from Hitler that Khar'kov be held at all costs, Lieutenant General P. Hausser, commander of SS Panzer Corps, while confronted with an uprising in the city on the evening of 14 February, requested permission from Lanz to withdraw from Khar'kov. Lanz rejected this request as well as a subsequent one by Hausser on the night of 14–15 February. Consequently, on 15 February Hausser independently ordered a withdrawal from the city. Reminded by Lanz of Hitler's orders, shortly before midnight on 15–16 February Hausser withdrew the order and decided "to hold Khar'kov to the last man." The change in mind was a bit late. SS "Das Reich" had begun withdrawing from its positions north of the city, and the Soviets had begun a night assault on Khar'kov in the early morning hours of 16 February, an assault which quickly occupied "Das Reich's" abandoned positions.[33]

While indecision reigned in the German camp, Golikov on 14 February ordered his armies to open a final assault on the city in the morning from the west, north, and southeast. 40th Army would advance into the city from the west and north, 69th Army from the northeast, 15th Tank Corps and 160th Rifle Division of 3d Tank Army from the east, and 62d Guards Rifle Division and 179th Tank Brigade from the south.

At dawn the Soviets pressed the German defenders from all sides. 40th Army's 340th Rifle Division, cooperating with 5th Guards Tank Corps, penetrated into western Khar'kov. Heavy snow in the densely wooded outskirts of the city held up the armor, and the infantry faced heavy going. On the morning of 16 February the 25th Guards Rifle Division and one motorized rifle brigade of 5th Guards Tank Corps advanced into Khar'kov on the 340th's right flank. Meanwhile, the 183d Rifle Division (40th Army) penetrated into the northwestern sector of the city, and 3d Tank Army's 62d Guards Rifle Division penetrated to the southwestern sector. To the south elements of the 184th Rifle Division marched southwest to reinforce the 111th Rifle Division in its drive to relieve beleaguered 6th Guards Cavalry Corps forces, at that time encircled at Okhocheye.[34]

The 62d Guards Rifle Division assault into the city threatened the German flank and rear and materially assisted the 69th Army's and 15th Tank Corps' assaults further north. 69th Army units assaulted on 15 February and occupied positions abandoned by SS Panzer Division "Das Reich." Meanwhile, 3d Tank Army's 15th Tank Corps and 160th Rifle Division entered eastern Khar'kov late on 15 February and engaged in heavy street fighting with SS Panzer Division "Das Reich" units. In all sectors of the city fighting raged into 16 February; but with their routes of egress shrinking steadily, German forces gave ground. At 1000 on 16 February the 15th Tank Corps and 160th Rifle Division entered Dzerzhinsky Square, there linking up with 40th Army's 183d Rifle Division. At the same time 5th Guards Tank Corps units joined with lead elements of 3d Tank Army on Sverdlov Street.[35] The German garrison, now fragmented and lacking any hope for restoring the situation, began a withdrawal from the city which it completed by noon on 16 February. Simultaneously, the 12th Tank Corps took Lizogubovka and reached the Udy River south of Khar'kov while the 111th Rifle Division took Borovaya on the south bank of the river.

Although Khar'kov had fallen to Soviet forces, the Soviets had failed to encircle any sizable German force. German communication lines were open westward to Poltava and south to Krasnograd; and Soviet forces, hopelessly snarled in the fighting for Khar'kov, now had to regroup and continue the offensive against a still coherent German defense.

Soviet Exploitation Toward Poltava (16–23 February)

Revised Soviet Plans

Even before Soviet forces took Khar'kov, urged on by the *STAVKA*, Golikov issued new orders to the Voronezh Front armies specifying that after the fall of Khar'kov, *front* forces would advance west and southwest to reach the Lebedin and Poltava areas by 20 February.[36] The earliest of these orders went to Moskalenko's 40th Army on 12 February. It displayed the continued optimism of both the *front* commander and the *STAVKA* and read, in part:

1. The army, after the fall of Khar'kov, no later than 13 February 1943, will begin regrouping and fulfilling a new operation – an offensive in the direction of Graivoron and Akhtyrka from a front from Kazach'ya Lopan and Dergachi. Immediate mission – no later than 17–2–1943 reach with the main force the line Krasnopol'ye, Slavgorod, Pozhnya, Spornoye. Distant mission – by 21 February reach a line through Lebedin.
2. Combat composition of the army – as before, except the 303d Rifle Division which will be subordinated to 38th Army after its arrival on a line from Oboyan to Verkhopen'ye. . . .
5. Have 5th Guards Tank Corps on the left flank which will, not later than 19 February, secure the town of Akhtyrka.[37]

Subsequently, Golikov ordered 69th Army to attack to Bogodukhov and Aktyrka, and the 3d Tank Army to advance toward Poltava in conjunction with 6th Army's advance on Krasnograd. Moreover, the orders mentioned a subsequent advance on a broad front ultimately designed to reach Kiev and Kremenchug on the Dnepr River.[38]

Soviet Regrouping of Forces

However, before these orders could be implemented Soviet units and staffs within Khar'kov had to be untangled. Because of the nature of the final assault on Khar'kov, in the city there were three army headquarters and staffs; three divisions of 40th Army; four rifle divisions and one rifle brigade of 69th Army; and two tank corps and two rifle divisions of 3d Tank Army.[39] Confusion created by the street fighting was rampant, and it compounded the problem of sorting out units and putting them on the correct path. 3d Tank Army formations took up positions outside the city to cover the complex task of regrouping and provide security for the city as well (see Map 43). Late on 16 February 15th Tank Corps moved through the city, occupied Zalyutino, and engaged German forces at Pesochnya on the road west to Lyubotin. The 160th Rifle Division advanced west toward Budy on the Mzha River north of Merefa. The 48th Guards Rifle Division occupied Osnovo Station and provided security for large amounts of captured rail stock and supplies. The 12th Tank Corps struck German forces at Vasishchevo, east of the Udy River, and the 111th Rifle Division occupied Borovaya, west of the river. Meanwhile, the 6th Guards Cavalry Corps with the 201st Tank Brigade and 37th Rifle Brigade attached concentrated at Sokolovo on the Mzha River west of Zmiyev and waited for the arrival of the 184th Rifle Division. To provide security within Khar'kov, Rybalko assigned the 62d Guards Rifle Division as a city garrison with the 179th Tank Brigade as a reserve.[40]

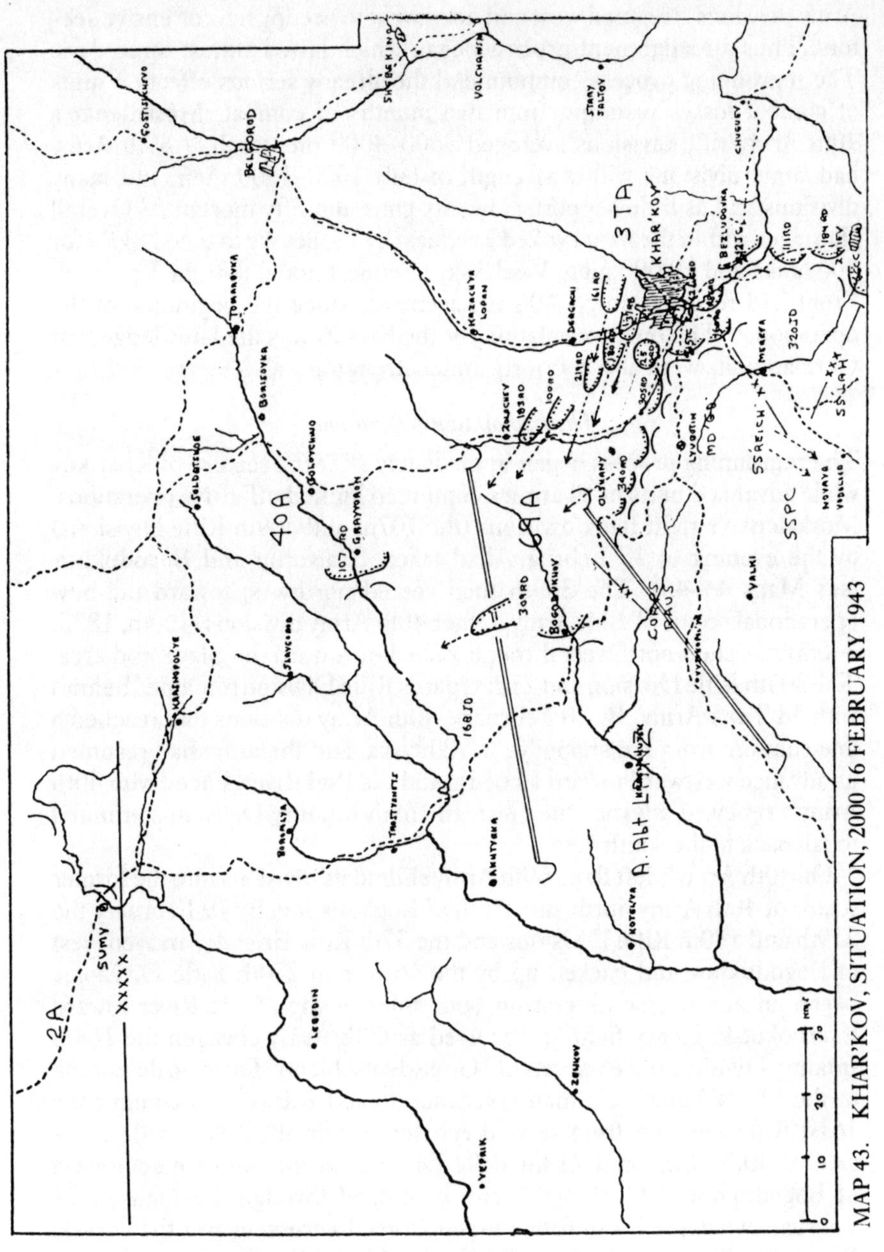

MAP 43. KHAR'KOV, SITUATION, 2000 16 FEBRUARY 1943

While 3d Tank Army covered the large-scale regrouping, 40th and 69th Army divisions streamed west and northwest to occupy new offensive sectors. Thus a realignment process began which lasted almost three days. The regrouping process compounded the already serious effect on units of combat losses resulting from two months of combat. Moskalenko's 40th Army rifle divisions averaged 3500–4000 men each.[41] 69th Army had some divisions with a strength of only 1000–1500 men, and many divisions had as little support as twenty guns and fifty mortars.[42] Overall shortages within the *front* evoked a request by Vasilevsky to the *STAVKA* for 300 tanks and 19,000 men. Vasilevsky's request noted that the Voronezh Front had received only 1,600 replacements since the beginning of the operation.[43] The only consolation for the Soviets was the knowledge that German units were also seriously under strength.

The Exploitation Operation

The regrouping process began immediately after the seizure of Khar'kov while advanced units of all armies continued limited offensive operations. Moskalenko's right flank divisions (the 107th and 309th Rifle Divisions) by the evening of 17 February had taken Graivoron and Bogodukhov (see Maps 44–45). The 309th then veered northwest toward the new operational sector of 40th Army. Other 40th Army divisions (100th, 183d, 340th) marched northwest through Zolochev toward the Slavgorod area. The 305th Rifle Division and 25th Guards Rifle Division remained behind with 3d Tank Army. By 20 February, 40th Army divisions had reached a line running from Krasnopol'ye to Akhtyrka, and the army had resumed its advance westward toward Lebedin and the Psel River. Faced with 40th Army's renewed advance the German 168th Infantry Division continued to fall back to the southwest.

On 40th Army's left flank 69th Army shifted its divisions into the former sector of 40th Army north and south of Bogodukhov. By 19 February the 219th and 180th Rifle Divisions and the 37th Rifle Brigade, arrayed west of Bogodukhov and backed up by the 161st and 270th Rifle Divisions, began an advance southwest on both sides of the Merla River toward Krasnokutsk. Heavy fighting occurred as 69th Army engaged the 168th Infantry Division and elements of "Grossdeutschland" Division defending in the Merla Valley. German resistance forced Kazakov to commit the 161st Rifle Division from second echelon to join the 309th Rifle Division of 40th Army and 219th Rifle Division in the advance southwest of Bogodukhov. 69th Army's drive continued through the night of 22 February when the 180th Rifle Division forced a crossing over the Vorskla River, 40 kilometers north of Poltava.[44] Meanwhile, Moskalenko's 40th Army expanded its offensive. The 309th Rifle Division occupied Akhtyrka and the banks of the Vorskla River north of 69th Army lines while the

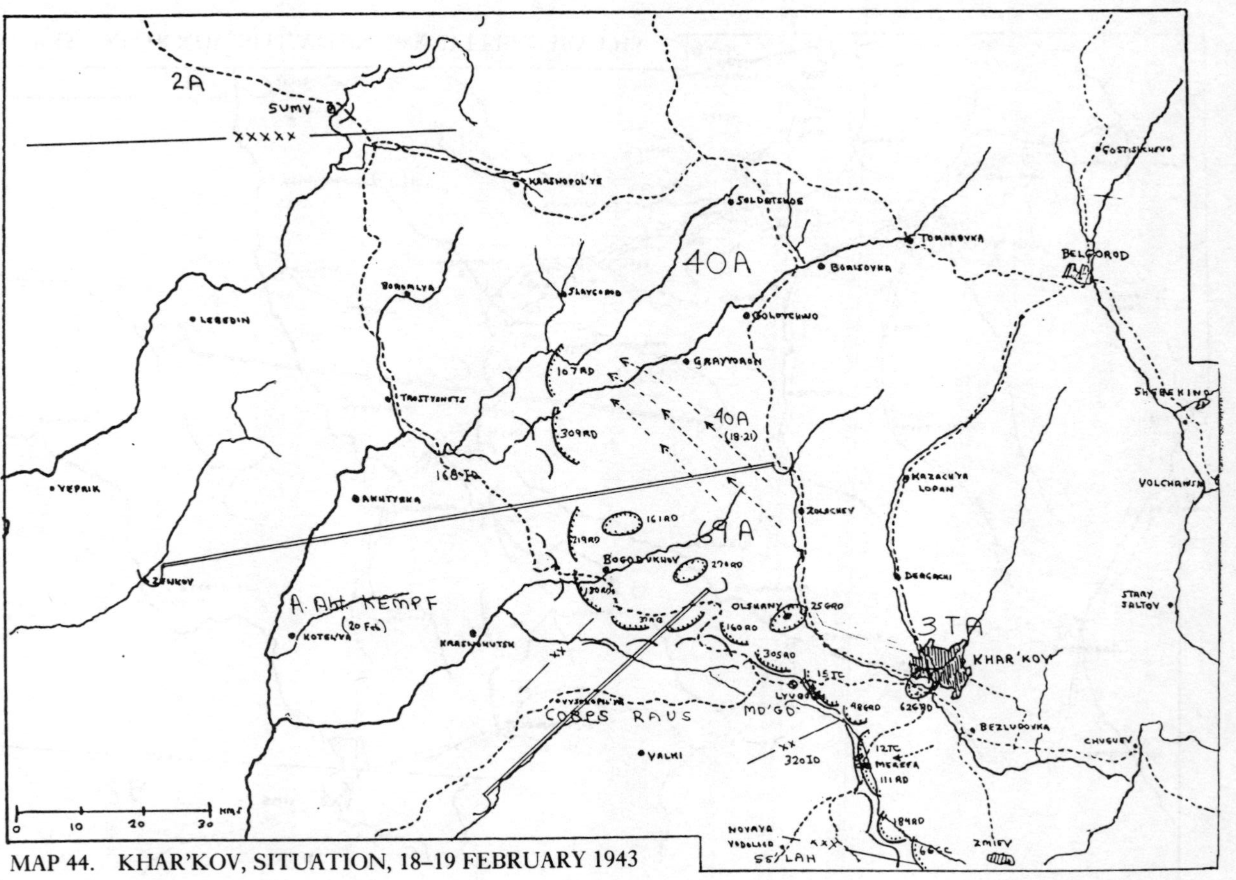

MAP 44. KHAR'KOV, SITUATION, 18–19 FEBRUARY 1943

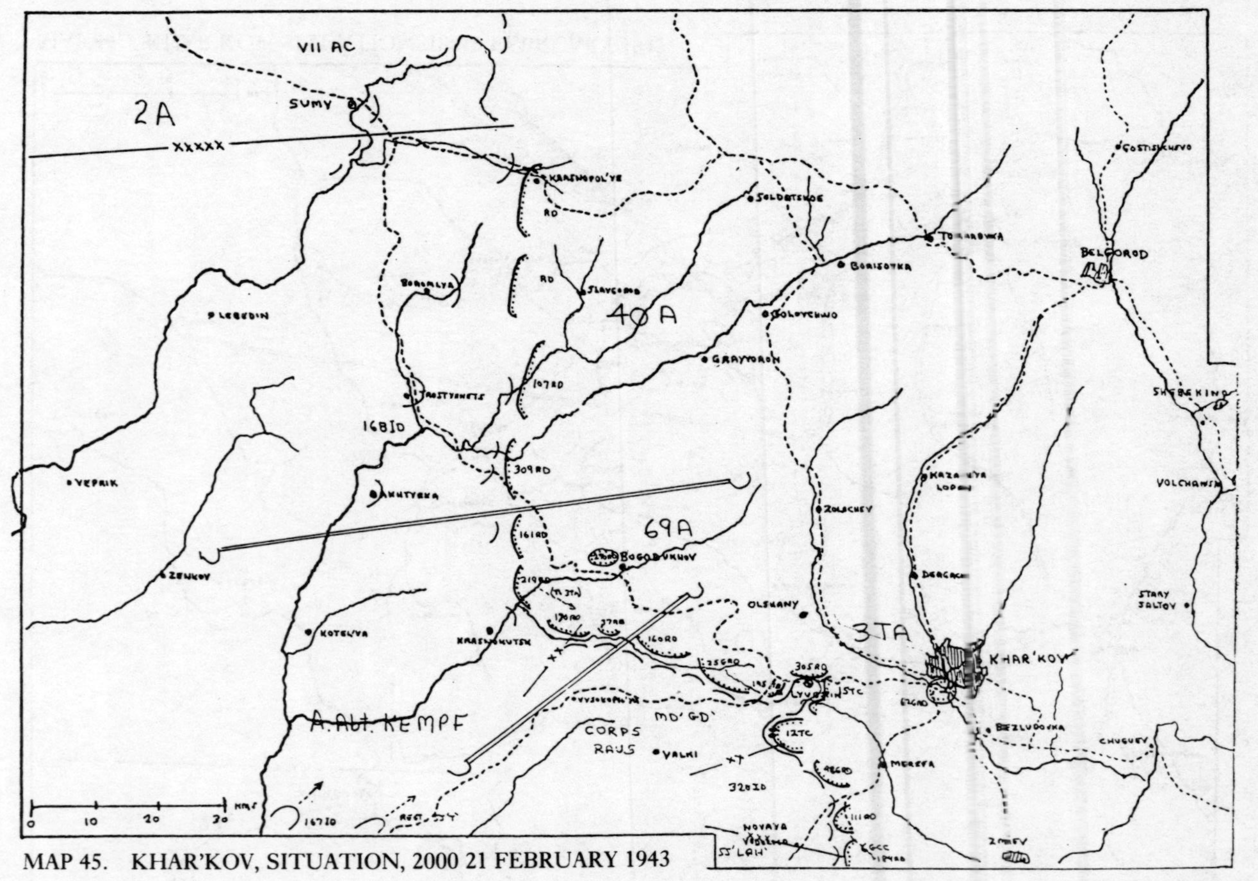

MAP 45. KHAR'KOV, SITUATION, 2000 21 FEBRUARY 1943

army's other divisions seized Lebedin and positions on the east bank of Psel River.

At this juncture events occurring in 3d Tank Army's sector and further south in the Southwestern Front's sector altered the situation in 40th and 69th Army's sectors. Rybalko's 3d Tank Army had resumed the offensive immediately after occupying positions covering Khar'kov. He ordered the 15th Tank Corps, 48th Guards, 25th Guards, and 160th Rifle Divisions to secure Valki; the 12th Tank Corps and the 111th Rifle Division to march on Novaya Vodolaga; and 6th Guards Cavalry Corps and the 184th Rifle Division to secure the army left flank.[45] Early on 17 February 3d Tank Army struck German defenses of Corps Raus ("Grossdeutschland" Division and 320th Infantry Division) deployed south and south-west of Khar'kov. The next day 15th Tank Corps secured Pesochnya and fought "Grossdeutschland" Division troops for Lyubotin. The 12th Tank Corps cracked German defenses at Merefa and, supported by 111th Rifle Division infantry secured the city after a full day of house to house fighting. With 15th Tank Corps tied down in heavy, yet inconclusive fighting for possession of Lyubotin, Rybalko ordered the 12th Tank Corps and 25th Guards Rifle Division to advance on Valki while the 160th Rifle Division and the 195th Tank Brigade of 15th Tank Corps prepared to bypass Lyubotin and seize Staryi Merchik. However, German 320th Infantry Division defenses along the Mzha River halted the 12th Tank Corps and forced it to turn westward toward Budy in an attempt to envelop Lyubotin from the south and southwest. On 21 February 12th Tank Corps battled German forces for possession of Ogult'sy, south of Lyubotin, while the main force of the 160th Rifle Division and the 195th Tank Brigade approached Lyubotin from the west.[46] With the noose tightening around Lyubotin, on 22 February Panzer Grenadier Division "Grossdeutschland" began to withdraw southward. The 15th Tank Corps pursued the withdrawing German units, occupied Lyubotin, and then joined forces with 12th Tank Corps to finally secure Ogult'sy. Meanwhile,the 48th Guards, 111th and 184th Rifle Divisions, and the 6th Guards Cavalry Corps continued to advance south of Khar'kov.

Rybalko's advance proceeded slowly across the entire front. German Corps Raus conducted a skillful delay operation in cooperation with SS Panzer Division "Leibstandarte Adolf Hitler," defending south of Novaya Vodolaga, in order to buy time necessary for Manstein to launch his planned counterstrokes further south. The German delaying tactics further eroded 3d Tank Army's strength (down to 110 tanks on 18 February). Likewise, the 168th Infantry Division and one regiment of SS Panzer Division "Totenkopf" delayed Soviet 69th Army units seeking to advance west of Vysokopol'ye.[47] Moreover, that German defense steadily firmed up with the arrival of reinforcements in the form of the 167th Infantry Division, which by 23 February occupied a defensive sector at the apex of the Soviet 69th Army's advance south of Kotel'va. By 23 February 40th Army's over-extended front from Sumy to Akhtryka also faced heavier resistance. VII Army corps of German 2d Army shifted forces into the Sumy area, and 4th Panzer Division arrived west of the Psel River opposite 40th Army positions at Lebedin.[48]

In essence, the Voronezh Front was becoming overextended just at the moment when Manstein was seeking to crush the Southwestern Front with the converging thrusts of 4th Panzer Army – this at a time when the Voronezh Front was unable to render credible assistance to its neighbor to the south.

Reorientation Southward: The Death Ride of 3d Tank Army (23 February–5 March)

The First Southward Shift of Soviet Forces – 23–28 February

Manstein's counterstroke against Vatutin's overextended 6th Army commenced on 19 February. Only by 28 February did the scope of the Soviet disaster finally become apparent to Vatutin and the *STAVKA* alike. However, Vatutin had made his first request for Voronezh Front assistance on 21 February.[49] Golikov responded by transferring the 219th Rifle Division from 69th Army to 3d Tank Army control. 3d Tank Army, locked in the battle for Lyubotin, could do little to aid 6th Army other than pressure German forces south of Khar'kov. While SS Panzer Corps, XXXXVIII Panzer Corps, and XXXX Panzer Corps chopped up 6th Army and Mobile Group Popov, Vatutin made more urgent calls for assistance.

By the evening of 22 February the *STAVKA* was sufficiently alarmed over the deteriorating situation to order the Voronezh Front to shift the attack of 3d Tank Army and 69th Army forces southward against German forces in the Krasnograd area (see Map 46). 3d Tank Army was to turn over the western portion of its sector to 69th Army and then advance to destroy German forces on its front and occupy Karlovka and Krasnograd. 69th Army, in its turn, would shift the direction of its advance toward the Poltava and Karlovka regions and would transfer its sector north and south of Kotel'va to 40th Army. However, 40th Army was still required to secure Sumy and the area west of the Psel River.[50]

These boundary changes forced a wholesale shifting of units. 40th Army divisions in the Akhtyrka region slid southward to the Merla River while 69th Army divisions likewise turned at right angles, crossed the Merla River, and occupied positions running from Vysokopol'ye westward past Krasnokutsk. 40th Army's sector expanded by 30 percent, and Moskalenko committed all of his divisions to first echelon in order

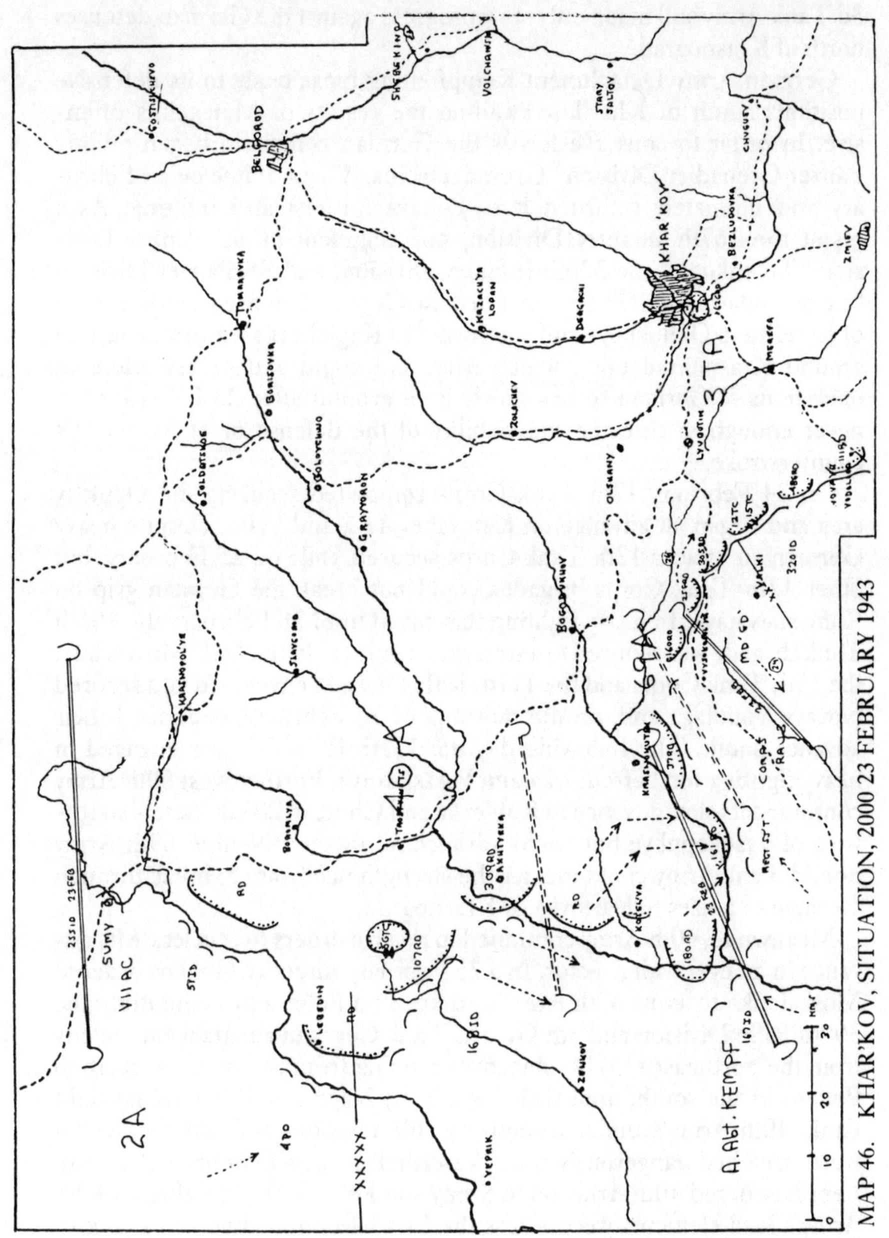

MAP 46. KHAR'KOV, SITUATION, 2000 23 FEBRUARY 1943

to cover the extensive region. Despite these movements, 69th Army and 3d Tank Army still made only slow progress against the German defenses north of Krasnograd.

German Army Detachment Kempf clung tenaciously to its defensive positions south of Khar'kov awaiting the results of Manstein's offensive. In order to conserve forces the German command began pulling Panzer Grenadier Division "Grossdeutschland" out of line on 24 February and ultimately returned it to Poltava for rest and refitting. As a result the 167th Infantry Division, one regiment of SS Panzer Division "Totenkopf," the 320th Infantry Division, and SS Panzer Division "Leibstandarte Adolf Hitler" manned the German defense line from south of Kotel'va to Okhocheye and southward to Kegichevka – a virtual bastion around Krasnograd upon which Manstein could anchor his offensive operations.[51] German forces slowly gave ground after 23 February but never enough to threaten the viability of the defense or of Manstein's counterstroke.

On 24 February 12th Tank Corps completed securing the Ogult'sy area and began an advance on Kamyshevataya and Valki. Despite heavy German air attacks 12th Tank Corps secured Valki on 25 February, but other 12th Tank Corps brigades could not break the German grip on Kamyshevataya. In heavy fighting that raged until 28 February the 106th Tank Brigade was reduced to a strength of only twelve tanks.[52] Meanwhile, the 15th Tank Corps and the 111th Rifle Division enveloped and secured Novaya Vodolaga and, on the morning of 26 February, continued their advance south. The following day the 111th Rifle Division engaged in heavy fighting for Yefremovka and Paraskovaya. Further west 69th Army continued its slow advance to Rublevka and Chutovo 20 kilometers southwest of Vysokopol'ye but could advance no further. Neither 69th Army nor 3d Tank Army could muster the strength necessary to break through German defenses to Karlovka or Krasnograd.

Meanwhile, 40th Army continued to receive orders to accelerate its advance in an ever wider sector. In a 25 February directive Golikov ordered Moskalenko to assist 69th Army's advance on Poltava by committing the 309th Rifle Division and 5th Guards Tank Corps in an attack on the city from the northeast.[53] With objectives ranging from Sumy in the north to Poltava in the south; and, with 38th Army lagging well behind its right flank, 40th Army's understrength six rifle divisions and one tank corps were stretched dangerously thin. Nevertheless, new *front* orders on 26th February urged 40th Army on to Sumy and Poltava. By 28 February 40th Army's lead elements were across the Psel River and almost to Zen'kov. Prodded by *front* headquarters Moskalenko sought to capture the key city of Sumy. He tasked the 20th Guards Tank Brigade (without tanks) of 5th Guards Tank Corps reinforced by the 59th Tank Regiment and 4th

Guards Tank Destroyer Regiment to seize the town in cooperation with the 183d Rifle Division, but all attempts to do so failed.[54]

The Demise of 3d Tank Army – 28 February–5 March

On 28 February, at a time when the Southwestern Front was in full collapse, the *STAVKA* issued new orders to the Voronezh Front. 1st Guards Army was withdrawing north toward the Northern Donets River while 6th Army elements were attempting to fight their way northward out of encirclement. In order to save the remains of 6th Army, the *STAVKA* ordered Golikov to relinquish control of 3d Tank Army to the Southwestern Front. 3d Tank Army was to wheel sharply southward toward Lozovaya to blunt the German advance and rescue 6th Army units (see Maps 30 and 47). Specifically, 3d Tank Army was to establish defenses in the bulk of its sector and then concentrate the army's main force by 1 March in the Kegichevka area. On 2 March 3d Tank Army was to attack south and southeast from Kegichevka to destroy advancing units of SS Panzer Corps.[55] To facilitate the shift 3d Tank Army gave up to 69th Army the 160th and 350th Rifle Divisions with their extended tactical sectors. 69th Army, with its two additional divisions, would cover the extended sector of the front from the Merla River to south of Valki and continue its attacks toward Poltava. When Kazakov questioned the feasibility of continuing the attack, Golikov sarcastically wrote: "To the Dnepr there remains 400–450 kilometers and to the spring thaw 30–35 days. Derive from this the corresponding conclusions and calculations. Golikov."[56] While 3d Tank Army concentrated for the southward thrust, 40th Army was to continue its offensive against earlier designated objectives.

On 1 March, after a long night march, the 15th Tank Corps and the 111th, 184th, and 219th Rifle Divisions reached the Kegichevka area and occupied defensive positions to await the arrival of 12th Tank Corps. The 6th Guards Cavalry Corps, which was concentrating at Yefremovka, ran into heavy enemy forces and immediately went on the defense. Late in the day 12th Tank Corps closed into its assembly area. At this critical point the combined tank strength of both 12th and 15th Tank Corps was only thirty tanks.[57] On 2 March, because the concentration of 3d Tank Army units was still incomplete and fuel and ammunition supplies were dangerously low, the offensive was postponed until the morning of 3 March.

Early on 3 March 3d Tank Army launched its desperate offensive directly into the teeth of the advancing SS Panzer Divisions "Totenkopf" and "Das Reich" (see Maps 31 and 47).[58] Reeling from the shock of the collision, 15th Tank Corps and its accompanying rifle divisions immediately went over to the defense. While SS Panzer Division "Totenkopf" struck 15th Tank Corps from the east, SS Panzer Division

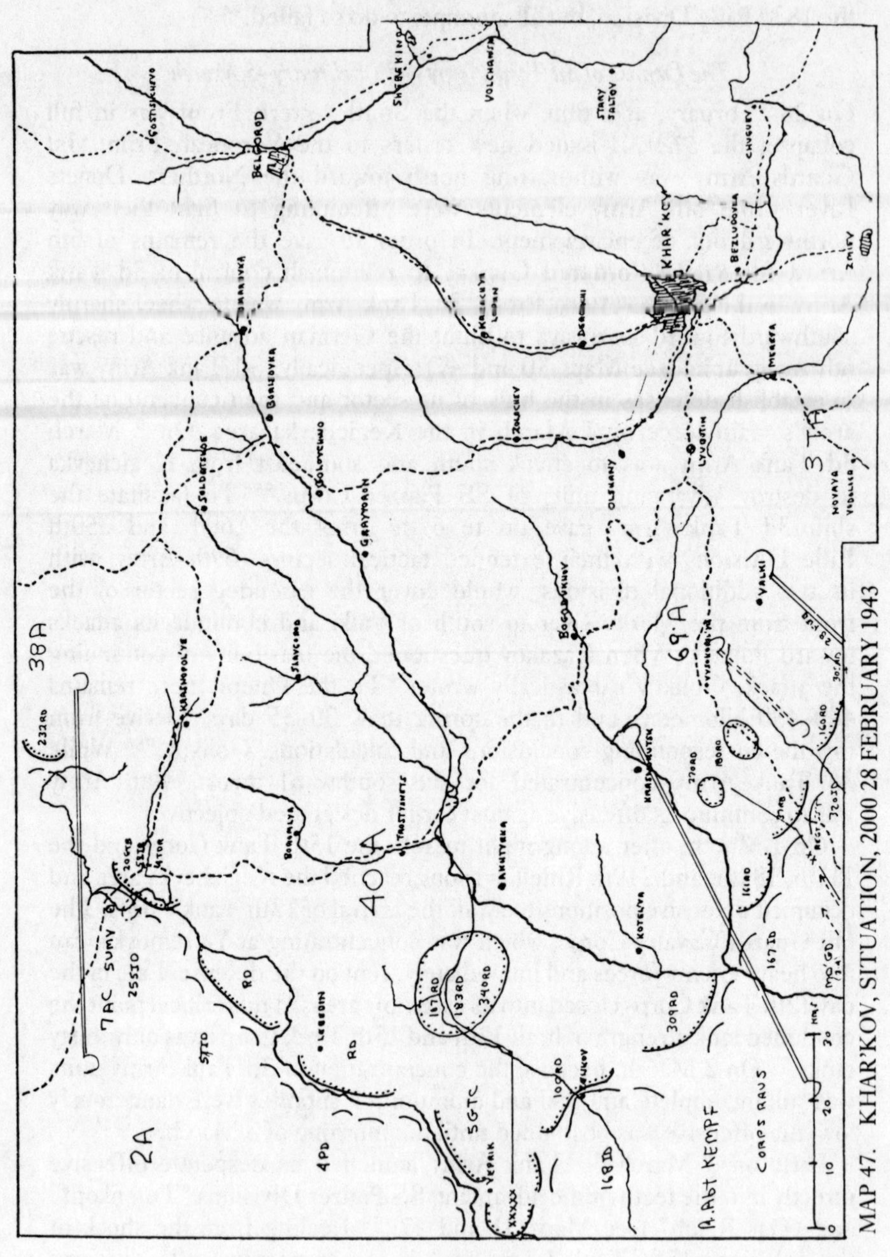

MAP 47. KHAR'KOV, SITUATION, 2000 28 FEBRUARY 1943

ERRATUM

p.191, line 1, *insert* "Leibstandarte Adolf Hitler" launched slashing attacks from Kegichevka' *before* 'and Staroverovka against the Soviet tank corps.'

ie Soviet tank corps. Ultimately the panzer
Corps' positions and linked up with SS Panzer
anced units at Paraskovaya and Yefremovka.
orps began a bitter and futile battle of survival
s.

k Corps began its eastward advance on the
106th Tank Brigade and 97th Tank Brigade
Zavod supported on the left by the 30th Tank
d Rifle Brigade. The advance immediately ran
zer Division "Totenkopf" and SS Panzer Divi-
r, the thrust by SS "Das Reich" on Yefremovka
th Guards Cavalry Corps and the 350th Rifle
and cut 3d Tank Army's supply lines. Under
of from twenty to thirty tanks, the 12th Tank
id defense.

Rybalko saw that further resistance was futile
its to break out of encirclement to the northeast
ps and its supporting divisions were unable to
kout. The corps commander, Major General
n 3 March; and his forces continued to struggle
h scattered groups made their way northward
e 12th Tank Corps reacted in more organized
M. I. Zin'kovich disengaged from contact with
and headed northwest (see Map 32).[60] The next day the corps ran into a series of German defensive positions. After heavy fighting, on 6 March corps' survivors, minus all of their equipment, reached Soviet defensive lines in the Okhocheye area.[61]

By 5 March 3d Tank Army was a shambles. Its two tank corps essentially were destroyed as were the three rifle divisions which accompanied the tank corps into what the Germans called the Kegichevka *Kessel* (cauldron). Although the Germans took until 5 March to reduce the encircled force, only small groups of Soviets and individual Soviet soldiers escaped northward or eastward. Meanwhile, Rybalko hastily tried to reconstruct Soviet defense lines anchored on Novaya Vodolaga and Okhocheye. He received as reinforcements from *front* the 253d Rifle Brigade, 195th Tank Brigade, and 179th Tank Brigade, as well as the 25th Guards Rifle Division and a Czechoslovak battalion. But Rybalko had only the brief period from 3–5 March to erect new defensive lines while SS Panzer Corps reduced the Kegichevka cauldron. All too soon the concentrated energy of the German counterattack would apply itself to the Voronezh Front's south flank.

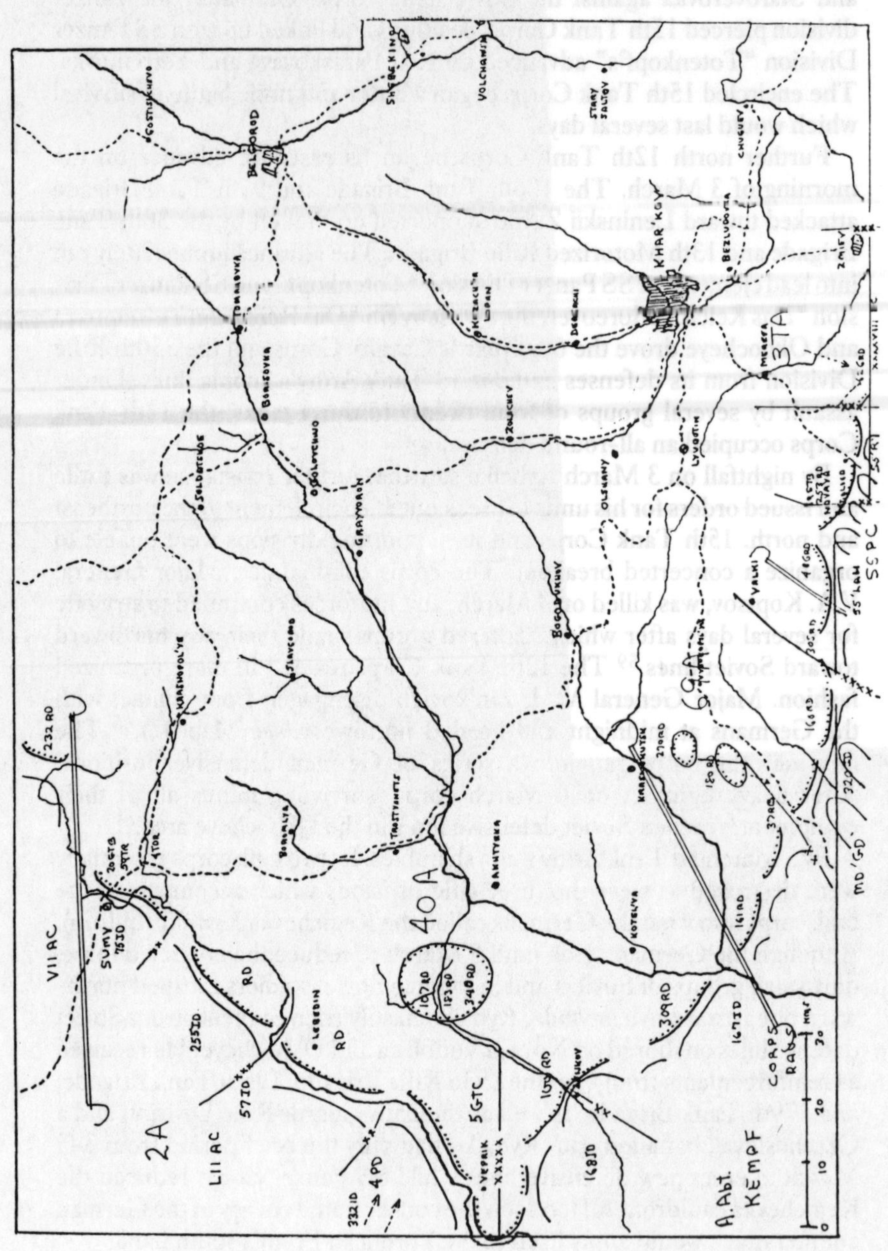

MAP 48 KHARKOV SITUATION 2000 5 MARCH 1943

Manstein's Counteroffensive (5–23 March)

The Situation on 5 March and German Offensive Plans

While SS Panzer Corps chewed up major elements of 3d Tank Army, Rybalko reorganized his defenses (see Maps 32 and 48). The 253d Rifle Brigade and 195th Tank Brigade anchored his defenses at Novaya Vodolaga. The 62d Rifle Division (replaced by the 17th NKVD Rifle Brigade at Khar'kov), 6th Guards Cavalry Corps, and 350th Rifle Division defended eastward to Okhocheye, and the 25th Guards Rifle Division supported by 24 tanks of the 179th Tank Brigade, occupied the sector from Taranovka to Zmiyev. In addition, *front* released to Rybalko's control the reinforced Czechoslovak battalion (900 men) of Colonel L. Svoboda which Rybalko placed in defensive positions around Sokolovo, west of the Mzha River, and along the east bank of the Mzha River north of Zmiyev. The 48th Guards Rifle Division held Rybalko's right flank west of Novaya Vodolaga to its boundary with 69th Army.[62]

In light of Rybalko's disaster south of Khar'kov and ominous signs of German preparations for an offensive against his sector, Kazakov withdrew his army's divisions to positions south of the Merla River from north of Chutovo to south of Valki. He reinforced these units with a tank brigade and several anti-tank rifle battalions plus the remaining seven or eight tanks available to his army.[63] On Kazakov's right flank Moskalenko's 40th Army also felt the shock waves created by the collapse of 3d Tank Army. By 1 March Moskalenko's forces had reached the line of the Psel River and controlled several bridgeheads along that river south of Sumy. South of Lebedin 40th Army forces reached Oposhnya, west of Kotel'va. Late that day Golikov finally ordered 40th Army to go on the defense but specified that 40th Army was to maintain its outposts west of the Psel. In addition, Golikov ordered Moskalenko to withdraw three rifle divisions into reserve and subordinate them to 69th Army for use in counterattacks against German forces operating against the Voronezh Front's left flank. Moskalenko pulled the 107th, 183d, and 340th Rifle Divisions out of his front lines and readied them to assist Kazakov.[64] This left Moskalenko just three rifle divisions and one tank corps to cover a 120 kilometer sector extending from Sumy to Oposhnya.

Already, by 5 March local German attacks were disrupting Soviet defensive adjustments; and German preparations for a major offensive northward against the Voronezh Front promised to capitalize on that disruption. In 3d Tank Army's sector 6th Panzer Division of XXXXVIII Panzer Corps engaged 25th Guards Rifle Division defenses at Taranovka while SS Panzer Division "Das Reich" drove the 6th Guards Cavalry Corps and the 350th Rifle Division from their positions at Okhocheye. Likewise, SS Panzer Division "Leibstandarte Adolf Hitler" forced Soviet defenders to withdraw north from Staroverovka toward Novaya Vodolaga. 4th Panzer Army, its offensive sector shifted west to include the region south of Khar'kov, awaited the release of the remaining elements of SS "Totenkopf" and SS "Leibstandarte Adolf Hitler" from the encirclement battle and the arrival of the remainder of XXXXVIII Panzer Corps (11th Panzer Division). Once these units assembled, 4th Panzer Army would launch a concerted drive northward.

West of Krasnograd, Army Detachment Kempf also concentrated its growing strength. It deployed its infantry divisions, the 168th, 167th, and 320th, in the sector from the Psel River to south of Valki and placed the somewhat refreshed "Grossdeutschland" Panzer Grenadier Division in the Chutovo area with orders to attack toward Valki and Bogodukhov. (The concentration of "Grossdeutschland" Division was completed on 6 March.) In addition, one regiment of SS Panzer Division "Totenkopf" deployed for an advance northeast along the road to Kolomak and Vysokopol'ye.[65]

Manstein's overall plan called for 4th Panzer Army to continue its drive northward against the Voronezh Front forces in the Khar'kov area. SS Panzer Corps and XXXXVIII Panzer Corps would spearhead 4th Panzer Army's drive north. 6th and 11th Panzer Divisions, concentrated southeast of Taranovka, would attack north in concert with SS Panzer Corps' attack, SS Panzer Corps with SS "Totenkopf" on the left, SS "Leibstandarte Adolf Hitler" in the center, and SS "Das Reich" on the right would regroup south of Novaya Vodolaga and launch a concerted attack through Novaya Vodolaga toward Valki and Merefa. Simultaneously, the right flank units of Army Detachment Kempf would join the attack and expand the assault to the west. Panzer Grenadier Division "Grossdeutschland" would advance toward Vysokopol'ye and Valki and then turn north toward Bogodukhov to split Soviet 69th Army from 3d Tank Army. A separate regiment of SS "Totenkopf" would thrust toward Krasnokutsk supported by the 320th Infantry Division. Ultimately, the 167th Infantry Division would attack Soviet 40th Army positions from Oposhnya to Akhtyrka as would VII Army Corps units of German 2d Army operating along the Psel River (the 33d Infantry Division, 57th Infantry Division, and 255th Infantry Division).[66]

German Advance to Khar'kov – 6–9 March

On 6 March German assaults commenced against Soviet defenses east and west of Novaya Vodolaga (see Map 49). SS Panzer Division "Das Reich" advanced northward along the railroad to Novaya Vodolaga against the Soviet 253d Rifle Brigade and 195th Tank Brigade and enveloped Soviet positions in the town from the east. SS Panzer Division "Leibstandarte Adolf Hitler" advanced north in two columns toward Valki and the region west of Novaya Vodolaga. After heavy fighting, in the evening Soviet forces withdrew to new defensive positions along the Mzha River and south of Lyubotin. By evening SS Panzer Division "Totenkopf," having mopped up encircled Soviet 3d Tank Army units, regrouped north of Krasnograd and prepared to join the advance on Valki.

Meanwhile, on SS Panzer Corps' right flank, 6th Panzer Division of XXXXVIII Panzer Corps struck the 25th Guards Rifle Division and the 179th Tank Brigade defending Taranovka and began a severe battle for the town which would last until early on 8 March when the decimated Soviet force finally abandoned the town and withdrew eastward to the Mzha River.* The following day 11th Panzer Division of XXXXVIII Panzer Corps joined the battle for Taranovka.[67]

The German drive widened and deepened on 7 March. While 6th Panzer Division struggled for Taranovka, SS Panzer Division "Das Reich" slowly drove Soviet forces from north of Novaya Vodolaga to Staraya Vodolaga. SS Panzer Division "Leibstandarte Adolf Hitler" cleared Valki of 48th Guards Rifle Division and 305th Rifle Division troops, and SS Panzer Division "Totenkopf" regiments moved into positions at Valki to take part in the subsequent advance on Lyubotin.

At 0500 that day Panzer Grenadier Division "Grossdeutschland" added its weight to the attack by slashing at positions held by the Soviet 69th Army's 180th, 160th, and 305th Rifle Divisions.[68] 69th Army slowly gave ground south of the Merla River. Kazakov knew that "Grossdeutschland" Division's advance threatened to split 69th Army from the neighboring fragments of 3d Tank Army. It would, in fact, be suicidal for the army to hold its positions at Kotel'va and Krasnokutsk while German forces plunged on toward Bogodukhov and Olshany.

Ominous signs were also appearing in 40th Army's sector indicating an impending German attack, this at a time when Moskalenko was in the process of dispatching three of his divisions to assist Kazakov. The growing confusion in the Soviet command was evidenced by Kazakov's and Moskalenko's conflicting accounts of the actions of those three divisions. Moskalenko claimed the counterattack of the three divisions was under Kazakov's control while Kazakov claimed Moskalenko organized the counterthrust.[69] Very simply, momentum was in the hands of the Germans. With the German counterattack unleashed, the Soviets could

*On 6 March 25th Guards Rifle Division was subordinated to 6th Army control. That army took over responsibility for the Zmiyev sector and began rushing reinforcements to the area.

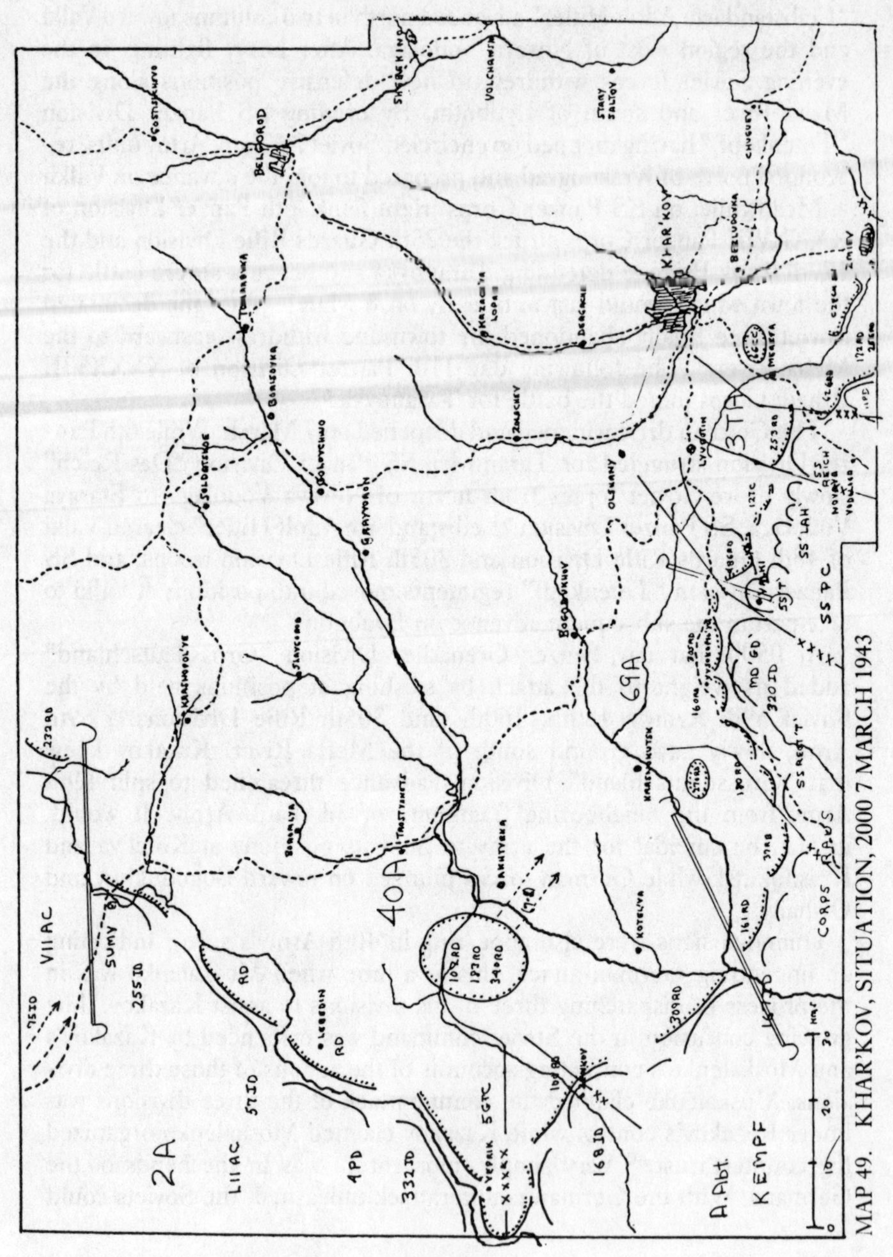

MAP 49. KHAR'KOV, SITUATION, 2000 7 MARCH 1943

only react and the Soviets' dispersed dispositions and the deteriorating situation made that reaction ineffective.

The following day the German juggernaut continued. XXXXVIII Panzer Corps finally smashed Soviet resistance at Taranovka and pushed its forces eastward to the Mzha River. 6th Panzer Division advanced to the Mzha River north and south of Sokolovo and assaulted the defensive positions of the 1st Czechoslovak Battalion at Sokolovo. The battalion clung to its positions at Sokolovo throughout 8 March and to its general defense lines on the Mzha River until 13 March when SS Panzer Corps' envelopment of Khar'kov made the position untenable.[70] On 6th Panzer Division's right flank the 11th Panzer Division advanced to the Mzha River at and south of Merefa where it faced the 62d Guards Rifle Division and portions of the 253d Rifle Brigade and 195th Tank Brigade.

SS Panzer Corps, with its three divisions on line, by the morning of 8 March had scattered the major portion of the 253d Rifle Brigade and 195th Tank Brigade north of Staraya Vodolaga and Valki. By 1600 SS Panzer Division "Das Reich" approached Lyubotin from the south. SS Panzer Division "Leibstandarte Adolf Hitler" pushed north, seized Ogult'sy, cut the railroad west of Lyubotin, and by 1600 enveloped Lyubotin from the north. Meanwhile, SS Panzer Division "Totenkopf" went into action north of Valki operating in tandem with a *kampfgruppe* of "Grossdeutschland." By 1700 "Totenkopf" drove back the 48th Guards Rifle Division and occupied Staryi Merchik just south of the rail line from Bogodukhov to Khar'kov.[71]

The following day SS Panzer Corps thrust northward to complete the job of splitting Soviet 69th Army from 40th Army; and, simultaneously, the corps swung eastward to isolate Khar'kov (see Map 50). Leaving XXXXVIII Panzer Corps to confront Soviet positions along the Mzha River from Merefa to Zmiyev, SS Panzer Division "Das Reich" secured Lyubotin early on 9 March and then advanced eastward along the rail line toward Khar'kov. Progress slowed as the Soviets dispatched the newly arrived 19th Rifle Division (released from *STAVKA* reserves) with orders to block the approach to Khar'kov from the southwest while the 86th Tank Brigade backed up remnants of 48th Guards Rifle Division, defending due west of Khar'kov. Simultaneously, the *front* commander ordered the 17th NKVD Rifle Brigade in Khar'kov to prepare the city for defense. While SS "Das Reich" thrust for Khar'kov proper, SS "Leibstandarte Adolf Hitler" fought its way to Udy River crossings at Peresechaya and dispatched an advanced element to Polevoye, west of Dergachi. SS "Totenkopf" thrust northward, seized Olshany, and wheeled eastward across the Udy River driving before it elements of Soviet 6th Guards Cavalry Corps, the only organized force covering the gap between 69th Army and 3d Tank Army.[72]

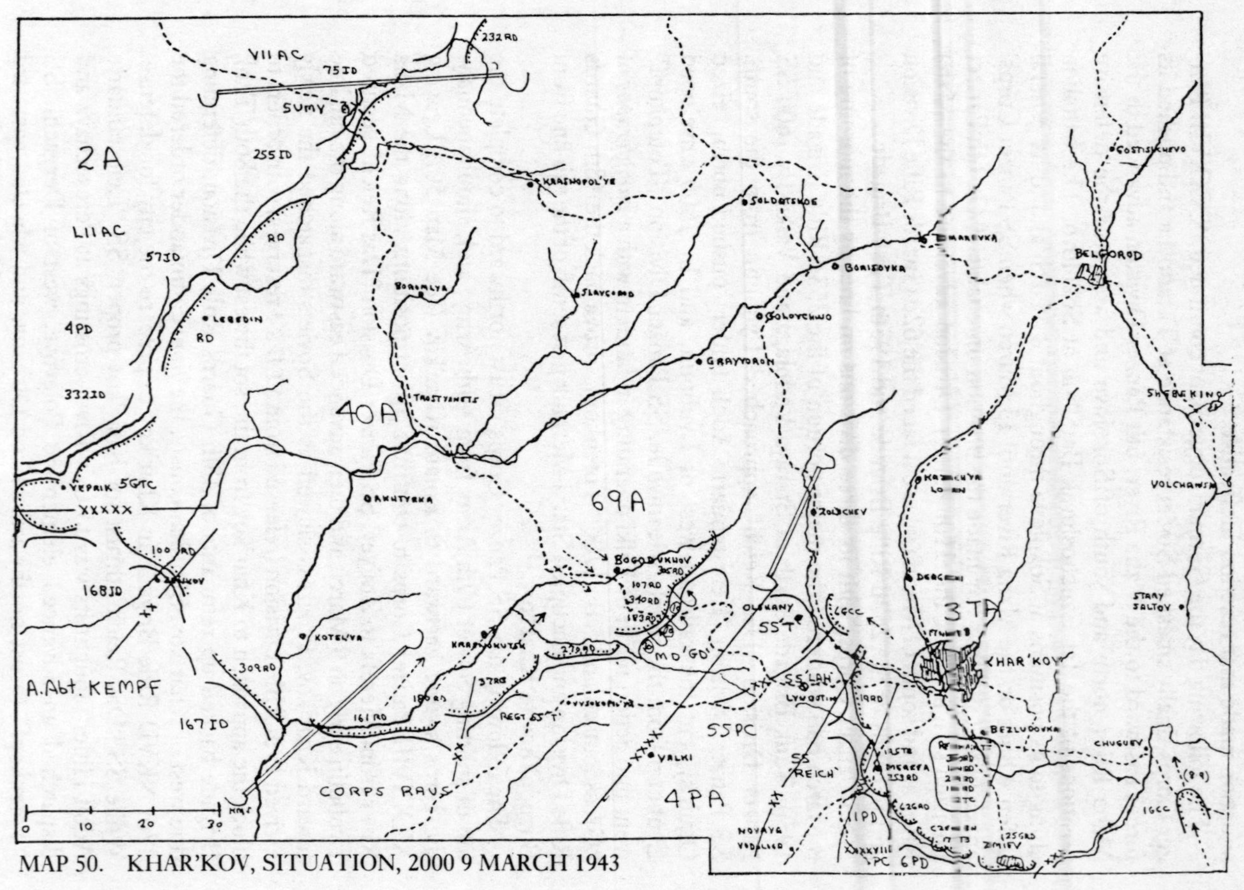

MAP 50. KHAR'KOV, SITUATION, 2000 9 MARCH 1943

While SS Panzer Corps conducted its northward penetrations and its turn eastward, Army Corps Raus accelerated its attacks on Soviet 69th Army. Panzer Grenadier Division "Grossdeutschland" continued its advance up the Merla River in close cooperation with SS "Totenkopf's" drive on Staryi Merchik. By 9 March, with the SS Panzer Corps firmly embedded in between Soviet 69th and 3d Tank Armies, "Grossdeutschland" Division turned northward toward Bogodukhov against 69th Army's 270th and 305th Rifle Divisions. That evening the 340th, 107th, and 183d Rifle Divisions of Moskalenko's 40th Army reached the Bogodukhov area and prepared to attack southward the following morning against "Grossdeutschland" Division's lead elements in one last attempt to restore communications with 3d Tank Army.[73] Both Moskalenko and Kazakov expressed continued concern over the fate of Soviet forces operating around Akhtyrka and at positions east of the Psel River. No withdrawal order would be issued, however, until the results were known of the counterattacks south of Bogodukhov.

Other elements of Army Corps Raus continued their pressure against 69th Army on 8 and 9 March. SS "Totenkopf's" regiment seized Vysokopol'ye from the Soviet 270th Rifle Division and 37th Rifle Brigade, then turned northward on "Grossdeutschland's" left flank. The 320th Infantry Division intensified its attacks on remaining 69th Army divisions (161st and 180th) south of the Merla River. Further westward the 167th Infantry Division prepared to attack from Zen'kov against Moskalenko's weakened 40th Army as did German 2d Army units deployed west of Psel River. Moskalenko shortened his defensive lines slightly by withdrawing his advanced elements back across the Psel River. However, his position was fragile, with three rifle divisions and a tank corps stretched across a front of over 100 kilometers, this at a time when the neighboring armies to the south were threatening to collapse.

The Battle for Khar'kov – 10–14 March.

On 10 March, as the Soviets launched a fruitless counterattack near Bogodukhov, German forces continued their offensive along the entire front from Khar'kov to Sumy (see Map 51). While XXXXVIII Panzer Corps' 11th and 6th Panzer Divisions pressed Soviet defenses along the Mzha River and waited for the 106th Infantry Division to join them, SS Panzer Corps continued its advance against Khar'kov.[74] SS "Das Reich" ground its way westward into the city's suburbs against Soviet 19th Rifle Division and 86th Tank Brigade. SS "Leibstandarte Adolf Hitler" thrust north of Khar'kov, and SS "Totenkopf" units smashed the Soviet 6th Guards Cavalry Corps, 160th Rifle Division, and 48th Guards Rifle Division, seized Dergachi, and occupied blocking positions facing north of Khar'kov from Dergachi to Russkaya Tishki. Meanwhile three

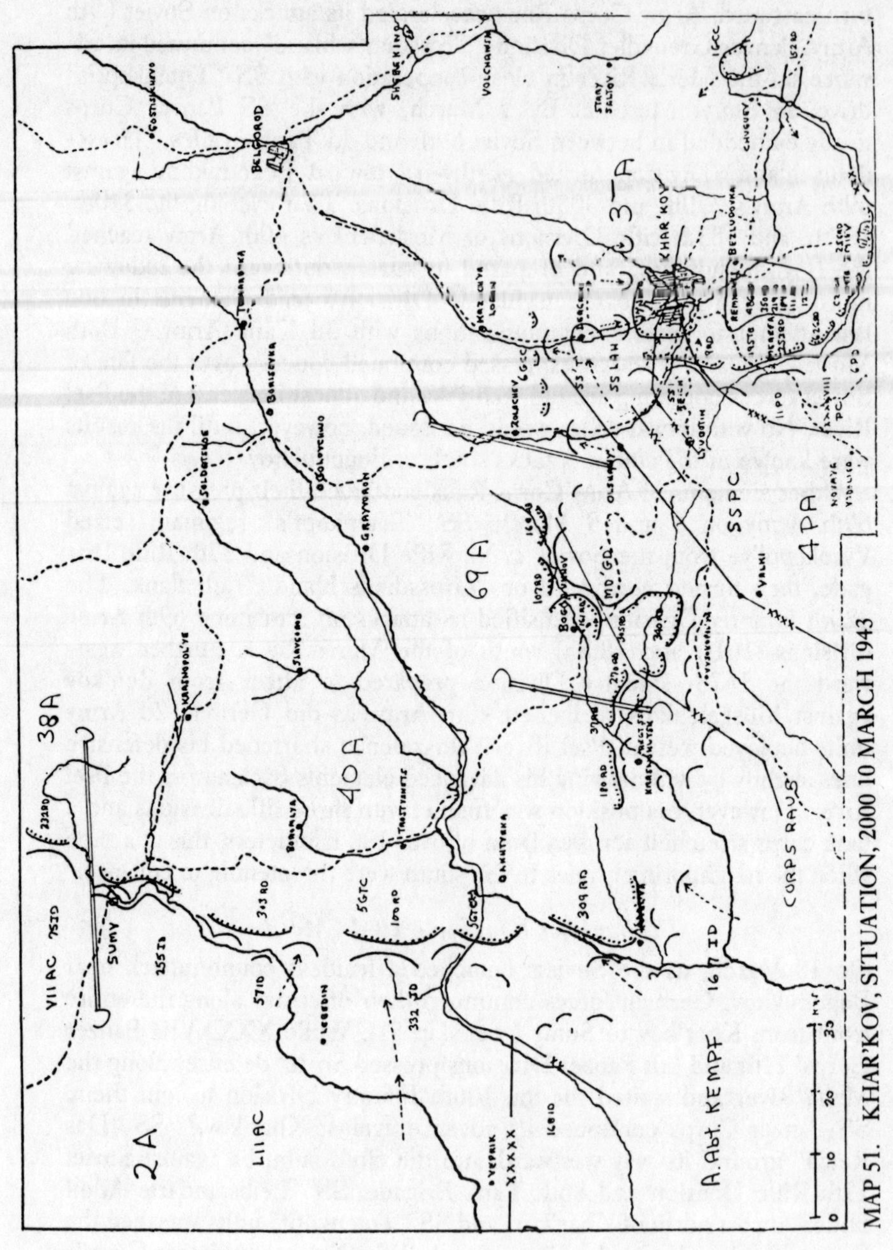

MAP 51. KHAR'KOV, SITUATION, 2000 10 MARCH 1943

kampfgruppen of SS "Leibstandarte Adolf Hitler" turned sharply south and penetrated into the northern and northeastern limits of the city by late afternoon on 10 March. Surprised by this turning movement Major General E.E. Belov, the commandant of Khar'kov, shifted elements of the 19th Rifle Division and 86th Tank Brigade northward, thus permitting SS "Das Reich" units easier entry into western sections of the city.

German pressure on Khar'kov continued to build. In heavy street fighting, SS "Das Reich" pushed through west Khar'kov; and pressure from SS "Leibstandarte Adolf Hitler," attacking through the northern and northeastern sections of the city, forced Belov's forces to withdraw across the Lopan River, blowing all bridges in their wake. The growing crisis at Khar'kov forced commitment of the last Soviet reserve forces in the region, the 179th Tank Brigade.[75] The heavy fighting in the city so tied up Soviet forces that by 13 March SS Panzer Corps could begin implementing a plan for a deep envelopment around Khar'kov by Panzer Division SS "Totenkopf."

While SS Panzer Corps fought for Khar'kov, German attacks collapsed the positions of the overextended Soviet 69th and 40th Armies. On the morning of 10 March the three Soviet divisions (340th, 107th, 183d) struck at "Grossdeutschland" units southeast and south of Bogodukhov; but, according to Kazakov and the war diary of Army Detachment Kempf, the attack virtually went unnoticed. Without a pause "Grossdeutschland" continued its advance. The next day it seized the southeastern outskirts of Bogodukhov, while SS "Totenkopf's" regiment occupied Krasnokutsk and Murafa in the Merla and Merchik valleys, further isolating 69th Army from its neighbors to the east.[76]

The failure of the Soviet counterattack forced Golikov to undertake major adjustments to his force. Golikov ordered Kazakov to regroup his forces, withdraw from the Kotel'va salient, and occupy defensive positions north of Khar'kov covering the road from Khar'kov to Belgorod. In addition, Kazakov retained responsibility for the defense of Bogodukhov. As this was clearly beyond his means, Kazakov proposed to transfer two of his divisions and one rifle brigade to 40th Army along with the responsibility for defending Bogodukhov. In return, two divisions of 40th Army presently defending south of Zolochev would be subordinated to 69th Army. Golikov approved this proposal and on the night of 10–11 March Kazakov began shifting his forces eastward to occupy his new defensive positions.[77]

Meanwhile, Moskalenko met Golikov at Khar'kov to discuss his new dispositions and later returned to Graivoron to supervise troop movements. The Germans greeted Moskalenko's arrival with heavy air attacks which forced him to move his headquarters further northeast.[78]

By 10 March the *STAVKA* undertook some measures to deal with the growing disaster. Two days earlier it had ordered Vatutin's Southwestern Front to launch an attack across the Mzha River from Zmiyev toward Taranovka and Novaya Vodolaga to catch the Germans in the flank. Vatutin's attack was repulsed, and on 11 March German forces pursued the Soviets back to Zmiyev. With its counterattacks parried, the *STAVKA* ordered new troop regroupings to counter the threat. It sent orders to the 1st Tank Army and 21st Army to concentrate north of Belgorod, and it ordered the 64th Army forward from Stalingrad.[79] However, these units would not be available until late March.

Late on 11 March "Grossdeutschland" troops drove the Soviet defenders from Bogodukhov. Soviet divisions of 40th Army in the Bogodukhov area (340th, 107th, 183d) withdrew northeast interspersed with regrouping divisions of 69th Army (180th, 270th, 161st, and 37th Rifle Brigade), themselves under pressure from the German 167th Infantry Division which on 10 March had opened its drive northeast toward Kotel'va and Akhtyrka. The 320th Infantry Division on its right and SS Group Thule cleared the sector from Murafa to north of Valki in the wake of "Grossdeutschland" Division spearheads.[80]

Simultaneous with the 167th Infantry Division advance, 2d Army's LII Army Corps' divisions struck Soviet 40th Army positions south of Sumy. The 75th, 255th, 57th, and 332d Infantry Divisions struck 40th Army's 100th Rifle Division and 5th Guards Tank Corps, occupied Lebedin, and forced Soviet units to withdraw toward the rail line from Sumy to Trostyanets. Moskalenko, with his attentions distracted by the withdrawal at Bogodukhov, sought to conduct an orderly withdrawal back through Akhtyrka and Graivoron. Meanwhile, his divisions in the Bogodukhov area withdrew north to regroup in the Graivoron–Borisovka area. On 13 March, however, a decisive German thrust into Moskalenko's flank and rear disrupted the orderly withdrawal of 40th Army.

The Voronezh Front's situation took a turn for the worse on 13 March when 4th Panzer Army and Army Detachment Kempf each undertook a major thrust to further disrupt Soviet efforts to restore the situation. In the Khar'kov area SS Panzer Corps, still fighting for possession of the city with its SS Panzer Divisions "Das Reich" and "Leibstandarte Adolf Hitler," undertook a deep envelopment of Soviet forces defending the city. On the night of 12–13 March SS Panzer Division "Totenkopf" struck east and south from its positions north of Khar'kov. By 1900 lead elements of the division reached Rogan, east of Khar'kov, and cut the main communications umbilical of 3d Tank Army with its rear area and the Northern Donets River. The following day SS "Totenkopf" cut the remaining 3d Tank Army lines of communication.

Meanwhile, on 14 March SS "Das Reich" and "Leibstandarte Adolf Hitler" completed clearing Khar'kov and emerged into the eastern outskirts of the city. The 11th Panzer Division advanced south of Khar'kov along the Udy River while the 106th Infantry Division cleared Merefa and, with 6th Panzer Division, secured a foothold over the Mzha River in the defensive sector of the Soviet 62d Guards Rifle Division.[81] 6th Panzer Division prepared to initiate a drive through Soviet defenses from the Mzha River line to the Udy River in order to link up with SS "Totenkopf" and to complete the encirclement of 3d Tank Army units south and southwest of Khar'kov.

German Exploitation to the Northern Donets River and Belgorod – 13–23 March

3d Tank Army's position was desperate. The 48th Guards, 62d Guards, and 350th Rifle Divisions; the 104th and 253d Rifle Brigades; and the 195th Tank Brigade were threatened by XXXXVIII Panzer Corps from the west and SS Panzer Corps from the north and east. On 14 March these Soviet units withdrew from the Mzha River defenses to the Osnovo–Bezlyudovka area. Fuel and ammunition supplies were low, and only a tenuous supply line existed southeastward toward the Northern Donets River. In the region east and southeast of Khar'kov the 17th NKVD Brigade, 19th Rifle Division, 25th Guards Rifle Division, and elements of the 350th and 152d Rifle Divisions defended, reinforced by the 58th Guards and 52d Guards Rifle Divisions. These forces faced SS Panzer Corps' SS "Das Reich" and SS "Leibstandarte Adolf Hitler" emerging from Khar'kov and SS "Totenkopf" operating in their rear. Further east two regiments of 48th Guards Rifle Division and the newly arrived 113th and 303d Rifle Divisions sought in vain to reestablish communications with encircled 3d Tank Army units. By the evening of 14–15 March Rybalko received permission from Golikov to abandon Khar'kov and withdraw his units to the Northern Donets River.[82] By this time that task would indeed be a difficult one.

A similar disaster befell 69th Army and 40th Army on 13 March. While Kazakov maneuvered his divisions to new defensive positions north of Khar'kov, and Moskalenko frantically sought to defend along the lower Vorskla Valley, on the morning of 13 March "Grossdeutschland" Division plunged northward against the junction of 40th and 69th Armies (see Map 52). By 1100 lead elements of "Grossdeutschland" turned northeast, traveled up the Vorskla Valley, and secured Golovchino and Borisovka.[83] Moskalenko's 100th and 309th Rifle Divisions, supported by 5th Guards Tank Corps, tried in vain to halt the advance and then withdrew to positions north of Graivoron. By late on 13 March Moskalenko committed

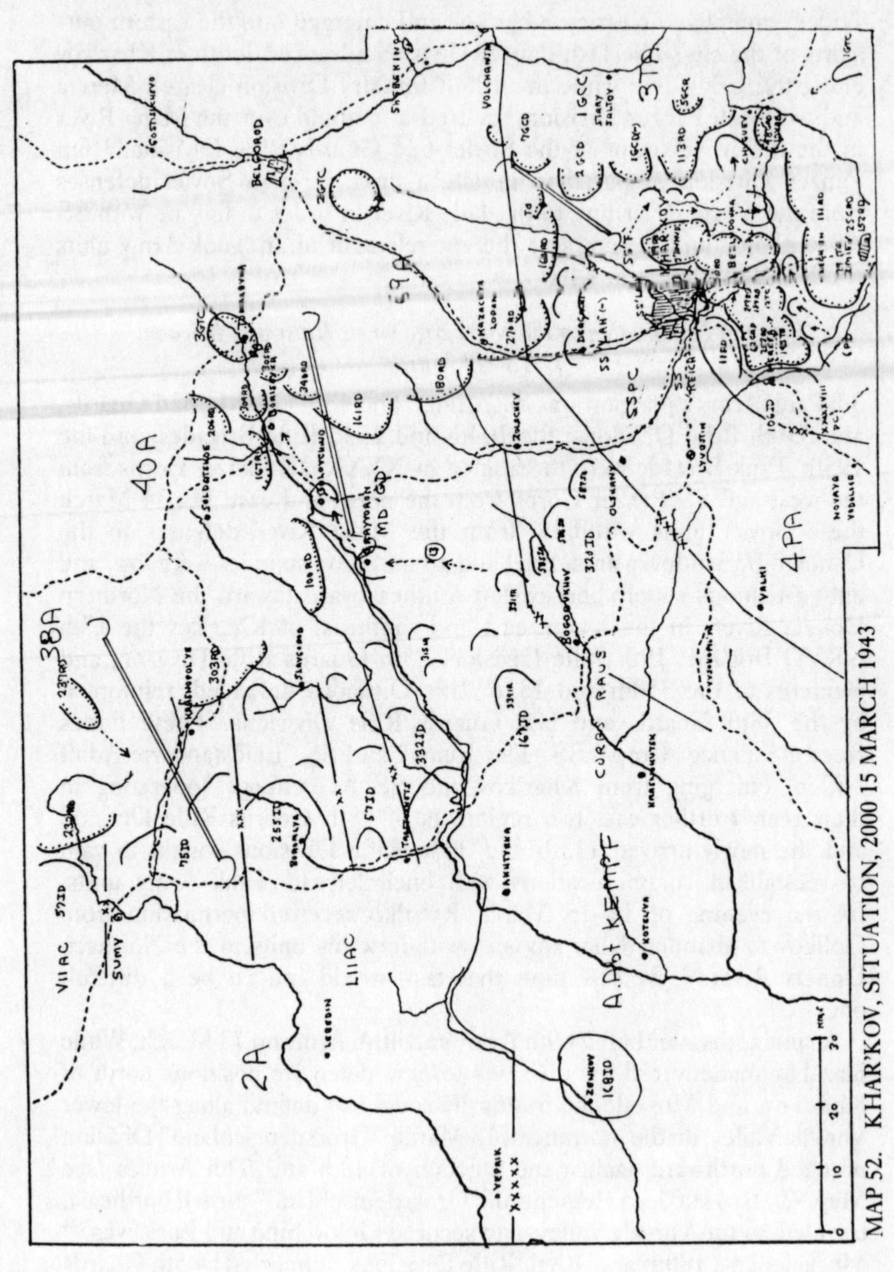

MAP 52. KHAR'KOV, SITUATION, 2000 15 MARCH 1943

3d Guards Tank Corps (released by *front*) to action in a running fight to defend Borisovka and Tomarovka.[84]

The attack of "Grossdeutschland" Division split the bulk of 40th Army from 69th Army. The latter now had to concern itself with a German advance from Khar'kov as well as an attack from the west. Kazakov's forces (161st, 180th, 320th, and 160th Rifle Divisions) occupied defenses from Udy through Kazach'ya Lopan to Ternovaya and were reinforced by the newly arrived 2d Guards Tank Corps whose full complement of 175 tanks were slowly arriving.[85] Kazakov's left flank units tied in with the 7th Guards Cavalry Division of 1st Guards Cavalry Corps, which the *STAVKA* had just committed east of Khar'kov to cover the withdrawal of 3d Tank Army from the city. Moskalenko's forces were not only cut off from 69th Army, they were also split in two by "Grossdeutschland's" advance. The 340th, 305th, and 309th Rifle Divisions withdrew up the Vorskla River and, along with 3d Guards Tank Corps, resisted "Grossdeutschland" Division's advanced units from south of Borisovka to Tomarovka. The 100th Rifle Division and portions of 5th Guards Tank Corps defended in positions north of Graivoron and Borisovka, simultaneously opposing the advance of German forces from the west and southwest. By 15 March the divisions of German Army Corps Raus (320th and 167th) cleaned up the area bypassed by Panzer Grenadier Division "Grossdeutschland." Meanwhile, German 2d Army divisions (75th, 255th, 57th, and 332d) steadily pivoted northeast of Sumy to a line running from south of Krasnopol'ye through Slavgorod to Bol'shaya Pisarevka.[86]

The German 2d Army's advance applied pressure to the junction of Soviet 38th Army and 40th Army and forced Golikov to adjust 38th Army's boundary southward to Krasnopol'ye and to dispatch additional divisions (released by *STAVKA* to the *front*) to reinforce the 100th Rifle Division on 40th Army's right flank. By 15 March 38th Army had shifted the 232d and 237th Rifle Divisions into the Krasnopol'ye area and dispatched the 167th and 206th Rifle Divisions to restore the defenses on Moskalenko's left flank.[87] These new divisions joined the fight against the north flank of "Grossdeutschland" Division in the Borisovka area.

On 15 March German 4th Panzer Army moved to crush resistance in the Khar'kov area. 6th Panzer Division lunged from its bridgehead across the Mzha River, south of Merefa, and cut directly across to the Udy River south of Bezlyudovka while a *kampfgruppe* of SS Panzer Division "Das Reich" headed down the Khar'kov–Chuguyev road and turned south to cross the Udy River near Vvedenka. SS "Totenkopf" tightened its grip on the highway from Rogan to Chuguyev. The following day 6th Panzer linked up with SS "Das Reich" while another *kampfgruppe* headed north along the Zmiyev–Khar'kov road and linked up with 11th Panzer Division units which advanced on Bezlyudovka from positions south of Khar'kov.

The same day SS "Das Reich" advanced eastward out of Khar'kov and drove Soviet forces out of the factory complex east of the city and toward the German blocking forces of SS Panzer Division "Totenkopf" and SS Panzer Division "Das Reich."[88] These Soviet forces, comprising the 19th Rifle Division, 86th and 179th Tank Brigades, and one battalion of the 17th NKVD Rifle Brigade under the supervision of General E. E. Belov, relinquished their grip on the tractor factory and conducted a fighting withdrawal northeast. By the afternoon of 16 March, after heavy fighting, these forces rejoined Soviet main forces (1st Guards Cavalry Corps) northeast of Khar'kov.

The combined thrusts of 6th, 11th, and SS Panzer Division "Das Reich" chopped up Soviet defenders southeast of Khar'kov (see Map 53). The 25th Guards and 62d Guards Rifle Divisions and the Czechoslovak Battalion withdrew to the Northern Donets River north of Zmiyev where the 25th Guards Rifle Division established a bridgehead west of the river. Pressed by the German 106th Infantry Division, the division finally relinquished its hold on the river's west bank on 22 March.[89] The 48th Guards Rifle Division, 253d Rifle Brigade, and 195th Tank Brigade with remnants of 12th Tank Corps and other fractured divisions, under the pressure of the 6th and 11th Panzer Divisions, withdrew to the southeast to join Soviet forces at Zmiyev or eastward over the Udy River. While many troops perished trying to break out of the SS Panzer Corps' cordon east of Khar'kov, some made it through gaps between SS "Das Reich" and 6th Panzer Division and finally rejoined the 113th Rifle Division, which was fighting advanced elements of SS "Totenkopf" near Chuguyev.

Although 3d Tank Army's position was hopeless, Golikov undertook some measures in order to hold on to positions east of the Northern Donets River and, if possible, relieve the encircled forces. His paucity of reserves forced him to seek assistance from the *STAVKA* which immediately began transferring relatively intact units from the Southwestern Front to Voronezh Front control. In addition, 6th Army moved new divisions into its new army sector south of the Udy River. These reinforcements began arriving east and southeast of Khar'kov on 10 March. Among these were the 152d, 244th, and 58th Guards Rifle Divisions which Vatutin used to reinforce 6th Army southeast of Khar'kov. Vatutin also committed the 113th Rifle Division to support 3d Tank Army units in the Chuguyev area and reinforced it on 13 March with the bulk of 1st Guards Cavalry Corps. 1st Guards Cavalry Corps, with two understrength cavalry divisions (7th Guards Cavalry and 2d Guards Cavalry), manned defensive positions along the Rogan River on 13 March and began delaying operations along with the 113th Rifle Division against elements of SS "Das Reich" and SS "Totenkopf." By

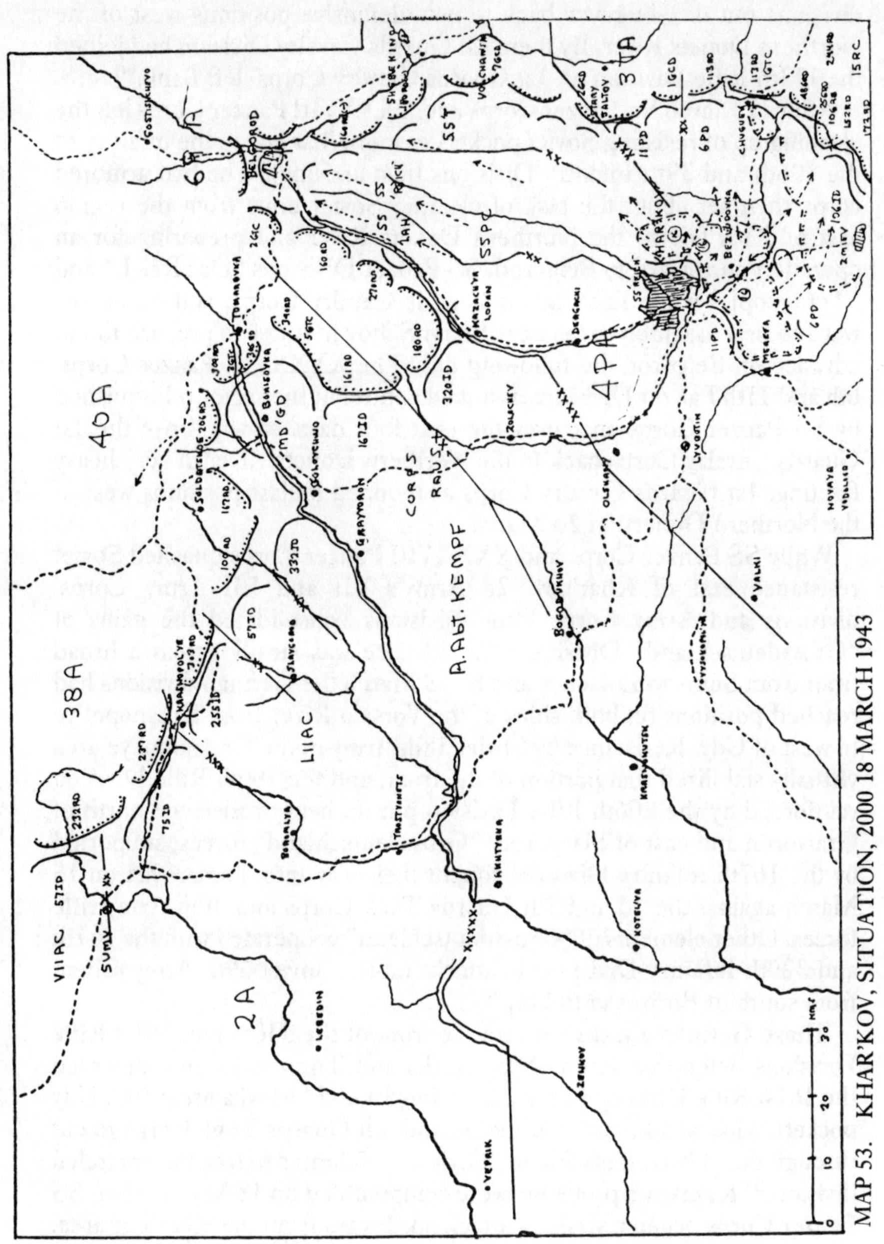

MAP 53. KHAR'KOV, SITUATION, 2000 18 MARCH 1943

16 March SS "Totenkopf" had pushed 1st Guards Cavalry Corps' two divisions out of Chuguyev back to new defensive positions west of the Northern Donets River. By then, 1st Guards Cavalry Division had joined the 113th Rifle Division on 1st Guards Cavalry Corps' left flank.[90]

After 17 March SS Panzer Corps and XXXXVIII Panzer Corps left the cleaning up of resisting Soviet pockets east of Khar'kov to the infantry of the 106th and 39th Infantry Divisions (just arriving). The two armored corps then set about the task of clearing Soviet units from the region east of Khar'kov to the Northern Donets River and preparing for an operation northward to Belgorod. SS Panzer Divisions "Das Reich" and "Totenkopf," while fighting 1st Guards Cavalry Corps, shifted northward to new assembly areas near Staryi Saltov in order to prepare for an advance on Belgorod the following day. The XXXXVIII Panzer Corps' 6th and 11th Panzer Divisions assumed control of the sector relinquished by SS Panzer Corps and, over the next four days, slowly drove the 1st Guards Cavalry Corps back to the Northern Donets River in very heavy fighting. 1st Guards Cavalry Corps abandoned its last positions west of the Northern Donets on 26 March.

While SS Panzer Corps and XXXXVIII Panzer Corps quashed Soviet resistance east of Khar'kov, 2d Army's VII and LII Army Corps' divisions and Army Corps Raus' divisions consolidated the gains of "Grossdeutschland" Division. The advance was steady across a broad front from Sumy to Zolochev and by 18 March the German divisions had reached positions on both sides of the Vorskla River from Krasnopol'ye to west of Udy. Resistance by Soviet 38th Army in the Krasnopol'ye area virtually stabilized that portion of the front, and the 100th Rifle Division reinforced by the 206th Rifle Division put up heavy resistance north of Graivoron and east of Slavgorod. "Grossdeutschland" forces, supported by the 167th Infantry Division, fought their way into Tomarovka on 15 March against the 3d and 5th Guards Tank Corps and 40th Army rifle forces. Other elements of "Grossdeutschland" cooperated with the 167th and 320th Infantry Divisions in attacks on the Soviet 69th Army salient from south of Borisovka to Udy.[91]

These German attacks cut into the front of the 340th and 161st Rifle Divisions defending south of Borisovka and Tomarovka and encircled the 161st Rifle Division in the Shchetinovka and Orlovka areas (the Udy pocket). Moskalenko ordered the 3d and 5th Guards Tank Corps to cut through the "Grossdeutschland" Division's columns to free the encircled division.[92] Kazakov's problems were compounded on 18 March when SS Panzer Corps began a slashing attack northward from the Khar'kov area. The attack commenced at 0400 with SS "Leibstandarte Adolf Hitler," SS "Das Reich," and SS "Totenkopf" advancing side-by-side from west to east between the Belgorod–Khar'kov rail line and the Northern Donets

River. The advance crushed Kazakov's weakened 270th and 160th Rifle Divisions, brushed aside the 2d Guards Tank Corps, and by 1900 SS Panzer Corps occupied Belgorod. SS Panzer Division "Leibstandarte Adolf Hitler" established blocking positions west of the rail line south of Belgorod facing the Udy pocket which consisted of 69th Army and 40th Army divisions. SS "Totenkopf" slowly cleared the western banks of the Northern Donets River south of Khar'kov, a process finally completed by 23 March.[93]

Caught between Corps Raus and SS Panzer Corps, Soviet forces in the Udy pocket fought for survival. Assisted by 3d and 5th Guards Tank Corps, on the night of 18–19 March the 161st Rifle Division fought its way west and then north and finally reached the Yakhontov area northwest of Belgorod on the morning of 19 March.[94] Other 69th Army units followed, while a few fought their way through the rear of SS Panzer Corps to Soviet bridgeheads across the Northern Donets River north of Shebekino. Although many of the army's personnel survived, it left virtually all of its heavier equipment behind. Those units who escaped north were immediately subordinated to 40th Army command.

From 19 to 23 March "Grossdeutschland" Division and SS Panzer Corps consolidated their hold on the Belgorod–Tomarovka area while German infantry moved up and cleaned out the remaining pockets of Soviet resistance (see Map 54). "Grossdeutschland" Division units fanned out around Tomarovka while SS Panzer Division "Leibstandarte Adolf Hitler" established contact with "Grossdeutschland" Division west of Belgorod. By 22 March Corps Raus' 167th and 320th Infantry Divisions moved north of Tomarovka and Belgorod and occupied defensive positions against stiffening Soviet resistance. Further west the 255th, 57th, and 332d Infantry Divisions pushed the Soviet 206th, 100th, and 167th Rifle Divisions back north toward the rail line from Sumy to Belgorod. The same day "Grossdeutschland" Division relocated to the rear to get a well earned rest.

After 21 March the *STAVKA* poured reinforcements into the Belgorod–Khar'kov area to bolster the seriously weakened 40th, 69th, and 3d Tank Armies. Lieutenant General I.M. Chistyakov's 21st Army began arriving on 22 March and deployed north and west of Khar'kov. The same day Lieutenant General M.S. Shumilov's 64th Army arrived to take over 69th Army's sector southwest of Belgorod and within days Lieutenant General M.E. Katukov's 1st Tank Army began arriving north of Belgorod.[95] Moreover, a stream of reinforcements changed the face of 3d Tank Army. Reflecting the German damage done to that army, the Soviets shortly renamed it the 57th Army.[96] By 23 March active operations in the Belgorod–Khar'kov area had ended just as the spring thaw set in.

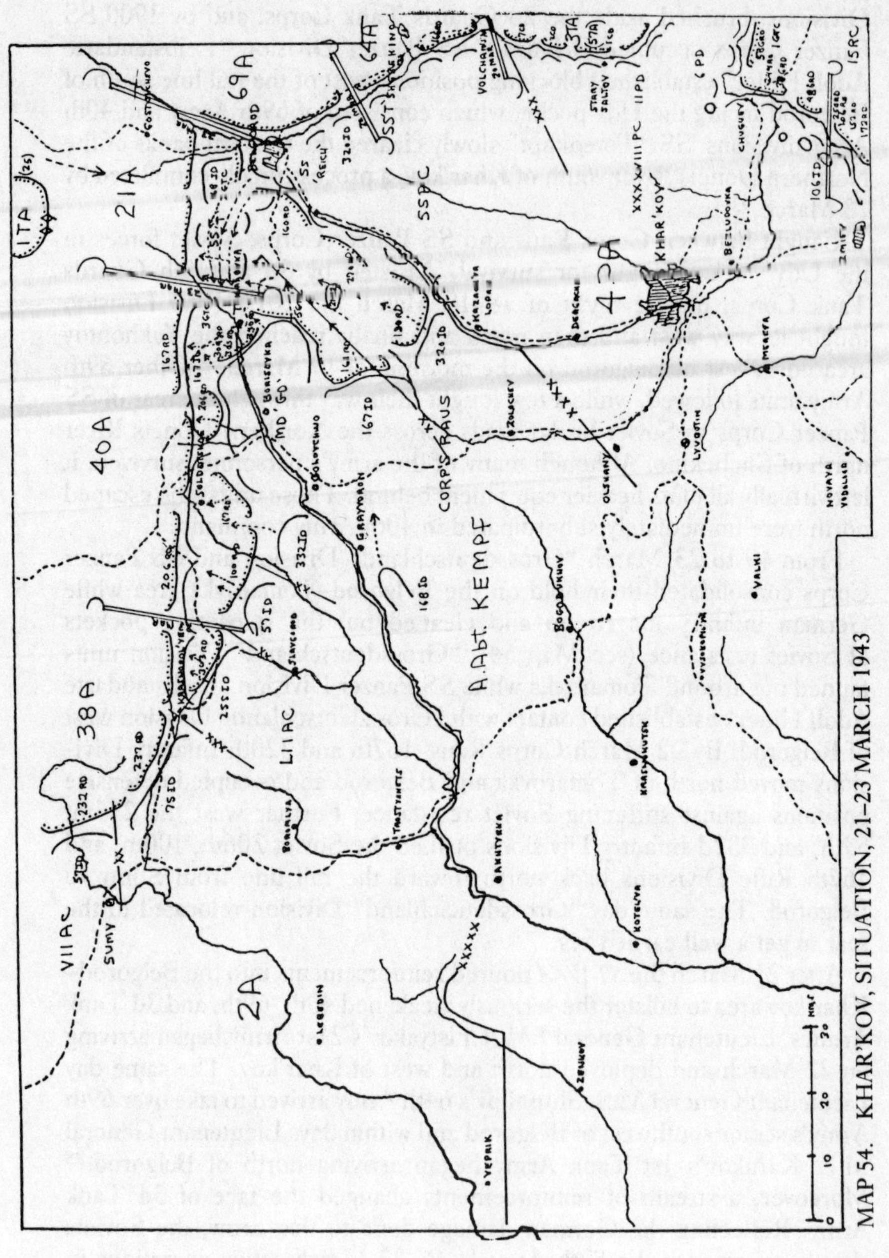

MAP 54. KHAR'KOV, SITUATION, 21–23 MARCH 1943

Conclusions

The Khar'kov–Kursk Operation, in reality the northern wing of the general Soviet winter offensive of February 1943, ended in an operational disaster for the Voronezh Front. In broad outline Soviet conduct of the operation suffered from the same faults as did the Southwestern Front's conduct of the Donbas operation. Over-optimism colored the conduct of the operation. Occurring as it did after the successful Ostrogozhsk–Rossosh' and Voronezh–Kastornoye operations which destroyed Hungarian 2d Army and damaged German 2d Army, the Voronezh Front began the operation with a significant superiority of forces. However, *front* forces were also tired and worn down, and a significant portion were unable to participate in the initial offensive because they were still involved in combat with encircled enemy units.

The Khar'kov operation began with virtually no operational pause and with the absence of any systematic regrouping or thorough resupply of forces. Moreover, supply bases remained 250–300 kilometers to the rear, making logistical support throughout the operation tenuous at best. *Front* mobile units were well below full strength (3d Tank Army – 165 tanks) and initially they did not spearhead the offensive. The Voronezh Front attacked in single echelon without significant *front* reserves, a condition which its initial superiority permitted, but which ultimately denied the *front* the flexibility to deal effectively with German counterattacks. Advancing armies also kept only small reserves. The Soviets had committed most of these reserves (except 40th Army) before the *front* reached the Northern Donets River.

Although German opposition was initially weak, the resistance of the German 168th Infantry Division delayed 40th Army operations as did the Panzer Grenadier Division "Grossdeutschland's" defense at Veliko–Mikhailovka. More important, SS Panzer Division "Reich's" active defense in the Prikolotnoye and Veliki Burluk area seriously disrupted the timing of the 3d Tank Army's advance. Only the decisive movement of 40th Army on Belgorod and 3d Tank Army's southerly advance to the Northern Donets River forced the withdrawal of German forces to the Northern Donets River line on 9 February. At this point the Voronezh Front's offensive was already four days behind schedule. This delay permitted SS Panzer Division "Leibstandarte Adolf Hitler" to erect strong defenses along the river from Staryi Saltov to Zmiyev. That fact, plus 3d Tank Army's hesitancy in mounting an assault across the river and its tardy attacks once the SS forces had withdrawn to the city defenses, resulted in a further Soviet delay in taking Khar'kov. Again, only 40th Army's rapid advance from Belgorod to Khar'kov made possible the ultimate Soviet seizure of Khar'kov, but seven days behind schedule.

3d Tank Army did attempt an operation to envelop Khar'kov by using 6th Guards Cavalry Corps. But that force, even though it neared its objective, was too weak to achieve success against German armor. Subsequently, 3d Tank Army undertook a direct frontal attack on the city which further reduced its armored strength.

The converging attacks on the city by 40th, 69th, and 3d Tank Armies generated requisite forces to seize it but in so doing created new problems. The disengagement of units from Khar'kov and the redeployment of armies on their proper axes took several precious days at a time when German counterstrikes were about to begin further south. After the fall of Khar'kov the *STAVKA* assigned the Voronezh Front overly ambitious missions which resulted in a dispersion of its forces and the dissipation of its strength. The converging Soviet attack on Khar'kov had left a gap of up to 80 kilometers between 40th Army and 38th Army operating in the Kursk area. By 21 February the Soviets closed this gap but at a cost of spreading *front* forces in a wide, thin fan west of Khar'kov. 40th Army advanced on a front of up to 80 kilometers; 69th Army, 30 kilometers; and 3d Tank Army, one of 60 kilometers. Expanding army objectives required a continuous widening of the front as the forces advanced.

When a crisis erupted further south the *STAVKA* gave the Voronezh Front a new mission without altering its old mission. On 23 February both 3d Tank Army and 69th Army shifted their axes of advance south to relieve German pressure on 6th Army of the Southwestern Front. Consequently, 40th Army's sector expanded to over 100 kilometers, and its offensive missions expanded as well. The 28 February decision to mass 3d Tank Army for an attack southward similarly expanded 69th Army's frontage, this at a time when German reserves were deploying forward against the Soviets in both armies' sectors.

The overall dispersal of *front* forces virtually negated the possibility of the *front* providing real assistance to its southern neighbor. The concentration of 3d Tank Army for an attack south came at a time when the army's presence was critical to the viability of the Voronezh Front. Its weakness in armor (50 tanks) and the already hopeless situation in 6th Army's sector spelled doom for 3d Tank Army in the form of immediate encirclement and destruction after it ripped itself away from other Voronezh Front forces and began its solitary advance into the teeth of SS Panzer Corps.

The destruction of 3d Tank Army and the absence of *front* reserves led to the collapse of the Voronezh Front's southern flank and the opening of a gap between 69th Army and the remnants of 3d Tank Army. The encirclement of Khar'kov resulted. In a rare instance of cavalry forces engaging armored units, 1st Guards Cavalry Corps conducted a three-day delay operation from east of Khar'kov back to the Northern Donets River. The remainder of the Voronezh Front did not regain its coherence until major reinforcements arrived. The commitment of 2d Guards Tank Corps and 3d Guards Tank Corps plus several reserve divisions sent by the *STAVKA* (206th, 167th, 113th) only slowed the German advance. The arrival of the 21st and 64th Armies and the imminent arrival of 1st Tank Army, as well as the onset of the thaw, finally brought operations to a halt.

The German command conducted a successful delay early in the operation and capped that delay with a successful counterattack, which was an expanded extension of Manstein's earlier Donbas counterstroke. Although the 168th Infantry Division and Panzer Grenadier Division "Grossdeutschland" conducted a fighting withdrawal in good order, it was SS Panzer Division "Reich" that disrupted Soviet hopes for a rapid advance. SS Panzer Division "Reich" seriously disrupted 3d Tank Army's advance, and SS Panzer Division "Leibstandarte Adolf Hitler" put up strong resistance at the Northern Donets River which, in part, made possible the extraction of the encircled 298th and 320th Infantry Divisions. SS Panzer Corps' controversial defense of Khar'kov produced the entanglement of Soviet forces at Khar'kov that took three days to sort out. This delay bought time for reinforcing divisions to contain the Voronezh Front's expanding offensive.

The stubborn German defense south of Valki and Merefa provided the western anchor for Manstein's offensive against Soviet forces advancing toward Zaporozh'ye and forced the *STAVKA* to decide to launch a desperate attack south by 3d Tank Army.

After the encirclement and liquidation of 3d Tank Army, the German advance north bore strong resemblance to Manstein's earlier drive. The shock group of Panzer Grenadier Division "Grossdeutschland," SS Panzer Corps, and XXXXVIII Panzer Corps, advancing north in tandem, irrevocably split apart Soviet 69th Army and 3d Tank Army. "Grossdeutschland" division's thrust to Graivoron and Bogodukhov likewise split 40th Army from 69th Army. SS Panzer Corps capitalized further on the chaos to advance on Belgorod and to force elements of 69th and 40th Army to emulate 3d Tank Army forces in a fight to escape encirclement. However, in the course of these operations, SS Panzer Division "Das Reich" paid heavily for its direct assault on and through Khar'kov.

While German forces threw the Soviet Voronezh Front back to the Northern Donets River and retook Khar'kov and Belgorod, they did so at a heavy price in fatigue and losses. SS Panzer Corps alone lost almost 12,000 casualties, and other units participating in the arduous days of delay and defense suffered likewise.[97] By early March both sides felt the effect of months of battle. However, it was the Soviet *STAVKA* which had at its disposal the relatively fresh armies freed for operational use by the destruction of German 6th Army at Stalingrad. Two of these armies fresh from victory filled the gap in Soviet ranks by 23 March. The German command had no reinforcements of similar magnitude available. In any case, the thaw put an end to prospects for continued operations.

The German counteroffensive, audaciously orchestrated in the midst of a potentially disastrous situation, rolled the Soviets back 150–200 kilometers and dealt a sobering blow to Soviet planners' hopes. It also offered a glint of hope to German commanders who had weathered a series of serious defeats during the winter of 1942–1943 in which German armies had lost from 300–600 kilometers of conquered territory.

Ironically, that glint of hope gave birth to even greater hopes on the part of the German High Command for renewed success in the summer of 1943. Thus it contributed in a major way to decisions which would lead to a new German disaster of strategic proportions – at Kursk – against a more realistic Soviet foe educated in part by the experiences at Khar'kov and in the Donbas in the winter of 1943.

5

OPERATION "POLKOVODETS RUMYANTSEV": The Belgorod–Khar'kov Operation August 1943

Strategic and Operational Context

German Planning for Operation "Citadel"

After the three month wave of Soviet offensives during the winter of 1942–43 and the German counterstroke of February and March an operational lull set in on the Eastern Front, dictated in part by the general exhaustion of forces on both sides and also by the onset of the spring thaw.

During the lull both sides intensely studied strategic and operational realities and developed future plans. Planners inexorably focused on the ominous or inviting (depending on one's perspective) bulge in the front around the city of Kursk. German planners, who despaired of launching another broad front strategic offensive because of the past attrition to their forces, viewed the Kursk bulge as an inviting target for renewed offensive action in a limited sector. It seemed a perfect target for future envelopment into which the Soviets would logically move large forces which the Germans could then eliminate in a repetition of the surgical blitzkreig style attacks used so successfully earlier in the war.

German planners confronted three major questions: First, was such an operation feasible or advisable? There were some at the army level who advised against such an offensive and urged the High Command to adopt a defensive posture in order to invite Soviet attack and chew up Soviet strength in defensive struggles and counterstrokes. Others in the High Command, including Hitler, advocated a sharp, yet limited offensive to smash Soviet operational reserves, deprive the Red Army of the capability of launching fresh offensives during the summer, and perhaps restore either the strategic or operational initiative into German hands. Understandably, Hitler's views prevailed.

The second question involved assembling forces necessary to launch such an offensive. German forces were weaker than in 1941–42, and the Germans would have to concentrate the bulk of their armor and virtually all of their operational reserves for such an offensive to succeed. The German assault forces would have to be equipped with the best, most modern equipment Germany's industrial arsenal could produce, in sufficient quantities for the Germans to achieve local superiority in firepower and armor required to cut through Soviet defenses. Experience seemed to demonstrate that even with inferior numbers, advanced technology and superior German technical skills would prevail against Soviet defenses which traditionally had been inflexible and prone to collapse when confronted by a concerted assault.

The third question – when should the attack be launched – was a critical one. Obviously, it should occur before substantial Soviet regrouping and reinforcement of their forces. However, time was required to restore German units to peak fighting strength, to regroup them, and to reequip them with new generations of armor and assault guns.

Arguments ensued over all three questions. Whereas the first two were answered fairly quickly, the third took considerably longer to answer. The German High Command issued Operational Order No. 5 on 13 March which laid down operational guidelines for offensive operations in the summer of 1943.[1] Army Group South of Field Marshal Erich von Manstein was assigned the task of planning the operation under close High Command (Hitler's) supervision. Operational Order No. 6 of 15 April spelled out in more detail the objectives and timing of the projected operation against the Kursk salient, codenamed Operation "Citadel." In it Hitler wrote:

> I have decided to launch the "Citadel" offensive, the first offensive this year, as soon as weather permits. . . . This offensive is of decisive significance. It must end in a quick and decisive success. It must give us the initiative for this spring and summer. . . . The victory at Kursk must have the effect of a beacon seen around the world.[2]

Hitler set 3 May as the date of attack. Immediately, however, a long series of postponements began, primarily associated with the problem of force preparation. First, participating headquarters asked for delays to carry out necessary redeployments. Later, the fielding and issuing of new equipment became a primary rationale for delays as Hitler insisted that new tanks (Panthers and Tigers) and assault guns (Ferdinands) were essential for the attacks to succeed. Ultimately, over the objections of the Operations Staff, OKW, Hitler set the attack date at 5 July.

The final concept for the "Citadel" offensive envisioned a two-pronged assault on the Kursk bulge from north and south by massed armored forces equipped with the hastily fielded new weaponry. The objective was to smash the large Soviet concentration in the Kursk bulge, demolish Soviet operational reserves, and hence deprive the Soviets of much of their future offensive capability. Implied in the objectives was an attempt to restore the strategic initiative to the German Army and make whatever subsequent territorial advances that success in the operation would make feasible.

Soviet STAVKA Planning

While the German High Command slowly sketched out plans for the Kursk offensive, Soviet planners went through a similar period of debate.[3] Characteristic of his earlier attitude, Stalin was inclined to resume the Soviet offensive in the early summer and apply pressure on the Germans along a broad front. Even after the Soviets detected German offensive preparations, Stalin thought about conducting a preemptive Soviet attack. Others in Soviet planning circles counseled greater caution. They argued that such blind Soviet dedication to the offensive produced failure and frustration in the winters of 1941–42 and 1942–43. Zhukov, Vasilevsky, and others urged Stalin to prepare a strategic defensive operation to entice the Germans into assaulting a well-prepared defense and to wear down German operational reserves. Only then should the Soviets launch a new offensive. In essence, they argued that the Red Army should do what the Germans had done in the spring of 1942 when they had smashed a Soviet offensive at Khar'kov and then had embarked on a major offensive of their own.

Increasing amounts of intelligence concerning German intentions (which almost certainly included Ultra material) reinforced the views of those who counseled caution. Stalin finally agreed with their recommendations and ordered extensive defensive preparations to begin in the Kursk region. Characteristically, however, Stalin insisted that planned Soviet counteroffensives be an integral part of that defensive plan.

Stalin directed the Central and Voronezh Fronts to construct defenses in considerable depth throughout the Kursk bulge to cover the main German advance axes on Kursk from the north and south. Stalin created a third *front* (Steppe) and positioned it to the rear of the bulge to insure the coherence of the defense and to participate in the large-scale counteroffensives.

Stalin's plan for strategic defense involved two stages. First, the Soviets would meet and defeat the German offensive. Then the Western, Bryansk, and Central Fronts would attack the German salient around Orel (north of Kursk) and the Voronezh and Steppe Fronts would strike German forces in the Belgorod–Khar'kov (south of Kursk) salient. The *STAVKA* developed the general concept of both counteroffensives before the defensive phase. Detailed planning on the Orel counteroffensive occurred before the German attack, but planning for the Belgorod–Khar'kov operation occurred during the defensive phase.[4] Thus the form and timing of the Belgorod–Khar'kov operation depended on the outcome of the defensive phase.

The German Offensive at Kursk and its Consequences

As Soviet intelligence predicted, the German offensive began on 5 July. By 11 July the northern prong of the German offensive ground to a halt after heavy German losses. The following day the Soviet Bryansk and Western Fronts began their counterstroke against German forces in the Orel salient thus virtually ending the German thrust to Kursk from the north. (The Central Front joined the offensive soon after.)

The southern prong of the German offensive, consisting of 4th Panzer Army and Army Detachment Kempf, made comparatively better progress than the northern force although at a heavy cost in material and manpower losses. By 12 July SS Panzer Corps and XXXXVIII Panzer Corps had chewed their way through the first three Soviet defensive belts. However, that day the *STAVKA* committed 5th Guards Tank and 5th Guards Armies of the Steppe Front to large scale counterattacks, which culminated in the major tank battle of Prohkorovka and virtually ended German hopes for success. The German defeat at Kursk, and Hitler's concern for the deteriorating situation in Italy (U.S.–British landing in Sicily 10 July), compelled cancellation of German offensive plans. From 13 to 23 July German forces slowly withdrew to defensive positions north of Belgorod in close proximity to positions from which the Germans had begun their offensive.

While battle raged for Orel in the north, after 23 July a short operational pause occurred on the southern flank of the Kursk bulge. The Soviets used the pause to regroup their forces and plan for a resumption of the offensive toward Belgorod and Khar'kov. The Germans, expecting a more lengthy pause, redeployed large forces to other threatened sectors of the Eastern Front. II SS Panzer Corps, which Hitler earmarked for use in Italy, left the Belgorod area on 17 July. Its planned movement to Italy, however, was postponed because of a renewed Soviet offensive further south along the Mius River. Thus, while SS Panzer Division "Leibstandarte Adolf Hitler" actually entrained for Italy, the other divisions remained on the Eastern Front although not in the Belgorod area. On 1 August von Manstein indicated he expected Khar'kov would be the next Soviet target. However, he believed the Soviets would require several weeks to make major necessary force adjustments and to regroup after the Kursk battle. Thus, on 2 August von Manstein decided to wait for more definite signs of an impending offensive before pulling back to the original German defense line (the present position was several kilometers in advance of the German pre-"Citadel" front).[5]

Soviet planners did not grant von Manstein's wish for a longer operational pause. On 3 August 1943, just nine days after operations south of Kursk ground to a halt, the Soviets launched a new massive offensive on unsuspecting German forces in the Belgorod–Khar'kov area.

Opposing Forces

Soviet Force Structure Changes in 1943

The Soviets used the winter and spring of 1943 to reconstruct their forces in accordance with the refined operational concepts enunciated in 1942 orders and directives and incorporated into the 1942 Field Regulations. These regulations updated the 1941 regulations and included comprehensive judgements derived from analysis of the experiences of the first two years of war.* Thus, force structure changes evolved in tandem with the written regulations which in turn reflected the real experience of war. By mid 1943, marked changes were evident in all areas of the force structure.

The combined arms army increased in size and sophistication throughout the winter and spring of 1943. Intermediate corps headquarters appeared in late 1942; and, by the winter of 1942–1943 many armies had two such headquarters. This process reflected the growing experience of army commanders and their ability to command larger, more sophisticated units. By August 1943 most armies were organized into two or three rifle corps consisting of from seven to twelve rifle divisions. Combat support within armies increased. The 10 April 1943 TOE specified each army would have four artillery regiments for fire support (one 152 gun regiment, one 76mm anti-tank regiment, one 37mm anti-aircraft regiment, and one 122mm mortar regiment). An integral signal regiment, a line communications battalion, a telegraph company, and an aviation communications troop within the army provided more extensive and reliable army communications. Overall army manpower strength rose from about 90,000 to up to 130,000 men.[6]

The *STAVKA* continued the practice of attaching supporting units to armies depending on the mission of the army, the nature of the enemy, and the terrain on which it would operate. By the summer of 1943 the average army operation on a main attack direction was supported

*The Soviets mandated the collection and analysis of war experiences in a specific General Staff Directive of 9 November 1942.

by:

- 1–2 artillery penetration divisions
- 3 artillery regiments
- 3 anti-tank regiments
- 3–4 tank or self-propelled gun-brigades (for infantry support)
- 10 separate tank or self-propelled gun regiments (for infantry support)
- 2 anti-aircraft artillery divisions
- 1–2 tank or mechanized corps (army mobile group)

These reinforcements increased the fire power of army artillery from up to 1,250 guns and mortars to up to 2,700 guns and mortars and the armor strength of armies from 250–450 tanks to 300–600 tanks per army. By summer most attacking armies had an operational maneuver (exploitation) force consisting of one, and in some cases two, tank or mechanized corps.

The Soviet rifle corps also became more sophisticated. These tactical headquarters increased in number from thirty-four on 1 January 1943 to 150 by 1 December 1943.[7] The combat composition of the rifle corps stabilized at an average strength of three rifle divisions. Most corps had their own signal and sapper battalions; and, by late 1943, some had artillery regiments as well.

The Soviet rifle division changed little from December 1942 to July of 1943. The division's 9,380 men were formed in three rifle regiments, each with an artillery battery of four 76mm guns and an anti-tank battery of twelve 45mm guns. (Most rifle divisions, however, until war's end were understrength in personnel, 20–30 percent in 1943 and up to 60 percent by 1945.) The division artillery regiment numbered twelve 122mm guns and twenty 76mm guns, while the divisional anti-tank battalion had twelve 45mm anti-tank guns. A full strength division totalled forty-four guns, 160 mortars, and forty-eight anti-tank guns and was more capable of establishing a credible anti-tank defense as the Kursk experience indicated.[8] While rifle divisions did not change, the number of guards rifle divisions with their higher strength of 10,670 men and forty-eight guns increased. Moreover, most rifle brigades were upgraded to the status of full rifle divisions.

Soviet tank forces were significantly improved during the spring of 1943. Tank and mechanized corps increased in strength, fire power, and combat support, and could better sustain offensive operations. Tank corps' strength increased from 7,800 to 10,977 men and from 168 (seventy T-70 and ninety-eight T-34) to 209 tanks (theoretically all T-34). The tank brigades (three) of the tank corps contained three battalions of sixty-five tanks, rather than the previous two battalions of fifty-three tanks. Tank corps firepower improved with the addition of a mortar regiment (January 1943), an anti-aircraft regiment (March 1943), a 76mm self-propelled artillery regiment (January 1943), a 45mm anti-tank artillery regiment (April 1943), and an 85mm anti-tank battalion (April 1943), increasing artillery strength from ninety-eight guns/mortars to 160 guns/mortars and twenty-one self-propelled SU-76 guns.[9] Improved corps logistical support also improved the sustainability of the formation as a whole. The mechanized corps similarly increased its strength to 15,018 men and 204 tanks.[10]

The most significant armored development in 1943 was the creation of a TOE tank army to replace the *ad hoc* tank armies which operated with mixed success from June 1942 to March 1943. The new tank army, created by GKO Order No. 2791 of 28 January 1943, in theory consisted of two tank corps, one mechanized corps, and supporting units (see table below) with a strength of 46,000–48,000 men, up to 800 tanks, and 500–600 guns/mortars.[11]

1943 SOVIET TANK ARMY

2	tank corps
1	mechanized corps
1	motorcycle regiment
1	anti-aircraft regiment
1	anti-tank regiment
1	howitzer artillery regiment
1	guards mortar regiment (multiple rocket launchers)
1	signal regiment
1	aviation communications regiment
1	engineer battalion
1	transport regiment
2	repair, reconstruction battalions
1	separate tank brigade or regiment

In April 1943 the tank army expanded with the addition of a second anti-tank regiment, two mortar regiments, a self-propelled artillery regiment, and an anti-aircraft regiment. By the summer of 1943 five such tank armies existed. Operating as the mobile group of the *front* commander, they promised to improve the Soviet capability for conducting and sustaining offensive operations into the operational depth.

While creating armored forces to act as mobile groups of armies and *fronts*, the Soviets also increased the number of tanks available for infantry support. Separate tank brigades which had performed that function since 1942 increased in number and strength. In addition, the Soviets formed new separate tank regiments to supplement those formed in the fall of 1942 for infantry support (74 existed by December 1942). The January 1943 separate tank regiment consisted of 3 tank companies totalling 39 tanks (32 T-34, 7 T-70). By June the Soviets had also formed tank penetration regiments of 21 KV heavy tanks and engineer tank regiments of 32 T-34 tanks and 18 PT-3 engineer vehicles.[12]

While the basic Soviet force structure matured in 1943, the Soviets also created a host of new supporting units for attachment to every level of command from *front* to rifle division.

The Soviets created new artillery units to complement the three and four-brigade artillery divisions of 1942 (11 of these divisions existed in December 1942, each with 168 guns and 80 mortars). In April 1943 the Soviets created artillery penetration divisions (6 brigades of 356 guns/mortars) and guards mortar divisions which they then combined into artillery penetration corps (2 artillery penetration divisions and 1 guards mortar division) with a strength of 712 guns/mortars and 864 multiple rocket launcher tubes. By June 1943 *STAVKA* artillery consisted of 5 artillery penetration corps; 11 artillery penetration divisions; 10 four-brigade artillery divisions; 4 three-brigade artillery divisions; 47 separate artillery, anti-tank, mortar, and multiple rocket launcher brigades; and 75 separate artillery, anti-aircraft, and multiple rocket launcher battalions.[13]

Anti-tank artillery went through a similar storm of development. To supplement the 240 "tank destroyer" regiments (a name adopted in July 1942 for anti-tank units) of November 1942, in April 1943 the Soviets created tank destroyer artillery brigades each numbering 1,850 men and from 60 to 72 anti-tank guns. These new units (20 existed by June 1943) were more balanced combined arms entities with 3 tank destroyer regiments (5 batteries each), a machine gun platoon for protection, a reconnaissance battalion, topographical engineer and signal platoons, and a transport element.[14] Similar expansion occurred in anti-aircraft artillery.

Soviet Forces

Within the context of these overall changes to force structure and military doctrine, in late July the Soviets began assembling forces to conduct the Belgorod–Khar'kov counteroffensive. The Voronezh Front had conducted the defensive operation against German forces south of Kursk. Its 38th, 40th, 6th Guards, and 7th Guards Armies and 1st Tank Army absorbed the German blow and, reinforced by the Steppe Front, drove the Germans back toward Belgorod. During the planning phase for the new operation Soviet forces regrouped. During regrouping the Steppe Front took control of the Voronezh Front's 69th and 7th Guards Armies and relinquished the 27th Army and the 2d and 10th Tank Corps to Voronezh Front control.

After regrouping, General N.F. Vatutin's Voronezh Front consisted of 38th, 40th, 27th, 5th Guards, and 6th Guards Armies deployed from the

Suzhda area northwest of Sumy to Gostishchevo, north of Belgorod, and 1st and 5th Guards Tank Armies deployed south of Oboyan as the *front* mobile groups (see Appendix 4, Order of Battle). In addition, Vatutin had the 2d, 10th, 4th Guards, and 5th Guards Tank Corps which he assigned to 40th, 27th, and 6th Guards Armies to serve as army mobile groups. The Voronezh Front's five combined arms armies consisted of ten rifle corps, twenty-eight rifle divisions, and four separate tank brigades. The *STAVKA* reinforced the Voronezh Front with significant supporting assets including one artillery penetration corps, five anti-aircraft artillery divisions, and a variety of separate artillery, tank destroyer, self-propelled artillery, mortar and engineer brigades and regiments. The 2d Air Army provided the *front* its air support. The Voronezh Front totalled 693,554 men, of which 458,167 were in the combat armies. It contained 1,859 tanks, 113 self-propelled guns, 8,728 guns/mortars, and 701 multiple rocket launchers. In spite of its heavy firepower, the *front's* armies were understrength in personnel due to losses which they had incurred during the Kursk defensive battles. Armies ranged from 10–30 percent understrength, and rifle divisions mustered an average strength of 7,180 personnel (75 percent).[15]

General I.S. Konev's Steppe Front contained the 53d, 69th, and 7th Guards Armies deployed from Gostishchevo south along the east bank of the Northern Donets River to Volchansk. The 1st Mechanized Corps and

10. Chief of Staff Lieutenant General M.V. Zakharov (left) and Steppe Front commander Colonel General I.S. Konev (right), August 1943.

several tank brigades provided support for Konev's armies. Konev's three combined arms armies contained five rifle corps, twenty-two rifle divisions, and three separate tank brigades. The *STAVKA* reinforced Konev's forces with one artillery division, three anti-aircraft artillery divisions, and other brigades and regiments. The 5th Air Army provided the Steppe Front with air support. The Steppe Front numbered 287,034 men, of which 198,034 were in the combat armies. These forces were supported by 454 tanks, 13 self-propelled guns, 4,881 guns and mortars, and 66 multiple rocket launchers. Personnel strength within the Steppe Front's armies was lower than those of the Voronezh Front. For example, Lt. General M.S. Shumilov's 7th Guards Army, by virtue of its defensive combat at Kursk, was 30,000 men below TO&E strength (at 65 percent). Individual rifle divisions averaged 6,070 men or 65 percent of full TOE strength.[16] This severely impeded the sustainability of the Steppe Front's infantry operations.

The *STAVKA* also planned to use the Southwestern Front's 57th Army in the late stages of the Belgorod–Khar'kov operation. Lt. General N.A. Gagen's army (the descendant of old 3d Tank Army), which numbered 60,000 men and 100 tanks, was deployed from Volchansk southward along the Northern Donets River to just south of Chuguyev. In addition, the *STAVKA* held in reserve Lt. General G.I. Kulik's 4th Guards Army and Lt. General P.P. Korzun's 47th Army to support the Voronezh Front should the need arise. Each army contained 75,000–80,000 men and one tank corps. Thus, the Soviet strike force assembled north and east of Belgorod–Khar'kov, although weakened by three weeks of heavy combat and forced to regroup and plan hastily for the new operation, was formidable. Moreover, German forces opposing them were also weakened and did not expect a major Soviet offensive so soon after the bitter combat at Kursk.

German Forces

German forces in the Belgorod–Khar'kov area consisted of 4th Panzer Army and Army Detachment Kempf. Colonel General Hermann Hoth's 4th Panzer Army, headquartered at Bogodukhov, was made up of two army corps and one panzer corps deployed from south of Rylsk (opposite Suzhda) to north of Belgorod.[17] VII Army Corps with three infantry divisions and a *kampfgruppe* formed from the 323d Infantry Division covered the front from Suzhda to west of Krasnopol'ye.* The XXXXVIII Panzer Corps, with one and one-half panzer divisions and one and one-third infantry divisions, defended from Krasnopol'ye to south of Soldatskoye. The LII Army Corps, consisting of two and one-half

*Transferred to 4th Panzer Army from 2d Army on 4 August.

OPERATION "POLKOVODETS RUMYANTSEV"

CORRELATION OF FORCES
BELGOROD–KHAR'KOV OPERATION – 7 AUGUST 1943

Soviet			*German*	
Voronezh Front				
38th Army	62,000	men	4th Panzer Army	120,000 men
40th Army	50,000	men		150 tanks (est)
	340	tanks		
27th Army	82,000	men	A. Abt. Kempf	80,000 men
	220	tanks		60 tanks (est)
6th Guards Army	85,000	men		
	180	tanks		
5th Guards Army	85,000	men	Initial reinforce-	
	70	tanks	ments: Panzer	
1st Tank Army	37,000	men	Grenadier Division	15,000 men
	542	tanks	"Grossdeutschland"	100 tanks
5th Guards Tank Army	37,000	men		
	503	tanks		
Front total strength	458,000	men	Subsequent reinforcements:	
	1,859	tanks	1 SS Panzer Grenadier Division	50,000 men
Steppe Front			2 SS Panzer	
53d Army	77,000	men	Divisions	250 tanks
	291	tanks	1 Panzer Division	
69th Army	60,000	men		
	70	tanks		
7th Guards Army	61,000	men		
	80	tanks		
Front total strength	198,000	men		
	454	tanks		
Southwestern Front				
57th Army	60,000	men		
	109	tanks		
Reserve				
4th Guards Army	80,000	men		
	200	tanks		
47th Army	75,000	men		
	210	tanks		
Total	900,000	men*	3:1	300,000* men
	2,832	tanks	5:1	560 tanks

*with logistical units and reserves

panzer divisions and two and two-thirds infantry divisions, defended in the remainder of the army sector from south of Soldatskoye to north of Belgorod. Thus, 4th Panzer Army controlled eight infantry divisions and four panzer divisions. After the heavy Kursk fighting all of the units were at reduced strength. Personnel strength of 4th Panzer Army included 120,000–130,000 men in combat units and an initial armored strength of approximately 220–260 serviceable tanks and assault guns. General Hoth deployed his infantry divisions forward with the bulk of his panzer divisions (6th, 7th, 19th, and half of the 11th) located to the rear.

General Werner Kempf's Army Detachment Kempf, headquartered west of Khar'kov, consisted of two army corps defending a sector from north of Belgorod southward along the Northern Donets River to south of Zmiyev.[18] The XI Army Corps with four infantry divisions covered the northern approaches to Khar'kov, held the Mikhailovka bridgehead across the Northern Donets River east of Khar'kov, and defended south along the river to north of Volchansk. The XXXXII Army Corps, with three infantry divisions, defended along the Northern Donets River south to the army boundary with 1st Panzer Army on Army Detachment Kempf's right flank. Army Detachment Kempf had just over 80,000 men in its combat units and was woefully short of armor. It had to depend on 4th Panzer Army's 6th Panzer Division located west of Belgorod for major armored assistance, should it be required. Panzer detachments available to the two German forces (such as Panzer Detachment 51, 52, and 503) added between 50 and 60 Panther and Tiger tanks to the German armored strength, much of it in the Belgorod area. Assault gun detachments (905, 228, 202) added about fifty guns to XI Army Corps' strength.

Thus the Soviets began the operation with clear superiority in manpower and weaponry. While the Germans could muster almost 300,000 men in both combat and logistical units, Soviet strength exceeded 900,000. The disparity in armor was even more pronounced, with the Soviets initiating the attack with over 2,300 tanks and self-propelled guns compared to the German tank and self-propelled gun strength of almost 350. During the course of the operation reinforcements on both sides reduced that disparity; but, by then, Soviet forces had done considerable damage to forward German units. Correlation of opposing force strengths is shown in the adjacent table.

Area of Operations

The Belgorod–Khar'kov area was familiar ground for both forces (see Map 55). Soviet armies had advanced through the same area in February

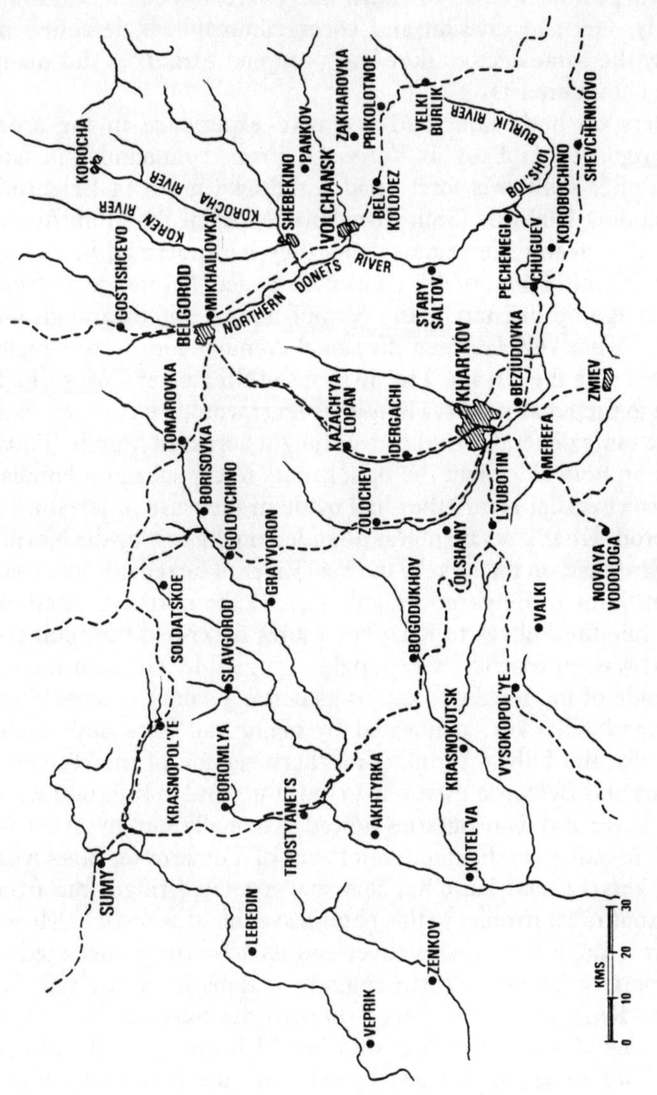

MAP 55. BELGOROD–KHAR’KOV AREA OF OPERATIONS

1943, and German forces had driven those Soviet units back across the region in March. In early July German forces had begun their Kursk offensive from positions close to those they were forced to withdraw to in late July. German division and corps commanders defended in approximately the same sectors they had occupied earlier, as did many of their Soviet counterparts.

Commanders on both sides had extensive experience in the area. Vatutin had replaced Golikov as Voronezh Front commander in late March 1943, after Golikov's forces had withdrawn north of Belgorod. Army commanders Chibisov (38th Army) and Moskalenko (40th Army) would operate in nearly the same sectors they had operated in during February and March. Hoth, of 4th Panzer Army, had led that army from Khar'kov to Belgorod in March, and Kempf had operated through the region west of Khar'kov. German divisional commanders were equally well acquainted with the terrain. The divisions of SS Panzer Corps which would return to the Khar'kov area in mid-August would be committed to combat in the same general area they had fought across in March. Thus, commanders on both sides had the opportunity to capitalize on familiar terrain or correct earlier errors they had made in their use of terrain.

The Belgorod–Khar'kov salient was bounded on the east by the Northern Donets River and on the west by the Psel River. The rail line and road network from Sumy to Belgorod roughly formed the northern extent of the salient, while the Poltava to Khar'kov routes described the southern limits of what was, in essence, a rectangle occupied by German forces. On the east side of the rectangle and in its corners were the large cities of Belgorod and Khar'kov, connected by major rail lines and roads. Topographically, the hilly and rolling northern section of the rectangle between Sumy and Belgorod gave way to lower ground to the southwest. The Vorskla River and its tributaries flowed diagonally southwest across the region. In its valley lay the important towns of Tomarovka, Borisovka, Graivoron, Akhtyrka, and Kotel'va. Sparsely vegetated ridges ran from northeast to southwest parallel to this natural avenue of approach. Movement southwest along the Vorskla River and its associated ridges led to the most important lateral German communications lines, the rail line from Sumy to Khar'kov which passed through the towns of Boromlya, Trostyanets, Bogodukhov, and Lyubotin in which the Germans placed much of their logistical support installations, and the Poltava–Khar'kov road and rail line which was critical for the movement of troops and supplies into the Khar'kov area.

OPERATION "POLKOVODETS RUMYANTSEV"

Planning

STAVKA *Deliberations*

On 24 July the *STAVKA* notified the Voronezh and Steppe Fronts to begin detailed preparations for the operation to liberate Belgorod and Khar'kov and gave subordinate headquarters and staffs ten days to prepare for the attack. General Zhukov coordinated preparations as representative of the *STAVKA* and, as such, kept in close touch with Stalin throughout the planning phase.[19] The *STAVKA* ordered Vatutin's Voronezh Front and Konev's Steppe Front to attack from northwest of Belgorod toward Bogodukhov, Valki, and Novaya Vodolaga to split German 4th Panzer Army from Army Detachment Kempf and then envelop and smash German forces in Khar'kov. Lt. General Gagen's 57th Army of the Southwestern Front would strike at Merefa south of Khar'kov while other *fronts* along the Eastern Front would launch secondary or diversionary attacks.

Zhukov supervised discussion of the *STAVKA's* plan with *front* and army commanders. During the discussions subordinate commanders aired their views. Lt. Gen. I.M. Chistyakov of 6th Guards Army voiced reservations about the hasty attack since his forces were understrength and required extensive regrouping.[20] Lt. Gen. K.S. Moskalenko of 40th Army suggested the main attack be launched from the Krasnopol'ye–Soldatskoye area toward Akhtyrka and Poltava in a wide envelopment of Khar'kov similar to the earlier Stalingrad operation. He warned of the dangers of a close envelopment of the city such as he had experienced in March.[21] Zhukov assuaged Chistyakov's concerns by stressing the need to catch the Germans unprepared. He rejected Moskalenko's suggestion, stating that both he and Stalin preferred the less complex blow at the point of the German salient because the Soviets had neither the men and weapons nor the energy to effect a bigger envelopment. Zhukov did agree to bolster 40th and 6th Guards Armies by inserting the reinforced 27th Army on 40th Army's left rather than on 6th Guards Army's left and by delaying 40th Army's attack until two days after the main *front* attack.

German Defenses

STAVKA plans took into account the objectives of the operation, the condition of Soviet forces, and the nature of German defenses. German forces opposing the Voronezh Front occupied prepared positions in or near locations they had defended since March 1943. North of Tomarovka and Belgorod the Germans occupied positions slightly north of their earlier positions (5–8 kilometers). Here there were weaker forward defenses but stronger defenses in depth. In most sectors the Germans had two well developed defensive belts of trenches and unit strongpoints covered by interlocking artillery and machine gun fire. Defenses were densest around large population centers and key communications or command centers such as Sumy, Tomarovka, Belgorod, and Khar'kov. The two defensive belts were up to 18 kilometers deep. The main defensive belt consisted of two positions, each 6–8 kilometers deep consisting of strongpoints linked by trenches and dotted with firing positions. Field trenches were interspersed between the two positions. The second defensive belt, 2–3 kilometers deep, consisted of trenches and a lesser number of strongpoints. The strongest German defenses were along the Northern Donets River from Belgorod to south of Chuguyev.[22]

Khar'kov proper was ringed with two defensive lines. An outer ring ran from Rogan, 10 kilometers east of Khar'kov, to south of Dergachi; and an inner ring covered the immediate suburbs of the city. Belgorod had one defensive ring based on the Northern Donets River, the chalk hills to the north of the city, and the factory suburbs and villages to the west of the city.

Although prepared German defenses were strong on paper, the actual force on hand was insufficient to man them fully. Thus, infantry divisions usually with all three infantry regiments on line, occupied forward positions. Division support units, reserve regiments (when they existed), and panzer divisions occupied assembly areas to the rear ready to reinforce threatened sectors, establish new defenses, or repel penetrations whenever necessary.

On 4th Panzer Army's front each of the eight infantry divisions defended a 10 kilometer sector. The bulk of the army's four panzer divisions were distributed throughout the rear area. Army Detachment Kempf's six infantry divisions occupied sectors averaging 13 kilometers wide, backed up in the Belgorod area by several smaller panzer detachments (primarily of Tiger and Panther tanks). The German command had no operational reserves in the Belgorod and Khar'kov area.[23]

Front Missions

The Belgorod–Khar'kov operational plan, codenamed "*Polkovodets Rumyantsev*" (General Rumyantsev), called for a frontal attack by the joined flanks of the Voronezh and Steppe Fronts from the region northwest of Belgorod in the general direction of Bogodukhov (see Map 56).[24] The Voronezh Front's 6th Guards, 5th Guards, 1st Tank, and 5th Guards Tank Armies would launch the *front* main attack supported by the 53d and 69th Armies and a portion of 7th Guards Army of the Steppe Front. The shock groups of the two *fronts* and the Voronezh Front's mobile groups (1st Tank Army, 5th Guards Tank Army) would advance on Khar'kov from the north and west and, in coordination with a Southwestern Front attack

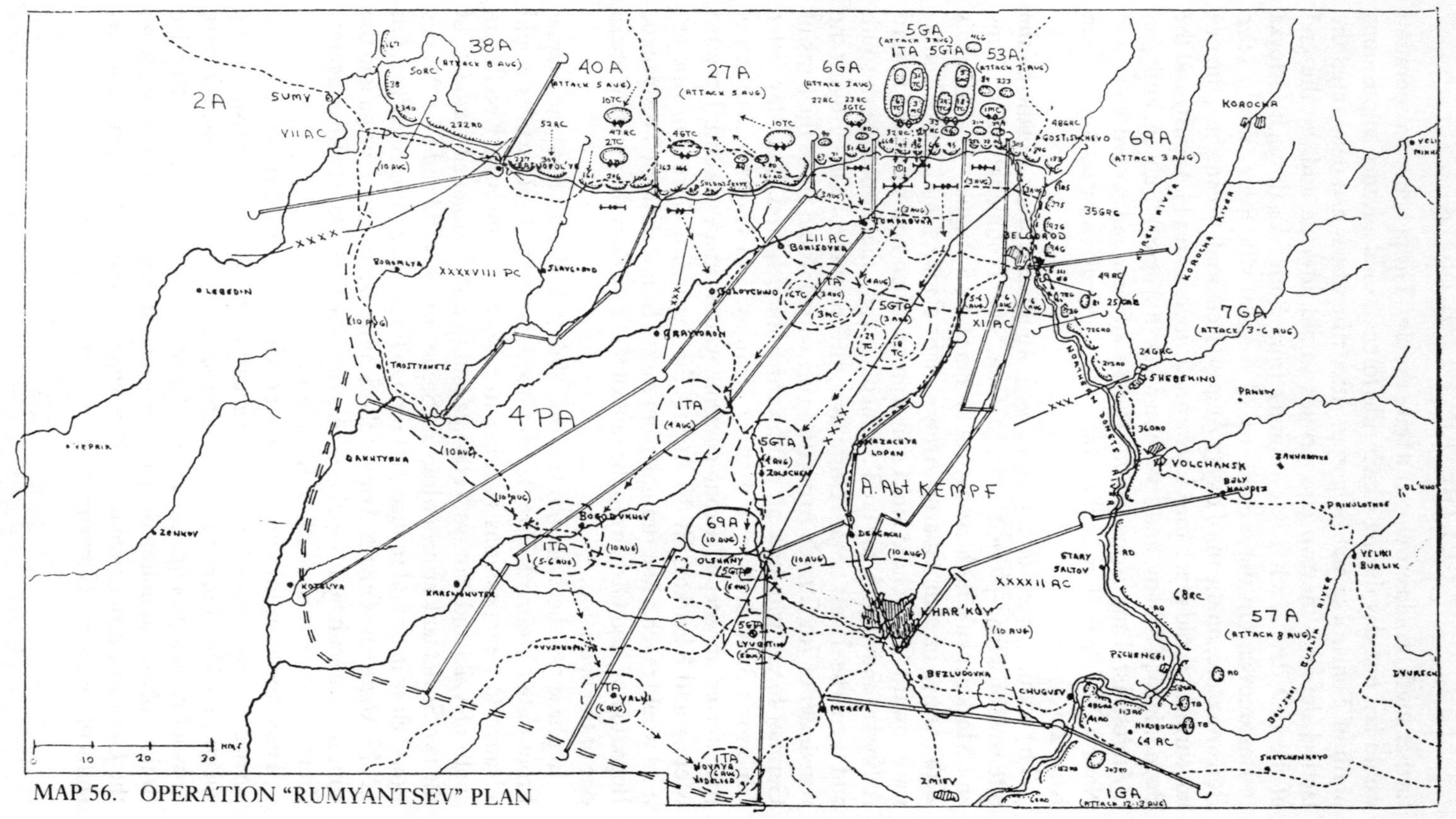

MAP 56. OPERATION "RUMYANTSEV" PLAN

further south, would envelop and seize the city. The penetration operation would last one day during which rifle forces would advance to positions north of Tomarovka and Belgorod. After rifle forces had penetrated the tactical defense, the two tank armies would advance and, by the end of the first day, reach a line running from Borisovka through Orlovka to Bessonovka. On the second day (4 August) rifle forces would seize Borisovka and, on the third day (5 August) Belgorod. Meanwhile, the two tank armies would reach the Graivoron–Zolochev area (4 August) and the Bogodukhov, Olshany, and Lyubotin areas (5 August). Subsequently, on 6 August 1st Tank Army would wheel southeast and secure Valki and Novaya Vodolaga thus sealing off the escape of German forces from Khar'kov.

The flank armies of the two *fronts* would add their weight to the offensive on a time-phased basis. Lt. Gen. S.G. Trofimenko's 27th Army and Moskalenko's 40th Army would attack on 5 August. Trofimenko's 27th Army, on 6th Guards Army's right flank, would strike southward toward Golovchino and Graivoron and then turn westward toward Akhtyrka, and 40th Army on Trofimenko's right flank would push south and then wheel west toward Boromlya and Trostyanets. On 6 August the remainder of 7th Guards Army (two rifle corps) would strike the flank of German forces withdrawing southward from Belgorod. Two days later Chibisov's 38th Army would strike at Sumy, and Gagen's 57th Army (transferred to Steppe Front control) would attack westward toward Merefa and Khar'kov. By 10 August the expanding torrent of rifle armies would reach a line running from east of Sumy, through Trostyanets, Bogodukhov, and Olshany to the outskirts of Khar'kov thus ending phase one of the operation.

In phase two the 27th, 6th Guards, 69th (transferred from the Steppe Front to the Voronezh Front), 5th Guards, and 1st Tank Armies would advance to new positions running from Akhtyrka through Kotel'va to south of Valki and Novaya Vodolaga and join the advanced elements of the two Soviet tank armies while the Steppe Front's 53d and 57th Armies would close in on and reduce the German forces defending Khar'kov. On 12–13 August 1st Guards Army of the Southwestern Front would join the concerted assault by advancing across the Northern Donets River against Zmiyev and Merefa, south of Khar'kov.

Thus, the plan involved a wider envelopment of Khar'kov than was carried out by Soviet forces in February. The envelopment was to be spearheaded by tank armies for greater speed, and both tank armies were to avoid combat in built-up areas. The rippling conduct of the offensive by time-phase commitment of armies would steadily increase pressure on the Germans, economize on artillery support, and take advantage of any shifts of forces the Germans made during their defense.

The Voronezh Front Plan

Vatutin deployed his armies in a single echelon with an exploitation echelon consisting of two tank armies. 5th and 6th Guards Armies were to conduct the *front* main attack. Lt. Gen. A.S. Zhadov's 5th Guards Army, on the left wing of the *front*, would penetrate enemy defenses west of Zhuravlinyi and secure the introduction into the penetration of 1st Tank Army and 5th Guards Tank Army. Thereafter, 5th Guards Army would develop the offensive toward Zolochev and Olshany and, by the end of the seventh day of the operation (9 August), reach the Bogodukhov, Olshany, and Dergachi area.[25]

Chistyakov's 6th Guards Army with 5th Guards Tank Corps serving as the army mobile group would penetrate the enemy defense near Gertsovka and Butovo, overcome German defenses at Tomarovka and Borisovka and, by the end of the seventh day, reach the area west from Bogodukhov.[26] Trofimenko's 27th Army with 4th Guards Tank Corps as the army mobile group would attack on 5 August, penetrate German defenses west of Soldatskoye, seize Golovchino and Graivoron, secure the right flank of the *front* main assault group, and occupy positions east of Akhtyrka by the end of the seventh day.[27] Moskalenko's 40th Army with the 2d Tank Corps as an army mobile group was to attack on 5 August, penetrate German defenses east of Krasnopol'ye, advance southwest, and by 10 August reach the Boromlya and Trostyanets area where it would establish a security line on the right flank of 27th Army.[28] Chibisov's 38th Army would attack on 8 August west of Krasnopol'ye to threaten the key town of Sumy and cover the right flank of 40th Army.[29]

Lt. Gen. M.E. Katukov's 1st Tank Army and Lt. Gen. P.A. Rotmistrov's 5th Guards Tank Army would serve key functions as the *front's* mobile groups. 1st Tank Army would develop the success of 5th Guards Army's right flank units toward Tomarovka and Valki. By the end of the first day Katukov's army would secure the Borisovka region and by the end of the fourth day the Bogodukhov, Valki, and Novaya Vodolaga regions 120 kilometers into the operational depth of the German defense. The tank army would advance into battle through advancing 5th Guards Army units in a 4 kilometer sector along four march routes at a depth of 6–8 kilometers into the German defenses.[30]

Rotmistrov's 5th Guards Tank Army would advance in a 6 kilometer sector through the left flank of 5th Guards Army's advancing units toward Bessonovka, Zolochev, and Olshany and, in coordination with 5th Army rifle forces, the army would reach the Orlovka, Shchetinovka, Bessonovka areas by the end of the first day. Subsequently, the army would smash German operational reserves, and, by the end of the third day of the operation, reach Olshany and Lyubotin and cut the roads running westward from Khar'kov, a distance of 100 kilometers from its start point.[31]

Maj. Gen. A. G. Kravchenko's 5th Guards Tank Corps, operating in 6th Guards Army sector on 1st Tank Army's right flank, would cooperate closely with 1st Tank Army and spearhead 6th Guards Army's advance on Tomarovka, Borisovka, and Graivoron. On 5th Guards Tank Army's left flank, Maj. Gen. M. D. Solomatin's 1st Mechanized Corps would lead 53d Army's advance to the west of Belgorod. As each additional army of the Voronezh Front joined the assault, tank forces would exploit the ensuing penetrations. Maj. Gen. P. P. Poluboyarov's 4th Guards Tank Corps would support 27th Army's advance and exploit toward Golovchino and Akhtyrka, and Major General A. F. Popov's 2d Tank Corps would support 40th Army's drive on Slavgorod and Trostyanets. An additional tank Corps, Major General V. M. Aleksysev's 10th, initially deployed in 27th Army's sector, after 5 August would shift westward to support 40th Army.

Thus, Vatutin concentrated his forces on his left flank and launched his main attack to the southwest along the Vorskla River and the major ridge to its south. As the main *front* shock group advanced into the depths of the German defense toward Bogodukhov, the other armies would join the attack on a time-phased basis. Vatutin's plan reflected the simplicity of the *STAVKA* order.

The Steppe Front Plan

General Konev's Steppe Front plan was a mirror image of Vatutin's. Konev deployed his forces in a single echelon of armies without a *front* mobile group and planned his main attack on the *front* right flank toward Belgorod. Subsequently, Konev's other armies would join in the assault on a time-phased basis culminating in an assault by all of his armies on Khar'kov after the city's envelopment by the Voronezh Front.

Lt. Gen. I. M. Managarov's 53d Army, Lt. Gen. V. D. Kryuchenkin's 69th Army, and the 49th Rifle Corps of Shumilov's 7th Guards Army would launch the initial assault on Belgorod on the morning of 3 August. 53d Army, supported by 1st Mechanized Corps, would strike south along the Belgorod–Oboyan road, secure the northwest section of Belgorod (in coordination with 69th Army and 7th Guards Army), develop the attack along the Khar'kov road toward Dergachi, relieve 5th Guards Army forces on a line from Olshany to Dergachi, and prepare to attack Khar'kov from the west and northwest.[32] 69th Army would attack on 53d Army's left, assist in reducing Belgorod, and subsequently advance to south of Belgorod where it would transfer some of its divisions to 53d Army and revert to *front* reserve. By phase two of the operation, 69th Army would redeploy to the Olshany area.[33] 7th Guards Army's 49th

Rifle Corps would attack westward against the German Mikhailovka bridgehead east of Belgorod to assist 69th Army in securing the city, and then advance south toward Brodok. As 49th Rifle Corps advanced the 25th and 24th Guards Rifle Corps would cross the Northern Donets River and join the attack against the right flank of withdrawing German units. Thereafter, the three rifle corps of 7th Guards Army would advance toward Khar'kov from the northeast and assist 57th Army in crossing the Northern Donets River in the vicinity of Staryi Saltov.[34]

While the Steppe Front advanced, General Gagen's 57th Army would shift from Southwestern to Steppe Front control and attack from Staryi Saltov across the Northern Donets River toward Khar'kov. By the end of phase one, 57th Army would reach the Rogan area, 10 kilometers east of Khar'kov.[35] By the end of phase one (on 10 August) all of Konev's armies would be arrayed on the close approaches to Khar'kov ready to open the second phase of the operation.

Before the second phase opened, Konev would transfer 69th Army to Voronezh Front control. In return, he would receive 5th Guards Tank Army which would join 53d Army in an attack on Khar'kov from the west and northwest. 5th Guards Tank Army would spearhead the advance from Olshany to the area east of Lyubotin. Simultaneously, 7th Guards Army would attack Khar'kov from the north and northeast while 57th Army attacked from the east and southeast.

Once reassigned to the Voronezh Front, 69th Army would deploy between 5th Guards Army and 53d Army in the Olshany area and attack south toward Valki in coordination with the remainder of the Voronezh Front's left flank. As the Steppe Front closed in on Khar'kov, the Southwestern Front's 1st Guards Army would advance across the Northern Donets River and then northwest along both banks of the Udy River toward Merefa, which dominated the approaches to Khar'kov from the south. Other 1st Guards Army forces would penetrate into the southern suburbs of Khar'kov via Chuguyev.

Armor Support

During the short time available for planning, the Soviets emphasized support of the simple plan with requisite amounts of armor, artillery, engineer, and logistical support. The Soviets realized that earlier operations had failed in part because of deficiencies in these areas. Now that the Soviets had an expanded force structure theoretically capable of conducting deep operations, that structure had to be coordinated to convert theory into practice.

For the first time, *front* and army commanders had well balanced, mobile groups to conduct operational maneuver. The two tank armies would serve as mobile groups of the Voronezh Front, and four separate tank corps would perform a similar role for 40th, 27th, and 6th Guards Armies. In addition, a mechanized corps would spearhead 53d Army's advance on Belgorod. Within the rifle armies and corps, an abundance of tank and self-propelled gun units were available for infantry support. The Voronezh Front had twelve tank and self-propelled gun regiments which it attached to first echelon rifle divisions in the main army attack sector for use in infantry support. The Steppe Front's three separate tank brigades and eight tank and self-propelled gun regiments were also used for infantry support at the rifle division level except in 57th Army. There, the two tank brigades (109 tanks) formed an army mobile group. Assignment of these armored assets created tactical densities of from 20 to 25 tanks per kilometer of front on main attack directions and operational densities including tank armies and tank and mechanized corps of 70 and 30 per kilometer in the Voronezh Front's and in the Steppe Front's main attack sectors.[36]

The *STAVKA* representative, Zhukov; the *front* commander, Vatutin; and the two tank army commanders took special care to coordinate operations of the tank armies and rifle forces, especially during the critical period of the passage of lines. Written orders, staff exercises, and personal coordination helped the process. The *front* commander organized air, artillery, and engineer support while the army commanders worked out the approach march routes, the order and schedule of the advance, and the operational formation of the armies. Each tank army and tank and mechanized corps created an operational group consisting of staff officers to advance with the first echelon of the armored force to react to rapidly changing conditions.

Artillery Support

Artillery support was essential to achieve a successful penetration and protect the exploiting force. In some earlier operations, the Soviets had only limited quantities of artillery or had poorly coordinated their artillery support. The introduction and use of the concept of the artillery offensive and the increased number of artillery units promised better artillery support in the Belgorod–Khar'kov operation.*

Extensive regrouping of *STAVKA* artillery assets occurred during the ten days prior to the new offensive. The Soviets transferred the 18th, 16th, and 17th Artillery Penetration Divisions and the 3d Guards Mortar Division from the Bryansk Front to the Voronezh and Steppe Fronts. In addition, the *STAVKA* shifted three separate brigades and twenty-eight artillery regiments to the Voronezh Front. The total of ninety additional

*The concept of the artillery offensive involved the planning and conduct of preparation fires, fires to accompany the infantry and armored assault, and fires to support exploiting forces.

artillery regiments provided the two fronts with a marked superiority over German forces (see Appendix 1). Operational densities of artillery in the 5th and 6th Guards Armies' sectors of the Voronezh Front reached 113 and 129 guns/mortars per kilometer and in the Steppe Front's 53d Army sector 242 guns/mortars per kilometer of front.[37]

Shifting of artillery units and movement of these units into position over that ten-day period was particularly difficult, for positions had to be built, reconnaissance and survey conducted, and resupply carried out (1.5 million shells and mines within *front* level and one-half million shells in the *front* artillery reserve). As a rule, in order to create requisite densities of artillery in penetration sectors, the *front* commander concentrated the artillery of second echelon rifle divisions, mobile groups, and armies operating on secondary attack axes. For example, the artillery of 1st Tank Army and 5th Guards Tank Army as well as four artillery regiments of 40th Army supported 5th Guards Army's attack and later had to relocate to support the attack of their parent unit. Likewise, the 5th Guards Tank Corps and 10th Tank Corps artillery and two divisional artillery regiments of 27th Army supported 6th Guards Army, and the artillery of 1st Mechanized Corps supported 53d Army's attack.[38]

Artillery support met the requirements of the artillery offensive: to assist in achieving the penetration, to support the introduction of the mobile group, and to facilitate the advance of infantry and tanks in the depth of the defense. The Voronezh Front's artillery preparation was to last 170 minutes and was organized as follows:

5 minutes – barrage fire on forward defenses and the near depth of the defense
30 minutes – pause
60 minutes – controlled fire and strikes by bomber aviation and guards mortars (rocket launchers)
70 minutes – methodical fire to destroy point targets
5 minutes – volleys of rocket artillery

Thereafter, artillery would fire on successive concentrations to a depth of two kilometers.[39] Thus, the barrage would transform itself smoothly into supporting fires for the advancing forces. The third period of the artillery offensive would involve fire by 5th Guards Army's long range corps* artillery groups at targets in the second line of German defenses to enable mobile groups to achieve penetration of the enemy's second defense line.

*Corps artillery groups were new. At this stage, they were under dual control of the corps commander and division commander.

Air Support

The growing power of Soviet aviation would make its presence felt on the battlefield. 1,311 aircraft supported the Voronezh and Steppe Fronts, as well as 200 aircraft of long range aviation attached to the *front* for the duration of the operation. About 50 percent of the air sorties would provide ground support for advancing forces against targets in the enemy tactical defense zone.[40] The Soviets conducted air strikes within the framework of an aviation offensive. This involved the sequential conduct of an air preparation, air strikes to assist the penetration, and strikes to accompany exploiting forces. The attack would begin with a massive, fifteen minute air preparation against enemy artillery positions beyond the range of artillery. Air strikes conducted during the penetration and exploitation would hit troop concentrations, artillery positions, and tanks in the tactical defense positions as well as enemy reserves reinforcing forward forces.[41]

Engineer Support

Engineer preparation of the battlefield during the defensive phase of the Kursk operation had been massive. Engineer work in support of the counteroffensive would also be extensive in light of the fairly well prepared German defenses, the river crossing requirements, and the necessity to reduce the German fortifications around Khar'kov. The *STAVKA* attached engineer units to the two *fronts*, and each *front* employed them differently. The Voronezh Front subattached most of its engineer assets to its armies while the Steppe Front kept such units under *front* control to support deploying units and units making the main attack.

Vatutin assigned the 14th Assault Engineer–Sapper Brigade to 5th Guards Army, the 42d Engineer Brigade (Special Purpose) to 6th Guards Army, the 6th Assault Engineer Brigade to 27th Army, and the 4th Engineer–Sapper Brigade to 40th Army. Combined arms armies provided engineer assistance for the commitment into the penetration of 1st Tank Army and 5th Guards Tank Army. The Steppe Front kept under *front* control the 5th, 8th, and 60th Engineer–Sapper Brigades; the 27th Special Purpose Engineer Brigade; four pontoon bridge battalions; and several specialized units. Most of these units supported the penetration operation.[42]

The primary task of Voronezh Front engineers was to conduct tactical and operational *maskirovka* (deception). Engineers prepared artillery positions, conducted engineer reconnaissance of German forward positions, and prepared dummy troop concentration areas to deceive the Germans as to the location of main attack areas. They also assisted in the *front* deception plan by simulating the assembly of an entire tank army in the Suzhda area north of Sumy.

Steppe Front engineers assisted the forward movement of troops into assault positions, and camouflaged troop positions in the swampy areas along the Northern Donets River and its tributaries east and northeast of Belgorod in order to mislead the Germans as to the main attack direction. They built or repaired ninety bridges, constructed sixty-two fords, built forty-seven kilometers of roads, and repaired 1,000 kilometers of roads in this difficult region.[43] Both *fronts* would also provide extensive engineer support to mobile forces operating in the depths of the enemy defenses during the course of the operation.

Command, Control and Communications

The Belgorod–Khar'kov operation would be the largest Soviet offensive since Stalingrad and would involve literally hundreds of units. The difficulty in commanding and controlling so extensive a force required that close attention be paid to communications. During the defensive phase of combat at Kursk the Soviets had relied heavily on wire communication. Now, in the offensive phase, the Soviets would have to rely primarily on radio links. A large scale wire net linked units while preparing for the offensive. After the offensive began *front* and army communications units created and restored communication lines with headquarters of advancing forces (as it turned out, three times for each *front* headquarters and five to seven times per army headquarters).[44]

Before the offensive began the Soviets organized radio communications between command posts and auxiliary command posts (V.P.U.s) by radio nets and by directions (i.e. along distinct axes of advance). Radio nets linked *fronts* to armies and cooperating armies on each attack direction. Mobile units operating in the operational depths of the defense would rely entirely on radio communications. For liaison with these forces the Soviets planned to use mobile communications centers for armies and *fronts* which could support an advance of up to 30 kilometers per day.

Signal communications also played a role in the pre-offensive deception plan. Prior to the operation *front* communications units simulated the assembly of a tank army in the Suzhda region by creating dummy radio nets complete with authentic call signs.[45] These and simultaneous engineer measures, the Soviets hoped, would fix the attention of German planners on the region west of Suzhda.

Logistical Support

Extensive logistical planning was also required in light of the huge expenditures of materiel during the Kursk defensive phase. The Voronezh

Front supply bases were 250 kilometers to the rear in the Kastornoye area. The chief resupply line for both the Voronezh and Steppe Fronts was a single rail line, constructed in late June, running from Staryi Oskol to Rzhava. Construction of this line and work on the Kastornoye–Kursk line went on despite constant German bombing raids. Prodigious efforts of the military authorities and civilian labor kept both lines functioning. Road communications to the *fronts* relied on only two good motor roads. Each army within the *fronts* had two 100–150 kilometer-long, dirt-surfaced roads for resupply. These roads, although good in dry weather, turned to deep mud in rain, requiring road maintenance teams to work around the clock to keep one-way traffic running on each road (one forward, one to the rear).[46]

Although adequate stocks of ammunition and fuel were on hand for the defensive phase, considerable resupply was necessary to undertake the counteroffensive. Resupply was completed only by 3 August, the day of the assault.

The Penetration Phase: The Creation of the Tomarovka–Borisovka Pocket and the Fall of Belgorod (3–5 August)

With *STAVKA* and *front* planning complete, army commanders drafted their plans and submitted them to the *front* commanders for approval. The most critical of these plans were those made by the four rifle armies, one rifle corps, and two tank armies making the initial assault to penetrate German defenses covering Belgorod (see Maps 57 and 58). Careful and detailed planning was required to carry out a successful penetration and to commit the two tank armies through the narrow penetration sector into the operational depths of the enemy defense.

German Defenses

The Germans defended in the designated penetration sector with elements of three infantry divisions and two panzer divisions of 4th Panzer Army's LII Army Corps and with two infantry divisions of Army Detachment Kempf's XI Army Corps.[47] West of the Soviet main attack sector, LII Army Corps' 255th Infantry Division defended the sector from Butovo to south of Soldatskoye with the bulk of its two infantry regiments deployed on line. The 332d Infantry Division defended the sector from Butovo to southwest of Bykovka with three regiments and kept two battalions of one of the regiments in reserve. The 167th Infantry Division defended with three regiments on line in positions stretching

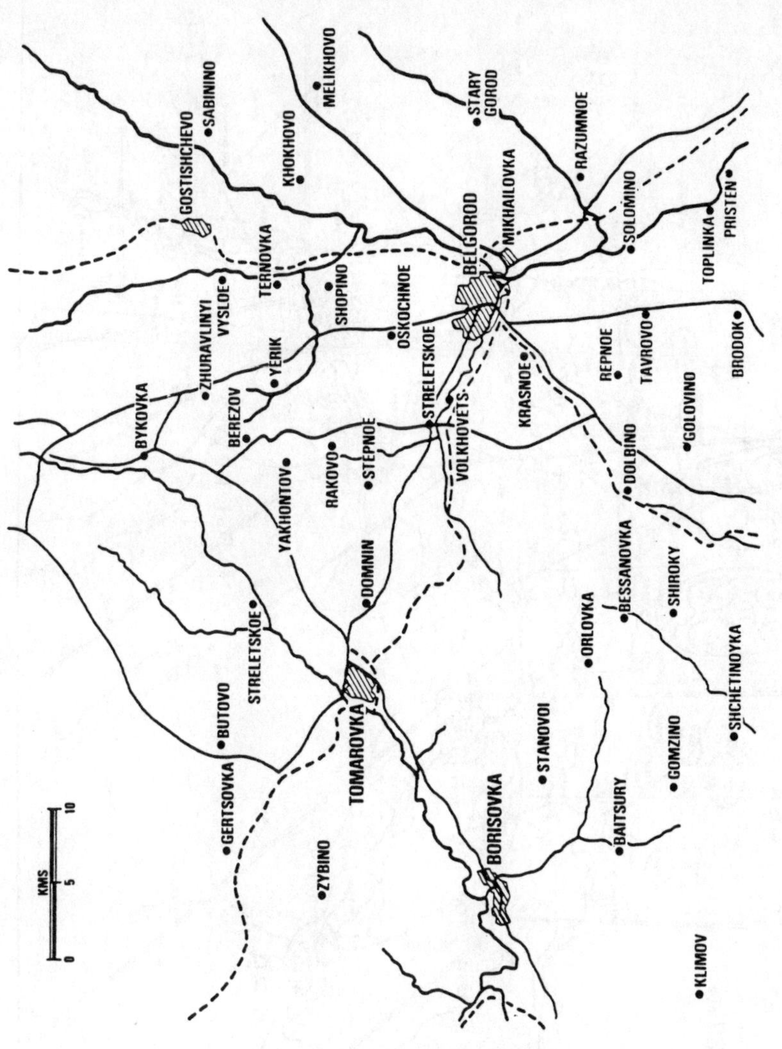

MAP 57. BELGOROD–TOMAROVKA AREA

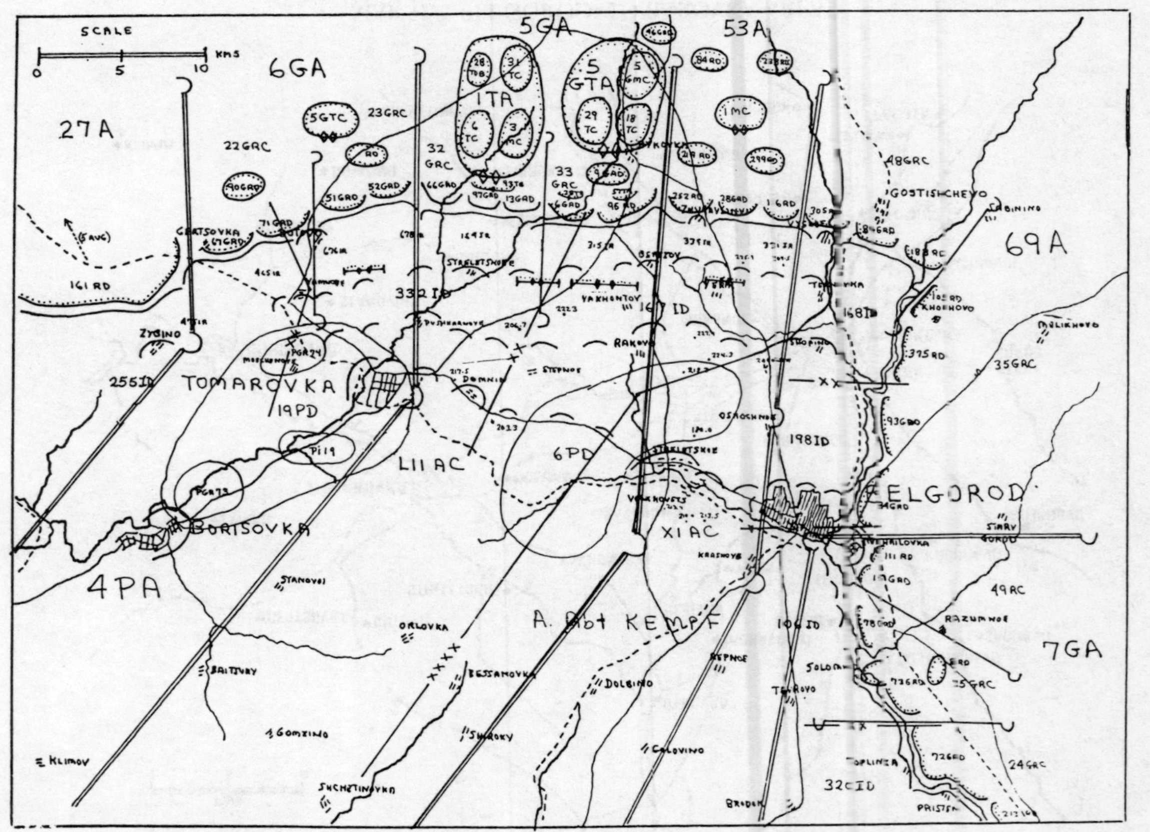

MAP 58. BELGOROD–KHAR'KOV, MAIN ATTACK SECTOR, 0500 3 AUGUST 1943

from southwest of Bykovka eastward to Vysloye on the Lipovyi Donets River. Each division's sector was approximately 14–16 kilometers wide. XI Army Corps' 168th Infantry Division defended the salient running east from the Lipovyi Donets River and south along the west bank of the Northern Donets River to the Shopino area. The 198th Infantry Division of XI Army Corps defended from the Shopino area south along the river through Belgorod, and the 106th Infantry Division defended the river sector south of Belgorod.

All defending infantry divisions had the bulk of their combat strength well forward with battalion-size reserves designated to reinforce threatened sectors. Both German corps relied on the two panzer divisions of LII Army Corps to provide strength necessary to repel Soviet penetrations. 19th Panzer Division with 49 tanks and assault guns was concentrated between Tomarovka and Borisovka, and 6th Panzer Division with twenty-eight tanks was located between Belgorod and Tomarovka. Reconnaissance elements of each division were located near the main infantry defense lines. In addition, Panzer Detachment 52 with about 10 Tiger tanks was co-located with 19th Panzer Division northwest of Tomarovka.[48]

5th Guards Army Planning

The most critical attack sector of the Voronezh Front was that of General Zhadov's 5th Guards Army through which both tank armies would advance into battle. Zhadov's army was to attack in a 16 kilometer sector west of Bykovka with his main attack occurring in a 6 kilometer sector on the army left flank.[49] By the end of the first day the army was to penetrate 12–15 kilometers (to the Tomarovka, Rakova area) and, by the end of the second day, to the Borisovka, Dolbino area 30–32 kilometers deep into the German defense. Zhadov's army consisted of two rifle corps (seven rifle divisions) supported by two tank regiments, one self-propelled gun regiment, an artillery penetration division, a guards mortar division, an anti-aircraft artillery division, two gun-howitzer and five tank destroyer artillery regiments, a tank destroyer brigade, a mortar regiment, and four guards mortar regiments. This formidable array of forces would strike portions of two German regiments (one regiment each from the 167th and 332d Infantry Divisions).

Zhadov deployed his army in a single echelon of rifle corps with one rifle division (42d Guards) in army reserve. The 32d Guards Rifle Corps, on the army right flank, formed in a single echelon of three rifle divisions supported by the 93d Tank Brigade, 1547th Self-Propelled Artillery Regiment, and one engineer battalion. The 33d Guards Rifle Corps, on the army left flank, formed in two echelons with two divisions in the first echelon supported by the 28th and 57th Tank Penetration Regiments and two engineer battalions and one division in the second.

From 25 July to 1 August 5th Guards Army conducted detailed planning and reconnaissance to determine precise enemy defensive positions. At 1600 on 1 August Zhadov ordered his corps forward to occupy jumping-off positions after dark. At 1800 on 2 August, just before darkness, each first echelon rifle division conducted a reconnaissance with a reinforced rifle battalion to gain a final picture of German defensive dispositions. Late that evening, Marshal Zhukov arrived at 5th Guards Army's observation post to supervise the conduct of the operation.[50]

1st Tank Army Planning

Both 1st and 5th Guards Tank Armies would join battle in 5th Guards Army's sector. Katukov's 1st Tank Army (6th Tank Corps, 31st Tank Corps, 3d Mechanized Corps, and 28th Tank Destroyer Brigade) was reinforced by a guards mortar regiment, an engineer assault battalion, and two anti-tank rifle battalions and would be supported by one assault and one fighter aviation division. The tank army was to advance into combat in a 4 kilometer wide sector after 5th Guards Army's right wing (32d Guards) rifle corps had penetrated the German first defensive belt to a depth of 6–8 kilometers.[51] Katukov's army would advance in two echelons with Major General A.L. Getman's 6th Tank Corps on the right and Major General S.M. Krivoshein's 3d Mechanized Corps (with two guards mortar regiments) on the left in first echelon. Major General D.Kh. Chernienko's 31st Tank Corps, in second echelon, would follow 3d Mechanized Corps and the army anti-tank reserve (28th Tank Destroyer Brigade) would advance behind 6th Tank Corps to cover the army's flank against enemy counter-attacks from the west.

Each first echelon mobile corps was to advance along two march routes in a two-echelon formation of brigades. 6th Tank Corps would lead with its 6th Motorized Rifle Brigade and 22d Tank Brigade, and 3d Mechanized Corps with its 1st Mechanized Brigade and 1st Guards Tank Brigade.* Each corps would designate a forward detachment consisting of a reinforced tank brigade (the 200th Tank Brigade for 6th Tank Corps and the 49th Tank Brigade for 3d Mechanized Corps) which would overcome enemy positions from the march and pave the way for exploitation by the advancing mobile corps. If necessary, they would also assist rifle units in overcoming resistance encountered in the enemy main defensive positions.

*Corps second echelon forces were the 112th Tank Brigade of 6th Tank Corps and the 3d and 18th Mechanized Brigades of 3d Mechanized Corps. 31st Tank Corps consisted of the 100th, 237th, and 242d Tank Brigades.

First echelon mobile corps also created a reconnaissance group of two reinforced tank platoons, and first echelon mobile brigades formed similar groups of up to one reinforced tank platoon. These groups would follow the advancing 5th Guards Army rifle regiments to determine the precise locations where the tank army forward detachments and first echelon brigades could best penetrate remaining enemy defenses. Katukov's advance into the penetration was to begin at 1300 on 3 August.

Katukov carefully tailored his supporting units and coordinated closely with 5th Guards Army to facilitate penetration and ensure the survivability of his units, especially during the passage of lines. The 8th Anti-Aircraft Artillery Division would provide air defense for his columns with two regiments integrated into his first echelon corps, one regiment defending the army command post, and a fourth regiment covering his rear installations. Katukov attached one motorized engineer battalion to 6th Tank Corps, an engineer assault battalion to 3d Mechanized Corps, and retained one engineer battalion in army reserve. On each march route, in advance of his main force, he deployed a movement security detachment of up to a reinforced sapper company.[52]

In numerous meetings Katukov, Zhadov, General P.A. Rotmistrov (5th Guards Tank Army commander), and General S.A. Krasovsky (2d Air Army commander) worked out the details of cooperation.[53] Together, they determined the precise location where tank armies' lead elements would begin their advance; the precise routes of advance; the maintenance responsibilities for those routes; the job of obstacle clearing; and signal, communications, and artillery support for the exploitation. Artillery support for the commitment of 1st Tank Army would be provided by the 13th Artillery Penetration Division, the 123d High Powered Artillery Brigade, the 628th Gun Artillery Regiment, and the artillery groups of 32d Guards Rifle Corps and its five rifle divisions. Katukov and Krasovsky determined key targets for air attack during commitment of the armored force and during the exploitation. Arrangements were made to locate the commander of the 264th Assault Aviation Division in the tank army command post and aviation division representatives with radios in the command posts of first echelon mobile corps in order to provide closer coordination of air support with the advancing armor. All staffs exchanged radio signal books and coordinated on the drafting of all planning documents and orders.

1st Tank Army corps and brigade commanders completed their planning in two days. On 30 July they conducted a personal reconnaissance of jumping-off positions and march routes into those positions. By 31 July all coordination with supported rifle divisions and all planning was complete. On 1 August it became necessary to revise the plan because 5th Guards

Army had been unable to throw the Germans back to positions south of the Vorskla River. Therefore, Vatutin had to commit 1st Tank Army in a narrower sector than planned (2 kilometers). Last minute coordination and refinement of orders took until day's end on 1 August. The final stage of planning was completed that day when battalion and company commanders conducted their on-site reconnaissance.[54]

After the bitter fighting and heavy losses of July, 1st Tank Army required considerable refitting and resupply before it could resume offensive operations. The army received 200 new tanks and repaired 1,215 vehicles during the planning period. By day's end on 2 August, refitting and resupply were complete. That day 1st Tank Army had 37,000 men, 542 tanks (417 T-34), 27 self-propelled guns, 432 guns and mortars, 55 BM-8 and BM-13 multiple rocket launchers, and 3,483 vehicles. This represented 82 percent of authorized personnel strength, 81 percent of tank strength, 67 percent of self-propelled gun strength, 85 percent of artillery strength, and 55 percent of vehicle strength.[55]

On the evening of 1 August first echelon corps began movement to their jumping-off positions 3–4 kilometers from the forward edge of the German defenses and closed in those positions by first light. On 2 August platoon leaders and tank and vehicle drivers studied the routes forward to the enemy defenses. That evening General Katukov; his artillery commander, Major General I.F. Frolov; and the operational group of the army staff (chief of operations, chief of reconnaissance, chief of signals and three staff officers) arrived at the 5th Guards Army's observation post where they were joined by General Vatutin and Marshal Zhukov. At the same time 1st Tank Army's first echelon corps commanders arrived with their operational groups and radios at the 32d Guards Rifle Corps observation post, and lead tank brigade commanders reported to rifle division observation posts in their respective sectors. The 1st Tank Army chief of staff, Major General M.A. Shalinyi, manned the 1st Tank Army main command post 1.5 kilometers northwest of Lukhanino.[56] In addition, 1st Tank Army established a secondary command point one kilometer from the Vorskla River to coordinate crossing of that river in the initial stages of the advance.

5th Guards Tank Army Planning

While Katukov planned the commitment of his army, General Rotmistrov did likewise for 5th Guards Tank Army. Rotmistrov's army (18th Tank Corps, 29th Tank Corps, and 5th Guards Mechanized Corps) would advance in a 5–6 kilometer wide sector on the left flank of 5th Guards Army through the advancing infantry of 33d Guards Rifle Corps once that corps had penetrated German defenses to a depth of 6–8 kilometers.[57] Rotmistrov's army would deploy with Colonel A.V. Yegorov's 18th Tank

Corps and Major General I.F. Kirichenko's 29th Tank Corps in first echelon and Major General B.M. Skvortsov's 5th Guards Mechanized Corps in second echelon. As was the case with 1st Tank Army, mobile corps would deploy in two echelons of brigades; and a forward detachment would lead the advance of each corps (110th Tank Brigade of 18th Tank Corps and 32d Tank Brigade of 29th Tank Corps). The army would advance at 1300 on the first day of the operation. In close coordination with Vatutin, Rotmistrov organized cooperation with 5th Guards Army and 2d Air Army in the same manner as Katukov. From 24 July to 2 August he task-organized his forces, developed detailed plans, and supervised the replenishment of his units. By 2 August the strength of 5th Guards Tank Army was approximately 37,000 men, 503 tanks, 40 self-propelled guns, 560 guns and mortars, and 45 BM-13 multiple rocket launchers.[58] Late that day 5th Guards Tank Army's staff relocated to the army command post. At 1900 hours, having established coordination with respective rifle corps and divisions, the 18th and 29th Tank Corps began movement into their jumping-off positions west of Bykovka where they closed into position at 0200 on 3 August.

6th Guards Army Planning

6th Guards Army, deployed on 5th Guards Army's right flank, was to attack directly against the German defenses around Tomarovka. Chistyakov's army was to attack in a 12-kilometer sector east of Gertsovka with its main attack concentrated in a 3-kilometer sector on the army's left flank. Due to the weakness of his rifle units, Chistyakov had tried unsuccessfully to give this sector to Zhadov's 5th Guards Army.[59] 6th Guards Army was to secure Tomarovka by the third day of the operation, cross the Vorskla River, commit 5th Guards Tank Corps to combat, and develop the attack toward Akhtyrka.

On 25 July Chistyakov submitted his plan to Vatutin. The following day Zhukov and Vatutin reviewed and approved Chistyakov's plan. The plan called for 6th Guards Army to deploy in a single echelon of two rifle corps with the main army shock group, the 23d Guards Rifle Corps, committed on the army's left flank. The 23d Rifle Corps deployed with two divisions in first echelon and one in second echelon. On the army's right flank the 22d Guards Rifle Corps also deployed in two echelons with two rifle divisions forward. General Kravchenko's 5th Guards Tank Corps, deployed behind 23d Guards Rifle Corps, had the mission of completing the tactical penetration of 3 August and developing the attack toward Tomarovka. On 1 August Chistyakov completed his planning. The following day, all army officers down to platoon level were briefed on the plans; and in the evening the four first echelon rifle divisions occupied their jumping-off positions. Sergeants and privates were briefed on the operation only during the artillery preparation.

While 5th and 6th Guards Army planned the penetration operation Vatutin regrouped his forces and inserted the newly arrived 27th Army into a sector between 40th Army and 6th Guards Army. On 19 July Trofimenko's 27th Army concentrated in the Voronezh Front's rear area, and by the night of 1 August the army's six rifle divisions and 4th Guards Tank Corps replaced 40th Army divisions in a 42 kilometer sector east and west of Soldatskoye. The 161st Rifle Division of 40th Army held its front line positions on 27th Army's left to cover the deployment. It shifted to 40th Army's new sector on 5 August.[60]

53d Army Planning

General Konev supervised the planning of his Steppe Front armies designated to participate in the penetration operation (53d Army, 69th Army, and 7th Guards Army). General Managarov's 53d Army and the 48th Rifle Corps of General Kryuchenkin's 69th Army formed the shock group of the Steppe Front. Their mission was to penetrate German defenses in an 11-kilometer sector north and northeast of Belgorod; attack south to envelop Belgorod from the west; and, in coordination with 49th Rifle Corps of 7th Guards Army, destroy German forces defending the city.[61] 69th Army's 35th Guards Rifle Corps would force the Northern Donets River near Khokhlovo and, by the end of the second day, deploy into second echelon positions to support 48th Rifle Corps' assault on Belgorod. General Managarov received his mission on 25 July. His army was to penetrate German defenses in an 8.5-kilometer sector from Zhuravlinyi to Vysloye, advance toward Streletskoye and Repnoye, and reach the Vezelka River west of Belgorod by the end of the second day. By the fourth day the army would advance southwest of Belgorod to secure the Dolbino area. Subsequently, it would develop the offensive through Dergachi to envelop Khar'kov from the west.[62]

Managarov's army (which lacked rifle corps headquarters) consisted of 7 rifle divisions, 1 mechanized corps, 3 separate tank penetration regiments, 28 artillery regiments, 15 separate artillery battalions, 4 mortar and 3 guards mortar regiments, an anti-aircraft artillery division, an anti-aircraft artillery regiment, and a separate anti-aircraft artillery battalion. Managarov originally planned to deploy his seven rifle divisions in two echelons with four divisions in the first echelon. After meetings with Konev and Zhukov on 26 and 27 July he decided to alter his formation and place three rifle divisions in his first echelon and four in his second to better sustain the offensive. Managarov weighted his attack in the 4 kilometer sector on his right flank.

Managarov designated General Solomatin's 1st Mechanized Corps as the army's mobile group. It would advance on the first day of the operation and develop the offensive through Streletskoye toward Khar'kov. 1st Mechanized Corps would deploy in two echelons of brigades with the 37th Mechanized Brigade on the right, the 19th Mechanized Brigade in the center, and the 219th Tank Brigade on the left in first echelon positioned to support the three first echelon rifle divisions during the penetration operation. The 35th Mechanized Brigade was in second echelon. After completing the penetration of German tactical defenses, the brigades would regroup into a corps-size mobile group and lead the exploitation. Each first echelon brigade would lead with a forward detachment consisting of a full tank regiment from each mechanized brigade and a tank battalion from the tank brigade, reinforced with automatic weapons, artillery, mortars, and sapper elements.[63]

To conduct the preparation, 53d Army had the support of an artillery division, an assault aviation corps, and a bomber aviation corps. Managarov assigned the army's separate tank regiments the mission of supporting the three first echelon rifle divisions.

Managarov completed his planning on 1 August, and the following day Konev and Zhukov approved his plan. On the evening of 1 August the divisions deployed into their jumping-off positions. 1st Mechanized Corps did likewise the following night. That same evening, Konev joined Managarov and prepared to watch the assault from 53d Army's observation post.

69th and 7th Guards Army Planning

The 48th Guards Rifle Corps of General Kryuchenkin's 69th Army would support Managarov's attack with an assault west of the Northern Donets River. The corps' three divisions deployed in single echelon formation and, supported by a tank brigade, would penetrate German defenses in the 4-kilometer sector from Vysloye to the Northern Donets River and advance on Belgorod from the north. 69th Army's 35th Guards Rifle Corps, with four divisions abreast, would clear the region east of the Northern Donets River, cross the river, and support 48th Rifle Corps in the reduction of Belgorod on the second and third days of the operation.[64]

General Shumilov's 7th Guards Army deployed on left flank of the Steppe Front. One of its three rifle corps (49th) would participate in the penetration operation against Belgorod while its remaining two corps (25th Guards and 24th Guards) would operate across the Northern Donets River against German units defending south of Belgorod.[65] 7th Guards Army's corps would widen its bridgeheads on the west bank of the river at Solomino and Toplinka on the first day of operations. By the

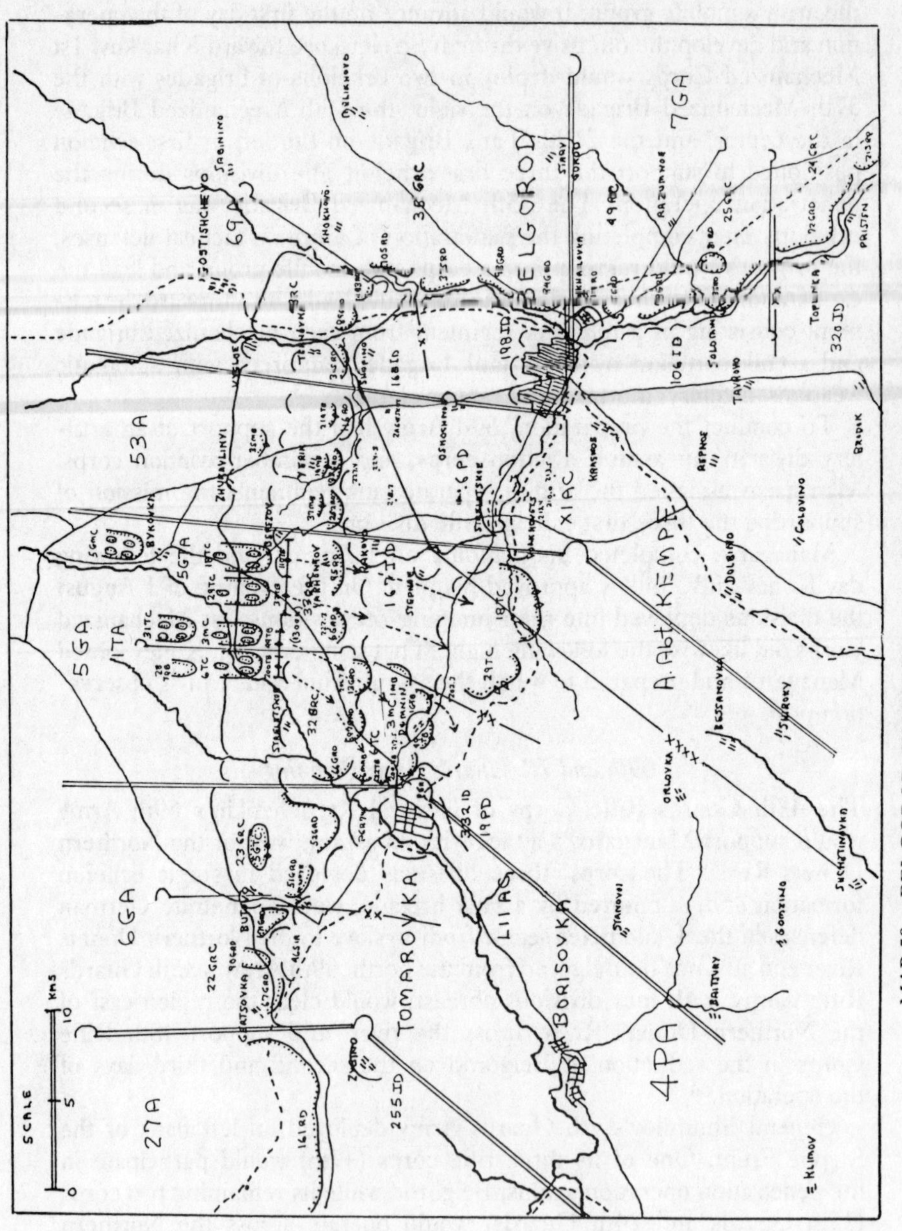

MAP 59. BELGOROD–KHAR'KOV, SITUATION, 2000 3 AUGUST 1943

end of the second day units would penetrate to the Tavrovo area and, in coordination with 69th Army and 1st Mechanized Corps, surround and destroy German forces in Belgorod.

The two rifle divisions of 49th Rifle Corps were to attack to reduce the Mikhailovka bridgehead and penetrate directly into Belgorod from the east. The 25th Guards Rifle Corps with two rifle divisions in first echelon and one in second would break out of the Solomino bridgehead, secure Tavrovo, and encircle German forces in Belgorod from the south. Two divisions of 24th Guards Rifle Corps would advance from the Toplinka bridgehead toward Brodok to secure the army's southern flank. Other 7th Guards Army divisions (two), deployed southward along the Northern Donets River to Volchansk, would join the attack as Soviet forces advanced towards Khar'kov.

Correlation of Forces: The Penetration Operation

The Soviets massed overwhelmingly superior forces in the penetration sector. 5th Guards Army, 1st Tank Army, and 5th Guards Tank Army, with a combined strength of 160,000 men and over 1100 tanks, would descend on four German infantry regiments, and the 85,000 men and 200 tanks of 6th Guards Army would strike two German infantry regiments. 53d Army of 77,000 men and 291 tanks would hit three German infantry regiments and 69th Army (60,000 men) two German infantry divisions. The 19th and 6th Panzer Divisions could intervene, but only after the initial damage was done; and the armored strength of these two divisions and Panzer Detachment 52 numbered only about ninety tanks, scarcely enough to slow the Soviet onslaught.

The First Day – 3 August 1943

At 0500 hours on 3 August, the Soviets passed the code word "*uregan*" (Hurricane) to their waiting units.[66] The summer morning silence dissolved in the ear shattering noise of the Soviet artillery preparation which systematically pulverized German defensive positions. The first five minute barrage tore apart the advanced positions of the 332d, 167th, and 168th Infantry Divisions before silence again descended on the battlefield. During the thirty minute pause Soviet sappers began their work, removing obstacles and clearing routes through the minefields, in particular on the main assault routes. At 0535 the preparation resumed, raining fire on German forward positions and point targets in the depth of the German defenses. Simultaneously, waves of aircraft struck German artillery positions, staffs, headquarters, and reserve concentrations. After two hours and ten minutes of intensive aimed fire, a final series of rocket mortar volleys brought the chorus of sound to an end to be replaced by the sounds of tanks and advancing infantry. (The Soviets estimate one round of artillery over 76mm landed every 15–18 meters.)

The artillery preparation tore gaping holes through the German infantry defenses, in particular at the junction of the 332d and 167th Infantry Divisions, and left the survivors of these divisions severely shaken and scarcely able to meet the infantry and armor onslaught (see Map 59). During the later stages of the preparation Soviet reconnaissance units and assault groups from lead battalions inched forward to capitalize on the sound and fury of the artillery assault. East of Butovo, in the main attack sector of 6th Guards Army, reconnaissance groups advanced 2–3 kilometers into the German 676th Infantry Regiment defenses. Further east, lead elements of 53d Army's 28th Guards Rifle Division advanced three kilometers and overwhelmed a battalion of the German 339th Infantry Regiment.[67]

Even while the artillery preparation was in progress, the Germans made some defensive adjustments. At 0700, 19th Panzer Division's 74th Panzer Grenadier Regiment (and 52d Panzer Detachment) moved northeast from their assembly areas near Tomarovka to reinforce the 332d Infantry Division defenses and 6th Panzer Division's reconnaissance battalion and elements of 4th Panzer Grenadier Regiment moved forward to reinforce the 167th Infantry Division, in particular in the sector where Soviet 28th Guards Rifle Division units were already into the forward German positions.

At 0755, as the sounds of the last rocket artillery rounds faded, Soviet infantry, supported by tanks, began their advance on a 40 kilometer front from Butovo to the Northern Donets River. The infantry assault occupied German outposts quickly and then tore into the first German defensive positions.

5th Guards Army's assault, of greatest concern to Soviet commanders because Rotmistrov's and Katukov's tank columns awaited its success, developed rapidly. On the army's right flank, Major General A.I. Rodimtsev's 32d Guards Rifle Corps (66th, 97th, and 13th Guards Rifle Divisions), reinforced by the 93d Tank Brigade, 1547th Self-Propelled Artillery Regiment, and two assault engineer battalions, streamed forward into and through the positions of the German 164th Infantry Regiment, 322d Infantry Division. On the army's left flank, Major General I.I. Popov's 33d Guards Rifle Corps (6th Guards Airborne Division, 9th Guards Airborne Division, and 95th Guards Rifle Division) supported by the 28th and 57th Tank Penetration Regiments, the 1440th and 1549th Self-Propelled Artillery Regiments and two assault engineer battalions struck the defensive positions of the 332d and 167th Infantry Divisions at the boundary of the two divisions.[68] The artillery preparation, with its planned pause and irregular pattern of fire, confused the Germans.

Many were still under cover as the advancing tank and infantry swept into their positions. The Soviets took the first three trench lines unimpeded by those defenders uninjured by the preparation and ran into opposition only after attack formations advanced out of range of supporting guns. There, at a depth of 3 kilometers, German aviation arrived to bomb advancing Soviet units.

In 32d Guards Rifle Corps' center, the 97th Guards Rifle Division plunged through positions of the 164th Infantry Regiment, quickly seized all forward trenches, and pushed on toward Streletskoye. At a depth of 3 kilometers lead regiment commanders committed their second echelon rifle battalions. Despite German air attacks, the two lead regiments steadily pressed on and overran the 164th Infantry Regiment headquarters on the north bank of the Vorskla River. At 1150, the forward detachments of 1st Tank Army passed through the advancing 97th Guards Rifle Division infantry and began their exploitation. Capitalizing on the impact of 1st Tank Army's commitment, the 97th Guards Rifle Division continued its advance, overran defensive positions of the 164th Infantry Regiment north of Streletskoye and secured a battery of heavy German guns. On approaching new German defensive positions near Streletskoye, the division commander committed his second echelon regiment and reestablished an offensive momentum that carried the 97th Guards Rifle Division by nightfall to German defensive positions 3 kilometers northeast of Tomarovka.[69]

The 13th and 66th Guards Rifle Divisions on the left and right flank of the 97th Guards kept pace. The 13th Guards overwhelmed forward German positions of the 164th Infantry Regiment and struck south across the Vorskla River under the cover of assault aviation aircraft. The division's first echelon regiments ran into strong opposition at a depth of 3 kilometers and came under heavy German air attack but, nevertheless, continued their advance. At 1140 1st Tank Army forward detachments passed through division positions and headed south. As the forward elements of 1st Tank Army passed from view the division commander committed his second echelon regiment. The three regiments then raced south, cut the Tomarovka–Belgorod road and dug in south of the highway in positions well ahead of other army divisions.[70] The 66th Guards Rifle Division, attacking straight down the road to Tomarovka, overran 164th Infantry Regiment positions; cleared several villages north of Tomarovka; and, by nightfall, joined the 97th Guards Rifle Division 4 kilometers northeast of Tomarovka.

Meanwhile, the 33d Guards Rifle Corps' attack progressed as successfully as that of the 32d Guards Rifle Corps. The 6th Guards Airborne Division struck and penetrated German 332d Infantry Division defensive positions already pulverized by the artillery and crossed the Vorskla

11. Tanks and infantry in the assault, Belgorod, August 1943.

12. Artillery firing over open sights, Belgorod, August 1943.

13. Combined infantry, tank assault on an objective, August 1943.

River by 0930. Lead regiments then committed their reserve battalions, and the division overcame the German second defensive position. At 1100 5th Guards Tank Army forward detachments passed through the advancing division. The tank army's main force cleared the area by 1500 and smashed remaining opposition in much of the division's sector. By nightfall, the division reached positions west of Yakhontov.

On the 6th Guards Airborne Division's left flank, the 95th Guards Rifle Division's attack progressed apace. While assisting passage of 5th Guards Tank Army units (1100–1300 hours), the division had to commit its second echelon regiment to support the 252d Rifle Division on its left whose advance had been held up by resisting German units. In spite of the delay, the 95th Guards Rifle Division penetrated to a depth of 8 kilometers on 3 August, reached Yakhontov and drove off elements of the German 114th Infantry Regiment defending in that location.[71]

5th Guards Army's assault on 3 August penetrated German defenses to depths of from 8 to 14 kilometers. The armor of 1st and 5th Guards Tank Armies, which by midday had crushed remaining enemy resistance, produced that high tempo of advance. While infantry units advanced through the forward German positions the lead brigades of the two tank armies followed 2–3 kilometers behind. At 1000, the 200th and 49th Tank Brigades, leading 1st Tank Army's two first echelon corps (6th Tank Corps and 3d Mechanized Corps), crossed the Vorskla River in the wake of the advancing infantry on routes prepared by the engineers.[72] The brigades formed in battalion and company columns and prepared to advance south at high speed. The 200th Tank Brigade and follow-on brigades of 6th Tank Corps were to sweep through Streletskoye, secure Tomarovka, and reach Borisovka by nightfall. The 3d Mechanized Corps would advance in tandem on the 6th Tank Corps' left flank. At 1330 the 200th and 49th Tank Brigades began their race south, bypassed the advancing Soviet rifle units, and pressed on toward Tomarovka. From 1420 to 1530 hours, nineteen groups of assault aircraft, in groups of six to eight aircraft, covered the commitment to battle of 1st Tank Army's first echelon corps. By 1700 the 200th Tank Brigade had cleared Streletskoye but met heavy opposition by the 164th Infantry Regiment northwest of Tomarovka. Meanwhile, the 49th Tank Brigade secured Domnin and cut the Belgorod–Tomarovka road east of Tomarovka.

1st Tank Army's first echelon corps were not able to exploit the forward detachments' success rapidly enough. A difficult crossing of the Vorskla River caused by hasty engineer preparations and the widespread smoke and confusion of the battle led to the corps' piecemeal commitment. Once across the Vorskla River, all corps units had to use the one road that ran toward Tomarovka. The 6th Motorized Rifle Brigade, which reached 200th Tank Brigade positions after 2000 hours, was immediately

14. Armor destroying a strongpoint, August 1943.

15. Grenade assault on German positions.

involved in repulsing German counterattacks. The 22d Tank Brigade arrived to assist 200th Tank Brigade at Pushkarnoye only at 2100 hours. Thereafter the Germans withdrew southwest to Tomarovka with 6th Tank Corps in pursuit. To the southeast, 1st Guards Tank Brigade finally joined the battle at 1800 in support of the 49th Tank Brigade at Domnin.

While 1st Tank Army units closed on Tomarovka and Domnin, German 19th Panzer Division units concentrated at Tomarovka to block the Soviet advance. The 74th Panzer Grenadier Regiment moved forward and reinforced 332d Infantry Division troops withdrawing to new positions north and north-east of Tomarovka, and the 73d Panzer Grenadier Regiment occupied defensive positions east of Tomarovka. That evening the two German regiments launched strong counterattacks against the

3d Mechanized Corps' brigades at Domnin in an attempt to reopen the Tomarovka–Belgorod road.

East of 1st Tank Army, in 33d Guards Rifle Corps' sector 5th Guards Tank Army followed the advancing Soviet infantry and prepared to commit its armored spearhead. The 32d and 110th Tank Brigades led 29th and 18th Tank Corps' columns toward German positions west of Stepnoye. The columns advanced gingerly across minefields, around obstacles, and through the debris of the overrun German positions. At 1400, the two forward detachments caught up with the 33d Guards Rifle Corps' infantry which, by that time, had cleared the German main defensive belt. With 5th Guards Army and 5th Guards Tank Army artillery firing in support and the 291st Assault Aviation Division and 10th Fighter Aviation Corps' aircraft covering their advance, the tanks charged ahead, through and around the last German strong-points. 5th Guards Tank Army's operational group followed and established its command post just east of Stepnoye. By nightfall, against dwindling opposition, 5th Guards Tank Army's corps assembled well south of the Belgorod–Tomarovka road 26 kilometers in the rear of initial German defense lines.[73]

While 5th Guards, 1st Tank, and 5th Guards Tank Armies ripped a gaping hole in German defenses, 6th Guards Army, on 5th Guards Army's right flank, attacked due south toward Tomarovka. The 23d Guards Rifle Corps of Maj. Gen. P.P. Bakhmareyev launched the army main attack east of Butovo supported by 5th Guards Army's 32d Rifle Corps on its left and the 71st Guards Rifle Division of 23d Guards Rifle Corps on its right. Capitalizing on the earlier success of reconnaissance groups, the 51st Guards and 52d Guards Rifle Divisions made rapid initial progress and penetrated the first defensive positions of the 332d Infantry Division. The 52d Guards Rifle Division, supported by a tank regiment, advanced with all three regiments on line. After seizing the first German trenches, the division's right flank regiment ran into heavy undestroyed German positions along a tributary of the Vorskla River which held up the advance for over an hour until the position was outflanked from the west. The 52d Guards Rifle Division continued its advance and, by evening, approached to within 4 kilometers north of Tomarovka. There counterattacks by 19th Panzer Division's 74th Panzer Grenadier Regiment slowed the division's progress and finally halted it, 3 kilometers north of Tomarovka.[74]

On the 52d Guards Rifle Division's right flank, at 0800 the 51st Guards Rifle Division and the 71st Guards Rifle Division of 22d Guards Rifle Corps attacked into the town of Butovo and drove the German 676th Infantry Regiment from it. However, the attack in this sector developed less favorably. German positions on the 71st Guards Rifle Division's right flank held firm; and, as the 71st and 51st Guards Rifle Divisions approached Tamnoye, south of Butovo, counterattacks rained down on the 71st right flank, bringing its progress to a halt short of the town. Simultaneously, the 52d Panzer Detachment, with its Tiger tanks supported by infantry of the 255th Infantry Division, struck the 51st Guards Rifle Division northeast of Tamnoye and halted its advance. Chistyakov reacted by ordering Major General N.B. Ibyansky of 22d Guards Rifle Corps to commit his second echelon division (90th Guards Rifle Division) to support the 71st Guards Rifle Division. Even that maneuver failed to break the German hold on Tamnoye.[75]

Zhukov visited Chistyakov to inquire whether he had committed 5th Guards Tank Corps to battle. That corps, according to the army plan, was to have joined battle in the 71st Guards Rifle Division sector once that division reached the Vorskla River. Chistyakov replied that in light of the 71st's lack of progress 5th Guards Tanks Corps was not yet engaged. Zhukov ordered him to commit the tank corps in 23d Guards Rifle Corps' sector.[76] By nightfall 5th Guards Tank Corps' brigades joined the infantry battling for German positions north of Tomarovka, but the effect of the reinforcements was negligible.

Managarov's 53d Army and 48th Rifle Corps of 69th Army, attacking on 5th Guards Army's left, faced German defenses covering the northern approaches to Belgorod. Each of Managarov's three first echelon divisions (252d Rifle Division, 28th Guards Rifle Division, and 116th Rifle Division) and the 305th Rifle Division and 89th Guards Rifle Division of 48th Guards Rifle Corps had a tank regiment in support. In addition, Major General D. M. Solomatin's 1st Mechanized Corps was posed to exploit the success of Managarov's advance. The three German regiments of the 167th Infantry Division defending this sector had some initial support from the reconnaissance battalions of 6th Panzer Division and other small tank elements from the panzer division which, on the morning of 3 August, were located 7–8 kilometers south of the front lines. German defenses were particularly strong in the 339th Infantry Regiment's sector where the Germans created strong points in a clump of woods near Zhuravlinyi which turned out to be located on the boundary between the Soviet 252d and 28th Guards Rifle Divisions.

At 0800 the Soviet infantry and tanks advanced, supported by regimental 45mm and 76mm guns, and quickly overran the already mostly destroyed German forward trenches. At a depth of 1 kilometer into the German defenses west of Zhuravlinyi, the 252d Rifle Division took heavy fire from the woods on their left. Simultaneously, the 28th Guards Rifle Division, advancing on to 252d Rifle Division's left received heavy fire from the same woods on its right flank. The 4-kilometer square woods, located at a point between the two divisions became a focal point of combat for both divisions on 3 August.[77] (It was defended by portions of the 2d and 3d Battalions, 315th Infantry Regiment, 167th Infantry Division, and by 6th Panzer Division tanks.) After heavy Soviet artillery and mortar fire failed to uproot the German defenders a combined infantry and tank assault finally rooted the German defenders out of the woods. The 252d Rifle Division was further delayed by a German counterattack supported by a few 6th Panzer Division tanks. Assistance from the 95th Rifle Division on the right and air strikes blunted the German counterattack.

Having overcome initial German resistance, the two Soviet divisions then ran into German defenses anchored on a string of villages east and west of Gonki south of Zhuravlinyi. The 89th Guards Rifle Regiment, 28th Guards Rifle Division attempted to envelop Gonki from the west; but, while the envelopment was in progress, German tanks sortied northward from Gonki. The regimental commander used his second echelon battalion and his anti-tank reserve to repel the attack. Meanwhile, other elements of the 28th Guards Rifle Division continued their advance into the valley of the Yerik River and ran into heavy defenses erected by withdrawing Germans and German reinforcements which had arrived from the rear. The division assaulted German positions along the river and secured a lodgement south of the river but was halted by heavy German fire on the outskirts of Yerik.[78] Simultaneously, the 252d Rifle Division to the west assaulted German positions from Berezov to Yakhontov.

While the 252d Rifle Division and 28th Guards Rifle Division struggled forward toward Berezov and Yerik, the 116th Rifle Division, supported by the 35th Tank Regiment, struck the 331st Infantry Regiment of 167th Infantry Division. Two rifle regiments led the attack followed by one rifle regiment in second echelon. The division's immediate objectives were 4 kilometers deep into the German defense. By 1030 the two lead regiments had penetrated to a depth of 2–2.5 kilometers and repelled several German counterattacks.[79] By 1300 the division had penetrated the second German position and was approaching new German positions in the Yerik River valley on a line with the 252d and 28th Guards Rifle Divisions on the left and somewhat in advance of the 305th Rifle Division of 48th Rifle Corps on the right.

At this juncture General Konev ordered Managarov to commit the 1st Mechanized Corps in order to speed up the advance rather than wait and use the corps for exploitation, thus Konev required the corps to provide infantry support. Solomatin's corps advanced into battle with his 219th Tank, 19th Mechanized, and 37th Mechanized Brigades deployed from left to right in first echelon, each supporting a first echelon division and each led by a forward detachment. 35th Mechanized Brigade remained in second echelon. Reinforced by the 37th Mechanized Brigade the 252d Rifle Division took Berezov and Yakhontov and, by evening, confronted new German defenses at Rakovo.[80]

Further east, the 19th Mechanized Brigade joined the 28th Guards Rifle Division's attack on Yerik. Although the division finally seized Yerik, it could not penetrate the German defenses on the south bank of the river; and the attacks died off at nightfall. Meanwhile, at 1300 the 219th Tank Brigade moved up to support the 116th Rifle Division, then fighting along the Belgorod road north of the Yerik River. By day's end this division also worked its way forward to the German defense lines at Yerik which had also been reinforced by elements of 6th Panzer Division. Thus, by nightfall on 3 August 53d Army forces had advanced up to 8 kilometers and had destroyed a major portion of the German 167th Infantry Division. However, early commitment of 1st Mechanized Corps deprived the army of its large tank maneuver force, and now 53d Army had run into heavy German defenses along the Yerik River.

On 53d Army's left flank, 48th Rifle Corps' 305th, 89th Guards, and 183d Rifle Divisions struck at German defenses from Vysloye to the Northern Donets River, a sector defended by a battalion of the 167th Infantry Division and a regiment of the 168th Infantry Division. These Soviet divisions, which lacked heavy armor support, found the going more difficult than their neighbors. The 305th Rifle Division by day's end had advanced 4 kilometers but was halted by heavy German defenses at Ternovka. However, the threat to the German left flank posed by 116th Rifle Division forced a German withdrawal to Yerik River positions during the night of 3–4 August. Likewise, the 89th Guards Rifle Division and 183d Rifle Division made limited progress, but the Germans withdrew in the evening to defense lines running in tandem with units defending to the west, generally from the Northern Donets River to Shopino.[81]

On 3 August, the remainder of 69th Army and 7th Guards Army divisions made numerous attempts to cross the Northern Donets River opposite Belgorod and to expand their bridgeheads at Solomino and Toplinka, but all efforts to do so failed. Numerous bridging attempts in the German 106th Infantry Division sector south of Belgorod failed due to heavy German artillery fire.[82]

Nevertheless, the Soviets achieved all of their major objectives for 3 August. 5th Guards Army's attack was successful, in particular that of the 13th Guards Rifle Division which punched through the tactical defenses and cut the Tomarovka–Belgorod road. Both tank armies (1st Tank Army, 5th Guards Tank Army) were in action, although German resistance was already diverting 1st Tank Army to combat in the Tomarovka area, thus making the exploitation more complicated than expected. 6th Guards Army and 53d Army also overcame the tactical defense zones. However, both armies had committed their mobile groups (5th Guards Tank Corps and 1st Mechanized Corps) to infantry support, and both had become bogged down in heavy fighting, the former at Tomarovka and the latter along the Yerik River. What remained to be seen on 4 August was whether that use of armor would provide the additional strength necessary for Soviet forces to take Tomarovka and Belgorod on schedule, that is by 5 August. In these initial attacks, the Soviets badly mauled the German 332d and 167th Infantry Divisions. Further German resistance depended on their ability to reform the remnants of these divisions into coherent units capable of defense and on the ability of 19th Panzer Division and 6th Panzer Division to fill the growing gaps in the German lines. Particularly threatening to German defense plans was the Soviet 5th Guards Tank Army's penetration 26 kilometers deep into the interval between German 4th Panzer Army and Army Detachment Kempf.

The Voronezh Front on the Second Day – 4 August 1943

On 4 August, Soviet forces sought to widen their offensive (see Map 60). Rifle forces of 6th Guards Army and 5th Guards Army, aided by infantry support tanks, strove to complete the penetration of the tactical defenses, in particular in the Tomarovka area where German defenders were making a deliberate defensive stand. Meanwhile, 1st Tank Army and 5th Guards Tank Army probed more deeply into the operational depths of the German defense in hopes of beginning a rapid exploitation toward Bogodukhov. However, as combat developed, 1st Tank Army units increasingly were attracted to combat with German units defending Tomarovka and Borisovka in the Vorskla River valley. 5th Guards Tank Army formations had broken cleanly through German defenses; but, as they began to exploit, their left flank units and 5th Guards Army rifle units began engaging German forces of Army Detachment Kempf which were erecting defenses north of Zolochev and north-west of Kazach'ya Lopan in a futile attempt to restore a continuous front with 4th Panzer Army. Meanwhile, against increasing resistance, Steppe Front forces of 53d, 69th, and 7th Guards Army continued their drive through the German tactical defenses north and east of Belgorod.

At 0400 the Voronezh Front commenced heavy air and artillery preparation against German positions north and east of Tomarovka. At 0430 the bombardment ceased, and tanks and infantry renewed their assaults on German positions which had been reinforced during the preceding night by 255th Infantry Division units and by the remainder of 19th Panzer Division. 6th Guards Army's 23d Guards Rifle Corps, supported by 5th Guards Tank Corps' tanks, repeatedly assaulted German positions but with only limited success. The 51st Guards and 71st Guards Rifle Divisions, in grinding battles lasting all day, pushed back the German units 4 kilometers to new defensive positions just south of the rail line running northwest from Tomarovka. The 52d Guards Rifle Division with 5th Guards Tank Corps support pushed the 74th Panzer Grenadier

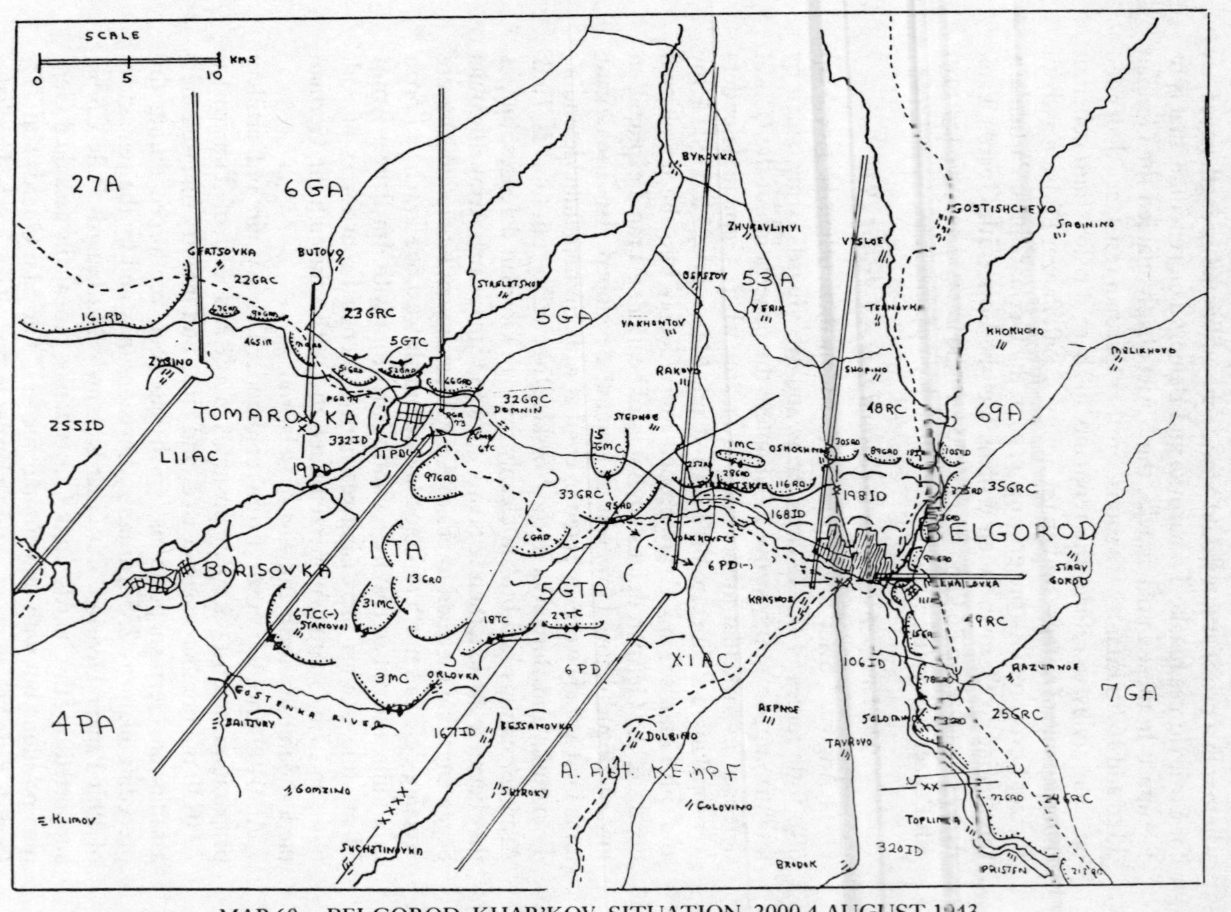

MAP 60 BELGOROD–KHAR'KOV. SITUATION. 2000 4 AUGUST 1943

Regiment and 255th Infantry Division infantry back about 2 kilometers to positions along the rail line north and northwest of Tomarovka.[83]

Meanwhile, 5th Guards Army's divisions of 32d Guards Rifle Corps continued to hammer away at German positions east of Tomarovka. At 0430, after a short artillery preparation, the 66th Guards and 97th Guards Rifle Divisions launched new assaults. The 66th drove the 19th Panzer Division's reconnaissance battalion and elements of the 164th Infantry Regiment back about 1.5 kilometers to defenses on the outskirts of Tomarovka where heavy German resistance again halted the division's advance. On the 66th Rifle Division's left, the 97th Guards Rifle Division repeatedly assaulted German positions only to be repulsed by 19th Panzer Division's 73d Panzer Grenadier Regiment. Only the 13th Guards Rifle Division was able to make appreciable gains in cooperation with 1st Tank Army units. Attacking from its positions south of the Belgorod–Tomarovka road, the division's regiments swept southwest in the wake of the 1st Tank Army advance. Unbeknownst to the Germans, the 13th Guards Rifle Division now threatened Tomarovka from the south as well as critical German communications lines running from Tomarovka to Borisovka.

On 32d Guards Rifle Corps' left flank, General Popov's 33d Guards Rifle Corps attacked south and southwest in the wake of 5th Guards Tank Army. The attacks struck the remnants of 167th Infantry Division, stiffened by 6th Panzer Division elements, and drove these German units south of the Tomarovka–Belgorod road. German defenses finally jelled in the Dolzhik area along the Borisovka–Belgorod road where the 6th Guards Airborne Division and 95th Rifle Division advance finally ground to a halt on the evening of 4 August.[84] The new German defense line now ran from Orlovka eastward to Dolzhik and northeastward toward Streletskoye, west of Belgorod. Although this new defense line emerged largely through 6th Panzer Division's efforts, it still left a sizable gap of about 20 kilometers between Army Detachment Kempf's left wing at Orlovka and 4th Panzer Army's right wing in the Tomarovka–Borisovka area.

While 6th Guards Army and 5th Guards Army pounded German defenses at Tomarovka, 1st Tank Army continued its exploitation. Katukov issued new orders on the night of 3–4 August.[85] Kravchenko's 5th Guards Tank Corps would cooperate with Getman's 6th Tank Corps in an attack on German positions at Tomarovka from the north and northeast while Krivoshein's 3d Mechanized Corps enveloped Tomarovka from the southeast. 6th Tank Corps' 6th Motorized Rifle Brigade and 200th Tank Brigade attacked on the morning of 4 August but made little progress. Nor could 5th Guards Tank Corps make a dent in the German defenses. However, the 3d Mechanized Corps had considerably more

16. Multiple rocket launchers [*katiushas*] of a guards' mortar battalion.

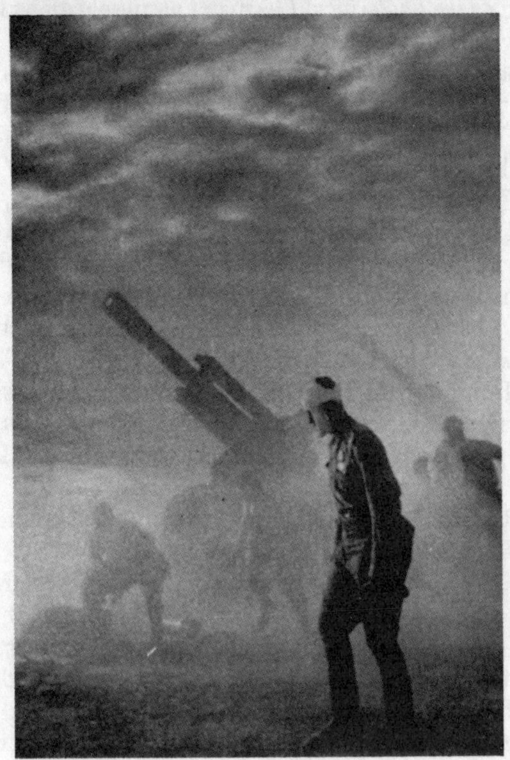

17. Firing an artillery preparation.

success. During the evening, the reconnaissance group of 1st Guards Tank Brigade discovered a gap in the German defenses east of Domnin. At first light, the brigade concentrated its forces and pushed through the gap. Krivoshein quickly shifted his 49th Tank Brigade and 1st Mechanized Brigade into the gap. The entire corps swept southwest through the German defenses, brushed aside a small German tank force along the Gostenka River southwest of Tomarovka, and thrust 20 kilometers south of the Gostenka River where the corps halted to consolidate its position and erect flank defenses.[86]

Katukov, bothered by the stalemate at Tomarovka, regrouped his forces to capitalize on Krivoshein's advance. His new orders to 6th Tank Corps read:

(1) The enemy stubbornly defends Tomarovka.
(2) Envelop Tomarovka from the east with the tank brigade and, with 6th Motorized Rifle Brigade, blockade it from the east and north [together with 5th Guards Tank Corps].[87]

Prodded into action by this order the 200th, 22d, and 112th Tank Brigades assembled east of Tomarovka; and, led by 22d Tank Brigade, on 4 August the force marched via Domnin into positions in the forests west of Stanovoi. Now both the 6th Tank Corps (less 6th Motorized Rifle Brigade) and 3d Mechanized Corps of 1st Tank Army were well into the German rear and located frighteningly close to the communications lines of the 19th Panzer, 255th and 332d Infantry Divisions still fighting around Tomarovka. 31st Tank Corps also continued its march forward. 1st Tank Army's position insured that the breach between 4th Panzer Army and Army Detachment Kempf could not be restored without a major German withdrawal to new positions in the south. German operational records noted the Soviet penetration but underestimated its scale. Thus, German 4th Panzer Army forces continued to defend Tomarovka, unaware of the serious threat to their flank and rear.

While 1st Tank Army exploited the gap in German defenses, Rotmistrov's 5th Guards Tank Army continued its southerly advance. At 0500 on 4 August Kirichenko's 29th Tank Corps set out toward Orlovka and Yegorov's 18th Tank Corps toward Bessonovka and Shchetinovka with 33d Guards Rifle Corps infantry now trailing over 10 kilometers to their rear. At 0900 the mobile corps' forward detachments approached the northern outskirts of Orlovka and Bessonovka, where they ran into deployed elements of 6th Panzer Division in defensive positions on the south bank of the Gostenka River. Heavy fighting raged all day as a skillful German defense using the river and village as obstacles limited 5th Guards Tank Army's gains to only 3–4 kilometers.[88] German aircraft attacks added to the discomfiture of Soviet tankers.

In late morning Rotmistrov decided to reinforce his two lead corps with Skvortsov's second echelon 5th Guards Mechanized Corps in order to crush German resistance and prevent the remnants of the 167th Infantry Division and 332d Infantry Division from escaping southward. 5th Guards Mechanized Corps was to outflank German defenders from the west, secure Zolochev by the evening of 4 August, and render 6th Panzer Division's defensive positions untenable. At 1100 5th Guards Mechanized Corps reached its jumping-off positions. However, a new order from Vatutin changed 5th Guards Mechanized Corps' mission and aborted Rotmistrov's plan. In light of the difficulty 53d Army was experiencing in its advance on Belgorod, Vatutin told Rotmistrov to release his mechanized corps to 53d Army control for an attack in coordination with 1st Mechanized Corps on the left rear of German forces defending positions west of Belgorod.[89] Deprived of 5th Guards Mechanized Corps' support, Rotmistrov's two tank corps tried several more times to smash through 6th Panzer Division's defenses at Orlovka only to fail in each attempt.

The success of 1st Tank Army, which Rotmistrov learned of on the evening of 4 August, opened new opportunities for 5th Guards Tank Army to circumvent 6th Panzer Division's defenses. He immediately ordered Yegorov to swing his 18th Tank Corps westward and southward around 6th Panzer Division's left flank to new positions northwest of Gomzino in what amounted to an envelopment of Orlovka from the west. Meanwhile, Kirichenko's corps would cooperate with approaching 33d Guards Rifle Corps troops and continue its attacks on the German front lines of Orlovka. Yegorov dispatched his reconnaissance detachments southwestward on the evening of 4 August while his main force prepared to march on the morning of 5 August. Thus, 5th Guards Tank Army prepared to participate fully in the offensive success of 1st Tank Army, adding to the growing threat to the integrity of German defenses.

With their front at Tomarovka under heavy attack and Soviet armored forces enveloping their right flank, German defenders at Tomarovka heard other disquieting news on 4 August. During the day General Trofimenko's 27th Army in the Soldatskoye–Gertsovka sector conducted reconnaissance operations in company to battalion strength. Particularly ominous were Soviet reconnaissance activities in 11th Panzer Division's sector west of Soldatskoye where Soviet reconnaissance units penetrated several kilometers and seized portions of the forward German trench lines. Similar Soviet reconnaissance efforts on a smaller scale occurred in 57th Infantry Division's sector westward toward Krasnopol'ye. This reconnaissance indicated an impending Soviet offensive in these sectors that would only add to the woes of German forces defending at Tomarovka. Moreover, a Soviet advance southward from Soldatskoye would threaten the left flank and rear of the German Tomarovka Group and render their positions untenable. This, in fact, was the Soviet plan, as the events of 5 August bore out.

The Voronezh Front on the Third Day – 5 August 1943: Formation of the Tomarovka–Borisovka Pocket

On 5 August 6th Guards and 5th Guards Armies continued hammering at German positions around Tomarovka while armored forces of 1st and 5th Guards Tank Armies plunged deeper and deeper into the rear of those defenders (see Map 61). Simultaneously 27th Army struck violently southward from the Soldatskoye area and penetrated perilously close to German communications links with the Tomarovka defenders. Chistyakov's 6th Guards Army divisions struck at dawn north and northwest of Tomarovka. The 23d Guards Rifle Corps' 52d Guards Rifle Division struck at the 19th Panzer Division's reconnaissance battalion and 74th Panzer Grenadier Regiment, but the 52d's attack stalled in the northern and northwestern outskirts of the town. The 51st Guards Rifle Division attacked positions of the 255th Infantry Division, and the 19th Panzer Division's Pioneer Battalion, penetrated 6 kilometers, and was halted only 4 kilometers north of the Tomarovka–Borisovka road by Tiger tanks of the 52d Panzer Detachment. Late in the day a regiment of 52d Guards Rifle Division, supported by a tank battalion, briefly cut through to the Borisovka road before being repulsed and driven back a short distance. The right wing of Chistyakov's army (22d Guards Rifle Corps with 67th Guards Rifle Division and 71st Guards Rifle Division) lunged southwest in an attempt to penetrate to Zybino, but its attacks halted 2 kilometers east of that town.[90] Try as he did, Chistyakov could not completely break the German defenses north of Tomarovka.

East of Tomarovka 32d Guards Rifle Corps' division of 5th Guards Army continued their attacks. The 66th Guards Rifle Division, supported by the 6th Motorized Rifle Brigade of 6th Tank Corps and heavy artillery strikes, made some headway; but counterattacks by 73d Panzer Grenadier Regiment drove the attackers back. Consequently, General Rodimtsev left the 66th Guards Rifle Division to blockade Tomarovka and shifted the other divisions of 32d Guards Rifle Corps westward in order to attack German communication routes running west from Tomarovka. The 97th Guards Rifle Division regiments reached out to cut the road from Borisovka to Tomarovka. The division's 289th and 292d Guards Rifle Regiments were halted short of the road while the 294th Guards Rifle Regiment moved against Borisovka proper. The 13th Guards Rifle Division made the greatest progress; and, by the evening of 5 August, its regiments, with 1st Tank Army units, concentrated in the Baitsury and Gomzino area south of Borisovka in positions

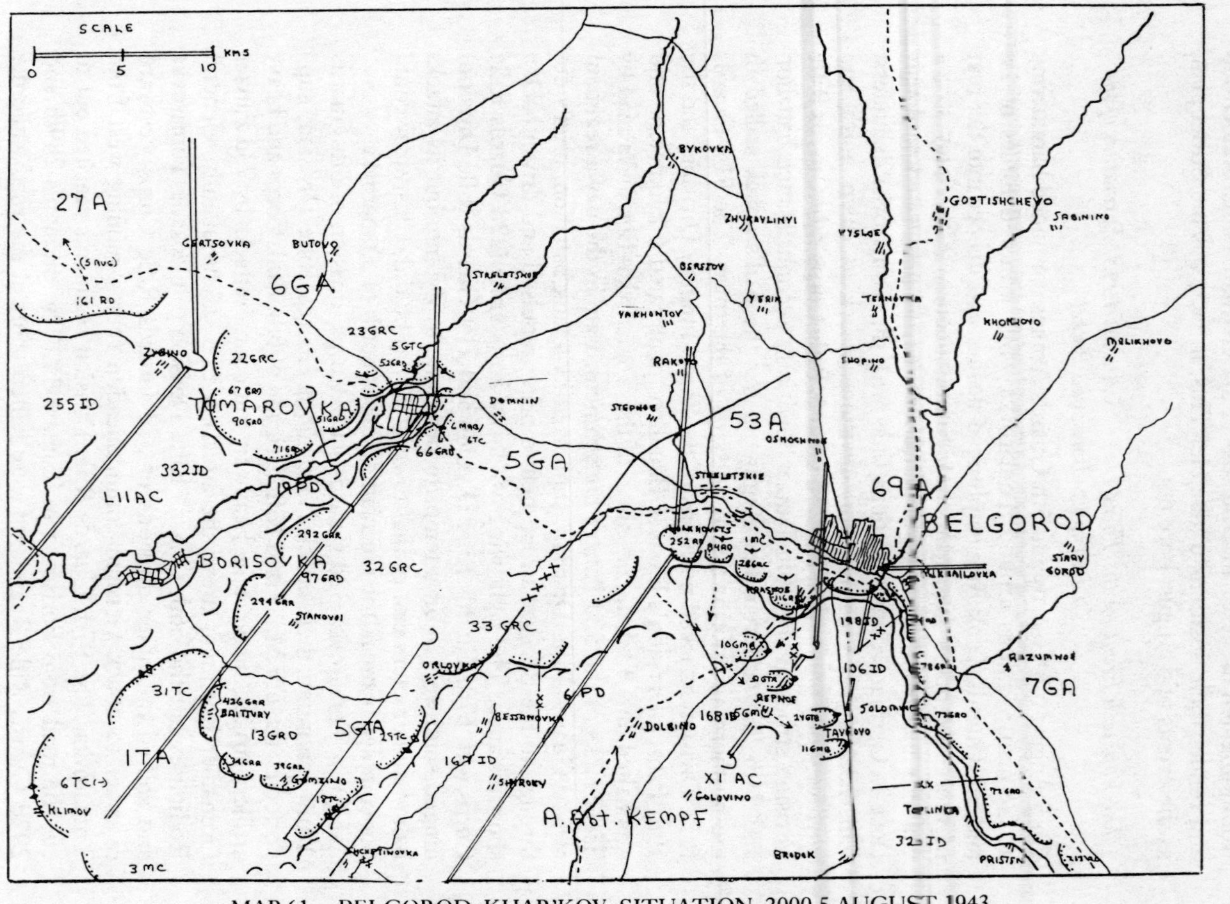

MAP 61. BELGOROD–KHAR'KOV, SITUATION, 2000 5 AUGUST 1943

from which it could strike even deeper against German communications.[91]

Meanwhile, 5th Guards Army's 33d Guards Rifle Corps' divisions struggled with the German 167th Infantry and 6th Panzer Divisions along the Orlovka–Dolzhik line. Progress in this area was minimal, but 33d Guards Rifle Corps' divisions prepared to take advantage of 5th Guards Tank Army's advances around the German defenders' left flank toward Zolochev.

With the German Tomarovka defenses and defenses from Orlovka to Dolzhik holding firm the Voronezh Front commander, Vatutin, pushed his tank army commanders to advance deeper into the German rear area to render those German defenses untenable. In the immediate future, Vatutin hoped 1st Tank Army and 27th Army could encircle the entire German Borisovka–Tomarovka Group. 1st Tank Army continued its southwestward advance on 5 August; and, by the end of the day, 6th Tank Corps and 2d Mechanized Corps neared the Klimov area south and southeast of Golovchino. During the day Katukov had detected German preparations to withdraw from Tomarovka. Consequently, he ordered 6th Motorized Rifle Brigade and 5th Guards Tank Corps (now under his control) to begin disengaging from Tomarovka and rejoin 1st Tank Army's main force preparatory to his army's advance on Golovchino, Graivoron, and his principal objective of Bogodukhov.[92] 31st Tank Corps was to assist 32d Guards Rifle Corps' assaults on German positions at Golovchino and Borisovka from the southeast.

The same day Rotmistrov's 5th Guards Tank Army, hindered by German air strikes, began its envelopment of 6th Panzer Division and 167th Infantry Division defenses at Orlovka. The Germans attempted to extend their lines southwest to forestall an envelopment, but as they did so their lines became thinner and thinner. They simply lacked the reserves necessary to plug the growing gaps in the defenses. By 1800 on 5 August, 5th Guards Tank Army reported to the *front* chief of staff:

(1) 18th Tank Corps – having enveloped Orlovka from the west at 1700 – two brigades (110th Tank Brigade and 32d Motorized Rifle Brigade) arrived at Gomzino and continued their advance on Shchetinovka. In the future the brigades will secure the operations of the corps on the left toward Zolochev.
(2) 29th Tank Corps at 1600 secured Orlovka with its main force. It is developing success to the southwest.
(3) 5th Guards Mechanized Corps is attacking Gryaznoye. It is cooperating with 1st Mechanized Corps units of General M.D. Solomatin.[93]

5th Guards Tank Army, although it had not crushed German defenses south of Orlovka, severely overlapped those defenses on the west and threatened Shchetinovka in the Germans' rear. German Army Detachment Kempf had few forces to hold back Rotmistrov's advance. III Panzer Corps headquarters had arrived at Zolochev, but its subordinate units had not yet arrived. The first of these, 3d Panzer Division, was assembling at Novaya Vodolaga, south of Khar'kov. Thus, 5th Guards Tank Army had at least a full day to continue its exploitation before being confronted with heavier opposition.

While 1st Tank Army concentrated its forces south of the Golovchino–Borisovka area and 5th Guards Tank Army threatened Army Detachment Kempf's left flank and rear, General Trofimenko's 27th Army and General Moskalenko's 40th Army launched their offensives against 4th Panzer Army defenses west of Tomarovka. Trofimenko's attack, together with 1st Tank Army's movements, threatened the very survival of 19th Panzer, 255th Infantry, and 332d Infantry Divisions in the Tomarovka–Borisovka pocket (see Map 62).

Trofimenko planned his army's main attack in the sector west of Soldatskoye.[94] This sector was defended by 11th Panzer Division which had half of the division forward and half located in assembly areas north of Graivoron. The 11th Panzer Division's armored strength was fifty tanks. Trofimenko's shock group, consisting of the 163d and 166th Rifle Divisions, would attack after a short artillery preparation and penetrate the main German defensive positions. General Poluboyarov's 4th Guards Tank Corps, the mobile group of the army, would then advance rapidly to secure Golovchino and cut German communications routes running from Graivoron to Tomarovka. Subsequently, the tank corps would exploit southwest toward Akhtyrka.

Poluboyarov's corps would pass through the advancing Soviet infantry in a 4 kilometer sector along two routes with its main force on the right flank. The 14th Guards Tank Brigade would operate as a corps forward detachment followed by the corps main body (12th Guards Tank Brigade and 3d Guards Motorized Rifle Brigade) and the 13th Guards Tank Brigade in corps reserve. Trofimenko ordered the 241st Rifle Division to cooperate closely with the advancing tank corps and attached two sapper battalions to the corps to assist in the advance and prepare crossings for Poluboyarov's corps over the Vorskla River. 27th Army artillery would fire artillery support for introduction of the corps into battle. In addition, each of Poluboyarov's brigades received a battery of anti-aircraft artillery beyond its authorized air defense assets.[95]

On 4 August advanced battalions of 27th Army had seized the first German defensive trenches and had cleared German mine fields on the north bank of the Vorsklitsa River thus enabling 4th Guards Tank Corps to deploy close to the remaining German positions. Early on 5 August, after an artillery preparation, the 163d and 166th Rifle Divisions crashed

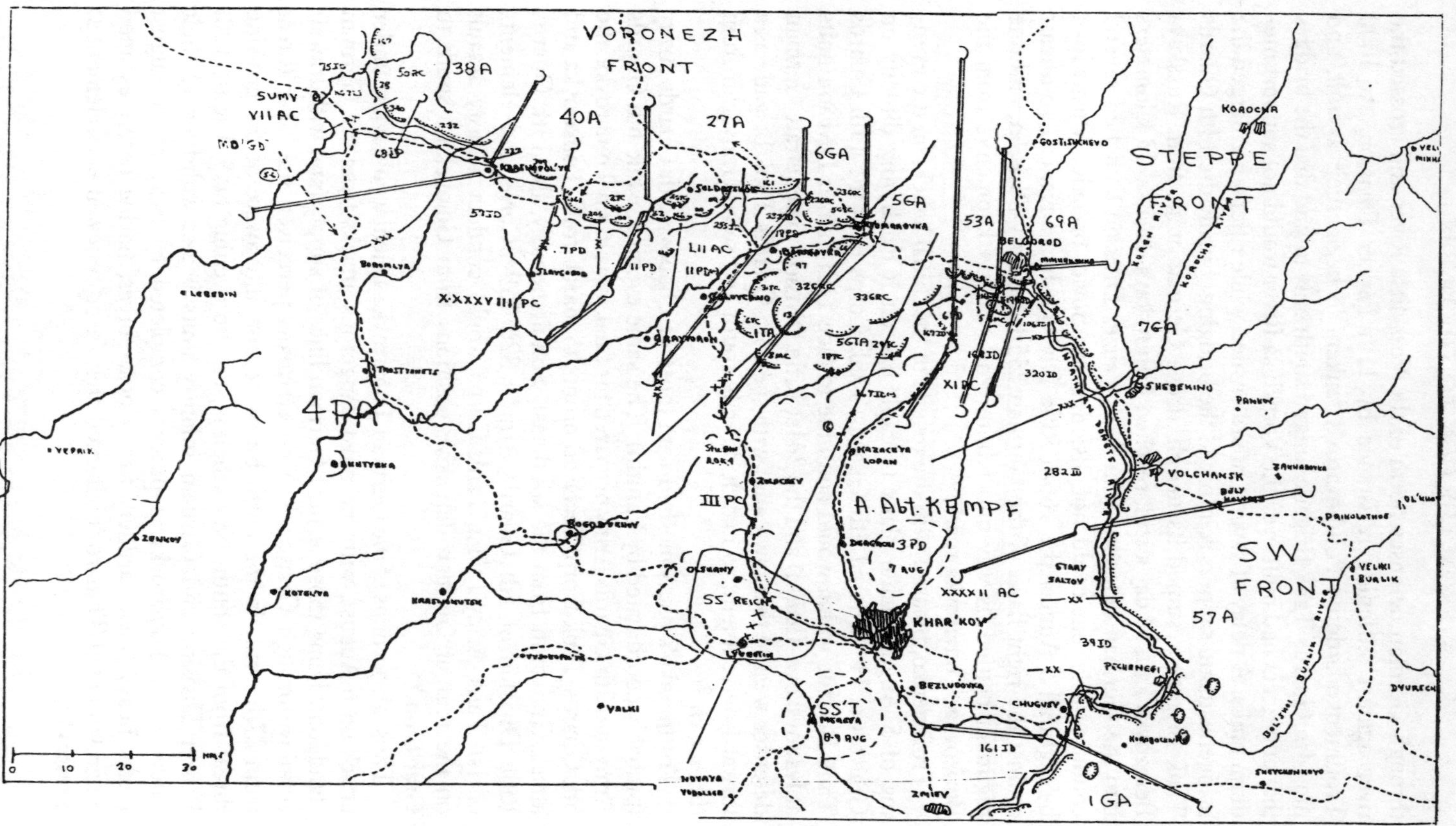

MAP 62. BELGOROD–KHAR'KOV, SITUATION, 2000 5 AUGUST 1943

through German defenses north of the Vorsklitsa River and crossed the river against stiffening resistance by 11th Panzer Division. At 1000 Trofimenko ordered Poluboyarov's tankers to begin their assault, and the 14th Guards Tank Brigade lunged south only to find that the bridges that engineers had built over the Vorsklitsa River would not support medium tanks. A delay of several hours ensued while riflemen enlarged the bridgehead and sappers reinforced the bridging. Finally the 14th Guards Tank Brigade resumed its march, drove German units from Russkaya Berezovka and, by day's end, reached Ivanovskaya–Lisitsa, 13 kilometers into the German defenses. The 11th Panzer Division launched several counterattacks but could not dislodge the Soviet brigade. Meanwhile, by nightfall 5 August the 166th Rifle Division had advanced southeast against the right flank of the German 255th Infantry Division, and one regiment battled its way into Khotmyzhsk, only 4 kilometers from the Borisovka–Tomarovka road.[96]

Trofimenko, pleased with the results of the initial attack, on the evening of 5 August made plans to capitalize on it by driving directly on Graivoron. He ordered 4th Guards Tank Corps (less the 14th Guards Tank Brigade which would continue to face 11th Panzer Division units at Ivanovskaya–Lisitsa) and the 241st Rifle Division to penetrate German defenses west of that town and, with the 13th Guards Tank Brigade as a forward detachment, to march directly south and seize Graivoron from the march.[97]

Trofimenko's plans meshed with those of Zhadov's 5th Guards Army (probably coordinated by Vatutin). The same evening, while 6th Guards Army and 5th Guards Army prepared for final assaults on Tomarovka, the 5th Guards Tank Corps received orders to march from Tomarovka and attack Graivoron from the southeast. Simultaneously, the 13th Guards Rifle Division of 5th Guards Army's 32d Rifle Corps and elements of 1st Tank Army's 31st Tank Corps would conduct a hasty assault on the rear of German defensive positions from Golovchino south to Graivoron.[98]

Thus, all portions of the German Tomarovka salient would come under attack on 6 August, with the most dangerous attacks from the German standpoint being those against German lines of supply (and withdrawal) running through Graivoron. The Germans perceived the clear threat from 27th Army in the north but were not fully aware of the growing threat from the south. Nevertheless, on the evening of 5 August 19th Panzer Division and German infantry units began withdrawing their forces from Tomarovka, a process completed by early on 6 August under heavy Soviet artillery fire. These forces, having barely escaped encirclement at Tomarovka, immediately faced renewed encirclement at Borisovka.

18. Artillery accompanying the assault.

19. Motorized infantry and armor advancing.

While the noose tightened around the German Tomarovka–Borisovka Group, on 5 August Moskalenko's 40th Army expanded the Soviet offensive westward. Moskalenko's army was to attack in a 7 kilometer sector along the Vorsklitsa River west of Soldatskoye, protect 27th Army's flank, and sweep southwest toward Boromlya and Trostyanets. After a two-hour artillery preparation 47th Rifle Corps' 100th and 206th Rifle Divisions would initiate the attack; and, after penetration of the defense, Major General A.F. Popov's 2d Tank Corps would begin the exploitation. The 161st Rifle Division, deployed on the left flank of 27th Army (in 40th Army's old sector from Gertsovka to Soldatskoye), would relocate westward on 5 August (after 27th Army attacked) and reinforce the 40th Army's 52d Rifle Corps. Only one rifle division (237th) would operate on 40th Army's right flank westward to Krasnopol'ye until the 309th Rifle Division's scheduled arrival on 7 August.[99] Vatutin also planned to reinforce Moskalenko's army with Major General V.M. Alekseyev's 10th Corps (from 27th Army's sector) shortly after Moskalenko's offensive began.

Opposite Moskalenko's lines, XXXXVIII Panzer Corps' 57th Infantry Division defended from Krasnopol'ye to Terebrino, west of Soldatskoye; and one regiment of the 332d Infantry Division faced Moskalenko's main attack. XXXXVIII Panzer Corps had made some defensive adjustments after the Soviet storm broke north of Belgorod on 3 August. That day 7th Panzer Division, in corps reserve in the Lebedin and Boromlya area (with a relatively heavy armored strength of fifty-eight tanks and twenty-four assault guns), moved forward to assembly areas around Slavgorod. The following day the division took up positions on the 57th Infantry Division's right flank and in the rear of the 11th Panzer Division.[100]

At 0515 5 August Moskalenko's artillery preparation tore at German defensive positions. Two hours later his rifle divisions went into action covered by a dense smoke screen laid by artillery during the final ten minutes of the preparation. The smoke screen completely blinded German strong points at Terebrino and masked the advancing infantry from German artillery fire. The 206th and 100th Rifle Divisions swept forward 4 kilometers, and at 1100 the 2d Tank Corps entered battle through positions of the 100th Rifle Division. By day's end the 100th Rifle Division and 2d Tank Corps approached Pochayevo, 8 kilometers deep, and the 206th Rifle Division Starosel'ye. 7th Panzer Division struck back with heavy counterattacks on the 206th Rifle Division's right flank. That evening the 161st Rifle Division arrived to bolster Moskalenko's attack. The division joined the 52d Rifle Corps, deployed on the left flank of the 237th Rifle Division, and prepared to advance to the southwest toward Boromyla. The 237th, 161st, and 206th Rifle Divisions would swing west and southwestward toward Boromyla while the 100th Rifle Division and 2d Tank Corps would take Pochayevo and advance southwest toward Trostyanets.[101] Moskalenko expected spirited German resistance as reports came in telling of increased German 7th Panzer Division support for the 57th Infantry Division.

Moskalenko's assault ruptured German defensive positions as far west as Krasnopol'ye. Occurring as it did during the most critical phases of the struggle for Tomarovka and Borisovka, it had the effect of tying down German forces and preventing reinforcement of the Tomarovka Group. In fact, it contributed to the growing threat of Soviet encirclement for all 4th Panzer Army forces operating east of Graivoron. By the evening of 5 August the stage was set for the swirling complicated battle around the Graivoron–Borisovka pocket.

The Steppe Front on the Second Day – 4 August 1943

While the Voronezh Front armies ripped into German defenses and pinned German forces into the narrow pocket along the Vorskla River, the Steppe Front continued its grinding approach to Belgorod against the stiff defense of Army Detachment Kempf's divisions (see Map 60). On 4 August 53d and 69th Army struggled to overcome German defenses covering the northern approaches to Belgorod. All of the two armies' armor assets had already been committed to battle, and the advance was still slow – so slow that Konev asked for and received assistance from the neighboring Voronezh Front. Soviet forces north of Belgorod were faced by three German divisions in prepared positions into which they had withdrawn during the previous night. 6th Panzer Division elements held Rakovo and anchored a line which slid away a considerable distance to the southwest (toward Orlovka and the advanced elements of Soviet 33d Guards Rifle Corps and 5th Guards Tank Army). On 6th Panzer Division's right flank the 168th Infantry Division held positions from Rakovo along the south bank of the Yerik River past the main road from Oboyan to Belgorod. The 198th Infantry Division occupied positions southeast to the Northern Donets River and along the right bank of the river to Belgorod.[102]

On the evening of 3 August while 1st Mechanized Corps' lead brigades sent out motorized rifle battalions with sappers and miners to clear lanes through mine fields and probe German defenses, Managarov assigned his units new missions. His rifle divisions (252d, 23d Guards, 116th) were to seize Rakovo and penetrate German defenses along the Yerik River near the Belgorod road. Subsequently, they were to advance toward Streletskoye and Belgorod and cut the Tomarovka–Belgorod road in the Vezelka River valley.[103] Meanwhile, the divisions of 69th Army's 48th Rifle Corps (305th and 89th Guards) would overcome German defenses between the Belgorod road and the Northern Donets River.

At first light (0500) Soviet infantry and tank assaults began on a broad front from Rakovo to the Northern Donets River. Artillery supported the attack, and Soviet aircraft struck German reserve positions from Streletskoye to Belgorod. The 252d Rifle Division and 37th Mechanized Brigade seized Rakovo and, in heavy fighting, by day's end, reached the Vezelka River just west of Streletskoye. The 28th Guards Rifle Division and 19th Mechanized Brigade at 0600 secured the heights east of Rakovo and advanced south until heavy German fire from northeast of Streletskoye halted its progress. After repulsing repeated German counterattacks, at 1800 the division's lead battalions secured the northern portion of Streletskoye but were halted in heavy street fighting and by German fire from the south bank of the Vezelka River. The 28th Guards Rifle Division commander then committed his second echelon regiment in a night attack to secure German strong points in southern Streletskoye. Supported by tanks of the 37th Mechanized Brigade, after a short artillery preparation the divisions overcame German positions in southwest Streletskoye and crossed the Vezelka River. In heavy fighting the entire division penetrated to the Belgorod road where German tank and artillery fire again halted its progress.[104]

On 28th Guards Rifle Division's left flank, the 116th Rifle Division, with the 219th Tank Brigade in support, attacked at 0600 after a short artillery preparation. Heavy opposition halted 116th Rifle Division's forward progress at noon; and, during the afternoon, the German 168th Infantry Division launched several counterattacks that kept the Soviet units tied down. Finally, the Soviet division commander committed his second echelon rifle regiment and the division managed to advance to the northern outskirts of Bolkhovets in the Vezelka Valley where it was again halted by new German defenses manned by the 320th Infantry Division which the Germans had shifted from the less threatened sector along the Northern Donets River south of Belgorod.[105] Overall, 53d Army divisions had advanced 6–9 kilometers on 4 August with the 28th Guards Rifle Division making the best progress. Nevertheless, German defenses, although pushed back, were still unbroken.

On 53rd Army's left flank, 48th Rifle Corps' progress was even more limited. By day's end the 305th Rifle Division had reached positions north of Oskochnoye to the rear of the neighboring 116th Rifle Division. The 89th Guards Rifle Division had advanced 3–4 kilometers, cleared Belomestnaya, and permitted 35th Guards Rifle Corps units to begin crossing to the west bank of the Northern Donets River. 48th Rifle Corps' divisions closed ranks in order to concentrate more power for the final thrust on Belgorod, which they hoped would occur on 5 August. At nightfall, the German 198th Infantry Division units facing 48th Rifle Corps fell back to the northern outskirts of Belgorod in order to align their

20. Advance to the outskirts of Belgorod

defenses with those of the 168th Infantry Division for a final defense of the city proper.

East of the Northern Donets River, 7th Guards Army units slowly reduced the German bridgehead at Mikhailovka, and tried to erect new bridges to expand their bridgeheads south of Belgorod. Progress, however, was limited. Frustration was evident in Soviet command channels. Konev himself had observed the attack from 28th Guards Rifle Division's observation post, and he was not satisfied with the progress.

Thus, Konev prepared new plans to complete destruction of German defenses covering Belgorod. He ordered 53d Army and 48th Rifle Corps to continue their attacks on Belgorod, and he sought to reinforce their attack by seeking the assistance of 5th Guards Tank Army. 1st Mechanized Corps' 219th Tank Brigade, in position along the Belgorod road, was to move westward and join with the 19th Mechanized Brigade. Together, the two brigades were to attack toward Bolkhovets and Krasnoye to cut German communications from Belgorod to the south. The 37th Tank Brigade was to continue to support the 252d Rifle Division, and the second echelon 35th Mechanized Brigade would relocate westward to Kazatskaya on the right flank and prepare to operate toward Gryaznoye, 10 kilometers southwest of Belgorod on the Khar'kov road.[106] More important, late on 4 August Vatutin transferred to Konev's control 5th Guards Mechanized Corps of 5th Guards Tank Army to help Konev reduce the Belgorod defenses. 5th Guards Mechanized Corps was to wheel eastward, secure Gryaznoye, leave one brigade there facing northeast, and move its main force along the Belgorod–Khar'kov road to the southwest to reach Kazach'ya Lopan by the morning of 6 August.[107]

The Steppe Front on the Third Day – 5 August: The Seizure of Belgorod

Konev's new assault began before first light on 5 August (see Map 61). The 28th Guards Rifle Division secured the remaining German strongpoints in Streletskoye. The 116th Rifle Division, led by the 219th Tank Brigade, approached Bolkhovets but could not force a crossing of the Vezelka River. Thwarted in its attempts to cross the river the 116th Rifle Division shifted its fires to support the 37th Tank Brigade and 84th Guards Rifle Division crossing operations west of Bolkhovets. Two battalions of the division made it across the river, and the 35th Mechanized Brigade followed to expend the attack on Gryaznoye. By 0900 1st Mechanized Corps' two lead brigades were across the Vezelka River, and the 219th Tank Brigade followed in corps second echelon. Meanwhile, the 28th Guards Rifle Division advanced south from its bridgehead at Streletskoye. The 116th Rifle Division, which by that time had seized the eastern part of Bolkhovets, crossed the Vezelka and moved on Krasnoye only to be stopped at 1100 by heavy fire from German positions north of the Belgorod–Khar'kov road. The fire also halted the forward movement of 28th Guards Rifle Division. At 1400 219th Tank Brigade tanks arrived and supported a successful attack on the German positions while the 37th Tank Brigade thrust south into Krasnoye.

On the 53d Army's right flank, the 252d Rifle Division and 35th Mechanized Brigade advanced in tandem with 5th Guards Tank Army's 5th Guards Mechanized Corps. The corps' 51st Guards Tank Regiment and infantry of 10th Guards Mechanized Brigade forced the Lopan River and, with 35th Mechanized Brigade, gained a foothold in Gryaznoye. Meanwhile, 5th Guards Mechanized Corps' 24th Guards Tank Brigade and 11th Guards Mechanized Brigade plunged on to Tavrovo.[108] By day's end, 53d Army and 5th Guards Mechanized Corps had secured Gryaznoye and Krasnoye and finally cut the Belgorod–Khar'kov road.

Meanwhile, 69th and 7th Guards Army divisions assaulted the city proper. After a thirty-minute preparation 48th Rifle Corps' 305th Rifle Division and 89th Guards Rifle Division advanced south against heavy resistance toward Belgorod's northern suburbs. The 305th attacked along both sides of the Oboyan–Belgorod road, and the 89th Guards Rifle Division struggled through the swampy land along both sides of the rail line. To project maximum firepower forward, both divisions deployed all three of their regiments into first echelon. East of Belgorod 7th Guards Army forces repeatedly attempted to build a bridge across the Northern Donets River under German artillery

21. Liberation of Belgorod.

fire. After several failures, the 156th Separate Bridge Construction Battalion finally installed the bridge (at Maslovyi Pristan) south of Belgorod.[109]

89th Guards Rifle Division led the assault into Belgorod from the north. Its regiments attacked using specially tailored assault groups from each first echelon battalion covered by fire support groups using direct fire to silence German machine guns and artillery positions. Under cover of smoke from artillery fire the division's assault groups overcame several key German positions and fought for the limestone chalk factory on the north edge of town. The first division unit to penetrate the town proper entered north of the railroad station. The 305th Rifle Division followed the 89th Guards Rifle Division into town.[110] Simultaneously, the 111th Rifle Division of 7th Guards Army followed by the 94th Guards Rifle Division entered the eastern section of the city. Konev, observing the progress of the battle from 53d Army's observation post, ordered a general assault to clear the city beginning at 1400. At 1330 an artillery preparation using Katyushas ripped at remaining German positions, and fifteen minutes later the general assault commenced. Threatened also from the southwest, the Germans had already begun a withdrawal. At 1400, elements of the 89th Guards Rifle Division proceeded down Narody and Lenin Streets.[111] Simultaneously, the 111th Rifle Division and 94th Guards Rifle Division of 7th Guards Army swept through the eastern portion of the city. By 1800 Belgorod was free of Germans.

By nightfall on 5 August Army Detachment Kempf had erected new defense lines south of Belgorod running from southwest of Bessonovka eastward to the Northern Donets River. Remnants of the 167th Infantry Division held positions southwest of Bessonovka, the 6th Panzer Division and 168th Infantry Division defended from Bessonovka to the Belgorod–Khar'kov road near Gryaznoye, and the 198th and 106th Infantry Divisions were located east of Gryaznoye and along the Northern Donets River.

The Soviet advance on Belgorod had been slow and costly, more so than Konev had expected. Although the German units defending the Belgorod sector had themselves suffered heavy casualties, they survived the battles without losing their cohesion. Consequently, the new defense line was still a formidable obstacle to the Soviet advance on Khar'kov – and until the German defenders further south along the river could be rolled back, 7th Guards Army and 57th Army forces east of the Northern Donets River could not be brought into action. The fighting for Belgorod and the tenacious German defense set a pattern that would endure. There would be no dramatic Soviet breakthrough on the Belgorod–Khar'kov axis.

Reduction of the Borisovka Pocket and Exploitation to Bogodukhov and Trostyanets (6–11 August)

The Situation on 6 August

On 6 August, with Tomarovka and Belgorod in Soviet hands, the Soviet High Command refined its operational plans. Believing that the German front was irreparably rent apart, representative of the *STAVKA,* Zhukov, and Steppe Front commander, Konev, sent the *STAVKA* new proposals for developing the offensive. They proposed a two-phased advance on Khar'kov by Steppe Front armies while Vatutin's Voronezh Front, spearheaded by its tank armies, enveloped Khar'kov from the west. The success of the Khar'kov operation and the speed of its development depended on the rapidity with which Vatutin crushed German resistance in his sector and propelled his tank armies into the operational depths of the German defense.

Vatutin was already developing new plans to overcome German resistance. Late on 5 August, while German forces were abandoning Tomarovka, he ordered his rifle armies to liquidate the German strong points which impeded their advance along the Vorskla River and his tank armies to expand the depth of their operations. He ordered Zhadov's 5th Guards Army to accelerate its advance, secure Borisovka, cut the road running south from that town, and cooperate with 6th Guards and 27th Armies in reducing the German Borisovka group.[112] 5th Guards Army's 32d Guards Rifle Corps would strike German positions southeast and south of the Vorskla River from Borisovka westward toward Graivoron and attempt to cut German withdrawal routes. 6th Guards Army's 22d and 23d Rifle Corps would attack northeast and north of Borisovka while 27th Army's divisions would advance toward Graivoron and Borisovka from the north and northwest.

German forces frantically sought to reestablish coherent defenses in the Borisovka area and secure their communications lines westward toward Graivoron and Trostyanets. The 255th Infantry Division occupied a semicircle of positions northwest, north, and east of Borisovka and covered the withdrawal of 19th Panzer Division units from Tomarovka. By the morning of 6 August, 19th Panzer units had closed on Borisovka and occupied defenses in the city proper and on the city's eastern and southern approaches. 11th Panzer Division defended positions north of Graivoron and Golovchino to block Soviet 27th Army's access to the main road. 7th Panzer Division defended on 11th Panzer Division's left flank to bar Soviet 40th Army's advance to the southwest. Small elements of 11th Panzer Division also patrolled south of Golovchino and Graivoron to keep track of Soviet forces operating in LII Army Corps' rear.[113] As yet, however, LII Army Corps did not realize the gravity of the threat to its rear area.

Voronezh Front Advance – 6–7 August: Reduction of the Borisovka Pocket

Early on 6 August Zhadov issued orders to achieve the tasks assigned him by Vatutin (see Maps 63–64). He ordered the 32d Guards Rifle Corps to move its divisions southwest toward Graivoron, and he reinforced Rodimtsev's corps with the 42d Guards Rifle Division which he specifically ordered to begin a drive on Zolochev. Rodimtsev set about the complicated task of disengaging his divisions from combat around Tomarovka, regrouping them, and dispatching them forward along new axes. The 66th Guards Rifle Division would operate against the eastern approaches to Borisovka, the 97th Guards Rifle Division would blockade Borisovka from the southeast and south, and the 13th Guards Rifle Division would sweep southwest to secure Khotmyzhsk Station, south of Golovchino, to strike at the southern part of Golovchino and cut the German withdrawal route southwest. Meanwhile, 42d Guards Rifle Division, along with 1st Tank Army elements, would attack southward toward Zolochev. Rodimtsev personally delivered the new orders to all of his divisions.[114] At 0100 on 6 August the

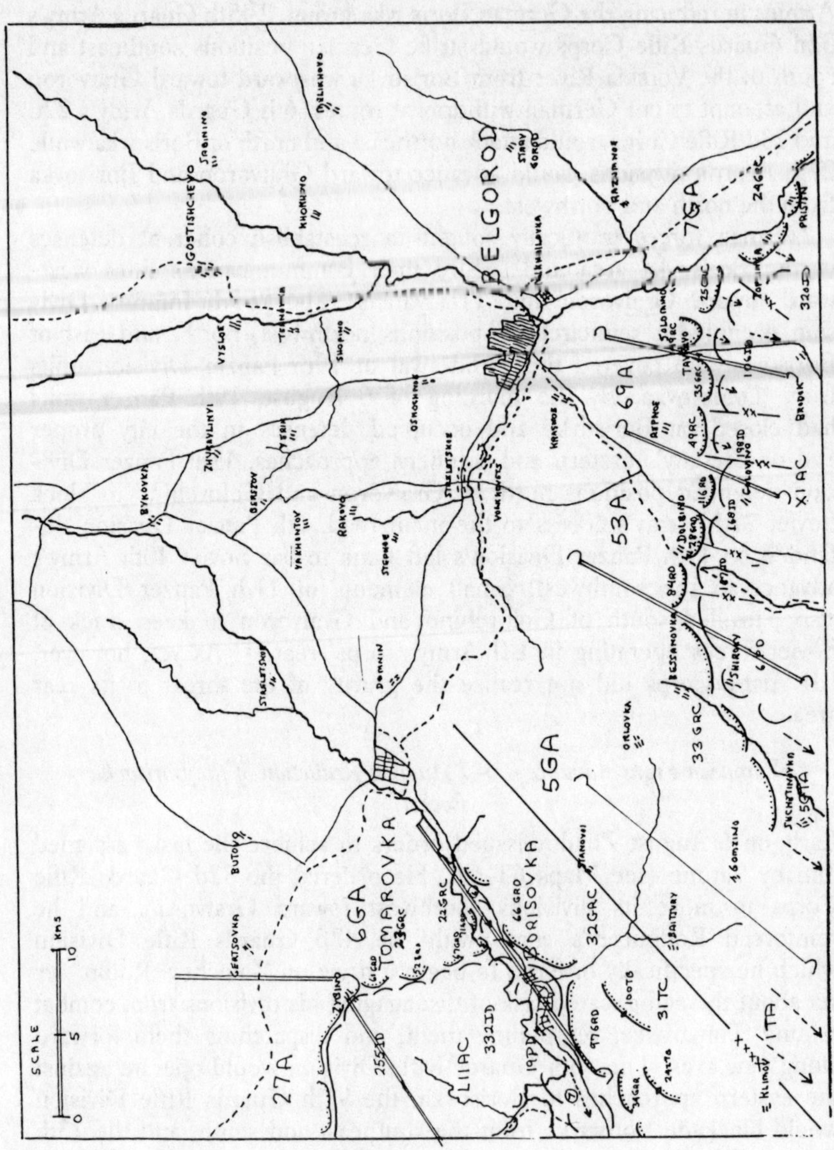

MAP 63. BELGOROD–KHAR'KOV, SITUATION, 2000 6 AUGUST 1943

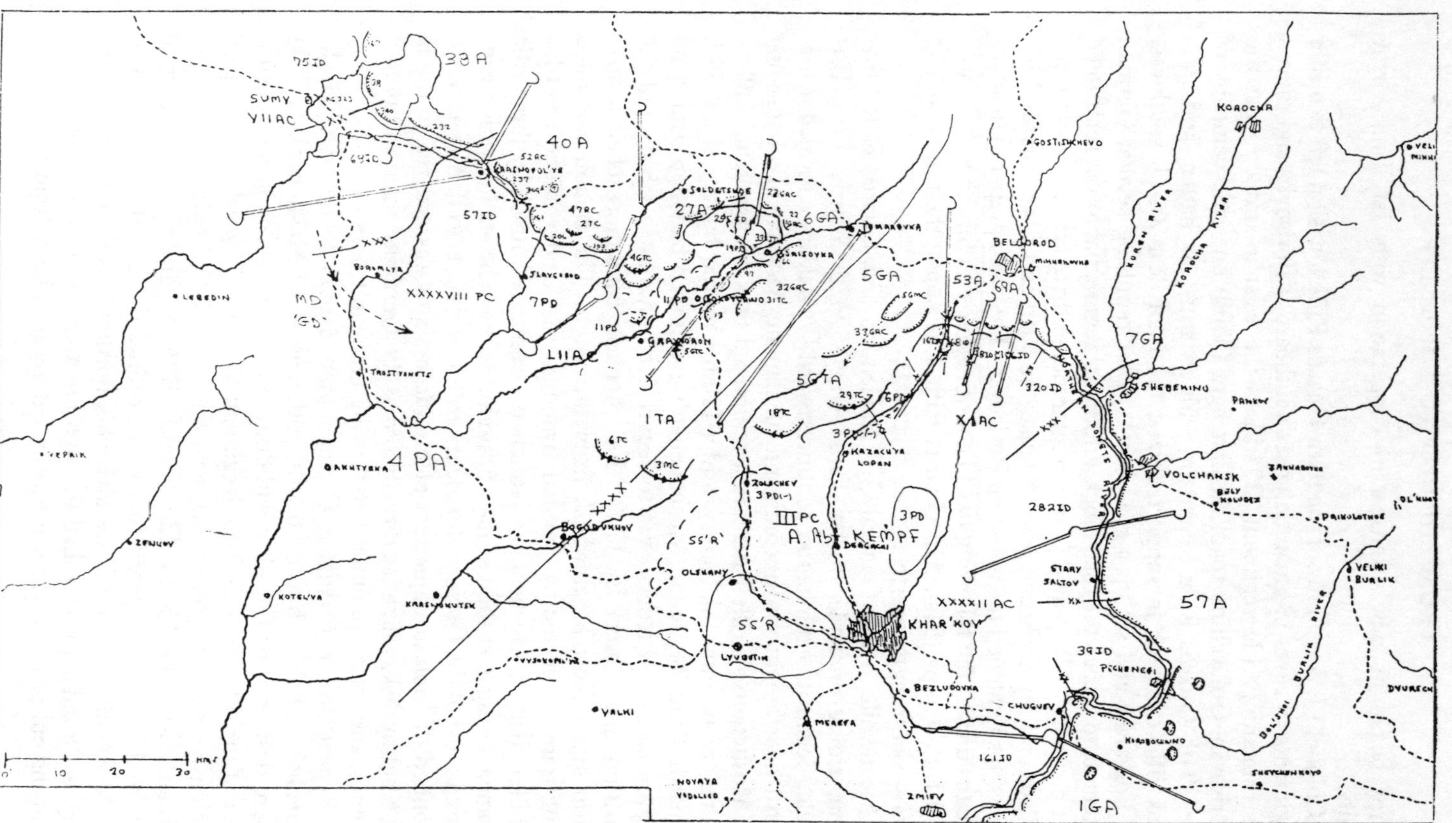

MAP 64. BELGOROD–KHAR'KOV, SITUATION, 2000 6 AUGUST 1943

corps began its new offensive in cooperation with 1st Tank Army units.

Colonel I.I. Antsiferov of the 97th Guards Rifle Division left two rifle regiments to cover German defenses southeast of Borisovka and moved his remaining rifle regiment (294th) to the west in order to cut the Borisovka–Golovchino road. At first light (0500) one rifle company of the 294th Guards Rifle Regiment, with an anti-tank battery and anti-tank rifle company in support, seized the road near Zozuli southwest of Borisovka and set up a road block. After repulsing several German attempts to breach the road block, additional regimental forces reinforced the position.[115] Repeated German attempts to drive off the Soviet force failed; and, by day's end on 6 August, the 97th and 66th Guards Rifle Divisions tightened the noose on Borisovka. They also prepared to attack the town itself the following day in coordination with 6th Guards Army's 23d Rifle Corps (51st, 52d Guards Rifle Divisions), then approaching Borisovka from the north.

Meanwhile, Major General G.V. Baklanov's 13th Guards Rifle Division, riding on tanks of 1st Tank Army's 242d Guards Tank Brigade, began its exploitation southwestward.[116] Baklanov formed a forward detachment under command of Captain Moshchenko consisting of Moshchenko's rifle battalion, a reinforced tank company, an artillery battalion, an anti-tank battery, and a 120mm mortar battery of the 39th Guards Rifle Regiment. Moshchenko's reinforced battalion, riding on eleven tanks and trucks, was to secure Khotmyzhsk in advance of the division main force. By 1700 Moshchenko's column reached a state farm overlooking Khotmyzhsk from the south. The station was filled with trains protected by German armed guards. Under the cover of his artillery battery Moshchenko launched a concerted attack by three rifle companies against the German positions around the station which captured most of the German defenders and the trains as well. Moshchenko notified division headquarters of his success and was ordered to dig in at Khotmyzhsk, which lay directly across the Germans' main withdrawal routes, and intercept other withdrawing German troops.

Repeatedly on 6 August German units sought to dislodge Moshchenko's battalion, but to no avail, although all of Moshchenko's tanks were destroyed or forced to withdraw. Finally, by evening, the remainder of the 39th Guards Rifle Regiment hastened forward and occupied defensive positions on the western outskirts of Golovchino. The 13th Guards Rifle Division's 42d Guards Rifle Regiment arrived east of Golovchino and prepared to attack northward while the 34th Guards Rifle Regiment covered the division's northern flank. Late that evening, as thunderstorms rolled through the area, German columns began moving out of Borisovka southwestward toward Golovchino.

With the 13th Guards Rifle Division in position to block German withdrawal routes Zhadov ordered the 66th and 97th Guards Rifle Divisions to assault Borisovka on the morning of 7 August. Simultaneously, Chistyakov's 6th Guards Army units would attack Borisovka from the northwest, north, and northeast. The German situation was becoming more precarious, for on 6 August 27th Army's thrust threatened Graivoron itself, deep in the German rear.

Early on 6 August, after a massive artillery preparation, 4th Guards Tank Corps and 241st Rifle Division lunged forward west of Ivanovskaya–Lisitsa and smashed through 11th Panzer Division defenses. By evening, 13th Guards Tank Brigade, the corps' forward detachment, reached Zamost'ye just north of Graivoron, where it was halted by 11th Panzer and 57th Infantry Division defenses. In a night battle the tank brigade secured Zamost'ye and a key bridge across the Vorskla River and repelled repeated counterattacks by 11th Panzer Division until the 4th Guards Tank Corps' main force arrived early on 7 August.[117] To further threaten Graivoron, late on the night of 6 August, Kravchenko's 5th Guards Tank Corps, under 1st Tank Army control, arrived southeast of Graivoron, having completed its march from the Tomarovka area.

Thus, by the night of 6 August the Soviets had encircled German forces in the Borisovka–Graivoron area; and the Germans had little choice but to fight their way out of encirclement or perish in place. The encirclement, however, was not contiguous; and German commanders had the task of finding the path of least resistance out of the area. The best path out seemed to be to the southwest and west, since heavy Soviet forces covered the northwest, north, and eastern regions. German commanders were unaware of the strength of Soviet units south of Borisovka and Graivoron, but they would soon detect that strength. Late in the evening German columns moved out of Borisovka, pressed by the patrols of 6th Guards Army's divisions and of 32d Guards Rifle Corps' 66th and 97th Guards Rifle Divisions. The organized withdrawal consisted of a 19th Panzer and 255th Infantry Division column traveling southwest along the highway and a 332d Infantry Division column moving further south. The withdrawal routes carried 19th Panzer directly into Soviet roadblocks at Khotmyzhsk and 332d Infantry Division straight into 13th Guards Rifle Division positions south of the road.[118] Meanwhile, 11th Panzer Division elements strove to hold off 27th Army forces north of Golovchino and at Graivoron.

At 0300 7 August 34th Guards Rifle Regiment's sapper company with four heavy machine guns, located east of Golovchino, detected German columns moving toward them through heavy fog from Zozuli. (These were from 57th Infantry Division and the reconnaissance battalion of 19th Panzer Division (without guns).) The division chief-of-staff, two machine gun platoons, and headquarters personnel joined the defense, and orders went to the remainder of the rifle regiment to close on the division headquarters. After heavy fighting the Germans veered off to the north after losing 300 men. Several kilometers to the northwest the 42d Guards Rifle Regiment defended against two battalions of the 332d Infantry Division and elements of 19th Panzer Division supported by four Tiger tanks. After a two-hour battle, in which two Tigers were destroyed, at 0500 the Germans turned northwest toward Khotmyzhsk Station.[119]

The morning of 7 August dawned sunny and warm (see Map 65). As 6th Guards Army divisions and the 66th and 97th Guards Rifle Divisions of 5th Guards Army continued to drive German units from Borisovka the Germans probed Soviet positions for suitable withdrawal routes.

From 0600 to 0900 German forces reconnoitered 13th Guards Rifle Division positions and then at 1000 launched a heavy assault against the 42d Guards Rifle Regiment and the right flank of the 39th Guards Rifle Regiment. The two regiments repulsed repeated German attacks over a three-hour period; and throughout the day, all along 13th Guards Rifle Division's front, heavy fighting raged at heavy cost to both sides. German columns ultimately funneled through Golovchino, there running a gauntlet of fire in front of the 39th Guards Rifle Regiment occupying defensive positions southwest of the town covering the Graivoron road. All the while the Soviets subjected the German columns to heavy air and artillery attacks. Having suffered heavy casualties the German columns left the road, worked their way north around Soviet positions, and finally regained the road to the southwest. There, however, the Germans ran into advancing 27th Army forces. 27th Army's 163d Rifle Division struck at Golovchino from the north, and the 166th Rifle Division and 93d Tank Brigade punched into Graivoron proper where they united with 1st Tank Army units advancing from the south. The hapless German columns turned south and smashed into Graivoron only to be driven back by 27th Army, 4th Guards Tank Corps, and 1st Tank Army forces. After repeated attempts to find an open route through Soviet lines, the beleaguered and heavily damaged German forces cut a gap through 1st Tank Army positions and marched south from Graivoron.

While the German columns were passing the 13th Guards Rifle Division positions, reports came in to Bakhlanov that a German headquarters column, escorted by armor, was approaching the division's positions. Bakhlanov ordered the 39th Guards Rifle Regiment to halt the column and capture the headquarters. After a sharp engagement the Soviet troops escorted to Bakhlanov's headquarters German prisoners possessing a photograph and papers from another officer. The papers turned out to belong to Lieutenant General F. Schmidt, 19th Panzer Division commander, who was presumed killed in the fighting.[120]

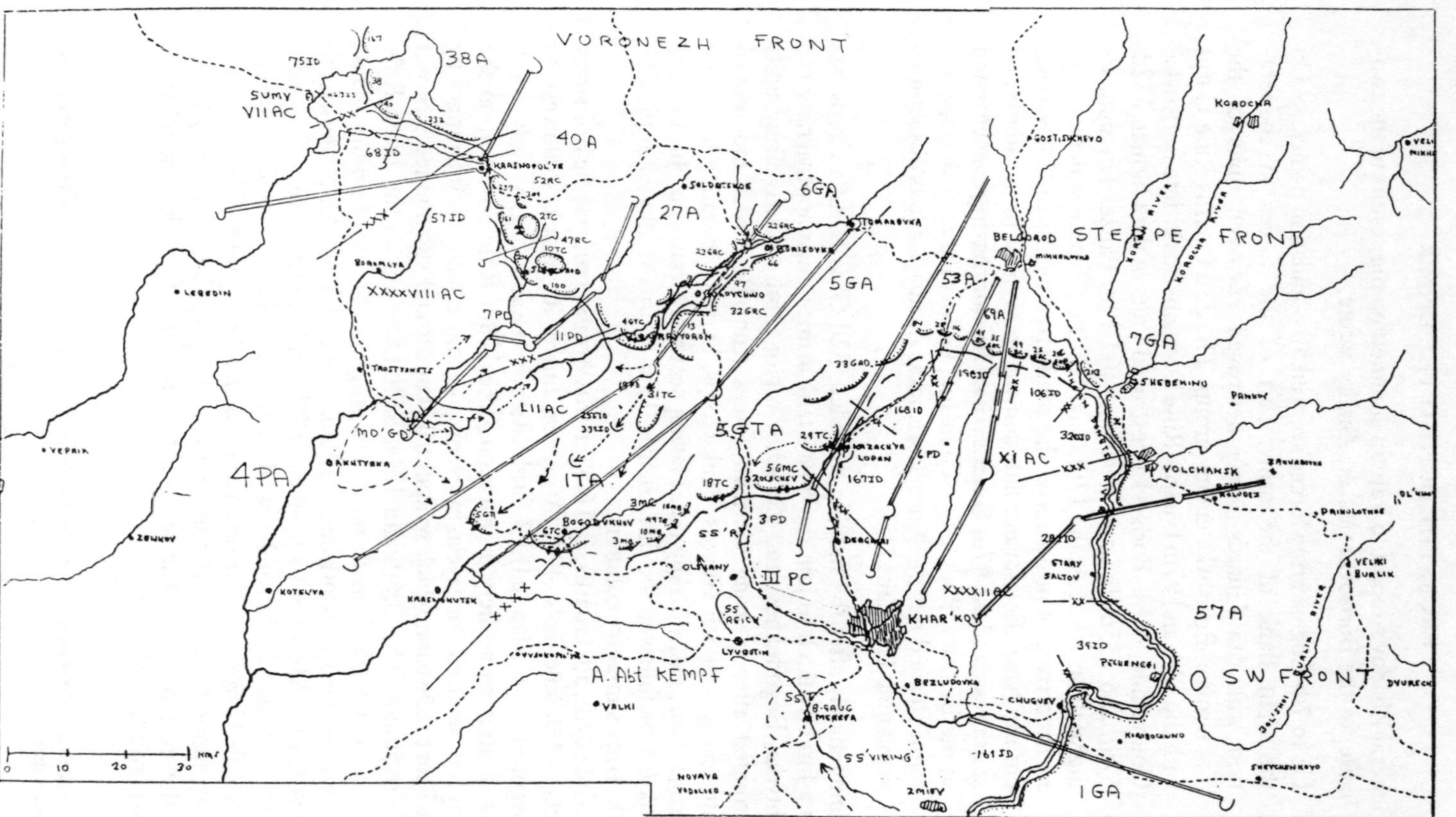

MAP 65. BELGOROD–KHAR'KOV, SITUATION, 2000 7 AUGUST 1943

General Zhadov's report to Vatutin summed up the results of the two-day battle for the Borisovka pocket. Zhadov wrote,

> Up to 7th August army forces secured 50 population points. . . .On the right flank of the army, part of the forces in cooperation with 6th Guards Army destroyed encircled units of the Tomarovka–Borisovka enemy group. The 32d Guards Rifle Corps with the 13th and 97th Guards Rifle Divisions on the line Borisovka, Golovchino, Novo-Borisovka destroyed units of the German 332d, 57th, and 255th Infantry Divisions and 19th Panzer Division. By nightfall on 7 August the 13th Guards Rifle Division with two regiments arrived in positions on the southern outskirts of Golovchino, cut the Novo-Borisovka road, denying movement to the south and southwest; and the 97th Guards Rifle Division, having concentrated in the Baitsury, Radchenki–Gomzino, Golovka area, with one regiment cleaned out the Novo-Borisovka, Zozuli–Kal'nitskii sector of remaining Germans.*[121]

Immediately after the fighting subsided, 32d Guards Rifle Corps began a forced march to join the *front's* tank armies, then approaching the Akhtyrka, Bogodukhov, and Zolochev regions. 6th Guards Army units regrouped after clearing German forces from Borisovka and moved southwest to join 5th Guards Tank Corps, by now operating far in the German rear, east of Akhtyrka. Having secured Graivoron, 4th Guards Tank Corps followed the 5th Guards Tank Corps southwest trailed by 27th Army's infantry columns.

While 27th, 5th Guards, and 6th Guards Armies reduced the Borisovka pocket, Moskalenko's 40th Army expanded its attack southwest to Slavgorod (see Map 64).[122] 40th Army's assault began early on 6 August after an artillery preparation. The 100th Rifle Division, on the army left, secured Pochayevo by evening despite a heavy counterattack by 7th Panzer Division which temporarily cut off and surrounded a Soviet rifle regiment. The 206th and 161st Rifle Divisions on the 100th Rifle Division's right flank made only slow progress. To speed up the attack, Vatutin assigned to Moskalenko Major General V.M. Alekseyev's 10th Tank Corps. Moskalenko would use 2d Tank Corps to lead 52d Rifle Corps' advance on Boromlya while 10th Tank Corps would spearhead 47th Rifle Corps' advance on Slavgorod and Trostyanets. The additional armor support accelerated the offensive and propelled 40th Army forces by the evening of 7 August to a line running from Krasnopol'ye to Slavgorod (see Map 65).

*Soviets claim 5,000 Germans killed and 2,000 prisoners along with 40 tanks destroyed and 500 vehicles destroyed.

The advance of 40th and 27th Armies prevented XXXXVIII Panzer Corps from assisting LII Army Corps' withdrawal from the Borisovka–Graivoron area. 7th Panzer Division had its hands full maintaining a continuous front opposite 40th Army. Meanwhile, LII Army Corps units filtered to the west and southwest, dodging Soviet blocking positions, and avoiding Soviet armored forces now operating in the depths of the German rear near Akhtyrka, Krasnokutsk, Bogodukhov, and Zolochev. 11th Panzer Division conducted a fighting withdrawal westward from Graivoron along the northern bank of the Vorskla River and ultimately occupied new defensive positions on 7th Panzer Division's right flank south of Slavgorod. Portions of 11th Panzer Division which had been cut off in Graivoron withdrew westward south of the Vorskla River toward LII Army Corps' new headquarters southeast of Trostyanets.

Remnants of the 19th Panzer, 332d Infantry, and 255th Infantry Divisions, which had fought their way out of Graivoron, assembled southwest of the town late on 7 August and, on 8 August, moved southwest and at 2000 entered the lines of "Grossdeutschland" Division east of Akhtyrka. "Grossdeutschland" Division, dispatched from the north, had begun arriving on 5 August in assembly areas around Akhtyrka. Rail movement of the division's 140 tanks and self-propelled guns was slow, and by 7 August only 50 of its armored vehicles had arrived.[123] Nevertheless, that day "Grossdeutschland" sent out detachments to assist the westward withdrawal of the badly mauled LII Army Corps. 4th Panzer Army's intention was to reestablish a defense line between Sumy and Akhtyrka and, hopefully, restore links with Army Detachment Kempf. Of course, the first task was to gather in the fragmented LII Army Corps units safely.

1st and 5th Guards Tank Army Exploitations to Bogodukhov and Zolochev – 6–7 August

The restoration of contact between 4th Panzer Army and Army Detachment Kempf would be a difficult task, for while the Soviet rifle armies were reducing the Borisovka–Graivoron pocket, the two tank armies had begun an exploitation toward Zolochev and Bogodukhov (see Map 64). Ironically, however, the German encirclement itself complicated the Soviet task. As the tank armies advanced, they inevitably became separated from Soviet rifle forces tied down by the encircled Germans. This provided the Germans the opportunity, if they could seize it, of dealing with the armored threat before the Soviet supporting infantry was available to protect the armor. Of course, on 6 August the Germans had no means of countering the two tank armies' advance. However, some new units were arriving in the Khar'kov area dispatched from other sectors of the front in an attempt to stem the tide of the Soviet advance. 3d Panzer Division began assembling in the Novaya Vodolaga area south of Khar'kov on the evening of 6 August. The following day it moved northward to new assembly areas and was assigned to III Panzer Corps (headquartered temporarily at Zolochev). III Panzer Corps was tasked to fill the breach in German defenses on 6th Panzer Division's (XI Army Corps) left flank from Kazach'ya Lopan southwest through Zolochev. SS Panzer Division "Das Reich," assembling on 6 August in the Olshany–Lyubotin area, also under III Panzer Corps control, was to seek out Soviet forces penetrating between 4th Panzer and Army Detachment Kempf and halt their progress, hopefully somewhere in the Zolochev area. Other divisions were also enroute to bolster German defenses.[124] SS Panzer Division "Totenkopf," enroute from the Mius River area, and due to reach Khar'kov on 8 and 9 August was also to join III Panzer Corps. Clearly these units could not arrive in time to affect the fate of encircled German LII Rifle Corps. The question was whether these forces could assemble in time to halt the penetration by a Soviet force as yet of unknown size.

The Soviet force penetrating deep in the German rear area was in reality the bulk of 1st Tank Army and 5th Guards Tank Army. Katukov's army, with Kravchenko's 5th Guards Tank Corps attached, regrouped southeast of Borisovka early on 6 August, retrieved the brigades engaged in the Tomarovka area, and began its advance southward with 6th Tank Corps and 3d Mechanized Corps in the lead followed by 31st Tank Corps. The 100th and 242d Tank Brigades of 31st Tank Corps became entangled in the fighting for Borisovka and Graivoron where they provided transport and support for 13th Guards Rifle Division's dash to Golovchino. 5th Guards Tank Corps skirmished with withdrawing 19th and 11th Panzer Division units for two days south of Graivoron and pursued German forces westward along the south bank of the Vorskla River to east of Akhtyrka where it encountered lead elements of German "Grossdeutschland" Division late on 7 August. Disengaging from contact with "Grossdeutschland," 5th Guards Tank Corps then swept southward on 1st Tank Army's right flank.

Meanwhile, 1st Tank Army's lead corps rolled southward. By mid-day on 6 August 6th Tank and 3d Mechanized Corps had advanced over 50 kilometers; and the 49th Tank Brigade, leading the tank army's advance, had intercepted a German troop train and scattered its occupants. Early on 7 August Katukov received orders from Vatutin to concentrate his forces for an advance on the important rail junction at Bogodukhov (see Map 65). During the day, after disengaging from combat along the Vorskla River, 31st Tank Corps units were to rejoin the main force of the army; and 5th Guards Tank Corps was to turn south and march on Kup'yevakha, west of Bogodukhov. 1st Tank Army's main force was to move through Bogodukhov, occupy positions south of the town, and push its forward detachments forward to Aleksandrovka and Staryi Merchik 15 kilometers south of Bogodukhov to threaten the rail line west of Khar'kov. Army reconnaissance units indicated that only German support units manned defensive positions at Bogodukhov. Simultaneously, Vatutin ordered Rotmistrov's tank army to complete an envelopment of German positions at Bessonovka from the west and seize Zolochev on 1st Tank Army's left flank.[125]

At midday on 7 August Katukov issued orders to his units. 6th Tank Corps would occupy Bogodukhov; and 3d Mechanized Corps, on its left, would seize Maksimovka station on the rail line southeast of Bogodukhov. 31st Tank Corps would cover the army's left flank against German counterattacks from the east and prepare to develop the success of 3d Mechanized Corps. At 1500 the advance began. By 1700 the 200th and 22d Tank Brigades of 6th Tank Corps had advanced 16 kilometers and reached the outskirts of Bogodukhov. The 22d Tank Brigades penetrated the town from the east, and the 200th Tank Brigade swept in from the northwest and occupied the railroad station. The sudden attack caught German units by surprise; and the two brigades, followed by the remainder of 6th Tank Corps, secured the entire town by 1800, in the process seizing large stocks of German supplies and 700 tons of fuel.[126] Having secured Bogodukhov, Katukov deployed three brigades of 6th Tank Corps in temporary defensive positions and prepared to resume the advance on 8 August.

While 6th Tank Corps marched virtually unopposed into Bogodukhov, further east 3d Mechanized Corps ran into advanced elements of SS Panzer Division "Das Reich," then deploying to cover Army Detachment Kempf's left flank. 3d Mechanized Corps had moved out at noon, led by 10th Mechanized Brigade and 1st Guards Tank Brigade. Simultaneously, SS Panzer Division "Das Reich," marching in two columns, moved north from Olshany. At 1700 the advanced guard of 1st Guards Tank Brigade ran into a German tank company (seventeen to eighteen tanks) and two companies of motorized infantry 10 kilometers north of Olshany. Meanwhile, 10th Mechanized Brigade's advanced guard and the German western column's advanced guard smashed into each other 10 kilometers east of Bogodukhov. Thus, the two units began a classic meeting engagement.

General Krivoshein deployed his 10th and 3d Mechanized Brigades to strike the western German column while 1st Guards Tank Brigade made a secondary attack against "Das Reich's" eastern column. The 49th Tank Brigade remained in corps' second echelon. To gain time and forestall the full concentration of SS "Das Reich," the corps' brigades were to launch their attacks consecutively. First, 10th Mechanized Brigade and

22. Shturmoviks covering the advance.

23. Shturmoviks attacking ground targets.

1st Guards Tank Brigade would attack then, from the right flank of 10th Mechanized Brigade, 3d Mechanized Brigade would conduct its attack. The engagement began on the evening of 7 August; and, by 2300, 1st Guards Tank, 10th Mechanized, and 3d Mechanized Brigades drove back forward elements of SS "Das Reich."[127] SS "Das Reich," with its main force still arriving, withdrew a few kilometers in order to establish new positions covering the approaches to Olshany. Thus, by the evening of 7 August, 1st Tank Army's 6th Tank Corps and 3d Mechanized Corps had secured Bogodukhov and a line running northwest toward Zolochev. To the west, Kravchenko's 5th Guards Tank Corps had advanced to within 10 kilometers of Krasnokutsk against virtually no resistance.

Further east, however, Rotmistrov's tank army continued to face heavier resistance. Operating in accordance with orders received on the evening of 5 August to envelop German positions at Bessonovka from the west, Yegerov's 18th Tank Corps swept westward, and his 110th and 170th Tank Brigades seized Shchetinovka and Udy, 15 kilometers northeast of Zolochev. After dark the second echelon 181st Tank Brigade pushed south and at 0400 attacked the small German force defending Zolochev. At dawn on 6 August the two remaining 18th Tank Corps brigades arrived, and a bitter contest ensued between the entire corps and lead elements of German 3d Panzer Division which had just arrived in the Zoloche area. By evening Soviet tankers had cleared the town but could advance no further than its southern outskirts because of increased German resistance.[128] In fact, German 3d Panzer Division, under III Panzer Corps' control, had occupied positions from Zolochev northeast to Kazach'ya Lopan to cover the right flank of XI Army Corps units still defending south of Belgorod and to tie in with SS Panzer Division "Das Reich," then fighting southwest of Zolochev.

Soon 5th Guards Tank Army's 29th Tank Corps also discovered the presence of 3d Panzer Division. Having seized Orlovka on 6 August the corps marched west of Kazach'ya Lopan hoping to smash the German XI Army Corps' right flank. Instead, it ran into 3d Panzer Division elements north of its objective and was stopped cold. To assist his two corps in securing Zolochev and Kazach'ya Lopan, Rotmistrov dispatched 5th Guards Mechanized Corps southward. By the morning of 7 August the corps, having returned to army control after completing its task of assisting in the reduction of Belgorod, moved southwest through Gomzino and Shchetinovka to envelop Zolochev from the east in coordination with 18th Tank Corps. Heavy fighting raged as 3d Panzer Division hung onto a foothold in Zolochev against 5th Guards Mechanized Corps' attacks from the east and 18th Tank Corps' assaults

24. Air attacks on German Borisovka pocket.

25. 5th Guards Tank Army Commander, Lieutenant General P.A. Rotmistrov, assigns missions to subordinate commanders.

from the west. By the morning of 8 August lead elements of 5th Guards Mechanized Corps fought their way south to Chernoglazovka (southeast of Zolochev); and 18th Tank Corps units penetrated to Rogozyanka (southwest of Zolochev), thus forcing German forces to abandon the key city.

Meanwhile, to the northeast, Kirichenko's 29th Tank Corps repeatedly tried to assault Kazach'ya Lopan under the anxious eyes of Rotmistrov and Vatutin who realized new German reinforcements were arriving in the Khar'kov area. All of Kirichenko's assaults, however, failed; and at nightfall on 7 August the town was still in 3d Panzer Division hands. Early the following morning Rotmistrov phoned Kirichenko and ordered him to withdraw his corps and move south to Zolochev. Kirichenko objected that leaving Kazach'ya Lopan in enemy hands would threaten his rear. Rotmistrov promised an airborne division would relieve him, and at 0900 on 8 August the 6th Guards Airborne Division of 33d Guards Rifle Corps took over 29th Tank Corps' positions. The tank corps marched rapidly southwest to the Zolochev area where it joined the remainder of the army and battled 3d Panzer Division elements along the rail line south of Zolochev.[129]

1st and 5th Guards Tank Army Exploitation South of Bogodukhov – 8–11 August

Early on 8 August 1st Tank Army and 5th Guards Tank Army had reached positions south of Bogodukhov and Zolochev (see Map 66). Although these tank armies were occupying the eastern shoulder of a large gap separating 4th Panzer Army from Army Detachment Kempf, German forces showed no evidence of collapse. Instead new units appeared to challenge the expanding Soviet offensive. 3d Panzer Division blocked the Soviet 5th Guards Tank Army's path between Kazach'ya Lopan and Zolochev, and SS Panzer Division "Das Reich" opposed 1st Tank Army's advance from southwest of Zolochev to southeast of Bogodukhov. Simultaneously, on 7 August SS Panzer Division "Totenkopf" moved into concentration areas south of Khar'kov with orders to move into the area west of Khar'kov the following two days.

The Soviet *STAVKA*, while noting the success of the operation, also took note of the problems that seemed to limit that success. In fact, major changes had occurred in the Voronezh Front's operational formation. The tank armies in their dash forward had become separated by large distances from the supporting infantry of 5th Guards Army and 6th Guards Army. Moreover, a shortage of tractors caused the tank armies' artillery to lag behind, preventing them from concentrating their firepower on German defenses. On 7 August Lieutenant General A.I.

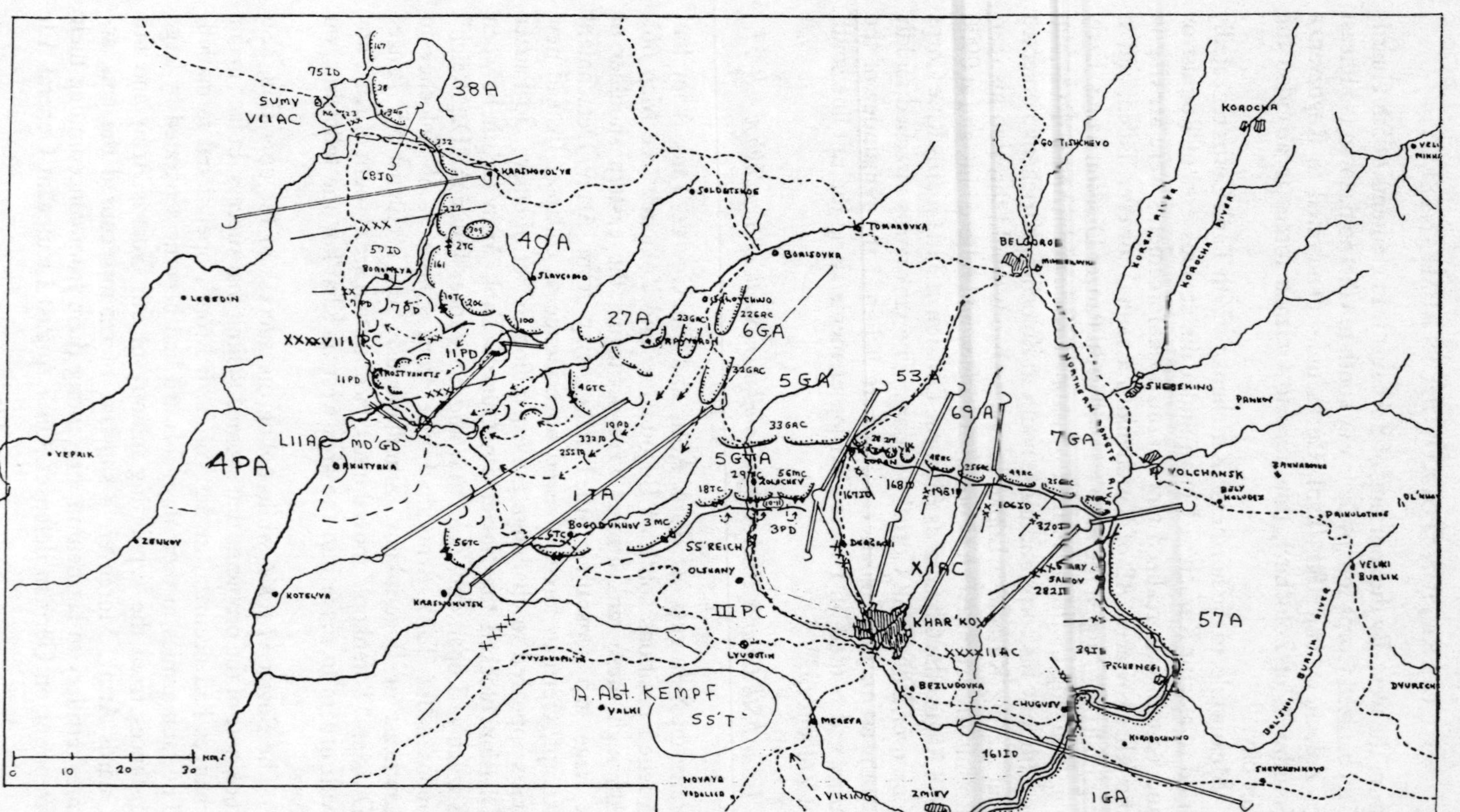

MAP 66. BELGOROD–KHAR'KOV, SITUATION, 2000 8 AUGUST 1943

Antonov, the Assistant Chief of the General Staff, sent Vatutin a telegram stating,

> From the position of 5th Guards Army forces it is clear that the army shock group is scattered and the army divisions are operating along diverse directions. Comrade Stalin orders you to keep the 5th Guards Army shock group compact. To an equal degree that applies also to 1st Tank Army.[130]

Vatutin urged his rifle units (6th Guards Army, 32d Guards Rifle Corps of 5th Guards Army), which were just completing the task of clearing the Borisovka–Graivoron area, to hasten their march forward. At the same time, he ordered Katukov's and Rotmistrov's armies to continue their advance. Katukov was to move his main force to the Vysokopol'ye area in order to cut the Poltava–Khar'kov rail line and dispatch forward detachments to Kolomak and Valki. 5th Guards Tank Corps would advance west of Krasnokutsk. Katukov decided to commit 31st Tank Corps southeast of Bogodukhov to cover his flank from attack from the east. 6th Tank Corps was to advance on Vysokopol'ye and 3d Mechanized Corps on Kovyagi, just north of Valki. Because of the corps' involvement in heavy fighting at Tomarovka and Borisovka, 31st Tank Corps was reduced to about fifty tanks while the other two corps had just over 100 tanks each.[131]

At first light on 8 August the three tank corps began their advance; and, almost immediately, 3d Mechanized and 31st Tank Corps ran into SS Panzer Division "Das Reich" which threw the two corps back and forced them to occupy defensive positions southeast and east of Bogodukhov. 6th Tank Corps, minus its 112th Tank Brigade which was still watching German forces withdrawing from Graivoron, left the 6th Motorized Rifle Brigade to defend Bogodukhov, moved southwest with its remaining two brigades, and sent out forward detachments to the south and southwest. The reconnaissance detachment of the corps drove off small German out-posts 20 kilometers south of Bogodukhov and occupied Aleksandrovka on the north bank of the Merchik River. Blocked in attempts to cross the river by blown bridges, the reconnaissance detachment pinpointed German defenses south of the river and determined from prisoners that large German reserves were deploying forward from the Donbas via the Poltava–Khar'kov rail line. Corps passed this information back to army, and it reinforced Katukov's resolve that 1st Tank Army must cut that critical rail line.[132] 6th Tank Corps received that mission, but could implement it only after all of its brigades had reassembled.

On the morning of 9 August 6th Tank Corps' reassembly was complete, and 6th Tank Corps advanced south in two columns with 200th and 112th Tank Brigades in the lead and the 22d Tank Brigade in second echelon. The newly arrived 163d Rifle Division of 6th Guards Army covered the corps' right flank, and 3d Mechanized Corps covered the left flank. During the afternoon the 200th Tank Brigade seized Murafa, 12 kilometers east of Krasnokutsk; and the 112th Tank Brigade reached its objective of Aleksandrovka, halfway between Bogodukhov and the rail line. 5th Guards Tank Corps still sparred with elements of 19th Panzer Division withdrawing from Graivoron. However, 6th Tank Corps ran into heavy opposition from lead elements of SS Panzer Division "Totenkopf" at the Merchik River and was unable to force a crossing.

Early on 9 August Katukov again ordered his army to renew its advance.[133] However, his plans foundered as all day on 9 August 6th Tank Corps units unsuccessfully sought passage across the Merchik River against determined German resistance. Concerned with the slowing rate of advance and believing that the Khar'kov operation was reaching a decisive phase, the *STAVKA* issued a new directive on the night of 9 August which read:

> The *STAVKA* of the High Command considers it necessary to isolate Khar'kov by means of a rapid cutting of the main rail and road lines of communications in the direction of Poltava, Krasnograd, and Lozovaya to speed the liberation of Khar'kov. For that aim, Katukov's 1st Tank Army will cut the main routes in the Kovyagi and Valki area and Rotmistrov's 5th Guards Tank Army, while enveloping Khar'kov from the southwest, will cut routes in the Merefa area.[134]

Consequently, Vatutin ordered Katukov, by day's end on 11 August, to secure the Vysokopol'ye area, cut the rail line from Khar'kov to Poltava and, with forward detachments, secure Valki (see Map 67). He ordered 5th Guards Tank Army to advance into the area west of Lyubotin by the evening of 11 August. 5th Guards Tank Army would revert to Steppe Front control, and its sector of operations would shift southeast. This rapid transfer of a major force between different headquarters illustrates the flexibility of Soviet planning and command structures.

Katukov now concentrated his army to force a crossing over the Merchik River. He replaced 31st Tank Corps with the newly arrived 13th Guards Rifle Division and moved 31st Tank Corps to new positions southeast of Bogodukhov to support the attack of 3d Mechanized Corps. On the afternoon of 10 August 6th Tank Corps' 112th Tank Brigade crossed the Merchik River at Aleksandrovka. Colonel M.T. Leonov, the brigade commander, formed a task force composed of a tank battalion of twenty-six tanks, an automatic weapons battalion, an anti-tank battery, a self-propelled battery, two anti-aircraft guns, and a sapper platoon to

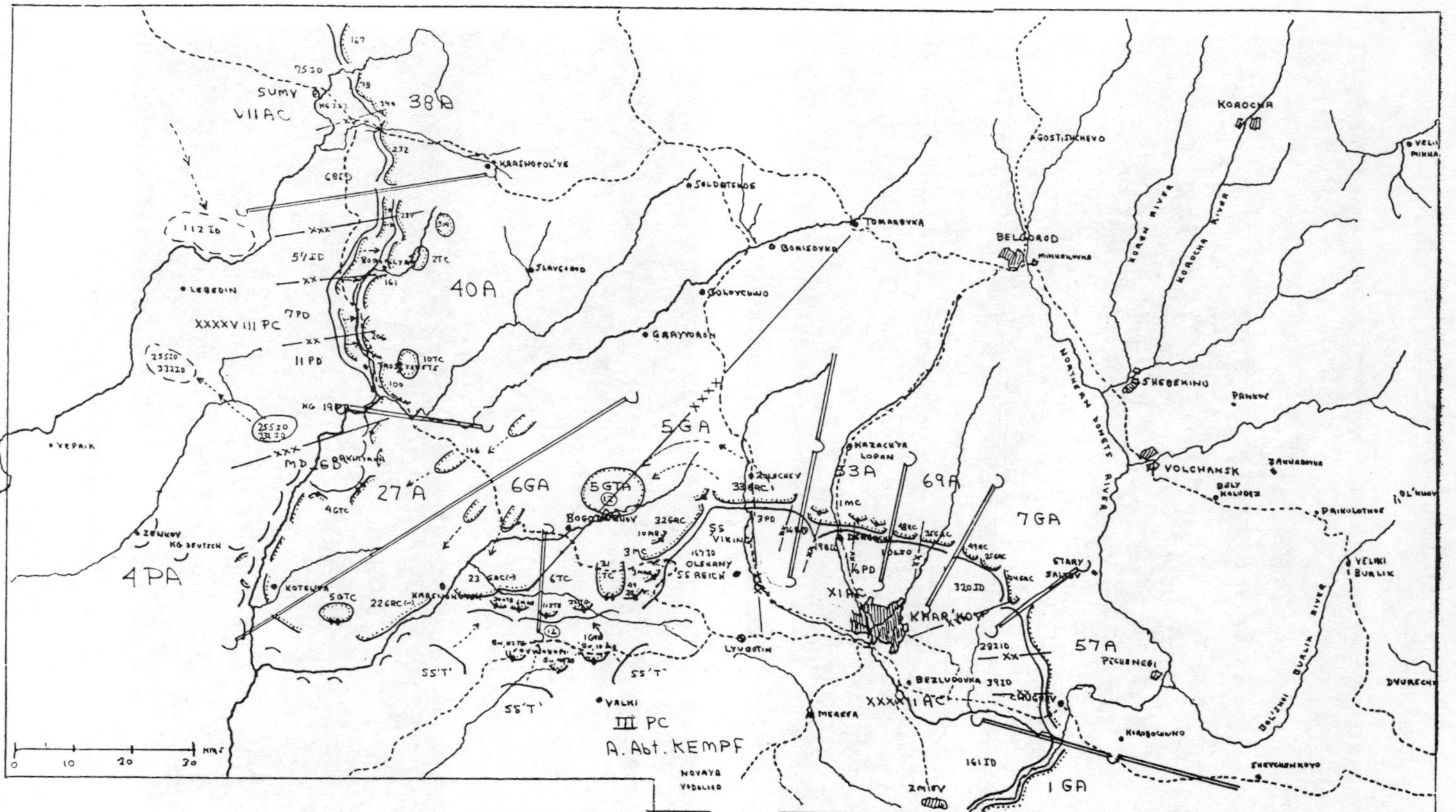

MAP 67. BELGOROD–KHAR'KOV, SITUATION, 11–12 AUGUST 1943

26. Motorized infantry mounted on tanks.

27. Advance south of Belgorod.

lead the advance. The task force, led by its tanks, plunged south out of the Aleksandrovka bridgehead and by dawn on 11 August reached Vysokopol'ye. At 0900 when the entire brigade arrived, it assaulted and seized Vysokopol'ye after several hours of fighting. However, more fighting occurred in the afternoon when German counterattacks cut off the brigade's withdrawal routes and inflicted heavy casualties on it (thirteen tanks, one self-propelled gun, two anti-aircraft guns, and 50 percent of the automatic weapons crews lost).[135] The strong German counterattacks forced the 112th Tank Brigade to withdraw to all-round positions just north of Vysokopol'ye until two battalions of the 6th Motorized Rifle Brigade reinforced it early on 12 August. Together, they again attacked and occupied Vysokopol'ye although they were immediately confronted with renewed German counterattacks.

Meanwhile, late on 10 August the right flank brigades of 3d Mechanized Corps resumed their attacks southward. 49th Tank Brigade's forward detachment (eleven tanks with infantry aboard) and the 10th Mechanized Brigade's forward detachment (nine tanks with infantry) crossed the Merchik River at Aleksandrovka and dashed for Kovyagi station east of Vysokopol'ye on the Poltava rail line. At 0600, the 1st Guards Tank Brigade and 17th Tank Regiment arrived at Kovyagi and immediately established all-round defensive positions to await the arrival of 3d Mechanized Corps' main force. 49th Tank Brigade's forward detachment continued on to the southwest and at 0900 occupied Levandalovka several kilometers south of Kovyagi.[136]

The advance of 6th Tank Corps' and 3d Mechanized Corps' forward detachments, however, was not properly supported since corps' main forces still battled along the Merchik River. Fighting was so heavy that the 31st Tank Corps had to support its two sister corps as well. These conditions paved the way for a new series of major German counterattacks launched by SS Panzer Divisions "Totenkopf" and "Das Reich," the first of which struck Vysokopol'ye late on 11 August. These counterattacks ultimately threatened 1st Tank Army with serious defeat.

Meanwhile, 5th Guards Tank Army sought to fulfill the *STAVKA* directives of 9 August. In orders issued at 1330 on 9 August, the *STAVKA* ordered 5th Guards Tank Army to attack "energetically and decisively" toward Lyubotin to cut enemy withdrawal lines from Khar'kov to the west.[137] Rotmistrov began his attacks toward Olshany late on 9 August but during two days of fighting Rotmistrov's forces made little progress. 3d Panzer Division, 167th Infantry Division remnants, and SS Panzer Division "Das Reich" gave little ground; and, by 11 August, SS Panzer Grenadier Division "Viking" elements had begun deploying into positions facing 5th Guards Tank Army north of Olshany. By the morning of 11 August 5th Guards Tank Army was still 10 kilometers from Olshany.

At that point, with the situation deteriorating in 1st Tank Army's sector, Zhukov ordered Rotmistrov's army to cease its futile attacks, concentrate north of Bogodukhov, and prepare to join 1st Tank Army in its growing struggle south of Bogodukhov.

Advance of Rifle Armies to Trostyanets, Akhtyrka, and Bogodukhov – 7–10 August

While 1st Tank Army and 5th Guards Tank Army developed the attack south, 33d Guards Rifle Corps of 5th Guards Army trailed 5th Guards Tank Army, fighting against the German 6th Panzer and 167th Infantry Divisions at Dessonovka, and then to the southwest (see Maps 65–67). By the evening of 7 August the 95th Rifle and 6th and 9th Guards Airborne Divisions had secured positions northeast along the rail line from Kazach'ya Lopan in tandem with 53d Army units on the left. A large gap, however, still existed between 33d Guards Rifle Corps' right flank and the 32d Guards Rifle Corps struggling for Borisovka. 5th Guards Tank Army to the southwest still fought for possession of the southern outskirts of Zolochev. Consequently, the *front* commander undertook measures to close that gap. 32d Guards Rifle Corps' 42d Guards Rifle Division began a march toward Zolochev, and 33d Guards Rifle Corps' divisions shifted southwest toward Kazach'ya Lopan. On 8 August the 95th Rifle Division and elements of 5th Guards Tank Army's 29th Tank Corps took the city from elements of 3d Panzer Division. Other elements of 33d Guards Rifle Corps pushed southwest to support 5th Guards Tank Army fighting south of Zolochev.

5th Guards Army's 32d Guards Rifle Corps disengaged from combat in the Borisovka–Graivoron area on 8 August; and, after regrouping and replenishing their supplies, they moved slowly southward toward Bogodukhov, engaging scattered remnants of German forces withdrawing southwest. The first elements of the corps arrived south of Bogodukhov late on 11 August when 1st Tank Army was attempting to parry the first series of German counterattacks. Only on 12 August were 5th Guards Army's two rifle corps reunited. By then, their assistance was required to stave off serious defeat for 1st Tank Army. The stage was set for several days of heavy see-saw combat in the Bogodukhov area as the German command sought to blunt the tank army's spearhead and drive it north of the critical Khar'kov–Poltava rail line.

Further west, 27th and 6th Guards Armies, having eradicated the Graivoron–Borisovka pocket, regrouped and headed southwest in the wake of their mobile groups to reach their objectives of Akhtyrka and Kotel'va (see Maps 66–67). Moskalenko's 40th Army, with two tank corps in support, pressed on toward its objectives of Trostyanets and Boromlya on the Sumy–Khar'kov rail line.

Chistyakov's 6th Guards Army required considerable time to regroup after the Borisovka fighting. Meanwhile, Vatutin attached Chistyakov's 5th Guards Tank Corps to 1st Tank Army; and 5th Guards Tank Corps began its exploitation southwest. By 8 August the corps had reached the area north of Krasnokutsk. Late that day, Chistyakov's infantry columns headed south in a long march which by late on 11 August brought his lead divisions to the Merla River southwest of Bogodukhov just in time to stiffen the 1st Tank Army's right flank. The bulk of 6th Guards Army forces were available for combat when German counterattacks opened against 1st Tank Army on 12 August.

Trofimenko's 27th Army cleared the Graivoron area on 7 and 8 August. Vatutin, concerned about the open flanks of his exploiting armored units, ordered Trofimenko to cover 6th Guards and 1st Tank Armies' right flank by securing Akhtyrka as soon as possible. Poluboyarov's 4th Guards Tank Corps, spearheading 27th Army's thrust, moved southwest along both banks of the Vorskla River on the afternoon of 7 August with 14th Guards Tank Brigade as a forward detachment followed by the 13th and 3d Guards Tank Brigades and the 12th Guards Tank Brigade in corps reserve. 14th Guards Tank Brigade ran into elements of "Grossdeutschland" Division at Bol'shaya Pisarevka, 30 kilometers northeast of Akhtyrka, and drove the German forces back to Novaya Ryabina along the rail line east of Akhtyrka. There, on the evening of 8 August, Poluboyarov's columns repeatedly attacked German defenses but were repulsed.[138]

After a thorough reconnaissance Poluboyarov concluded the defenses were too strong to engage frontally. Therefore, he dispatched the 13th Guards Tank Brigade southward around the German right flank to strike at Akhtyrka from the southeast while the 12th and 14th Guards Tank Brigades kept up pressure on the eastern and northeastern approaches to Akhtyrka. The 13th Guards Tank Brigade, having just missed intercepting the withdrawing German columns of 19th Panzer Division, 255th Infantry Division, and 332d Infantry Division, late in the afternoon of 9 August drove "Grossdeutschland" Division's elements westward toward Akhtyrka. The remainder of Poluboyarov's corps attacked German positions further north, cut the Trostyanets–Bogodukhov road, and threatened to cut off "Grossdeutschland" units in Novaya Ryabina.

On 10 August Poluboyarov's brigades assaulted "Grossdeutschland's" positions from all directions and by evening penetrated German defenses in the south. "Grossdeutschland" then conducted a phased withdrawal back to defensive positions around Akhtyrka. The following day Poluboyarov attempted a coordinated assault to take the city. After a short artillery preparation, tank units carrying infantry with automatic weapons attacked under cover of direct fire artillery. The 12th Guards Tank

Brigade attacked from the east and penetrated into the city; but the 14th Guards Tank Brigade and 3d Guards Mechanized Brigade, advancing from the southeast, were stopped short of the town. By late on 11 August the Germans had cleared Poluboyarov's troops from the town and forced him to look elsewhere for success.[139]

Thwarted in his initial attempt to take the town by storm, Poluboyarov's 13th Guards Tank Brigade attacked the town from the southwest, drove German forces from Gai–Mashenka in Akhtyrka's southern suburbs, but still could not penetrate into the town. By this time lead rifle divisions of 27th Army were approaching the city from the northeast. Poluboyarov gave the infantry forces the task of blockading the city and moved southward along the Vorskla River seeking another way to prise the German defenders from their positions at Akhtyrka.

Trofimenko ordered Poluboyarov to cross the Vorskla River south of Akhtyrka and isolate the German defenders by cutting the road running from Zen'kov to Akhtyrka. 27th Army rifle divisions were to seize Kotel'va to restore a continuous front with 5th Guards Army to the east and cover Poluboyarov's advance.[140] Trofimenko was especially concerned over German troop concentrations south of Bogodukhov and at Akhtyrka, for they had the potential of threatening his army's flanks.

On 27th Army's right flank Moskalenko's 40th Army continued its advance on 8 August against XXXXVIII Panzer Corps' 57th Infantry, 7th Panzer, and 11th Panzer Divisions. 10th and 2d Tank Corps and Moskalenko's two rifle corps forced the Germans to conduct delaying operations back to more defensible lines north and south of Boromlya and Trostyanets on line with "Grossdeutschland" Division's defensive positions at Akhtyrka. By day's end 10th Tank Corps' advanced guard had penetrated 11th Panzer Division defenses east of Trostyanets and entered the town well ahead of the supporting infantry of the 100th and 206th Rifle Divisions (47th Rifle Corps). 2d Tank Corps, with 52d Rifle Corps in its wake, pushed toward Boromlya against 7th Panzer and 57th Infantry Divisions and reached the eastern outskirts of Boromlya by nightfall.

To add to XXXXVIII Panzer Corps' discomfiture, Chibisov's 38th Army joined the Soviet offensive by attacking German VII Army Corps' positions from north of Sumy to Krasnopol'ye. Chibisov sought to capitalize on 40th Army's success by penetrating German defenses east of Sumy, crossing the Psel River, and threatening Sumy itself. Chibisov's 50th Rifle Corps with three rifle divisions (38th, 167th, 340th) would make the main attack northeast of Sumy. Chibisov would use his left flank 232d Rifle Division to strike the German 68th Infantry Division which had already been flanked by 40th Army's attack.[141]

Chibisov's assault began on the morning of 8 August after a strong artillery preparation. 50th Rifle Corps drove 2–5 kilometers into the German defenses on the first day of the attack and forced the German VII Army Corps commander to commit all of his reserves. The following day the 232d Rifle Division penetrated German defenses and forced a general German withdrawal to new defense lines adjacent to 57th Infantry Division defenses north of Boromlya. Meanwhile, 50th Rifle Corps' divisions threatened German strongholds east of Sumy and the Psel River.

Heavy fighting also raged on 40th Army's front. On 9 August 10th Tank Corps and 100th Rifle Division fought for possession of Trostyanets against 11th Panzer Division and elements of 19th Panzer Division, which had just conducted their harrowing withdrawal from Graivoron. 11th Panzer Division counterattacks drove the Soviets from the western sections of Trostyanets but could not clear them from the town proper. Ten kilometers to the north the 206th Rifle Division cut the rail line, seized the town of Belka, and threatened the flanks of 11th Panzer and 7th Panzer Divisions. Further north, around Boromlya, 2d Tank Corps and the 161st and 237th Rifle Divisions forced 7th Panzer and 57th Infantry Divisions to withdraw to new defenses west of Boromlya along the highway to Sumy, thus freeing 7th Panzer Division to deal with the dangerous Soviet penetration at Belka.

At dawn on 10 August, 7th Panzer Division attacked 206th Rifle Division positions at Belka from the north. Simultaneously, the reconnaissance battalion of 11th Panzer Division struck from the south; and the two forces drove the 206th back to positions east of Belka. At the same time, other elements of 11th Panzer Division regained most of Trostyanets from the 10th Tank Corps and 100th Rifle Division. These actions signaled XXXXVIII Panzer Corps' intentions of holding firmly to the Boromlya–Trostyanets defensive line. To reinforce this defense VII Army Corps sent one regiment of the 88th Infantry Division from its left flank to the Boromlya area. In addition, 19th Panzer Division remnants formed into a *kampfgruppe* which deployed in the rear of German lines south of Trostyanets to deal with any threatened Soviet penetration in that region.[142]

One last threat surfaced to XXXXVIII Panzer Corps on 10 August. The Soviet 161st and 237th Rifle Divisions capitalized on the 57th Infantry Division's withdrawal west of Boromlya by attacking to within 1 kilometer of the rail line. Over the next two days, however, 57th Infantry Division counterattacks supported by 7th Panzer Division tanks drove the 161st Rifle Division back to positions along the Boromlya River and in the town itself.[143] Here the front temporarily stabilized. XXXXVIII Panzer Corps' defensive adjustments discouraged further attack by Moskalenko's army until 13 August when he again tried to crack German defenses in the Boromlya sector. It was clear that, until the Soviets completed a major regrouping or received significant reinforcements, the front from Sumy to Akhtyrka would remain stable. For the time being all eyes were on events in the south at Bogodukhov and in the immediate environs of Khar'kov.

The Situation on 11 August

From 6 to 11 August Soviet forces had advanced 60–100 kilometers. In the German center, 1st Tank and 5th Guards Tank Armies had exploited to the Bogodukhov–Zolochev area, while on the German left flank 40th and 27th Armies had pushed to the outskirts of Akhtyrka and secured Trostyanets. By prodigious efforts, the Germans, although unable to close the gap between 4th Panzer Army and Army Detachment Kempf, had managed to marshal enough forces to extend their flanks and keep the Soviet advance in contact if not under control. The deployment of 3d Panzer Division, SS "Das Reich," SS "Totenkopf," and finally, SS "Viking" had checked the uncontrolled advance of 5th Guards Tank Army and had finally met advance elements of 1st Tank Army south of Bogodukhov. Meanwhile, LII Army Corps' fighting withdrawal from Borisovka and Graivoron and XXXXVIII Panzer Corps' defensive wheeling movement southwest of Krasnopol'ye had kept the German front intact, tied down Soviet infantry elements so critical to 1st Tank Army and 5th Guards Tank Army's ultimate success, and succeeded in re-establishing a credible front from Sumy to Akhtyrka.

Now the German command sought to accomplish what it had so often achieved before, namely a repulse and defeat of those advanced Soviet elements. The Germans chose Bogodukhov and Akhtyrka as the points where counterattacks would pay the greatest dividends. Unlike earlier years, however, the bulk of German counterattack forces had already been worn down in heavy fighting. Only time would tell if they could succeed in attacks planned to begin late on 11 August.

The Advance on Khar'kov (6–11 August)

The Situation on 6 August

While the Voronezh Front reduced the Borisovka pocket and drove on Bogodukhov, the Steppe Front, after securing the city of Belgorod on 5 August, set about the grinding task of moving directly on Khar'kov. That the advance would be difficult was no surprise. Fighting for Belgorod proper had been indicative of the resistance the Soviets would face.

On 6 August the Steppe Front commander, Konev, and *STAVKA* representative, Zhukov, sent a proposal to the *STAVKA* detailing their plans for developing the offensive to Khar'kov. 53d Army would launch the *front* main attack along the Belgorod–Khar'kov road toward Dergachi. 69th Army initially would attack on 53d Army's left flank and then would revert to *front* reserve. 7th Guards Army's 49th Rifle Corps would advance south along the west bank of the Northern Donets River, and as it progressed the 25th and 24th Guards Rifle Corps would also cross the Northern Donets. When the army reached the Staryi Saltov area it would assist 57th Army's passage of the river. Subsequently, 57th Army would shift from Southwestern Front to Steppe Front control and would attack from Staryi Saltov and Pechenegi toward Khar'kov.[144] In light of previous losses Zhukov and Konev requested the *STAVKA* furnish replacements and material amounting to 35,000 men, 200 T-34s, 100 T-70s, and 35 KV tanks, 90 fighters, 40 PO-2 aircraft, 60 IL-2 as well as four self-propelled artillery regiments and two engineer brigades.[145] For the time being, however, the offensive would continue without those reinforcements.

When Army Detachment Kempf withdrew from Belgorod on 5 August it established its new defensive positions south of the city on both sides of the Khar'kov road. XI Army Corps' 6th Panzer and 167th Infantry Divisions held the left wing of the defense line running from Bessonovka southwest along the Udy River toward Zolochev facing Rotmistrov's 5th Guards Tank Army and 5th Guards Army's 33d Guards Rifle Corps. The threat to this flank remained a constant problem for Army Detachment Kempf, for an eastward push by either Soviet force could threaten defending units along the Khar'kov road with envelopment and encirclement. Thus, Army Detachment Kempf placed all newly arrived reinforcements, including 3d Panzer Division, on its left flank under III Panzer Corps' control along a line extending southwest toward Zolochev. On its critical northern front, Army Detachment Kempf deployed XI Army Corps' 168th and 198th Infantry Divisions into defenses eastward from Bessonovka across the Khar'kov road and reinforced them with all available assault gun and armor units. The 106th Infantry Division defended from Repnoye, south of Belgorod, to the Northern Donets River and watched over the menacing Soviet bridgehead on the west bank of the river at Solomino. Further south along the river, the 320th Infantry Division held in check the Soviet bridgehead at Toplinka and defended crossings opposite Shebekino. The XXXXII Army Corps with the 282d, 39th and 161st Infantry Divisions defended positions along the Northern Donets River from Volchansk to south of Zmiyev and watched for threats from Soviet 57th and 1st Guards Armies.[146]

Army Detachment Kempf planned to defend and delay in successive positions along the Khar'kov road while closely watching Soviet activity on both flanks. Relying on firepower, strong defensive positions, and a lack of room for Soviet maneuver, Kempf intended to make the Soviets pay in blood for their advance. The Soviets, who would have to pay that price, were confronted with the task of maintaining pressure on all German defensive positions and attempting maneuver in limited spaces. At first, 53d, 69th, and those few 7th Guards Army divisions which had crossed the Northern Donets River would have to apply pressure in narrow army, corps, and division attack sectors. As the advance progressed and the front widened, other 7th Guards Army divisions from the east bank of the Northern Donets River could join the effort. The primary armor support for the Steppe Front remained Solomatin's 1st Mechanized Corps supporting 53d Army and separate tank regiments and brigades supporting the other armies.

The Steppe Front Advance – 6–11 August

Early on 6 August Konev's armies resumed their offensive. Managarov's 53d Army made its main attack between the road and rail line to Khar'kov and conducted secondary attacks on both flanks (see Maps 64–67). Managarov's initial objective was Mikoyanovka, 25 kilometers southwest of Belgorod. Solomatin's 1st Mechanized Corps supported the advance with two brigades forward (35th and 37th Mechanized) and one in reserve (219th Tank) while the 19th Mechanized Brigade in the rear engaged German stragglers fleeing Belgorod and covered the army left flank.

Although heavy rains and flooded streams assisted the defenders, Soviet pressure forced German units to fall back. The 116th and 28th Guards Rifle Division pushed the German 168th Infantry Division to the south, however, Solomatin's armor was unable to penetrate German defenses and break through to Mikoyanovka. Consequently, he committed his 219th Tank and 37th Mechanized Brigades to support a 28th Guards Rifle Division assault on the town. On the evening of 6 August, the combined assaults of Soviet infantry and armor finally forced the German 168th and 198th Infantry Divisions to withdraw to new defenses south of Mikoyanovka. The following day 53d Army divisions pressed forward another 12–14 kilometers confronted by skillful German rear guard actions that stymied a more rapid advance.[147]

Late on 7 August, to accelerate the pace of the offensive, Managarov created a new shock group from the 219th Tank Brigade, 32d Separate Armored Battalion, 57th Separate Motorcycle Battalion, 75th Tank Destroyer Regiment, and one motorized rifle battalion of the 19th Mechanized Brigade. He ordered the group to attack and seize Dergachi and cut enemy withdrawal routes to Khar'kov. Despite the careful arrangements, the group succeeded in penetrating the 168th Infantry Division defenses but only advanced as far as the Kazach'ya Lopan area by the evening of 8 August.[148] Meanwhile, the 19th and 35th Mechanized Brigades shifted westward to support 33d Guards Rifle Corps units also battling for possession of Kazach'ya Lopan. East of Kazach'ya Lopan the 28th Guards and 84th Guards Rifle Divisions and 219th Tank Brigade attacked at 0700 along the Khar'kov road, but heavy German air attacks and firm resistance by 6th Panzer Division supported by Ferdinand assault guns slowed the Soviet advance.[149] The only positive news of the day for Managarov came in late evening when Kazach'ya Lopan finally fell to the 19th and 35th Mechanized Brigades.

Still smarting over the slow advance, at 0500 on 10 August Managarov ordered Solomatin to assemble his corps southwest of Kazach'ya Lopan and launch an attack at 0800 southward west of Dergachi to occupy Korotich, 12 kilometers west of Khar'kov, by nightfall (a depth of 40 kilometers). Solomatin, with only three hours to assemble his corps over the rain-drenched terrain, decided to initiate his attack with his two available brigades, the 19th and 35th Mechanized Brigades. The 219th Tank Brigade and 37th Mechanized Brigade would assemble as soon as possible and support the attack in its later stages. The overly ambitious plan aborted from the start. The lead brigades penetrated only 5 kilometers against particularly heavy resistance from 3d Panzer Division. By nightfall, the two brigades, cooperating with the 84th Guards Rifle Division, took Bezrukovka, less than 10 kilometers north of Dergachi, while to the east the 28th Guards Rifle Division, operating along the rail line, advanced against heavy resistance to German defense lines covering the approaches to Russkaya Lozovaya, 6 kilometers northeast of Dergachi.[150]

On the evening of 10 August the Steppe Front Chief of Staff, General M.V. Zakharov, issued new orders to Managarov. 53d Army was to attack at 0900 and, by day's end, cut the rail line from Khar'kov to Zolochev near Peresechnaya, 10 kilometers northeast of Lyubotin. Simultaneously, 1st Mechanized Corps was to advance to Gavrilovka on the Udy River, 10 kilometers west of Khar'kov. Again the mission proved unrealistic. In Managarov's words,

> To destroy the enemy on the approaches to Khar'kov in the field – such was the demand of the front commander. I.S. Konev, in this decision, departed from the real correlation of forces and existing conditions. Battle in Khar'kov itself, a large industrial center, could take on a bitter character and cost us large casualties.[151]

By the evening of 11 August Managarov's army had advanced several kilometers through Russkaya Lozovaya to the northeastern outskirts of

Dergachi, in essence reaching the outer defenses of Khar'kov. However, the German defense held firm, promising that Managarov's concerns over a bloody approach to Khar'kov would prove true.

On 53d Army's left flank Kryuchenkin's 69th Army advanced south from Belgorod in a narrow sector between Repnoye and the Belgorod–Brodok road against remnants of the German 198th Infantry Division and the left flank of the 106th Infantry Division. The 111th and 15th Guards Rifle Divisions of 7th Guards Army's 49th Rifle Corps filled the gap from the Brodok road to the Northern Donets River. Kryuchenkin's army was to participate in the initial penetration and thereafter become the *front* reserve. However, its advance was as difficult as Managarov's; and, consequently, the army was kept in its narrow offensive sector for the remainder of the Khar'kov operation.

On 6 August the 111th Rifle Division advanced toward Tavrovo, while the 15th Guards Rifle Division attacked and secured Solomino. The following day the two divisions seized Tavrovo and Brodok, and forces from 7th Guards Army's 25th and 24th Guards Rifle Corps broke out of their bridgeheads across the river at Toplinka and Pristen driving the German 320th Infantry Division before them.[152]

On 8 August 69th Army's two corps (48th Guards and 35th Guards) and the three corps of 7th Guards Army (49th, 24th Guards, 25th Guards), in tandem with 53d Army commenced a concerted advance against heavy resistance. As they advanced south and southwest against delaying German forces, they uncovered the right flank of Soviet 57th Army which on 8 August was transferred from Southwestern to Steppe Front control.* 69th Army's 35th Guards Rifle Corps (94th Guards and 93d Guards Rifle Divisions) drove back the German 320th Infantry Division and, at 1300 on 10 August, occupied Liptsy, 30 kilometers northeast of Khar'kov, while the 48th Guards Rifle Corps kept pace to the east. The following day the two corps advanced almost 20 kilometers, seized Tsirkuny, and approached the outer German defense line of Khar'kov.[153]

Meanwhile, 7th Guards Army's 49th Rifle Corps marched southward abreast of 69th Army while the 25th Guards and 24th Guards Rifle Corps to the east took Murom and Ternovaya and headed toward Staryi Saltov on the west bank of the Northern Donets. 7th Guards Army's steady advance continued until 11 August when the three corps reached Khar'kov's outer defense line. There 24th Guards Rifle Corps occupied the main attack sector of the army opposite German 320th Infantry Division defenses while the other two corps held the flanks and

*The Southwestern Front was then participating with the Southern Front in the Donbas operation.

cleared out pockets of German resistance in their rear area west of the Northern Donets River.

On 9 August Lieutenant General N.A. Gagen's 57th Army, now under Steppe Front control, launched its offensive across the Northern Donets River, just as 7th Guards Army forces were threatening Staryi Saltov from the north. 57th Army was to attack across the Northern Donets River, envelop Khar'kov from the southeast, and cut German withdrawal routes running south from Khar'kov. Gagen's right flank corps (68th) was to begin the offensive to secure bridgeheads on the west bank of the Northern Donets River and support a 64th Rifle Corps attack further south which was to occur one or two days later, depending on the success of the main attack.[154] On the morning of 9 August the 68th Rifle Corps crossed the river near Staryi Saltov and Pechenegi, and the German 282d and 39th Infantry Divisions began a fighting withdrawal to Khar'kov's outer defense lines. The following day 64th Rifle Corps joined the assaults with attacks north and south of Chuguyev. The 41st Guards Rifle Division led the attack to secure Chuguyev and advance westward to Bezlyudovka.

The 41st Guards Rifle Division's assault across the Northern Donets River occurred at first light while a heavy fog hung over the river. The division attacked with all three regiments forward and eschewed the firing of an artillery preparation in order to achieve surprise. By 1500 on 10 August the division had attained all of its immediate objectives. The following morning sappers constructed bridges across the Northern Donets River, and other divisions of 64th Rifle Corps deployed forward. Although the 113th Rifle Division, on the division's right flank, became bogged down in fighting north of Chuguyev, the 41st Guards Rifle Division cleared the city of Germans by 1000. To speed up the advance Gagan committed the 303d Rifle Division to battle late on 11 August in the 113th Rifle Division's sector. Subsequently, the two divisions assaulted German strong points along the road to Khar'kov.[155]

The Soviet commitment of 57th Army to the offensive brought German positions at Khar'kov under assault from a semi-circle of Soviet armies running from Dergachi in the northwest to Chuguyev in the southeast. The rapid progress of 57th Army forces along the Chuguyev–Khar'kov road threatened German communication routes with the city, especially if Soviet forces kept the axis of their advance south of Khar'kov and avoided repeating the mistake made by 3d Tank Army in February, when it dashed its strength to pieces against the eastern approaches to the city. To forestall a further Soviet advance in that sector, Army Detachment Kempf shifted the 6th Panzer Division to the southeastern approaches to the city thereby weakening German defenses in the north.[156]

The Struggles at Bogodukhov (11–17 August)

Prelude

By 11 August a critical stage loomed before both participants in the developing Khar'kov operation. Vatutin's two tank armies had plunged up to 100 kilometers into the German operational rear area and were preparing to consolidate their gains, concentrate their forces, and move decisively against the communications lines of German forces defending Khar'kov. Although Katukov's and Rotmistrov's tank armies were separated from their infantry support, the infantry could join them within 24 hours. When that occurred, it would be exceedingly difficult for German forces to reverse the tide of the Soviet offensive. As if to make this threat clearer, on 11 August 1st Tank Army's lead brigades had plunged south out of the Bogodukhov area and cut the Poltava–Khar'kov rail line at several locations.

The Germans, however, had detected the threat and were undertaking measures to strike back at the Soviet armor and perhaps destroy it. Since 6 August the rail lines south and southwest of Khar'kov were jammed with tanks, assault guns, and combat paraphernalia of German armored units returning to the Khar'kov area – the scene of glorious victory in March and disastrous defeat in July. Between 6 and 11 August 3d Panzer Division, SS Panzer Division "Das Reich," and finally SS Panzer Division "Totenkopf" arrived. III Panzer Corps took operational control of these units and fed them into battle piecemeal, first against Soviet 5th Guards Tank Army northeast of Zolochev (3d Panzer Division) then against 1st Tank Army southeast and east of Bogodukhov (SS "Das Reich"). While these stop gap measures channeled and slowed the Soviet advance, the manner of commitment produced no fundamental change in the situation. It was to achieve just such a fundamental change that the German command approved new plans to use III Panzer Corps units, together with additional reinforcements, to strike decisively at the Soviet armored spearheads.

German Counterattack Planning

In general concept the Germans' counterattack plan envisioned the creation of two panzer shock groups which would deliver converging blows against the flanks of the Soviet penetration to cripple the Soviet advance. The first of the panzer shock groups, under control of III Panzer Corps, would strike north and northwest from the Vysokopol'ye–Kovyagi area through Bogodukhov to join ultimately with a thrust by a second panzer shock group formed around "Grossdeutschland" Division and under XXIV Panzer Corps' control, which would attack southeast from Akhtyrka. The sequence, timing, and composition of the two attacks was dependent upon Soviet actions. Thus, the Soviet advance south of Bogodukhov on 11 August forced the Germans to begin the southern counterstroke before either of the panzer shock groups was fully assembled. In essence, the ensuing extended period of battle around, first, Bogodukhov and, later, Akhtyrka resembled a meeting engagement more than a well-coordinated counterstroke. The ensuing complex series of battles ultimately wore down the combat strength of both participants and provided victory to that side that could employ "the last battalion."

III Panzer Corps prepared for its counterstroke on 10–11 August just as 1st Tank Army resumed its attacks south from Bogodukhov. The corps had at its disposal SS Panzer Division "Das Reich," defending south and southwest of Zolochev, 3d Panzer Division, defending southeast of Zolochev, and SS Panzer Division "Totenkopf," assembling south of the Khar'kov–Poltava rail line due south of Bogodukhov. In addition, SS Panzer Grenadier Division "Viking" was assembling near Khar'kov preparatory to moving northwest to join III Panzer Corps. III Panzer Corps' plan was to strike at 1st Tank Army advanced elements south of Bogodukhov with SS Panzer Division "Totenkopf." Simultaneously, Panzer Division "Das Reich" would turn over its sector north and northwest of Olshany to SS Panzer Grenadier Division "Viking" and would then attack 1st Tank Army's left flank east of Bogodukhov.

On 11 August the combat strength of SS Panzer Division "Das Reich" and SS Panzer Division "Totenkopf" was about 70 and 60 tanks and assault guns, respectively. SS "Viking" added about 50 more to that total. (3d Panzer Division at the same time had about 20–30 tanks and assault guns.)[157] At that time, 1st Tank Army numbered 268 tanks and self-propelled guns and 5th Guards Tank Army, 115.[158] The superior Soviet armored strength made it imperative that German panzer commanders strike the most vulnerable portion of the Soviet armored force. On 11 August this turned out to be the reinforced forward detachments operating in the vanguard of 1st Tank Army.

Battle of Bogodukhov: The German Counterattack of 11 August

On 11 August forward detachments of 1st Tank Army's lead corps had crossed the Merchik River and raced to the Poltava–Khar'kov rail line (see Map 67). Colonel Leonov's 112th Tank Brigade (6th Tank Corps) had secured Aleksandrovka, and its forward detachment (reinforced tank battalion with 26 tanks) had occupied Vysokopol'ye and scattered German rear service units defending along the rail line. Further east the 49th Tank Brigade's forward detachment (11 tanks) and 10th Mechanized Brigade's forward detachment (9 tanks) had crossed the Merchik and occupied Kovyagi. Later the 1st Guards Tank Brigade and 17th Tank Regiment had arrived at Kovyagi and had established all round defenses while awaiting the arrival of the corps' main force. Meanwhile, 49th Tank Brigade's forward detachment had moved on and occupied Levandalovka.

Although these forces had cut the critical rail line west of Khar'kov, they also offered a ripe opportunity for German counterattack, because remaining 1st Tank Army units still fighting along the Merchik River had lagged behind their forward detachments. Moreover, the bulk of 31st Tank Corps' brigades were assisting 5th Guards Army's 13th Guards Rifle Division and 3d Mechanized Corps, then under attack southeast of Bogodukhov.

At 1100 on 11 August SS Panzer Division "Totenkopf" assaulted 1st Tank Army's lead elements along the rail line just as SS Panzer Division "Das Reich" opened its drive from the east. The attacks swept around and isolated Katukov's forward detachments and drove the main forces to the rear. The 112th Tank Brigade withdrew toward Sharovka on the Merchik River early on 12 August and ordered its battalion at Vysokopol'ye to do likewise. The isolated tank battalion fought a savage battle in encirclement before breaking out northwest to join the main force at Sharovka. The fighting cost the battalion thirteen tanks, all of its self-propelled guns, both anti-aircraft guns, and 50 percent of its automatic weapons battalion. Another five tanks fell behind during the withdrawal only to be swallowed by SS "Totenkopf's" advance.[159] 1st Guards Tank Brigade, encircled at Kovyagi, also succeeded in breaking out to the north by nightfall on 11 August, although also with heavy losses. The 49th Tank Brigade and 17th Tank Regiment in the Kovyagi area and the battalion of the 49th Tank Brigade at Levandalovka were not as fortunate. For several days the units fought in encirclement, but ultimately they were destroyed with only a few personnel escaping.

SS "Totenkopf's" attack had isolated or driven off 1st Tank Army forward elements along the rail line. In addition, an assault by twenty-five SS "Totenkopf" tanks south of Krasnokutsk had struck the right flank of 6th Tank Corps south of the Merchik River and forced the unit to withdraw to the north bank of the river. Katukov reinforced 6th Tank Corps' right flank brigade (200th) with the 6th Motorized Rifle Brigade, sent forward from Bogodukhov, and with the 163d Rifle Division of 27th Army. He also dispatched the 22d Tank Brigade to support the 112th Tank Brigade at Aleksandrovka.

On 1st Tank Army's left southeast of Bogodukhov, the situation had also deteriorated. There, 3d Mechanized Corps came under heavy pressure by SS Panzer Division "Das Reich" attacks which penetrated Soviet positions from Aleksandrovka north toward the Bogodukhov–Khar'kov rail line. Katukov committed his second echelon 31st Tank Corps to close the breach, and by nightfall the German attack stalled.

Battle of Bogodukhov: The German Counterattack of 12 August

By nightfall on 11 August 1st Tank Army's main force occupied positions along the north bank of the Merchik River through Aleksandrovka and northeast to Skovorodinovka, 20 kilometers east of Bogodukhov. In the course of one day the tank army had lost over one-third of its strength and now possessed 134 tanks (plus several units still encircled to the south).[160] What had begun as a decisive advance on a broad front early on 11 August turned into a severe crisis by that evening. 1st Tank Army had experienced severe losses; its right flank was open and the bulk of 6th Guards and 27th Army rifle units still well to the rear; air support was lacking; several of its units were encircled, and the Germans gave no indication of ceasing their attacks.

Nevertheless, Vatutin continued to display his characteristic optimism. He had known of the growing German armored concentration since early on 8 August, yet he had chosen to believe that its purpose was to cover a German withdrawal to the Psel and Vorskla Rivers. Even the events of 11 August failed to change his mind.[161] Hence, during the night he ordered 1st Tank Army to continue its attacks and to push one brigade toward Merefa to cut German withdrawal routes from Khar'kov. Prudently, however, Vatutin also ordered 5th Guards Tank Army to regroup and prepare to support 1st Tank Army. Already on 10 August, Vatutin had ordered 5th Guards Tank Army to abandon its costly attacks south of Zolochev and to concentrate northeast of Bogodukhov. Rotmistrov moved his army 40 kilometers to its new assembly area on the evening of 11 August. There he received orders to advance southward on the morning of 12 August, in tandem with 1st Tank Army, toward Valki and Novaya Vodolaga to cut German communications lines west of Khar'kov.

At 0400 on 12 August 5th Guards Tank Army moved out in column formation and at 0600 occupied positions south of Bogodukhov. The 18th and 29th Tank Corps deployed in jumping-off positions behind the defenses of the 71st Guards and 97th Guards Rifle Divisions of 5th Guards Army's 32d Guards Rifle Corps. 5th Guards Mechanized Corps remained in the concentration area as the tank army second echelon. Other 32d Guards Rifle Corps' divisions defended to the northeast on 5th Guards Tank Army's left flank. Katukov's 1st Tank Army, with 6th Guards Army divisions in support, defended along the Merchik River on 5th Guards Tank Army's right flank.[162]

As Rotmistrov's forces occupied their jumping-off positions, the tank corps' forward detachments arrived at Aleksandrovka expecting to find 1st Tank Army units in position south of the Merchik River. Instead, the forward detachments ran into SS Panzer Division "Totenkopf" units deploying for an attack. Rather than "beginning the attack at 0800" through the friendly positions of 1st Tank Army, 5th Guards Tank Army units now became the focus of a major German attack.

Meanwhile, during the night of 11–12 August Katukov regrouped his forces, brought up his remaining artillery and prepared to resume the offensive the next morning. At 0930 on 12 August Katukov's corps lunged forward against SS Panzer Division "Totenkopf." 6th Tank Corps' 200th Tank Brigade and 6th Motorized Rifle Brigade thrust across the Merchik River and attacked toward Vysokopol'ye. Simultaneously, 3d Mechanized Corps' 22d and 112th Tank Brigade on 6th Tank Corps' left flank advanced southward from positions west of Aleksandrovka. The 1st and 3d Battalions, 6th Motorized Rifle Brigade, supported by sixteen tanks, reached Vysokopol'ye by passing through gaps in SS Panzer Division "Totenkopf" lines and at 1300 seized a small section of the rail line. However, "Totenkopf" cut these battalions off as well. Reinforced by anti-tank guns from 6th Tank Corps, the two battalions received orders to hold their positions. Soon one rifle regiment of the 163d Rifle Division and a tank battalion of the 200th Tank Brigade tried to relieve the two battalions but failed, losing eight of its twelve tanks in the futile attempt. The remaining four tanks broke through and joined the encircled battalions.[163] On 14 August the remnants of 6th Motorized Rifle Brigade's force, on Katukov's orders, withdrew from Vysolopol'ye after suffering heavy losses.

3d Mechanized Corps' attack had no sooner begun when SS Panzer Division "Das Reich" began its own heavy attacks from the east against 1st Tank Army's left flank. The attacks struck the 112th Tank Brigade, 49th Tank Brigade, and 3d Mechanized Brigade of 31st Tank and 3d Mechanized Corps. The German Tiger tanks proved especially damaging in light of 1st Tank Army's shortage of self-propelled artillery and the ineffectiveness of its 45mm anti-tank guns. By day's end "Das Reich" had pushed 3d Mechanized and 31st Tank Corps units 3–4 kilometers westward. The 31st Tank Corps commander, General Chernienko, was killed in the attack.[164] 32d Guards Rifle Corps units finally reinforced 1st Tank Army's defenses and halted the German drive.

Meanwhile, 5th Guards Tank Army adjusted to the surprising situation. After withdrawing its forward detachments from the Aleksandrovka area, the 18th and 29th Tank Corps and two divisions of 5th Guards Army's 32d Guards Rifle Corps (97th, 13th Guards) assembled in combat positions to the rear of 1st Tank Army's embattled forces; and at 1200, on Zhukov's orders, they joined the attack, literally advancing through the fractured remains of 1st Tank Army's 31st Tank and 3d Mechanized Corps. Confused battle raged throughout the remainder of the day as German aircraft repeatedly struck at 5th Guards Tank Army units. The 29th Tank Corps and the 13th Guards Rifle Division met the main German attack near Kiyany and Krysino on both sides of the rail line 6 kilometers south of Bogodukhov and finally halted the German advance. To the south the 18th Tank Corps, cooperating with 1st Tank Army's 22d Tank Brigade and the 97th Guards Rifle Division, at day's end halted the German drive 10 kilometers south of Bogodukhov. During the battle, Rotmistrov was forced to commit two brigades of 5th Guards Mechanized Corps (10th and 12th Mechanized) to reinforce the 18th Tank Corps' defenses.[165]

At nightfall on 12 August fighting died down, and Soviet commanders took stock of the battlefield where elements of four armies lay intermingled in the darkness. 5th Guards Army's 32d Guards Rifle Corps' infantry occupied positions southwest of Bogodukhov interspersed with units of 3d Mechanized Corps of 1st Tank Army and 29th and 18th Tank Corps of 5th Guards Tank Army. 31st Tank Corps of 1st Tank Army defended west of 18th Tank Corps to the Merchik River backed up by two brigades of 5th Guards Mechanized Corps. Remaining 1st Tank Army units of 6th Tank Corps, supported by the 163d Rifle Division of 27th Army and newly arriving divisions of 6th Guards Army's 22d Guards Rifle Corps, deployed in defenses west along the Merchik River to its confluence with the Merla River. That evening Rotmistrov met with his corps commanders at the army observation post east of Bogodukhov. After discussing the day's activities, Rotmistrov, like Katukov of 1st Tank Army, ordered his exhausted corps to go on the defense. SS Panzer Division "Das Reich" would again test that defense on 13 August.

Battle of Bogodukhov: The Soviet Counterattack on 13 and 14 August

Despite the frustrations of 11–12 August Vatutin did not give up his idea of renewing offensive operations to reach the Khar'kov–Poltava rail line. He drafted new plans and issued new orders on the night of 12–13 August to capitalize on the arrival of fresh units of Chistyakov's 6th Guards Army, then occupying positions south of the Merla and Merchik Rivers from Lyubovka south of Krasnokutsk through Kachalovko to Merchik. Chistyakov's 51st Guards Rifle Division reported German infantry and armor advancing along the Poltava road and rail line northeast toward Vysokopol'ye. Thinking it an enticing target, Chistyakov reported his find to Vatutin. Despite warnings from Zhukov of the dangers from other German forces in the area, namely the panzer divisions, Vatutin successfully argued for a new plan of attack using 6th Guards Army's rifle divisions reinforced by 5th Guards Mechanized Corps of 5th Guards Tank Army in a flank attack against the Germans along the rail line. Simultaneously, 6th Tank Corps of 1st Tank Army would renew its attack across the Merchik River southward toward Vysolopol'ye and Kovyagi. Two divisions of 6th Guards Army would remain in defensive positions south of Bogodukhov to stiffen 1st Tank and 5th Guards Tank Army defenses against renewed German attacks toward Bogodukhov from the east. In addition, Vatutin ordered the 33d Guards Rifle Corps to undertake diversionary attacks eastward against German positions north of Olshany (a sector now defended by SS Panzer Grenadier Division "Viking").[166] The necessary regrouping of forces occurred under cover of darkness.

At 0530 on 13 August the concerted 6th Guards Army attack began, and it immediately forced SS "Totenkopf" to withdraw its overextended regiments (see Map 68). The 52d Guards Rifle Division struck SS "Totenkopf's" left flank and secured the rail line north and south of Alekseyevka 8 kilometers west of Vysokopol'ye. 6th Tank Corps' 6th Motorized Rifle and 200th Tank Brigades advanced 10 kilometers and again occupied Vysokopol'ye, thus forcing German reinforcements moving from Poltava (223d and 355th Infantry Divisions) to take a more circuitous route to Khar'kov. 5th Guards Mechanized Corps' two brigades forced the Merchik River at 0400 but were recalled later in the day to help repulse new German attacks south of Bogodukhov.[167]

Soviet success southwest of Bogodukhov on 13 August was tempered by the continuing serious situation south and east of Bogodukhov where SS Panzer Division "Das Reich," joined by the left wing of SS Panzer Grenadier Division "Viking," resumed attacks toward that town. At 0900 the Germans fired a 60-minute artillery preparation at Soviet defensive positions and followed the preparation with heavy tank and infantry attacks. 97th Guards Rifle Division, supported by 1st Tank Army tanks, fell back to new positions northeast of Khrushchevaya–Nikitovka, 10 kilometers south of Bogodukhov, while 29th Tank Corps relinquished its grip on Gavrishi State Farm just 8 kilometers southeast of Bogodukhov. The limited withdrawal of 1st Tank Army units and the 97th Guards Rifle Division uncovered 5th Guards Tank Army's right flank, which Rotmistrov struggled to cover with elements of his remaining 100 tanks.[168]

Ironically the fighting was punctuated by orders from higher headquarters, most of them unrealistic. Konev ordered 5th Guards Tank Army to form a "fist" and smash through to Novaya Vodolaga, and Vatutin likewise urged Rotmistrov on. Rotmistrov replied that if he moved his forces, the enemy would take Bogodukhov.[169] Despite the *front* commander's orders, 5th Guards Tank Army would remain riveted to its defenses until 17 August when, after fighting in the Bogodukhov sector quieted down, Rotmistrov received new orders to resume offensive operations.

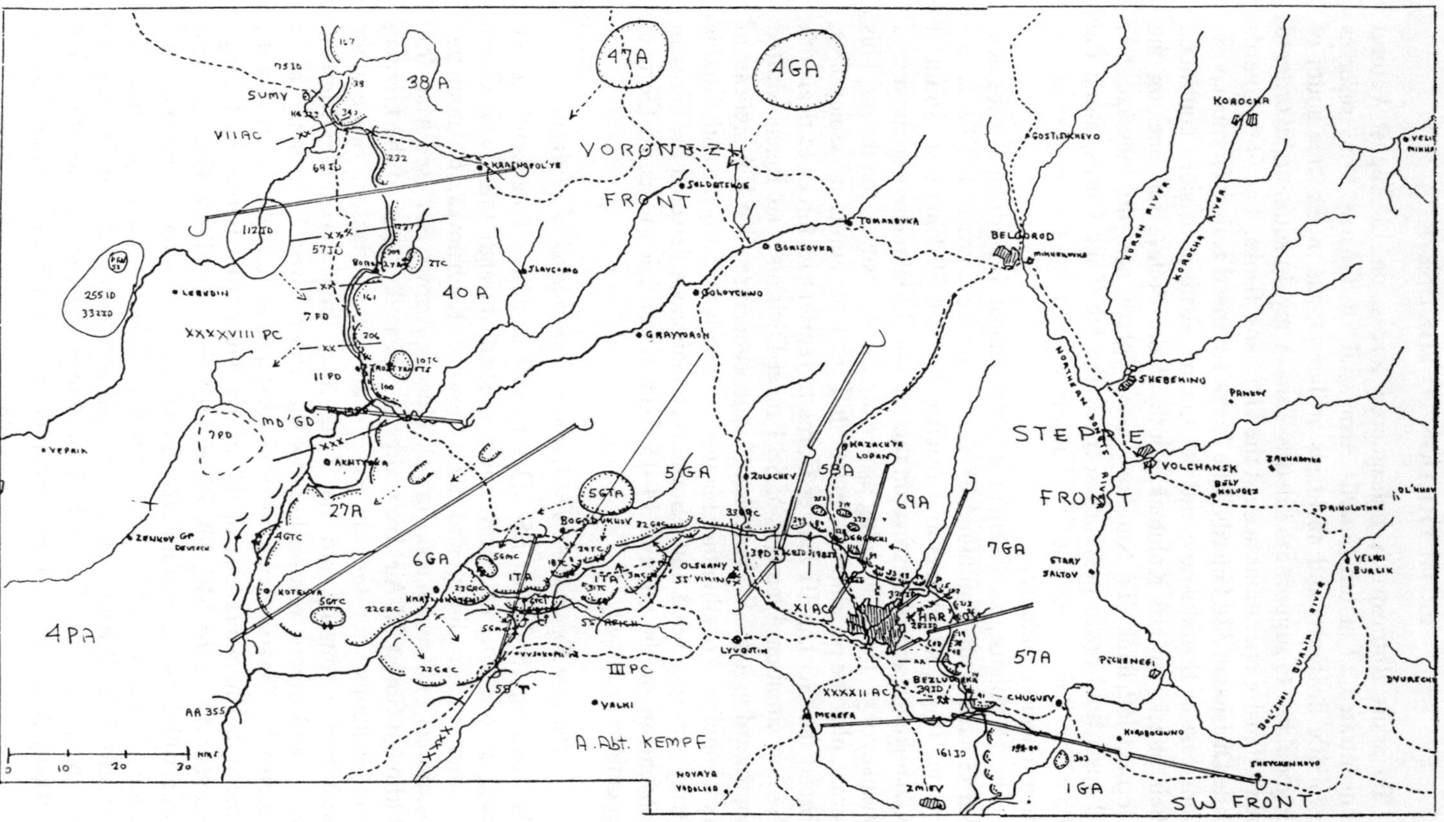

MAP 68. BELGOROD–KHAR'KOV, SITUATION, 13–14 AUGUST 1943

To assist Rotmistrov's beleaguered forces, on 13 August Vatutin concentrated all of 6th Guards Army and 5th Guards Army reserves (two rifle divisions) and all of his artillery assets in the area south of Bogodukhov to support 5th Guards Tank Army. In addition, he ordered new offensive operations against the Germans' flanks. The 66th Guards Rifle Division of 32d Guards Rifle Corps advanced against German positions east of Bogodukhov, and 6th Guards Army's divisions continued their attacks toward Kolomak, south of the Poltava rail line, on the German left flank. To Katukov's army Vatutin sent the message, "At all costs hold on to positions secured [by 6th Tank Corps] along the Khar'kov–Poltava rail line."[170] Vatutin ordered other units to continue their tenacious defense.

On 14 August, as German attacks against Bogodukhov subsided, 6th Guards Army continued its assault on the German left flank, advanced 10–12 kilometers and reached Otrada, 30 kilometers south of Krasnokutsk, and Shelestovo on the rail line 12 kilometers southwest of Vysokopol'ye, but in so doing dispersing the intensity of the thrust. This threat, plus the presence of Soviet 6th Tank Corps units at Vysolopol'ye, forced the German III Panzer Corps to reorient its forces to deal with the new situation. Elements of SS Panzer Division "Das Reich" shifted southward to join SS "Totenkopf" units concentrated at Kovyagi east of Vysokopol'ye. Together they planned a westerly thrust against 6th Guards Army's overextended units. Soviet reconnaissance detected the German movements on the night of 14–15 August, but failed to assess German intentions accurately.[171]

Battle of Bogodukhov: The German Counterattack of 15 August

At dawn on 15 August SS "Das Reich" and SS "Totenkopf" struck hard at 6th Guards Army units, slashed through 6th Tank Corps communications lines, and raced toward Kachalovka, 6 kilometers southwest of Krasnokutsk, in 6th Guards Army's rear (see Map 69). Although Soviet 2d Air Army aircraft repeatedly battered the German tank columns, 6th Guards Army's defenses collapsed. Some units withdrew northward into 1st Tank Army lines across the Merchik River and others westward across the Merla River. By evening on 15 August 6th Guards Army divisions reestablished a stable defense in the forests 6 kilometers east of the Merla River from Berezovka through Kachalovka to the Merchik River. However, not all 6th Guards Army units withdrew successfully. 52d Guards Rifle Division was encircled and fought its way out with heavy casualties while one regiment of the 90th Guards Rifle Division was surrounded and destroyed near Alekseyevka on the Poltava rail line. 6th Tank Corps units at Vysokopol'ye were virtually destroyed, and the remnants of the two brigades filtered out of

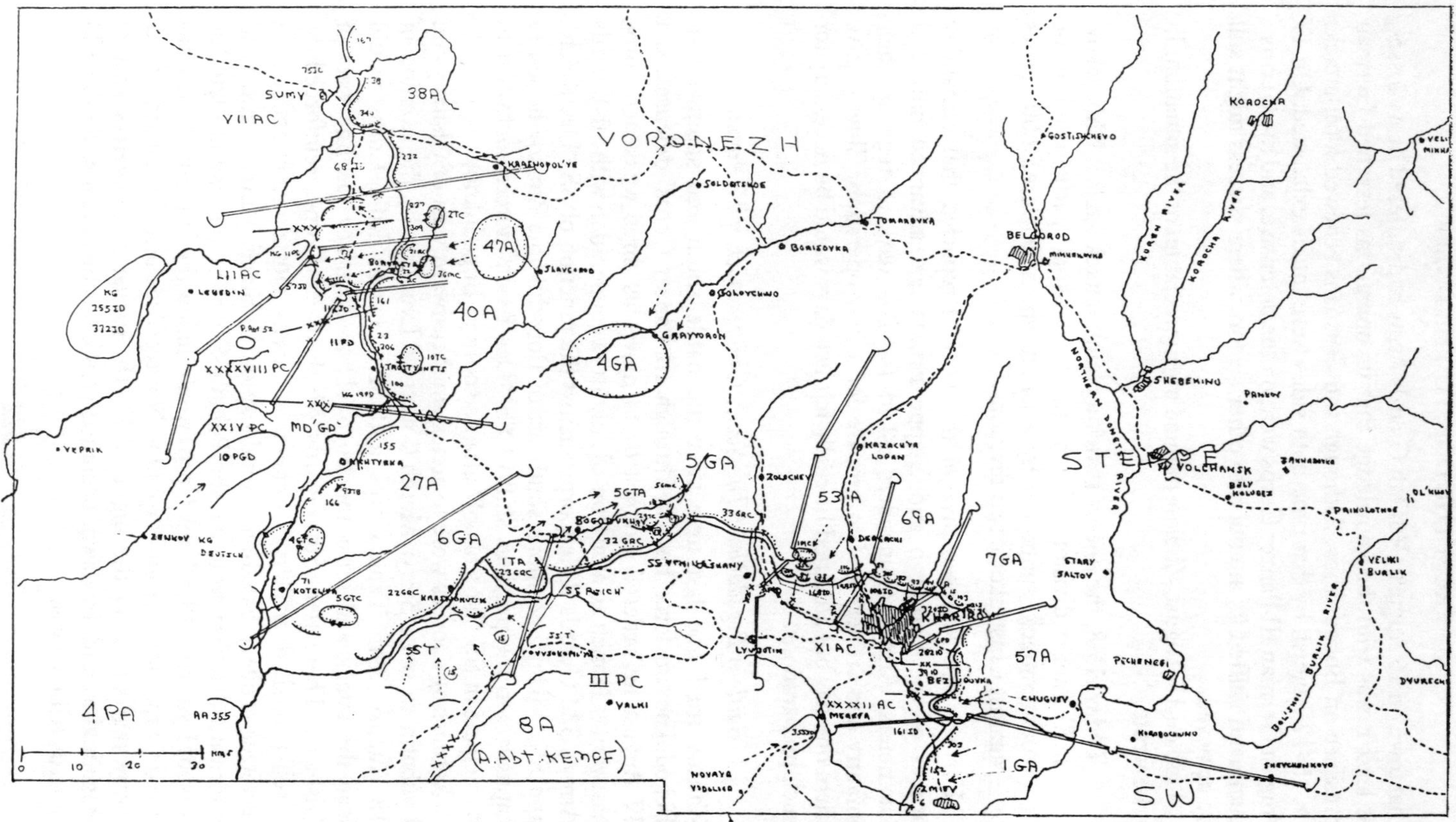

MAP 69. BELGOROD–KHAR'KOV, SITUATION, 16–17 AUGUST 1943

that town on 16 August.[172] If 6th Guards Army had suffered heavy losses, at least it was with the knowledge that its operations lessened German pressure on Bogodukhov. Although the Germans renewed local attacks on 16–17 August, by that time both sides were totally exhausted. On 17 August German III Panzer Corps went on the defensive, and the German command shifted its attention to other sectors where success might still be achieved.

Late on 15 August, Zhukov penned an appreciation of the situation. In it he wrote,

> Today, 15.8, the enemy struck a counterattack against Chistyakov. [SS] Panzer divisions 'Reich' and "Totenkopf' participated in the counterattack, supported by aviation which delivered 600 sorties against Chistyakov's two divisions.[173]

Further, the representative of the *STAVKA* reported that remaining armies of the Voronezh and Steppe Fronts had advanced only 2–3 kilometers. Army commanders asked for 2–3 days to regroup their infantry and artillery and to prepare for a new operation. Zhukov gave them one day but admitted he really felt two days would be necessary for such preparations.

Battle of Bogodukhov: The Soviet Counterattack of 17 August

Zhukov tried one last time after the battle south and southwest of Bogodukhov to force his way through III Panzer Corps' defenses. On 17 August he ordered Rotmistrov to move his three weakened corps eastward to launch an attack on 18 August in cooperation with 5th Guards Army's 32d Guards Rifle Corps against the junction of SS "Das Reich" and SS "Viking" positions southeast of Bogodukhov. Zhukov hoped to capitalize on the previous shift of SS "Das Reich" forces southwest to participate in SS "Totenkopf" attacks south of Bogodukhov.

Rotmistrov's forces were to attack southeastward west of Olshany and Lyubotin to seize Staryi Merchik west of Lyubotin by the evening of 18 August. 29th Tank Corps and 32d Guards Rifle Corps would lead the attack and cross the Bogodukhov–Khar'kov rail line west of Olshany. Thereafter, 5th Guards Mechanized Corps, reinforced by a self-propelled artillery regiment, a guards mortar regiment, and a howitzer artillery battalion, would exploit to Staryi Merchik and send a forward detachment to cut the Poltava–Khar'kov railroad at Ogult'sy, west of Lyubotin. 18th Tank Corps would follow the 5th Guards Mechanized Corps' advance and exploit to Novaya Vodolaga. 5th Guards Tank Army regrouped on the night of 17–18 August 6 kilometers east of Bogodukhov and, by dawn, occupied attack positions alongside the 32d Guards Rifle Corps.

At 0600 the artillery and air bombardment began; and one hour later the 32d Guards Rifle Corps attacked, supported by 29th Tank Corps armor. However, the artillery preparation had been ineffective; and heavy German fire halted the attack in the forward German defenses short of the Bogodukhov–Khar'kov rail line. To speed the attack, Rotmistrov ordered Skvortsov's 5th Guards Mechanized Corps into battle. Skvortsov's assault ran into heavy fire and German reinforcements arriving from Olshany. At noon Skvortsov reported, "Secured height 288.1, approaching the grove north of Kadnitsa. The enemy strongly resists and separate groups of tanks are counterattacking. The corps is suffering heavy losses."[174]

It was clear that German defenses were too strong, and further attacks would be futile. Therefore, Rotmistrov passed word to 18th Tank Corps to halt its attack just as that corps was about to join 5th Guards Mechanized Corps' futile efforts. Rotmistrov withdrew his armor and replaced it with all of his anti-tank weapons. That very day word arrived of a crisis to the west at Akhtyrka. Rotmistrov hurriedly dispatched 29th Tank Corps west, regrouped 18th Tank Corps northeast of Bogodukhov, and left 5th Guards Mechanized Corps to support the exhausted 32d Guards Rifle Corps.

The Situation on 17 August

In essence, combat in the immediate vicinity of Bogodukhov had ended. The swirling series of battles had reduced the combatant forces to exhaustion. By 15 August 1st Tank Army's armored strength had fallen to about 100 tanks; and after its battles on 17 August, 5th Guards Tank Army was at about the same strength. Moreover, casualties in the command echelons of both armies had been high; and ammunition and fuel supplies were low. The supporting infantry of 5th Guards Army and 6th Guards Army had also been weakened; units like the 52d Guards Rifle Division, 13th Guards Rifle Division, and 97th Guards Rifle Division were well below 50 percent strength. German units had suffered as well. Strength returns for 15 August placed SS Panzer Division "Das Reich" armored strength at 32 tanks and 19 assault guns, and SS "Viking" at 18 tanks and 4 assault guns.[175] Some rest was required for these units to be brought up to more effective combat strength.

The German attacks had succeeded in halting the long advance of 1st Tank and 5th Guards Tank Armies. Moreover, the Germans had seriously reduced the capability of those armies to have a major impact on future operations. In the 6-day struggle Soviet forces had been driven back 20 kilometers to the Bogodukhov area. However, German units had been unable to penetrate the Soviet defenses, destroy the overall coherence of the front, or threaten Soviet forces advancing on Khar'kov. In fact, while the Germans had fought 1st Tank Army and 5th Guards Tank Army to a standstill, their position at Khar'kov had worsened. Soon, the Germans would face a new threat to the northwest around Trostyanets. They would attempt to parry that threat with a new advance of their own in the Akhtyrka area – the belated delivery of the northern attack designed to envelop Voronezh Front forward units which the Germans had hoped could have been launched in synchronization with the Bogodukhov assaults.

The Advance on Khar'kov (11–18 August)

German Defenses on 11 August

While the seesaw struggle raged around Bogodukhov the Soviet Steppe Front conducted an agonizingly slow advance toward Khar'kov (see Map 67). Konev lamented the lack of maneuver space and the continued erosion of his forces' strength against the skillful German delaying tactics. Kempf had to cope with four Soviet armies advancing on an increasingly narrow front. By 11 August all of Kempf's divisions defended in a semicircle from Olshany northwest of Khar'kov to the Northern Donets River south of Chuguyev, and Kempf's force possessed no reserves.

The XI Army Corps defended the northwestern and northern approaches to the city with 3d Panzer Division deployed along both sides of the rail line north of Olshany and *kampfgruppen* formed from remnants of the 167th, 168th, and 198th Infantry Divisions defending north of Dergachi. Further east, the 106th and 320th Infantry Divisions defended approaches west of the main Belgorod–Khar'kov road to the Staryi Saltov–Khar'kov road. The XXXXII Army Corps defended the eastern and southeastern approaches to the city with primary emphasis on the dangerous Chuguyev–Khar'kov axis. The 282d Infantry Division faced east in defenses along the Roganka River and, on its right, the 39th Infantry Division covered the section north of the Chuguyev–Khar'kov road. Further south, the 161st Infantry Division defended in the wide sector across the Udy River to south of Zmiyev. 6th Panzer Division backed up German defenses north and east of the city and proposed to meet crises elsewhere wherever they arose (although its strength seldom exceeded twenty tanks).[176]

Army Group "South" had earmarked reinforcements for Army Detachment Kempf, specifically the 223d and 355th Infantry Divisions transferred from other sectors of the front. However, the Voronezh Front's repeated cutting of the Khar'kov–Poltava rail line delayed the ultimate arrival in Khar'kov of both units. Meanwhile, Army Detachment

Kempf had to cling to its defenses on the outer approaches to Khar'kov as best it could by shifting forces from sector to sector to meet and repel Soviet attacks.

By the evening of 11 August Steppe Front forces had finally reached the outer defense line of Khar'kov, 10–15 kilometers from the city. This defense line consisted of a series of strong points anchored on villages and towns on the outskirts of the city. Between these towns, the Germans artfully wove a system of anti-tank obstacles, minefields, barbed wire barriers, and fortifications all covered by anti-tank guns, artillery, and machine gun fire. The heart of the defensive system was the interconnected anti-tank strong points. German positions were skillfully constructed and well protected against the effects of Soviet artillery fire.

Between the forward defense line and Khar'kov's inner defense line were a series of intermediate defense positions in which the Germans could assemble reserves and from which they could launch counterattacks. All roads and bridges in the Khar'kov vicinity were mined and blocked by obstacles as were the forests covering the western and northwestern approaches to the city. The inner defense line, 3–5 kilometers from the city, ran from the wooded hills west of town (Kholodnaya Gora) through Severnyi Post and Sokolniki through the factory district east of town to Osnovo in the southwest. This line was anchored on the stone buildings of the suburbs which had been converted into firing points and strong points. The Germans also threw up networks of barricades across the major streets leading from the city.

Steppe Front Planning

As had been the case in February the Khar'kov defenses were formidable and would require considerable force to overcome. Hence, the Soviets sought to envelop the city, if at all possible. The failure of 1st Tank and 5th Guards Tank Armies to effect a wide envelopment made it obvious that the Soviets would have to go after Khar'kov proper, either by direct attack or by close envelopment to the west or south. This is in essence what the Steppe Front set about doing after 11 August.

Konev's plan, prepared late on 10 August, required his forces to thrust rapidly into the city and overcome the garrison before it could fully man the city's prepared defenses. Although Konev's earlier orders to achieve such a rapid penetration from a distance had failed, his new optimism was based on Zhukov's assignment to the Steppe Front of 5th Guards Tank Army. Konev's plan called for 5th Guards Tank Army to penetrate Khar'kov's western defenses and envelop the city from the west and 57th Army to conduct a similar envelopment from the south.

While 53d, 69th, 7th Guards, and 57th Armies attacked Khar'kov proper and drove German forces back to the city's inner defenses, 5th

Guards Tank Army was to attack toward Korotich and Ogult'sy east and west of Lyubotin and cut the rail line from Khar'kov to Poltava. Shortly thereafter, 57th Army would strike the southern outskirts of the city and cut German withdrawal routes to Merefa.[177]

Steppe Front Assaults North of Khar'kov – 11–18 August

Events of 11 August, however, disrupted Konev's plan. Heavy German attacks at Bogodukhov forced Zhukov to retain Rotmistrov's 5th Guards Tank Army in Vatutin's sector. The loss of 5th Guards Tank Army condemned Konev to 11 days of heavy combat around Khar'kov. Deprived of his major strike force, on 11 August Konev's Steppe Front armies launched their assaults on German defenses but with very limited effect. On the first day of the attack Steppe Front armies closed on the German outer defense line but were unable to penetrate it. Managarov's 53d Army, ordered to attack to Peresechnaya west of Khar'kov in cooperation with Solomatin's 1st Mechanized Corps, attacked at 0900, but immediately ran into heavy resistance north of Dergechi and was halted after advancing less than 1 kilometer. Kryuchenkin's 69th Army, its divisions deployed on frontages of less than 2 kilometers, smashed into Tsirkuny, 15 kilometers northeast of Khar'kov, and finally seized the town after twelve hours of house-to-house fighting against the German 320th Infantry Division.[178] 7th Guards Army made virtually no gains while the 57th Army's 41st Guards Rifle Division cleared Chuguyev and prepared to advance with the 303d Rifle Division on German positions east of Khar'kov.

The following day all Steppe Front armies resumed their attacks after an extensive artillery preparation, but again made only limited gains. Managarov attacked west of Dergachi with three rifle divisions (299th, 84th, and 252d) concentrated in a 3-kilometer sector supported by 1st Mechanized Corps while the 28th Guards Rifle Division continued its attack on Dergachi proper. Heavy fighting raged all day; and by nightfall the 28th Guards Rifle Division had gained a toehold in northern Dergachi but no more, as elements of 6th Panzer Division reinforced the 198th Infantry Division *kampfgruppe* defending the city. The 84th and 299th Rifle Divisions, supported by 1st Mechanized Corps, took several villages and advanced 3–4 kilometers to the northwest outskirts of Dergachi, in doing so finally penetrating a narrow sector of the Khar'kov outer defense line.[179]

At 0700 on 13 August Managarov's 28th Guards and 84th Guards Rifle Divisions resumed their attacks after a 30-minute artillery preparation, widened the penetration, and by nightfall finally occupied the key city of Dergachi (see Map 68). Managarov's 13 August report to Konev read:

> To 2100 the army battles along the following lines: 299th Rifle Division with 1st Mechanized Corps conducts battle for Polevoye; the 84th Rifle Division secured Dergachi and fights to the south along an unnamed river; the 28th Guards Rifle Division secured Luzhok and fights south of Kuzhok; the 116th Rifle Division secured Karavan and Lozoven'ka and continues the offensive to the south; the 233rd, 214th, and 252d Rifle Divisions occupy anti-tank regions and prepare to attack and counterattack.
>
> The enemy [3rd Panzer Division, 168th, 198th, and 106th Infantry Divisions] continues to offer strong opposition and, by counterattacks and artillery and mortar fire, tries to stop the offensive of our army's formations.[180]

Having secured Dergachi on 13 August, Managarov's attacks faltered the next day in the forested areas to the south in the face of heavy German counterattacks. Managarov's divisions were tired and worn down (as were their German counterparts). The 28th Guards Rifle Division, representative of the problem, had only 40 percent of its initial rifle strength or roughly 20 to 30 percent of its authorized strength.[181] Just as German divisions had to fight as reinforced battalion *kampfgruppen,* Soviet divisions were equivalent in strength to rifle regiments. The Soviet advance tested the limits of its divisions while also testing the limits of defending German units.

After 13 August 53d Army's attack waned. For the next five days the army conducted reconnaissance and limited attacks to feel out German positions and made only minimal gains in the Polevoye area west of Dergachi. During the period Managarov, with Konev's supervision, regrouped his forces and prepared for a new offensive to begin on 18 August.

Kryuchenkin's 69th Army attacked on 12 August and, like 53d Army, managed to penetrate the outer defenses of Khar'kov and advance about 10 kilometers before exhausting its offensive strength. The 183d Rifle and 93d Guards Rifle Divisions, spearheading the army advance against the German 320th Infantry Division seized the important strongpoint of Bol'shaya Danilovka, only 2 kilometers from Khar'kov's inner defense lines; and division reconnaissance elements reached into the factory district and park region on the northeastern outskirts of the city. However, these attacks also faltered against the German inner defense lines. It was clear a period of regrouping was necessary before 69th Army's attack could resume. Offensive operations in Kryuchenkin's sector ceased and would not resume until 18 August.

7th Guards Army, its sector telescoped against the northeastern defenses of the city, assisted the 69th Army in reducing German defenses at Bol'shaya Danilovka and in two days of fighting also advanced about 10 kilometers. Advanced elements of the army late on 14 August battled with the German 282d Infantry Division for possession of Kulinichi, 5 kilometers east of Khar'kov. There the army's front stabilized for the next four days.

The 57th and 1st Guards Army Assault East of Khar'kov – 12–18 August

During the 12 August Steppe Front offensive the greatest threat to the Germans developed in the sector southeast of Khar'kov. There Gagen's 57th Army resumed its attacks westward from Chuguyev, and 1st Guards Army of the Southwestern Front opened an offensive across the Northern Donets River to secure Zmiyev and advance westward between the Udy and Mzha Rivers to envelop Khar'kov from the south. The German 39th and 161st Infantry Divisions were soon confronted with a major attack that threatened to cut the main German communications lines south of Khar'kov.

On 12 August Gagen's army initiated the attack and struck westward from Chuguyev. During the day the 41st Guards and 303d Rifle Divisions of 64th Rifle Corps drove west along the Khar'kov–Chuguyev road while further north four divisions of 68th Rifle Corps (36th Guards, 19th, 52d, 14th Guards), supported by two tank brigades and a tank regiment, thrust westward along the Khar'kov road. The attack pushed the German 39th Infantry Division back to positions along the Rogan River 15 kilometers east of Khar'kov. So tenuous was the 39th Infantry Division's defense that Army Detachment Kempf shifted remnants of 6th Panzer Division into the area to bolster the sagging lines. The following day the 41st Guards and 118th Rifle Divisions took Novo Pokrovskoye and Ternovaya, on the northern bank of the Udy River, from the German 161st Infantry Division.

On 41st Guards Rifle Division's left flank, 1st Guards Army commenced its attack on 12 August and crossed the Northern Donets River between Chuguyev and Zmiyev. On the evening of 13 August 1st Guards Army, with the 152d Rifle Division in the lead, prepared to attack westward along the south bank of the Udy River to cut the Khar'kov–Zmiyev road.[182]

The concerted 57th and 1st Guards Army drive accelerated on 14 August. 57th Army's 68th Rifle Corps penetrated the German 39th Infantry Division defenses along the Rogan River and advanced 8 kilometers toward Osnovo. While 64th Rifle Corps' 41st Guards Rifle Division fought west of Ternovaya near the junction of the Rogan and Udy Rivers, the 303d and 113th Rifle Divisions veered northwest to strengthen 68th Rifle Corps' thrust. South of the Udy River 1st Guards Army's 152d Rifle Division kept pace with 41st Guards Rifle Division's advance.

While most of Konev's armies ceased their attacks late on 14 August, southeast of Khar'kov the 57th and 1st Guards Armies pushed their forces forward the next day and created a critical situation for Army Detachment Kempf (redesignated as 8th Army) (see Map 66). 68th Rifle

Corps thrust westward 10 kilometers in the sector north and south of the Khar'kov–Chuguyev road, propelled in part by the commitment of one more division and by the arrival of the 113th Rifle Division on the corps' left flank south of the road. By day's end on 15 August the 6th Panzer and 39th Infantry Divisions had stabilized their defenses 8 kilometers east of Khar'kov, but the right flank of the 39th Infantry Division and the left flank of 161st Infantry Division were forced to withdraw to new positions just east of Bezlyudovka. 41st Guards Rifle Division advanced west over 10 kilometers and, in heavy fighting, took Lizogubovka on the Khar'kov–Zmiyev road. The same day, the 152d Rifle Division took Krasnaya Polyana south of the Udy River on the Khar'kov–Zmiyev road and beseiged Zmiyev.

By the evening of 16 August, although General Gagen had thrown yet another division into combat along the Khar'kov–Chuguyev road (48th Guards Rifle), it was clear his offensive had expended its strength. German defenses from Zaikin to Bezlyudovka on the Udy River held firm. Indicative of the strong German defense, the 41st Guards Rifle Division north of the Udy River repeatedly tried in vain to take Bezlyudovka.[183] Thus, Gagen halted his attacks and made plans to resume the general offensive on order of the Steppe Front commander.

Although 57th Army's attack had died out by 16 August, 1st Guards Army continued to expand its offensive south of the Udy River in the Zmiyev region. On 17 August the 152d Rifle Division, in conjunction with an assault across the Northern Donets River by 6th Guards Rifle Division took Zmiyev and launched an attack westward through the forests on the north bank of the Mzha River. South of Zmiyev the 1st Guards Army launched a major attack spearheaded by the 24th Guards Rifle Division from a bridgehead on the west bank of the Northern Donets River which they had seized on 16 August. Although the 161st Infantry Division fought bitterly on 17 August to contain the penetration, the assault opened a 10-kilometer gap in its defenses and threatened to carry all the way to Taranovka on the Khar'kov–Lozovaya rail line. On 18 August, the newly arrived German 355th Infantry Division joined the 161st Infantry Division; and, with heavy counterattacks, they halted the Soviet advance just 5 kilometers east of Taranovka.[184]

The Situation on 18 August

From 12 to 18 August Konev's armies had hammered German positions around Khar'kov. Having failed to punch directly through the city's defenses, Konev had first tried to envelop the city from the south using 57th Army. When that drive expired on 16 August 1st Guards Army continued the attempted envelopment in the south only to have its attacks contained by 18 August. Frustrated in these attempts to crack the German defenses, Konev planned to renew his attacks on 18 August with a general assault on the city proper. He still sought the assistance of 5th Guards Tank Army, as Zhukov had promised in earlier discussions.

The condition of Konev's Steppe Front eloquently testified to the need for reinforcements before the new operation commenced. After 15 days of combat his units were threadbare and had lost much of their punch. 7th Guards Army divisions averaged 3,000–4,000 men each, with some regiments at strengths of only 200–300 men. The entire army had only 20 tanks for support. 53d Army's divisions averaged 50–60 percent strength, and 1st Mechanized Corps numbered only 44 tanks.[185] 69th Army was in an even worse state. However, the Steppe Front did have the relatively strong and fresh 57th Army available, fresh strength that enabled it to make its major gains from 12–16 August.

German units were in equally poor condition with companies counting 30 to 40 men and divisions fighting as regimental or battalion *kampfgruppen.* 8th Army's few panzer divisions were pitifully weak. 3d Panzer Division had but ten tanks; 6th Panzer Division, four tanks; and the 905th and 228th Assault Gun Detachments had 5 and 17 guns, respectively.[186]

In spite of the mutual exhaustion of both sides the exigencies of the situation prevailed. On 18 August Konev would again launch Steppe Front forces in another wave of attacks to seize Khar'kov. By then, events to the west presented a new, equally serious challenge to the German command.

Thrust and Counterthrust: The Soviet Advance to the Psel River and the German Counterattack at Akhtyrka (13–23 August)

While Soviet and German forces fought one another to a standstill in the Bogodukhov area and Soviet forces inched forward toward Khar'kov's inner defense lines, opposing forces west of Bogodukhov tested one another's positions and planned future operations to take advantage of available maneuver space (see Map 69).

4th Panzer Army Planning for the Akhtyrka Counterattack

By 13 August 4th Panzer Army had established a fairly stable defense line running from Sumy through Boromlya and Trostyanets to Akhtyrka, manned by VII Army Corps, XXXXVIII Panzer Corps, and Panzer Grenadier Division "Grossdeutschland." The VII Army Corps' 88th, 75th, and 68th Infantry Divisions defended from north of Sumy to 10 kilometers north of Boromlya. XXXXVIII Panzer Corps' 57th Infantry and 7th Panzer Divisions defended from north of Boromlya to Belka and the 11th Panzer Division and a *kampfgruppe* of 19th Panzer Division defended from Belka through Trostyanets to north of Akhtyrka. The bulk of "Grossdeutschland" Division occupied defenses around Akhtyrka, and a single *kampfgruppe* of the division (Group Deutsch) covered the west bank of the Vorskla River southward to Kotel'va. LII Army Corps with *kampfgruppen* formed from remnants of 255th and 332d Infantry Divisions remained in rest areas around Lebedin while a *kampfgruppe* of the 112th Infantry Division north of Lebedin provided a meager reserve for 4th Panzer Army.[187]

Although 4th Panzer Army's divisions were severely worn down, only the 255th and 332d Infantry Divisions were so badly damaged that they had to be pulled out of combat. The three VII Army Corps infantry divisions were battle worthy as were the 57th Infantry, 7th Panzer, and 11th Panzer Divisions, even though the armor strength of the latter was reduced to seventeen and six tanks, respectively. 19th Panzer Division had enough strength left to form a combat-worthy *kampfgruppe* while "Grossdeutschland" Division, having received a slow but steady supply of tanks, had an armored strength of almost seventy tanks and assault guns, some of which were Tiger and Panther tanks. In addition, the 503d and 52d Panzer Detachments with 13 Tigers backed up 4th Panzer Army units.[188]

4th Panzer Army planned to stabilize its defense, gather reinforcements, and establish a panzer shock group which could cooperate with Army Detachment Kempf in an attack on the Voronezh Front's exploiting tank forces. The panzer army sought to assemble its panzer group in the Akhtyrka area and launch it southeastward toward Bogodukhov to cut off and destroy Soviet forces in the Akhtyrka–Kotel'va–Bogodukhov salient.[189] Ideally, the Akhtyrka shock group would link up with III Panzer Corps' shock group operating toward Bogodukhov.

However, the timing of the attack depended on the activity of Soviet forces facing 4th Panzer Army and the timely arrival of German reinforcements, primarily the 112th Infantry and the 10th Panzer Grenadier Divisions. The former was required to replace 7th Panzer Division in its defensive sector so that 7th Panzer Division could participate in the Akhtyrka attack. The 112th arrived and occupied 7th Panzer Division's sector on 16 August. The 10th Panzer Grenadier Division arrived in Poltava on 14 August and began moving north the following day. XXIV Panzer Corps, the headquarters designated to control the Akhtyrka shock group, moved north from 6th Army and arrived in 4th Panzer Army's sector on 15 August. Upon its arrival, XXIV Panzer Corps took control of Panzer Grenadier Division "Grossdeutschland," 7th Panzer Division, and 10th Panzer Grenadier Division, the nucleus of the Akhtyrka shock group.

Soviet Attacks at Boromlya – 13–17 August

While 4th Panzer Army strengthened its defenses, regrouped, and planned the Akhtyrka attack, Vatutin watched developments at Bogodukhov, conducted local attacks, and planned a large-scale operation against 4th Panzer Army. The operation originally was intended to counter the German build-up at Akhtyrka and then, in the light of Soviet failures at Bogodukhov, to break the growing operational stalemate along the front. Initially, Vatutin ordered 40th Army to resume attacks near Boromlya.

Moskalenko's army, after a two day rest to regroup and refit, was to initiate new attacks on 13 August against the junction of German VII Army and XXXXVIII Panzer Corps north of Boromlya (see Map 68). Reinforced by one additional rifle division (23d) and additional artillery units, Moskalenko intended to attack with his 52d Rifle Corps to smash German defenses, exploit to the Psel River, and seize Lebedin. 52d Rifle Corps' 237th, 309th, 23d, and 161st Rifle Divisions deployed north of Boromlya would conduct the main attack, supported by 38th Army's 232d Rifle Division attacking on 40th Army's right flank. 10th Tank Corps would exploit 52d Rifle Corps' success. 206th and 100th Rifle Divisions would defend the rest of the army sector south of Boromlya.

From the very start Moskalenko's plans encountered difficulty. First, Vatutin took 10th Tank Corps from his control and gave it, instead, to 47th Army which was just entering the Voronezh Front's rear area. Second, the army attack, which began after a strong artillery and air preparation, quickly ran into heavy resistance and withering German artillery fire. In three days of heavy fighting the 161st, 309th, and 237th Rifle Divisions penetrated German defenses north of Boromlya to a depth of only 4 kilometers after which Moskalenko's attack stalled.[190] By now, it was clear to *front* headquarters that a greater effort was required if German defenses along the Boromlya river were to be pierced.

Reckoning that it would take several days to a week for German forces to create a shock group at Akhtyrka of sufficient size to conduct a successful offensive, Vatutin decided to deliver a preemptive blow in the Boromlya-Trostyanets area to shatter German defenses and outflank and destroy the German Akhtyrka group before it became a danger to the Soviet 27th and 6th Guards Army and perhaps to turn the flank of the entire German force defending west of Khar'kov. Vatutin outlined his concept of the operation in Voronezh Front Directive No. 16 of 15 August 1943 which ordered Lieutenant General R.R. Korzun's 47th Army, together with 40th Army elements, to attack on the morning of 17 August from the Boromlya area toward the southwest and strike the flank and rear of the German Akhtyrka group.[191] Simultaneously, 27th Army forces would attack westward toward Kotel'va and Zen'kov to assist 47th Army's envelopment of the German Akhtyrka group. 38th Army would also support 47th Army with an assault toward the Psel River and Sumy. 2d Air Army would provide support for all three attacking armies.

Although the attack by 47th and 40th Army was feasible, the secondary attack by 27th Army was clearly beyond its means. Earlier, on 12 August, Poluboyarov's 4th Guards Tank Corps had received orders to occupy Kotel'va, cross the Vorskla River, and again strike the southern flank of the German Akhtyrka force (see Map 68). At the time 27th Army divisions were just beginning to arrive at Akhtyrka from the Graivoron area. 4th Guards Tank Corps turned over its sector at Akhtyrka to the 166th Rifle Division, swept southwest, took Kotel'va, and crossed the Vorskla River. Late on 14 August Poluboyarov's lead brigade (14th Guards Tank) reached Grun, 16 kilometers east of Zenkov, with other corps elements close behind. The Germans initially committed Group Deutsch of Panzer Grenadier Division "Grossdeutschland" against Poluboyarov's corps. Late on 15 August lead elements of 10th Panzer Grenadier Division arrived and forced 4th Guards Tank Corps back to defensive positions along the Vorskla River north of Kotel'va.[192]

Meanwhile, 27th Army's rifle divisions filtered into the Akhtyrka area (see Map 69). Several of the army's divisions (including the 163d Rifle Division) had been temporarily commandeered for use by 1st Tank Army in its defensive battles on 11–12 August at Bogodukhov. By 16 August the 71st, 166th, and 241st Rifle Divisions and two regiments of the 155th Rifle Division were deployed in extended fashion from Akhtyrka south to Kotel'va and east to Krasnokutsk. By no stretch of the imagination was this force capable of launching a coordinated attack across the Vorskla River south of Akhtyrka. Thus, on 17 August only the northern wing of Vatutin's offensive would swing into action, as it turned out too late to affect German offensive plans at Akhtyrka.

Vatutin closely supervised Moskalenko's and Korzun's operational planning. Because of geographical considerations and the configuration of the German defense, the two commanders agreed to give 47th Army an attack sector in the center of 40th Army's operational formation. Korzun deployed his two rifle corps (21st and 22d Rifle Corps), backed up by Major General V.T. Obukhov's 3d Guards Mechanized Corps (213 tanks), in a 9-kilometer sector just north of Boromlya facing the junction of the 68th and 57th Infantry Divisions. His rifle corps would penetrate enemy defenses, and then Obukhov's mechanized corps would exploit toward Lebedin. By the end of the first day of operations 3d Guards Mechanized Corps was to reach the area southeast of Lebedin and prevent the Germans from conducting an orderly withdrawal to the Psel River. Meanwhile, army rifle forces would reach the Ol'shanka River east of Lebedin. Ultimately by 23 August 47th Army was to reach and fortify the Psel River line.[193]

40th Army's 52d Rifle Corps (237th and 309th Rifle Divisions), supported by Alekseyev's 10th Tank Corps, would attack in a 4-kilometer sector on 47th Army's right flank against one regiment of the 68th Infantry Division. Moskalenko's 47th Rifle Corps (23d and 206th Rifle Divisions), on 47th Army's left flank, would advance in a 4-kilometer sector south of Boromlya against one regiment of the 112th Infantry Division. Other 40th Army divisions in the Boromlya area and south of Trostyanets would support the main thrust (161st Rifle Division) or defend in place (100th Rifle Division). 2d Tank Corps, already worn down in heavy fighting, would support the 100th Rifle Division local attacks against the German 11th Panzer Division defenses at Trostyanets.

These elaborate offensive preparations would pit 10 Soviet divisions, many of them fresh, and about 250–300 tanks against two and one-third combat weary German infantry divisions which had virtually no armor support. The blow would strike only days after the 112th Infantry Division took over the defensive sector of 7th Panzer Division. Clearly, the attack would smash through the German defenses. The only question was whether the attack would carry deep enough fast enough to disrupt the planned German offensive at Akhtyrka.

At 0700 on 17 August a massive Soviet artillery preparation tore apart German positions opposite 40th and 47th Army assault forces (see Map 69). At 0800 the lead divisions of 47th Army's 21st and 23d Rifle Corps advanced, supported by tanks of 3d Guards Mechanized Corps' 44th Guards Tank Regiment. The attacks overwhelmed the German 68th and 57th Infantry Division defenses. At 1100 the brigades of 3d Guards Mechanized Corps, in column formation, passed through the advancing infantry and began the exploitation. On the right flank of 47th Army, the 7th Mechanized and 35th Guards Tank Brigades smashed 68th Infantry Division defensive positions along the rail line and at 1700 secured Velikii Istorop, 8 kilometers from the Psel River. During the evening 11th Panzer Division tanks, sent north to restore the situation, together with 112th Infantry Division infantry, counterattacked but failed to halt the Soviet advance. On 47th Army's left flank, the 8th and 9th Guards Mechanized Brigades also cut the rail line by 1600 although the German 112th and 57th Infantry Divisions still manned coherent defenses to the southwest.[194]

Thus, on 17 August 47th Army smashed through German tactical defenses to a depth of 12 kilometers in the north and 8 kilometers in the south. The attack in the north, in conjunction with 52d Army Corps' assault, opened a 6-kilometer gash in those defenses which the German defenders could not repair. To compound the Germans' problems, elements of Chibisov's 38th Army, on 52d Rifle Corps' right flank, advanced to within 3 kilometers of the Psel River driving before it two regiments of the 68th Infantry Division. South of 47th Army, 40th Army's 47th Rifle Corps' attack became bogged down north of Trostyanets against the defenses of the 112th Infantry Division. However, unless the Germans contained the major Soviet penetration to the north, the firm defense in the south seemed irrelevant.

The German Counterattack at Akhtyrka – 17–18 August

On the night of 17–18 August Hoth's 4th Panzer Army faced some hard choices. It could curtail its Akhtyrka attack and instead use those forces to help restore the situation further north, or it could go on with the attack and hope its left flank could delay the Soviet advance sufficiently to permit the major German attack at Akhtyrka to proceed without interruption. While Hoth made minor adjustments in the north, he opted for the second choice – that of attacking at Akhtyrka.

Thus, on the morning of 18 August, two separate offensives unfolded in opposite directions within a distance of 100 kilometers. This pinwheel effect had Soviet forces attacking west and southwest at the western extremity of the front while German forces attacked east and southeast at the southern extremity. In essence, it was a race to see whose offensive would have the greatest effect in the shortest time.

By the evening of 17 August, despite the cacophony of battle to the north, the Germans completed their attack preparations at Akhtyrka (see Map 69). Hoth planned to use XXIV Panzer Corps to control his shock group in the attack, while III Panzer Corps of 8th Army (former Army Detachment Kempf) would form its own shock group to advance from the southeast. The heart of XXIV Panzer Corps' force was Panzer Grenadier Division "Grossdeutschland" with a strength of 46 tanks (of which 15 were Tigers) and 22 assault guns. "Grossdeutschland" was joined by 7th Panzer Division with 23 tanks, 10th Panzer Grenadier Division, and by the 239th Assault Gun Detachment. 51st Panzer Detachment with about 15 Tigers and Panthers was attached to "Grossdeutschland."[195]

Hoth ordered XXIV Panzer Corps to attack on a narrow front southeast from Akhtyrka, cut across the base of the Kotel'va salient, sever the communication lines of 27th and 6th Guards Armies, and destroy as many of those units as possible. "Grossdeutschland" would spearhead the attack by advancing toward Kaplunovka and Koz'yevka, 10 kilometers north of Krasnokutsk, to link up with columns of 8th Army's III Panzer Corps moving up from the southeast. 7th Panzer Division was to defend Akhtyrka and cover "Grossdeutschland's" left flank; and 10th Panzer Grenadier Division, advancing in "Grossdeutschland's" wake, would deploy on the shock groups' right flank and form a barrier to prevent the escape of encircled Soviet units. Smaller elements of 10th Panzer Grenadier Division would deploy along the west bank of the Vorskla River south of Akhtyrka, and the 355th Infantry Division's reconnaissance battalion would deploy south of Kotel'va, to prepare for the northward advance of 34th Infantry Division, then assembling at the Poltava railhead.

While XXIV Panzer Corps struck from Akhtyrka, III Panzer Corps was to strike from the south using SS Panzer Division "Totenkopf" which was deployed along the south bank of the Merla River southwest of Krasnokutsk. SS "Totenkopf," with two regiments of the newly arrived 223d Infantry Division attached, would use its armor (thirty-nine tanks and sixteen assault guns) to thrust northward across the Merla River and unite with "Grossdeutschland" forces.

Soviet forces in the Kotel'va bulge between Akhtyrka and Krasnokutsk consisted of the bulk of Trofimenko's 27th Army and elements of Chistyakov's 6th Guards Army. 27th Army was deployed on a front of 170 kilometers with four of its five rifle divisions concentrated against the German Akhtyrka group. The 147th, 241st, and 155th Rifle Divisions occupied positions northeast and east from Akhtyrka. The 166th Rifle Division, supported by 93d Tank Brigade, covered the southeastern approaches to Akhtyrka; and the 71st Rifle Division, backed up by Poluboyarov's 4th Guards Tank Corps, was deployed in extended formation south along the Vorskla River through Kotel'va. On the eastern side of the salient Chistyakov's 6th Guards Army defended positions facing south along the Merla River and a bridgehead on the south bank of the Merla and Merchik Rivers facing SS "Totenkopf" and 223d Infantry Division. Chistyakov defended the Merla River southwest of Krasnokutsk with the 52d Guards and 71st Guards Rifle Divisions. The 163d and 51st Guards Rifle Divisions covered the bridgehead south of Krasnokutsk while the 90th Guards and 67th Guards Rifle Divisions defended along the Merchik River southwest of Bogodukhov interspersed with units of 1st Tank Army's three corps. Kravchenko's 5th Guards Tank Corps had three brigades (21st, 22d Guards Tank, and 6th Guards Motorized Rifle Brigade) concentrated in the rear of Chistyakov's right flank and the 20th Guards Tank Brigade screening 6th Guards Army's far right flank.[196]

27th Army, and to some extent 6th Guards Army, was vulnerable to a coordinated German attack. Soviet *ex post facto* critiques noted some of the problems as follows:

The 27th Army commander did not undertake necessary measures to strengthen his newly occupied positions, and he scattered his forces across a wide front.

Although it knew of enemy counterattack preparations, the 27th Army staff, up to the time of the German offensive, did not possess the necessary information concerning the grouping and plans of the enemy. The staffs of rifle divisions and regiments conducted reconnaissance very poorly.

The wide front that 27th Army occupied did not permit creation of necessary troop and weapon densities on the Akhtyrka direction.

On the night of 17–18 August 27th Army conducted a partial regrouping for a future offensive in the area west of Kotel'va.

This regrouping was incomplete when the Germans attacked, and no compact force was available for a counterattack.

A considerable portion of reinforcing artillery was located in the Kolontayev–Krasnokutsk area and could not take part in repulsing the enemy counterattack. That artillery in the Akhtyrka region was short of ammunition.

The force of 2d Air Army was, to a large measure, concentrated to support 40th and 47th Armies. Thus forces in the Akhtyrka area on the first day of the operation had weak air support.[197]

For these reasons and because of careful German preparations, the German assault achieved immediate success (see Map 70). At 0900 18 August, after a short but violent artillery and air preparation, the armored columns of "Grossdeutschland" Division, under air cover, struck the Soviet 166th Rifle Division's forward positions; tore a gap through the defenses of the 517th and 735th Rifle Regiments; and, within forty minutes, penetrated deep into the 166th Rifle Division's rear area. At 1000 a second *kampfgruppe* joined the first, and at 1130 a third group followed the second. This time-phased assault crushed the 517th Rifle Regiment, surrounded a battalion of the 423d Rifle Regiment which had been sent to reinforce it, and drove the remainder of the two regiments southeast. By 1300 "Grossdeutschland" tanks had penetrated to the division headquarters at Udarnik, 12 kilometers southeast of Akhtyrka. Shortly after 1400 German advanced detachments reached Kaplunovka and virtually severed communications of 27th Army units in the Kotel'va area with their headquarters in the rear.[198] Late on 18 August the 166th Rifle Division commander gathered remnants of his regiments and portions of 93d Tank Brigade and occupied new defensive positions facing northeast 8 kilometers southeast of Akhtyrka.

With major Soviet forces now encircled in the Kotel'va salient, Soviet commanders quickly reacted. Zhukov, then at Vatutin's headquarters,

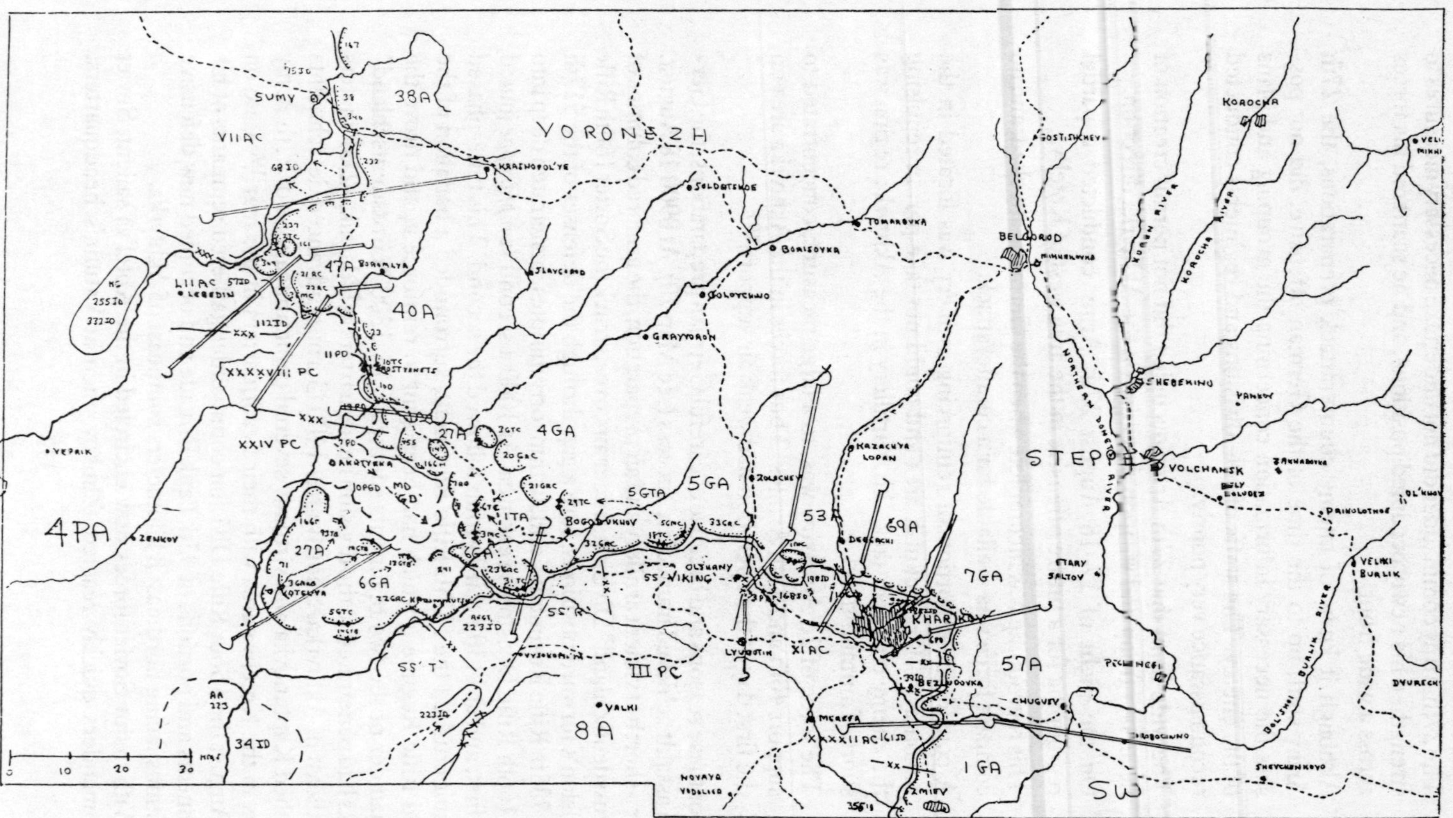

MAP 70. BELGOROD–KHARKOV, SITUATION, 2000 18 AUGUST 1943

was under intense pressure from the *STAVKA* to liquidate the threat as soon as possible. He ordered both Vatutin and Trofimenko to prepare counterthrusts. Ultimately, they worked out a broad plan involving the reinforcement of 27th Army with *front* and *STAVKA* reserves, the movement of other units to the Akhtyrka sector, and counterattacks by 27th Army to restore the situation.[199]

Specifically, Vatutin ordered Trofimenko to assemble the 4th Guards and 5th Guards Tank Corps and the 166th Rifle Division and 93d Tank Brigade, isolated south of Akhtyrka, and launch them in a coordinated attack against the base of the German penetration. Trofimenko was to use his 147th Rifle Division in a supporting attack from the north. Late on 18 August Trofimenko moved up his artillery and anti-tank reserves and regrouped his artillery and engineers. Zhukov also effected a higher level regrouping of forces by ordering Lt. General G.I. Kulik's 4th Guards Army (under Voronezh Front control since 16 August) and Maj. General I.A. Vovchenko's 3d Guards Tank Corps to prepare to launch counterattacks in 27th Army's sector. He ordered 1st Tank and 5th Guards Tank Armies to move all available units toward Akhtyrka to support Trofimenko's army. At noon on 18 August 1st Guards Tank Brigade of 3d Mechanized Corps (1st Tank Army) headed west for Kaplunovka. That evening the remainder of 3d Mechanized Corps and all of 6th Tank Corps moved to Kup'yevakha and Polkovaya Nikitovka, 15 kilometers west of Bogodukhov, to block further eastward movement of "Grossdeutschland's" shock group. On the evening of 18 August Zhukov also ordered 5th Guards Tank Army's 29th Tank Corps (minus 25th Tank Brigade) to move westward to participate in the Akhtyrka counterattacks.

Already, on 18 August new German assaults interfered with the Soviet regrouping efforts as III Panzer Corps attacked across the Merla River and tied down portions of 4th Guards and 5th Guards Tank Corps. That day SS Panzer Division "Totenkopf," supported by two 223d Infantry Division regiments assaulted 6th Guards Army Merla River defenses and the bridgehead south of Krasnokutsk. 6th Guards Army forces in the bridgehead held off the assaults, and the 71st Guards, 241st, and 52d Guards Rifle Divisions, reinforced first by the 20th Guards Tank Brigade and later by all remaining elements of 5th Guards Tank Corps, gave little ground along the Merla River. Meanwhile, Poluboyarov's 4th Guards Tank Corps left its 3d Guards Motorized Rifle Brigade in defensive positions along the Vorskla River and moved its 12th and 13th Guards Tank Brigades into positions to support the 166th Rifle Division and 93d Tank Brigade south of Akhtyrka. However, his 14th Guards Tank Brigade became entangled in the defense against SS "Totenkopf" and could not assemble in time to join the counterattack to the north.[200]

By nightfall on 18 August the German thrust from Akhtyrka had penetrated 24 kilometers southeast on a 7 kilometer front and had severed communications between 27th Army and its units in the Kotel'va area. As yet, however, the northerly advance of SS "Totenkopf" had failed to link up with "Grossdeutschland" Division's advance. Meanwhile, significant Soviet forces were assembling to parry this new threat.

The Struggle at Akhtyrka – 19–21 August

On 19 August, with regrouping partially complete, the Soviets launched their first counterattacks at the same time that German forces also resumed their offensive (see Map 71). Poluboyarov's 4th Guards Tank Corps and the remnants of the 166th and 71st Rifle Divisions struck the southern flank of the German penetration. After confused fighting, during which the 166th Rifle Division commander was killed, the Soviet units withdrew to a shrinking defensive perimeter and fended off repeated German air attacks.[201] Further south 4th Guards Tank Corps' 3d Guards Motorized Rifle Brigade withdrew slowly from Kotel'va, and the 14th Guards Tank Brigade with 5th Guards Tank Corps units and the 241st Rifle Division continued to fend off attempts by SS "Totenkopf" to cross the Merla River and join "Grossdeutschland" to the north. Because the attention of Panzer Grenadier Division "Grossdeutschland" and 10th Panzer Grenadier Division was focused on the northern and eastern sectors of the penetration, 27th Army units continued to hold out throughout 19 August.

North of the German penetration, Soviet forces erected defenses and launched counterattacks in piecemeal fashion. East of Akhtyrka the 155th Rifle Division and one regiment of the 166th Rifle Division prepared defenses against an advance of 7th Panzer Division eastward from the town. Trofimenko ordered the 147th Rifle Division to counterattack early on the morning of 19 August, but the Germans handily repulsed the attack. The night before, Vatutin had ordered Kulik to move his 4th Guards Army forward into defensive positions and to prepare an attack on the German penetration from the northeast. Consequently, Kulik moved Major General N.I. Biryukov's 20th Guards Rifle Corps into positions east of Novaya Odessa, 10 kilometers northwest of Krasnokutsk and ordered Vovchenko's 3d Guards Tank Corps to assemble 15 kilometers east of Akhtyrka and prepare to attack southwest toward Udarnik State Farm (on the same axis as the 147th Rifle Division's unsuccessful attack).[202] While 4th Guards Army deployed for the attack, 1st Tank Army units arrived and prepared to support the 20th Guards Rifle Corps' assault.

Soviet assaults began late on 18 August when 20th Guards Rifle Corps committed the 8th Guards Airborne Division to battle to aid 27th Army divisions in their fight against lead elements of "Grossdeutschland." Early on 19 August the 7th Guards and 5th Guards Airborne Divisions and

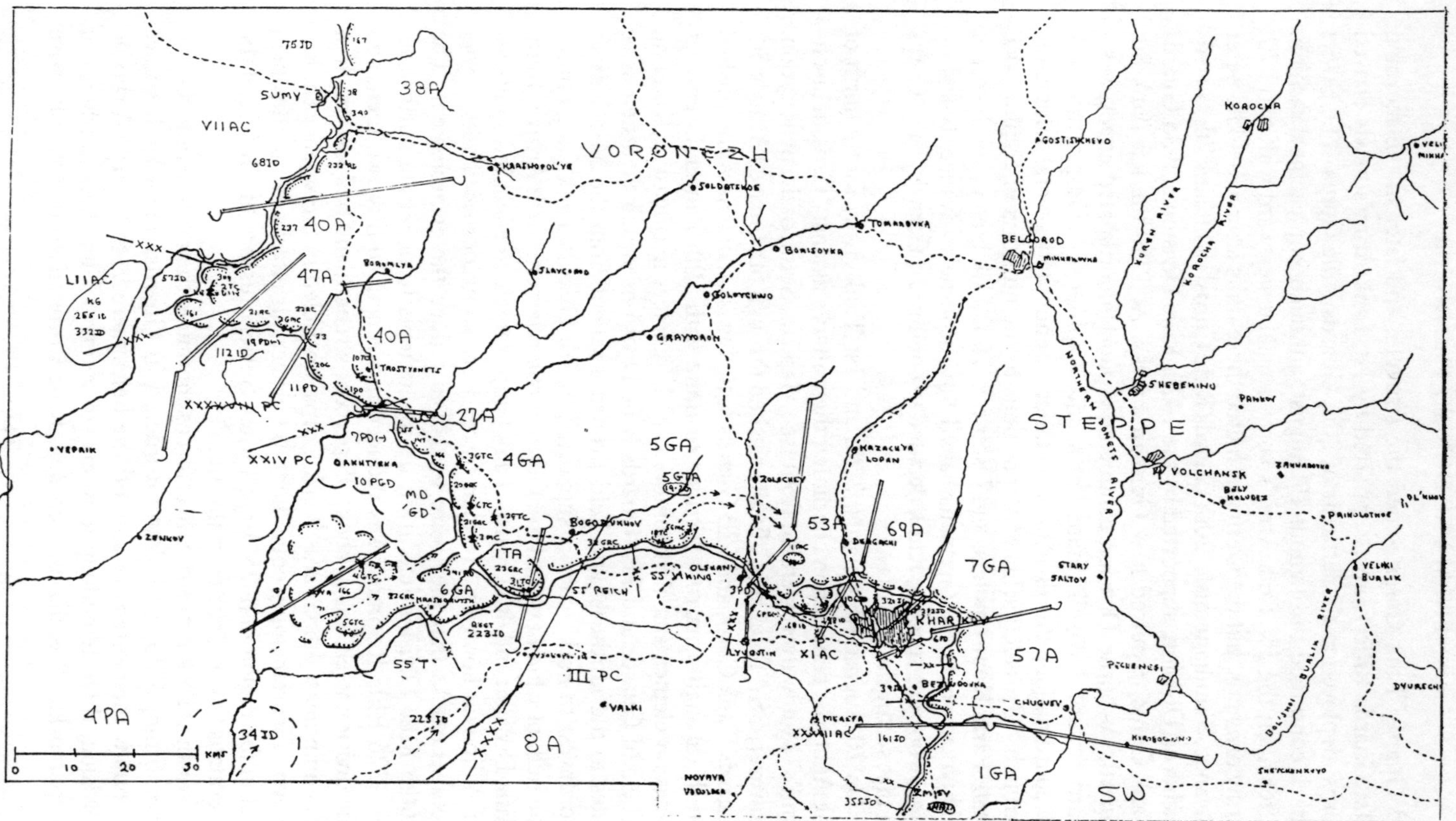

MAP 71. BELGOROD–KHAR'KOV, SITUATION, 2000 19 AUGUST 1943

3d Guards Tank Corps joined the struggle; and later in the morning 21st Guards Rifle Corps, supported by 1st Tank Army's newly arrived corps, deployed to the left rear of 20th Guards Rifle Corps. The Soviet attack continued throughout 19 August, although in piecemeal fashion. After noon the 1st Tank Army's corps attacked westward with two 27th Army divisions, but the Germans halted these units after a 3–4 kilometer advance. Simultaneously, 20th Guards Rifle Corps' right flank 7th Guards Airborne Division, supported by the 147th Rifle Division and 3d Guards Tank Corps, repulsed new German attacks. At 1730 the left flank 8th Guards Airborne Division conducted a poorly coordinated attack westward toward Udarnik State Farm and Kaplunovka. Despite the lack of coordination, the division's battalions penetrated several kilometers through "Grossdeutschland's" positions to the outskirts of Kaplunovka, State Farm Komsomolets, and Osetnyak, 16–20 kilometers southwest of Akhtyrka, where the Germans halted 8th Airborne's advance. Based on 8th Airborne's success, Kulik decided to commit 3d Guards Tank Corps in that sector the next day.[203]

On 20 August 4th Guards, 27th, and 1st Tank Army forces north of the Akhtyrka penetration continued their attacks against "Grossdeutschland's" by now overextended front (see Map 72). South of the penetration, however, SS "Totenkopf" finally slashed through 6th Guards Army's 5th Guards Tank Corps and 52d Guards Rifle Division defenses and pushed north through a narrow corridor to unite with 10th Panzer Grenadier Division elements at Parkhomovka, 17 kilometers northeast of Kotel'va. The 52d Guards and 71st Guards Rifle Divisions swung their defensive lines to the northeast and held firm to a salient from the Merla River northwest to Parkhomovka supported by 5th Guards Tank Corps units, the bulk of which avoided the German encirclement. 27th Army's 166th Rifle Division and 4th Guards Tank Corps remained encircled southeast of Akhtyrka; however, German forces were so preoccupied with Soviet counterattacks that they were unable to reduce the encirclement. The 166th Rifle Division had given up its attempts to penetrate northward. Its 432d Rifle Regiment was reduced in strength to fifty-two men, and the division itself was at about 35 percent strength and had lost much of its equipment. 4th Guards Tank Corps, encircled in the same area, lost much of its remaining equipment to German air attacks. Both units held out in the region until 25 August when Soviet pressure finally forced the Germans to withdraw from the area.[204]

North of Parkhomovka Soviet forces continued their counterattacks. On the morning of 20 August Vatutin ordered 4th Guards and 1st Tank Armies to renew their offensive and aid the beleaguered 8th Guards Airborne Division, then defending positions stretching 6 kilometers northeast of Kaplunovka.[205] Kulik ordered 20th Rifle Corps to resume the offensive

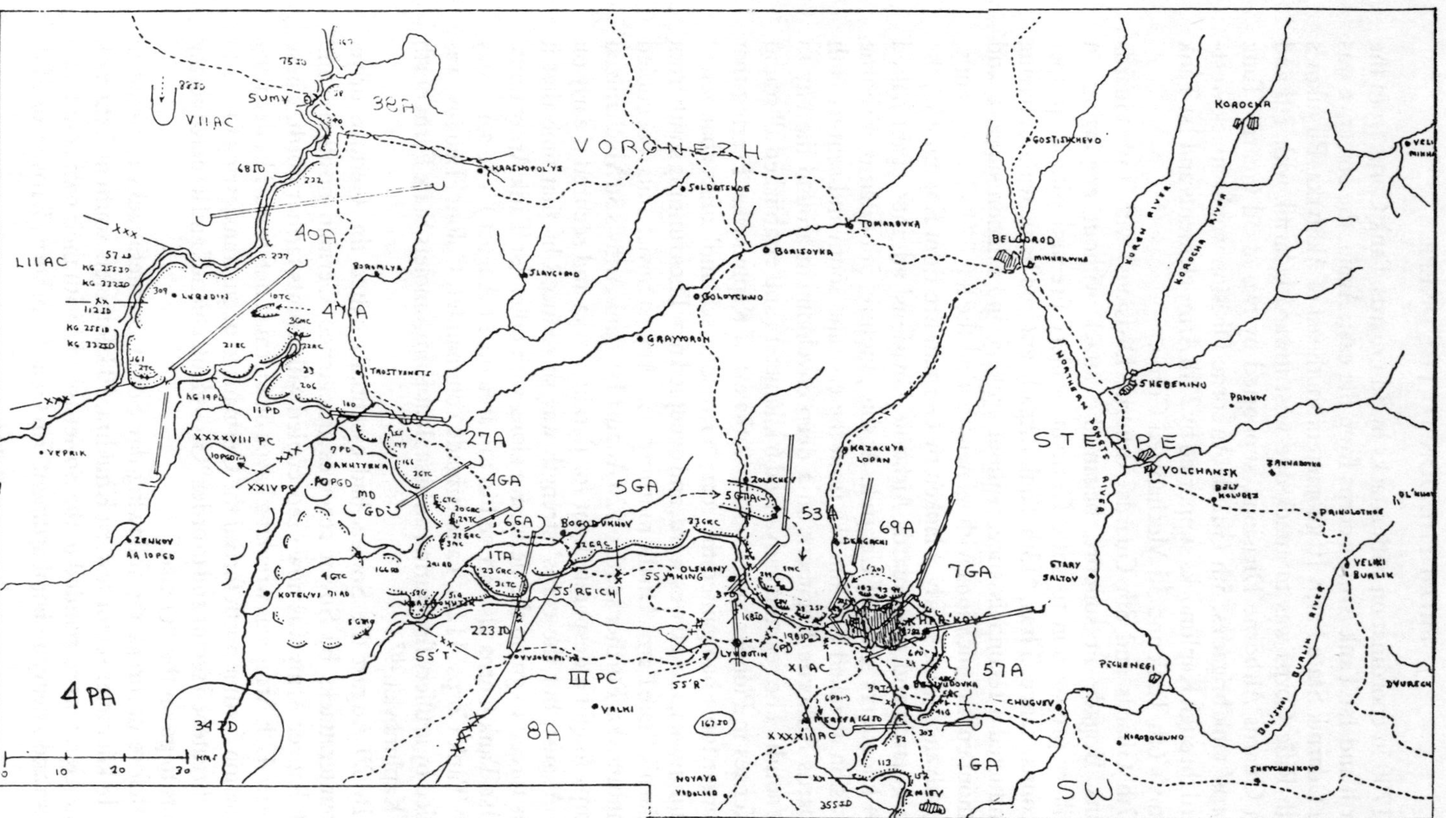

MAP 72. BELGOROD–KHAR'KOV, SITUATION, 20–21 AUGUST 1943

at 1700 in coordination with attacks by 3d Guards Tank Corps from the north and 1st Tank Army's corps from the east. Again, the objective was the Udarnik State Farm 10 kilometers southeast of Akhtyrka. Biryukov's 20th Rifle Corps was to attack due west toward Udarnik with 7th and 8th Guards Airborne Divisions, supported by two of 3d Guards Tank Corps' tank brigades. 5th Guards Airborne Division would attack westward through Kaplunovka supported by 27th Army elements and 1st Tank Army's 6th Tank and 3d Mechanized Corps.

7th Guards and 8th Guards Airborne Divisions, with 13th Guards Tank Brigade in support, began the attack without employing an artillery preparation to stifle German artillery fire and without proper reconnaissance. Thus, "13th Tank Brigade entered battle without having conducted a reconnaissance, without artillery and aviation support, and without communications with its neighbor on the left."[206] Consequently, the advance went slowly. Flanked by German fire from Kaplunovka, the 7th Guards and 8th Guards Airborne Divisions' advance again halted 1–4 kilometers short of Udarnik. At this juncture, 5th Guards Airborne Division attacked Kaplunovka from the east and south and sent its 16th Guards Airborne Regiment on a deep envelopment around the city to the south. The regiment advanced 6 kilometers and established all round defenses in Pioneer State Farm, southwest of Kaplunovka. Fearing that a larger force had gained the rear, "Grossdeutschland" units abandoned Kaplunovka, moved westward, and occupied new lines running south from Udarnik State Farm. On the morning of 21 August Soviet units reoccupied Kaplunovka. Further south on 20 August 1st Tank Army's 3d Mechanized Corps fought a desperate fight for Parkhomovka and secured it early on 21 August, but the corps' strength was so reduced by that time that it was forced to go on the defensive along with other 1st Tank Army units. (31st Tank Corps also arrived in the area on 21 August.) The same day 6th Tank Corps' 112th Tank Brigade commander, Colonel Leonov, was killed by artillery fire during an assault at Komsomolets State Farm north of Kaplunovka.[207]

By 20 August the Soviets had essentially halted the German drive. Counterattacks by Soviet reserves threatened German positions, and 4th Panzer Army was now preoccupied with events farther north, where Soviet 47th Army was wreaking havoc on German defenses. The decaying situation further north forced the Germans to begin transferring forces to the threatened sector and to order "Grossdeutschland" and its neighboring units to go on the defense.

Before daybreak the following day Soviet counterattacks resumed in an 18 kilometer sector toward Khukhra, 10 kilometers south of Akhtyrka. The Germans responded to the Soviet assaults with their own counterattacks and a heavy air bombardment. 7th Guards Airborne Division on 20th

Guards Rifle Corps' right flank made the greatest progress. A night attack by its 29th Guards Airborne Regiment penetrated German defenses; and at 0230, in cooperation with 2d Guards Motorized Rifle Brigade, the regiment took the Udarnik State Farm, only to be encircled by German forces at daybreak. Heavy German attacks killed the regimental commander and most of his battalion commanders. However, the remnants of the regiment held Udarnik until relieved by 4th Guards Army units on 23 August.[208] Farther south the 5th Guards Airborne Division attacked west of Kaplunovka against 10th Panzer Grenadier Division defensive positions but made only minimal gains.

By evening on 21 August fighting east of Akhtyrka had ground to a halt. 1st Tank Army units were used up; and 4th Guards Army, because of the piecemeal nature of its attack and its poor attack preparations, had also lost much of its offensive punch. Consequently, Kulik ordered the army to go on the defense. For his poor performance at Akhtyrka and his decision to halt the offensive he was soon replaced on Stalin's orders. By rights, 4th Guards Army should have crushed "Grossdeutschland's" counterattack, especially with the assistance of the large reinforcements sent by Zhukov and Vatutin. Instead, Kulik's army stopped "Grossdeutschland's" advance, but did little else. The attack cost 20th Guards Rifle Corps heavy casualties; for example, only 723 men of the 29th Guards Airborne Regiment survived.[209] One of Kulik's division commanders was relieved (8th Guards Airborne Division) for twice losing control of his division, and 3d Guards Tank Corps squandered away much of its armored strength with poor effect. Among the mistakes made, as admitted by the 20th Guards Rifle Corps commander Biryukov, were: a failure to allocate artillery and anti-tank support to combat divisions and regiments, an uncoordinated commitment of army units to battle, improper reconnaissance, and a failure to concentrate forces to deliver a decisive blow.

Part of these problems resulted from new tactics the Germans used at Akhtyrka after they made their initial lunge eastward. In a message sent by Zhukov to the *STAVKA* on 20th August he stated:

> In the Akhtyrka-Kaplunovka region the enemy is using the following tactical defensive measures: He deploys his tanks behind the infantry and behind the anti-tank artillery and hides them in areas covered from fire. Against our attacking units, mainly against Kulik, the enemy used artillery and mortar fire, aviation, and infantry counterattacks with groups of 20–30 tanks. It can be seen he wishes to preserve his tanks and destroy our tanks, and then, having weakened us, try to resume the offensive. Considering the nature of enemy operations I gave an order to Vatutin and army commanders to strike the enemy,

without separating their tanks from his artillery and infantry, to strike mainly with aviation, artillery, and all infantry and anti-tank weapons systems.[210]

Although the Soviets repelled 4th Panzer Army's counterattack at Akhtyrka, the German counterstroke reduced the capability of the Voronezh Front to outflank German forces by a wide envelopment west of Khar'kov. Now, while the *STAVKA* drafted orders for a resumption of 4th Guards Army assaults east of Akhtyrka, Soviet hopes lay in their expanding offensive northwest of Akhtyrka. That offensive's success had already contributed in part to the German decision to halt "Grossdeutschland's" counterattack.

The Soviet Offensive at Boromlya – 18–21 August: Advance to the Psel River

The concerted attack of 47th, 40th, and 38th Armies on 17 August north of Trostyanets had ripped a gaping hole in German defenses. The next day, as German guns to the south announced the opening of their Akhtyrka counterattacks, Moskalenko and Korzun resumed their assaults and threatened to collapse all German defenses east of the Psel River. Even before the renewed Soviet attack began, German VII Army Corps had received orders to withdraw its forces opposite Soviet 38th Army to new positions west of the Psel River. The Germans now concentrated their defensive efforts on holding Soviet forces near Trostyanets in order to protect the left flank of their Akhtyrka force.

Early on 18 August 47th Army units, spearheaded by 3d Guards Mechanized Corps, attacked on a 12-kilometer front along the Lebedin–Boromlya road (see Map 70).[211] The German 57th Infantry Division delayed 3d Guards Mechanized Corps' advance through Malyi Istorop and then fought a three-hour defensive battle for possession of Seblyankin, 20 kilometers east of Lebedin. The 35th Guards Tank Brigade led an infantry assault along the Boromlya–Lebedin road while the remainder of 3d Guards Mechanized Corps swept north around the German 57th Infantry Division's strongpoints along the road near Seblyankin and threatened the German strongpoint at Gruzchevo on the main road 13 kilometers east of the Lebedin in the 57th and 112th Infantry Divisions' rear area.

Further north 40th Army's 52d Rifle Corps reached the Psel River and the outskirts of Revki and Karavan, 15 kilometers east of Lebedin, and the 38th Army closed on the Psel River. Progress was slower on 47th Army's left flank where 40th Army's 47th Rifle Corps was unable to penetrate 11th and 19th Panzer Division defenses southwest of Boromlya and at Belka and Trostyanets. Any further advance by Soviet forces to the north, however, would seriously threaten the left flank and rear of those defending divisions.

The headlong advance of 47th Army southwest of Lebedin continued the next day without any change in the army's operational formation (see Map 71). 3d Mechanized Corps' brigades and supporting infantry advanced to within 7 kilometers of Lebedin and then turned south and reached Pushkary, 10 kilometers southwest of Lebedin. The hardpressed German 57th and 112th Infantry Divisions formed battalion size *kampfgruppen* and conducted a slow delaying operation westward toward Lebedin. By 1700 on 19 August *kampfgruppen* of 57th Infantry Division manned defenses just east of Lebedin against forward elements of 3d Guards Mechanized and 2d Tank Corps. The bulk of 3d Guards Mechanized Corps, followed by 47th Army rifle forces, swung south and drove 19th Panzer Division units toward Dolzhik, 18 kilometers southwest of Lebedin. The 112th Infantry Division also withdrew in stages south of Lebedin via Budylka and ultimately occupied defensive positions along the west bank of the Psel River south of Lebedin.[212]

40th Army's 52d Rifle Corps, reinforced by the 161st Rifle Division, pursued along the south bank of the Psel River toward Lebedin while its 237th Rifle Division remained along the Psel River west of Veliki Istorop and cleared the forests of German stragglers. The corps' 309th Rifle Division, led by elements of 2d Tank Corps, advanced due west on Lebedin against 57th Infantry Division's *kampfgruppen.* By evening the 161st Rifle Division had approached to within 5 kilometers of Lebedin's southern outskirts. At 2000 German forces withdrew across the Psel River, and the 309th and 161st Rifle Divisions and 2d Tank Corps entered the city.[213] The 52d Rifle Corps ceased offensive action at the Psel River and thereafter simply covered 47th Army's right flank. The 161st Rifle Division marched southward along the Psel River, supported by 2d Tank Corps, and by 21 August occupied a defensive sector along the river south toward Veprik.

Meanwhile, on 19 August 40th Army's 47th Rifle Corps increased its pressure on the 11th and 19th Panzer Divisions at Trostyanets (part of their forces had shifted westward). By day's end the 206th Rifle Division penetrated German defenses northwest of Trostyanets, and the 100th Rifle Division did likewise south of the town. Outflanked from the north and south, 19th Panzer Division's defenses in Trostyanets became untenable. On the evening of 19 August 19th Panzer abandoned the city to the 126th Rifle Division and 10th Tank Corps and slowly withdrew southwest.[214]

After the fall of Lebedin German attention focused on 47th Army and 40th Army's 47th Rifle Corps, both poised dangerously close to the left flank and rear of 4th Panzer Army's Akhtyrka group. It was clear that VII and LII Army Corps' divisions west of the Psel River were essentially out of the operational picture, and XXXXVIII Panzer Corps' 11th and 19th Panzer Divisions could not halt the massive Soviet forces descending on them from the Lebedin and Trostyanets areas. As the threat to 4th Panzer Army's left flank grew, so also did the threat to the entire German force defending Khar'kov.

The threat increased on 20 August as Korzun's two rifle corps, spearheaded by 3d Guards Mechanized Corps, advanced toward Dolzhik and Oleshnya, 15–20 kilometers southwest of Akhtyrka (see Map 72). 19th and 11th Panzer Divisions, reduced to a combined strength of thirteen tanks and sixteen assault guns, deployed on a 20-kilometer front from Dolzhik to south of Trostyanets covering the approaches to Oleshnya and Akhtyrka and relied on heavy air strikes to compensate for their dwindling ground force strength. The air strikes hit the 47th Rifle Corps' 100th and 206th Rifle Divisions particularly hard. German aircraft also destroyed the communications center of 52d Rifle Corps and destroyed the 206th Rifle Division's command post, killing the chief-of-staff and wounding the division commander.[215] Nonetheless, the Soviet forces pressed the attack. 3d Guards Mechanized Corps (whose commander, General Obukhov, had been wounded in an air attack the previous day and replaced by the corps chief-of-staff) seized remaining German positions around Kostev, 10 kilometers north of Dolzhik, early on 20 August and pushed on south engaging 19th Panzer Division *kampfgruppen* in constant battle.[216] At noon on 20 August 3d Guards Mechanized Corps' main force and 47th Army rifle forces cleared 19th Panzer Division troops from Razsokhovatyi, 4 kilometers northeast of Dolzhik. 3d Guards Mechanized Corps' left wing by late evening pushed the 11th Panzer Division south toward Oleshnya. To the east, 47th Rifle Corps' 206th and 100th Rifle Divisions continued a painful advance through the forests southwest of Trostyanets and reached the Vorskla River only 6 kilometers northwest of Akhtyrka.

During the night of 20–21 August 4th Panzer Army hastily began shifting forces westward from Akhtyrka to assist the hard pressed 19th and 11th Panzer Divisions. 10th Panzer Grenadier Division, preceded by its reconnaissance battalion, marched west and occupied positions north of Zen'kov on 19th Panzer Division's left flank.[217] Lead elements (one regiment) of 34th Infantry Division pushed north from Poltava to Oposhnya south of Kotel'va while the remainder of the division was arriving by rail in Poltava.

That same evening Vatutin ordered 47th Army and 3d Guards Mechanized Corps to continue its offensive on the morning of 21 August, penetrate German defenses at Dolzhik and Oleshnya, and sever German communications lines between Zen'kov and Akhtyrka. Further west, in 40th Army's sector, Vatutin ordered 2d Tank Corps to probe southwest toward Veprik and Zen'kov in the gap between German LII Army Corps and XXXXVIII Panzer Corps in order to support the advance of 47th Army's right wing.[218]

Overnight, Korzun's forces regrouped and replenished their fuel and ammunition. Before dawn on 21 August the 29th Rifle Division, supported by the 45th Guards Tank Regiment and 9th Guards Mechanized Brigade, approached Dolzhik from the north. Sappers of the mechanized brigade cleared mines from the open fields surrounding the town; the brigade fired a short artillery preparation; and three tank companies, supported by infantry, attacked 19th Panzer defenses. Fire from 19th Panzer Division defenders separated the infantry from the tanks and halted the attack. Another preparation preceded a second Soviet attack, this time from the flanks. By 1100 hours the 3d Guards Mechanized Corps units had cleared Dolzhik and pressed on southward, only to encounter stronger German defenses at Alenino and Chupakhovka, southwest of Oleshnya, manned by 19th Panzer Division and the 94th Assault Gun Battalion. Repeated attacks over the next three days by the 9th Guards and the 7th Guards Mechanized Brigades failed to break 19th Panzer Division's grasp on these key defensive positions.[219]

Farther east the 8th Guards Mechanized Brigade and 35th Guards Tank Brigade with supporting infantry of the 337th Rifle Divisions broke through 11th Panzer Division defenses north of Oleshnya but before noon on 21 August ran into heavy opposition and violent German air strikes west and southwest of Oleshnya. The brigades dug in and for two days were subjected to heavy German air and artillery attacks and frequent counterattacks. 47th Army's offensive stalled late on 21 August in front of the tenacious 19th and 11th Panzer Division defenses extending from Alenino through Oleshnya eastward to the Vorskla River. Farther west 2d Tank Corps reached the outskirts of Zen'kov but was thrown back by 10th Panzer Grenadier Division units. The imminent arrival of the main body of 10th Panzer Grenadier Division with its supporting 239th Assault Gun Battalion (with thirty-one guns) and two regiments of 34th Infantry Division at Zen'kov temporarily ended the grand flank march of 47th Army.

The Situation on 22 August

4th Panzer Army, by tremendous exertions, had fought Soviet forces to a standstill on a front westward from Bogodukhov, but at a considerable cost (see Map 73). A *STAVKA* message to Vatutin on the night of 22 August reflected growing Soviet frustration. It said:

> The desire to attack everywhere and to secure as much territory as possible without consolidating success and closely securing the flanks of the shock groups gives the offensive an indiscriminate character. Such an offensive leads to a scattering of forces and

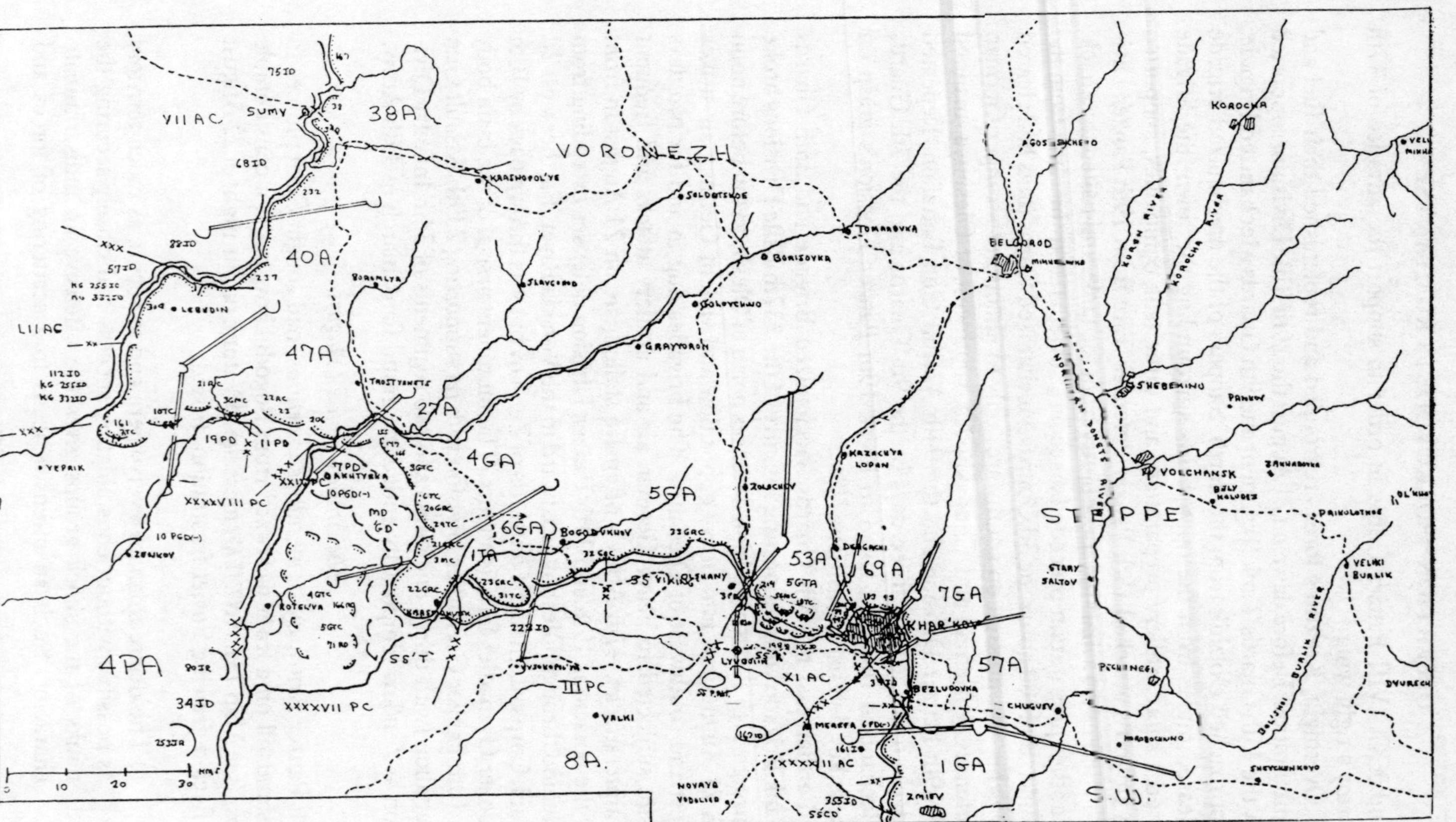

MAP 73. BELGOROD–KHAR'KOV, SITUATION, 2000 22 AUGUST 1943

> material and provides the enemy the opportunity to strike blows on the flanks and rear of our overextended forces with unprotected flanks and defeat them piecemeal.

Stalin reiterated the prime importance of liquidating the Akhtyrka group, and added:

> I ask you not to become infatuated by the mission of enveloping the Khar'kov bridgehead from the Poltava area, but concentrate all attention on the real and concrete mission – the liquidation of the enemy Akhtyrka group, for without the liquidation of that enemy group serious success of the Voronezh Front will become impracticable.[220]

By 22 August Vatutin had not liquidated the German Akhtyrka group; but he had seriously weakened it and, in doing so, had attracted the bulk of German reinforcements to his sector. More important, Vatutin planned a new offensive to begin on 23 August. Knowledge of what had occurred and what would probably occur in the near future prevented the Germans from shifting any forces from the Akhtyrka area to Khar'kov. With virtually all forces fully committed, additional pressure on Khar'kov or sectors adjacent to Khar'kov would threaten not only a loss of the city but also collapse of 4th Panzer Army's and 8th Army's defenses. The Soviets began applying that pressure east of Bogodukhov on 17 August and increased it against German defenses at Khar'kov proper shortly thereafter.

The Battle for Khar'kov – 18–23 August

Steppe Front Planning

While the right wing of the Voronezh Front struggled with 4th Panzer Army, Konev's Steppe Front resumed operations to seize the ultimate objective of the operation, Khar'kov. The tough and skillful German resistance forced Konev to avoid direct assaults on the city and instead nibble away at 8th Army's flanks west and southwest of the city to force a German withdrawal or encircle 8th Army by cutting its communications lines. Konev repeatedly appealed to the *STAVKA* to release Rotmistrov's 5th Guards Tank Army to his control to reinforce 53d Army west of Khar'kov; but because of the intense fighting around Akhtyrka, Konev had to settle for an assault on Khar'kov without Rotmistrov's immediate assistance.

Managarov's 53d and Gagen's 57th Armies led Konev's attempt to envelop Khar'kov. Konev described his intent as follows:

> I calculated in my mind all pluses and minuses, having viewed Khar'kov from all sides and from various directions and finally arrived at a final decision: the most favorable direction to strike the main blow was the northwest where 53d Army was located. . . . Here were the best approaches to the city, forests, and commanding heights from which you could see all of Khar'kov well. Now one had to decide the question of securing that army from the west, from the Lyubotin area from where enemy tank divisions constantly counterattacked. We decided to oppose tanks with tanks and conduct the offensive on the city with two armies: 53rd Army and P.A. Rotmistrov's tank army. . . . My forward command post was located in the sector of General Managarov's 53rd Army, that is, on the main attack direction.[221]

Konev and Managarov jointly planned a 53d Army thrust southward toward Peresechnaya and the woody hill mass northwest of Khar'kov. Ultimately 53d Army would cross the Udy River and cut the Poltava–Khar'kov rail line near Korotich, 10 kilometers west of Khar'kov. 69th Army, on 58th Army's left, would shift the bulk of its forces to the southwest to cooperate with 53d Army divisions in a concerted assault on Khar'kov from the west and northwest. All night of 16–17 August and until noon on 17 August Managarov's army regrouped for the new offensive (see Map 69). The 299th Rifle Division seized Polevoye, 8 kilometers southwest of Dergachi, and deployed south of the town alongside the 84th and 116th Rifle Divisions, supported by the 219th and 19th Tank Brigades of 1st Mechanized Corps. The 252d Rifle Division and the remainder of 1st Mechanized Corps deployed in second echelon to exploit the army's offensive successes.

Managarov and Konev were convinced by earlier experiences that new offensive techniques were required. Previously, Soviet attacks had occurred in the morning after an artillery preparation which usually ended with Katyusha volleys followed by the infantry assaults. Consequently, German defenders went under cover during the preparation but emerged in time to face the advancing infantry. Managarov reasoned that an attack launched later in the day using a different artillery pattern would confuse the Germans. Moreover, Managarov learned from prisoners that at 1700 about 50 percent of the German officers and men left the forward trenches and went to the vicinity of the battalion command post for supper. Hence, Managarov arranged to fire his preparation at 1645 using Katyusha rocket volleys to strike German battalion command posts and communications trenches. After the initial preparation, artillery fire and air strikes would hit forward German positions. The infantry assault would begin at 1700 and go on into the night.[222] By the afternoon of 18 August Managarov's army was poised to attack. The mechanized corps commander, aviation commander, army artillery commander, operations officer, and the chief of reconnaissance were at Managarov's headquarters while nearby, Konev occupied his *front* forward command post from which he could observe the progress of the attack.

German dispositions facing Managarov had changed little since 14 August. XI Army Corps' 3d Panzer Division defended the sector from Olshany to west of Polevoye with the 168th Infantry Division on its right defending a 4-kilometer sector centered south of Polevoye. The 198th Infantry Division covered a 4-kilometer front south of Dergachi, and the 106th Infantry Division occupied positions farther east across the Dergachi–Khar'kov road and rail line. On XI Corps' right flank, the 320th Infantry Division deployed across the Belgorod–Khar'kov road facing Soviet forces at Bol'shaya Danilovka.[223]

The Steppe Front Assault – 18–20 August

At 1645 on 18 August Soviet artillery opened fire on German defenses at the junction of 3d Panzer Division and 168th Infantry Division. Katyusha volleys preceded the massed gun fire (see Map 70). At 1730 assault battalions of the 299th, 84th, and 116th Rifle Divisions, covered by the direct fire of all tanks and artillery, stormed through German defenses south of Polevoye and plunged into the heavy woods in the German rear. 84th Rifle Division's 41st Rifle Regiment made the deepest initial penetration and advanced 3 kilometers. Into its sector Managarov then committed his 252d Rifle Division. By the morning of 19 August, after heavy night fighting, the 299th, 84th, and 252d Rifle Divisions cleared the Germans from the forest and approached to within 2 kilometers of Peresechnaya on the Udy River (see Map 71). 3d Panzer Division, its armored strength down to 13 tanks, could do little but delay the concerted assault.[224]

Once into the forests northwest of Khar'kov Soviet forces were covered from German observation and, to some extent, from German air attack. With this added advantage Managarov pressed his assaults throughout 19 August. The 84th and 299th Rifle Divisions occupied the suburbs of Peresechnaya and the heights to its north and east and cut the Dergachi–Khar'kov road as well. The 252d Rifle Division forced 3d Panzer Division troops westward toward Olshany and reached the rail line east of town. Farther west SS Panzer Grenadier Division "Viking," its right flank threatened by 53d Army's advance, withdrew 8 kilometers on 33d Guards Rifle Corps' front to new positions just north of Olshany.[225]

Battles raged throughout the night of 19–20 August, and by morning a reinforced battalion from each of Managarov's first echelon divisions smashed into Peresechnaya and Gavrilovka while farther east a lead battalion of 28th Guards Rifle Division reached the forests along the Udy River north of Korotich (see Map 72). Motorized infantry of 1st Mechanized Corps, operating with the 299th Rifle Division, crossed the Udy River south of Peresechnaya; and the 214th Rifle Division, operating on the army right flank, secured a small bridgehead at Andreyevka and Peresechnaya. (The 18th Separate Motorized Engineer Battalion built a bridge for tanks.) 28th Guards Rifle Division, on the army's left flank, battled throughout 20 August for possession of Gavrilovka and finally reached the Udy River at Podnika, 5 kilometers west of Khar'kov, but could not cross because of heavy German fire from the south bank.

To capitalize on 53d Army's success, on 20 August Konev subordinated 69th Army's 48th Rifle Corps to Managarov's control. Managarov moved the corps' 89th Guards Rifle Division and 107th Rifle Division southwest toward the wooded hills northwest of Khar'kov to increase pressure on the Germans from the west and northwest and to join the attacks on the western approaches of the city by the 116th Rifle Division. Meanwhile, 69th Army's 305th and 183d Rifle Divisions covered the shift of the two divisions by attacking German 106th Infantry Division positions and seizing several villages on the northern outskirts of Khar'kov.[226] 7th Guards Army, northeast of Khar'kov, also struck at 282d Infantry Division defenses north of the factory sector east of the city.

5th Guards Tank Army Attacks West of Khar'kov – 21–23 August

On 20 August Zhukov finally released 5th Guards Tank Army to Konev's control. Konev ordered Rotmistrov to move east, concentrate his remaining armor north of the Udy River, attack German defenses south of the Udy River, occupy Korotich and Lyubotin, and cut the Poltava–Khar'kov rail line in order to block the transfer of German troops to Khar'kov from the west. Rotmistrov's columns of tanks, artillery, and vehicles headed southeast on the night of 20–21 August, and in the morning Yegorov's 18th Tank Corps concentrated in the forests east of Peresechnaya. Skvortsov's 5th Guards Mechanized Corps, in march columns, hastened forward to join Yegorov (29th Tank Corps was still located west of Bogodukhov). The hasty march prevented any maintenance work or regrouping, and there was only minimum time to refuel and coordinate artillery and aviation support.[227] At 0900 on 21 August lead elements of 18th Tank Corps joined 53d Army's attack but immediately experienced difficulties.

Meanwhile, on 18 August 57th Army had renewed its attack southeast of Khar'kov and immediately had run into heavy resistance (see Map 70). Farther south 1st Guards Army's drive on Taranovka had stalled in the face of resistance from the German 355th Infantry Division and the newly arrived SS Cavalry Division. The next day the 152d, 303d, and 6th Rifle Divisions made limited gains north and west of Zmiyev against the 161st and 355th Infantry Divisions; and the 41st Guards Rifle Division, north of the Udy River, pounded German positions east of Bezlyubovka, but with little effect.[228] The German 39th Infantry and 6th Panzer Divisions clung fast to their defenses against 57th Army's main forces east of Khar'kov. By late on 20 August it was apparent to Konev that 5th Guards Tank Army's progress would be key to future Steppe Front success in wresting Khar'kov from German hands.

Rotmistrov's two corps prepared for action on the morning of 21 August (see Map 72). At 0900 forward units of 18th Tank Corps tried to cross the Udy River. However, the wheeled vehicles in the march columns of the lead brigades were immediately bogged down in the muddy banks of the river under heavy German artillery fire. Nor had sappers cleared mines from the river bank. Consequently, fifteen of Yegorov's tanks were either bogged down in the mud or went up in flames from German artillery fire.[229] Even more severe was the loss of time which forced Rotmistrov to postpone the attack until the next day.

Thus, the task of crossing the Udy River and creating a bridgehead large enough to deploy 5th Guards Tank Army fell to Managarov's exhausted infantry. During the night 28th Guards Rifle Division expanded its bridgeheads and assisted the 252d and 84th Rifle Divisions to cross the river. The 19th Pontoon Bridge Battalion installed a sixty ton bridge near Gavrilovka, 7 kilometers west of Khar'kov, despite heavy German artillery fire; and, in the early morning hours, Rotmistrov finally moved his two corps across the river.[230]

German 8th Army's defenses west of Khar'kov were now stretched almost to the breaking point. XI Army Corps' 106th Infantry Division defenses covered the Dergachi road on the northern outskirts of Khar'kov, and swung southwest and south along the outskirts of Khar'kov to the Udy River. The 168th and 198th Infantry Divisions, now reduced to regimental *kampfgruppe* size, defended the southern bank of the Udy River from Khar'kov westward to Peresechnaya. On III Panzer Corps' right flank 3d Panzer Division occupied the sector from Olshany to Peresechnaya with its remaining nine tanks. To bolster these defenses and contain Soviet forces in bridgeheads south of the Udy River 8th Army dispatched SS "Das Reich" from the Bogodukhov area to reinforce the threatened III Panzer Corps' sector. On the evening of 21 August "Das Reich" moved its 38 tanks and 19 self-propelled guns to Lyubotin in the rear of the 168th Infantry Division. In addition, 8th Army moved the 393d Assault Gun Battery (two guns) and the 905th Battalion (six guns) into the area along with "SS Panzer Detachment" with 42 Panther tanks.[231]

In essence 8th Army concentrated virtually all of its armored and anti-tank assets in the Lyubotin–Korotich areas in a desperate attempt to keep the roads from Khar'kov open. For it was no longer just a question of holding the city. It was now a question of permitting an orderly withdrawal and the survival of XI Army Corps' units in the city proper. On 22 August fighting began whose desperation and intensity rivaled the bitterest struggles which had occurred earlier in the operation. Rotmistrov, driven by Zhukov's and Konev's orders, threw his army at the Poltava–Khar'kov road and Korotich. Forces of German 3d Panzer, 168th Infantry, 198th Infantry, and SS "Das Reich" Panzer Division clung equally desperately to their defenses.

Early on 22 August Soviet forces occupied jumping off positions in a 10-kilometer sector south of the Udy River, 6 to 8 kilometers from their objectives of Lyubotin and Korotich which lay across the road and rail line from Khar'kov to Poltava (see Map 73). In the bridgehead, the 233d Rifle Division deployed for combat on the right flank with 5th Guards Mechanized Corps and the 107th and 28th Guards Rifle Divisions deployed on the left with 18th Tank Corps. The 299th and 252d Rifle Divisions deployed for the assault north along the Udy River toward Peresechnaya while the 84th Rifle Division formed in second echelon north of the river. The German 3d Panzer and 168th Infantry Divisions defended along the road and rail line with SS "Das Reich" units deployed between Lyubotin and Korotich, tied in with the fixed defenses around those towns and ready to intervene should Soviet forces make a penetration.

After a heavy artillery barrage, at 0500 Rotmistrov's tanks (111 at the time) and those of 1st Mechanized Corps struck. On the tank army's right flank two of Skvortsov's mechanized brigades led the attack backed up by 24th Guards Tank Brigade.[232] Fighting raged all day with unmatched ferocity as Rotmistrov launched attack after attack. SS "Das Reich" responded with repeated counterattacks, and German aviation pounded Soviet troop and armored concentrations. In the afternoon the 24th Guards Tank Brigade enveloped Korotich from the northwest, and a tank company of 1st Mechanized Corps' 219th Tank Brigade penetrated the town but was itself encircled and destroyed by German counterattacks. SS "Das Reich" drove 5th Guards Mechanized Corps' tank brigade from the town as both sides expended their remaining strength. The seesaw fighting persisted into the evening with Soviet tanks and infantry hammering at the northeast approaches to Lyubotin and at the northern outskirts of Korotich. 5th Guards Tank Army succeeded in cutting the Poltava–Khar'kov road and repeatedly assaulted across the fields and rail line just north of Korotich but simply could not take the town. But with each Soviet assault, German strength also ebbed. Only by prodigious efforts did the German defenders of Korotich hold off the armoured onslaught. In early evening, when it became apparent Rotmistrov would not be able to break the German defense lines, Konev ordered his Steppe Front armies to commence a general assault on Khar'kov later in the evening.

The Fall of Khar'kov – 23 August

By 1800 22 August Konev learned that German forces were beginning a withdrawal from the city. Seeking to catch as many Germans in the city as possible and compensate for Rotmistrov's failure to cut off the city, Konev ordered his armies to launch a concerted attack against the weakened German defenses (see Map 74).[233] Gagen's 57th and Kuznetsov's 1st Guards Army had already pushed their advanced elements (113d and

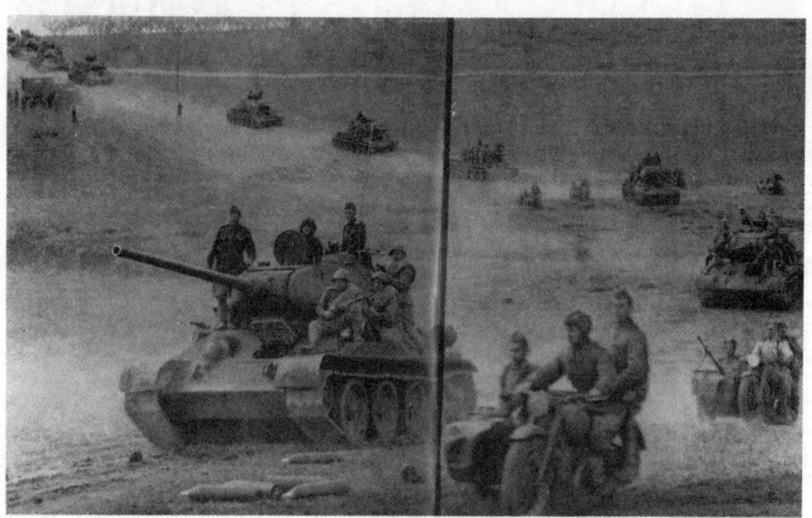

28. An armored column advances.

152d Rifle Divisions) to Konstantovka only 13 kilometers east of Merefa. The Germans countered by moving 6th Panzer Division into the area. On 22 August Kuznetsov's army continued its advance toward Merefa while Gagen's main force crept westward into Khar'kov's southeastern suburbs. 69th Army, on Konev's orders, sent the 94th Guards Rifle Division and a tank brigade by forced march to positions just northwest of Khar'kov. Once in position the 94th Guards plunged southward on Khar'kov's western outskirts on the left flank of 53d Army in a shorter

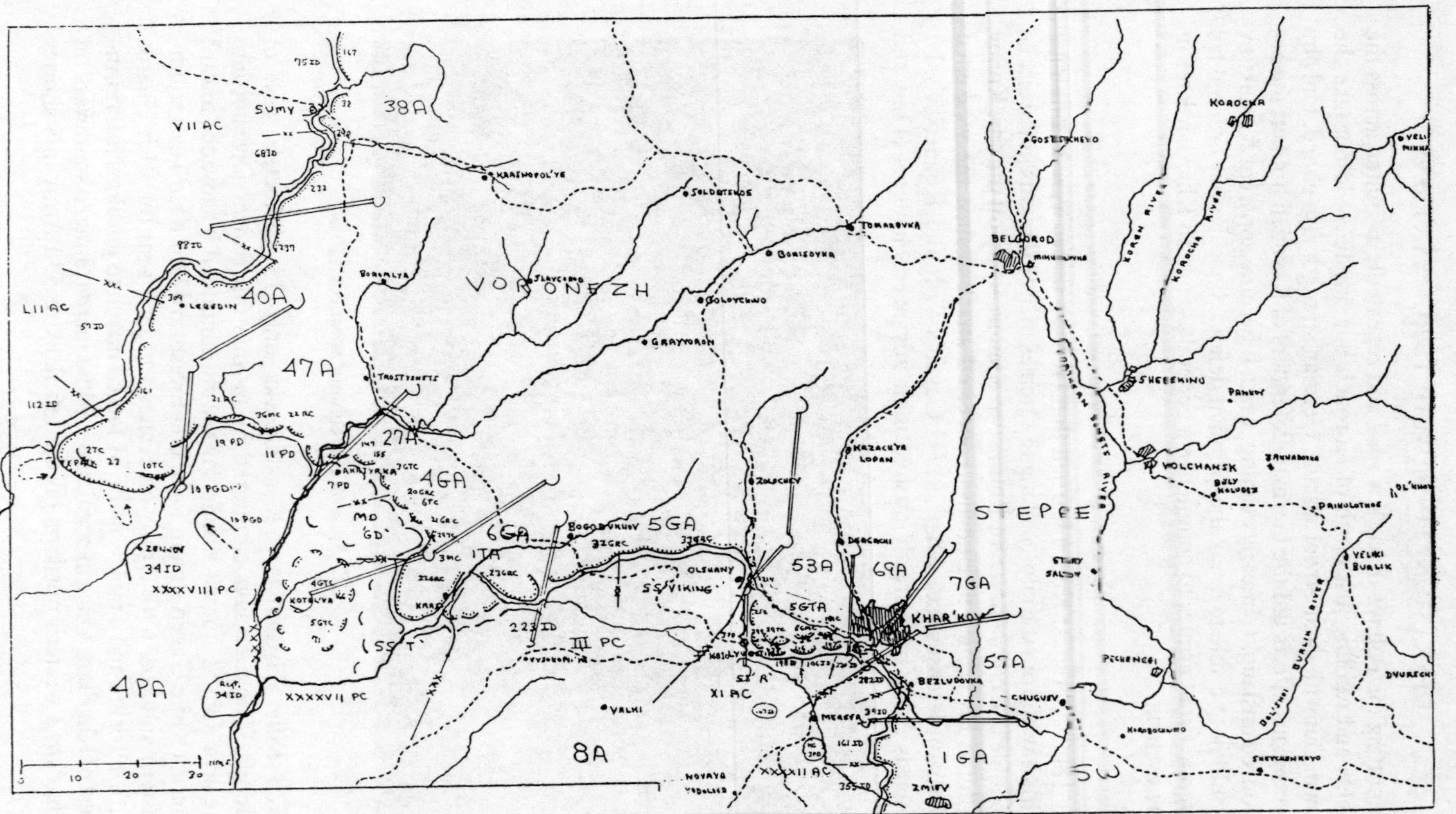

MAP 74. BELGOROD–KHAR'KOV, SITUATION, 2000 23 AUGUST 1943

29. German prisoner

version of Rotmistrov's earlier attempt to envelop the city. The 94th Guards Rifle Division ground to a halt short of the Udy River.[234]

During the night other 53d, 69th, and 7th Guards Army divisions penetrated Khar'kov's inner defense lines. 53d Army's 89th Guards and 107th Rifle Divisions entered the western section of the city. At 2200 69th Army and 7th Guards Army sent forward detachments into the city followed at 0200 by army main forces. The 183d Rifle Division advanced south on Sumy Street into Dzerzhinsky Square. German rear guards set fires and delayed the Soviet occupation until 1100 on 23 August when German forces completed their withdrawal and occupied defensive positions south of the Udy River.[235]

Although the fall of Khar'kov formally meant the end of the Belgorod–Khar'kov operation, heavy fighting continued for several days west of Khar'kov. Rotmistrov's 5th Guards Tank Army, now reinforced by his 29th Tank Corps, continued futile attacks on German positions at Korotich. By 25 August his once proud army was a shell of its former self with a combat strength of only fifty tanks.[236] Farther west, Vatutin resumed his offensive and on 25 August forced 4th Panzer Army to relinquish its hold on Akhtyrka.

German forces successfully avoided collapse, even after the loss of Khar'kov. But as Soviet assaults began anew and as Soviet reinforcements poured in from the north, the German command knew it had no choice but to conduct a major withdrawal, this time to the Dnepr River line. (The army group decision to abandon Khar'kov had been made on 18 August.)

Conclusions

The Belgorod–Khar'kov operation (and its sister operation at Orel) was the first "modern" Soviet operation of the Great Patriotic War in terms of Soviet operational intent and the force structure they relied on to achieve their offensive aims. By August 1943 the Soviets had developed a force structure which, in theory, possessed the capability of conducting deep operations. Creation of the tank army to supplement the existing tank and mechanized corps provided *front* commanders with their own mobile groups with which they could conduct operational maneuver. Although early use of these *front* mobile groups was often flawed, in time Soviet commanders learned how to use them with great effect. The starting point in that learning process occurred in August 1943.

In terms of both scale and scope of operations, Operation *Rumyantsev* surpassed earlier Soviet offensive operations in 1943. Although launched only a short time after the German Kursk offensive had ground to a halt, Soviet planning for the Belgorod–Khar'kov operation was thorough, and the array of assembled forces was impressive.

Preliminary planning for the Belgorod–Khar'kov operation occurred simultaneously with Soviet planning for the Kursk defense. During this period the Soviets designated the *fronts* which would conduct the counteroffensive and set the general time frame during which the offensive would occur. Precise timing of the assault and definitive troop lists of attacking forces, of course, depended upon the outcome of the German attacks. Detailed planning for Operation *Rumyantsev* occurred during the short three-week period after German attacks at Kursk had subsided.

For the first time in the war the *STAVKA* intended to conduct a major offensive operation (at Orel) while a German offensive was in progress and then expand that offensive (at Belgorod) once German attacks had ceased. In essence, the *STAVKA* took a calculated risk that German forces would be weakened significantly in battles against Soviet defenses and that Soviet forces would retain enough combat punch to conduct a successful counteroffensive. The Soviets hoped to achieve surprise in both the Orel and Belgorod–Khar'kov offensives. Of course, all Soviet plans were predicated on the assumption that their Kursk defense would succeed. The Soviet Kursk counteroffensive took place within the context of other major offensives at Smolensk (7 August) and in the Donbas (13 August), thereby posing a dilemma for the Germans who were forced to redistribute scarce reserves.

Since the Soviets in the counteroffensive would have to rely heavily on forces that had taken part in the repulse of German attacks, considerable regrouping and refitting of their forces within a short period of time was required. The Soviets also had to make a conscious decision to launch the offensive in spite of marked shortages of men and material in many units. 5th Guards Tank Army, reduced to a strength of 150–200 tanks after the major tank battle at Prokhorovka (12 July), was reinforced to a strength of over 500 tanks by 3 August. The Soviets similarly refitted 1st Tank Army and other tank and mechanized corps. These tank forces, with a high percentage of new weapons, new crews, and new small unit commanders, spearheaded the Belgorod–Khar'kov offensive.

The Soviets had to replenish the strength of rifle units as well, in particular those which, like the 69th and 7th Guards Army, had absorbed the brunt of the German attack and were now required to conduct penetration operations. Even after reinforcement 7th Guards Army was 30,000 men understrength at the time of the new offensive. The Soviet command accepted these shortfalls in manpower and equipment realizing that German units were also understrength and that Soviet forces would still maintain a significant overall numerical superiority.

Because of the weakened condition of Soviet forces the *STAVKA* deliberately eschewed use of a wide envelopment to secure Khar'kov. Stalin assumed that complicated maneuvers by new tank armies and tired rifle forces would court disaster and thus opted for a direct time-phased assault on the German Belgorod salient followed by a close envelopment of Khar'kov. Such a direct attack would also take advantage of terrain conditions by using the northeast to southwest ridge lines as the principal axes of advance.

At the operational level the Soviets made major strides during the counteroffensive. The Soviets launched the offensive in a time-phased manner, first conducting the penetration operation, then expanding the offensive with a series of army attacks along the shoulders of the penetration. This ripple effect steadily built up pressure on German defenses and economized on the use of available artillery and air assets, much of which the Soviets used successively in each sector.

Because of their expanded force structure, the Soviets adopted a flexible operational formation which generated initial penetrating power and possessed enough depth to strengthen the offensive as it developed. For the first time, a *front* had a second echelon army (47th Army of Voronezh Front) as well as large mobile forces to exploit success (1st and 5th Guards Tank Armies). Armies on main attack axes formed in a single echelon of rifle corps, but the corps themselves often formed in two echelons of rifle divisions. Every Voronezh Front army commander (except 38th Army) had at his disposal a mobile group composed of a tank or mechanized corps. The presence of mobile groups and second echelons improved the Soviet capability of sustaining the offensive and reacting to German counterattacks.

Fronts and armies attacked in narrower sectors than in earlier operations. Armies on main attack axes operated in sectors of from 8.5–20 kilometers and created much higher than usual operational densities of men and weaponry. Likewise, the depth of *front* and army operational formations shrank from 30–40 kilometers to 20–25 kilometers and 12–20 to 10–15 kilometers respectively. This increased both the force and the sustainability of the attack. The use of larger artillery units in greater number provided overwhelming Soviet artillery superiority in main attack sectors.

Soviet mobile forces played a significantly increased role in the counteroffensive. The Soviets used their new tank armies for the first time in the Kursk counteroffensive. At Belgorod–Khar'kov they used two such armies in tandem, committed to action on the first day of the offensive in an extremely narrow sector (6 kilometers). This massive use of armor so early in the attack caught German commanders by surprise and led to larger than usual German losses. Tank and mechanized corps, under army control, also entered battle on the first day of the operation. Subsequent operations by these mobile forces demonstrated that the Soviets still had lessons to learn about the coordination of combined arms forces battling in the operational depths.

During the preparation phase the Soviets made widespread use of deception. They successfully masked offensive preparations and simulated a tank army concentration at Suzhda to lull the Germans into a false sense of security. When the attack occurred it clearly came as a surprise to the Germans. Before the Germans could react, the Soviets had done considerable damage to their units.

Careful Soviet planning of the initial penetration operation paid dividends. The Soviets effected the penetration on schedule and did considerable damage to the German 332d, 167th, and 168th Infantry Divisions. By the end of the first day both Soviet tank armies had successfully penetrated German forward defenses. German armored units backing up front line infantry divisions reacted quickly and deprived the Soviets of some of the fruits of their initial victory. 19th Panzer Division's stand at Tomarovka severely disrupted 6th Guards and 5th Guards Army's offensive timetable and also tied up some of the exploiting 1st Tank Army armor. 6th Panzer Division's quick reaction permitted reestablishment of defenses north of Belgorod and forced the Steppe Front's armies to fight their way into the city. Even so, Belgorod fell by the third day of the operation.

The strong German defense at Tomarovka and Borisovka had a mixed impact on both sides. Initially, it slowed the progress of Soviet attacks. However, the Germans did not properly assess the Soviet capability for injecting large armored forces into their rear area. 1st Tank Army's appearance at Golovchino caught the Germans by surprise and resulted in the encirclement of virtually all of LII Army Corps. The subsequent escape from encirclement cost the Germans high losses and rendered at least two divisions (255th and 332d Infantry Divisions) combat ineffective. 19th Panzer Division also lost much of its combat strength. The Germans were forced to withdraw to Boromlya and Trostyanets before the arrival of "Grossdeutschland" Panzer Grenadier Division permitted them to reestablish a stable defensive line.

Reduction of the Tomarovka–Borisovka pocket also had an adverse effect on subsequent Soviet operations. 1st Tank Army continued its offensive to Bogodukhov while 5th Guards Army lagged well behind. The absence of infantry and artillery support made 1st Tank Army vulnerable to the German armored counterstrokes which began on 11 August. In addition, Vatutin's aggressiveness encouraged Katukov to push his forces too far. The advanced brigades of the overextended 1st Tank Army fell victim to III Panzer Corps' initial counterattacks which deprived 1st Tank Army of about one-third of its armored strength. Compounding that situation, 5th Guards Tank Army was tied up first by 6th Panzer Division and then by 3d Panzer Division, and it arrived in the Zolochev area too late to stave off the damage to 1st Tank Army. By the time Soviet rifle forces and 5th Guards Tank Army arrived at Bogodukhov III Panzer Corps had enough forces in the area (SS "Totenkopf," SS "Das Reich," SS "Viking") to fight Soviet exploitation forces to a standstill.

The delay in the advance of 27th and 6th Guards Armies from Borisovka and Graivoron also adversely affected their operations. The lead tank corps of both armies (4th Guards and 5th Guards Tank Corps) advanced unsupported while rifle forces were clearing the Graivoron area, and although the tank corps reached the Kotel'va–Krasnokutsk area, they were unable to take Akhtyrka. When rifle forces did arrive, some divisions were diverted to support 1st Tank Army at Bogodukhov while the other divisions deployed in extended formation throughout the exposed salient southeast of Akhtyrka. Thus, on 18 August the German XXIV Panzer Corps struck at this exposed salient and severely damaged 27th Army. Although the Soviets assembled large forces to launch a counterattack (4th Guards Army, 1st Tank Army), the counterattacks were poorly coordinated and again German XXIV Panzer Corps fought the Soviets to a standstill. Farther east 6th Panzer Division and XI and XXXXII Army Corps conducted a skillful delaying operation back to Khar'kov which sapped the strength of Konev's Steppe Front and left it unable to seize Khar'kov by a single deep strike. In the end the battle for Khar'kov became one of attrition.

It was the Soviet operation on the German left flank that sealed the fate of German forces at Khar'kov. 47th Army's attack at Boromlya threatened the flank of the German force at Akhtyrka and forced the Germans to commit most newly-arrived units (10th Panzer Grenadier and 34th Infantry Divisions) to that sector. Although the Germans eventually halted the attack, by that time Soviet pressure along the entire front was so great that a fatal penetration could occur anywhere. The Soviet attacks west and southwest of Khar'kov on 22 August, although also halted, demonstrated to the Germans the dangers of continuing the struggle with their depleted units. The decision to withdraw to the Dnepr River followed.

Both sides suffered high losses during the operation. Konev's Steppe Front rifle divisions decreased in strength to from 3,000 to 4,000 men per division, and divisions in 5th Guards Army and 40th Army were in a similar state. 27th Army lost virtually all its equipment and a majority of the personnel of two rifle divisions (71st, 166th) and a tank corps (4th Guards). 6th Guards Army's 52d Guards and 90th Guards Rifle Divisions suffered similar losses. Soviet mobile forces also suffered heavy attrition although rear service units performed prodigious feats in keeping tanks operational. 1st Tank Army began the operation with 542 tanks and during the operation lost 1,042 tanks of which 289 were repairable. By 23 August the army's tank strength was 120. 5th Guards Tank Army also suffered heavy losses. It began the operation with 503 tanks but by 25 August had but fifty remaining. During the same period the army lost 60–65 percent of its staff officers, 85 percent of its company and battalion commanders, and 75 percent of its radios.[237] At the end of the operation the army had the effective strength of only a single tank brigade, mute testimony to the ferocity of the fighting in which it was involved. Soviet command casualties were also high and included many regimental commanders, the commander of 1st Tank Army's 31st Tank Corps and 112th Tank Brigade, 4th Army's 52d Rifle Corps commander, and the deputy commander of the Voronezh Front.

German losses were equally severe; and, since German strength was initially one-third that of the Soviets, the losses were even more critical. The 255th, 332d, and 57th Infantry Divisions lost over two-thirds of their strength, reaching by the end of the operation 3336, 342, and 1791 men, respectively. One regiment of the 112th Infantry Division had 1 officer and 45 men survive. The 167th, 168th, 106th, and 252d Infantry Divisions of 8th Army likewise suffered heavy losses. The 11th Panzer Division by 23 August had 820 infantrymen, 15 tanks, and 4 assault guns while the 19th Panzer Division lost its division commander and was reduced to a strength of 760 infantrymen and 12 tanks.[238] The strength of the SS panzer divisions remained remarkably stable throughout the operation, attesting in part to the priority in resupply these units had. For example, SS "Das Reich" had 51 tanks and assault guns on 15 August, and by 23 August that number had grown to 55. In the same period, SS "Totenkopf" increased its strength from 44 to 61 armored vehicles and assault guns.[239] Even so, the extended combat wore down unit personnel and reduced overall unit effectiveness.

Soviet armored superiority flagged as the operation progressed. The Soviets began the offensive with around 2300 tanks to the Germans' 220 tanks (less "Grossdeutschland"). By the end of the offensive, Soviet tank strength was about 500, while German armor and assault gun strength stood at about 330 (counting reinforcements).

The Soviets achieved their operational objectives in Operation *Rumyantsev,* but at a heavy cost. Both Belgorod and Khar'kov fell into Soviet hands, but more important, the offensive chewed up German front line units and the already thin German operational reserves. For the first time Soviet mobile forces fought German armored units to a standstill and were not forced to make significant withdrawals. Moreover, the damage done to German operational reserves and the German 4th Panzer and 8th Armies in general, virtually mandated further German withdrawals back to the Dnepr River. The damage done to German mobile forces at Kursk and during the counteroffensive stifled any future German hopes of conducting strategic offensive operations on the Eastern Front.

6

CONCLUSIONS

The Situation from December 1942 to August 1943

The eight month period from December 1942 to August 1943 was one of intense struggle which exacted a heavy toll on both contending parties. For the Soviets, accustomed in previous years to even larger losses amidst grievous defeats, this period had the redeeming feature that the Axis forces had finally begun to pay a terrible price for their Russian venture. That price was measurable in terms of casualties, lost ground, and the changing momentum of war. A less tangible aspect of that price was wounded German pride and an inevitable erosion in German faith that the war was winnable. By August 1943 there was little doubt as to the military outcome of the war if political allegiances persisted. The only question was how long it would take for the Soviets to achieve victory.

The period was a costly one for the Germans involving, as it did, the loss of one complete army (6th), the dismemberment of a second army (2d), and the almost total ruin of four allied armies. Moreover, it was a period when Soviet forces ground up Germany's best units and an increasing number of experienced officers, non-commissioned officers, and soldiers. These losses were irreplaceable; and, although units still functioned and retained their cohesion, the proud and victorious German Army of 1941–1942 slowly disappeared from the battlefield. Clearly the process had begun even earlier, perhaps as early as Smolensk in July 1941 but certainly by the winter of 1941–1942. Although Stalingrad made that process visible to the world at large, the German operational victories of February and March 1943 blinded Hitler and a portion of the military to those realities. As a result the battle of Kursk compounded the damage already done by smashing, once and for all, the concept of German offensive invincibility. Whereas, after Stalingrad, optimistic military figures could realistically ponder a stalemate, after Kursk prospects for future stalemate were all but dead. The trail of battle after August 1943 pointed inexorably westward.

Strategic Assessment

Strategically, during the winter of 1942–1943 the Soviets conducted war with an offensive abandon reminiscent of operations in the winter of 1941–1942. The *STAVKA* discounted the ability of the German Army to recover after the Stalingrad debacle and ordered a series of first consecutive and then simultaneous *front* operations aimed at collapsing the southern wing of the German eastern front and driving the Germans west of the Dnepr River or beyond. The Soviets planned and conducted the operations on the assumption that German forces would collapse at any moment and were determined to escape from the Soviet grasp before that collapse. This Soviet misreading of German intentions blinded the Soviets to true German capabilities and produced the operational disasters of late February and March 1943 in the Donbas and at Khar'kov.

The principal strategic aim of the Soviet military in November 1942 was to secure the strategic initiative by defeating the German strategic drive into southern Russia and the Caucasus and then to maintain that initiative. The Soviets conducted their strategic counteroffensive by employing several *fronts* in tandem on the most critical strategic direction – that of Stalingrad. The continued Soviet practice of committing strategic reserves to combat at the critical place and time played a key role in their achieving strategic success. Those reserves spearheaded the Soviet drive at Stalingrad, helped repel German relief attempts at Stalingrad, and launched Soviet forces westward in December 1942. Conversely, an absence of strategic reserves after January 1943 materially contributed to Soviet failures in February and March, a lesson not lost on the *STAVKA* in August 1943.

The Soviet strategic counteroffensive at Stalingrad was larger in scale than any previous offensive and involved simultaneous and consecutive blows delivered across a broad front. The winter offensive was of even larger geographical scope and involved 4 *fronts* and 18 combined arms armies advancing in a sector 700–800 kilometers wide to a depth of from 120–400 kilometers. Unlike the Stalingrad operation where planning time was adequate, the winter campaign involved hasty, essentially *ad hoc* planning; and the offensive began with little or no regrouping or resupply of forces. Soviet conduct of the winter offensive resembled in many ways the haphazard offensive of the winter of 1941–1942. Although the Soviet force structure was more mature in the winter of 1942–1943 than in 1941–1942, the erosion of unit strengths compensated for that maturity and contributed to the ultimate demise of the offensive.

The Soviets failed to achieve their full offensive aims in the winter of 1942–1943 for a number of reasons besides their overambition and haste. *STAVKA* coordination was either poor or totally lacking. Individual *STAVKA* representatives coordinated single *front* operations, thus producing a fragmentation of aim and objective that contrasted with the well-coordinated Stalingrad operation. In the future that experience would produce changes in how the Soviets coordinated major operations. Henceforth, the Soviets would rely on greater use of *STAVKA* representatives to coordinate distinct groups of *fronts* operating along strategic directions.

In the winter offensive the Soviets sought to achieve too many strategic (and operational) objectives. This phenomenon was indicative of their insufficient grasp of operational realities. Close study of the operations indicates that the Soviet grasp of the nature of "operations" was maturing during the winter. However, the Soviets had not yet fully comprehended the shadowy line between the art of the possible and the reckless. In that regard the lessons of February and March were instructive.

By seeking to achieve ever wider objectives Soviet forces became overextended. In part this explained the rapid collapse of the apparently victorious Soviet westward advance in February. The Soviet force structure in early 1943 was also in the middle stages of reconstruction. The *STAVKA* was experimenting with a new rifle corps structure, but most armies had only one or two rifle corps, and those corps lacked significant organic fire support and logistic capabilities. The Soviet army's armored force had expanded; but the new tank and mechanized corps were capable of only limited operational exploitation, had weak support organizations, and were vulnerable to counterattack, especially when at the end of their logistical tether. Similar weaknesses plagued large unit artillery and air support where logistical problems wrought even greater havoc.

The lessons of February and March produced sober reflection by the Soviet military leadership, and the strategic operations of the summer of 1943 bore mute testimony to the value of that reflection. By summer the Soviets adopted a more realistic view of the situation evidenced by Stalin's willingness to undertake a strategic defensive stance in order to entice Germany into a costly battle of attrition. Meanwhile, the Soviets studied the experiences of the winter of 1942 and 1943 and made necessary adjustments to their force structure and doctrine in order to make that battle of attrition even more deadly for the Germans. Kursk was the result of those efforts.

The Soviet strategic defense of 1943, unlike those of 1941 and 1942, did not occur along the entire front or in the equivalent of a theater of military operations (several strategic directions). Instead, it occurred along one strategic direction. In the summer of 1943 at Kursk, a group of *fronts* backed up by a strategic reserve (the Steppe Front) constructed a strategic defense which turned out to be a virtual strategic killing zone. Unlike earlier defensive operations, sufficient time existed for the Soviets to prepare and fully man a deeply echeloned and fortified defense extending over 100 kilometers deep. For the first time the Soviets integrated into that strategic defense a well planned strategic counteroffensive with its own large scale objectives (again using strategic reserves – the Steppe Front). After commencing at Orel and Belgorod–Khar'kov with a force of five *fronts*, ultimately the summer offensive involved 10 *fronts*, 40 combined arms armies, and 5 tank armies operating on a 2,000 kilometer front to a depth of 600–700 kilometers. The momentum of that strategic offensive ultimately propelled Soviet forces to the Dnepr River and the borders of Belorussia.

Operational Assessment

Equipped with an almost completely revitalized force structure manned by an increasingly experienced command cadre and guided by new regulations based upon generalized war experiences, the Soviet Army used 1943 to experiment in the operational realm. Of particular importance was the problem of coordinating the more elaborate forces and evolving operational techniques for their use. The Soviets sought to create a capability for conducting large scale offensive operations on a broad front in order to penetrate German defenses in multiple sectors. To achieve the penetrations the Soviets increasingly relied on concentration and the use of tailored shock groups.

From December 1942 to March 1943 the Soviets used rifle forces to produce initial penetrations and mobile groups (tank and mechanized corps) to exploit penetrations and conduct operational maneuver. However, inadequate quantities of artillery and infantry support tanks and improper coordination of forces often forced the Soviets to use their armored mobile groups to complete tactical penetrations. This weakened the tank and mechanized forces and increased their vulnerability when they finally began the exploitation phase. In addition, procedures and techniques for coordinating and supporting exploiting forces were insufficiently developed. In December 1942 the *STAVKA* committed multiple tank and mechanized corps to combat along separate axes. These corps lacked common command and control headquarters, were often unable to support one another, and were deficient in infantry and fire support. Throughout these operations logistical problems and the limited experience of commanders further reduced the effectiveness of these armored exploitation forces.

By February 1943 the Soviets had remedied some of these problems. They created large mobile group headquarters (Mobile Group Popov), reinforced the corps with heavier fire support, and mandated their cooperation with truck-mounted or tank-mounted infantry. However, subsequent experience in the Donbas in February 1943 clearly pointed out the need for an all new *front* level exploitation echelon organized under a single TOE and containing those elements necessary to sustain deep armored operations. The 1943 tank army met this need, and by April the Soviets had fielded five such armies.

By the summer of 1943 the Soviets had developed the force structure and doctrine which, with minor modification, would endure until war's end. Mobile groups of armies (tank and mechanized corps) and *fronts* (tank armies, cavalry-mechanized groups) would develop tactical success into operational success. The Soviet rifle force structure was larger and better organized. The rifle corps link within armies had developed and would continue to mature. In addition, a wide array of larger, more powerful artillery, tank destroyer, and armor units evolved, designed to provide necessary support to rifle forces seeking to produce a penetration and to support deep operations. The logistical structure also expanded, permitting the Soviets to sustain operations to greater depths, although some logistic problems would remain until war's end.

The primary characteristics of 1943 offensive operations were the decisive conduct of the penetration and the subsequent use of maneuver to envelop and encircle the enemy. Successful Soviet use of the envelopment and Soviet mastery of the complexities of coordinating such types of operations, although experimented with in 1943, would be more characteristic of operations in 1944. Unlike the first period of the war, when attack sectors were wide and penetration sectors imprecise, in the second period these sectors were narrow and well defined. The transformation was evident in the course of operations from December 1942 to August 1943. Along the middle Don River the Southwestern Front operated in a sector of about 400 kilometers with its armies in sectors of 145, 84, and 150 kilometers. Concentration of forces in main attack sectors improved with up to 80 percent of army forces massed on 12–15 percent of an army's front. This produced tactical densities of 3–3.5 kilometers of front per rifle division and 70 to 75 guns/mortars and 6 to 8 tanks per kilometer of front.

In the Donbas the Southwestern Front attacked on a front of 350 kilometers and armies operated on frontages of 60, 130, 100 and 50 kilometers. The Voronezh Front advanced on a front of about 300 kilometers with its armies in sectors of 60–80 kilometers each. However, operational densities fell because of the general erosion of unit strengths.

In August 1943 *fronts* attacked in sectors 180 to 200 kilometers wide and armies in 20 to 35 kilometer sectors, with *front* penetration sectors 25 to 30 kilometers wide and army penetration sectors 6 to 12 kilometers wide. Consequently, tactical densities in penetration sectors increased to

2.5 to 3 kilometers per rifle division and 150–180 guns/mortars and 30 to 40 tanks per kilometer of front.

Operational formations also evolved. During the winter offensive of 1942–1943 *fronts* deployed in a single echelon and usually maintained a small combined arms reserve. However, the single echelon was stronger than it had been in early 1942, and it sometimes included a tank army of mixed composition, as in the Middle Don and Khar'kov operations. In the summer of 1943 the Soviets responded to the maturation of German defenses by forming their *fronts* in two echelons with the mobile groups (tank army) following the first echelon on the main attack axis. During the winter offensive Soviet combined arms armies organized in one or two echelons with an army mobile group (tank or mechanized corps). By the summer of 1943 combined arms armies often formed in a single echelon of rifle corps with artillery and anti-aircraft artillery groups, mobile obstacle detachments, and reserves in order to fulfill the close mission of the *front* at depths of from 60 to 90 kilometers. Before launching the offensive, armies increasingly used cover and deception and more refined techniques for operational reconnaissance.

Throughout 1943 mobile groups increased in importance and expanded the scope of their offensive operations. The Soviets usually planned to commit army and *front* mobile groups on the first day of the offensive in order to complete the tactical penetration and to exploit the penetration. The Soviet ability to commit these forces as planned improved throughout the period. By August tank armies experimented with uninterrupted operations deep in the operational depth (100 to 120 kilometers), and these first experiences (Belgorod–Khar'kov) served as a basis for subsequent use of tank armies, singly or in combination. In sectors where mobile groups were not available, *front* and army commanders used second echelons to develop the attack, although at a slower pace.

Soviet use of artillery and air power in offensive operations markedly improved in 1943 because of the development of the concept of the artillery and air offensive and the fielding of larger and more numerous support units. The Soviets used artillery more systematically by forming artillery groups under centralized control at higher levels of command and by effecting better coordination of air support, in particular between mobile units and air units. However, air-ground coordination in 1943 remained spotty and fragile. The centrally controlled artillery offensive provided closer support of ground troops by subdividing army artillery groups into support groups for first echelon rifle corps. Fires were designed to precede the attack, accompany the attack through the tactical defenses, and provide artillery coverage for the advance into the operational depths. The aviation offensive provided similar phasing of air support throughout the duration of the offensive.

During offensive operations to an increasing extent the Soviets regrouped forces and tailored them to meet the concrete requirements of the operation. Regrouping during the Stalingrad and Middle Don operations (2d Guards Army, four tank corps, the creation of 1st Guards Army) materially contributed to Soviet success. Regrouping was very limited during the winter offensive because of the haste necessary in planning and the constantly changing situation. The negative outcome of that operation underscored the necessity of careful regrouping before each offensive operation. In August 1943 the Soviets resumed the shifting and tailoring of forces on a large scale (such as the forward deployment of the Steppe Front and the shifting of artillery assets during early stages of the Belgorod–Khar'kov Operation). Regrouping during offensive operations (47th Army, 4th Guards Army, 5th Guards Tank Army) allowed the Soviets to switch the impetus of attack to secondary directions or to repulse German counterattacks.

Throughout 1943 the Soviets increased their use of forward detachments, in particular in advance of mobile forces to increase attack and pursuit tempos. Forward detachments would race ahead of main forces and secure key terrain features, river crossings and road junctions, and hold them until the arrival of the main force. The technique worked well in the Middle Don operation, but in the Donbas it had less success because Soviet tank forces were fragmented and of limited strength. The Soviets used the technique at Belgorod–Khar'kov, although in that operation forward detachments tended to become overextended. Thus, south of Bogodukhov the Germans smashed the relatively isolated forward detachments of 1st Tank Army and hence inhibited the future operations of that army.

Soviet command and control of operational forces improved throughout 1943 with the reintroduction of the rifle corps link and use of better communications security (though still weak, by Soviet admission). The Soviets deployed command posts closer to operating troops by using main and reserve command posts, secondary command posts, and observation points.

However, while the scale of operations grew and tempos of advance increased, the corresponding growth of German defenses limited the scale of Soviet offensive success as did the systematic German destruction of the regions they abandoned.

Tactical Assessment

During this period Soviet tactics broke away from the linear forms of the earlier war years when forces were more equally distributed across the front, and Soviet commanders began to mass forces in distinct sectors and rely on more secret and rapid maneuver. In accordance with Order

No. 306 and the 1942 *Field Regulations*, the Soviets launched the Stalingrad operation with rifle divisions attacking in a single echelon of regiments against shallow and relatively weak enemy defenses. A rifle division in the army main attack sector attacked on a frontage of 4 to 5 kilometers (regiment 1.5 to 2 kilometers, battalion 500 to 700 meters). Reinforced by artillery and infantry support tanks, the division was to achieve an immediate mission to a depth of 4 kilometers and a subsequent mission to a depth of 20 kilometers in the course of a single day (the entire tactical depth of the defense). This depth turned out to be excessive, and divisions seldom accomplished their missions.

By the time of the Middle Don Operation changes were already occurring. There divisions in army main attack sectors advanced in two echelons of regiments on a frontage of roughly 3 to 4 kilometers. During the winter offensive, however, division frontages again expanded because of the weakening of operational formations. By the summer of 1943 enemy defenses were deeper and better prepared. Thus, the Soviets decreased rifle divisions missions to 3 to 4 kilometers of depth for immediate missions and 12 to 15 kilometers for the mission of the day. To accomplish these missions, divisions in main attack sectors were more deeply echeloned, and the attack sector decreased to about 3 kilometers (in some cases at Belgorod–Khar'kov 2 kilometers). This produced a correspondingly higher tactical density.

Tactical combat by August 1943 involved greater use of maneuver, increased reliance on night operations, and more systematic reconnaissance. By the summer of 1943 divisions conducted reconnaissance using a reinforced rifle battalion from each first echelon regiment. Several days prior to the main attack these battalions conducted local attacks to determine enemy defensive dispositions, clarify the enemy intent to hold those positions, and to avoid firing an artillery preparation on weakly held enemy positions.

Soviet tactical use of artillery, tanks, and self-propelled artillery also became more sophisticated. Although infantry support artillery groups (*poderzhka pekhoty*) of divisions supported each first echelon regiment, and long range artillery groups (*dalnyi deistvii*) supported each division and rifle corps, an increasing number of infantry support artillery groups were subordinated directly to regimental commanders. The Soviets also assigned an increased number of tanks and self-propelled guns to first echelon rifle regiments operating on main attack axes. Tank brigades and regiments and self-propelled artillery regiments were echeloned in support of rifle divisions and rifle corps beginning in the summer of 1943 to provide direct assault and covering fire for advancing infantry units. Engineer support for rifle divisions also doubled in 1943, thus improving jumping-off positions, clearance of obstacles, and installation and removal of minefields. The cumulative effect of this increased fire and engineer support was an improved capability on the part of rifle divisions to overcome the first two enemy defensive positions. However, limited quantities of infantry support tanks and the reduced effectiveness of artillery fire at greater ranges left enemy third positions intact. Thus, army mobile groups often had to overcome enemy third defensive positions and the second defensive belt by attack from the march. The Soviets crossed water obstacles by makeshift means or by using forward detachments to seize bridges and crossing sites from the march.

Soviet tactical command and control improved through greater use of radios, vehicles, aircraft, and command points near the front. Armored forces often created special operational staff groups to control mobile operations at great distances. Especially important was the assembly of all participating force commanders at a single command post.

Soviet Leadership

Improvements in Soviet force capabilities in 1943 paralleled the general improvement in leadership within the Red Army, in particular at the operational level. Leadership improved in part because of the war experiences of Soviet commanders and in part because of the four month operational pause after March 1943. The tank brigade commanders of late 1941 and early 1942 became the tank corps commanders of late 1942 and the tank army commanders of 1943 (Rotmistrov, Kravchenko, Katukov). Division commanders of 1941 and corps commanders of early 1943 became the army commanders of later years. Those who learned – and survived – commanded until war's end. While Soviet commanders were still hard pressed to match the tactical prowess and expertise of German commanders, at the operational level (*front*-army) commanders emerged who could fight German commanders on an equal footing. This fact, combined with the growing strength and sophistication of the Soviet Army force structure, portended ill for German fortunes.

Soviet Problems

Amidst this generally improving climate, there were still gnawing problems which the Soviet military had to address. Some of these were old, a product of the army of 1941; and some were new, a product of the changing nature of the war. Some leaders were thrust into command positions for which they were not prepared (Kulik). Some were still inhibited by the specter of Stalin and failed to display necessary flexibility. The Soviets still had much to learn about the full coordination of combined arms (armor, artillery, engineers, and infantry), particularly in the conduct of deep operations. Much testing was necessary in order to instill in commanders the flexibility necessary to carry out deep offensives. This required a balance between initiative and obedience that was hard to achieve. Some commanders inclined toward the latter (Rybalko at Khar'kov) while many evidenced a degree of initiative that bordered on recklessness (for example, Katukov at Bogodukhov, Vatutin in the Donbas). It would involve several operations of the scale of Belgorod–Khar'kov for the Soviets to begin mastering this problem. Soviet equipment immeasurably improved, in particular armor and artillery where the Soviets stressed simplicity, durability, and quantity (such as the T-34). The Soviet lack of a true armored infantry vehicle severely inhibited Soviet armored operations until war's end and gave the Germans a marked tactical edge. Other problems like that of logistical support would persist until war's end.

The German Army at Mid War

From the German perspective, during the period from December 1942 to August 1943, the pendulum of German fortunes swung wildly from near disaster in December, January, and February, to victory in February and March, to disaster again in July and August. During the winter the Germans avoided wholesale defeat largely due to the flexibility and initiative of commanders at all levels, the high cohesion and morale of units, and a deeper understanding by von Manstein of the nature of operations. German commanders at the tactical level performed stunning feats to forestall even larger operational disasters than occurred from December to February. Of particular significance during the winter was the erosion of German strength, especially the strength of those experienced mobile forces which had produced victory for Germany earlier in the war.

An inhibiting factor throughout this period was the interference of Hitler which adversely affected German flexibility and stifled operational imagination. Yet, the German military command, which had lived with Hitler during victorious years and shared the glory of those victories had also to share the fruits and gloom of defeat.

In the summer, after intense preparations and at the insistence of Hitler, Germany made a last attempt to regain the initiative. However, the pause in operations from April to July, accepted by the Germans in order to rebuild their forces, permitted the Soviets to prepare for the offensive and to inflict a disastrous defeat on the German Army. The German defeat at Kursk and the subsequent Soviet counteroffensive deprived the German Army of the capability of launching future major offensives. Likewise, it seriously hindered the German ability to defend against ever larger and better equipped Soviet forces.

The transitional year of 1943 was decisive for the Soviet war effort. Seizing the strategic initiative, the Soviets would never again lose it. By year's end, the Soviet force structure had matured to the form it would emerge in at war's end. Only minor adjustments to that structure would occur in 1944 and 1945. The operational failures of 1943 produced smoother operations in 1944. The patient conduct of the strategic defense of 1943 insured that ensuing years would be offensive ones. The *front* and multi-*front* offensives of 1943 paved the way for the successive offensives of 1944 and the simultaneous offensives of 1945. Operational and tactical techniques the Soviets tested and improved in 1943, they refined and perfected in 1944 and 1945. The elementary education which the Red Army received in 1941–1942 gave way to the secondary education of 1943. In 1944 and 1945 the Soviets would accomplish graduate and postgraduate study in the conduct of war.

1

APPENDIX
Order of Battle: Middle Don Operation
December 1942

SOVIET FORCES

Voronezh Front

```
6th Army  Lt. Gen. F.M. Kharitonov
   15th Rifle Corps  Maj. Gen. P.F. Privalov
     172d Rifle Division  Col G.S. Sorokin
     350th Rifle Division  Maj. Gen. A.P. Grishchenko
     267th Rifle Division  Col. A.K. Kudryashov, 18 Dec - Col. V.A. Geramisov
  127th Rifle Division  Col. G.M. Zaitsev
  160th Rifle Division
   8th Artillery Division (9 artillery regiments)
   17th Tank Corps  Maj. Gen. P.P. Poluboyarov - 168 tanks (98 T-34, 70 T-70)
      66th Tank Brigade
      67th Tank Brigade
     174th Tank Brigade
      31st Motorized Rifle Brigade
  115th Tank Brigade
   82d Separate Tank Regiment
  212th Separate Tank Regiment
    5 tank destroyer artillery regiments
    2 antiaircraft artillery regiments
    3 multiple rocket launcher regiments
    5 separate multiple rocket launcher batteries
    3d Mixed Aviation Corps (support)

  Strength - 60,200 men
             250 tanks
             966 guns/mortars
```

Southwestern Front

```
1st Guards Army  Lt. Gen. V.I. Kuznetsov
   4th Guards Rifle Corps  Maj. Gen. N.A. Gagen
      35th Guards Rifle Division  Col. I. Ya. Kulagin (13,049 men)
      41st Guards Rifle Division  Maj. Gen. N.P. Ivanov
     195th Rifle Division  Col. V. P. Karuna
   6th Guards Rifle Corps  Maj. Gen. I.P. Alferov
     38th Guards Rifle Division
     44th Guards Rifle Division  Maj. Gen. V.A. Kupriyanov
      1st Rifle Division  Maj. Gen. A.I. Semenov
 153d Rifle Division
   9th Artillery Division (7 artillery regiments), arrived late;
      only 2 regiments present
   4th Artillery Division (PVO) (6 antiaircraft artillery regiments)
  18th Tank Corps  Maj. Gen. B.S. Bakharov - approx 160 tanks
     110th Tank Brigade
     170th Tank Brigade
     181st Tank Brigade
      32d Motorized Rifle Brigade
  24th Tank Corps  Maj. Gen. V.M. Badanov   - 159 tanks
      4th Guards Tank Brigade
      54th Tank Brigade
     130th Tank Brigade
      24th Motorized Rifle Brigade
```

25th Tank Corps Maj. Gen. P.P. Pavlov - approx 160 tanks
- 111th Tank Brigade
- 162d Tank Brigade
- 175th Tank Brigade
- 16th Motorized Rifle Brigade

126th Separate Tank Regiment
141st Separate Tank Regiment
407th Tank Destroyer Regiment
12 - M-30 MRL battalions
3d Mixed Aviation Corps (support)

<u>Strength</u> 110,796 men
504 tanks
1,523 guns/mortars

3d Guards Army Lt. Gen. D.D. Lelyushenko (average division strength - 7000 men)
- 14th Guards Rifle Corps Maj. Gen. F.E. Sheverdin
  - 159th Rifle Division Col. M.B. Anashkin
  - 203d Rifle Division Col. I.F. Zdanovich
  - 266th Rifle Division Maj. Gen. L.V. Betoshnikov
  - 14th Guards Rifle Division Maj. Gen. A.S. Gryaznov
- 197th Rifle Division Maj. Gen. M.I. Zaporozhsenko
- 278th Rifle Division Col. D.P. Monakhov
- 50th Guards Rifle Division Maj. Gen. A.I. Belov
- 90th Separate Rifle Brigade
- 94th Separate Rifle Brigade Col. I.A. Kranov
  - 5 artillery regiments
  - 8 tank destroyer artillery regiments
  - 4 antiaircraft artillery regiments
  - 2 mortar regiments
- 58th Guards Mortar Regiment
- 1st Guards Mechanized Corps Lt. Gen. I.N. Russiyanov
  - 1st Guards Mechanized Brigade
  - 2d Guards Mechanized Brigade
  - 3d Guards Mechanized Brigade
  - 16th Guards Tank Regiment
  - 17th Guards Tank Regiment
- 22d Motorized Rifle Brigade
- 243d Separate Tank Regiment
- 114th Separate Tank Regiment
- 119th Separate Tank Regiment
- 1st Mixed Aviation Corps (support)

<u>Strength</u> - approx 110,000 men
234 tanks
1,321 guns mortars

5th Tank Army Lt. Gen. Romanenko
- 40th Guards Rifle Division
- 47th Guards Rifle Division
- 119th Rifle Division Col. I. Ya. Kulgin
- 321st Rifle Division Maj. Gen. I.A. Makarenko
- 333d Rifle Division
- 346th Rifle Division
  - 5 artillery regiments
  - 6 tank destroyer regiments
  - 6 antiaircraft artillery regiments
  - 2 mortar regiments
  - 2 multiple rocket launcher regiments
- 1st Tank Corps
  - 89th Tank Brigade
  - 117th Tank Brigade
  - 159th Tank Brigade
  - 44th Motorized Rifle Brigade

8th Cavalry Corps Maj. Gen. M.D. Borisov
21st Cavalry Division
55th Cavalry Division
112th Cavalry Division
5th Mechanized Corps Maj. Gen. M.V. Volkov (183 tanks)
45th Mechanized Brigade
49th Mechanized Brigade
50th Mechanized Brigade
168th Tank Regiment
188th Tank Regiment

Strength about 90,000 men
182 tanks
1213 guns/mortars

Total 6A, SW Front

425,476 men (370,000 in armies)
1,170 tanks
5,625 guns/mortars
309 aircraft

GERMAN, ITALIAN, RUMANIAN FORCES

8th Italian Army Gen of Army I. Gariboldi
2d Army Corps Gen. G. Zanghieri
5th Infantry Division "Cosseria" Gen. D. Gazzale
3d Infantry Division "Ravena" Gen. F. Dupont
318th Infantry Regiment (G) (132 guns)
"23 March" Blackshirt Brigade (6 battalions)
14th Police Regiment (G)
1 corps artillery regiment
35th Army Corps Gen. F. Zingales
9th Motorized Division "Pasubio" Gen. G. Boselli
298th Infantry Division (G) (525, 526, 527 IRs) (156 guns)
"3 January" Blackshirt Brigade (6 battalions)
1 corps artillery regiment
29th A y Corps
52d Motorized Division "Torino" Gen. R. Lerici
3d Infantry Division "Celere" Gen. E. de Blasio (170 guns)
2d Infantry Division "Sforzesca" Gen. C. Pellegrini (50 tanks)
57th Tank Battalion
1 corps artillery regiment
Alpine Corps Gen. G. Nasci
2d Alpine Division "Tridentina" Gen. L. Reverberi
3d Alpine Division "Julia" Gen. U. Ricagno
4th Alpine Division "Cuneense" Gen. E. Battisti (216 guns)
156th Infantry Division "Vicenza" Gen. E. Pascolini
Blackshirt Brigade (6 battalions)
1 corps artillery regiment
4 independent heavy artillery batteries
6 independent mortar battalions

Strength 135,000* (100,000 in attack sector)
624 guns (over 75 mm)
50 tanks

*Soviet estimate. Italians official strength at 220,000

A. Abt. Hollidt
- 1st Army Corps
  - 7th Infantry Division (R) (-)
  - 9th Infantry Division (R) (-)
  - 11th Infantry Division (R) (-)
  - 62d Infantry Division (G), regiment
- 17th Army Corps
  - 62d Infantry Division (G) (-)
  - 294th Infantry Division (G)
- 2d Army Corps
  - 22d Panzer Division (G)
  - 1st Panzer Division (R)(-)
  - 7th Cavalry Division (R)(-)
  - 14th Infantry Division (R)(-)

3d Rumanian Army
- Group Spang
  - 619th Security Regiment
  - 354 Group
- Group Stahel
  - 8th Luftwaffe Field Division (18 Dec)
- Group Stumpfeld
  - 3d Army hdqtrs (R)
  - 403d Security Division (-)
  - 1 regiment, 336th Infantry Division (G)
  - 4th Army Corps (R) remnants
  - 5th Army Corps (R) remnants
  - 403d Security Division
  - 213th Security Division

48 Panzer Corps (4th Panzer Army)
- 336th Infantry Division (G) (-)
- 11th Panzer Division (G) (30 tanks - 16 Dec)
- 7th Luftwaffe Field Division (G)
- 24th Panzer Division rear

<u>Strength</u> 60,000 Germans
50,000 Rumanians
110,000

<u>Arrivals</u>

<u>8th Italian Army Sector</u>
- 27th Panzer Division (G) 16 Dec (50 tanks)
- 385th Infantry Division (G) 16 Dec
- 387th Infantry Division (G) 20 Dec
- 24th Panzer Corps headquarters

<u>Strength</u> about 30,000

- 30th Army Corps (Fretter-Pico) 23 Dec
- 3d Mountain Division (G) 23 Dec
- 304th Infantry Division (G) 24 Dec
- 19th Panzer Division (G) 25 Dec

<u>Strength</u> about 35,000

<u>A. Abt. Hollidt Sector</u>
- 306th Infantry Division (G) 21 Dec
- 7th Panzer Division (G) 29 Dec
- 6th Panzer Division (G) 25 Dec
- 11th Panzer Division (G) 22 Dec to Morozovsk
- Group "Pfeiffer" (G) 26 Dec
- 48th Panzer Corps 25 Dec to Morozovsk

<u>Strength</u> about 40,000 (less 11th PD)

Correlation of Forces initial and reinforcements

8th Italian Army		6th Army / 1st Guards Army
	100,000	171,000
Reinforcements	70,000	30,000
A. Abt. Hollidt / 3d Rum Army		**3d Guards Army / 5th Tank Army**
	110,000	200,000
Reinforcements	40,000	30,000
Total (initial)	220,000	Total (initial) 371,000
Reinforcements	110,000	Reinforcements 60,000

2, 3

APPENDIX
Order of Battle: Khar'kov-Donbas Operation and Manstein's Counterattack
January – March 1943

SOVIET FORCES

Voronezh Front Col. Gen. F.I. Golikov

40th Army Lt. Gen. K.S. Moskalenko
- 100th Rifle Division Maj. Gen. F.I. Perkhorovich
- 183d Rifle Division Maj. Gen. A.S. Kostitsin (4 Mar to 6 A)
- 305th Rifle Division Col. I.A. Danilovich (17 Feb to 3 TA, 28 Feb to 69 A)
- 309th Rifle Division Maj. Gen. M.I. Men'shikov
- 340th Rifle Division Maj. Gen. S.S. Martirosyan (4 Mar to 6 A)
- 107th Rifle Division Maj. Gen. P.M. Bezhko (4 Mar to 6 A)
- 303d Rifle Division Col. K.E. Fedorovsky (12 Feb to 38 A)
- 25th Guards Rifle Division Maj. Gen. P.M. Shafarenko (19 Feb to 3 TA)
- 129th Rifle Brigade
- 4th Tank Corps (5th Guards TC) Maj. Gen. A.G. Kravchenko (about 50 tanks)
  - 45th Tank Brigade
  - 64th Tank Brigade
  - 102d Tank Brigade
  - ____ Motorized Rifle Brigade
- 116th Tank Brigade
- 192d Tank Brigade
- 59th Separate Tank Regiment (9 Feb)
- 60th " " " "
- 61st " " " "

Strength - approx 90,000 men
100 tanks

69th Army Lt. Gen. M.I. Kazakov
- 161st Rifle Division Maj. Gen. P.V. Tertyshny
- 180th Rifle Division Maj. Gen. I.Ya. Maloshitsky
- 219th Rifle Division Maj. Gen. V.P. Kotel'nikov
- 270th Rifle Division Col. N.D. Polyakov
- 37th Rifle Brigade Col. P.G. Moskovsky
- 137th Tank Brigade
- 292d Tank Regiment

Strength - approx 40,000 men
50 tanks

3d Tank Army General P.S. Rybalko
- 12th Tank Corps Maj. Gen. M.I. Zen'kovich
  - 30th Tank Brigade
  - 97th Tank Brigade
  - 106th Tank Brigade
  - 13th Motorized Rifle Brigade
- 15th Tank Corps Maj. Gen. V.A. Koptsov (killed 3 Mar)
  - 88th Tank Brigade

113th Tank Brigade
195th Tank Brigade
__ Motorized Rifle Brigade
6th Guards Cavalry Corps Maj. Gen. S.V. Sokolov
48th Guards Rifle Division Maj. Gen. N.M. Mokovchuk
62d Guards Rifle Division Maj. Gen. G.M. Zaitsev
111th Rifle Division Col. S.P. Khoteev
184th Rifle Division Col. S.T. Koida
179th Tank Brigade
201st Tank Regiment

Reinforcements

25th Guards Rifle Division (19 Feb)
253d Rifle Division (23 Feb)
219th Rifle Division (25 Feb)
1st Czech Battalion (1 Mar)
19th Rifle Division Col. G.A. Golilitsyn (1 Mar)
86th Tank Brigade (1 Mar)
17th Rifle Brigade (NKVD) (1 Mar)
1st Guards Cavalry Corps (1, 2, 7th Cav Divs) (13 Mar)
113th Rifle Division (10 Mar)

Strength 57,577 men
165 tanks

Tank Strength - 29 Jan - 165
14 Feb - 100
18 Feb - 110
27 Feb - 39
16 Mar - 22

Front Reserve
86th Tank Brigade
150th Tank Brigade
3d Guards Tank Corps (150 tanks)
2d Guards Tank Corps (175 tanks)

Voronezh Front (40th, 69th, 3d Tank Armies) (less 38 and 60th Armies)

Strength 190,000 men
315 tanks (less reserve)

Southwestern Front General N.F. Vatutin

6th Army Lt. Gen. F.M. Kharitonov
15th Rifle Corps
6th Rifle Division
172d Rifle Division
350th Rifle Division
267th Rifle Division
106th Rifle Brigade
115th Tank Brigade
212d Tank Regiment

Strength 40,000
40 tanks

1st Guards Army - Lt. Gen. V.I. Kuznetsov
4th Guards Rifle Corps Maj. Gen. N.A. Gagen (19 Feb to 6A)
35th Guards Rifle Division Col. I.Ya. Kulagin
41st Guards Rifle Division Maj. Gen. N.P. Ivanov (wounded 26 Feb)
195th Rifle Division Col. V.P. Karuna
6th Guards Rifle Corps Maj. Gen. I.P. Alferov
44th Guards Rifle Division
58th Guards Rifle Division
78th Rifle Division
244th Rifle Division

Strength 70,000 men

Mobile Group Popov: Lt. Gen. M.M. Popov
- 4th Guards Tank Corps - Maj. Gen. P.P. Poluboyarov
  - 12th Guards Tank Brigade
  - 13th Guards Tank Brigade
  - 14th Guards Tank Brigade
  - 3d Guards Motorized Rifle Brigade
- 3d Tank Corps - Maj. Gen. M.D. Sinenko
- 10th Tank Corps - Maj. Gen. V.G. Burkov
- 18th Tank Corps
- 57th Guards Rifle Division
- 38th Guards Rifle Division
- 52d Rifle Division
- 9th Tank Brigade
- 11th Tank Brigade
- 7th Ski Brigade
- 5th Ski Brigade (18 Feb)
- 10th Ski Brigade (18 Feb)

Strength 55,000 men
212 tanks

Tank Strength

25 Jan	212
30 Jan	180
7 Feb	140
16 Feb	145
21 Feb	25
22 Feb	50
26 Feb	50

3d Guards Army Lt. Gen. D.D. Lelyushenko
- 14th Guards Rifle Corps
  - 14th Guards Rifle Division
  - 50th Guards Rifle Division
  - 61st Guards Rifle Division
- 18th Guards Rifle Corps
  - 59th Guards Rifle Division
  - 243d Rifle Division
  - 279th Rifle Division
- 60th Guards Rifle Division
- 266th Rifle Division (16 Feb to 5 TA)
- 203d Rifle Division (16 Feb to 5 TA)
- 2d Guards Tank Corps Maj. Gen. V.M. Badanov
- 23d Tank Corps (16 Feb to 5 TA)
- 2d Tank Corps Maj. Gen. H.F. Popov
- 1st Guards Mechanized Corps
- 8th Guards Cavalry Corps (21, 55, 112 Cav Divs) Maj. Gen. M.D. Borisov

Strength 100,000 men
110 tanks

5th Tank Army Lt. Gen. I.T. Shlemin
- 321st Rifle Division
- 47th Guards Rifle Division
- 333d Rifle Division
- 266th Rifle Division (16 Feb)
- 203d Rifle Division (16 Feb)
- 23d Tank Corps (16 Feb)

Strength 40,000 men

Front reserve
- 1st Guards Tank Corps Maj. Gen. A.V. Kukushkin 150 tanks on 19 Feb
- 25th Tank Corps Maj. Gen. P.P. Pavlov
- 1st Guards Cavalry Corps

Front strength 320,000
362 tanks (reserve of 267 tanks on 16 Feb)

APPENDICES

GERMAN FORCES

3 February 1943

A. Abt. Lanz
- 24th Panzer Corps
  - 385th Infantry Division
  - 387th Infantry Division
  - 213d Security Division
- 320th Infantry Division
- 298th Infantry Division
- regiment, SS Panzer Division "Das Reich"
- Corps Cramer
  - Panzer Grenadier Division "Grossdeutschland"
  - 2 regiments, 168th Infantry Division
  - 1 regiment, 88th Infantry Division
  - remnants 1st, 10th, 13th Infantry, 23d Light, 1st Panzer Division (H)

Strength - approx 50,000 Germans

OKH Reserves (enroute)
- SS Panzer Corps
  - SS Panzer Division "Das Reich"
  - SS Panzer Division "Liebstandarte Adolf Hitler"

Strength - approx 20,000

1st Panzer Army
- 40th Panzer Corps Headquarters
- 30th Army Corps
  - Group Kreising (3d Mountain Division)
  - 2 regiments, 335th Infantry Division
- 3d Panzer Corps
  - 7th Panzer Division
  - 19th Panzer Division w/Lehr-Regiment 901
  - 27th Panzer Division

Strength - approx 40,000

A. Abt. Hollidt

- 29th Army Corps
  - Group 79 (2d Rum Army Corps hqdts)
  - Group Security Regiment 177
- Group Mieth
  - 384th Infantry Division
  - 336th Infantry Division
- 17th Army Corps
  - 62d Infantry Division
  - 306th Infantry Division
  - 294th Infantry Division
  - 8th Luftwaffe Field Division
- 48th Panzer Corps
  - 5th Panzer Division
  - 304th Infantry Division
  - Group Schuldt
  - Group von Hundersdord
  - 22d Panzer Division

Strength 100,000

4th Panzer Army
- 5th Army Corps
  - 444th Security Division
  - Kos Regiment

111th Infantry Division
15th Luftwaffe Field Division
57th Panzer Corps
23d Panzer Division
SS Panzer Grenadier Division "Viking"
17th Panzer Division
3d Panzer Division
16th Panzer Grenadier Division
11th Panzer Division

<u>Strength</u> 70,000

11 February 1943

A. Abt. Lanz

24th Panzer Corps
385th Infantry Division
387th Infantry Division
213d Security Division
Corps Cramer
Panzer Grenadier Division "Grossdeutschland"
168th Infantry Division
1 regiment, 88th Infantry Division
SS Panzer Corps
SS Panzer Division "Das Reich"
SS Panzer Division "Liebstandarte Adolf Hitler"
298th Infantry Division
320th Infantry Division

1st Panzer Army
30th Army Corps
335th Infantry Division
Group Kreising (3d Mountain Division; regiment, 304th Infantry Division)
3d Panzer Corps
17th Panzer Division
Group Schmidt (19th Panzer Division; Lehr-Regiment 901)
one regiment, 7th Panzer Division (with 27th Panzer Division)
3d Panzer Division
40th Panzer Corps
11th Panzer Division; regiment, 333d Infantry Division
7th Panzer Division
2 regiments, 333d Infantry Division
SS Panzer Grenadier Division "Viking"

A. Abt. Hollidt

Group Mieth
384th Infantry Division
336th Infantry Division
17th Army Corps
62d Infantry Division
8th Luftwaffe Field Division
294th Infantry Division
48th Panzer Corps
6th Panzer Division (-)
Group Schuldt
306th Infantry Division
302d Infantry Division
2 regiments, 304th Infantry Division
1 regiment, 6th Panzer Division (with 22d Panzer Division)

4th Panzer Army
5th Army Corps
444th Security Division
Kos. Regiment

57th Panzer Corps
- 23d Panzer Division
- 16th Panzer Grenadier Division
- 15th Luftwaffe Field Division
- 111th Infantry Division

29th Army Corps
- Group 79
- Group 177

16 February 1943

A. Abt. Lanz

SS Panzer Corps
- SS Panzer Division "Das Reich"
- SS Panzer Division "Liebstandarte Adolf Hitler"
- 320th Infantry Division
- 1 regiment, SS Panzer Division "Totenkopf"

Corps Raus
- Panzer Grenadier Division "Grossdeutschland"
- 168th Infantry Division
- 1 regiment, 88th Infantry Division

SS Panzer Division "Totenkopf" (-)

1st Panzer Army

30th Army Corps
- Group Kreising (3d Mountain Division)
- 335th Infantry Division

3d Panzer Corps
- Group Schmidt (19th Panzer Division, Lehr-Regiment 901)
- 7th Panzer Division (with 27th Panzer Division)
- 3d Panzer Division
- 17th Panzer Division

40th Panzer Corps
- 11th Panzer Division; 1 regiment, 333d Infantry Division; 19th Panzer Division (part); 7th Panzer Division (part)
- 7th Panzer Division
- 333d Infantry Division (-)
- SS Panzer Grenadier Division "Viking"

A. Abt. Hollidt

Group Mieth
- 384th Infantry Division
- 336th Infantry Division

17th Army Corps
- 62d Infantry Division
- 8th Luftwaffe Field Division
- 294th Infantry Division

48th Panzer Corps
- 6th Panzer Division
- 306th Infantry Division
- Group Schuldt
- 302d Infantry Division
- 304th Infantry Division
- 6th Panzer Division (with 22d Panzer Division)

24 February 1943

A. Abt. Kempf

Corps Raus
Panzer Grenadier Division "Grossdeutschland"
1 regiment, SS Panzer Division "Totenkopf"
320th Infantry Division
167th Infantry Division
SS Panzer Division "Liebstandarte Adolf Hitler"
168th Infantry Division
1 regiment, 88th Infantry Division

4th Panzer Army
57th Panzer Corps (headquarters)
48th Panzer Corps
17th Panzer Division
6th Panzer Division (-)
153d Field Training Division
SS Panzer Corps
SS Panzer Division "Das Reich"
SS Panzer Division "Totenkopf" (-)
15th Infantry Division
Group Steinbauer

4th Panzer Army
5th Army Corps
454th, 444th Security Divisions
Kos. Regiment
111th Infantry Division
57th Panzer Corps
23d Panzer Division
16th Panzer Grenadier Division
15th Luftwaffe Field Division
29th Army Corps
Group 79
Group 177

1st Panzer Army
30th Army Corps
Group Kreising (3d Mountain Division)
Group Schuldt
304th Infantry Division
335th Infantry Division
3d Panzer Corps
19th Panzer Division; 1 regiment, 7th Panzer Division
(with 27th Panzer Division)
3d Panzer Division; 1 regiment, 333d Infantry Division
40th Panzer Corps
11th Panzer Division; 2 regiments, 333d Infantry Division
SS Panzer Grenadier Division "Viking"
7th Panzer Division (-)

A. Abt. Hollidt

5th Army Corps
454th, 444th Security Divisions
Kos. Regiment
29th Army Corps
15th Luftwaffe Field Division
16th Panzer Grenadier Division
79th Infantry Division
23d Panzer Division
Group Mieth
384th Infantry Division
336th Infantry Division

17th Army Corps
1 regiment, 6th Panzer Division (with 22d Panzer Division)
294th Infantry Division
306th Infantry Division
302d Infantry Division

Arriving
46th Infantry Division
198th Infantry Division
332d Infantry Division

2d Army
7th Army Corps
255th Infantry Division
57th Infantry Division
4th Panzer Division

4 March 1943

A. Abt. Kempf
Panzer Grenadier Division "Grossdeutschland"
Corps Raus
1 regiment, SS Panzer Division "Totenkopf"
167th Infantry Division
168th Infantry Division
320th Infantry Division
1 regiment, 88th Infantry Division

4th Panzer Army
57th Panzer Corps
15th Infantry Division
17th Panzer Division
48th Panzer Corps
6th Panzer Division
11th Panzer Division
SS Panzer Corps
SS Panzer Division "Das Reich"
SS Panzer Division "Totenkopf" (-)
SS Panzer Division "Liebstandarte Adolf Hitler"
Group Steihbauer: 1 regiment, 46th Infantry Division;
1 regiment, 153d Field Training Division
1st Panzer Army
30th Army Corps
304th Infantry Division, Group Schuldt
Group Kreising and 1 regiment, 3d Mountain Division
335th Infantry Division
3d Panzer Corps
62d Infantry Division (with 8th Luftwaffe Field Division)
19th Panzer Division; 1 regiment 7th Panzer Division
(with 27th Panzer Division); Lehr Regiment 901
3d Panzer Division; 333d Infantry Division
40th Panzer Corps
SS Panzer Grenadier Division "Viking"
7th Panzer Division (-)

A. Abt. Hollidt
5th Army Corps
454th, 444th Security Division
111th Infantry Division
29th Army Corps
15th Luftwaffe Field Division
79th Infantry Division
16th Panzer Grenadier Division
Group Mieth
23d Panzer Division
384th Infantry Division
336th Infantry Division

17th Army corps
294th Infantry Division
306th Infantry Division
302d Infantry Division
6th Panzer Division (with 22d Panzer Division)
2d Army
7th Army Corps
75th Infantry Division
52d Army Corps
57th Infantry Division
332d Infantry Division
4th Panzer Division
255th Infantry Division

17 March 1943

A. Abt. Kempf
Corps Raus
320th Infantry Division
167th Infantry Division
Panzer Grenadier Division "Grossdeutschland"
168th Infantry Division

4th Panzer Army
57th Panzer Corps
15th Infantry Division
17th Panzer Division
48th Panzer Corps
106th Infantry Division
6th Panzer Division
11th Panzer Division
SS Panzer Corps
SS Panzer Division "Das Reich"
SS Panzer Division "Totenkopf"
SS Panzer Division "Liebstandarte Adolf Hitler"
39th Infantry Division
1 regiment, 153d Field Training Division

1st Panzer Army
30th Army Corps
304th Infantry Division; Group Schuldt
Group Kreising; 1 regiment 3d Mountain Division
335th Infantry Division
3d Panzer Corps
62d Infantry Division
3d Panzer Division; Lehr-Regiment 901
333d Infantry Division
40th Panzer Corps
SS Panzer Grenadier Division "Viking"
7th Panzer Division
19th Panzer Division
3d Mountain Division

A. Abt. Hollidt
24th Panzer Corps
Koruck 200; 444th; 445th Security Divisions
111th Infantry Division
29th Army Corps
15th Luftwaffe Field Division
16th Panzer Grenadier Division
Group Mieth
23d Panzer Division
336th Infantry Division
Group de Salengre

17th Army Corps
294th Infantry Division
306th Infantry Division
302d Infantry Division
Group Burgstaller

2d Army
7th Army Corps (-)
75th Infantry Division

52d Army Corps
57th Infantry Division
332d Infantry Division
255th Infantry Division

4

APPENDIX
Order of Battle: Belgorod–Khar'kov Operation
August 1943

SOVIET FORCES

VORONEZH FRONT
CO General N.F. Vatutin   Frontage: 160 kms
Member of Soviet Lt. Gen. N.S. Khrushchev
C/S Lt. Gen. S. P. Ivanov

38th Army Lt. Gen. N.E. Chibisov
50th Rifle Corps Maj. Gen. S.S. Martirosyan   Frontage: 72 kilometers
38th Rifle Division   Strength: 62,000 men
167th Rifle Division   991 guns/mortars
340th Rifle Division
232d Rifle Division
180th Rifle Division

40th Army Lt. Gen. K.S. Moskalenko
47th Rifle Corps Maj. Gen. A.S. Gryaznov
100th Rifle Corps   Frontage: 32 kilometers
206th Rifle Division   Strength: 50,000 men
52d Rifle Corps Maj. Gen. F.T. Pekhorovich   (70,000 12 Aug)
237th Rifle Division   985 guns/mortars
161st Rifle Division (5 Aug)   340 tanks (+10TC)
309th Rifle Division (7 Aug)
23d Rifle Division (12 Aug)
2d Tank Corps Maj. Gen. A.F. Popov
10th Tank Corps (6 Aug) Maj. Gen. V.M. Alekseev
27th Army Lt. Gen. S.G. Trofimenko
26th Guards Rifle Corps
155th Rifle Division
163d Rifle Division   Frontage: 42 kilometers
166th Rifle Division   Strength: 82,000 men
27th Guards Rifle Corps   1816 guns/mortars
147th Rifle Division   220 tanks (-10TC)
241st Rifle Division
161st Rifle Division (5 Aug to 40 A)
4th Guards Tank Corps - 180 tanks 9 Aug 97 tanks
Maj. Gen. P.P. Poluboyarov
10th Tank Corps (6 Aug to 40 A)
93d Tank Brigade

6th Guards Army Lt. Gen. I.M. Chistyakov   Frontage: 10 kilometers
22d Guards Rifle Corps Maj. Gen I.B. Ibyansky   3 kilometer penetration sector
67th Guards Rifle Division
71st Guards Rifle Division
90th Rifle Division   Strength: 85,000
23d Guards Rifle Corps   1291 guns/mortars
Maj. Gen. P.P. Bakhrameev   180 tanks

51st Guards Rifle Division
52d Guards Rifle Division
53d Guards Rifle Division
5th Guards Tank Corps Maj. Gen. A.G. Kravchenko

5th Guards Army Lt. Gen. A.S. Zhadov
32d Rifle Corps Maj. Gen. A.I. Rodimtsev
13th Guards Rifle Division
66th Guards Rifle Division
97th Guards Rifle Division

Frontage: 16 kilometers
6 kilometer penetration sector
Strength: 85,000
1085 guns/mortars
approx 70 tanks

33d Rifle Corps Maj. Gen. M.I. Kozlov
95th Guards Rifle Division
6th Guards Airborne Division
9th Guards Airborne Division
42d Guards Rifle Division
93d Tank Brigade
28th Tank Regiment
57th Tank Regiment
13th Artillery Penetration Division

1st Tank Army Lt. Gen. M.E. Katukov
6th Tank Corps Maj. Gen. A.L. Getman
31st Tank Corps Maj. Gen. D.Kh Chernienko (killed 18 Aug)
3d Mechanized Corps Maj. Gen. S.M. Krivosnein
28th Tank Destroyer Brigade
316th Guards Mortar Regiment
69th Battalion, 14th Engineer Assault Brigade
138th Antitank Rifle Battalion
139th Antitank rifle Battalion
8th Antiaircraft Artillery Division
71st Motorized Engineer Battalion
69th Engineer Assault Battalion
267th Motorcycle Battalion

Frontage of Commitment: 3 kilometers
Strength: 37,000 men
542 tanks
(417 T34)
27 SP guns
432 guns/mortars
55 BM-8, BM-13 MRLs
3483 vehicles

Tank Strength: 9 Aug 260 tanks/SP guns
11 Aug 268 tanks/27 SPs
12 Aug 134 tanks
17 Aug 160 tanks/SPs
18 Aug 120 tanks/SPs
repaired 657 in operation

5th Guards Tank Army Lt. Gen. P.A. Rotmistrov
18th Tank Corps Col. A.V. Yegorov
29th Tank Corps Maj. Gen. I.F. Kirichenko
5th Guards Mechanized Corps Maj. Gen. B.M. Skvortsov

Frontage of Commitment: 6 kilometers
Strength: 37,000 men
503 tanks
40 SP guns
560 guns/mortars
45 M-13 MRLs
11 Aug 106 tanks
12 Aug 113 tanks
13 Aug 100 tanks
18 Aug 130 tanks (less 5th GMC)
24 Aug 111 tanks (97 T34 - 14 T30)
25 Aug 50 tanks

VORONEZH FRONT STRENGTH

5 Combined arms armies
10 rifle corps
28 rifle divisions
(22 - 1st echelon, 5 - 2d echelon, 1 - reserve)
2 tank armies
8 tank corps (4 separate)
4 separate tank brigades
2 mechanized corps
1 artillery corps
2 artillery divisions
5 antiaircraft artillery divisions
1 guards mortar division
3 separate artillery brigades
4 separate tank destroyer brigades
6 separate tank regiments
8 separate self-propelled artillery regiments
6 separate artillery regiments
18 separate mortar regiments
35 separate tank destroyer artillery regiments
9 separate guards mortar regiments
9 separate antiaircraft regiments
1 engineer sapper brigade (4th)
2 road engineer sapper brigades
1 separate engineer brigade
1 pontoon bridge brigade
17 separate engineer battalions
1 air army
1 separate fighter brigade

693,554 men - total
458,167 combat-armies
1859 tanks
113 self-propelled guns
8728 guns/mortars
2269 field
1491 anti-tank
4408 mortars
560 anti-aircraft
701 multiple rocket launchers

average rifle division strength 7,180 men

STEPPE FRONT
CO General I.S. Konev
Member of Soviet Lt. Gen. I.Z. Susaikov
C/S Lt. Gen. M.V. Zakharov

Frontage: 100 kilometers

53d Army Lt. Gen. I.M. Managarov
252d Rifle Division
28th Guards Rifle Division
116th Rifle Division
84th Rifle Division
214th Rifle Division
233d Rifle Division
299th Rifle Division
35th Tank Regiment
148th Tank Regiment
_____ Tank Regiment
_____ Heavy Tank Regiment
1st Mechanized Corps Maj. Gen. M.D. Solomatin (212 tanks)

Frontage: 8.5 kilometers
Strength: 77,000 men
2088 guns/mortars
291 tanks
11 SP guns

69th Army Lt. Gen. V.D. Kryuchenkin
48th Guards Rifle Corps (20 Aug to 53 A)
89th Guards Rifle Division
305th Rifle Division
183d Rifle Division

Frontage: 21.5 kilometers
Strength: 60,000 men
1006 guns/mortars
about 70 tanks

35th Guards Rifle Corps
105th Rifle Division
375th Rifle Division
93d Guards Rifle Division
94th Guards Rifle Division

7th Guards Army Lt. Gen. M.S. Shumilov
- 49th Rifle Corps
  - 15th Guards Rifle Division
  - 111th Rifle Division
- 25th Guards Rifle Corps
  - 78th Guards Rifle Division
  - 73d Guards Rifle Division
  - 81st Guards Rifle Division
- 24th Guards Rifle Corps
  - 72d Guards Rifle Division
  - 36th Guards Rifle Division
  - 213th Rifle Division

Frontage: 45 kilometers
Strength: 61,000
1250 guns/mortars
about 80 tanks

STEPPE FRONT STRENGTH

3 combined armies (4 on 8 Aug)
5 rifle corps
22 rifle divisions
(17 - 1st echelon, 5 - 2d echelon)
(29 on 8 Aug)
3 separate tank brigades
1 mechanized corps
1 artillery division
3 antiaircraft artillery divisions
1 separate artillery brigade
1 separate tank destroyer brigade
(2 on 8 Aug)
10 separate tank regiments
2 separate self-propelled artillery regiments
2 separate armored trains
3 separate artillery regiments
4 separate mortar regiments
10 separate tank destroyer regiments
5 separate guards mortar regiments
2 separate antiaircraft artillery regiments
1 separate artillery regiment
3 engineer sapper brigades
1 engineer battalion
4 flame engineer battalions
4 antiobstacle-mine battalions
1 air army
2 separate fighter brigades

287,034 men-total
(350,000 on 8 Aug)
198,034 combat-armies
454 tanks
13 self-propelled guns
4881 guns/mortars
1453 field
854 antitank
2152 mortars
422 antiaircraft
66 multiple rocket launchers

average rifle division strength
6,070 men

SOUTHWEST FRONT

57th Army Lt. Gen. N.A. Gagen (8 Aug to Steppe Front)
- 68th Rifle Corps
  - 19th Rifle Division
  - 38th Guards Rifle Division
  - 48th Guards Rifle Division
- 64th Rifle Corps Maj. Gen. G.G. Karzhavin
  - 14th Guards Rifle Division
  - 41st Guards Rifle Division (25 Aug - 2845 men)
  - 52d Rifle Division
  - 113th Rifle Division
- 173d Tank Brigade
- 179th Tank Brigade
  - 1st Tank Destroyer Brigade

Frontage: 50 kilometers
Strength: 60,000 men
109 tanks

STAVKA RESERVE

4th Guards Army Lt. Gen. G.I. Kulik (16 Aug to Voronezh Front)
20th Guards Rifle Corps Maj. Gen. N.I. Biryukov
5th Guards Airborne Division — Strength: 80,000 men
7th Guards Airborne Division — approx 200 tanks
8th Guards Airborne Division
21st Guards Rifle Corps Maj. Gen. P.I. Fomenko
68th Guards Rifle Division
69th Guards Rifle Division — average rifle division
80th Guards Rifle Division — strength
9,000 men

3d Guards Tank Corps Maj. Gen. I.A. Vovchenko

47th Army Lt. Gen. P.P. Korzun (3 Aug to Voronezh Front)
21st Rifle Corps
218th Rifle Division — Strength: 75,000 men
Rifle Division — approx 210 tanks
Rifle Division
23d Rifle Corps
Rifle Division
Rifle Division
Rifle Division
3d Guards Mechanized Corps Maj. Gen. V.T. Obukhov (wounded 19 Aug)
(213 tanks)
Maj. Gen. A.A. Poshkus (19 Aug)

German Forces: 3 August 1943

2d Army - General W. Weiss

VII Army Corps (3 Aug to 4th Panzer Army)
68th Infantry Division
75th Infantry Division
88th Infantry Division
Kampfgruppe 323 Infantry Division

4th Panzer Army - Colonel General H. Hoth

LII Army Corps
167th Infantry Division
255th Infantry Division
332d Infantry Division
6th Panzer Division
19th Panzer Division

XXXXVIII Panzer Corps
57th Infantry Division
11th Panzer Division
7th Panzer Division

A. Abt. Kempf - General W. Kempf

XI Army Corps
168th Infantry Division
198th Infantry Division
106th Infantry Division
320th Infantry Division

XXXXII Army Corps
282d Infantry Division
39th Infantry Division
161st Infantry Division

German Forces: 5 August 1943

4th Panzer Army

VII Army Corps
68th Infantry Division
75th Infantry Division
88th Infantry Division
Kampfgruppe 323d Infantry Division

LII Army Corps
167th Infantry Division
255th Infantry Division
1/3 332d Infantry Division
1/3 57th Infantry Division
6th Panzer Division
19th Panzer Division
1/2 11th Panzer Division

XXXXVIII Panzer Corps
2/3 57th Infantry Division
2/3 332d Infantry Division
7th Panzer Division
1/2 11th Panzer Division.
III Panzer Corps (enroute)

A. Abt. Kempf

XI Army Corps
168th Infantry Division
198th Infantry Division
106th Infantry Division
320th Infantry Division

XXXXII Army Corps
282d Infantry Division
39th Infantry Division
161st Infantry Division
3d Panzer Division (enroute)

German Forces: 14 August 1943

4th Panzer Army

LII Army Corps
Kampfgruppe 255th Infantry Division
Kampfgruppe 332d Infantry Division

VII Army Corps
68th Infantry Division
75th Infantry Division
88th Infantry Division
Kampfgruppe 323d Infantry Division

XXXXVIII Panzer Corps
57th Infantry Division
7th Panzer Division
Kampfgruppe 11th Panzer Division
Kampfgruppe 19th Panzer Division

"Grossdeutschland" Panzer Grenadier Division
Kampfgruppe, 112th Infantry Division
10th Panzer Grenadier Division (enroute)

A. Abt. Kempf

- XI Army Corps
  - *Kampfgruppe* 167th Infantry Division
  - *Kampfgruppe* 168th Infantry Division
  - *Kampfgruppe* 106th Infantry Division
  - *Kampfgruppe* 198th Infantry Division
  - 320th Infantry Division
  - 3d Panzer Division
- XXXXII Army Corps
  - 282d Infantry Division
  - 39th Infantry Division
  - 161st Infantry Division
  - *Kampfgruppe* 6th Panzer Division
- III Panzer Corps
  - SS Panzer Division "Das Reich"
  - SS Panzer Division "Totenkopf"
  - SS Panzer Grenadier Division "Viking"
- XXIV Panzer Corps
  - 223d Infantry Division (enroute)
  - 355th Infantry Division (enroute)

German Forces: 21 August 1943

4th Panzer Army

- LII Army Corps
  - 57th Infantry Division
  - *Kampfgruppe* 112th Infantry Division
  - *Kampfgruppe* 255th Infantry Division
  - *Kampfgruppe* 332d Infantry Division
- VII Army Corps
  - 68th Infantry Division
  - 75th Infantry Division
  - 88th Infantry Division
  - *Kampfgruppe* 323d Infantry Division
- XXIV Panzer Corps
  - 10th Panzer Grenadier Division
  - "Grossdeutschland" Panzer Grenadier Division
  - 7th Panzer Division
- XXXXVIII Panzer Corps
  - *Kampfgruppe* 11th Panzer Division
  - *Kampfgruppe* 19th Panzer Division

8th Army (former *A. Abt.* Kempf)

- XI Army Corps
  - 320th Infantry Division
  - 106th Infantry Division
  - 167th Infantry Division
  - *Kampfgruppe* 168th Infantry Division
  - *Kampfgruppe* 198th Infantry Division
  - 3d Panzer Division
  - 6th Panzer Division

XXXXII Army Corps
- *Kampfgruppe* 282d Infantry Division
- *Kampfgruppe* 39th Infantry Division
- 161st Infantry Division
- 355th Infantry Division
- *Kampfgruppe* 6th Panzer Division

III Panzer Corps
- 223d Infantry Division
- SS Panzer Division "Das Reich"
- SS Panzer Division "Totenkopf"
- SS Panzer Division "Viking"

XXXXVII Panzer Corps (enroute)
- 34th Infantry Division (enroute)

CORRELATION OF FORCES

2d Army (7th Army Corps) 4th Panzer Army			Voronezh Front; 53d Army, Steppe Front
	120,000 men	1:4.5	537,000
	150 tanks	1:13.7	2050 tanks
A. Abt. Kempf			Steppe Front (-53d Army); 57th Army, Southwestern Front
	80,000 men	1:2.3	180,000
			260 tanks
	TOTAL		
Initial Strength	200,000 men	1:3.6	717,000
	150 tanks	1:15	2310 tanks
Reinforcements			
	130,000 men		155,000
	280 tanks		410 tanks
Total Committed			
	330,000 men	1:2.6	872,000
	430 tanks	1:6.3	2720 tanks

Notes

INTRODUCTION

1. A.A. Strokov, ed. *Istoriya voennogo isskustvo* (A history of military art) (Moskva: Voenizdat, 1966), 323–324.
2. S.K. Skorobogatkin, ed., *50 Let vooruzhennykh sil SSSR* (50 Years of the Soviet Armed Forces) (Moskva: Voenizdat, 1968), 269–271.
3. For this process, see *Directive of the General Staff Concerning the Study and Application of War Experience, 9 November 1942, No. 1005216, Inclosure: Instructions Concerning the Study and Application of War Experience in Front and Army Staffs*, translated by US Army General Staff, G-2.
4. Strokov, 389; N.Kh. Bagramyan, ed., *Istoriya voin i voennogo iskusstva* (A history of war and military art) (Moskva: Voenizdat, 1970), 185–186.
5. N.A. Sbytov, "Stavka verkhovnogo glavnokomandovaniya" (The Stavka of the High Command) *Sovetskaya voennaya entsiklopediya* (Soviet military encyclopedia), 1979, 7:511–512. Hereafter cited as *S.V.E.*
6. Strokov, 389–391; Bagramyan, 187–189.
7. A. Radzievsky, "Proryv oborony v pervom periode voiny" (Penetration of a Defense in the First Period of War) *Voenno-istoricheskii zhurnal* (Military-historical journal), March 1972, 17–18. Hereafter cited as *VIZh*.
8. Strokov, 391; Bagramyan, 189–190. More detail found in S. Lototsky, "Iz opyta vedeniya armeiskikh nastupatel'nykh operatsii v gody Velikoi Otechestvennoi voiny" (From the Experience of Conducting Army Offensive Operations in the Years of the Great Patriotic War) *VIZh*, December 1965, 3–14.
9. "Prikaz NKO No. 325 ot 16 Oktyabrya 1942 g" (Order of the Peoples Commissariat of Defense No. 325 of 16 October 1942) *VIZh*, October 1974, 68–73.
10. Bagramyan, 192–193; Strokov, 391–392.
11. "Prikaz NKO No. 306 ot 8 Oktyabrya 1942 g" (The Order of the Peoples Commissariat of Defense No. 306 of 8 October 1942) *VIZh*, September 1974, 62–66.
12. Bagramyan, 193–194; Lototsky, 4–8.

CHAPTER TWO

1. The best Soviet accounts of the Stalingrad operation are K.K. Rokossovsky, ed., *Velikaya pobeda na Volge* (The great victory on the Volga) (Moskva: Voenizdat, 1960); A.M. Samsonov, *Stalingradskaya bitva* (The Stalingrad Battle) (Moskva: Izdatel'stvo Akademii Nauk SSSP, 1960); A. M. Samsonov, ed., *Stalingradskaya epopeya* (The Stalingrad epic), (Moskva: Izdatel'stvo "Nauka," 1968). For the German view see M. Kehrig, *Stalingrad: Analyse und Dokumentation einer Schlacht* (Stalingrad: Analysis and Documentation of a Battle) (Stuttgart: Deutsche Verlags-Anstalt, 1974).
2. A.M. Vasilevsky, *Delo vsei zhizni* (Life's work) (Moskva: Izdatel'stvo politicheskoi literatury, 1983), 227–228.
3. Ibid., 227.
4. Samsonov, *Stalingradskaya bitva* claims the Soviets encircled twenty German and Rumanian divisions totaling 300,000 men. Kehrig cites German strength in the encirclement as being 260,000 men including 9,590 Rumanians and 20,300 "Hilfswillige" (Russian auxiliaries), Kehrig, 271.
5. Vasilevsky, *Delo*, 228–231.
6. Ibid., 232.
7. Rokossovsky, 303–304; Vasilevsky, 237–238.
8. Soviet 5th Tank Army strength is unclear. Rokossovsky, 307, states: "At the beginning of December, 5th Tank Army's *shock group* numbered up to 50,000 men, nearly 900 guns and mortars and seventy-two tanks [in 1st Tank Corps]." However, on 6 December, the *STAVKA* reinforced the army with 5th Mechanized Corps with a strength of 193 tanks,

see M. Shaposhnikov, "Boevye deistviya 5-go mekhanizirovannogo korpusa zapadnee Surokovino v dekabre 1942 goda" (The combat operations of 5th Mechanized Corps west of Surokovino in December 1942). *Voenno–Istoricheskii Zhurnal* November 1982, 33. The total strength of 5th Tank Army shown in the text is taken from V. Gurkin, "Razgrom nemetsko–fashistskikh voisk na Sredem Dony (operatsiya "Mal'yi Saturn") (Destruction of German–Fascist forces on the Middle Don (operation "Little Saturn")). *VIZh*, May 1975, 26. Gurkin does not count 5th Mechanized Corps in the total figure.

9. H. Scheibert, *Panzer Zwischen Don and Donez: Die Winterkämpfe 1942/1943* (Panzers between the Don and Donets) (Friedberg, Podzun–Pallas–Verlag, 1979), 27.
10. Rokossovsky, 307–309, gives one of the few Soviet versions of 5th Tank Army's ill-fated attempts to cross the Chir River. The best German accounts are found in F.S. von Mellenthin, *Panzer Battles: A Study of the Employment of Armor in the Second World War* (Norman, Okla.: University of Oklahoma Press, 1968), 175–183 and H. Schneider, "Breakthrough by the V Russian Mechanized Corps on the Khir River from 10 to 16 December 1942" *Small Unit Tactics: Tactics of Individual Arms, Examples from World War II*. MS #P–060f (Historical Division, European Command, 1951).
11. A. Vasilevsky, "Nezabyvaemye dni" (Unforgettable days) *VIZh*, March 1966, 26–28.
12. Ibid., 29–30.
13. M.I. Kazakov, "Operatsiya 'Saturn'" (Operation Saturn) *Stalingradskaya epopeya* (The Stalingrad Epoch) (Moskva: Izdatel'stvo "Nauka" 1968), 509–511; M.I. Kazakov, *Nad kartoi bylykh srazhenii* (On the map there were battles) (Moskva: Voenizdat, 1965) 137.
14. For details of the operational plan of "Little Saturn" see Rokossovsky, 313–340. The Soviets confirm these details in their own wartime study of the operation found in *Sbornik Materialov po izucheniyu opyta voyny, No. 8, August-Oktyabr' 1943g.* (Collections of materials for the study of war experiences, No. 8, August–October 1943.) Department of Research into and Application of Wartime Experiences, General Staff of the Red Army. (Moskva: Voenizdat, 1943) 8–14, translated by The Directorate of Military Intelligence, Army Headquarters, Ottawa, Canada. This volume was one of many which resulted from a General Staff Directive of 9 November 1942 which mandated the collection and processing of war experiences. The four volumes of this series available in the west offer a candid view of Soviet successes and failures. They also provide a source for much of the information contained in post-war studies of Soviet operations. Hereafter cited as *Sbornik materialov*.
15. Ibid., see also D.D. Lelyushenko, *Moskva–Stalingrad–Berlin–Praga* (Moskva–Stalingrad–Berlin–Prague) (Moskva: Izdatel'stvo "Nauka", 1973), 146–149.
16. See also Kazakov, "Operatsiya Saturn", 505–507; A.V. Kuz'min, I.I. Krasnov, *Kantemirovtsy: boevoi put 4-go gvardeiskogo tankovogo Kantemirovskogo ordena Lenina Krasnoznamennogo Korpusa* (Kantemirovtsy: The combat path of the Kantemirovka, Order of Lenin, Red Banner 4th Guards Tank Corps) (Moskva: Voenizdat, 1971), 36–38.
17. *Sbornik materialov*, 5.
18. G. Derr, *Pokhod na Stalingrad* (Approach to Stalingrad) (Moskva: Voenizdat, 1957), 102–106, is a translation of a German volume by Hans Doerr; Scheibert, 27, Ministero della Guerra, Stato Maggiore Esercito–Ufficio Storico, *L'8'Armata Italiana nella Seconda Battaglia Difensiva Del Don* (*11 Decembre 1942–31 Gennaio 1943*) (The Italian 8th Army in the Second Defensive Battle of the Don, 11 December 1942–31 January 1943) (Roma, 1946). Hereafter cited as L'8' Armata; Ministero Della Difesa, Stato Maggiore dell' Esercito, Ufficio Storico, *Le Operationi della Unita Italiane Al Fronte Russo* (*1943–1944*) (Roma, 1977), 324–327. Hereafter cited as *Le Operationi.*
19. *Sbornik Materialov*, 40–42.
20. *Le Operationi*, 326.
21. Rokossovsky, 323. Counting 17th Tank Corps, tank density was 31.6 per 1 kilometer of front. Calculations in Gurkin, 26, include tank and mechanized corps and division equivalents, thus unit densities are greater than found in Rokossovsky.
22. Ibid., 325. Inclusion of the three tank corps increased total tank density to thirty-three per 1 kilometer.
23. Ibid., 326. Consideration of 1st Mechanized Corps in the calculations raised the tank density to eighteen per kilometer.

24. Ibid., 327–328; *Sbornik materialov*, 18, 45–46.
25. *Sbornik materialov*, 19; Rokossovsky, 328, cites lower overall ratios in penetration sectors of 3.3 : 1 in 6th Army, 2.2 : 1 in 1st Guards Army, 2.8 : 1 in 3d Guards Army and 3.3 : 1 in 5th Tank Army. Rokossovsky takes into account artillery which did not arrive in time for the preparation, while the *Sbornik* cites planning figures.
26. Rokossovsky, 328–329; *Sbornik materialov*, 46–50.
27. *Sbornik materialov*, 48–50.
28. Ibid., 55; Rokossovsky, 330.
29. *Sbornik materialov*, 53.
30. Ibid., 62.
31. Rokossovsky, 330.
32. Ibid., 332.
33. *Sbornik materialov*, 22–23.
34. Ibid., 24; Rokossovsky, 336.
35. *Sbornik materialov*, 25, 53–56.
36. Rokossovsky, 337.
37. *Sbornik materialov*, 21–22.
38. *Le Operationi*, 339–348.
39. Kazakov, "Operatsiya Saturn," 510–511.
40. V.S. Vylitok, S.F. Leskin, *Novomoskovskaya Krasnoznamennaya*: *boevoi put' 195–i Novomoskovskoi Krasnoznamennoi strelkovoi divizii* (The Red Banner 195th Rifle Division) (Moskva: Voenizdat, 1979), 29–30; *Le Operationi*, 339, 342, cites Italian casualties on 11 December as 50 dead, 175 wounded and 126 captured. On 12 December, Ravenna Division lost 80 killed, 283 wounded and 135 captured.
41. *Le Operationi*, 343, 345, 346, 349–352, 356–358.
42. Rokossovsky, 344.
43. Vylitok, 33–35.
44. Ibid., 35–37; *Le Operationi*, 356–361.
45. A.A. Yaroshenko, *V boi shla 41-ya gvardeiskaya*: *boevoi put' 41–i gvardeiskoi strelkovoi Korsun'sko–Dunaiskoi ordena Suvorova divisii* (Into battle went the 41st Guards: the combat path of the Korsun–Danube, Order of Suvorov 41st Guards Rifle Division) (Moskva: Voenizdat, 1982), 55–57; *Le Operationi*, 359–361.
46. *Sbornik materialov*, 59, 89; Rokossovsky, 345; A. Zheltov, "Yugozapadnom front v kontranastuplenii pod Stalingradom" (The Southwestern Front in the counteroffensive at Stalingrad) *VIZh*, November 1967, 66.
47. G.S. Zdanovich, *Idem v nastuplenie* (On the offensive) (Moskva: Voenizdat, 1980), 43–45. Combat history of the 203d Rifle Division.
48. A.V. Tuzov, *V ogne voiny*: *boevoi put' 50–i gvardeiskoi dvazhdi krasnoznamennoi ordena Suvorova i Kutuzova strelkovoi divizii* (In the fire of battle: the combat path of the twice Red Banner, Order of Suvorov and Kutuzov 50th Guards Rifle Division) (Moskva: Voenizdat, 1970), 69–70; Lelyushenko, *Moskva –*, 149–150.
49. *Le Operationi*, 363–373.
50. Ibid.; Kuz'min, 41; Vylitok, 38–39; Rokossovsky, 346–347.
51. Yaroshenko, 57–58.
52. D.D. Lelyushenko, "1-ya i 3-ya gvardeiskie armii v kontranastuplenii pod Stalingradom" (The 1st and 3d Guards Armies in the Counteroffensive at Stalingrad) *Stalingradskaya epopeya* (Stalingrad epic) (Moskva: Izdatel'stvo "Nauka," 1968), 698–699; Rokossovsky, 349–350.
53. *L'8 Armata Italiana*, 22–25; *Le Operationi*, 373–375.
54. Kuz'min, 42.
55. *L'8 Armata Italiana*, 25–29.
56. Rokossovsky, 350–351; Lelyushenko, *Berlin–*, 151.
57. Shaposhnikov, 33–38; Mellenthin, 178–182; *Lagenkarte XXXXVIII PzKps*, 18.12.
58. Rokossovsky, 353–354. A security line was designed to protect a force's flank from enemy counterattacks.
59. Ibid., 354–355.

NOTES

60. Kuz'min, 43–45; *Le Operationi,* 381–383.
61. Ibid., 45–46; Rokossovsky, 356.
62. Rokossovsky, 356.
63. A. Krull, *Das Hannoversche Regiment 73: Geschichte des Panzer–Grenadier–Regiments 73* (The Hanoverian Regiment 73: A History of Panzer Grenadier Regiment 73). (Hannover: Regimentskameradschaft 73, undated), 254. 19th Panzer Division units began arriving in the combat area on 25 December.
64. *Sbornik materialov,* 58–99; Rokossovsky, 357.
65. H.I. Vasil'ev, *Tatsinskii reid* (The Tatsinskaya raid) (Moskva: Voenizdat, 1969), 26–62.
66. Rokossovsky, 359–360.
67. Vylitok, 41–42.
68. Ibid., 43; Yaroshenko, 58.
69. N.I. Afanas'yev, *Ot Volgi do Shpree: boevoi put' 35–i gvardeiskoi strelkovoi Lozovskoi Krasnoznamennoi ordenov Suvorova i Bogdan Khmel'nitskogo divizii* (From the Volga to the Spree: the combat path of the Lozovaya, Red Banner, Orders of Suvorov and Bogdan Khmel'nitsky 35th Guards Rifle Division) (Moskva: Voenizdat, 1982), 85–95.
70. Ibid., 93.
71. Rokossovsky, 361; *Sbornik materialov,* 72.
72. Rokossovsky, 362.
73. A.M. Chmelev, "Proshla s boyami . . ." (Passing through battles) (Kishinev: Kartya Moldevenyaske, 1983) 22–25. Combat history of the 197th Rifle Division.
74. I. Sazonov, "Derzkii reid tankistov–pozolotintsev" (The daring raid of the gilded tankers) *VIZh,* September 1971, 49–53; N.N. Popel', V.P. Savel'yev, P.V. Shemansky, *Upravlenie voiskami v gody Velikoi Otechestvennoi* (Troop control during the Great Patriotic War) (Moskva: Voenizdat, 1974), 150–152, contains the following operational summary from 1st Guards Mechanized Corps Records.

CHIEF OF STAFF OF THE 3d GUARDS ARMY
OPERATIONS SUMMARY No 38 as of 0400 HOURS 21 DEC 42,
CORPS STAFF HEADQUARTERS 1, MAP SCALE 100,000

1. Under attack by units of the 1st Guards Mechanized Corps, the enemy is withdrawing in continuous columns to the west and southwest, leaving strong covering detachments behind. During 20 Dec 42, after stiff battles, corps units liberated the communities of Kalinovskiy, Karginskaya, Arkhipovaka, Fedorovka, Gusynka, Klimovskiy, Nizhnii Yablonovskiy, Stoyanov, Budanovskiy, Kamenskiy, Popovka and Pervomayskiy. The German 190th, 183d, and 179th infantry regiments and the 162d Artillery Regiment of the 62d Infantry Division were totally destroyed and the Rumanian 11th, 7th and 9th infantry divisions partially destroyed.

Enemy aviation bombed Bokovskaya, Dulenskiy and Astakhov during the day. Our aviation bombed the enemy locations and the withdrawing columns.

Our air patrols over the corps' units are inadequate.

2. On 20 Dec 42 the 1st Guards Mechanized Brigade, after stiff battles, advanced and liberated the communities of Karginskaya, Arkhipovaka, Fedorovka and Gusynka.

Losses: 12 killed and 23 wounded.

Captured by our forces: 9 guns, 13 vehicles, 8 motorcycles, 2 clothing depots, 2 food depots, 1 wine depot. A regimental standard was captured, more than 1,000 enemy soldiers and officers destroyed and 250 prisoners taken (data for 2400 hours 20 Dec 42). The count continues.

3. During 20 Dec 44 [sic] the 3d Guards Mechanized Brigade advanced and liberated the communities of Klimovskiy, Nizhnii Yablonovskiy, Stoyanov, Budanovskiy, Kamenskiy, Popovka and Pervomayskiy.

Losses are being determined.

Captured by our troops: 67 guns of various systems, 53 mortars and 40 horses, more than 1500 soldiers and officers destroyed and up to 600 soldiers and officers taken prisoner (data for 2400 hours 20 Dec 42). The count continues.

4. During 20 Dec 44 [sic] the 2d Guards Mechanized Brigade engaged in fierce battles with the enemy on a line running through hills 191.1, 182.0, 176.2 and 173.1.

Losses: 300 men killed or wounded, 6 T-34 tanks, two of them non-recoverable, 25 motor vehicles.

Captured by our troops: 2 tanks and 3 motor vehicles, 1 German aircraft shot down and 1 field artillery battalion wiped out.

5. By decision of the command the 17th Guards Tank Regiment was sent on 19 Dec 42 to the enemy rear in the area of the Krasnayaarya and Verkhnii Yablonobskiy sovhozes to paralyze the enemy rear and destroy withdrawing columns. As a result of 2 days of combat activities in the enemy rear (19–20 Dec 42) the regiment destroyed: hundreds of enemy soldiers and officers (headquarters of an Italian infantry regiment and a colonel killed; documents of the latter seized and preserved in their entirety), 200 wagons, 100 loaded motor vehicles, 30 guns of various caliber and 1 mortar battery. Captured without damage: 20 guns, 5 motor vehicles, 21 motorcycles, 30 bicycles, 50 rifles, 10 submachine guns, 300 horses, 1700 head of cattle, sheep and hogs, 3 depots, of which 2 were food warehouses and 1 a liquor warehouse, 1200 kilograms of gasoline and a great deal of other booty, the count of which continues.

Losses: 1 T-34 tank (burned), 1 T-70 tank (burned), 8 killed and 2 wounded. 20 submachine gun personnel killed or wounded. Regiment continues to fulfill the assigned combat mission.

6. 116th Guards Artillery Regiment is operating on a battalion basis within brigades. Destroyed during 20 Dec 42: 1 four-gun antitank battery (50-mm, including team), 1 three-gun 75-mm battery, up to an enemy battalion dispersed or destroyed, up to 100 wagons. Neutralized: 2 75-mm three-gun batteries and 1 mortar battery (81-mm). No loss of personnel or materiel.

7. The 16th Guards Tank Regiment remains in the same area. During 20 Dec 42 it did not conduct active combat operations. There were no losses of personnel or materiel.

8. The corps had the following provisions for 20 Dec 42: bread rations for 1.5 days, groats for 3.5 days, sugar for 8 days, a one-day ration of meat, 50-mm mortar shells – 2.1 units of fire, 82-mm mortar shells – 0.7 units of fire, 122-mm mortar shells – 2 units of fire, 37-mm rounds – 1.5 units of fire, 45-mm rounds – 1.4 units of fire, 76-mm regimental artillery – 2.7 units of fire, 76-mm division artillery – 2.7 units of fire, 122-mm rounds – 0.5 units of fire;

fuel and lubricants: second grade gasoline – 0.7 fuelings, KB-70 – 0.3 fuelings, diesel fuel – 0.6 fuelings and oil – 1.5 servicings.

9. Communications operating without interruption (breaks in the telephone lines). There are telephone communications with the army staff and communications officers, as well as with corps units.

10. Weather: cloudy – 10 points, low cloud cover, horizontal visibility – 7 kilometers.

Corps command post at 1800 hours 20 Dec 42 – Visslogubov.

Chief of Staff of the 1st Guards
Mechanized Corps, Guards Lieutenant Colonel
(signature)

For chief of the first staff section,
Guards Lieutenant Colonel
(signature)

75. N.I. Zav'yalov, *Versty muzhestva* (Versts of Courage) (Kiev: Izdatel'stvo politicheskoi literatury Ukrainy, 1981), 102–194; Lelyushenko, *Berlin–*, 155–156.
76. Scheibert, 37–42.
77. F. Schulz, *Reverses on the Southern Wing* (1942–1943) MS # T-15 Headquarters, United States Army, Europe, Historical Division, 325–327; K. Ruef, *Odyssee einer Gebirgsdivision: Die 3 Geb. Div. im Einsatz* (The Odyssey of a Mountain Division: The 3d Mountain Division in Action) (Stuttgart: Leopold Stocker Verlag, 1976), 299–303.
78. Badanov, *Tatsinskii,* 66–77; V.M. Badanov, "Glubokii tankovyi reid" (Deep tank raid) *Stalingradskaya epopeya* (Moskva: Izdatel'stvo "Nauka," 1968), 631–635; *Lagenkarte, XXXXVIII Pz.Kps.* 25–26.12.42; Schulz, 268.
79. The Soviets claimed to have destroyed 350 aircraft on the airfields and 50 more on rail cars; Schulz, 319–320 states:

 > In the morning of 24 December the enemy overran the airfields at Morozovsky [sic] and Tatsinskaya from the north. Although there had been definite indications for such an enemy thrust several days in advance, the formations were forbidden to effect a transfer in time. The writer of this annex does not know whether the supreme command underestimated the danger because it did not want the daily aircraft tonnage carried to drop further. The HE-III formations were able to take off for Novocherkassy comparatively intact. The airworthy Ju 52's took off from Tatsinskaya, visibility below 1000 meters, and under fire from Russian tanks that had rolled onto the field itself – This interruption of aircraft traffic, in itself already insufficient, was bad enough. But beyond that, a large number of planes on these fields, among them those in for repairs, were lost.

 Scheibert, 54, quotes a report of Panzer Grenadier Regiment 4 that forty destroyed Ju's littered the airfield.
80. Scheibert, 48, cites reports placing 6th Panzer Division tank strength on 26 December at forty-eight. By 30 December, it had fallen to about twenty. 11th Panzer Division's strength was somewhat lower.
81. *Lagenkarte XXXXVIII Pz. Kps.* 25–26.12.42; *Kriegs–Tagebuch Gen. Kdo. XXXXVIII Panzer Korps,* 25.12.42, 26.12.42. German reports on 26 December place Russian tank strength at Uryupin at eighteen tanks (this would have been 25th Tank Corps).
82. *Kriegs-Tagebuch Gen. Kdo. XXXXVIII Panzer Korps* 27.12.42; Badanov, *Tatsinskii,* 101–106.
83. *Sbornik materialov,* 72; for the exchange of messages, see Samsonov, *Stalingradskaya bitva,* 522–525; Badanov, 109–114. Badanov claimed that during his operations his unit killed 11,292 enemy, took 4,769 prisoner and destroyed eighty-four enemy tanks, 106 guns and 431 aircraft. The *Kriegs-Tagebuch Gen. Kdo. XXXXVIII Panzer Korps,* 28.12.42, stated that at 0430 the enemy with a mass of his tanks tried to break out from Tatsinskaya to the northwest. In heavy battle, the Germans destroyed numerous tanks. However, the enemy succeeded in breaking through the unobserved area between Panzer Grenadier Regiment 4 and Panzer Regiment 15 with "more tanks and 200 vehicles (lorries)." A subsequent German report on 28 December claimed the destruction of forty-two Soviet tanks.
84. Rokossovsky, 361.
85. Yaroshenko, 61–62; Afanas'yev, 94–95; Krull, 256–257. (On 29 December 19th Panzer Division's armored strength was about thirty operating tanks.)
86. *Lagenkarte XXXXVIII Pz. Kps.*, 28.12.; Tuzov, 71–72.
87. Zdanovich, 47–53; *Lagenkarte XXXXVIII Pz. Kps.*, 29.12; *Kriegs-Tagebuch Gen. Kdo. XXXXVIII Panzer Korps,* 28.12.42, 29.12.42.
88. Lelyushenko, *Berlin–*, 159.
89. Zdanovich, 53–54.
90. Scheibert, 34, notes that on 28 December 5000 men, the remnants of XXIX Army Corps, filtered through German lines south of Skosyrskaya; *Lagenkarte XXXXVIII Pz. Kps.*, 27.12; 28.12.
91. *L'8 Armata,* Allegato 1.
92. Soviet examination of tank operations in November and December concluded that this lost rate was typical. This may account for the high TOE tank strength of the Soviet tank armies

created in 1943.

93. Zdanovich, 46; J. Erickson, *The Road to Berlin* (Boulder, Colorado: Westview Press, 1983), 18–19.
94. *Sbornik materialov,* 63.
95. Ibid., 66.
96. G.K. Zhukov, *Vospominaniya i razmyshleniya* (Memoirs and Reflections) (Moskva: Novosti, 1970), 125.
97. Kazakov, "Operatsiya Saturn," 514–515.

CHAPTER THREE

1. For a thorough survey of the Ostrogozhsk–Rossosh' operation, see V.P. Morozov, *Zapadnee Voronezha* (west of Voronezh) (Moskva: Voenizdat, 1956) 23, 90. A briefer account is in M. Kazakov, "Ot verkhnego Dona k Dnepry" (From the Upper Don to the Dnepr) *Voenno–Istoricheskii Zhurnal* (Military History Journal) November 1965, 55–62.
2. See Morozov, *Zapadnee,* 90–112.
3. S. M. Shtemenko, *General'nyi Shtab v Gody Voiny* (The General Staff in the War Years) (Moskva: Voenizdat, 1981), 161–162.
4. A.G. Yershov, *Osvobozhdenie Donbassa* (The liberation of the Donbas) (Moskva: Voenizdat, 1973), 11. For planning details, see also S. Shtemenko, *General'nyi shtab v gody voiny* (The General Staff during the war years) (Moskva: Voenizdat, 1968), 100–102; *Istorii Vtoroi Mirovoi Voiny 1939–1945* (History of the Second World War) (Moskva: Voenizdat, 1976) 6:127–129. (Hereafter cited as I.V.M.V.)
5. Yershov, 20.
6. *I.V.M.V.* 6:128; Yershov, 10.
7. Shtemenko, 158.
8. *Ibid.*, 159.
9. E. von Manstein, *Lost Victories* (Chicago: Henry Regnery Company, 1958), 399.
10. Yershov, 19–20, 25, 34–35, 46–47, 56.
11. For example, see A.V. Kuz'min, I.I. Krasov, *Kantemirovtsy*: *boevoi put 4–go gvardeiskogo tankovogo kantemirovskogo ordena Lenina Krasnoznammennogo korpusa* (Kantemirovtsy: The combat path of the Kantemirovsky Order of Lenin and Red Banner 4th Guards Tank Corps) (Moskva: Voenizdat, 1971), 50–51 (hereafter cited as Kuz'min). I.E. Krupchenko, ed., *Sovetskie tankovye voiska 1941–1945* (Soviet tank forces 1941–1945) (Moskva: Voenizdat, 1973), 100, cites the Southwestern Front's tank strength in late January as being 362, without specifying whether this figure counted 25th Tank Corps and 1st Guards Tank Corps. It is likely that by early February the *front* armored strength was about 500 tanks.
12. For an excellent summary of the German Order of Battle of Army Group South for the entire period from 3 February to 29 March, see E. Schwarz, *Die Stabilisierung in Süden der Ostfront nach der Katastrophe von Stalingrad und dem Rückzug aus dem Kaukasus* (The stabilization in the south of the eastern front after the catastrophe at Stalingrad and the withdrawal from the Caucasus) (Köln: University of Köln, 1981), 364–372.
13. For example, see *Auszug aus Anl. zum KTB Pz. AOK 1-Kampfwert der Divisionen der 1. Pz Armee* (Combat Worth of 1st Panzer Army Divisions) Stand: 20.2.1943, Dok 31555/2; Stand: 27. 2.1943, Dok 31444/3 (originals).
14. Kuz'min, 56.
15. Yershov, 20, 34.
16. Ibid., 25.
17. Ibid., 34–36 outlines the specific missions of each tank corps in Popov's group. Shtemenko, 163, notes that Popov's Group formed on 27 January and began operations only two days later.
18. Kuz'min, 56.
19. Yershov, 46–47; D.D. Lelyushenko, *Moskva–Stalingrad–Berlin–Praga* (Moscow–Stalingrad–Berlin–Prague) (Moskva: Izdatel'stvo "Nauka," 1973), 167–170.

20. *I.V.M.V.* 6:132.
21. Yershov, 20–21; Schwarz, 376–378.
22. Yershov, 22; *Befehl des Gewissens: Charkow Winter 1943* (Dictate of Conscience: Khar'kov, Winter 1943) (Osnabruck: Munin–Verlag GmbH, 1976) 10–46. Contains the War Diary and maps of Army Detachment Lanz (1 February to 18 March) with references to adjacent units (298th Infantry Division and 320th Infantry Division). Subsequent accounts of these divisions' operations are from this source.
23. Yershov, 24–25.
24. V.S. Vylitok, S.F. Leskin, *Novomoskovskaya Krasnoznamennaya: boevoi put' 195–i Novomoskovskoi Krasnoznamennoi strelkovoi divizii* (The Novo-Moskovsk Red Banner: the combat path of the Novomoskovsk Red Banner 195th Rifle Division) (Moskva: Voenizdat, 1979), 60–63 (hereafter cited as Vylitok); A. Krull, *Das Hannoversche Regiment 73* (The Hanoverian Regiment 73) (Hannover: Regimentskameradschaft 73, undated) 272–278.
25. N.I. Afanas'yev. *Ot Volgi do Shpree: boevoi put' 35–i gvardeiskoi strelkovoi Lozovskoi Krasnoznamennoi Ordenov Suvorova i Bogdana Khmel' nitskogo divizii* (From the Volga to the Spree: The combat path of the Lozovaya Red Banner, Order of Suvorov and Bogdan Khmel'nitsky 35th Guards Rifle Division) (Moskva: Voenizdat, 1982) 99.
26. Ibid., 101–102.
27. Vylitok, 64–66; Yershov, 29–30; *Lagenkarten der K.T.B. des III Pz. Korps* Lage 2.2.43–6. 2.43 (original).
28. An excellent account of 1st Panzer Army and, specifically, 40th Panzer Corps operations during February is found in Carl Wagener, "Der Gegenangriff des XXXX. Panzerkorps gegen den Durchbruch der Panzergruppe Popow im Donezbecken Februar 1943" (The counterstroke of 40 Panzer Corps against the breakthrough of Mobile Group Popov in the Donets Basin, February 1943). *Wehrwissenschaftliche Rundschau,* January 1954, 21–36, translated by Richard Simpkin.
29. A.A. Yaroshenko, *V boi shla 41–ya gvardeiskaya: boevoi put' 41–i gvardeiskoi strelkovoi Korsun'sko–Dunaiskoi Ordene Suvorova divizii* (Into battle went the 41st Guards: the combat path of the Korsun–Danube, Order of Suvorov 41st Guards Rifle Division) (Moskva: Voenizdat, 1982), 64; Krull, 279.
30. Yershov, 28–29; *Anlagenband 1a KTB Gen. Kdo. XXX AK. Abt* 1a 3.2. 1943 (original).
31. Krull, 279–282; *Lagenkarten der K.T.B. des III Pz. Korps.* Lage 2.2.43–6.2.43, Lage 7.2.43–8.2.43 (original).
32. Yershov, 34. *I.V.M.V.* 6:132 puts Popov's strength at 137 tanks.
33. Kuz'min, 57.
34. Wagener, 21.
35. Ibid., 72.
36. Ibid.
37. Vylitok, 67.
38. Wagener, 25.
39. Ibid., 25–26; A. J. Donnhauser, W. Drews, *Der Weg der 11 Panzer Division* (The Path of the 11th Panzer Division) (Bad Worishofen: Holzman–Druck–Service, 1982), 102–104; Yershov, 37–38.
40. Afanas'yev, 102–103. The counterattacks at Barvenkovo of the 333d Infantry Division's 680th Infantry Regiment, according to 35th Guards Rifle Division reports, occurred on 8 February; Yershov, 31–32.
41. Yershov, 31, 37; Kuz'min, 57. Germans picked up this order to Popov's Group. See Wagener, 26.
42. Yershov, 32.
43. Ibid., 32–33.
44. Kuz'min, 57–59.
45. Wagener, 27; F. Schulz *Reverses on the Southern Wing (1942–43) MS–T–15*, Historical Division, Headquarters, United States Army, Europe (undated), 171, states:

    At 0200 on 11 February it was reported to the Army [1st Panzer Army] that strong Russian elements had "burrowed their way" to within Postyshevo [Grishino area]. The decision to move the "Viking" SS Division to this area proved to have been completely correct. The orders to move the division had been issued just in time.

46. Wagener, 26.
47. Ibid., 27.
48. Ibid., 27–29.
49. Kuz'min, 60–61; Yershov, 38–39; Wagener, 29–30.
50. Wagener, 29; Yershov, 32–33 dated the engagement as 13 February as did Yaroshenko, 65. On the other hand Vylitok, 67–68, dated the engagement on 11 February.
51. Wagener, 29–30; *Kartenband zum K.T.B. Nr. 8 der 11. Panzer Division*, Lage am 11.2.1943, Lage am 12.2.1943, Lage am 12.2.1943, Lage am 13.2.1943, Lage am 14.2. 1943 (originals).
52. Yershov, 33.
53. Ibid., 33–34.
54. Ibid., 39–40; Kuz'min, 60–61.
55. Yershov, 43–44.
56. Afanas'yev, 103–104; Yaroshenko, 65.
57. Wagener, 30–31.
58. Yershov, 45, stated: "On that day [17 February] 1st Guards Army units after a decisive assault, liberated Slavyansk." Vylitok, 69–72, also described heavy fighting for possession of Slavyansk.
59. Yershov, 46; Vylitok, 72–73.
60. Kuz'min, 62.
61. Wagener, 31.
62. Wagener, 31–32; Yershov, 85–86; Kuz'min, 62–66.
63. Kuz'min, 43, 86.
64. Yershov, 75.
65. Wagener, 33; *Kartenband zum K.T.B. Nr. 8 der 11. Panzer Division*, Lage am 19.2.32 (original).
66. Kuz'min, 66.
67. V. Morozov, "Pochemu ne zavershilos' nastuplenie v Donbasse vesnoi 1943 goda" (Why was the offensive in the Donbas not completed in the spring of 1943) *Voenno–Istoricheskii Zhurnal* (Military History Journal) March 1963, 16.
68. Ibid., 16–17.
69. Ibid.
70. Ibid., 23.
71. Ibid., 17.
72. Ibid.
73. For Manstein's plans, see Manstein, 420–429, and O. Hackl, "Problems of Operational Command of Army Group Don/South in Defensive Operations Between the Donets and the Dnieper, February/March 1943" *Truppenpraxis* 3/1982, 191–200; 4/1982, 268–274, translated by Richard Simpkin 1, 24.
74. 16 February – Army Group South over to *A. Abt.* Hollidt to take over 4th Panzer Army's sector. 4th Panzer Army to reform at Dnepropetrovsk.
    17 February – Army Group South to *A. Abt.* Lanz. Push SS Panzer Corps with two divisions to Lozovaya. With one division, hold Merefa line.
    18 February – Army Group South to *A. Abt.* Lanz. Push SS Panzer Corps from Krasnograd via Pereshchepino to Novo Moskovsk.
    19 February – Army Group South order to 4th Panzer Army: Destroy enemy in gap between *A. Abt.* Lanz and 1st Panzer Army. *A. Abt.* Lanz cover north flank – pass control of SS Panzer Corps to 4th Panzer Army. Meanwhile, continue attack on Novo Moskovsk. 4th Panzer Army to control SS Panzer Corps and 48th Panzer plus 15th Infantry Division (arrived from France) and 57th Panzer Corps' headquarters. 40th Panzer Corps continue attack on Krasnoarmiskoe.
    Hackl, 13, summarizes. Original documents in *Abschrift aus Anlagen zum KTB AOK 8*, Dok 36188/9.
75. *Befehl des Gewissens*, 128–133.
76. Ibid., 132–134.

77. Morozov, "Pochemu . . ." 23–26, gives 25th Tank Corps and 1st Guards Tank Corps strength as 150 medium tanks, without mentioning what light tanks they possessed. At the same time, Morozov states that Mobile Group Popov strength was 13,000 men and 53 medium tanks. By the end of 20 February, Popov's strength was 25 tanks.
78. Yershov, 81–84; Morozov, 27–28.
79. *Befehl des Gewissens,* 135–141.
80. Afanas'yev, 105–108; Yaroshenko, 65–66. 41st Guards Rifle Division on 21 February had a strength of slightly more than 3,000 men and was almost out of ammunition.
81. Yershov, 84.
82. *Befehl des Gewissens,* 141–146, 153.
83. F. von Senger und Etterlin, *Panzer Retreat to Counteroffensive,* Headquarters, United States Army, Europe, Historical Division, 1956, 1–2; *Lagenkarte, 4 Pz. Armee,* Stand. 24.2.43, 2200 (original).
84. Morozov, 30; Yershov, 84.
85. Yershov, 84–85; Vylitok, 72–73.
86. *Befehl des Gewissens,* 147–150.
87. Afanas'yev, 107–110; Yaroshenko, 66.
88. von Senger, 4–6; *Lagenkarte 4. Pz. Armee,* Stand. 24.2.1943, 2200 (original).
89. Vylitok, 73–74.
90. Yershov, 87.
91. Morozov, "Pochemu . . .," 26.
92. Ibid., 27.
93. Wagener, 30–31; Yershov, 88; *Kartenband zum K.T.B. Nr. 8 der 11. Panzer Division,* Lage am 21.2.1943; Lage am 22.2.1943; Lage am 23.2.1943; Lage am 24.2.1943 (original).
94. Morozov, "Pochemu . . .," 31.
95. *Befehl des Gewissens,* 151–162; Afanas'yev, 109–111.
96. von Senger, 7–10; Vylitok, 73–74.
97. von Senger, 10–12.
98. Morozov, "Pochemu . . .," 32.
99. *Befehl des Gewissens,* 163–173.
100. von Senger, 13–18.
101. Wagener, 35–36; *1. Pz. Armee Lage* 26.2.43; *1. Pz. Armee Lage* 28.2.43 (original).
102. Morozov, "Pochemy . . .," 32; A. M. Zvartsev, *3-ya gvardeiskaya tankovaya: boevoi put' 3–i gvardeiskoi tankovoi armii* (3d Guards Tank: The combat path of 3d Guards Tank Army) (Moskva: Voenizdat, 1982), 50–51.
103. *Befehl des Gewissens,* 187–199.
104. Afanas'yev, 110–111.
105. Precise Soviet losses during the operation are difficult to determine. It is clear that many units, in particular those of 6th Army, 1st Guards Army's 4th Guards Rifle Corps, and of the *front's* mobile groups suffered heavily. However, understrength German forces were able to break the cohesion of Soviet units but were unable to inflict the casualties and encircle the number of prisoners they had been able to in 1941. Manstein's report to the OKH summarized Russian losses after 1 February as follows:

> Destroyed: XXV Tank Corps with the 111th, 162d, 187th Tank Brigades, 16th Motorized Brigade, 35th Guards Rifle, 267th Rifle Division, 106th Rifle Brigade.
> Smashed: III Tank Corps with 50th, 51st, 103d Tank Brigades, 57th Motorized Brigade, IV Guards Tank Corps with 12th Guards Tank, 13th, 14th Guards Tank Brigades, 3d Guards Motorized Brigade.
> V Tank Corps with 178th, 183d, 186th Tank Brigades, 11th Motorized Brigade, 9th Separate Guards Tank Brigade, 78th Rifle Division, 7th Ski Brigade.
> Heavily Damaged: I Guards Tank Corps with 15th, 16th, 17th Guards Tank Brigades, 1st Guards Motorized Brigade. XVIII Tank Corps with 110th, 170th, 181st Tank Brigades, 32d Motorized Brigade. 6th Rifle Division, 38th Guards Rifle Division, 41st Guards Rifle Division, 57th Guards Rifle Division, 172d Rifle Division, 244th Rifle Division, 5th Ski Brigade, and 10th Ski Brigade.

The report listed Soviet losses as follows:

	1st Panzer Army	*4th Panzer Army*	*Total*
Prisoners	1,187	7,884	9,071
Dead	8,000	15,200	23,200
Tanks	406	209	615
Armored Cars	31	25	56
Guns	100	264	364
AA guns	22	47	69
AT guns	255	337	592
Multiple Rocket Launchers	2	14	16

The total personnel casualties amount to between fifteen and twenty percent of 6th Army, 1st Guards Army and Group Popov's strength. Obviously, wounded and evacuated troops would add significantly to that total, but even so the major portion of those forces manpower survived the operation. This explains why Soviet reconstitution of damaged units was so rapid. The armored losses were more severe. Vatutin's two mobile groups lost virtually all of the tanks they possessed at the beginning of the operation, as well as the armor the *STAVKA* sent forward as reinforcements.

106. von Senger, 29.

CHAPTER FOUR

1. S.M. Shtemenko, *General'nyi Shtab v Gody Voiny* (The General Staff in the War Years) (Moskva: Voenizdat, 1981), 158.
2. K.S. Moskalenko, *Na Yugo-zapadnom napravlenii* (On the southwestern direction) (Moskva: Izdatel'stvo "Nauka," 1969), 1:418; I.E. Krupchenko, ed., *Sovetskie tankovye voiska 1941–1945* (Soviet tank forces 1941–1945) (Moskva: Voenizdat, 1973), 107.
3. Order of battle for 69th Army reconstructed from N.I. Kazakov, *Nad kartoi bylykh srazhenii* (There were battles upon the map) (Moskva: Voenizdat, 1971), 163–179; V.P. Morozov, *Zapadnee Voronezha* (West of Voronezh) (Moskva: Voenizdat, 1966), 113–197.
4. A.M. Zvartsev, *3-ya gvardeiskaya tankovaya: boevoi put' 3-i gvardeiskoi tankovoi armii* (3d Guards Tank: the combat path of 3d Guards Tank Army) (Moskva: Voenizdat, 1982), 42–43.
5. E. Schwarz, *Die Stabilisierung im Süden der Ostfront nach der Katastrophe von Stalingrad und dem Rückzug aus dem Kaukasus* (The stabilization in the south of the eastern front after the catastrophe at Stalingrad and the withdrawal from the Caucasus) (Köln: University of Köln, 1981), 364, 377–378; *Befehl des Gewissens: Charkov Winter 1943* (Dictate of Conscience: Khar'kov, Winter 1943) (Osnabruck: Munin-Verlag GmgH, 1976), 8–14.
6. Morozov, *Zapadnee*, 118–120.
7. Zvartsev, 42–43.
8. Kazakov, 162.
9. Moskalenko, 1:420.
10. *K.T.B. Ia Anl. Bd. B.* . . ., Lage bei SS-Pz Kps 31.1.1943; *Befehl des Gewissens*, 15–17.
11. Morozov, *Zapadnee* . . ., 122–123; *Befehl des Gewissens*, 18–21.
12. Zvartsev, 43.
13. N.G. Nersesyan, *Kievsko–Berlinskii: boevoi put' 6-go gvardeiskogo tankovogo korpusa* (Kiev–Berlin: the combat path of 6th Guards Tank Corps) (Moskva: Voenizdat, 1974), 31; Zvartsev, 43.
14. *K.T.B. Ia. Bd. B.* . . ., Lage bei SS-Pz Kps, 3.2.1943; *Befehl des Gewissens*, 22–26.
15. Zvartsev, 44; *K.T.B. Ia. Bd. B* . . ., Lage bei SS. Pz. Kps. 4.2.1943.
16. M.K. Smol'nyi, *7000 kilometrov v boyakh i pokhodakh: boevoi put' 161-i strelkovoi Stanislavskoi Krasnoznamennoi Ordena Bogdana Khmel'nitskogo divisii 1941–1945* (7000 kilometers in battles and marches: the combat path of the Stanislav, Red Banner, Order of Bogdan Khmel'nitsky 161st Rifle Division 1941–1945) (Moskva: Voenizdat, 1982), 49; *Befehl des Gewissens*, 18–40.
17. Morozov, *Zapadnee*, 128–129.

18. Zvartsev, 44; *K.T.B. Ia. Bd. B* . . ., Lage bei SS. Pz. Kps. am 6.11.1943; *Befehl des Gewissens,* 40–46.
19. Morozov, *Zapadnee,* 142–143.
20. Ibid., 141.
21. Morozov, *Zapadnee,* 125, 138–139; Zvartsev, 44; *Befehl des Gewissens,* 34–40; *K.T.B. Ia. Bd. B* . . ., Lage bei SS-Pz. Kps. am 5.2.1943.
22. Kazakov, 165; *K.T.B. Ia. Bd. B* . . ., Lage bei SS-Pz. Kps. am 5.2.1943; *Befehl des Gewissens,* 34–40.
23. Smol'nyi, 50; *Befehl des Gewissens,* 40–54.
24. Morozov, *Zapadnee,* 135; Moskalenko, 421.
25. Moskalenko, 1:422–423; Morozov, *Zapadnee,* 136–138; *Befehl des Gewissens,* 47–63.
26. Morozov, *Zapadnee,* 143–144; Zvartsev, 45; N.G. Nersesyan, *Fastovskaya Gvardeiskaya: boevoi put' 53-i gvardeiskoi Ordena Lenina Krasnoznamennoi Ordenov Suvorova i Bogdana Khmel'nitskogo Tankovoi Brigady* (Fastov Guards: the combat path of the Order of Lenin, Red Banner, Order of Suvorov and Bogdan Khmel'nitsky, 53d Tank Brigade) (Moskva: Voenizdat, 1964), 39–41; *Befehl des Gewissens,* 66–70.
27. Zvartsev, 45–46; Morozov, *Zapadnee,* 149–150.
28. Zvartsev, 46; Nersesyan, *Fastovskaya,* 41–42; *Feindlage-Karte der Armee-Abt. Lanz,* 14.2.1943; *Befehl des Gewissens,* 79–102.
29. Smol'nyi, 52.
30. Moskalenko, 1:425.
31. Morozov, *Zapadnee,* 146–147; Moskalenko, 427–428; P.M. Shafarenko, *Na raznykh frontakh* (On different fronts) (Moskva: Voenizdat, 1978), 132–133. A history of the 25th Guards Rifle Division.
32. Morozov, *Zapadnee,* 147; Moskalenko, 429; Shafarenko, *Na paznykh* . . ., 133–134; P.M. Shafarenko, *My vse byli soldatami* (We were all soldiers) (Khar'kov: "Prapor," 1983), 77–80; *Feindlage-Karte der Armee-Abt. Lanz,* 14.2.1943.
33. E. Ziemke, *Stalingrad to Berlin: The German Defeat in the East* (Washington, D.C.: Office of the Chief of Military History, United States Army, 1968), 90; *Befehl des Gewissens,* 95–108; *K.T.B. Ia. Bd. B* . . ., Lage bei SS-Pz. Kps. am. 15.2.1943.
34. Morozov, *Zapadnee,* 155–158; Zvartsev, 47.
35. Moskalenko, 1:433.
36. *I.V.M.V.* 6:134; Morozov, *Zapadnee,* 167.
37. Moskalenko, 1:437.
38. Kazakov, 171.
39. Ibid., 168.
40. Zvartsev, 48.
41. Moskalenko, 1:438.
42. Kazakov, 169.
43. Moskalenko, 1:440.
44. Kazakov, 171; Smol'nyi, 51–53; *Befehl des Gewissens,* 126, 130.
45. Zvartsev, 48–49.
46. Ibid., 49; Nersesyan, *Kievsko* – 32–33; Nersesyan, *Fastovskaya—*, 43–44; *Lagenkarte 4. Pz. Armee,* Stand. 21.2.43, 2200.
47. Zvartsev, 50; S.I. Mel'nikov, *Marshal Rybalko* (Kiev: Izdatel'stvo politicheskoi literatury Ukrainy, 1980), 85. States on 21 February 3d Tank Army had 96 tanks and 0.5 loads of fuel.
48. *Befehl des Gewissens,* 135–145.
49. Morozov, "Pochemu ne Zavershilos' nastuplenie v Donbasse vesnoi 1943 goda" (Why was the offensive in the Donbas not completed in the spring of 1943) *Voenno-Istoricheskii Zhurnal* (Military History Journal) March 1963, 30.
50. Zvartsev, 50–51; Kazakov, 173; Moskalenko, 1:444–445.
51. *Befehl des Gewissens,* 146–149; *Lagenkarte 4 Pz. Armee,* Stand. 26.2.43, 22*00*.
52. Nersesyan, *Fastovskaya—*, 45–47; *Lagenkarte 4 Pz. Armee,* Stand. 28.2.43, 22*00*.
53. Moskalenko, 1:447. The order read:

    With the arrival of Kravchenko [5th Guards Tank Corps commander] and Men'shikov [309th Rifle Division commander] in the Oposhnya area, favourable conditions are created to secure Poltava from the north and northwest without damaging the fulfilling of my main directive No. 130/DP. This provides the opportunity to not only secure Poltava but also cut off a considerable portion of enemy forces, who have begun to withdraw to Poltava from the Valki, Kovyagi and Kolomak regions and to help Kazakov quickly cope with the mission of reaching Poltava.

54. Ibid., 451.
55. Zvartsev, 51.
56. Kazakov, 173–174.
57. Zvartsev, 52.
58. Ibid., 51–52, Nersesyan, *Kievsko* . . ., 35–36, Nersesyan, *Fastvoskaya* . . ., 48–50; *Lagenkarte 4. Pz. Armee,* Stand. 3.3.43, 22*00; Gen. Kdo. XXXXVIII Pz. Kps. Abt. Ic.*, Kartenanlagen 2.4.3 Februar 1943; *Befehl des Gewissens,* 187–198.
59. Zvartsev, 52.
60. Nersesyan, *Fastovskaya* . . ., 51–56; Nersesyan, *Kievsko* . . ., 35–36. A detailed description of the battle for survival of 15th Tank Corps and the death of its commander is found in A.A. Vetrov, *Tak i bylo* (Thus it was) (Moskva: Voenizdat, 1982), 121–129.
61. Ibid., *Gen. Kdo XXXXVIII Pz. Kps. Abt. Ic.*, Kartenanlagen 4.3–6.3.43; *Befehl des Gewissens,* 200–214.
62. Zvartsev, 53–54; N. Gladkov "Boi s tankami pod Taranovkoi" (Battle with tanks at Tarnovka) *Voenno-Istoricheskii Zhurnal* (Military History Journal), January 1963, 35, 40–41; V. Kashits, *Do poslednikh rubezhei* (Up to the last boundary line) (Moskva: Ordene "Znak Pocheta" Izdatel'stvo DOSAAF SSSR, 1980), 82–94. Brief account of 48th Guards Rifle Division action.
63. Kazakov, 175.
64. Moskalenko, 1:451–452.
65. *Lagenkarte 4. Pz. Armee* Stand. 6.3.43 22*00*, Stand. 7.3.43, 22*00*.
66. For a good summary of Manstein's plans, see: O. Hackl, "Problems of Operational Command of Army Group Don/South in Defensive Operations Between Donets and Dniepr, February/March 1943" *Truppenpraxis,* 3/1982, 4/1982 translated by R. Simpkin, 16–18. Individual unit deployments appear in detail in *Befehl des Gewissens,* 215–228.
67. *Befehl des Gewissens,* 215–228; *K.T.B. Ia. Bd. B* Verlauf des 6.3.1943; Gladkov, 36–40; A.P. Dikan', *Gvardeitsy dvadtsat' pyatoi: boevoi put' 25-i gvardeiskoi strelkovoi Sinel'nikovsko-Budapeshtskoi Krasnoznamennoi ordenov Suvorova i Bogdana Khmen'nitskogo divizii* (Guardsmen of the 25th: the combat path of the Sinel'nikovo'–Budapest, Order of Suvorov and Bogdan Khmen'nitsky Red Banner 25th Guards Rifle Division), (Moskva: Voenizdat, 1984), 52–79.
68. *Befehl des Gewissens,* 221–228; *Lagenkarte 4. Pz. Armee,* Stand. 7.3.43, 22*00*.
69. Moskalenko, 1:452; Kazakov, 177.
70. Gladkov, 40–45; *Gen. Kdo. XXXXVIII Pz. Kps. Abt. IC,* Kartenlagen, 7.3–9.3.43; *Lagenkarte 4. Pz. Armee,* Stand. 8.3.43, 22*00*; Zvartsev, 54–56.
71. *Befehl des Gewissens,* 229–236; *K.T.B. Ia Bd. B,* Verlauf des 8.3.1943; Zvartsev, 53–54.
72. *Befehl des Gewissens,* 238–246; Zvartsev, 57–58; *Lagenkarte 4. Pz. Armee,* Stand. 9.3.43, 22*00*.
73. The Soviet concentration was noted in *Anlage zu Gen. Kdo. XI A.K. Ia,* Lagenkarte zum K.T.B. 10.3. früh, 11.2 früh.
74. Ibid., *Lagenkarte 4. Pz. Armee,* Stand. 11.3.43, 22*00*.
75. Zvartsev, 57–58.
76. Kazakov, 177.
77. Ibid., 177–178.
78. Moskalenko, 1:453.
79. *I.V.M.V.* 6:139–140; *Gen. Kdo. XXXXVIII Pz. Kps. Abt. Ic.*, Kartenlagen, 10.3–11.3.43.
80. *Anlage zu Gen. Kdo XI AK Ia,* Lagenkarte zum K.T.B., 12.3, früh.
81. *Befehl des Gewissens,* 278–293; Zvartsev, 58–59; Mel'nikov, 88 reports that during the fighting Maj. Gen. S.P. Zaitsev, commander of the 62d Guards Rifle Division died as did Col. I.A. Tonkopiev, commander of the 17th Rifle Brigade.
82. Zvartsev, 58.

83. *Befehl des Gewissens*, 279–281; *Anlage zu Gen. Kdo. XI AK Ia*, Lagenkarte zum K.T.B. 14.3 früh, 15.3 früh.
84. Moskalenko, 1:453–454.
85. Kazakov, 178–179; Smol'nyi, 54–55.
86. *Befehl des Gewissens*, 282–283.
87. I.Ya. Vyrodov, ed., *V srazheniyakh za Pobedu: boevoi put' 38-i armii v gody Velikoi Otechestvennoi voiny 1941–1945* (In battles for victory: the combat path of 38th Army in the years of the Great Patriotic War 1941–1945) (Moskva: Izdatel'stvo "Nauka," 1974), 219.
88. *Befehl des Gewissens*, 295–304; *Gen. Kdo. XXXXVIII Pz. Kps. Abt. Ic.*, Kartenlagen, 14.3, 15.3.43.
89. Shafarenko, *My vse . . . .*, 109–113.
90. A detailed account of 1st Guards Cavalry Corps operations is found in, "The Cavalry on the Defense," *Sbornik Materialov po Izuchenyu Opyta Voyny, No. 8, August–Oktyabr' 1943g* (Collection of Materials for the Study of War Experiences, No. 8, August–October 1943) (Moskva: Voennoe Izdatel'stvo, 1943), 110–117.
91. *Anlage zu Gen. Kdo XI AK Ia*, Lagenkarte zum K.T.B., 15.3–18.3 früh.
92. Smol'nyi, 55–57.
93. *Befehl des Gewissens*, 319–329.
94. Smol'nyi, 57.
95. *I.V.M.V.* 6:140; Shtemenko, 170. 21st Army left the Central Front on 13 March and closed into positions north of Belgorod on 20 March. The 64th Army arrived by 23 March. War diary maps of German XI AK confirm those arrival times.
96. Mel'nikov, 91–95. In late March 3d Tank Army was transferred from the Voronezh to the Southwestern Front. The two tank corps remnants moved to Tambov for refitting. At the end of April, the *STAVKA* redesignated 3d Tank Army the 57th Army. On 14 May Rybal'ko took command of the resurrected 3d Guards Tank Army made up of its former two tank corps and a new mechanized corps.
97. C.W. Sydnor, Jr., *Soldiers of Destruction: The SS Death's Head Division 1933–1945* (Princeton, New Jersey: Princeton University Press, 1977), 278.

CHAPTER FIVE

1. E. Ziemke, *Stalingrad to Berlin: The German Defeat in the East* (Washington, D.C.: Office of the Chief of Military History, United States Army, 1968), 124–125.
2. *Kriegstagebuch der OKW, 1940–1945*, Vol. III, 1425.
3. For a good summary of Soviet planning debates, see G. Zhukov, "In the Kursk Bulge," *The Battle of Kursk* (Moscow: Progress Publishers, 1974), 33–59; A. Vasilevsky, "Strategic Planning of the Battle of Kursk," *The Battle of Kursk*, 59–76.
4. M. Zakharov, "O sovetskom voyennom iskusstve v bitve pod Kurskom" (Concerning Soviet military art in the battle of Kursk) *Voenno-Istoricheskii Zhurnal* (Military History Journal) July 1963, 12–13. Hereafter cited as *VIZh*.
5. Ziemke, 151.
6. P.A. Kurochkin, *Obschevoiskovaya armiya v nastuplenii* (The combined arms army in the offensive) (Moskva: Voenizdat, 1966), 22.
7. S.F. Begunov, "Strelkovye voiska" (Rifle forces) *Sovetskaya voyennaya entsiklopediya* (Soviet Military Encyclopedia) (Moskva: Voenizdat, 1979), 7:570. Hereafter cited as *S.V.E.*
8. A.I. Radzievsky, *Taktika v boevykh primerakh: diviziya* (Tactics by combat example: division) (Moskva: Voenizdat, 1976), Skhema 1; Kurochkin, 205.
9. O.A. Losik, ed. *Stroitel'stvo i boevoe primenenie Sovetskykh tankovykh voisk v gody Velikoi Otechestvennoi voiny* (The construction and combat use of Soviet tank forces in the years of the Great Patriotic War) (Moskva; Voenizdat, 1979), 65.
10. Radzievsky, *Taktika . . .*, Skhema 2, Skhema 3.
11. A.I. Radzievsky, *Tankovyi udar* (Tank blow) (Moskva: Voenizdat, 1977), 26.
12. Losik, 58; "Tankovyi polk" (The Tank Regiment) *S.V.E.* 7:674.
13. K. Malan'in, "Razvitie organizatsionnykh form sukhoputnykh voisk v Velikoi Otechestvennoi voine" (The development of the organizational form of the ground forces in the Great Patriotic War) *VIZh*, August 1967, 34; K. Kazakov, "Razvitie sovetskoi artillerii v

gody Velikoi Otechestvennoi voiny" (The development of Soviet artillery in the years of the Great Patriotic War) *VIZh,* November 1975, 14–17.

14. F. Samsonov, "Iz istorii razvitiya sovetskoi artillerii" (From the history of the development of Soviet artillery) *VIZh,* November 1971, 65; Malanin, 36.
15. "Kurskaya bitva v tsifrakh" (The Kursk battle in figures) *VIZh,* July 1968, 79–81.
16. Ibid.
17. Gen. St. d. H. Op. Abt. III *Schematische Kriegsgliederung,* Stand. 25.7.43; Stand. 5.8.43. Provides the organization of both 4th Panzer Army and *A. Abt.* Kempf; *Lagenkarte 4. Pz. Armee,* Stand. 3.8.43, 2200.
18. *Lagenkarte A.A. Kempf,* Stand. 3.3.43.
19. Zhukov, 53–55; K. Moskalenko, "The Voronezh Front in the Battle of Kursk," *The Battle of Kursk* (Moscow: Progress Publishers, 1974), 105.
20. I.M. Chistyakov, *Sluzhim Otchizne* (In the service of the fatherland) (Moskva: Voenizdat, 1975), 169–171.
21. K.S. Moskalenko, *Na yugo-zapadnom napravlenii 1943–1945* (On the southwest direction 1943–1945) (Moskva: Izdatel'stvo "Nauka," 1972) 2:81–82.
22. G.A. Koltunov; B.G. Solov'ev, *Kurskaya Bitva* (The battle of Kursk) (Moskva: Voenizdat, 1970), 275. For an example of German defensive deployment, see *Lagenkarte, LII A.C.* 31.7.43, 2000, 1.8, 2000.
23. *Lagenkarten* of 4th Panzer Army and *A. Abt.* Kempf for 3 August show precise unit positions down to division level. Similar corps maps show the location of units subordinate to divisions.
24. Overall plan and phasing found in many works including Koltunov, 277, and I.Kh. Bagram'yan, ed., *Istoriya voin i voennogo isskustva* (A history of war and military art) (Moskva: Voenizdat, 1970), 223–224.
25. A.S. Zhadov, *Chetyre goda voiny* (Four years of war) (Moskva: Voenizdat, 1978), 99–100.
26. Chistyakov, 172–174.
27. A.V. Kuz'min, I.I. Krasnov, *Kantemirovtsy: boevoi put' 4-go gvardeiskogo tankovogo kantemirovskogo Ordena Lenina Krasnoznamennogo corpusa* (Kantemirovtsy: the combat path of the Kantemirovsky, Order of Lenin, Red Banner, 4th Guards Tank Corps) (Moskva: Voenizdat, 1971), 75.
28. Moskalenko, *Na yugo-zapadnom . . .*, 2:82.
29. I.Ya. Vyrodov, ed., *V srazheniyakh za Pobedu: boevoi put' 38-i armii v gody Velikoi Otechestvennoi voiny 1941–1945* (In battles for victory: the combat path of the 38th Army in the Years of the Great Patriotic War 1941–1945) (Moskva: Izdatel'stvo "Nauka," 1974), 234–236.
30. A.Kh. Babadzhanyan, N.K. Popel, M.A. Shalin, I.M. Kravchenko, *Lyuki otkryli v Berline: boevoi put' 1-i gvardeiskoi tankovoi armii* (They opened the hatchway to Berlin: the combat path of the 1st Guards Tank Army) (Moskva: Voenizdat, 1973), 63.
31. P.Ya. Yegorov, I.V. Krivoborsky, I.K. Ivlev, A.I. Rogalevich, *Dorogami pobed: boevoi put' 5-i gvardeiskoi tankovoi armii* (By the roads of victory: the combat path of 5th Guards Tank Army) (Moskva: Voenizdat, 1969), 58.
32. I.M. Managarov, *V srazhenii za Khar'kov* (In the battles for Khar'kov) (Khar'kov: Prapor, 1978), 60.
33. I. Konev, *Zapiski kommanduyushchego frontam, 1941–1944* (Notes of a *front* commander, 1941–1944) (Moskva: Voenizdat, 1972), 23–24.
34. D.A. Dragunsky, ed., *Ot Volgi do Pragi* (From the Volga to Prague) (Moskva: Voenizdat, 1966), 91–92.
35. Konev, 24.
36. I.E. Krupchenko, ed., *Sovetsckie tankovye voiska 1941–1945* (Soviet tank forces, 1941–1945) (Moskva: Voenizdat, 1973), 138; P. Rotmistrov, "Bronetankovye i mekhanizirovannye voiska v bitva pod Kurskom" (Armored and mechanized forces in the battle at Kursk) *VIZh,* January 1970, 20.
37. K.P. Kazakov, *Vsegda s pekhotoi vsegda s tankami* (Always with the infantry, always with the tanks) (Moskva: Voenizdat, 1969), 166–167.
38. A.I. Radzievsky, *Proryv* (Penetration) (Moskva: Voenizdat, 1979), 56–57.
39. Koltunov, 282.

40. S. Rudenko, "The Gaining of Air Supremacy and Air Operations in the Battle of Kursk," *The Battle of Kursk* (Moscow: Progress Publishers, 1974), 194.
41. Radzievsky, *Proryv,* 58.
42. A.D. Tsirlin, P.I. Biryukov, V.P. Istomin, E.N. Fedoseyev, *Inzhenernye voiska v boyakh za sovetskiyu rodinu* (Engineer forces in battles for the Soviet homeland) (Moskva: Voenizdat, 1970), 171.
43. A. Tsirlin, "Engineer Troops," *The Battle of Kursk* (Moscow: Progress Publishers, 1974), 224–226.
44. I.P. Grishin, et. al., *Voennye svyazisty v dni voiny i mira* (Military communicators in the days of war and peace) (Moskva: Voenizdat, 1968), 194–195.
45. Moskalenko, "The Voronezh Front," 107; Koltunov, 284–285.
46. N. Antipenko, "Logistics," *The Battle of Kursk* (Moscow: Progress Publishers, 1974), 240–248.
47. *Lagenkarte, LII A.K.* 2.8.20*00; Lagenkarte, A.A. Kempf,* Stand. 3.8.43, *Lagenkarte 4. Pz. Armee,* Stand. 3.8.43, 22*00.*
48. H. Reinhardt, *German Army Group Operations on the Eastern Front 1941–1943, Southern Area,* MS No. P-114C, Vol. Vi (USAREUR, Historical Division, 1954), 26.
49. A.S. Zhadov, "Prorvy gluboko eshelonirovannoi oborony protivnika" (Penetration of deeply echeloned enemy defense), *VIZh,* January 1978.
50. I.A. Samchuk, P.G. Skachko, Yu N. Babikov, I.L. Gnedoi, *Ot Volgi do El'by i Pragi* (From the Volga to the Elbe and Prague) (Moskva: Voenizdat, 1970), 78.
51. Babadzhanyan, *Lyuki otkryli . . .,* 63–65.
52. Ibid., 65–66.
53. Zhadov, *Chetyre goda voiny,* 102–104; Babadzhanyan, *Lyuki otkryli . . .,* 66.
54. Babadzhayan, *Lyuki otkryli . . .,* 67.
55. Ibid., 67–71; Koltunov, 283, states: 1st Tank Army armored strength on 3 August was 549 tanks, including 412 T-34, 108 T-70 and 29 T-60.
56. Ibid., 72–73.
57. A.P. Ryazansky, *V ogne tankovykh srazhenii* (In the fire of tank battles) (Moskva: Izdatel'stvo "Nauka," 1975), 86–87; A. Yegorov, "Yuzhnee Kurska" (South of Kursk) *VIZh,* July 1968, 60–61; P.Ya Yegorov, *Dorogami . . .,* 60–61.
58. P.Ya. Yegorov, *Dorogami . . .,* 56; Koltunov, 283, cites 5th Guards Tank Army strength on 3 August as being 445 tanks and 64 armored cars.
59. Chistyakov, 171–173; Yu.N. Babikov, I.A. Samchuk, *Kotel pod Tomarovkoi* (The cauldron of Tomarovka) (Moskva: Voenizdat, 1967), 6–10.
60. Babikov, *Kotel,* 7–8; M.K. Smol'nyi, *7000 kilometrov v boyakh i pokhodakh: boevoi put' 161-i strelkovoi Stanislavskoi Krasnoznamennoi Ordena Bogdena Khmel'nitskogo divizii 1941–1945 gg.* (7000 kilometers in marches and battles: the combat path of the Stanislav, Red Banner Order of Bogdan Kheml'nitsky 161st Rifle Division, 1941–1945) (Moskva: Voenizdat, 1972), 69–70.
61. Koltunov, 281.
62. Managarov, 60, covers all 53d Army planning considerations. See also Yu. Sukhinin, B. Frolov, "Proryv oborony protivnika 116-i strelkovoi divisiei v Belgorodsko– Khar'kovskoi operatsii (3–5 Avgusta 1943 g)" (Penetration of the enemy defense by the 116th Rifle Division in the Belgorod–Khar'kov operation, 3–5 August 1943) *VIZh,* August 1977, 52–54.
63. M.D. Solomatin, *Krasnogradtsy* (Krasnogradtsy) (Moskva: Voenizdat, 1963), 51–53.
64. Koltunov, 281.
65. Dragunsky, 92; Koltunov, 281; 7th Guards Army planning from a division's perspective in I.K. Morozov, *Ot Stalingrada do Pragi* (From Stalingrad to Prague) (Volgograd: Nizhne-Volzhsko Knizhnoe Izdatel'stvo, 1976), 119–121.
66. I.Ya. Vyazankin, *Za strokoi boevogo doneseniya* (Across the lines of combat messages) (Moskva: Voenizdat, 1978), 35.
67. *Lagenkarte LII A.K.* 2.8.2000–3.8.2000 display all Soviet attacks and German troop movements in the corps sector on 3 August. For 19th and 6th Panzer Division reactions to the assault see W. Paul, *Brennpunkte; Die Geschichte der 6. Panzerdivision (1937–1945)* (Focal point, the history of the 6th Panzer Division 1937–1945) and A. Krull, *Das Hannoversche*

Regiment 73: Geschichte des Panzer-Grenadier-Regiments 73 1943–1945 (The Hanoverian Regiment 73: A history of the Panzer Grenadier Regiment 73, 1939–1945) (Hannover: Regimentskameradschaft 73, undated), 321–322.
68. Samchuk, *Ot Volgi,* 77–80; Zhadov, *Chetyre goda voiny,* 106–108.
69. I.A. Samchuk, *Gvardeiskaya Poltavskaya: kratkii ocherk o boevom puti 97-i gvardeiskaya. Poltavskoi Krasnoznamennoi ordena Suvorova i Bogdana Khmel'nitskogo strelkovoi divizii* (Guards Poltava: A short survey about the combat path of the Poltava, Red Banner, Order of Suvorov and Bogdan Khmel'nitsky 97th Guards Rifle Division) (Moskva: Voenizdat, 1965), 72–73.
70. I.A. Samchuk, *Trinadtsataya gvardeiskaya: boevoi put' Trinadtsatoi gvardeiskoi Poltavskoi ordena Lenina dvazhdy Krasnoznamennoi ordena Suvorova i Kutuzova strelkovoi divizii (1941–1945)* (Thirteenth Guards: the combat path of the Poltava, Order of Lenin, twice Red Banner, Order of Suvorov and Kutozov, 13th Guards Rifle Division (1941–1945)) (Moskva: Voenizdat, 1971), 188–189.
71. N.D. Sebezhko, "Poverzhennyi bastion" (The overcome bastion), *Kurskaya Bitva* (The Battle of Kursk) (Voronezh: Tsentral'no-Chernozemnoye Knizhnoye Izdatel'stvo, 1982), 256–258.
72. Koltunov, 288; Babadzhanyan, *Lyuki otkryli,* 74; A.L. Getman, *Tanki idut na Berlin* (Tanks advance on Berlin) (Moskva: Izdatel'stvo "Nauka," 1973), 116; D.A. Dragunsky, *Gody v brone* (Years in Armor) (Moskva: Voenizdat, 1975), 108–110.
73. Koltunov, 289; P.Ya. Yegorov, 63–64; A. Yegorov, 62–63.
74. Babikov, *Kotel,* 10–13.
75. Chistyakov, 177.
76. Ibid., 177–178.
77. Managarov, *V srazhenii,* 65–66; Vyazankin, 39–41; Sebrezhko, 260.
78. Vyazankin, 38–47.
79. Sukhinin, 55–56.
80. Solomatin, 54–55.
81. *Lagenkarte A.A. Kempf,* Stand. 3.8.43.
82. The persistence of Soviet bridging efforts is portrayed in Department of the Army Pamphlet No. 20–269 *Small Unit Actions During the German Campaign in Russia* (Department of the Army, July 1953), 220–228.
83. Babikov, *Kotel,* 19; *Lagenkarte LII AK* 3.8.20*00*–4.8.20*00*; *Lagenkarte 4. Pz. Armee,* Stand. 3.8.43.22*00*.
84. Samchuk, *Gvardeiskaya Poltavskaya,* 73–74; Samchuk, *Trinadtsataya gvardeiskaya,* 189.
85. Babadzhanyan, 77–78.
86. Ibid.
87. Getman, 118.
88. P.Ya. Yegorov, 65–66; *Lagenkarte A.A. Kempf,* Stand. 4.8.43.
89. P.Ya. Yegorov, 65–66; Ryazansky, 88.
90. Koltunov, 293; Babikov, 21–29; Chistyakov, 180–181; *Lagenkarte LII K.*, 4.8.2000–5.8.2000; *Lagenkarte 4 Pz. Armee,* Stand. 5.8.43, 22*00*.
91. Zhadov, 108–109; Samchuk, *Gvardeiskaya Poltavskaya,* 73; Samchuk, *Trinadtsataya gvardeiskaya,* 189–190; Krull, 323.
92. Getman, 119.
93. P.Ya. Yegorov, 66–67.
94. Babikov, 29–30; Koltunov, 292–293.
95. Kuz'min, 75–81.
96. Ibid., 82–86; Babikov, 29–32; *Lagenkarte LII A.K.* 4.8.2000–5.8.2000.
97. Kuz'min, 86.
98. Zhadov, 108–109; Babikov, 35–37.
99. Moskalenko, 2:82.
100. Reinhardt, 26; *Lagenkarte 4. Pz. Armee,* Stand. 3.8.43 22*00*; Stand. 4.8.43 2200; Stand. 5.8.43 2200.
101. Moskalenko, 2:83–89; Smol'nyi, 70.
102. *Lagenkarte A.A. Kempf,* Stand. 4.8.43.
103. Managarov, 70; Vyazankin, 48; Sukhinin, 56.

104. Vyazankin, 48–56; Solomatin, 56.
105. Sukhinin, 56.
106. Konev, 27–28; Solomatin, 56.
107. Ryazansky, 88.
108. Ibid., 89–90; Managarov, 71–72; Vyazankin, 49–57; Smol'nyi, 57; Solomatin, 58.
109. Koltunov, 294–295.
110. G.A. Sepeda "Shturm Belgorodskikh pozitsii" (The storming of the Belgorod position), *Kurskaya Bitva* (The Battle of Kursk) (Voronezh: Tsentral'no Chernozemnoye Knizhnoye Izdatel'stvo, 1982) 268–271.
111. Ibid.
112. Babikov, 35.
113. *Lagenkarte LII A.K.*, 4.8.2000–5.8.2000; *Lagenkarte LII A.K.*, 5.8.2000–6.8.2000.
114. Babikov, 35–37.
115. Samchuk, *Gvardeiskaya Poltavskaya*, 74–75.
116. Samchuk, *Trinadtsataya gvardeiskaya*, 190–192; Babikov, 45–65.
117. Kuz'min, 86–88; *Lagenkarte, 4. Pz. Armee*, Stand. 6.8.43 22*00*; Stand. 7.8.43 22*00*.
118. *Lagenkarte LII A.K.* 6.8.2000–7.8.2000; Krull, 326–328.
119. Babikov, 65–89, details the course of battle on 7 August; *Lagenkarte LII A.K.* 6.8.2000–7.8.2000; Koltunov, 305–306; Samchuk, *Trinadtsataya Gvardeiskaya*, 191–193.
120. Babikov, 90–91; Krull, 327.
121. Babikov, 91–92. The Soviets claim 5,000 Germans were killed and 2,000 became prisoners in the Borisovka encirclement. They also claim to have destroyed 40 tanks and 500 vehicles.
122. Moskalenko, *Na yugo-zapadnom...*, 2:85; Smol'nyi, 71–72; *Lagenkarte, 4. Pz. Armee*, Stand. 6.8.43 22*00*.
123. Reinhardt, 37.
124. *Lagenkarte A.A. Kempf*, Stand. 5.8.43; Stand. 6.8.43; *Anlage zum K.T.B. Armee Abt. Kempf* vom 5.8.43.
125. Babadzhanyan, 79–81.
126. Ibid., 81; Getman, 119–120.
127. Koltunov, 309; I. Kravchenko "Vstrechnye boi tankovykh i mekhanizirovannykh korpusov v Velikoi Otechestvennoi voine" (Meeting engagements of tank and mechanized corps in the Great Patriotic War) *VIZh*, May 1963, 29.
128. P.Ya. Yegorov, 67–69; A. Yegorov, 64.
129. P.Ya. Yegorov, 69–72; Ryazansky, 89–90; *Lagenkarte A.A. Kempf* Stand. 7.8.43.
130. Koltunov, 310.
131. Babadzhanyan, 83.
132. Getman, 121–122.
133. Babadzhanyan, 84.
134. Koltunov, 315.
135. Getman, 39; Karavayev, 39–40.
136. Babadzhanyan, 84–85.
137. P.Ya. Yegorov, 73.
138. Kuz'min, 89–91. On 8 August Poluboyarov's corps had 97 tanks. *Lagenkarte, 4. Pz. Armee*, Stand. 8.8.43 22*00*; *Lagenkarte LII A.K.* 7.8.2000–8.8.2000.
139. Kuz'min, 91–94; *Lagenkarte LII A.K.*, 9.8.43. 2000–10.8.43 2000; 10.8.43 2000–11.8.43 2000.
140. Kuz'min, 95.
141. Vyrodov, 236–237.
142. *Lagenkarte LII A.K.* 7.8.43 2000–8.8.43.2000; 8.8.43.2000–9.8.43.2000; *Lagenkarte, 4. Pz. Armee*, Stand. 10.8.43 0600.
143. Smol'nyi, 74–76.
144. Koltunov, 303–304.
145. Ibid.
146. *Lagenkarte A.A. Kempf*, Stand. 6.8.43.
147. Managarov, 74–75; Solomatin, 61–62; Vyazankin, 63–64.
148. Solomatin, 62–63.

149. Vyazankin, 67–72; *Lagenkarte A.A. Kempf,* Stand. 8.8.43.
150. Solomatin, 65–66; Managarov, 77–80.
151. Ibid., 80.
152. Dragunsky, 94; S.I. Vasil'ev, A.P. Dikan', *Gvardeitsy pyatnadtsatoi: boevoi put' pyatnadtsatoi gvardeiskoi strelkovoi divizii* (The Guards 15th: the combat path of the 15th Guards Rifle Division) (Moskva: Voenizdat, 1960), 88; S.N. Pikrovsky, *Kazakhstanskie soedineniya v bitva na Kurskom Duge* (Kazakh formations at the battle of Kursk) (Alma-Ata: Izdatel'stvo "Nauka," Kazakhstan, SSP, 1973), 100–102; I.K. Morozov, 119–139 relates the role of the 81st Guards Rifle Division.
153. S.G. Goryachev, *Ot Volgi do Al'p* (From the Volga to the Alps) (Kiev: Izdatel'stvo politicheskoi literatury Ukrainy, 1982), 73.
154. A.A. Yaroshenko, *V boi shla 41-ya gvardeiskaya: boevoi put' 41-i gvardeiskoi strelkovoi Korsun'sko–Dunaiskoi Ordena Suvorova divizii* (Into battle went the 41st Guards: the combat path of the Korsun–Danube, Order of Suvorov 41st Guards Rifle Division) (Moskva: Voenizdat, 1982), 68–69; Koltunov, 314.
155. Yaroshenko, 71–74.
156. A.A. Kempf sent 6th Panzer Division to reinforce the 282d Infantry Division, one of whose regiments (848th) broke under the weight of the Soviet assault. See P. Carell, *Scorched Earth: The Russian–German War, 1943–1944* (New York: Ballantine Books, 1972), 355.
157. Reinhardt, 33, 36. Third Panzer Division at that time had a strength of 30 tanks and assault guns.
158. B. Frolov, "Tankovoe srazhenie v raione Bogodukhova (1943 g)" (The tank battle in the Bogodukhov region (1943)) *VIZh,* September 1978, 18, 21; Koltunov, 320.
159. For details of this complex engagement see Karavayev, 37–41; Getman, 124–127; M.E. Katukov, *Na Ostrie glavogo udara* (On the point of the main attack) (Moskva: Voenizdat, 1976), 246–248; Frolov, 18–20; Babadzhanyan, 86–87.
160. Koltunov, 320.
161. Frolov, 20.
162. P.Ya. Yegorov, 73–74; Samchuk, *Gvardeiskaya Poltavskaya,* 77–78.
163. Frolov, 21–22; Karavayev, 40–41; Getman, 127.
164. Katukov, 248.
165. P.Ya. Yegorov, 75–76.
166. Frolov, 22; Chistyakov, 188–189.
167. Chistyakov, 189; Frolov, 22; *Lagenkarte 4. Pz. Armee,* Stand. 13.8.43 22*00*.
168. P.Ya. Yegorov, 77.
169. Ibid., 77–78.
170. Koltunov, 322.
171. *Lagenkarte Armee-Abt. Kempf,* Stand. 15.8.43. Früh; O. Weidinger, *Division "Das Reich."* (Germany: Publisher unknown), 291–293. Gives "Das Reich's" strength as 70 tanks on 12 August and 80 tanks on 13 August; Frolov, 23.
172. Frolov, 23; Koltunov, 323; *Lagenkarte Hgr. Sud. Gen. StdH Op Abt. III*[b], Stand. 15.8.43 abds.
173. Koltunov, 323–324.
174. P.Ya. Yegorov, 78–79; Ryazansky, 91–92.
175. *Unterstellungen und Kampfgruppen Hgr. Sud.,* Stand. 15.8.43.
176. *Armee-Abt. Kampf,* Stand. 15.8.43 Früh.
177. Konev, 33–34.
178. Managarov, 80–81; Solomatin, 66; Vyazankin, 75; Goryachev, 74.
179. Managarov, 81; Vyazankin, 75–78.
180. Managarov, 82.
181. Vyazankin, 83.
182. Yaroshenko, 74–76; G.A. Koltunov, "Donbasskaya Operatsiya 1943" (The Donbas Operation 1943) *Sovetskaya Voennaya Entskiklopediya* (Soviet Military Encyclopedia) (Moskva: Voenizdat, 1977), 3:240–241.
183. Yaroshenko, 75–76; *Karten K.T.B. XXXXII A.K. Ia.,* 14.8.43, 15.8.43, 16.8.43.
184. A.G. Yershov, *Osvobozhdenie Donbassa* (Liberation of the Donbas) (Moskva: Voenizdat, 1973), 126–128.

185. Koltunov, 332.
186. *Unterstellungen u. Kampfgruppen Hgr. Sud,* Stand. 17.8.43.
187. *Hgr. Sud. Gen. StdH Op. Abt. IIIb,* Stand. 17.8.43 abds; *Lagenkarte LII A.K.,* 14.8.43.2000–15.8.43.2000.
188. *Unterstellungen u. Kampfgruppen Hgr. Sud.,* Stand. 17.8.43.
189. Reinhardt, 43–44.
190. Moskalenko, 2:90–91; *Lagenkarte LII A.K.* 14.8.43.2000–15.8.43.2000, 15.8.43.2000–16.8.43.2000; Smol'nyi, 76–77.
191. Koltunov, 334.
192. Kuz'min, 96–98.
193. Moskalenko, 2:91–93; A.M. Samsonov, *Ot Volgi do Baltiki: ocherk istorii 3-go gvardeiskogo mekhanizirovannogo korpusa 1942–1945 gg* (From the Volga to the Baltic: A sketch of the history of 3d Guards Mechanized Corps 1942–1945) (Moskva: Izdatel'stvo "Nauka," 1973), 121–123.
194. Moskalenko, 2:93–94; Samsonov, 123–126; *Lagenkarte LII A.K.,* 16.8.43.2000– 17.8.43.2000; *Lagenkarte A.O.K.8.* Lage vom 18.8.1943, Früh; *Hgr Sud Gen. StdH Op. Abt. IIIb,* Stand. 17.8.43 abds; Reinhardt, 45–46; Krull, 332–333.
195. *Hgr. Sud Gen. Stuh Op. Abt. IIIb,* Stand. 19.8.43, Reinhardt claims German tank strength on 16 August was 7th Panzer Division 23 tanks and "Grossdeutschland" Division 55 tanks.
196. A.I. Radzievski, *Armeiskie operatsii* (Army operations) (Moskva: Voenizdat, 1977), 72–74; F. Utenkov, "V boyakh pod Akhtyrkoi" (In the battle at Akhtyrka) *VIZh,* August 1981, 38–39; *Hgr Sud Gen StdH, Op. Abt. IIIb,* Stand. 17.8.43 abds.
197. Koltunov, 337–338.
198. Ibid., 335–337; Utenkov, 39–41.
199. Radzievsky, 75; Babadzhanyan, 88; Getman, 128; P.Ya. Yegorov, 79–80. Soviet regrouping recorded in *Hgr. Sud. Gen. StdH. Op. Abt. IIIb,* Stand. 19.8.43 abds.
200. Kuz'min, 99–100.
201. Utenkov, 41.
202. T.F. Vorontsov, N.I. Biryukov, A.F. Smekalov, et. al., *Ot Volzhshikh Stepei do Avstriiskikh Al'p: boevoi put' 4-i gvardeiskoi armii* (From the Volga Steppes to the Austrian Alps: the combat path of 4th Guards Army) (Moskva: Voenizdat, 1971), 28–29; N.I. Biryukov, *Trudnaya Nauka Pobezhdat'* (Hard science prevails) (Moskva: Voenizdat, 1968), 12–14.
203. Biryukov, 15–18; Koltunov, 338–339; Babadzhanyan, 88; *Hgr, Sud. Gen. StdH Op. Abt. IIIb,* Stand. 19.8.43 abds.
204. Utenkov, 41–42.
205. Biryukov, 17.
206. Ibid., 21.
207. Ibid., 21–22; Babadzhanyan, 88–89; Getman, 129.
208. Biryukov, 23–26.
209. Ibid., 30.
210. Koltunov, 341.
211. Moskalenko, 2:77–78; Samsonov, 127–134; *Lagenkarte LII A.K.* 18.8.43. 2000–18.8.43.2000.
212. Samsonov, 134–137; *Lagenkarte LII A.K.* 18.8.43.2000–19.8.43.2000.
213. Smol'nyi, 78–79.
214. Moskalenko, 2:97.
215. Ibid., 98.
216. Samsonov, 136–139.
217. Reinhardt, 45–46; *Hgr. Sud. Gen. StdH Op. Abt. IIIb,* Stand. 21.8.43 abds.
218. Samsonov, 139.
219. Ibid., 139–140.
220. Koltunov, 341–342.
221. Konev, 31–32.
222. Managarov, 83.
223. *Lagenkarte A.O.K.8.* Lage vom 18.8.1943 früh; Lage vom 19.8.1943 früh.
224. Managarov, 86; Solomatin, 67; Vyazankin, 84–88; *Unterstellungen u. Kampfgruppen Hgr Sud,* Stand. 19.8.1943.

225. *Lagenkarte A.O.K.8,* Lage vom 20.8.1943 früh.
226. Managarov, 87; Goryachev, 76.
227. P.Ya. Yegarov, 80; Managarov, 87.
228. *Lagenkarte A.O.K.8,* Lage vom 20.8.1943 früh.
229. P.Ya. Yegorov, 80–81.
230. Koltunov, 345.
231. *Hgr. Sud. Gen. StdH Op. Abt. IIIb,* Stand. 21.8.43 abds.
232. P.Ya. Yegorov, 80–81; Ryazansky, 93–94; Solomatin, 68; see also Department of the Army Pamphlet No. 20–230 *Russian Combat Methods in World War II* (Department of the Army, 1950), 52–57.
233. Vyazankin, 86; Konev, 37.
234. Goryachev, 77–78.
235. Koltunov, 346–349; Managarov, 87–88.
236. P.Ya. Yegorov, 83.
237. A.I. Radzievsky, *Tankovyi udar* (Tank blow) (Moskva: Voenizdat, 1977), 212. In 1st Tank Army, the 242d Tank Brigade (31st Tank Corps) lost 80 percent of its tanks and 65 percent of its personnel. 3d Mechanized Corps lost 90 percent of its command cadre while 6th Motorized Rifle Brigade (6th Tank Corps) emerged with 7–10 percent of its original strength.
238. Reinhardt, 47.
239. *Unterstellungen und Kampfgruppen Hgr Sud,* Stand. 15.8.43, Stand. 23.8.43.

Index

All children have a great ambition to read to themselves...

and a sense of achievement when they can do so. The **read it yourself** *series has been devised to satisfy their ambition. Since many children learn from the Ladybird Key Words Reading Scheme, these stories have been based to a large extent on the Key Words List, and the tales chosen are those with which children are likely to be familiar.*

The series can of course be used as supplementary reading for any reading scheme.

Ananse and the Sky God *is intended for children reading up to Book 5c of the Ladybird Reading Scheme. The following words are additional to the vocabulary used at that level –*

many, stories, Ananse *(An-an-see)*, spider, Africa, world, tells, went, Sky, God, Earth, once, spun, web, laughed, Osebo *(Oss-ee-boh)*, leopard, terrible, teeth, Mmoboro *(Mmm-oh-borr-oh)*, hornets, sting, Aboatia *(Ab-wa-tee-ay)*, fairy, if, such, nothing, first, tie, feet, banana, took, hard, gourd, shell, leaf, over, head, poured, rest, raining, cork, mouth, doll, bowl, hand, glue, cooked, yams, vine, stuck, end, round, hide, angry, slap, happened, could, kicked, adventures

A list of other titles at the same level will be found on the back cover.

Published by Ladybird Books Ltd Loughborough Leicestershire UK
Ladybird Books Inc Lewiston Maine 04240 USA

Ananse and the Sky God

adapted by Fran Hunia
from the traditional tale
illustrated by Angie Sage

Ladybird Books

There are many stories about Ananse, the Spider man. They come from Africa, but are known to children all over the world.

This is one of the stories. It tells how Ananse went to the Sky God to ask for some stories for the children of Earth, and it tells how the Sky God's stories came to be known as "Spider Stories".

Once the children of Earth had no stories. The Sky God had all the stories and he kept them by his chair in his house up in the sky.

Ananse the Spider man knew about the Sky God's stories, and he wanted them for the children of Earth.

"I know what I will do," said Ananse. "I will go up to see the Sky God and ask him if I can have some of his stories."

Ananse spun a web that went up into the sky. Up and up and up it went, to the house of the Sky God.

Up went Ananse the Spider man, up the web to see the Sky God.

The Sky God was big. He looked down at little Ananse. "What do you want, little Spider man?" he asked.

Ananse looked up at the Sky God. He said, "Please, Sky God, I know you have some stories, and I want some of them for the children of Earth. What can I give you for the stories?"

The Sky God laughed at Ananse. "You are a funny little man," he said.

"I will tell you what I want for my stories, little Spider man," said the Sky God. "I want Osebo, the leopard with the terrible teeth, Mmoboro, the hornets that sting like fire, and Aboatia, the fairy that no man sees. If you will get them for me, then I will give you some stories for the children of Earth," and the Sky God laughed and laughed.

"Yes," said Ananse. "I will do as you ask."

The Sky God laughed more and more. ''How can a little man like you get me such things?'' he asked. ''Osebo the leopard will eat you, or Mmoboro the hornets will sting you. As for Aboatia the fairy, no man can see her, so how can you get her for me?''

Ananse said nothing. He went down the web. Down and down and down he went, down to Earth to look for Osebo the leopard with the terrible teeth, Mmoboro the hornets that sting like fire, and Aboatia the fairy that no man sees.

"I can get them," he said. "I know I can."

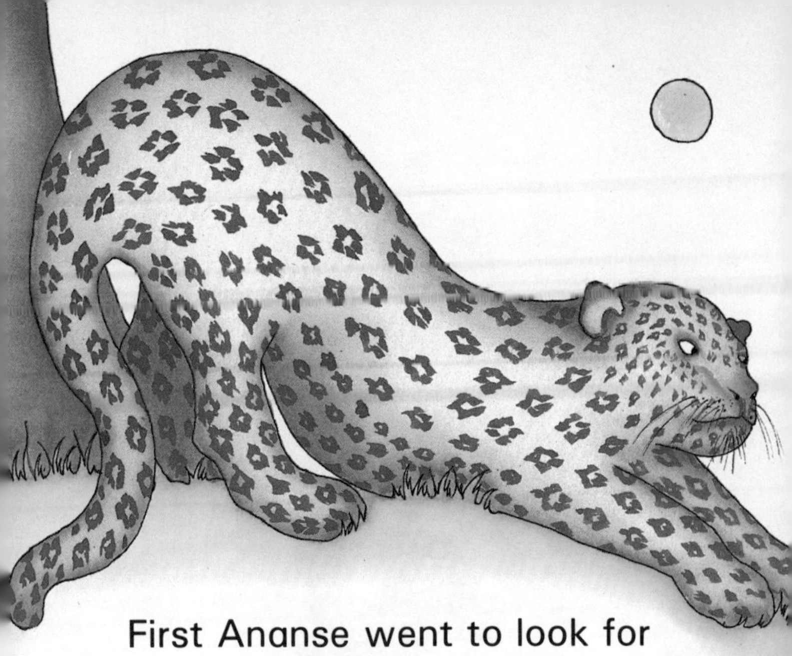

First Ananse went to look for Osebo the leopard with the terrible teeth. He saw him sitting by a tree.

''Have you come for tea, little Spider man?'' asked Osebo.

''We will see about that,'' said Ananse, ''but first I want to play a game with you.''

Osebo liked playing games. ''What game do you want to play?'' he asked.

''This is the game,'' said Ananse. ''I will tie you up by the feet, then I will let you go and you can tie me up.''

"This will be fun," said Osebo. (He wanted to tie Ananse up and then eat him.) But Ananse tied Osebo up first, and then he tied his feet to a tree.

"Soon I will take you to see the Sky God," said Ananse. "But first I must go and look for Mmoboro the hornets that sting like fire. Do not run away, Osebo," and he laughed at the leopard tied to the tree.

Ananse walked on. Soon he came to a banana tree.

"This will help me," he said. He took a big leaf from the banana tree. Then he went to get a hard gourd and put some water in it.

"Now I will look for Mmoboro, the hornets that sting like fire," he said.

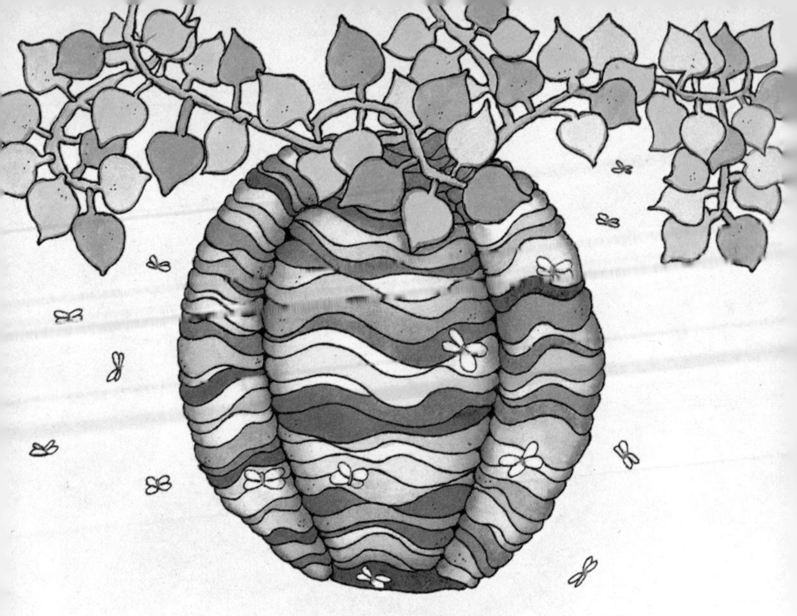

Ananse walked on. Soon he saw Mmoboro, the hornets that sting like fire. He put the banana leaf up over his head and poured some of the water from his gourd on to the banana leaf. It looked as if it was raining.

Ananse poured the rest of the water over the hornets.

"It is raining, it is raining," he said to the hornets. "Get into my gourd, little hornets, to keep out of the rain."

"Thank you, Ananse," said the hornets, and in they went, one after the other, to keep out of the rain.

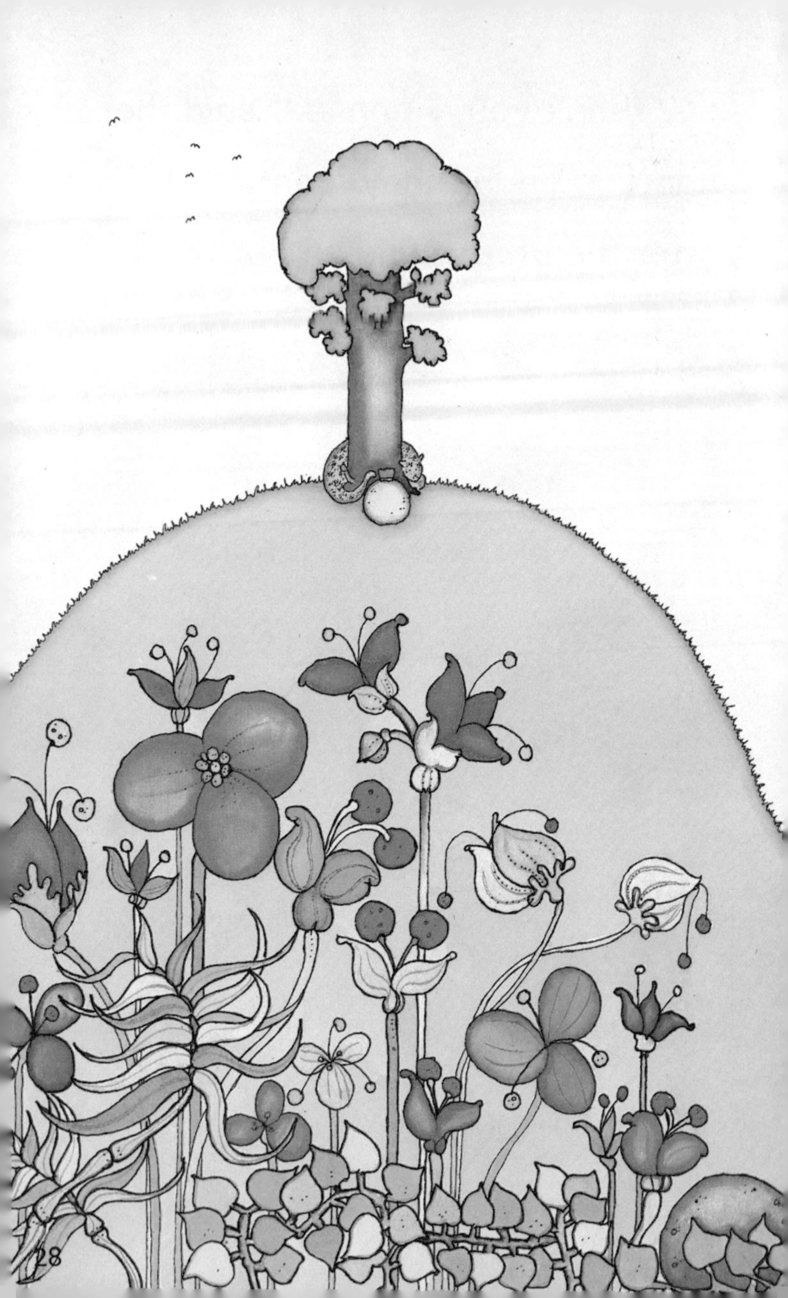

"Now all I have to do is to keep you in there," said Ananse, and he put a cork in the mouth of the gourd. He took the gourd to the tree where he had tied Osebo, the leopard with the terrible teeth.

He tied the gourd to the tree.

"Soon I will take you to see the Sky God," said Ananse, "but first I must go to look for Aboatia, the fairy that no man sees."

Ananse made a little doll with a bowl in her hand. He put glue all over the doll and then he put some cooked yams into the bowl.

He took a vine and stuck one end of it to the little doll's head. Then he put the doll down by the tree with red flowers round it, where the fairies like to play.

Ananse took the other end of the vine and went off to hide.

Soon Aboatia, the fairy that no man sees, came to the tree with red flowers round it.

She saw the doll sitting by the tree and stopped to see what was in the bowl.

Aboatia looked at the yams and her mouth watered. She liked yams!

"Please let me have some yam," said Aboatia to the doll.

Ananse pulled the vine and

made the doll's head go up and down. It looked as if the doll was saying, ''Yes.''

Aboatia took some yam and put it into her mouth. It was good! Aboatia took some more yam, then more and more.

Soon Aboatia had eaten all the yams. "Thank you," she said to the doll. The doll said nothing.

"Thank you," said Aboatia again. Once more the doll said nothing. Aboatia was getting angry. "Talk to me!" she said, but the doll said nothing.

"Talk to me. Talk to me, or I will slap you!" said Aboatia, but the doll said nothing.

So Aboatia slapped the doll and do you know what happened? Her hand stuck to the glue that Ananse had put all over the doll.

Aboatia was getting more and more angry. ''Let go of my hand, or I will slap you with my other hand,'' she said.

But the doll could not let go, so Aboatia slapped her again and her other hand stuck to the glue.

Now Aboatia was as angry as a fairy could be. She kicked at the doll with her feet, and her feet stuck to the glue. She looked so funny with her two hands and her

two feet stuck to the doll!

Ananse looked out from where he was hiding and saw that Aboatia was stuck.

Ananse laughed at Aboatia. ''Now I will take you to see the Sky God,'' he said. ''But first come with me to get the other things that I have to take with me.''

Ananse took Aboatia to the tree where he had tied Osebo the leopard and Mmoboro the hornets. Then he spun a web that went up into the sky.

Ananse pulled Osebo, Mmoboro, and Aboatia up the web and into the sky. He put them down at the Sky God's feet.

"Here are the things you asked for," said Ananse. "Osebo, the leopard with the terrible teeth, Mmoboro the hornets that sting like fire, and Aboatia the fairy that no man sees. Now will you give me some stories for the children of Earth?"

The Sky God saw Osebo, the leopard, Mmoboro the hornets, and Aboatia the fairy. Then he looked down at little Ananse, the Spider man.

"Yes, Ananse," said the Sky God. "You have given me all the things I asked for. Now I will give you all my stories. From now on they will be known as 'Spider Stories'."

Ananse was pleased to have the stories. He took them down to the children of Earth.

Now children all over the world know about Ananse, the Spider man, and all his adventures.

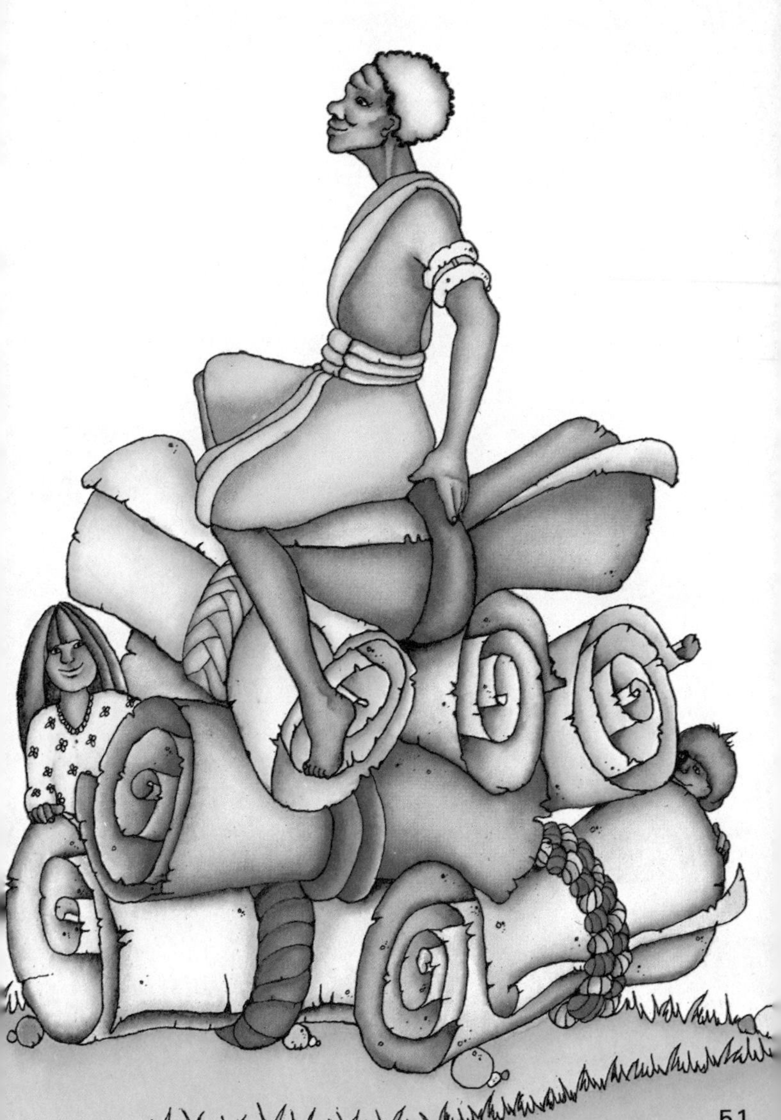